Revenue Statistics 2020

1965-2019

OECD
BETTER POLICIES FOR BETTER LIVES

Please cite this publication as:
OECD (2020), *Revenue Statistics 2020*, OECD Publishing, Paris, *https://doi.org/10.1787/8625f8e5-en*.

ISBN 978-92-64-95556-1 (print)
ISBN 978-92-64-54583-0 (pdf)

Revenue Statistics
ISSN 2522-7696 (print)
ISSN 2522-770X (online)

Photo credits: Cover © some of the graphic elements in the main cover illustration were adapted from Freepik.com.

Corrigenda to publications may be found on line at: *www.oecd.org/about/publishing/corrigenda.htm*.

Foreword

This annual publication provides information on tax levels and tax structures in OECD countries. It was prepared under the auspices of the Working Party on Tax Policy Analysis and Tax Statistics of the Committee on Fiscal Affairs and is published under the responsibility of the Secretary-General of the OECD.

Acknowledgements

Revenue Statistics 2020 has been produced by the Organisation for Economic Cooperation and Development (OECD)'s Centre for Tax Policy and Administration (CTPA) under the auspices of Working Party No.2 on Tax Policy Analysis and Tax Statistics (WP2) of the Committee on Fiscal Affairs. The authors of this edition were Michelle Harding, Nicolás Miranda and Michael Sharratt. The special feature was written by Hannah Simon and Michelle Harding.

The authors would like to thank colleagues in the OECD for their invaluable comments and practical support in finalising the publication, including David Bradbury, Karena Garnier, Natalie Lagorce, and Violet Sochay in CTPA; Nadim Ahmad, Peter Van de Ven, Bettina Wistrom and Jorrit Zwijnenburg in the Statistics and Data Directorate; and the Statistical Editors and Content Management Team in the Press and Communications Directorate. Marie-Aurélie Elkurd at CTPA assisted with the production and publication of this report and Stephanie Coic in the Development Cooperation Directorate (DCD) designed the cover. The authors would also like to thank WP2 delegates and their colleagues working in national administrations for their input and comments.

Table of contents

FIGURES

TABLES

Executive Summary

In 2019, the average OECD tax-to-GDP ratio was 33.8%, a decrease of 0.1 percentage points since 2018. This is the first decrease in the OECD average tax-to-GDP ratio that has been observed since 2009, following the global financial crisis (GFC) in 2008 (except in 2017, which was an exceptional case due to the one-off stability contributions in Iceland in the preceding year). The most recent data on the structure of tax revenues in OECD countries shows that corporate tax revenues reached 10% of total tax revenues in 2018: this is the first time they have returned to this level since the GFC, although it remains lower than the pre-GFC peak of 11.5%.

In this publication, taxes are defined as compulsory, unrequited payments to the general government or to a supranational authority. They are unrequited in that the benefits provided by governments to taxpayers are not normally allocated in proportion to their payments. Taxes are classified by their base: income, profits and capital gains; payroll; property; goods and services; and other taxes. Compulsory social security contributions (SSCs) paid to general government are also treated as taxes. Revenues are analysed by level of government: federal or central; state; local; and social security funds. Detailed information on the classifications applied is set out in the Interpretative Guide in Annex A.

Tax levels in 2019

Across OECD countries, tax-to-GDP ratios in 2019 ranged from 16.5% in Mexico to 46.3% in Denmark. Between 2018 and 2019, the OECD average tax-to-GDP ratio decreased from 33.9% to 33.8%, due to falls in 15 countries that were larger, on average, than the increase in the remaining countries:

- The largest fall was seen in Hungary (1.7 percentage points), partially due to a decrease in corporate income taxes following the removal of the compulsory tax advance supplement on business taxes, as well as smaller decreases in a number of other taxes. Other large decreases were seen in Iceland (1.1 percentage points), Belgium and Sweden (1.0 percentage points in both countries). Eleven other countries had decreases of less than one percentage point.
- An increase in tax-to-GDP ratios from 2018 to 2019 is observed in the remaining 20 of the 35 countries for which preliminary 2019 data is available. The increase in the tax-to-GDP ratio was largest in Denmark (2.0 percentage points) due to higher than expected payments of income taxes in 2019. There were no other increases above one percentage point.

Across the last decade, 31 OECD countries reported higher tax-to-GDP ratios in 2019 than in 2009, with the greatest increases in Greece and the Slovak Republic (8.0 and 5.8 percentage points, respectively). Among the remaining six countries, tax levels in 2019 were more than five percentage points lower than in 2009 in Ireland and more than three percentage points lower in Hungary.

Tax structure in 2018

In 2018, the latest year in which final data is available for all countries, social security contributions (SSCs) amounted to the largest share of tax revenues in the OECD, at just over one-quarter (25.7%), on average. Together with personal income taxes (23.5%), these two tax types amounted to nearly one-half of tax revenues in OECD countries. Value Added Tax (VAT) accounted for a further one-fifth of total revenues (20.4%). Other consumption taxes and taxes on corporate income accounted for smaller shares of tax revenues (12.3% and 10.0% respectively), with property taxes (5.6%) and residual taxes accounting for the remaining share.

Since 2017, the average share of income taxes in total tax revenues has increased by 0.4 percentage points. This was largely due to increases in the share of corporate income taxes, which continued their recent upward trend from 9.2% of total tax revenues in 2014 and 2015, 9.4% in 2016, 9.7% in 2017 and 10.0% in 2018. However, this is still lower than the peak recorded share of corporate income taxes at 11.5% of total revenues in 2007. By contrast, the average share of tax revenues from taxes on goods and services decreased by 0.3 percentage points in 2018: although VAT revenues were unchanged at 20.4% of total revenues, excise tax revenues fell by 0.4 percentage points.

Changes by level of government

On average, subnational governments received a slightly higher share of tax revenues in 2018 relative to 2017. The central government's average share of revenues in 2018 fell from 53.7% to 53.4% of general government revenue in federal countries and from 63.6% to 63.5% in unitary countries. In federal countries, 25.1% of tax revenues were received at subnational level on average (ranging from 4.5% in Austria to 49.6% in Canada), with roughly two-thirds of revenues being received by state governments and one-third by local governments. In unitary countries, the share of local government revenues was 11.1% on average, ranging from less than 0.9% in Estonia to 35.1% in Sweden.

Consumption tax revenues under COVID-19

A special feature in this publication examines the drivers of recent changes in consumption tax revenues in OECD countries by disentangling their policy and macroeconomic drivers. It examines the global financial crisis of 2008 (GFC) to identify the channels through which consumption tax revenues are affected during an economic downturn and to provide initial insights into how the COVID-19 crisis and the policy actions taken in response to it will affect tax revenues.

It concludes that VAT systems are vulnerable to economic shocks, particularly if the crisis directly affects private consumption rather than investment. During the GFC, the level of consumption remained relatively stable, while consumption tax revenues decreased sharply due to a shift in consumer spending towards necessity goods and services and increases in government consumption – changes which have not since fully reversed. The COVID-19 crisis is likely to have an even bigger impact on consumption tax revenues than the GFC, because the current crisis has affected consumption directly and to a far greater extent as a result of lockdowns, including the forced closure of businesses in certain sectors (e.g. tourism and hospitality). Some of the other changes in consumption patterns observed in the current crisis mirror those from the 2008 crisis, including an increase in household spending on necessities and in government spending. As these areas of expenditure are often exempt from VAT, consumption tax revenues are expected to increase less than proportionally to the increase in government spending. Over time, it is expected that consumption tax revenues will gradually increase as a share of GDP and will return to their pre-crisis levels, as private spending returns to pre-crisis patterns and governments take action to restore lost revenues.

Consumption taxes will remain an important part of the toolkit that governments have to facilitate the economic and fiscal recovery after the COVID-19 crisis. In considering consumption tax policy after the crisis, governments may wish to give careful consideration to how the structure of their VAT systems will affect the resilience of their tax system and its revenues in future economic downturns. This will also require careful consideration of the complexity of VAT systems, and the likely behavioural and distributional impacts of any changes to improve resilience.

Introduction

The purpose of this annual publication is to provide internationally comparative data on tax levels and tax structures in member countries of the OECD. The taxes imposed in each country are presented in a standardised framework based upon the OECD classification of taxes and its Interpretative Guide as contained in Annex A to this Report.

The data for the Report has, for the most part, been provided by Delegates to Working Party No.2 on Tax Policy Analysis and Tax Statistics of the Committee on Fiscal Affairs. The OECD acknowledges the co-operation of the International Monetary Fund, whose classification of tax revenues — although in a number of respects less detailed — is in many respects similar to that of the OECD.[1] The most important of the other classifications currently in use is the System of National Accounts (henceforth referred to as SNA) and the European System of Integrated Economic Accounts of EU member states (henceforth referred to as ESA), which is primarily an elaboration of SNA, though differing from it in certain respects. Subject to a few exceptions, SNA/ESA figures can be reconciled with the figures in the present Report, since SNA criteria and definitions have been adopted unless the contrary is specifically indicated.

The material is organised in six chapters. Chapter 1 summarises tax trends of the past 50 years focusing in turn on tax-to-GDP ratios (section 1.1), tax structures (section 1.2) and taxes by level of government (section 1.3). Section 1.4 discusses the impact of alternate treatments of non-wastable tax credits and section 1.5 provides information on financing of social security-type benefits. This year's issue also carries in Chapter 2 a special feature on "Drivers of consumption tax revenues in OECD countries". Chapter 3 contains a set of comparative statistical tables for years 1965-2019. Chapter 4 provides country tables with tax revenue and tax-to-GDP ratios broken down by selected tax categories and by level of government for years between 1990 and 2018 (section 4.1).[2] Two memorandum tables show how countries finance their social benefits, and report taxes and social security contributions paid by general government (section 4.2). Chapter 5, which is available on line only provides statistical tables with a detailed breakdown of tax revenues by country for years between 1965 and 2018 (section 5.1). Two memorandum tables show how countries finance their social benefits, and report taxes and social security contributions paid by general government (section 5.2). Chapter 6, which is also only available on line, attributes tax revenues to general government by the following sub-sectors: central, state; local and social security funds. It contains a set of tables with a detailed breakdown of tax revenues by country for years between 1975 and 2018 (section 6.1).

Notes

[1] See IMF, *Government Finance Statistics Manual 2014* (Washington D.C.: International Monetary Fund, 2014).

[2] Because of space limitations, data are shown for selected years between 1965 and 2018. Data for years not shown are available online.

1 Tax revenue trends 1965-2019

Chapter 1 provides information on trends in tax revenues in OECD countries, including changes in tax-to-GDP ratios, tax structures, taxes by level of government and non-wastable tax credits.

Revenue Statistics 2020 presents detailed internationally comparable data on tax revenues of OECD countries for all levels of government. The latest edition provides final data on tax revenues in 1965-2018. In addition, provisional estimates of tax revenues in 2019 are included for almost all OECD countries.[1]

Box 1.1. Revenue Statistics in OECD Countries – definitions & classifications

In *Revenue Statistics 2020*, taxes are defined as compulsory, unrequited payments to the general government or to a supranational authority. Taxes are unrequited in the sense that benefits provided by government are not normally in proportion to their payments.

In the OECD classification, taxes are classified by the base of the tax:

- Income and profits (heading 1000)
- Compulsory social security contributions paid to general government, which are treated as taxes (heading 2000)
- Payroll and workforce (heading 3000)
- Property (heading 4000)
- Goods and services (heading 5000)
- Other (heading 6000)

Much greater detail on the tax concept, the classification of taxes and the accrual basis of reporting is set out in the OECD Interpretative Guide at annex A of *Revenue Statistics 2020*.

All of the averages presented in this summary are unweighted.

Tax-to-GDP ratios

Tax ratios for 2019 (provisional data)

New OECD data in the annual *Revenue Statistics 2020* publication show that on average, tax revenues as a percentage of GDP (i.e. the tax-to-GDP ratio) were 33.8% in 2019, a decrease of 0.1 percentage points (p.p.) of GDP relative to 2018. This is the first decrease observed in the OECD average since the impact of the global financial crisis in 2009 (excluding 2017, which was a special case due to the one-off stability contributions in Iceland in 2016).[2] Although the tax-to-GDP ratio increased in 20 of the countries for which 2019 data are available, the scale of the decrease in the remaining 15 countries was larger, leading to the decrease in the average. If the largest decrease, in Hungary, is excluded, the OECD average tax-to-GDP ratio would have remained unchanged.

Figure 1.1. Trends in tax-to-GDP ratios, 1965-2019p (as % of GDP)

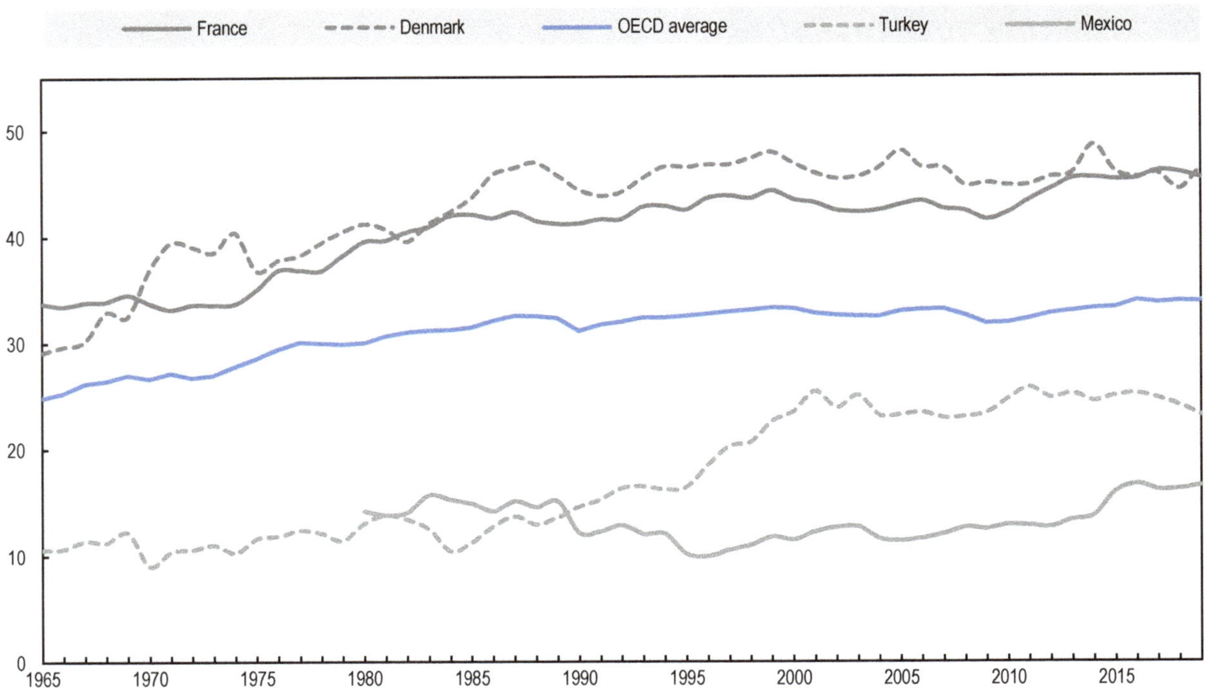

Notes: Data for 2019 are preliminary. The OECD average in 2019 is calculated by applying the unweighted average percentage change for 2019 in the 35 countries providing data for that year to the overall average tax to GDP ratio in 2018.
The 2016 OECD average tax-to-GDP ratio includes the one-off revenues from stability contributions in Iceland. Without these revenues included, the OECD average tax-to-GDP ratio in 2016 would have been 33.5%.
Source: Table 3.1.

StatLink https://doi.org/10.1787/888934209381

Table 1.1. Revenue Statistics: overview

	Tax revenue as % of GDP				Tax revenue as % of total tax revenue in 2018						
	2019p	2018	2017	2000	1100 Taxes on income, individuals (PIT)	1200 Taxes on income, corporates (CIT)	2000 Social security contributions (SSC)	4000 Taxes on property	5111 Value added taxes	Other consumption taxes[4]	All other taxes[5]
OECD - Average[1]	**33.8**	**33.9**	**33.7**	**33.3**	**23.5**	**10.0**	**25.7**	**5.6**	**20.4**	**12.3**	**2.4**
Australia	..	28.7	28.5	30.5	41.1	19.1	0.0	9.5	11.7	13.8	4.8
Austria	42.4	42.2	41.8	42.3	22.2	6.4	34.8	1.3	18.0	9.7	7.6
Belgium[2]	42.9	43.9	43.8	43.8	27.0	9.8	30.2	7.8	15.4	9.8	0.0
Canada	33.5	33.2	33.1	34.7	36.2	11.3	14.0	11.6	13.6	9.9	3.3
Chile	20.7	21.1	20.2	18.8	6.7	22.1	6.9	5.2	40.2	13.0	5.8
Colombia	19.7	19.3	19.0	15.7	6.4	25.5	9.6	8.0	29.4	13.4	7.7
Czech Republic	34.9	35.0	34.4	32.3	12.2	10.4	43.8	1.3	21.6	10.7	0.0
Denmark[2]	46.3	44.4	45.8	46.9	54.4	6.5	0.1	4.1	21.5	11.4	2.0
Estonia	33.1	32.9	32.5	31.0	16.5	6.1	34.9	0.7	27.3	14.5	0.0
Finland	42.2	42.4	42.9	45.8	28.9	6.0	27.9	3.4	21.6	12.2	0.0
France[2]	45.4	45.9	46.1	43.4	20.5	4.6	34.9	9.0	15.4	11.2	4.4
Germany	38.8	38.5	37.8	36.4	27.2	5.6	37.7	2.7	18.2	8.6	0.0
Greece	38.7	38.9	38.6	33.4	16.1	5.6	29.9	7.7	21.3	18.2	1.3
Hungary	35.8	37.5	38.3	38.6	14.6	3.6	31.6	2.6	25.8	18.9	2.8
Iceland	36.1	37.2	37.6	36.0	39.7	6.5	9.5	5.5	23.6	9.7	5.5
Ireland	22.7	22.7	22.8	30.8	31.2	14.2	17.3	5.8	19.3	11.5	0.8
Israel	30.5	30.9	32.5	34.8	20.6	10.4	16.8	10.3	24.2	12.2	5.6
Italy	42.4	41.9	41.9	40.5	25.6	4.5	31.0	6.1	14.8	13.9	4.1
Japan	..	32.0	31.4	25.8	19.1	12.9	40.2	8.1	12.8	6.7	0.3
Korea	27.4	26.8	25.4	20.9	18.4	15.7	25.4	11.6	15.3	11.0	2.6
Latvia	31.2	31.2	31.4	29.1	19.2	3.4	29.3	3.0	27.0	18.1	0.0
Lithuania[2]	30.3	30.2	29.5	30.8	13.5	5.1	42.1	1.0	25.8	12.6	0.0
Luxembourg[2]	39.2	39.7	37.6	36.9	23.5	15.9	27.1	9.7	15.4	8.3	0.1
Mexico[3]	16.5	16.2	16.1	11.5	21.2	21.3	13.4	2.0	24.3	12.1	5.7
Netherlands	39.3	38.8	38.7	36.9	20.5	9.0	36.0	4.0	17.6	12.6	0.3
New Zealand	32.3	32.9	31.6	32.5	37.5	15.6	0.0	5.8	29.6	8.3	3.2
Norway	39.9	39.6	38.8	41.7	25.3	16.4	25.5	3.1	21.3	8.2	0.1
Poland	35.4	35.2	34.1	32.9	15.1	5.9	37.2	3.7	23.1	14.1	0.8
Portugal	34.8	34.8	34.1	31.1	18.7	9.6	26.9	4.0	25.1	14.7	1.0
Slovak Republic	34.7	34.3	34.2	33.6	10.5	9.6	43.0	1.2	20.5	14.5	0.7
Slovenia	37.7	37.4	37.1	37.7	14.3	5.2	41.4	1.6	22.0	15.4	0.1
Spain	34.6	34.6	33.9	33.1	22.2	7.1	33.9	7.3	19.0	10.5	0.0
Sweden	42.9	43.9	44.3	48.8	29.4	6.5	21.8	2.2	21.0	7.1	12.0
Switzerland[2]	28.5	28.0	28.4	27.6	30.7	11.4	23.6	7.3	11.7	9.1	6.1
Turkey	23.1	24.0	24.7	23.5	15.4	8.7	29.9	4.3	19.8	20.7	1.1
United Kingdom	33.0	32.9	32.8	32.8	27.3	8.0	19.1	12.5	21.1	11.5	0.4
United States	24.5	24.4	26.7	28.3	41.1	4.1	24.9	12.3	0.0	17.6	0.0

1. 2019 provisional average calculated by applying the unweighted average percentage change for 2019 in the 35 countries providing data for that year to the overall average tax to GDP ratio in 2018.
2. The total tax revenue has been reduced by the amount of any capital transfer that represents uncollected taxes.
3. 2019 provisional: Secretariat estimate, including expected revenues collected by state and local governments.
4. Calculated as 5000 Taxes on goods and services less 5111 Value added taxes.
5. Includes 1300 Unallocable between personal and corporate income tax, 3000 Taxes on payroll and workforce and 6000 Other taxes.

StatLink https://doi.org/10.1787/888934209590

Country tax-to-GDP ratios in 2019 varied considerably (Table 1.1), both across countries and since 2018. Key observations include:

- Denmark had the highest tax-to-GDP ratio in 2019 (46.3%), and with the exceptions of 2017 and 2018, in which France was higher, has had the highest tax-to-GDP ratio of OECD countries since 2002. France had the second-highest tax-to-GDP ratio in 2019 (45.4%). Mexico had the lowest tax-to-GDP ratio (16.5%).
- Of the 35 countries for which data for 2019 are available, the ratio of tax revenues to GDP compared to 2018 rose in 20 and fell in 15.
- Between 2018 and 2019, the largest tax ratio increase was in Denmark, at 2.0 percentage points of GDP. This was due to an increase in income taxes (2.4 percentage points, offset by a fall in consumption tax revenues other than VAT). There were no other countries with increases of more than 1 percentage points. (Figure 1.2).
- The largest fall in the tax-to-GDP ratio between 2018 and 2019 was in Hungary, at 1.7 p.p.. The decrease in Hungary was due to a reduction in revenues from corporate income taxes (0.6 percentage points of GDP) following the removal of the compulsory tax advance supplement on business taxes, as well as smaller decreases in a number of other taxes, which increased in nominal terms by less than the rate of nominal GDP. This lead to a decrease across all categories as a share of GDP.
- Decreases of over one percentage points were also seen in Iceland (1.1 p.p.), Belgium and Sweden (1.0 p.p. each). In Belgium, this was due to decreases in personal and corporate income taxes. The decrease in corporate income taxes was the result of higher advance payments in 2017 and 2018 following an increase in the base rate of the tax surcharge in the event of insufficient advance payments. This temporarily inflated corporate tax revenues in 2017 and 2018, resulting in a decrease in 2019.

Figure 1.2. Changes in tax-to-GDP ratios, p.p., 2018-19p and 2009-19p

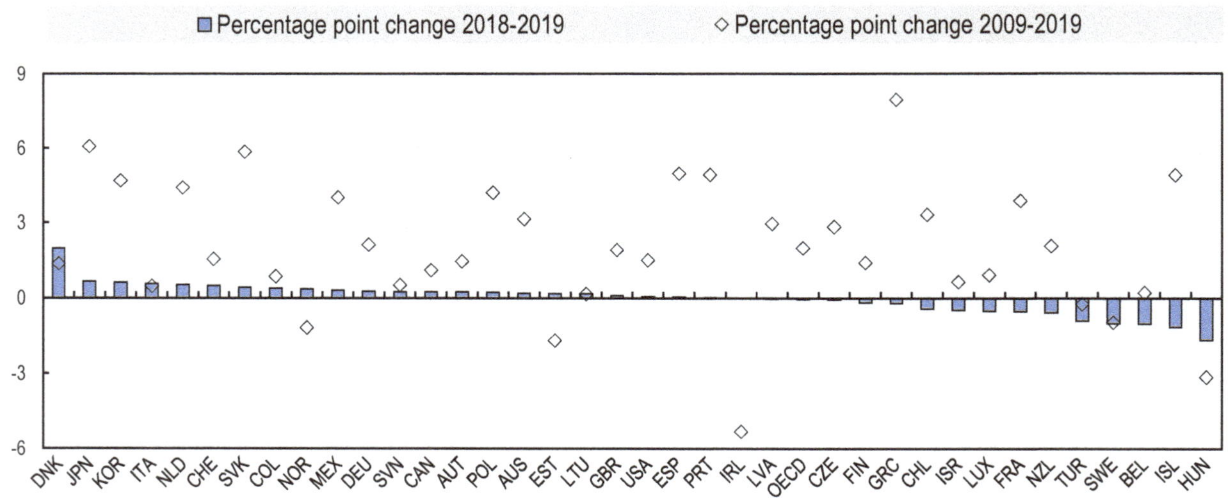

Note: Preliminary data for 2019 was not available for Australia and Japan. For these countries the comparison shown is 2017-2018 and 2009-2018 data.
Source: Secretariat calculations based on Table 3.1.

StatLink https://doi.org/10.1787/888934209400

Over a longer timeframe, the OECD average tax-to-GDP ratio was higher in 2019 than in 2009, when it was 31.8% of GDP on average. Across countries, the tax-to-GDP ratio was higher in 2019 than in 2009 in 31 countries. The largest increase was seen in Greece (8.0 percentage points) and increases of over 5 percentage points were also seen in Japan (2018 data) and the Slovak Republic. Decreases since 2009 were seen in the remaining 6 countries. The largest fall has been in Ireland, from 28.0% in 2009 to 22.7% of GDP in 2019, largely due to the exceptional increase in GDP in 2015. The next largest decrease was seen in Hungary (3.1 percentage points) (Figure 1.2).

Changes in the tax-to-GDP ratio are driven by the relative changes in nominal tax revenues and in nominal GDP. From one year to the next, if tax revenues rise more than GDP (or fall less than GDP) the tax-to-GDP ratio will increase. Conversely, if tax revenues rise less than GDP, or fall further, the tax-to-GDP ratio will go down. Therefore, the tax-to-GDP ratio does not necessarily mean that the amount of tax revenues have increased in nominal, or even real, terms.

In 2019, 20 OECD countries had an increase in their tax-to-GDP ratio relative to 2018. In all of these countries, GDP growth was positive, although to a lesser degree than tax revenue growth. Of the 15 OECD countries that experienced a decline in their tax-to-GDP ratio in 2019, thirteen had higher levels of tax revenues in nominal terms than the preceding year, but the increase in nominal tax revenues was less than the increase in nominal GDP levels. One country (New Zealand) had positive nominal GDP growth and negative tax revenue growth; no countries experienced declines in nominal GDP (Figure 1.3). In Figure 1.3, changes between 2017 and 2018 are shown for Australia and Japan, where the tax-to-GDP ratio is not available in 2019. In both countries, nominal tax revenues grew faster than GDP, leading to increases in the tax-to-GDP ratio.

Box 1.2. Methodology: the tax-to-GDP ratio

The tax-to-GDP ratios shown in *Revenue Statistics 2020* express aggregate tax revenues as a percentage of GDP. The value of this ratio depends on its denominator (GDP) as well as its numerator (tax revenue), and that the denominator – GDP – is subject to historical revision.

The numerator (tax revenue)

- For the numerator, the OECD Secretariat uses revenue figures that are submitted annually by correspondents from national Ministries of Finance, Tax Administrations or National Statistics Offices. Although provisional figures for most countries become available with a lag of about six months, finalised data become available with a lag of around one and a half years. Final revenue data for 2018 were received during the period May-August 2020.
- In thirty-four OECD countries the reporting year coincides with the calendar year. Three countries — Australia, Japan and New Zealand — have different reporting years. Reporting year 2018 includes Q2/2018–Q1/2019 (Japan) and Q3/2018–Q2/2019 (Australia, New Zealand) respectively (Q = quarter).

The denominator (GDP)

- For the denominator, the GDP figures used for *Revenue Statistics 2020* are the most recently available in September 2020. By that time, the 2018 and 2019 GDP figures were available for all OECD countries.
- Using these GDP figures ensures a maximum of consistency and international comparability for the reported tax-to-GDP ratios.
- The GDP figures are based on the OECD Annual National Accounts (ANA – SNA) for the thirty-four OECD countries where the reporting year is the actual calendar year.
- Where the reporting year differs from the calendar year, the annual GDP estimates are obtained by aggregating quarterly GDP estimates provided by the OECD Statistics Directorate for those quarters corresponding to each country's fiscal (tax) year.

The average shown in this publication is an unweighted average for all countries in which data is available. The 2019 provisional average calculated by applying the unweighted average percentage change for 2019 in the 35 countries providing data for that year to the overall average tax to GDP ratio in 2018. The historical series for the OECD average shown in this publication is lower than that shown in previous editions due to the inclusion of Colombia in the OECD average for the first time in this edition, after Colombia became an OECD member in April 2020.

Figure 1.3. Relative changes in nominal tax revenues and nominal GDP (%), 2018-19p

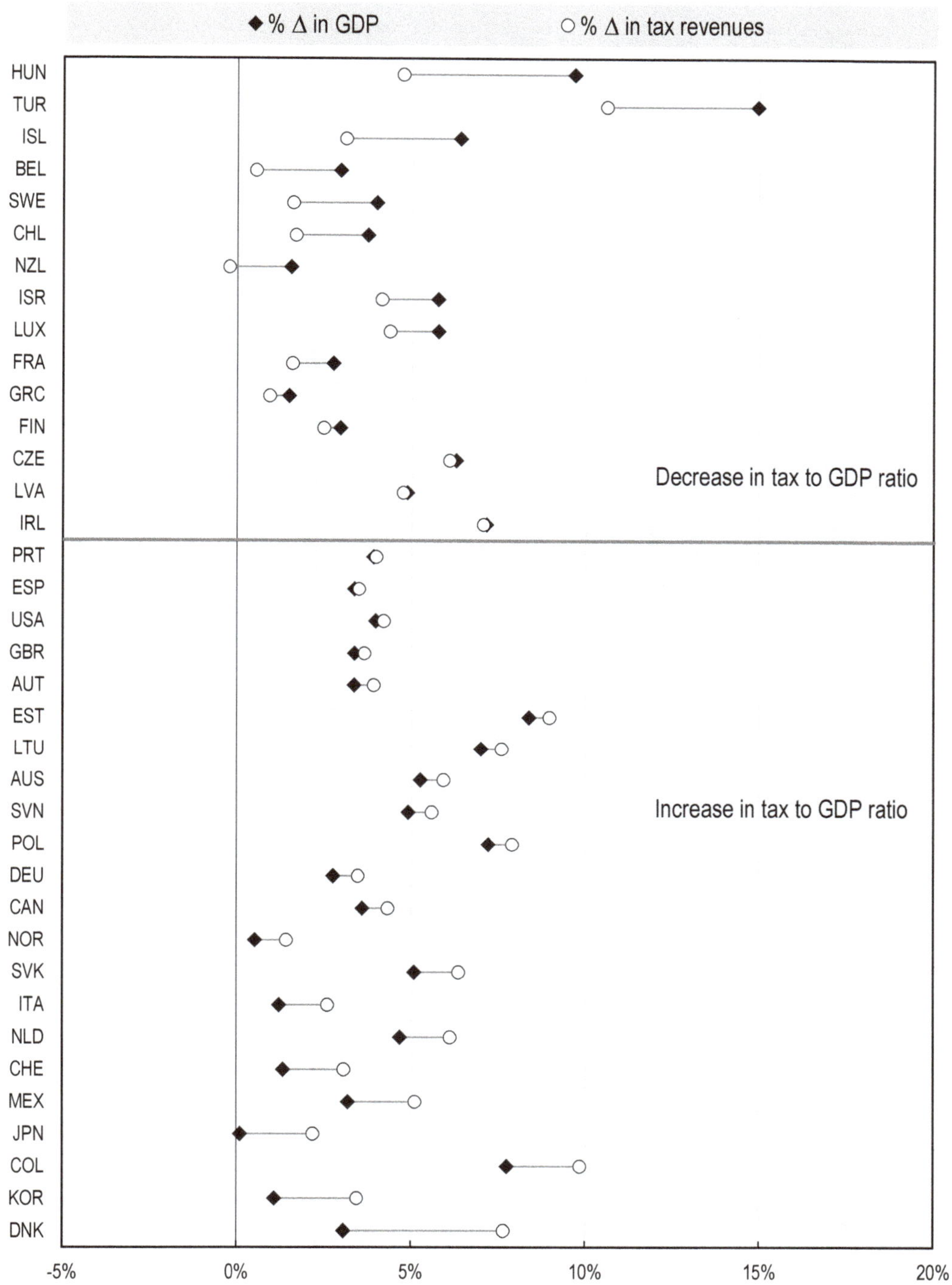

Note: Data for Australia and Japan show the change between 2017 and 2018, as preliminary data for 2019 was not available for Australia and Japan. Data for Mexico in 2019 show a Secretariat estimate, including expected revenues collected by state and local governments.
Source: Secretariat calculations based on chapter 4 (tax revenues) and table 3.19 (GDP).

StatLink https://doi.org/10.1787/888934209419

Figure 1.4. Tax to GDP ratios in 2018 and 2019p (as % of GDP)

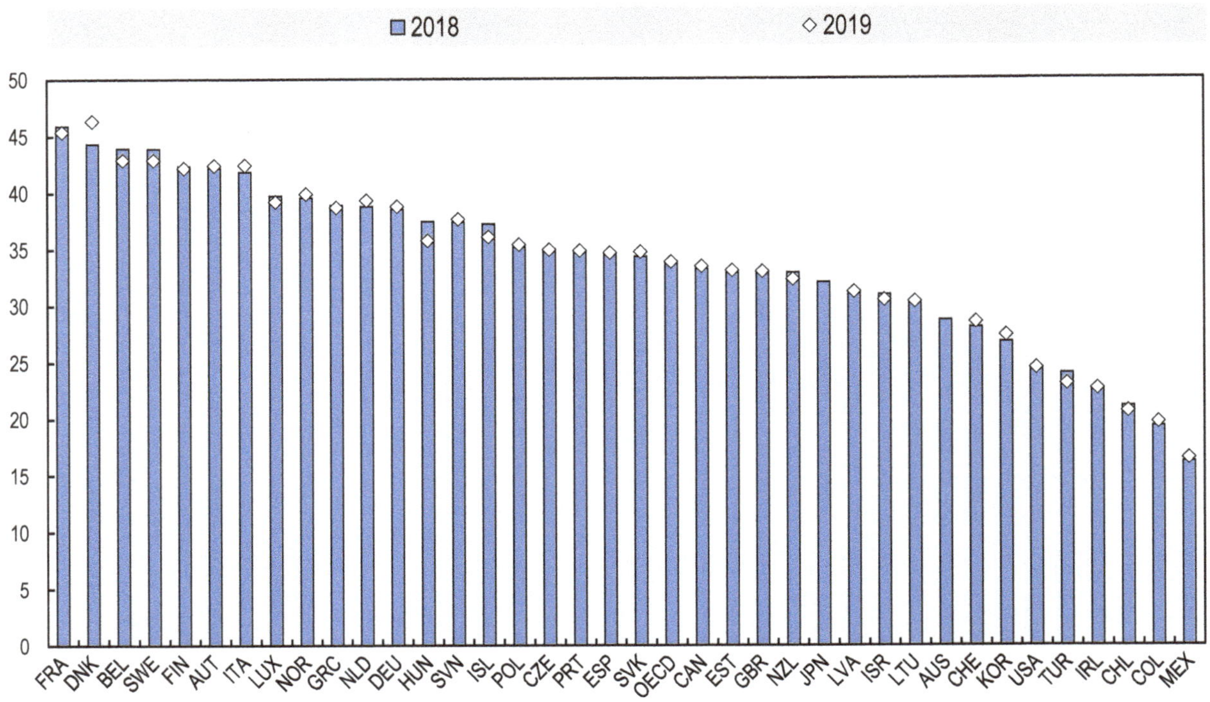

Note: Preliminary data for 2019 were not available for Australia and Japan.
Source: Secretariat calculations based on Table 3.1

StatLink https://doi.org/10.1787/888934209438

Tax-to-GDP ratios for 2018 (final data)

The latest year for which tax-to-GDP ratios are based on final revenue data and available for all OECD countries is 2018 (Figure 1.4). These data show that tax ratios vary considerably across countries:

- In 2018, France had the highest tax-to-GDP ratio (45.9%), followed by Denmark (44.4%). Five other countries also had tax-to-GDP ratios above 40% (Belgium, Sweden, Finland, Italy and Austria).
- Mexico had the lowest ratio at 16.2% followed by Colombia (19.3%), Chile (21.1%), Ireland (22.7%) Turkey (24.0%) and the United States (24.4%). No other countries had a tax-to-GDP ratio of less than 25% in 2018, but three other countries had ratios below 30% (Korea, Switzerland and Australia).
- The tax-to-GDP ratio in the OECD area as a whole (un-weighted average) was 33.9% in 2018. In 2017, it was 33.7%.
- Relative to 2017, overall tax ratios rose in 24 OECD member countries and fell in 13.
- The largest increases in the tax-to-GDP ratio were in Luxembourg (2.1 percentage points), Korea (1.4 p.p.), New Zealand (1.3 p.p.) and Poland (1.0 p.p.).
- The largest reductions were in the United States (2.3 p.p.), Israel (1.6 p.p.) and Denmark (1.5 p.p.).

Between 2017 and 2018, the key changes in the average tax-to-GDP ratio were driven by increases in revenues from income taxes (both personal and corporate income taxes), social security contributions and value-added taxes (0.1 p.p. each), offset by a fall in property tax revenues (0.1 p.p.).

Table 1.2. Tax structures in the OECD area, selected years (unweighted average as % of GDP)

Per cent

	1965	1990	2000	2007	2010	2015	2016	2017	2018
Total tax revenue	24.8	31.1	33.3	33.2	31.9	33.3	34.0	33.7	33.9
1000 Taxes on income, profits and capital gains	8.7	11.8	11.7	11.9	10.4	11.1	11.1	11.4	11.5
of which:									
1100 Taxes on income, profits and capital gains of individuals	6.8	9.3	8.5	8.0	7.4	8.1	8.0	8.1	8.1
1200 Taxes on income, profits and capital gains of corporates	2.1	2.4	3.2	3.6	2.7	2.8	2.9	3.0	3.1
2000 Social security contributions (SSC)	4.5	7.1	8.4	8.3	8.7	8.8	9.0	8.9	9.0
3000 Taxes on payroll and workforce	0.3	0.3	0.4	0.3	0.3	0.4	0.4	0.4	0.4
4000 Taxes on property	1.9	1.7	1.7	1.8	1.7	1.9	2.3	1.9	1.9
5000 Taxes on goods and services	9.4	9.9	10.8	10.7	10.6	10.9	11.0	11.0	10.9
of which:									
5111 Value added taxes	0.4	5.1	6.3	6.5	6.4	6.7	6.7	6.8	6.8
5121 Excises	3.5	2.6	2.8	2.6	2.6	2.5	2.6	2.5	2.4
6000 Other Taxes	0.1	0.3	0.2	0.2	0.2	0.2	0.2	0.1	0.1

Note: Percentage share of major tax categories in GDP. Data are included from 1965 onwards for Australia, Austria, Belgium, Canada, Denmark, Finland, France, Germany, Greece, Iceland, Ireland, Italy, Japan, Luxembourg, the Netherlands, New Zealand, Norway, Portugal, Spain, Sweden, Switzerland, Turkey, United Kingdom and United States; from 1972 for Korea; from 1980 for Mexico; from 1990 for Chile and Colombia; from 1991 for Hungary and Poland; from 1993 for the Czech Republic and from 1995 for Estonia, Israel, Latvia, Lithuania, the Slovak Republic and Slovenia. The figures for the 2016 OECD average includes the one-off revenues from stability contributions in Iceland.
Source: OECD (2020), "Revenue Statistics: Comparative tables", OECD Tax Statistics (database), DOI: http://dx.doi.org/10.1787/data-00262-en.

StatLink https://doi.org/10.1787/888934209609

Tax ratio changes between 1965 and 2018

Between 1965 and 2018, the average tax-to-GDP ratio in the OECD area increased from 24.8% to 33.9% (an increase of 9.0 percentage points, with the difference due to rounding) (Figure 1.1).

Before the first oil shock (1973 to 1974), strong, almost uninterrupted income growth enabled tax levels to rise in all OECD countries. In part, tax levels rose automatically through the effect of fiscal drag on personal income tax schedules. From 1975 to 1985, the tax burden in the OECD area increased by 2.9 percentage points. After the mid-1970s, the combination of slower real income growth and higher levels of unemployment apparently limited the revenue raising capacity of governments. But during and after the deep recession following the second oil shock (1980), countries in Europe saw tax levels rise further, to finance higher spending on social security and rein in budget deficits.

After the mid-1980s, most OECD countries substantially reduced the statutory rates of their personal and corporate income tax, but the negative revenue impact of widespread tax reforms was often offset by reducing or abolishing tax reliefs. By 1999, the average OECD tax-to-GDP ratio had risen to 33.3%, the highest recorded level at that time. It fell back slightly between 2001 and 2004, but then rose again between 2005 and 2007 before falling back following the crisis. Taking these changes together the average tax level in the OECD area increased by 1.3 percentage points between 1995 and 2018 (Figure 1.1).

The OECD average conceals the great variety in national tax-to-GDP ratios. In 1965, tax-to-GDP ratios in OECD countries ranged from 10.6% in Turkey to 33.7% in France. By 2018 the corresponding range was from 16.2% in Mexico to 45.9% in France. The trend towards higher tax levels over this period reflects the need to finance a significant increase of public sector outlays in almost all OECD countries.

Tax structures

Tax structures are measured by the share of major taxes in total tax revenue. In 2018, the tax structures of OECD countries varied. Sixteen countries raised the largest part of their revenues from income taxes (both corporate and personal), twelve countries raised the largest part of their revenues from SSCs, and nine countries raised the largest part of their revenues from consumption taxes (including VAT). Taxes on property and payroll taxes played a smaller role in the revenue systems of OECD countries in 2018, both on average and within most countries (Figure 1.5).

Figure 1.5. Tax structures in 2018 (as % of total tax revenue)

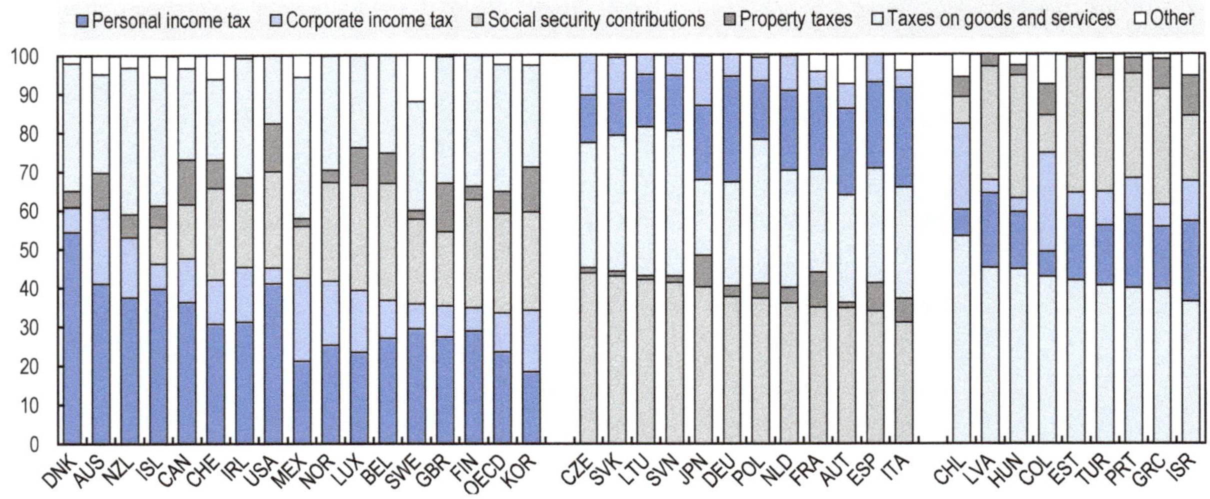

Note: Countries are grouped and ranked by those where income tax revenues (personal and corporate) form the highest share of total tax revenues, followed by those where social security contributions, or taxes on goods and services, form the highest share.
Source: Secretariat calculations based on data in chapter 4.

StatLink https://doi.org/10.1787/888934209457

While on average tax levels have generally been rising, the tax structure or tax 'mix' has been remarkably stable over time. Nevertheless, several trends have emerged up to 2018 – the latest year for which data is available for all 37 OECD countries. These trends are discussed further below.

Taxes on income and profits

On average, in 2018, OECD countries collected 34.3% of their tax revenues through taxes on income and profits (personal and corporate income taxes taken together). Taxes on personal and corporate incomes remain the most important source of revenues used to finance public spending in 16 OECD countries, and in eleven of them – Australia, Canada, Denmark, Iceland, Ireland, Luxembourg, Mexico, New Zealand, Norway, Switzerland and the United States – the share of income taxes in the tax mix in 2018 exceeded 40%.

Figure 1.6. Trends in tax structures (1965-2018, as % of total tax revenue)

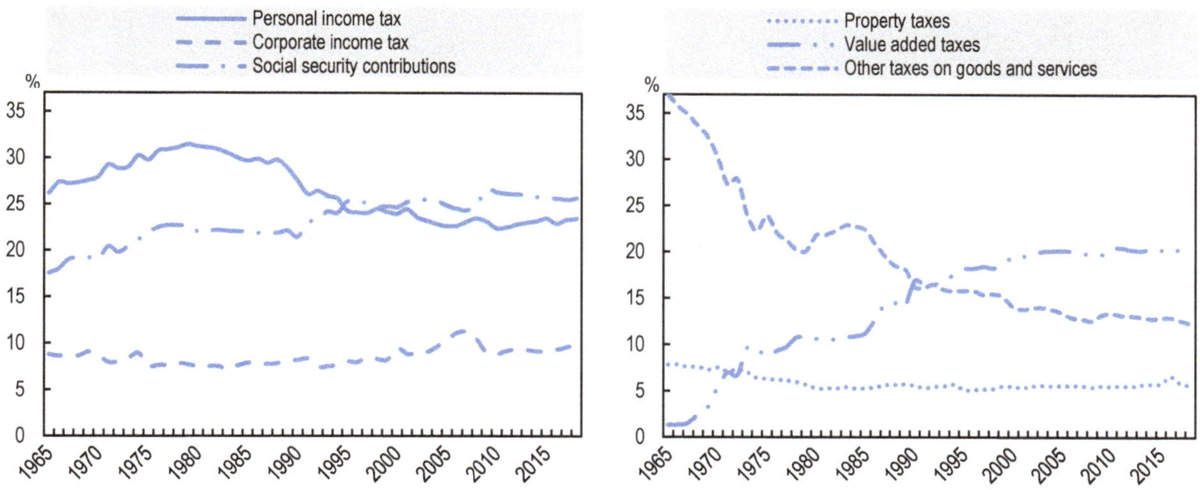

Note: The OECD average tax revenue in 2016 from main categories includes the one-off revenues from stability contributions in Iceland. This predominately affects the average revenues from property taxes, as a percentage of total tax revenues, in that year only.
Source: Secretariat calculations based on tables 3.8 to 3.14.

StatLink https://doi.org/10.1787/888934209476

Within taxes on income and profits, the share of PIT and CIT varies:

- Revenues from personal income taxes are 23.5% of total taxes on average in 2018 compared with around 30% in the 1980s. About two percentage points of this reduction can be attributed to the impact on the average of a number of relatively new entrants to the OECD from Eastern Europe for which tax revenue data is only available from the 1990s onwards. These countries tend to have relatively low personal income tax revenues and high revenues from social security contributions, but this impact is observed in the post 1990 data only.
- The variation in the share of the personal income tax between countries is considerable. In 2018, it ranged from a low of 6.4% in Colombia to 41.1% in Australia and the United States, and 54.4% in Denmark (Figure 1.5).
- Corporate income tax revenues represented between 7% and 9% of total tax revenues, on average, throughout the period 1965 to 2003. They then increased to a high of 11.3% in 2007, before dropping to 8.9% in 2010, directly after the financial crisis. They remained at between 9.0% and 10.0% of total revenues until 2018, when they were 10.0% of total tax revenues, on average.
- The share of the corporate income tax in total tax revenues varied considerably across countries from less than 5% (France, Hungary, Italy, Latvia and the United States) to over 20% in Mexico (21.3%), Chile (22.1%) and Colombia (25.5%) in 2018. Apart from the spread in statutory rates of the corporate income tax, these differences are at least partly explained by institutional and country specific factors, for example:
  - the degree to which firms in a country are incorporated,
  - the breadth of the corporate income tax base, for example some narrowing may occur as a consequence of generous depreciation schemes and of tax incentives,
  - the degree of cyclicality of the corporate tax system, for which one of the important elements are loss offset provisions,
  - the extent of reliance upon tax revenues from the exploitation of oil and/or mineral deposits, and

- other instruments to postpone the taxation of earned profits.

Social security contributions

Social security contributions as a share of total tax revenues on average across the OECD accounted for 25.7% in 2018. They were highest in the Czech Republic and the Slovak Republic (43.8% and 43.0%, respectively). In contrast, Australia and New Zealand do not levy social security contributions.

There is also wide variation across OECD countries in the relative proportions of social security contributions paid by employees and employers (Figure 1.7):

- Nine countries (Chile, Denmark, Greece, Israel, Japan, Luxembourg, the Netherlands, Poland, and Slovenia) raise more revenues from employee SSCs, whereas the remainder raise more from employer SSCs.
- The highest share of employee SSC revenues are found in Slovenia, at 20.4% of total revenues. Germany, Greece, Hungary, Japan and Poland also have employee SSC revenues of over 15% of total tax revenues. Denmark had the lowest share, at 0.1% of total revenues. Apart from Denmark, only Estonia had revenues from employee SSCs of less than 5% of total revenues.
- The highest share of employer social security contribution revenues are found in Estonia, at 33.2% of total revenues. Lithuania (28.5%), the Czech Republic (28.1%) and the Slovak Republic (25.6%) also had employer SSC revenues of over 25% of total tax revenues. Denmark and Chile had the lowest shares, at 0.03% and 0.2% of total revenues respectively.
- The highest share of self-employed or non-employed social security contribution revenues are found in the Netherlands and Poland, at 8.5% and 7.1% of total revenues respectively.

Figure 1.7. Composition of social security contributions, as % of total social security contributions, 2018

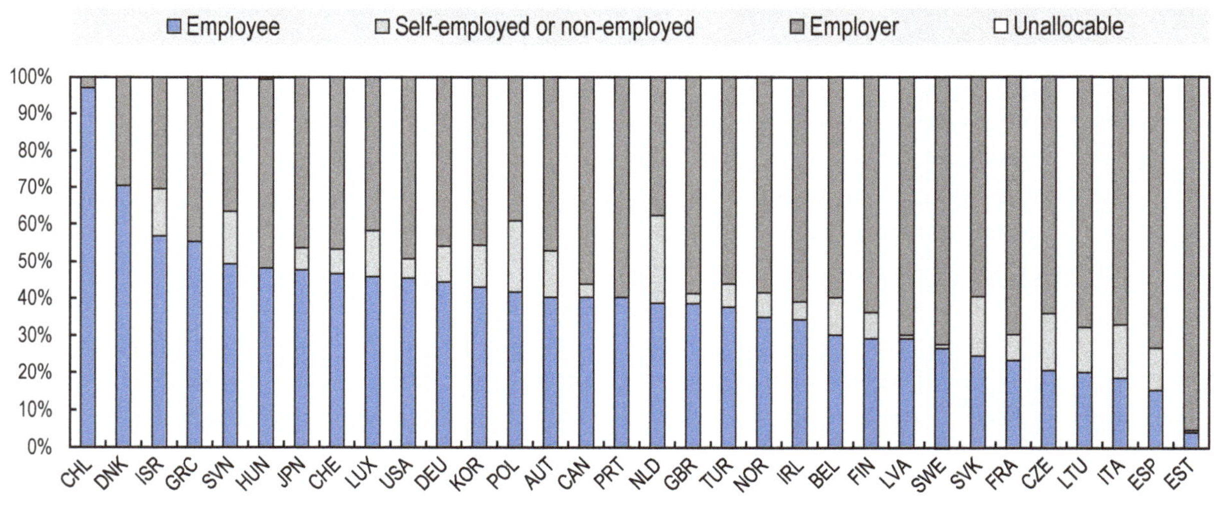

Note: Australia, Colombia, Iceland, Mexico and New Zealand are not included within figure 1.7. Although Colombia, Iceland and Mexico collect social security contributions, disaggregated data is not available. New Zealand and Australia do not levy social security contributions.
Source: Secretariat calculations based on data in chapter 4.

StatLink https://doi.org/10.1787/888934209495

Property taxes

Between 1965 and 2018, the share of taxes on property fell from 7.9% to 5.6% of total tax revenues on average across the OECD (Figure 1.6). Canada, Israel, Korea, the United Kingdom and the United States had property tax revenues that amounted to more than 10% of total tax revenues. By contrast, property taxes accounted for 0.7% of total revenues in Estonia, and were also less than 2% in Austria, the Czech Republic, Lithuania, Slovenia and the Slovak Republic.

Consumption taxes

- The share of taxes on consumption (general consumption taxes plus specific consumption taxes) fell from 38.4% to 32.7% between 1965 and 2018 (Figure 1.6).
- During this period, the composition of taxes on goods and services has fundamentally changed. A fast-growing revenue source has been general consumption taxes, especially the value-added tax (VAT) which is imposed in thirty-six of the thirty-seven OECD countries.[3]
- General consumption taxes presently account for 21.2% of total tax revenue, compared with only 11.5% in the mid-1960s. In 2018, the vast majority of this was from VAT (20.4% of total tax revenues) (Figure 1.6)
- The substantially increased importance of the value-added tax has served to counteract the diminishing share of specific consumption taxes, such as excises and custom duties.
- Between 1975 and 2018 the share of specific taxes on consumption (mostly on tobacco, alcoholic drinks and fuels, as well as some environment-related taxes) have almost halved from 17.7% to 9.6% of total revenues. In 2018, excises were the largest single category of total revenues, accounting for 7.2% of total revenues (Figure 1.8).
- Rates of taxes on imported goods were considerably reduced across all OECD countries, reflecting a global trend to remove trade barriers.
- Nevertheless, countries such as Estonia, Greece, Hungary, Latvia Mexico, Poland, Portugal, the Slovak Republic, and Slovenia (between 12-13%) and Turkey (around 19%) still collect a relatively large proportion of their tax revenues through taxes on specific goods and services.

Taxes by level of government

This section discusses the relative share of tax revenues attributed to the various sub-sectors of general government in 2018. The different sub-sectors are:

- Central government
- State government (federal and regional countries only)
- Local government
- Social security funds
- Supranational authorities (EU countries only)

The guidelines for attributing these revenue shares to the different levels of government are based on the final version of the 2008 System of National Accounts. These guidelines are discussed in the special feature S.1 in the 2011 edition of OECD *Revenue Statistics*.

Figure 1.8. Share of general consumption tax revenues (left panel) and specific consumption revenues (right panel) as % of total revenues, 1975-2018

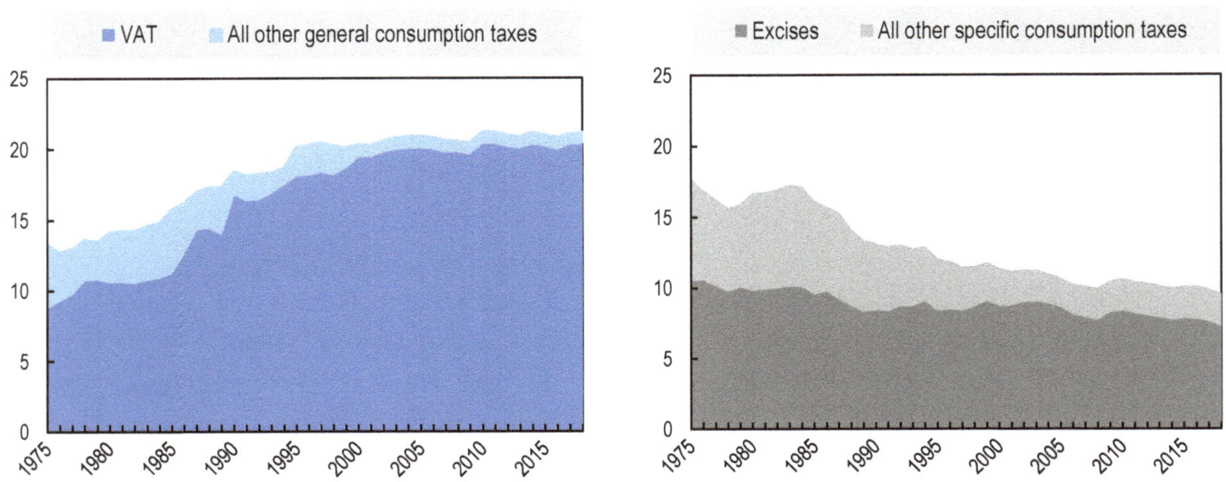

Note: The unweighted average for each year includes all countries which report revenue in the categories shown in that year. The OECD averages for 2016 include the one-off revenues from stability contributions in Iceland.
Source: Secretariat calculations based on chapter 4.

StatLink https://doi.org/10.1787/888934209514

Revenues of sub-national governments in federal and unitary countries

Eight OECD countries have a federal structure. Among these countries, central governments received 53.4% of total revenues in 2018 on average. The second-highest share of revenues on average was received by social security funds, which are a sub-sector of general government, at 21.2% of total revenues, followed by 17.5% at the state level and 7.7% at the local level (Table 1.3). However, within countries there was considerable variation around these means:

- In 2018, the share of central government receipts in the eight federal OECD countries varied from 29.5% in Germany to 81.2% in Australia.
- In 2018, the share of the states varied from 1.6% in Austria, 4.0% in Mexico and 10.2% in Belgium to 39.5% in Canada. The share of local government varied from 1.6% in Mexico to 15.2% in the United States and 15.5% in Switzerland.
- Between 1975 and 2018 the share of federal government revenues declined by nearly thirteen percentage points in Belgium and by around six percentage points in Canada and the United States.
- The share of federal government revenues increased in Austria by around 14 percentage points. There was little change in Australia and Mexico.
- Of the seven federal countries with social security funds, five increased the share of revenue between 1975 and 2018. The exceptions were Canada and Mexico, where the share slightly declined between 1975 (1980 for Mexico due to data availability) and 2018.

Colombia and Spain are classified as regional rather than unitary countries because of their highly decentralised political structure, and have very different compositions by level of government. In Colombia, the share of central government receipts was 73.2% in 2018, with regional governments receiving 5.0% of total revenues and local governments receiving 12.3%. In Spain, the share of central government receipts in 2018 was 41.7% compared with 15.3% for regional governments and 9.3% for local governments.

Table 1.3. Attribution of tax revenues to sub-sectors of general government as % of total tax revenue, federal countries

Per cent

	Supranational			Central government			State or Regional government			Local government			Social Security Funds		
	1975	1995	2018	1975	1995	2018	1975	1995	2018	1975	1995	2018	1975	1995	2018
Federal countries															
Australia	..	..	..	80.1	77.5	81.2	15.7	19.0	15.5	4.2	3.4	3.4	0.0	0.0	0.0
Austria	..	0.4	0.4	51.7	64.7	65.8	10.6	1.8	1.6	12.4	4.1	3.0	25.3	29.0	29.2
Belgium[1]	1.4	1.0	0.9	65.3	60.1	52.5	..	1.8	10.2	4.4	4.8	4.6	28.8	32.2	31.7
Canada	..	..	..	47.6	39.1	41.5	32.5	37.1	39.5	9.9	9.8	10.0	10.0	14.0	8.9
Germany	1.2	0.6	0.5	33.5	31.4	29.5	22.3	21.6	23.6	9.0	7.4	8.6	34.0	39.0	37.7
Mexico	..	..	..	..	73.9	80.9	..	2.8	4.0	..	1.5	1.6	..	21.8	13.4
Switzerland[1]	..	..	..	30.7	31.4	35.9	27.0	24.2	24.9	20.3	17.6	15.5	22.0	26.8	23.6
United States	..	..	..	45.4	41.4	39.3	19.5	20.0	20.6	14.7	13.3	15.2	20.5	25.2	24.9
Unweighted average	1.3	0.7	0.6	50.6	52.4	53.4	21.3	16.0	17.5	10.7	7.7	7.7	20.1	23.5	21.2
Regional countries															
Colombia[2]	..	..	..	..	63.2	73.2	..	5.5	5.0	..	8.6	12.3	..	22.7	9.6
Spain[2]	..	0.8	0.6	48.2	51.1	41.7	..	5.0	15.3	4.3	8.6	9.3	47.5	34.6	33.1

1. The total tax revenue has been reduced by the amount of any capital transfer that represents uncollected taxes.
2. Colombia and Spain are not constitutionally federal countries, but both have a highly decentralised political structure, with high autonomy of their territorial entities.

StatLink https://doi.org/10.1787/888934209628

The remaining twenty-seven OECD countries have a unitary structure. In these countries, an average of 63.5% of revenues were derived at the central level, with 25.0% accounted for by social security funds. A further 11.1% were raised by local governments. Among unitary OECD countries:

- The share of central government receipts in 2018 varied from 33.6% in France to 93.4% in New Zealand.
- The local government share varied from 0.8% in Estonia to 35.1% in Sweden.
- Between 1975 and 2018 there have been shifts to local government of 5 percentage points or more in six countries – France, Iceland, Italy, Korea, Portugal and Sweden and a smaller increase in the Netherlands. Shifts of 5 percentage points or more in the other direction occurred in three countries – Ireland, Norway and the United Kingdom.[4]
- Between 1975 and 2018, there were increases in the share of social security funds of 7 or more percentage points in four countries – Finland, France, Japan and Korea and corresponding decreases in four other countries – Italy, Norway, Portugal and Sweden.

Table 1.4. Attribution of tax revenues to sub-sectors of general government as % of total tax revenue, unitary countries

Per cent

	Supranational			Central government			State or Regional government			Local government			Social Security Funds		
	1975	1995	2018	1975	1995	2018	1975	1995	2018	1975	1995	2018	1975	1995	2018
Unitary countries															
Chile	..	..	..	..	89.9	86.4	..	..	..	..	6.5	7.9	..	3.6	5.7
Czech Republic	..	..	0.4	..	57.7	54.7	..	..	..	..	0.9	1.0	..	41.4	43.8
Denmark[1]	1.0	0.5	0.3	69.1	68.2	72.7	..	..	..	29.8	31.3	27.0	0.1	0.0	0.0
Estonia	..	..	0.6	..	84.3	82.1	..	..	..	..	0.8	0.8	..	14.9	16.5
Finland	..	0.4	0.2	56.0	46.6	49.2	..	..	..	23.5	22.3	22.7	20.4	30.8	27.9
France[1]	0.7	0.7	0.4	51.2	42.5	33.6	..	..	..	7.6	11.0	13.5	40.6	45.8	52.5
Greece	..	0.6	0.5	67.1	66.3	67.2	..	..	..	3.4	2.0	2.4	29.5	31.0	30.0
Hungary	..	..	0.4	..	63.8	61.7	..	..	..	..	2.5	5.8	..	33.6	32.2
Iceland	..	..	..	81.3	79.2	72.5	..	..	..	18.7	20.8	27.6	0.0	0.0	0.0
Ireland	2.3	1.5	0.6	77.4	83.1	82.8	..	..	..	7.3	2.7	2.1	13.1	12.7	14.5
Israel	..	..	..	..	79.6	75.3	..	..	..	..	6.4	7.9	..	14.0	16.8
Italy	..	0.4	0.5	53.2	62.7	56.8	..	..	..	0.9	5.4	11.7	45.9	31.5	31.0
Japan	..	..	..	45.5	41.2	36.6	..	..	..	25.6	25.2	23.2	29.0	33.6	40.2
Korea	..	..	..	89.0	69.2	58.0	..	..	..	10.1	18.7	16.6	0.9	12.1	25.4
Latvia	..	..	0.7	..	43.5	52.8	..	..	..	..	19.5	18.1	..	36.9	28.4
Lithuania[1]	..	..	0.9	..	71.7	55.9	..	..	..	..	2.3	1.2	..	26.1	42.1
Luxembourg[1]	0.8	0.4	0.6	63.6	66.4	68.4	..	..	..	6.7	6.5	4.5	29.0	26.6	26.4
Netherlands	1.5	1.3	1.1	58.9	56.0	59.4	..	..	..	1.2	3.1	3.5	38.4	39.5	36.0
New Zealand	..	..	..	92.3	94.7	93.4	..	..	..	7.7	5.3	6.6	0.0	0.0	0.0
Norway	..	..	..	50.6	57.6	84.7	..	..	..	22.4	20.0	15.3	27.0	22.4	0.0
Poland	..	..	0.5	..	61.2	49.5	..	..	..	..	8.5	12.7	..	30.3	37.2
Portugal	..	0.8	0.5	65.4	72.3	66.8	..	..	..	0.0	5.4	7.2	34.6	21.5	25.4
Slovak Republic	..	..	0.5	..	62.6	56.0	..	..	..	..	1.3	1.8	..	36.1	41.7
Slovenia	..	..	0.4	..	50.5	49.7	..	..	..	..	6.2	9.0	..	43.3	40.9
Sweden	..	0.8	0.6	51.3	46.8	52.2	..	..	..	29.2	30.8	35.1	19.5	21.6	12.1
Turkey	..	..	..	..	75.1	60.5	..	..	..	..	12.8	9.6	..	12.1	29.9
United Kingdom	1.0	1.0	0.5	70.5	77.5	75.3	..	..	..	11.1	3.7	5.1	17.5	17.8	19.1
Unweighted average	1.2	0.4	0.5	65.2	65.6	63.5	..	..	..	12.8	10.4	11.1	21.6	23.7	25.0

1. The total tax revenue has been reduced by the amount of any capital transfer that represents uncollected taxes.

StatLink https://doi.org/10.1787/888934209647

Composition of central and sub central revenues

Figure 1.9 shows the revenues from each major category of tax revenue for central and sub central governments. For federal and regional countries, the sub central level includes revenues received by both state and local governments. Figure 1.9 demonstrates that:

- Central government revenues in almost all OECD countries are predominantly derived from income and goods and services taxes, with a negligible share from property taxes.
- At the subnational level, revenue from property taxes provides a much larger share of revenues than at the central level, and accounts for over 90% of revenues in four countries (Israel, Ireland, Greece and the United Kingdom).

- By contrast, the share of income taxes and goods and services taxes is lower at the sub-central level, the exceptions being Finland, Luxembourg and Sweden, where over 90% of sub-central revenues are derived from income taxes.

Figure 1.9. Composition of revenues of federal or central government (left) and sub-national government (right), 2018

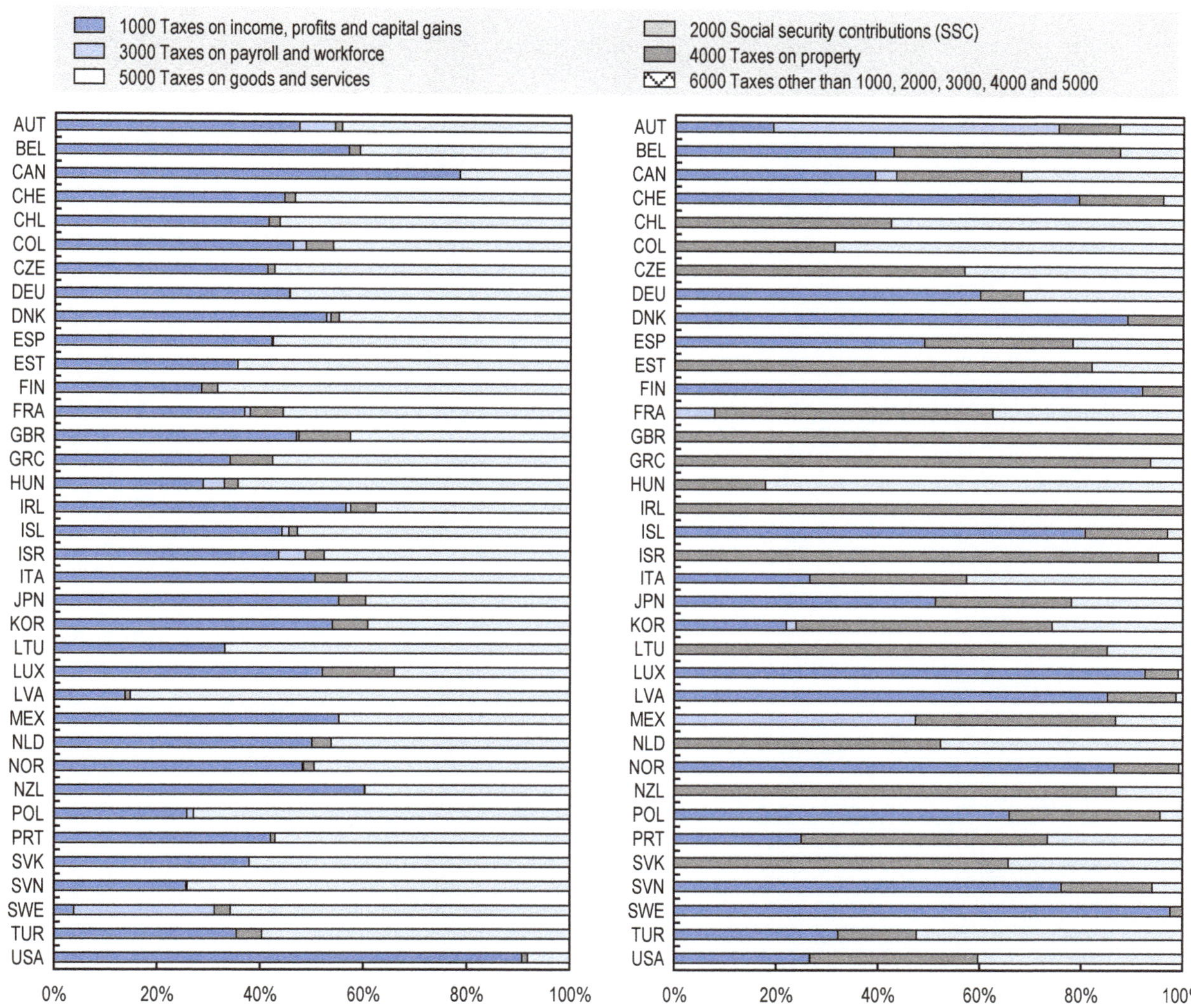

Note: The left-hand panel (a) refers to only those taxes which are classified as central government taxes. Social security contributions paid to social security funds are excluded. The right-hand panel (b) refers only to those taxes which are classified as sub-central taxes (local and (where relevant) state taxes). Social security contributions paid to social security funds are excluded.
Source: Secretariat calculations based on tables 3.16 to 3.18.

StatLink https://doi.org/10.1787/888934209533

Revenues paid to a supranational authority

The twenty-two EU member states that are also members of the OECD collect taxes on behalf of the European Union (EU), as did the United Kingdom prior to 2020. These taxes primarily consist of customs duties and Single Resolution Fund contributions.[5] Both taxes are collected on behalf of the EU by national tax administrations and are included in the total tax figures under headings 5123 and 5126 at the SUPRA level of government. In addition, they are shown as a memorandum item separately from the main figures since they represent a tax imposed by the EU and collected by national administrations.

Table 1.5 shows the level of taxes collected on behalf of supranational governments in EU countries that are also OECD members, divided into those countries in the Euro area and other EU member countries.

Table 1.5. Levies collected on behalf of the European Union, as % of GDP

Per cent

	2000	2005	2007	2010	2014	2015	2016	2017	2018	2019p
Euro area										
Austria, total supranational	0.2	0.1	0.1	0.1	0.1	0.2	0.2	0.2	0.2	0.2
of which: Customs duties	0.2	0.1	0.1	0.1	0.1	0.1	0.1	0.1	0.1	0.1
of which: SRF contributions	..	..	..	..	..	0.1	0.1	0.1	0.1	0.1
Belgium, total supranational	0.4	0.4	0.4	0.4	0.3	0.4	0.4	0.4	0.4	0.4
of which: Customs duties	0.4	0.4	0.4	0.3	0.3	0.3	0.4	0.4	0.4	0.4
of which: SRF contributions	..	..	..	..	0.0	0.1	0.1	0.1	0.1	0.1
Estonia, total supranational	..	0.2	0.2	0.2	0.2	0.2	0.2	0.2	0.2	0.2
of which: Customs duties	..	0.2	0.2	0.2	0.2	0.2	0.2	0.2	0.2	0.2
of which: SRF contributions	..	..	..	..	..	..	0.0	0.0	0.0	0.0
Finland, total supranational	0.1	0.1	0.1	0.1	0.1	0.1	0.1	0.1	0.1	0.2
of which: Customs duties	0.1	0.1	0.1	0.1	0.1	0.1	0.1	0.1	0.1	0.1
of which: SRF contributions	..	..	..	..	..	0.0	0.1	0.1	0.0	0.1
France, total supranational	0.1	0.1	0.1	0.1	0.1	0.1	0.2	0.2	0.2	0.2
of which: Customs duties	0.1	0.1	0.1	0.1	0.1	0.1	0.1	0.1	0.1	0.1
of which: SRF contributions	..	..	..	..	..	0.0	0.1	0.1	0.1	0.1
Germany, total supranational	0.2	0.2	0.2	0.2	0.2	0.2	0.2	0.2	0.2	0.2
of which: Customs duties	0.2	0.2	0.2	0.2	0.2	0.2	0.2	0.2	0.2	0.1
of which: SRF contributions	..	..	..	..	..	0.1	0.1	0.1	0.1	0.1
Greece, total supranational	0.2	0.1	0.1	0.1	0.1	0.1	0.2	0.2	0.2	0.2
of which: Customs duties	0.1	0.1	0.1	0.1	0.1	0.1	0.1	0.1	0.1	0.2
of which: SRF contributions	..	..	..	..	..	..	0.1	0.0	0.1	0.0
Ireland, total supranational	0.2	0.1	0.1	0.1	0.1	0.1	0.2	0.1	0.1	0.1
of which: Customs duties	0.2	0.1	0.1	0.1	0.1	0.1	0.1	0.1	0.1	0.1
of which: SRF contributions[1]	..	..	..	..	..	..	0.1	0.0	0.0	0.0
Italy, total supranational	0.1	0.1	0.1	0.1	0.1	0.3	0.2	0.3	0.2	0.2
of which: Customs duties	0.1	0.1	0.1	0.1	0.1	0.1	0.1	0.1	0.1	0.1
of which: SRF contributions[2]	..	..	..	..	..	0.1	0.0	0.1	0.1	0.0
Lithuania, total supranational	..	0.2	0.3	0.2	0.2	0.3	0.3	0.3	0.3	0.3
of which: Customs duties	..	0.2	0.2	0.2	0.2	0.3	0.2	0.2	0.3	0.3
of which: SRF contributions	..	..	..	..	..	0.0	0.0	0.0	0.0	0.0
Latvia, total supranational	..	0.2	0.2	0.1	0.2	0.2	0.2	0.2	0.2	0.2
of which: Customs duties	..	0.2	0.2	0.1	0.2	0.2	0.2	0.2	0.2	0.1
of which: SRF contributions	..	..	..	..	..	0.0	0.0	0.0	0.0	0.0
Luxembourg, total supranational	0.1	0.1	0.1	0.0	0.0	0.1	0.2	0.2	0.3	0.3
of which: Customs duties	0.1	0.1	0.1	0.0	0.0	0.0	0.0	0.0	0.0	0.0
of which: SRF contributions	..	..	..	..	..	0.1	0.1	0.2	0.2	0.2
Netherlands, total supranational	0.4	0.3	0.3	0.3	0.4	0.4	0.4	0.4	0.4	0.4
of which: Customs duties	0.3	0.2	0.3	0.3	0.3	0.3	0.3	0.3	0.3	0.3
of which: SRF contributions	..	..	..	..	..	0.1	0.1	0.1	0.1	0.1
Portugal, total supranational	0.2	0.1	0.1	0.1	0.1	0.1	0.2	0.2	0.2	0.2
of which: Customs duties	0.2	0.1	0.1	0.1	0.1	0.1	0.1	0.1	0.1	0.1
of which: SRF contributions	..	..	..	..	..	..	0.1	0.1	0.1	0.1

Slovak Republic, total supranational	..	0.1	0.2	0.2	0.2	0.1	0.2	0.2	0.2	0.2
of which: Customs duties	..	0.1	0.2	0.2	0.2	0.1	0.2	0.2	0.2	0.1
of which: SRF contributions	..	..	..	..	..	..	0.0	0.0	0.0	0.0
Slovenia, total supranational	..	0.1	0.2	0.2	0.1	0.2	0.2	0.2	0.1	0.1
of which: Customs duties	..	0.1	0.2	0.2	0.1	0.1	0.1	0.1	0.1	0.1
of which: SRF contributions	..	..	..	..	..	0.0	0.0	0.0	0.0	0.0
Spain, total supranational	0.2	0.2	0.2	0.1	0.2	0.2	0.2	0.2	0.2	0.2
of which: Customs duties	0.2	0.2	0.2	0.1	0.2	0.2	0.2	0.2	0.2	0.2
of which: SRF contributions	..	..	..	..	..	0.1	0.1	0.1	0.1	0.1
Non-euro area										
Czech Republic, total supranational	..	0.2	0.2	0.2	0.2	0.2	0.2	0.2	0.2	0.2
of which: Customs duties	..	0.2	0.2	0.2	0.2	0.2	0.2	0.2	0.2	0.2
Denmark, total supranational	0.2	0.2	0.2	0.2	0.2	0.2	0.1	0.1	0.1	0.1
of which: Customs duties	0.2	0.2	0.2	0.2	0.2	0.2	0.1	0.1	0.1	0.1
Hungary, total supranational	..	0.1	0.2	0.1	0.1	0.1	0.1	0.1	0.1	0.1
of which: Customs duties	..	0.1	0.1	0.1	0.1	0.1	0.1	0.1	0.1	0.1
Poland, total supranational	..	0.1	0.1	0.1	0.1	0.2	0.2	0.2	0.2	0.2
of which: Customs duties	..	0.1	0.1	0.1	0.1	0.2	0.2	0.2	0.2	0.2
Sweden, total supranational	0.3	0.3	0.3	0.3	0.3	0.3	0.3	0.3	0.3	0.3
of which: Customs duties	0.1	0.1	0.2	0.2	0.1	0.1	0.1	0.1	0.1	0.1
United Kingdom, total supranational	0.2	0.2	0.2	0.2	0.2	0.2	0.2	0.2	0.2	0.2
of which: Customs duties	0.2	0.1	0.1	0.2	0.2	0.2	0.2	0.2	0.2	0.2

Note: SRF figures may differ slightly from those published on the SRB website. These differences are primarily due to timing. Details on these revenues for each country can be found in chapters 4 and 5.

1. In 2016, the figure includes the 2016 payment of 99.12 and also a payment of 75.89 which was due in quarter 4 of 2015 but was paid in quarter 1 of 2016. The figures in this table were reported by the Central Statistics Office and are gross amounts and therefore due to adjustments will differ from the figures reported on the SRB website, which are net figures.

2. The "Bank contribution to the unique European Resolution Fund" amount includes not only the European but the National resolution fund yet, as required by Eurostat classification. Source: Revenue Statistics 2019, supplemented by discussions with delegates

Source: *Revenue Statistics 2020*, supplemented by discussions with delegates.

StatLink https://doi.org/10.1787/888934209666

In 2018, the combined total of payments collected for the EU was highest in Belgium and the Netherlands, at over 0.4% of GDP. Levels above 0.2% of GDP were also seen in Latvia, Lithuania, Luxembourg, Spain, Sweden and Germany. All other EU countries that are also members of the OECD collected revenues on behalf of the EU equivalent to between 0.1 and 0.2% of GDP. In all countries except France and Luxembourg, customs duties were the majority source of these revenues.

Non-wastable tax credits

There are two kinds of tax credits that apply to income taxes (both personal and corporate):

- Non-payable or wastable tax credits are those that can only ever be used to reduce or eliminate a tax liability. They cannot be paid out to either taxpayers or non-tax payers as a benefit. They are, therefore, the same as a tax allowance or relief.
- In contrast, payable or non-wastable tax credits can be partitioned into two parts. One part is used to reduce or eliminate a tax liability in the same way as a wastable tax credit. The other part can be paid directly to recipients as a benefit payment, when the benefit exceeds the tax liability.

The OECD methodology for classifying non-wastable tax credits is set out in paragraphs 19 and 20 of the *Interpretative Guide*. This states that only the part of a non-wastable tax credit that is used to reduce or eliminate a taxpayer's tax liability should be subtracted in the reporting of tax revenues. This is referred to as the 'tax expenditure component' of the credit. In contrast, the part of the tax credit that exceeds the taxpayer's tax liability and is paid to that taxpayer is treated as an expenditure item and not subtracted in the reporting of tax revenues. This part is referred to as the 'transfer component'.

Table 1.6. Effect of alternative treatments of non-wastable tax credits, 2018

	Non-wastable tax credits in billlions of national currency			Total tax revenue in billions of national currency			Total tax revenue as a percentage of GDP		
	Total value	Transfer component	Tax expenditure component	Net basis	Split basis (per current guidance)	Gross basis	Net basis	Split basis (per current guidance)	Gross basis
Australia	9.8	7.4	2.4	551.0	558.5	560.9	28.3	28.7	28.8
Austria[1]	0.3	0.1	0.2	162.7	162.8	163.0	42.2	42.2	42.3
Belgium[2]	0.9	0.3	0.6	201.7	202.0	202.6	43.9	43.9	44.1
Canada[3]	13.8	11.4	2.4	727.4	738.7	741.1	32.7	33.2	33.3
Chile[4]	251.6	186.8	64.8	40 314.7	40 501.5	40 566.3	21.1	21.2	21.2
Czech Republic	39.1	8.7	30.3	1 883.7	1 892.4	1 922.7	34.8	35.0	35.5
Denmark[2]	3.7	0.2	3.5	996.0	996.2	999.7	44.3	44.4	44.5
France[2]	35.8	19.7	16.1	1 064.5	1 084.2	1 100.3	45.1	45.9	46.6
Germany	43.9	14.7	29.2	1 279.0	1 293.7	1 322.9	38.1	38.5	39.4
Iceland	3.1	2.5	0.6	1 035.1	1 037.6	1 038.2	37.1	37.2	37.2
Ireland	0.5	0.0	0.5	..	73.5	73.9	..	22.7	22.8
Israel	0.8	0.8	0.0	410.8	411.6	411.6	30.9	30.9	30.9
Italy	11.8	2.6	9.1	736.9	739.5	748.7	41.7	41.9	42.4
Luxembourg[2, 5]	0.2	..	..	..	..	23.9	..	..	39.7
Mexico	49.1	1.2	47.9	3 796.7	3 797.9	3 845.8	16.2	16.2	16.4
New Zealand	2.8	1.2	1.5	98.6	99.8	101.4	32.5	32.9	33.4
Norway	4.0	3.2	0.8	1 394.0	1 397.2	1 398.0	39.5	39.6	39.6
Slovak Republic[5]	0.3	..	..	..	..	30.8	..	..	34.3
Spain	3.1	2.2	1.0	414.5	416.7	417.7	34.4	34.6	34.7
United Kingdom[6]	29.0	25.0	4.0	680.2	705.2	709.2	31.7	32.9	33.1
United States	194.7	137.0	57.7	4 894.8	5 031.7	5 089.5	23.7	24.4	24.7

Note: In *Revenue Statistics 2020*, the tax revenue data are reported on a split basis, unless indicated otherwise.
1. The children's tax credit is not regarded as a tax credit in the *Revenue Statistics 2020* and is treated entirely as an expenditure provision.
2. The total tax revenue has been reduced by the amount of any capital transfer that represents uncollected taxes.
3. Some non-wastable tax credits cannot be split into the transfer and tax expenditure components. Their total values have been added to the transfer component.
4. In *Revenue Statistics*, the tax revenue data for Chile are reported on a net basis.
5. In *Revenue Statistics*, the tax revenue data for Luxembourg and Slovak Republic are reported on a gross basis.
6. Please note that the non-wastable tax credit data for the United Kingdom is on a cash basis and includes estimates in some years. Please see the footnotes in the table for the United Kingdom in chapter 5 for more information.

StatLink https://doi.org/10.1787/888934209685

Table 1.6 provides information on the non-wastable tax credits in 2018 for those countries reporting them in the *Revenue Statistics 2020* (though it may be that some countries with non-wastable tax credits do not appear in the table). It shows the amounts of the non-wastable tax credits and their two components together with the results of using the figures to calculate tax revenue values and the associated tax-to-GDP ratios. Table 1.6 also shows two alternative treatments:

- The 'net basis' which treats non-wastable tax credits entirely as tax provisions, so that the full value of the tax credit reduces reported tax revenues, as shown in columns 4 and 7.

- The 'gross basis' is the exact opposite, treating non-wastable tax credits entirely as expenditure provisions, with neither the transfer component nor the tax expenditure component being deducted from tax revenue, as shown in columns 6 and 9. This is the approach followed by the GFSM and the SNA.

Table 1.6 shows that, with some exceptions, the choice of method for reporting non-wastable tax credits has only a small impact on the ratio of total tax revenue to GDP. For the countries with available data, the differences between the ratios on a net basis and on a gross basis are one percentage point or more in only France, Germany and the United Kingdom, and between half a percentage point and one percentage point in Australia, Canada, Czech Republic, Italy, New Zealand and the United States.

Financing of social security-type benefits in OECD countries

A memorandum item[6] in *Revenue Statistics 2020* describes the financing of social security-type benefits in OECD countries. Unlike social assistance benefits, which are funded from general government revenues, social security-type benefits are funded via contributions to social security or to private insurance schemes, or by other earmarked sources of funding. These sources of financing include:

- Earmarked financing from tax revenues:
  1. Social security contributions (SSCs, category 2000 in the OECD classification)
  2. Other taxes earmarked for social security-type benefits
- Earmarked financing from non-tax revenues:
  3. Voluntary contributions to the government (VCG)
  4. Compulsory contributions to the private sector (CCPS)

Figure 1.10 shows the relative contribution of each of these sources to financing for social security-type benefits in OECD countries, based on data provided by countries for inclusion in the memorandum item in *Revenue Statistics 2020.*

Figure 1.10. Composition of earmarked financing for social security-type benefits, 2018

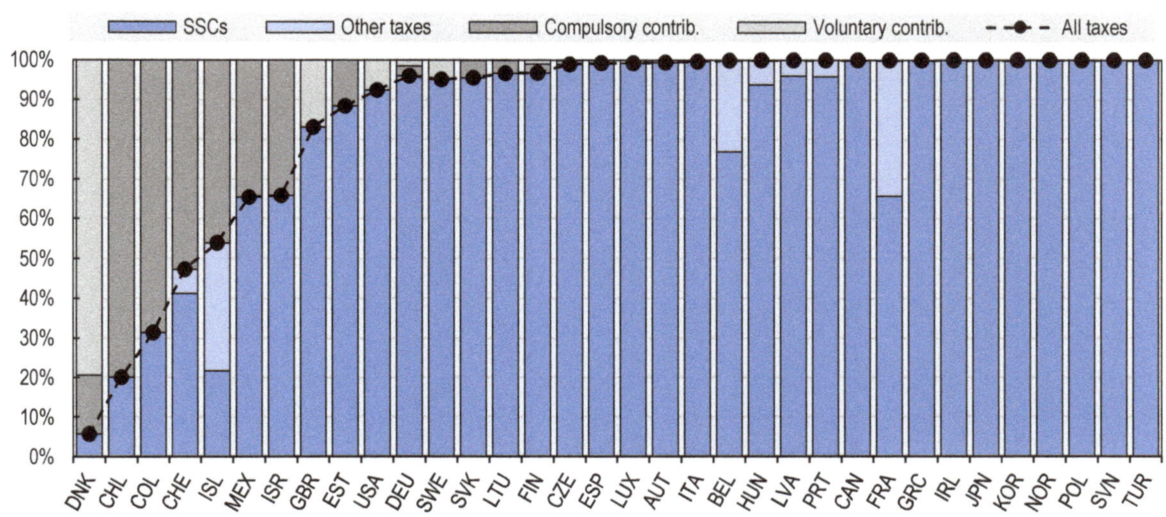

Note: Two countries (Australia and New Zealand) provide social benefits via social assistance rather than via social security, so are not included in the table. In addition, the Netherlands are also not included in the figure as complete data on mandatory contributions was not available in Revenue Statistics. The figures for Denmark should be interpreted with care as the level of social security-type benefits is very small compared to the level of social assistance benefits. Further, there may be borderline issues in some countries when distinguishing between quasi-compulsory and voluntary schemes.

Source: Secretariat calculations based on chapter 4.

StatLink https://doi.org/10.1787/888934209552

Taxes represent the largest source of earmarked financing for social security-type benefits, predominantly via social security contributions. Together, SSCs and other earmarked taxes account for over 90% of the financing of social security-type benefits in 25 OECD countries and 100% in 13 countries. In the remaining nine OECD countries that provide this data, compulsory contributions to the private sector play a larger role, at 79.9% in Chile, 68.6% in Colombia and 52.7% in Switzerland, with smaller shares in Iceland, Mexico, Israel, Denmark and Estonia. Few countries received significant shares of voluntary contributions: only in the United Kingdom and Denmark do these exceed 10% of financing.

Figure 1.11 shows tax-to-GDP ratios (as in Table 1.1 and Figure 1.4) both *exclusive* of earmarked funding for social security-type benefits (i.e. tax-to-GDP ratios *less* SSCs and other earmarked taxes) and *inclusive* of all non-tax earmarked financing for social security-type benefits (i.e. tax-to-GDP ratios - including SSCs and other earmarked taxes - *plus* compulsory contributions to the private sector and voluntary contributions to government).

Countries with the largest share of social security-type schemes financed by non-tax earmarked contributions are Switzerland (8.5% of GDP), Iceland (7.5%) and Chile (5.8%), which materially affects their rankings:

- Switzerland has a relatively low tax-to-GDP ratio among OECD countries, at 28%, but its combined ratio is roughly halfway in the OECD distribution;
- Iceland has a tax-to-GDP ratio of 37.2%, in the top-third of OECD countries, and a combined ratio of 44.7%, which is the third-highest in the OECD.
- Chile has the third-lowest tax-to-GDP ratio and the seventh-lowest combined ratio.

Figure 1.11. Tax-to-GDP ratios and earmarked social security financing (% of GDP, 2018)

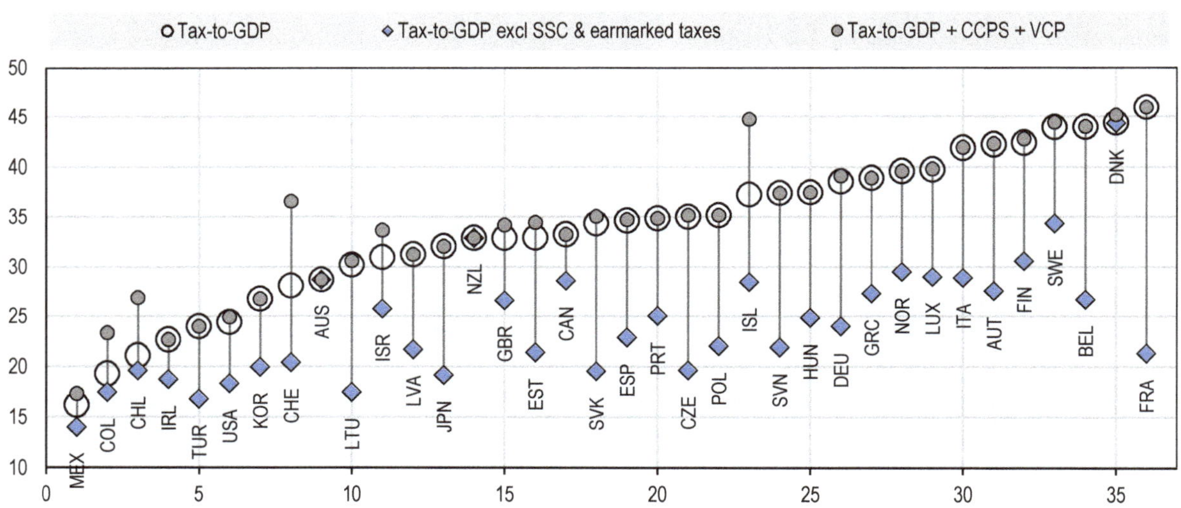

Note: The Netherlands are not included in the figure as complete data on social security financing in the Netherlands were not available.
Source: Secretariat calculations based on data in chapter 4.

StatLink https://doi.org/10.1787/888934209571

Excluding earmarked financing for social security benefits from the tax-to-GDP ratio does not affect Australia, Denmark and New Zealand, where benefits are funded out of general taxation. Figure 1.11 highlights that the largest share of earmarked funding for social security-type benefits is seen in France, at 24.6% of GDP, as indicated by the difference between the highest and lowest points on the figure. Belgium, Iceland and Switzerland have the next highest shares, at between 16% and 18% of GDP.

Notes

[1] Provisional 2019 figures are not available for Australia and provisional figures on social security contributions in Japan are also not available as at the time *Revenue Statistics 2020* was published.

[2] In 2016, Iceland received revenues from one-off stability contributions from entities that previously operated as commercial or savings banks and were concluding operations. The revenue from these contributions led to unusually high tax revenues for a single year and consequently, Iceland's tax-to-GDP ratio rose from 35.4% in 2015 to 50.8% in 2016, before dropping to 37.6% in 2017. This led to an artificial high in the OECD average tax-to-GDP ratio in 2016 of 34.0%. Without these one-off revenues in Iceland, the OECD average tax-to-GDP ratio would have been 33.5%, an increase of 0.2 p.p. relative to 2015.

[3] The terms "value added tax" and "VAT" are used to refer to any national tax that embodies the basic features of a value added tax by whatever name or acronym it is known e.g. "Goods and Services Tax" ("GST").

[4] For 1975, please see Table 1.4 of *Revenue Statistics 2020*.

[5] The Single Resolution Fund (SRF) has been in place since 2015 and countries in the Eurozone are required to make SRF contributions under the Single Resolution Mechanism (Regulation (EU) No 806/2014). Contributions are paid on an ex-ante basis and contributions are transferred from the national authorities to the SRF. So far, contributions have been collected for the years 2015 to 2019

[6] The financing of social security-type benefits is shown in Table 4.75 on a comparable basis (percentage of GDP) and in Table 5.38 on a national currency basis.

2 Special feature: Consumption tax revenues under COVID-19: lessons from the 2008 global financial crisis

Chapter 2 analyses the drivers of changes in consumption tax revenues during economic downturns, with the global financial crisis (2007-09) as a case study, and uses these insights to understand how the COVID-19 crisis will affect tax revenues.

Introduction

The fight against COVID-19 has forced many countries to impose unprecedented measures, shutting down large parts of the economy and isolating a significant proportion of the population. As a result, public life has been severely impeded or halted and consumer spending has plummeted, with wide-ranging implications for tax revenues. (Simon and Harding, 2020[1]) analyses the impacts of major economic downturns on consumption tax revenues, particularly during the global financial crisis (GFC) of 2007-09, providing important insights on how the COVID-19 crisis is likely to affect consumption tax revenues.

During the GFC, tax revenues in OECD countries fell considerably, with most countries experiencing the lowest point in their tax revenues as a share of GDP for several decades. Meanwhile, revenues from taxes on consumption were typically less affected and have been seen to be more stable over time than revenues from other bases such as corporate income (Simon and Harding, 2020[1]).

As countries navigate the COVID-19 crisis, government spending programmes and tax policy measures, including consumption tax measures, are playing an important role in supporting individuals and businesses. With all OECD countries strongly relying on consumption taxes, which represent on average around one-third (32.7%) of total tax revenues and 10.9% of GDP, monitoring and understanding what drives changes in revenues from consumption taxes is key. This is particularly the case in light of the COVID-19 crisis relief packages and their implications for fiscal policy and public debt levels in many countries.

This Special Feature is based on the analysis in (Simon and Harding, 2020[1])[1], which examines the drivers of recent changes in consumption tax revenues in OECD countries by disentangling their policy and macroeconomic drivers. This Special Feature identifies the channels through which consumption tax revenues are affected during an economic downturn, using the GFC as a case study to draw initial insights into how the COVID-19 crisis and the policy actions taken in response to it will affect tax revenues.

Trends in consumption tax revenues

As detailed in chapter 1, taxes on consumption[2] are an important source of tax revenue in all OECD countries. In 2018, they ranged from less than 6% of GDP in the United States, Canada and Mexico to more than 15% in Greece and Hungary.

The overall share of taxes on consumption in total tax revenue has remained relatively stable since 1995, except during the GFC. During the GFC, consumption tax revenues as a share of GDP declined by 0.36 percentage points on average (between 2007 and 2009) and reached their lowest point since 1992. This decrease was largely driven by a fall in VAT revenues in those countries that have a VAT in place, with both consumption tax and VAT revenues only returning to their pre-GFC level in 2012.

In 2018, countries fell into three groups with different levels of consumption taxes as a share of GDP (Figure 2.1): low (consumption tax-to-GDP ratios below 9%); mid (between 9% and 13%) and high (greater than 13%). The high consumption tax-to-GDP group in 2018 was entirely composed of European Union (EU) countries, while all countries with low consumption tax-to-GDP ratios except for Ireland were non-EU countries. With the exception of the highest group, the composition of these groups was broadly stable between 1995 and 2018, particularly since 2000.

Across the period, countries with the most marked changes in the level of consumption tax revenues as a share of GDP included Greece and Turkey, where the consumption tax-to-GDP ratios increased by 3.6 percentage points in both countries; and Canada and Ireland, where consumption taxes as a share of GDP decreased by more than 3 percentage points. In Canada, Greece and Turkey, these changes were largely driven by corresponding changes in the standard VAT rates, whereas the decrease in revenues in Ireland resulted from a change in the composition of GDP (Simon and Harding, 2020[1]).

Figure 2.1. Consumption tax-to-GDP ratios in OECD countries: 1995, 2018; minimums and maximums between these dates

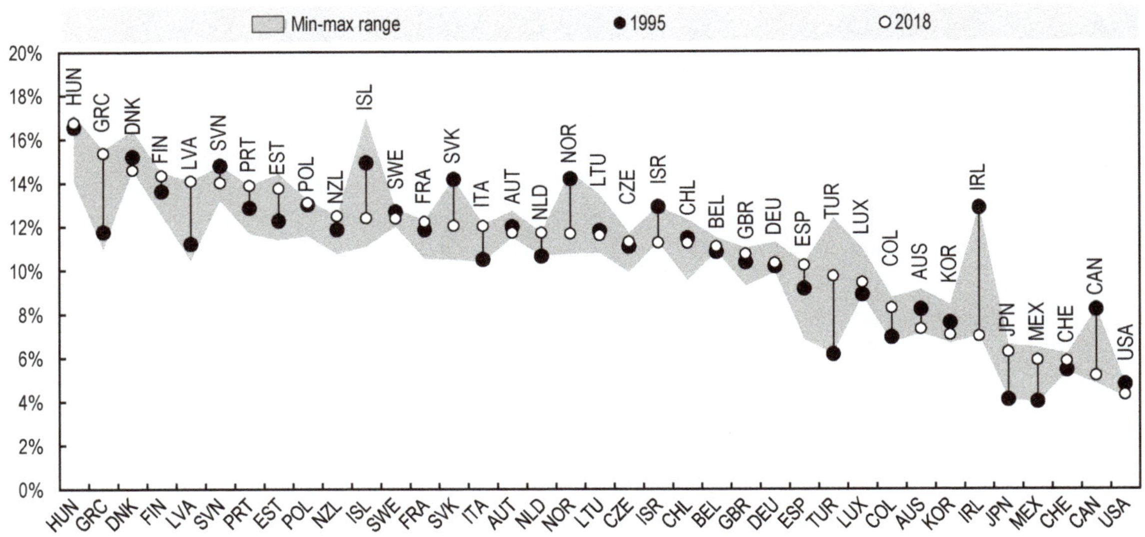

Note: The shaded area shows the minimum and maximum consumption tax-to-GDP ratio for each country, regardless of year.
Source: Authors' calculations based on OECD Revenue Statistics (2020).

StatLink https://doi.org/10.1787/888934209704

The mix of consumption taxes has changed markedly over the last 40 years, as the growing share of value-added taxes (VAT)[3] has displaced other forms of consumption taxes in most OECD countries (see chapter 1). In 2018, VAT revenues as a share of total consumption tax revenues accounted for almost two-thirds (61.3%) on average and more than 50% in all but three OECD countries, Australia, Turkey and the United States (which does not have a VAT). Excises accounted for, on average, 22.1% of total consumption tax revenues in 2018.

Box 2.1. Decomposing consumption tax revenues as a share of GDP

Following (Simon and Harding, 2020[1]), consumption tax revenues as a share of GDP are decomposed using the corresponding conceptual tax base[4], as set out in equation (1).

$$\frac{consumption\ tax\ revenues}{GDP} = \underbrace{\frac{consumption\ tax\ revenues}{consumption}}_{\text{Consumption tax revenues as a share of the corresponding conceptual tax base, the ITR on consumption.}} \times \underbrace{\frac{consumption}{GDP}}_{\text{The conceptual tax base as a share of GDP.}} \qquad (1)$$

The decomposition in equation (1) allows the impact of a change in the conceptual tax base, consumption, to be isolated. The Implicit Tax Rate (ITR) on consumption demonstrates the effect of changes in the consumption tax itself, i.e., base broadening (including for domestic and cross-border trade) and changes in the headline rates, as well as the effect of changes in compliance or informality on consumption tax revenues as a share of GDP. Consumption as a share of GDP captures all other changes in the economic environment that affect the consumption tax-to-GDP ratio, i.e., changes in GDP and its components.

To understand what drives the changes in consumption as a share of GDP, data from the OECD National Accounts is used to illustrate changes in the different elements of GDP as well as in the composition of consumption, which in turn can influence the level of the ITR.

In a second step, a decomposition of VAT revenues provides further insights into the drivers of consumption tax revenues. Using the standard VAT rate, τ_S, the VAT-Revenue-Ratio (VRR)[5] and consumption as a share of GDP, equation (2) serves to illustrate the impact of changes in tax rates and in tax bases on VAT revenues and hence on consumption tax revenues more generally (Simon and Harding, 2020[1]):

$$\frac{VAT\ revenues}{GDP} = \tau_s \times \underbrace{\left[\frac{VAT\ revenues}{consumption \times \tau_s}\right]}_{\text{VAT-Revenue-Ratio (VRR)}} \times \frac{consumption}{GDP} \qquad (2)$$

The drivers of consumption tax revenues in OECD countries

The ITR on consumption is the primary determinant of overall levels of consumption tax revenues to GDP in most OECD countries, although its importance varies across countries (Figure 2.2). Within the consumption tax-to-GDP groups identified above, countries vary widely with respect to their levels of consumption as a share of GDP, while their ITRs are more similar, with the exception of Luxembourg and Ireland.[6] Nevertheless, the drivers of these ratios can differ significantly among countries with similar levels of consumption taxes as a share of GDP.

Figure 2.2. Decomposition of consumption tax revenues as a share of GDP, 2018

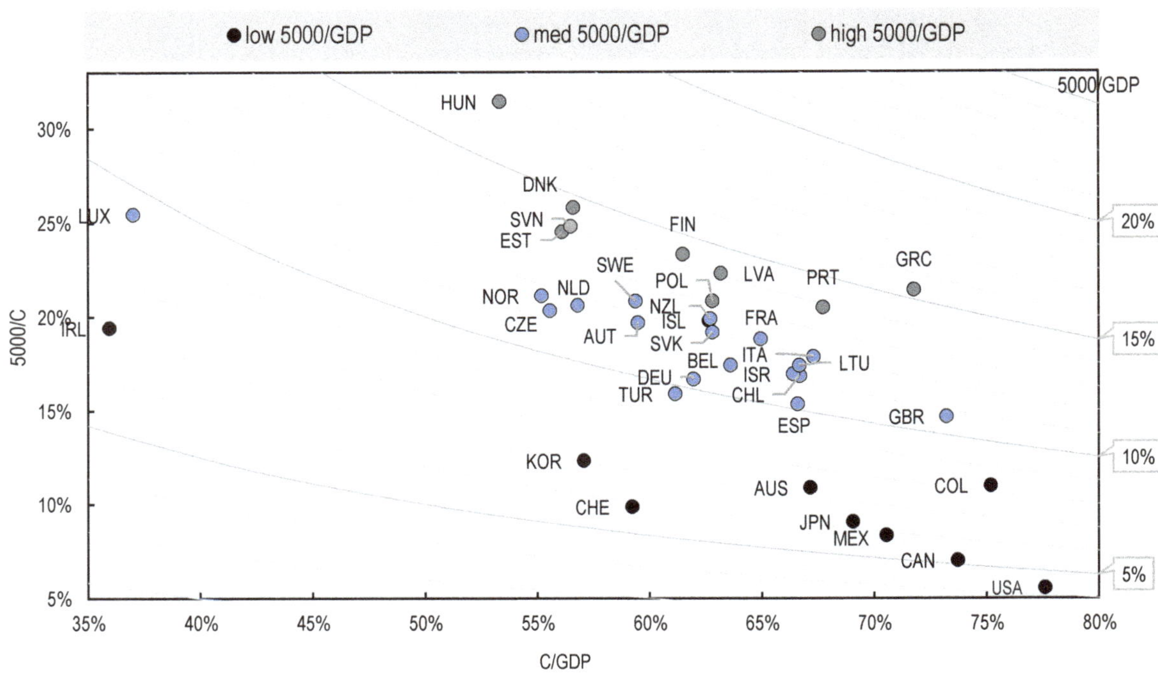

Note: The graph shows the decomposition of consumption tax revenues across OECD countries according to equation (1). The horizontal axis shows consumption as a share of GDP and the vertical axis shows the ITR on consumption. Consumption tax revenues as a share of GDP, given by the product of the two shares, are equal to the area under and to the left of each dot. Therefore, countries along each of the curved lines have the same level of consumption tax revenues as a share of GDP (as indicated on the right side of the graph). The Czech Republic and the United Kingdom, for example, have similar levels of consumption taxes as a share of GDP (11.3% and 10.7%), but for different reasons: the Czech Republic has a higher ITR on consumption but lower consumption as a share of GDP.

Source: Authors' calculations based on OECD National Accounts and OECD Revenue Statistics (2020).

StatLink https://doi.org/10.1787/888934209723

Changes in the OECD average consumption tax-to-GDP ratio and its components between 1995 and 2018 can be segmented into four distinct periods (Figure 2.3):[7]

- Prior to 2003, average consumption tax revenues as a share of GDP (5000/GDP) remained relatively stable, despite small fluctuations in consumption expenditure relative to GDP (C/GDP).
- In the years leading up to the GFC, average consumption as a share of GDP fell from 64.9% to 62.3%, while a slight increase in the ITR on consumption led the average consumption tax-to-GDP ratio remaining relatively stable around 10.8% until 2007.
- During the GFC, the ITR on consumption decreased in every OECD country in at least one year, causing the OECD average ITR to decrease from 17.6% to 16.0%. Despite a strong increase in average consumption as a share of GDP, the average consumption tax-to-GDP ratio fell by more than 3.5%, reaching a low of 10.2% in 2009.
- Since then, consumption tax revenues as a share of GDP have returned to their 1995 level, while consumption as a share of GDP was slightly lower (2.6 percentage points) and ITRs were slightly higher (1.0 percentage points) in 2018 than in 1995, on average.

Figure 2.3. Consumption tax revenues as a share of GDP and its components in percentages, OECD average, 1995-2018

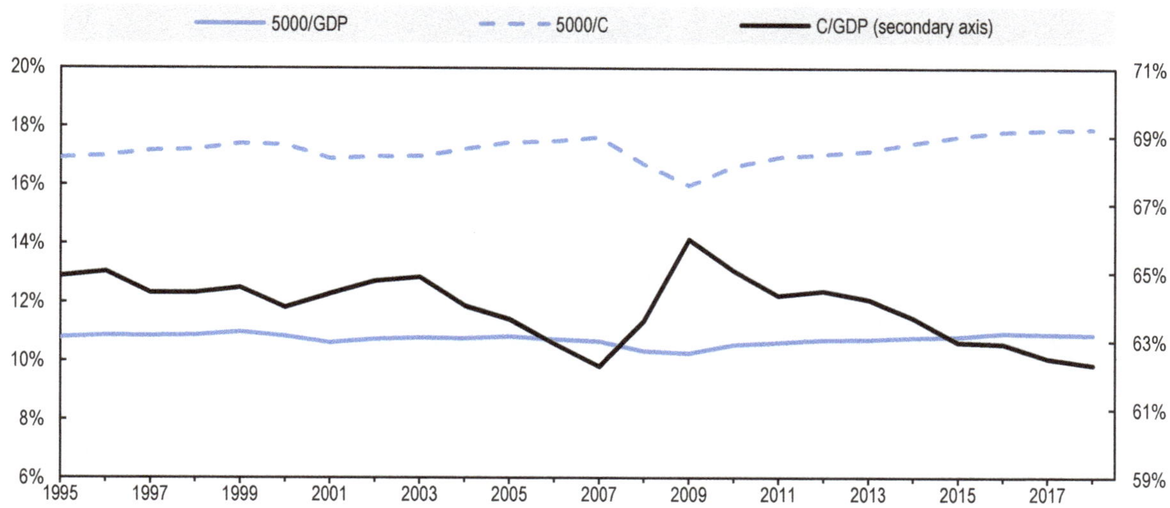

Note: Consumption tax revenues are decomposed according to equation (1).
Source: Authors' calculations based on OECD National Accounts and OECD Revenue Statistics (2020).

StatLink https://doi.org/10.1787/888934209742

During the GFC, changes in consumption tax revenues were larger than in other years and significantly different in terms of composition. Over the period from 1995 to 2018, changes in consumption taxes as a share of GDP were driven primarily by changes in the ITR on consumption, as shown in Figure 2.4. However, while the direction of change in average consumption taxes as a share of GDP was the same as the ITR on consumption in almost every year, the magnitude of change in consumption tax revenues was strongly influenced by average consumption expenditure as a share of GDP. In all but five years, the changes in the consumption tax base and in the implicit tax rate went in opposite directions, offsetting each other. In contrast to other years, the average ITR on consumption fell in 2008 and 2009 to a significant extent, while the share of consumption to GDP increased sharply in the same years.

This implies that the key avenue through which the GFC impacted consumption tax revenues was by decreasing ITRs, rather than consumption – and that an increasing share of consumption in GDP offset the fall in ITRs and stabilised consumption tax revenues during the GFC.

Figure 2.4. Annual growth rates (logged) in consumption taxes as a share of GDP and its components, OECD average, 1995-2018

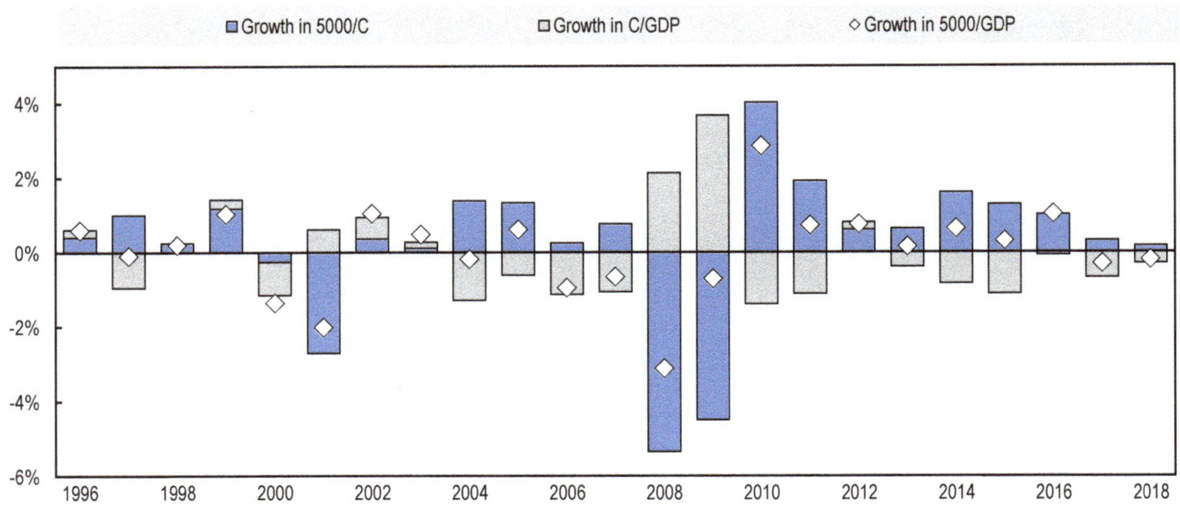

Note: Consumption tax revenues are decomposed according to equation (1).
Source: Authors' calculations based on OECD National Accounts and OECD Revenue Statistics (2020).

StatLink https://doi.org/10.1787/888934209761

Changes in consumption as a share of GDP during the GFC

The increase in consumption as a share of GDP during the GFC resulted from a change in the level of other GDP aggregates, rather than due to an increase in the level of consumption. Figure 2.5 reveals marked differences in the composition of GDP prior to, during and after the GFC. Between 2004 and 2007, higher growth in investment than in consumption in the majority of countries caused consumption as a share of GDP to decrease, on average. During the GFC, investment as a share of GDP decreased by 5.4 percentage points on average, primarily due to decreases in inventories and in machinery investment [8], while government consumption raised average total consumption to a temporary high of 76.2% of GDP in 2009.

After the GFC, average net exports as a share of GDP have been increasing, while both private and government consumption have, on average, slightly decreased relative to GDP, causing total consumption as a share of GDP to return to around its pre-GFC level in 2015. In fact, total consumption as a share of GDP has remained stable over time in most OECD countries, with an average country standard deviation of 2.3% over the period. Compared to 1995, the average composition of GDP in 2018 showed higher levels of government consumption (0.1 percentage points) and lower levels of private consumption (2.7 percentage points).

Figure 2.5. Major expenditure aggregates as a share of GDP (non-cumulative), OECD average, 1995-2018

As % of GDP

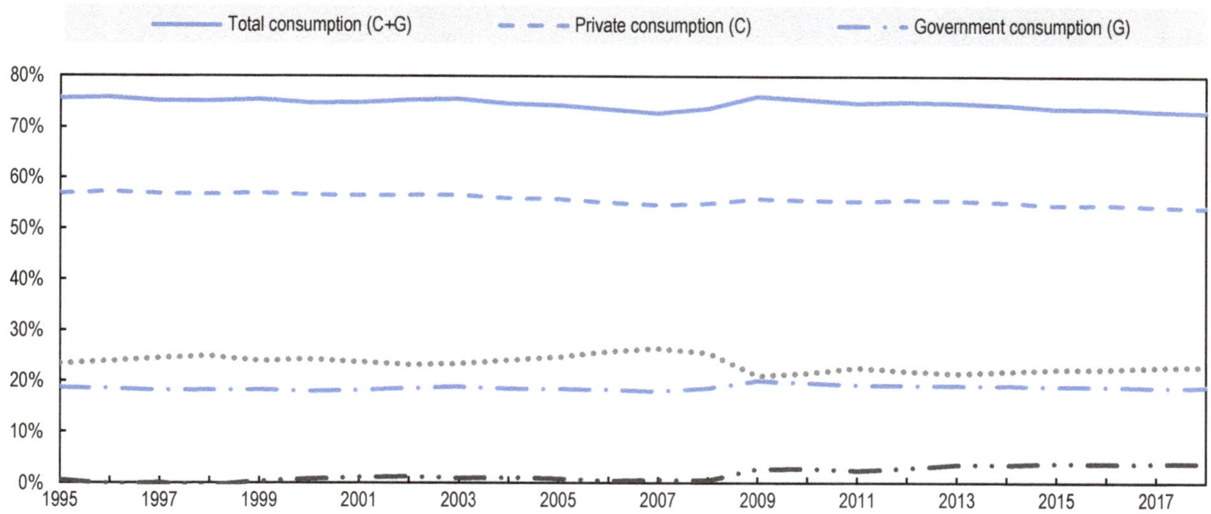

Note: Decomposition of GDP according to the expenditure approach: $GDP = C + G + I + (EX - IM)$. Private consumption expenditure includes private household consumption and final consumption expenditure of non-profit institutions serving households (NPISH). Unweighted average of all OECD countries. For Turkey, where data on investment as a share of GDP was not available, the share was approximated as the residual of the equation.

Source: Authors' calculations based on OECD National Accounts.

StatLink https://doi.org/10.1787/888934209780

Changes in the ITRs on consumption

The main driver of changes in the OECD average ITR on consumption is VAT (Simon and Harding, 2020[1]). To provide additional insights on the drivers of changes in consumption tax revenues, Figure 2.6 separates changes in the VAT revenues as a share of GDP (5111/GDP) in those countries that have a VAT system in place into changes in VAT rates and structures, as well as changes in the consumption base.

Both on average and in the individual countries, changes in the VRR have been the main driver of changes in VAT revenues as a share of GDP across the period, and can explain most of the drop in ITRs during the GFC. During the GFC, the average VRR dropped by 6.8 percentage points, as VAT revenues fell back to their level from 1995, before increasing again slowly post GFC.

Figure 2.6. VAT revenues as a share of GDP and its components in percentages, OECD average, 1995-2018

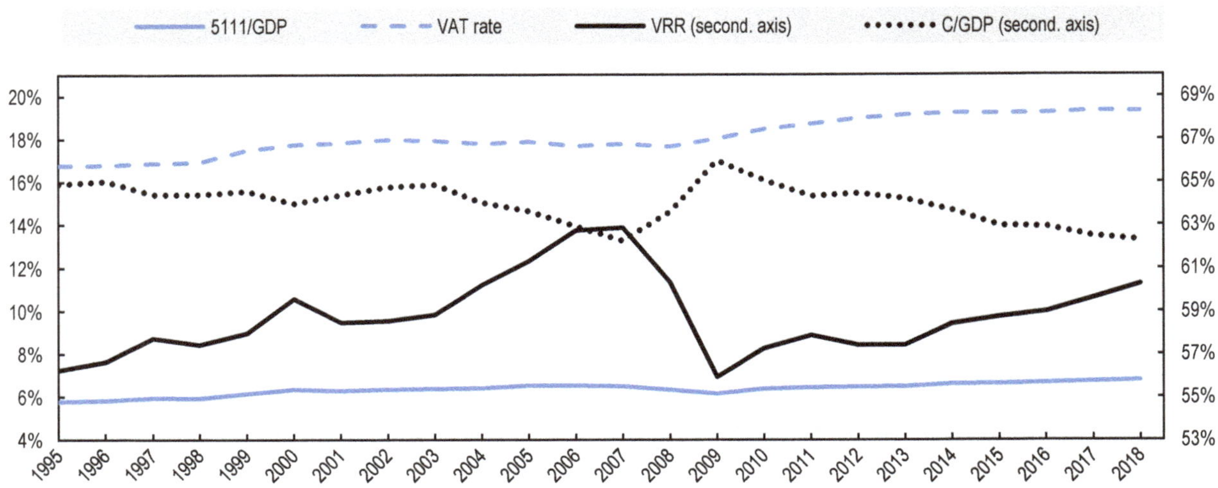

Note: VAT revenues are decomposed according to equation (4).
Source: Authors' calculations based on OECD National Accounts and OECD Revenue Statistics (2020).

StatLink https://doi.org/10.1787/888934209799

In light of significant fluctuations in the VRR, changes in standard VAT rates as well as in the consumption base relative to GDP stabilised VAT revenues. The average standard VAT rate increased from 2008 onwards and reached a plateau of 19.2% in 2014, when average VAT revenues as a share of GDP exceeded their pre-GFC level. In 2018, average VAT revenues reached their highest level throughout the period, at 6.8% of GDP. These developments in the average standard VAT rate over time reflect a number of important policy changes in OECD countries, as explained in more detail in Box 2. Although changes in standard rates in the individual countries have been much less frequent than for the OECD average, they have contributed considerably to the stability in consumption tax revenues as a share of GDP.

Nevertheless, the average ITR on consumption in 2018 was only slightly above its pre-GFC level, while standard VAT rates are, on average, 1.5 percentage points higher than prior to the GFC. This is the result of a number of macroeconomic and policy changes that narrowed the VAT base, namely: i) the implementation of new or additional reduced VAT rates (see Box 2); ii) changes in the composition of consumption expenditure; and iii) changes in VAT compliance.

Box 2.2. VAT rates and structures in OECD countries between 1995 and 2018

The Value Added Tax (VAT) (and its equivalent in several jurisdictions, the Goods and Services tax, or GST) is a specific type of turnover tax levied at each stage in the production and distribution process. Although the liability for VAT falls on the suppliers of goods or services, the tax burden is designed to fall on final consumers, making the VAT a tax on final consumption of goods or services.

Standard VAT rates

In 2018, standard VAT rates in the OECD ranged from 27% in Hungary to less than 10% in Japan, Switzerland and Canada[9]. Compared to 2005, nearly two thirds of OECD countries (22) increased their standard rates.[10]

The developments in the average standard VAT rate over time reflect a number of important policy changes in OECD countries. Four OECD countries introduced their VAT after January 1995: Latvia and Switzerland (both in 1995), Slovenia (in 1999) and Australia (in 2000). Prior to the GFC, the standard VAT rate remained stable in most countries, with the majority of countries maintaining a rate between 15% and 22%.

From 2007 to 2009, six OECD countries (Estonia, Hungary, Israel, Ireland, Latvia and Lithuania) increased their standard VAT rates as part of their fiscal consolidation efforts, while Portugal and the United Kingdom temporarily decreased their standard rates to stimulate the economy. These changes in VAT rates (both positive and negative) across OECD countries caused the average standard rate to decrease temporarily, from 17.7% in 2007 to 17.6% in 2008, but to increase again to 18.0% in the following year.

Between 2009 and 2014, and in large part as a response to the GFC, 23 countries raised their standard VAT rate at least once, 17 of which were EU member countries. This resulted in an increase in the OECD average standard rate to 19.2% in 2014, since when it has slowly increased to 19.3% in 2018. The average standard VAT rate of the 22 OECD countries that are members of the EU was at 21.7% in 2018, which is significantly higher than the OECD average. The standard VAT rate generally applies to all goods and services, unless advised differently by legislation. However, most OECD countries continue to apply a wide variety of reduced rates and exemptions to support various policy objectives.

Reduced rates and exemptions

During the period from 1995-2018, most OECD countries have relied primarily on increases in standard VAT rates rather than base-broadening reforms. A number of countries (France, Hungary, Ireland and the Slovak Republic) implemented new or additional reduced VAT rates between 2009 and 2014, and most countries that have increased their standard VAT rate since the GFC have also increased their reduced rates, although generally to a lesser extent. In Japan, an increase in the standard VAT rate from 8% to 10% in October 2019 was accompanied by the introduction of a reduced rate of 8%. To date, all OECD countries that have a VAT system in place apply one or more reduced rates, with the exception of Chile.

In most OECD countries, a number of goods of services are exempt from VAT, i.e., they are taxed on their inputs rather than their outputs. Common exemptions across most OECD countries include financial services, expenditure on education and the letting of immovable property. Government consumption is exempt from VAT in all OECD countries except for New Zealand, where government activities are fully taxable under the VAT.[11] For further information on VAT rates and structures in OECD countries, see OECD Consumption Tax Trends (2020).

Source: OECD Consumption Tax Trends (2020).

The pattern of consumption, i.e., the composition of consumption expenditure, typically changes over the economic cycle. As can be seen from Figure 2.7, shifts in consumption patterns affected consumption tax revenues through two main channels during the GFC: by increasing both the share of government consumption and the share of private consumption of necessity goods relative to total consumption.

On average across OECD countries, government expenditure fluctuated between 24.4% and 25.1% of total consumption until 2007 inclusively, before it increased sharply to 26.5% in 2009. In those countries where government consumption is exempt from VAT, these increases in public spending increase the share of the VAT base that is input- rather than output-taxed, which reduces the VRR and, ceteris paribus, decreases VAT revenues as a share of GDP.

The composition of private consumption also changed over the economic cycle, as consumers decreased their expenditure on luxury goods and services, which increased the share of expenditure on necessities[12,13] (Sancak, Velloso and Xing, 2010[2]). The average private expenditure on luxury goods increased from 62.9% of total consumption in 1995 to its peak of 65.2% in 2007, before dropping by nearly two percentage points in the following two years. Meanwhile, the average share of expenditure on necessities in total consumption increased relatively steadily between 2007 and 2015, resulting in a 8.3% increase in the average share across this period. In the presence of reduced VAT rates on necessity goods, these shifts in private consumption reduce the share of the tax base that is subject to the standard VAT rate, thereby reducing the VRR.

Between 2007 and 2009, when the average expenditure on necessity goods as well as government services as a share of consumption increased sharply, the average VAT collection efficiency, as measured by the VRR, dropped significantly. Even though total consumption expenditure (in constant prices) stayed, on average, relatively stable during the GFC, these shifts in the consumption base, combined with reduced rates and exemptions in the VAT, contributed to a decrease in the VRR and thereby in consumption tax revenues.

In addition to changes in the pattern of consumption, an increase in taxpayer VAT noncompliance during the GFC adversely affected the VRR, thereby putting further downward pressure on VAT revenues ((Ueda, 2017[3]); (Sancak, Velloso and Xing, 2010[2])).[14]

After the GFC, the shares of both government consumption and private consumption of necessities in total consumption have remained elevated. Government consumption has remained on a new higher level of around 25.8% of total consumption expenditure, with the majority of OECD countries (23) having higher levels of government consumption as a share of total consumption in 2018 than in 1995, by 2.0 percentage points on average. Average expenditure on necessity goods and services as a share of total consumption has decreased slightly following its increase between 2007 and 2015. As a result, increases in standard rates do not translate fully into increases in the average implicit VAT rate, causing VAT revenues as a share of GDP to remain close to their long-run average, despite standard VAT rates in OECD countries being significantly higher now than prior to the GFC.

Figure 2.7. Shares of major consumption expenditures (non-cumulative), OECD average, 1995-2018

As % of total consumption expenditure

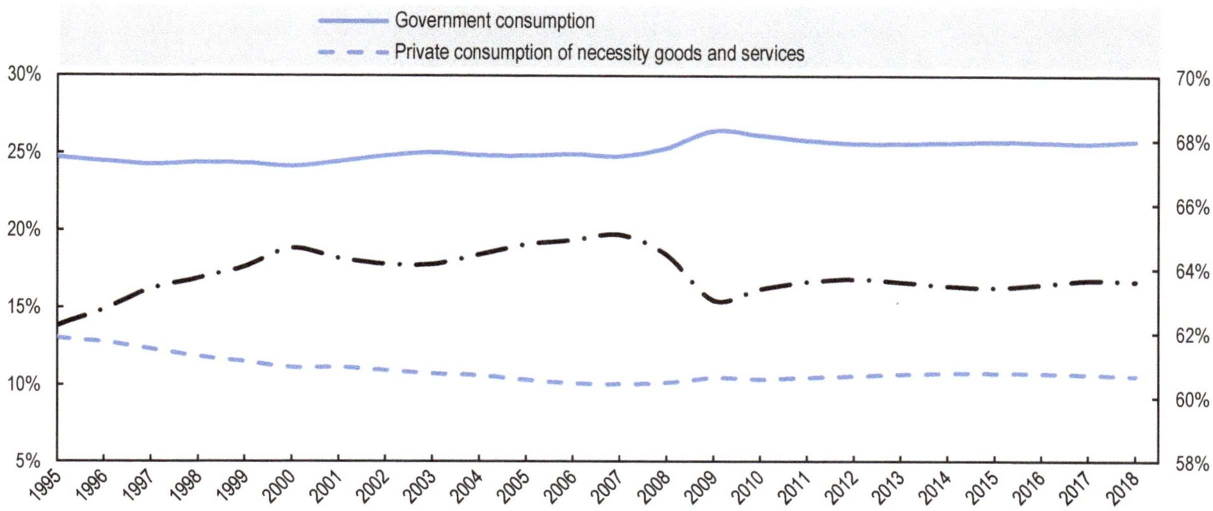

Note: The share of expenditure on food and non-alcoholic beverages in private consumption expenditure has been used as a proxy of the share of necessity goods and services. The residual has been used as a proxy for the expenditure on luxury goods and services. Data on necessity goods and services was not available for Colombia until 2005, Chile until 2012, Korea until 1999 and Turkey until 2008 inclusively.
Source: Authors' calculations based on OECD National Accounts.

StatLink https://doi.org/10.1787/888934209818

Consumption tax revenues during COVID-19

Consumption tax revenues are affected both by macroeconomic and policy changes, including changes in the level and composition of expenditure and to the rate and base of VAT. During crises, these forces affect consumption tax revenues in multiple ways.

This Special Feature has considered the impact of the GFC on consumption tax revenues as a case study, which can provide insights into the likely impact of the COVID-19 crisis. On average across the OECD, during the GFC, the overall level of consumption remained relatively stable, while consumption tax revenues and VAT revenues in particular decreased sharply. This fall in revenues was primarily due to a shift in consumer spending towards necessity goods and services, often exempt or taxed at lower or zero VAT rates, as well as an increase in the consumption of government and public sector services, which are exempt from VAT. In addition, a temporary increase in taxpayer non-compliance decreased VAT revenues. However, partly offsetting these impacts, the size of the consumption tax base actually increased as a share of GDP, largely due to strong decreases in investment. Since the GFC, many of the changes to consumption patterns have not reversed, which has left VAT systems more exposed to economic shocks, particularly in countries with low VRRs and high shares of government consumption, and especially if a crisis directly affects private consumption rather than investment.

The current COVID-19 crisis is likely to have an even bigger impact on consumption tax revenues than the GFC had, because it affects consumption directly and to a far greater extent. Countries imposed unprecedented health measures that have effectively shut down large parts of the economy and eroded business and consumer confidence, which caused a sharp decrease in economic activity. These combined effects of the health crisis and the policy response decrease consumption tax revenues through a number of channels.

During the emergency phase of the COVID-19 crisis, when shops and restaurants were closed and consumers were asked to stay at home, consumer spending in OECD countries decreased significantly. In major advanced economies, consumer spending is projected to have plummeted by up to one-third during this period (OECD, 2020[4]), which, despite possible increases in online sales, has a direct and immediate impact on VAT revenues. In the face of a combined supply-side and demand-side shock (reduced or delayed spending), governments in many countries introduced various measures to improve business liquidity, including deferring VAT payments and accelerating VAT refunds (OECD, 2020[5]). While these measures are an important short-term response, they will likely lead to a reduction in VAT revenues in the short-run.

At the onset of the COVID-19 crisis, some of the changes in consumption patterns mirrored the GFC. The earliest data from household surveys (see e.g. (CBS, 2020[6]), (Insee, 2020[7])) and from household bank account transaction data (Baker et al., 2020[8]) show that households spent a larger share of their total expenditure on necessities, which directly reduced VAT revenues as these items are often taxed at reduced or zero VAT rates. At the same time, many governments increased their healthcare spending and introduced large-scale expenditure initiatives, with government spending projected to rise by, on average, between 4.0% and 4.5% in 2020 (OECD, 2020[9]). As these areas of expenditure are often exempt from VAT, consumption tax revenues are expected to increase less than in proportion to the increase in government spending.

The COVID-19 crisis will also likely cause a temporary increase in business insolvencies and bankruptcies, further decreasing revenues, and unlike during the GFC, excises and fuel taxes are also falling as a result of confinement, travel bans and the closure of bars and restaurants.

The reopening of economies has reversed some of the fall in consumption, and revenues are starting to pick up again. As consumer restrictions have been lifted, private spending, particularly on durable goods, has risen, increasing both total consumption and tax revenues. However, private spending on services – such as a haircut or a restaurant meal – is unlikely to increase enough to make up for the falls during the shutdown. To spur consumer spending, some countries (e.g. Germany and Norway; see (OECD, 2020[10])) have introduced temporary reductions in standard and reduced VAT rates, similarly to the GFC. Nevertheless, in some sectors such as tourism and travel, spending is likely to remain depressed into the medium term.

Over the course of the year 2020, the level of consumer spending in OECD countries is projected to be, on average, around 8.5% lower than in the previous year (10.8% lower if a second outbreak occurs in all OECD countries towards the end of 2020), before picking up through 2021 (OECD, 2020[9]). Meanwhile, the average level of investment in OECD countries in 2020 is projected to decrease by around 10.5% compared to 2019 (by 12.8% in case of a second outbreak) (OECD, 2020[9]). With investment decreasing more strongly than consumption expenditure, consumption will increase as a share of GDP. As was the case during the GFC, this offsets part of the fall in the ITR and helps stabilise consumption tax revenues as a share of GDP. However, in the event of a renewed virus outbreak, uncertainty would intensify further and for an extended period, with additional precautionary saving, lower household spending and substantially weaker investment prospects.

Consumption taxes are an important part of the toolkit that governments have to facilitate the economic and fiscal recovery after the COVID-19 crisis. Over time, consumption tax revenues will gradually increase as a share of GDP to regain their pre-crisis levels, as private spending returns to pre-crisis patterns and governments take action to restore lost revenues. In doing so, governments may wish to give careful consideration to how the structure of their VAT systems will affect the resilience of their tax system and its revenues in future economic downturns. Any changes to improve resilience will need to account for the complexity of VAT systems and consider likely behavioural responses as well as potential distributional impacts.

References

Baker, S. et al. (2020), "How Does Household Spending Respond to an Epidemic? Consumption During the 2020 COVID-19 Pandemic", *Becker Friedman Institute and the University of Chicago* Working Paper No 2020-30, https://bfi.uchicago.edu/wp-content/uploads/BFI_WP_202030.pdf. [8]

CASE and IHS (2018), *Study and Reports on the VAT Gap in the EU-28 Member States - 2018 Final Report TAXUD/2015/CC/131*, Directorate General Taxation and Customs Union. [12]

CBS (2020), *Biggest contraction ever in household consumption*, https://www.cbs.nl/en-gb/news/2020/20/biggest-contraction-ever-in-household-consumption (accessed on 2 July 2020). [6]

Cevik, S. et al. (2019), "Structural Transformation and Tax Efficiency", *IMF Working Paper Fiscal Affairs Department*, No. WP/19/30, International Monetary Fund. [13]

Insee (2020), *Informations rapides No133*, https://www.insee.fr/en/statistiques/4500961 (accessed on 2 July 2020). [7]

OECD (2020), *Evaluating the initial impact of COVID-19 containment measures on economic activity*, https://read.oecd-ilibrary.org/view/?ref=126_126496-evgsi2gmqj&title=Evaluating_the_initial_impact_of_COVID-19_containment_measures_on_economic_activity. [4]

OECD (2020), *OECD Economic Outlook, Volume 2020 Issue 1*, OECD Publishing, Paris, https://dx.doi.org/10.1787/0d1d1e2e-en. [9]

OECD (2020), *Tax and Fiscal Policy in Response to the Coronavirus Crisis: Strengthening Confidence and Resilience*, https://read.oecd-ilibrary.org/view/?ref=128_128575-o6raktc0aa&title=Tax-and-Fiscal-Policy-in-Response-to-the-Coronavirus-Crisis. [5]

OECD (2020), *Tax policy responses to COVID-19; table with measures takes by countries*, http://www.oecd.org/tax/covid-19-tax-policy-and-other-measures.xlsm (accessed on 2 July 2020). [10]

OECD (2018), *Consumption Tax Trends 2018: VAT/GST and Excise Rates, Trends and Policy Issues*, OECD Publishing, Paris, https://dx.doi.org/10.1787/ctt-2018-en. [11]

Sancak, C., R. Velloso and J. Xing (2010), "Tax Revenue Response to the Business Cycle", *IMF Working Papers* WP/10/71, http://dx.doi.org/10.5089/9781451982145.001. [2]

Simon, H. and M. Harding (2020), "What drives consumption tax revenues? : Disentangling policy and macroeconomic drivers", *OECD Taxation Working Papers*, No. 47, OECD Publishing, Paris, https://dx.doi.org/10.1787/94ed8187-en. [1]

Ueda, J. (2017), "The Evolution of Potential VAT Revenues and C-Efficiency in Advanced Economies", *IMF Working Papers* WP/17/158, http://dx.doi.org/10.5089/9781484305874.001. [3]

Annex 2.A. – Data on Implicit Tax Rates (ITRs) on consumption

Annex Table 2.A.1. ITRs on consumption (in %) across OECD countries, selected years

	1995	2000	2005	2007	2009	2011	2013	2015	2017	2018
AUS	12.2	13.0	12.8	12.1	11.4	10.8	11.8	11.1	11.1	10.9
AUT	19.2	20.4	19.7	19.4	18.9	19.4	19.4	19.7	19.8	19.7
BEL	17.1	18.3	18.4	18.5	17.0	17.3	17.1	16.9	17.3	17.4
CAN	11.9	11.8	11.3	10.5	7.0	6.8	6.7	6.9	7.0	7.0
CHL	19.3	18.7	18.2	17.9	15.7	16.9	16.7	16.9	16.6	16.8
COL	9.3	9.2	11.1	11.9	11.1	12.0	10.8	10.9	10.9	11.0
CZE	19.2	17.0	18.9	18.9	18.5	19.6	20.3	20.5	21.1	20.3
DNK	25.6	28.3	28.6	29.6	24.9	25.5	25.2	25.1	25.9	25.8
EST	18.0	19.5	21.2	24.0	23.9	23.7	22.9	24.4	24.9	24.5
FIN	23.0	24.6	23.1	22.3	20.5	22.1	22.6	21.9	22.9	23.3
FRA	18.0	17.5	16.5	16.2	15.2	16.8	17.1	17.7	18.3	18.8
DEU	15.6	16.0	16.0	17.5	17.3	17.4	16.8	17.0	16.3	16.7
GRC	15.9	16.0	14.9	15.7	13.8	16.9	18.3	19.3	21.0	21.4
HUN	27.5	26.0	23.4	24.7	25.6	27.6	30.7	32.8	30.1	31.4
ISL	23.5	24.0	25.2	24.6	17.0	17.6	17.7	18.5	20.7	19.8
IRL	22.5	23.9	23.4	21.9	17.0	17.3	18.4	20.2	20.2	19.4
ISR	18.7	17.6	17.8	17.6	17.2	17.9	17.9	18.3	17.1	16.9
ITA	15.9	17.1	15.2	15.8	14.9	16.3	16.8	17.5	18.0	17.8
JPN	6.4	7.5	7.4	7.2	6.8	6.9	6.9	9.2	9.6	9.0
KOR	14.0	14.0	12.8	12.7	12.2	12.4	12.2	11.7	12.6	12.3
LVA	14.4	15.6	17.3	17.2	16.7	17.2	18.6	20.3	21.0	22.3
LTU	15.5	16.1	15.5	16.8	14.8	16.6	15.7	16.6	17.3	17.4
LUX	17.8	22.8	25.6	27.2	26.3	27.8	28.4	25.6	24.6	25.4
MEX	5.6	6.6	5.9	6.1	6.4	6.5	5.9	8.6	8.2	8.3
NLD	17.4	18.3	18.9	19.4	18.0	18.1	18.3	19.2	20.3	20.6
NZL	19.3	18.1	18.2	16.9	16.8	18.6	18.8	19.7	19.6	19.9
NOR	25.5	27.1	23.8	25.4	22.0	22.2	21.8	21.0	21.1	21.1
POL	20.0	16.6	18.4	20.2	17.0	19.1	17.4	18.4	20.2	20.8
PRT	18.5	18.2	19.0	18.8	15.7	17.9	17.9	19.0	20.1	20.5
SVK	22.5	19.3	20.5	18.8	15.4	18.0	18.2	19.0	19.2	19.1
SVN	23.9	22.6	23.0	24.0	21.7	21.9	24.3	25.3	24.9	24.8
ESP	13.2	15.3	15.5	14.5	9.6	11.9	14.0	15.2	15.2	15.3
SWE	20.8	20.3	20.8	21.3	21.1	21.0	20.1	20.4	20.9	20.8
CHE	8.5	9.6	9.9	10.3	10.0	10.3	10.2	10.0	10.0	9.9
TUR	9.0	14.3	17.8	16.9	16.0	18.0	18.2	17.6	17.2	15.9
GBR	14.6	14.5	13.3	13.2	12.0	14.8	14.6	14.8	14.7	14.7
USA	6.4	6.0	5.8	5.6	5.1	5.4	5.6	5.6	5.4	5.5
OECD average	16.9	17.3	17.4	17.6	16.0	16.9	17.1	17.6	17.9	17.9

Source: Authors' calculations based on OECD National Accounts and OECD Revenue Statistics (2020).

StatLink https://doi.org/10.1787/888934209837

Notes

[1] (Simon and Harding, 2020[1]) is a recent OECD Taxation Working Paper that decomposes consumption tax revenues in OECD countries over the period 1995-2017 into the implicit tax rate (ITR) and consumption relative to GDP. Using the GFC as a case study, the paper identifies how economic downturns affect consumption tax revenues.

[2] This analysis covers data from 1995 until 2018, the latest year for which comprehensive *Revenues Statistics* data is available for all OECD countries.

[3] The acronym "VAT" refers to any national value-added tax (VAT) and its equivalent in several jurisdictions (goods and services tax, or GST), as described in (OECD, 2018[11]). Currently, 36 of the 37 OECD member countries operate a VAT, the only exception being the United States.

[4] The conceptual tax base is approximated by using final consumption expenditure in the OECD National Accounts (NAs) under item P3, measured according to the domestic concept. The numerator of the ITR on consumption comprises all revenues under the *Revenue Statistics* heading *5000 Taxes on goods and services* except for *5124 Taxes on exports*, *5125 Taxes on investment goods* and *5127 Other taxes on international trade and consumption*. For a discussion of this methodology as well as a review of other existing literature, see (Simon and Harding, 2020[1]).

[5] The VRR is a widely-used tool for evaluating the efficiency of a VAT system that normalises VAT revenues by reference to a theoretical situation where the standard VAT rate is applied to all final consumption (see for example (OECD, 2018[11]) and (CASE and IHS, 2018[12])). For a technical discussion on the factors influencing the VRR, see (OECD, 2018[11]).

[6] (Simon and Harding, 2020[1]) explain the causes of the relatively low levels of consumption as a share of GDP in Luxembourg and Ireland.

[7] See Annex C for ITRs on consumption for all OECD countries in selected years. For individual country results for the period 1995-2017, see (Simon and Harding, 2020[1]).

[8] Data on the major components of investment expenditure is available from the NAs for all countries except for Chile, Israel and Turkey.

[9] This is the GST rate at the federal level only. The combined federal GST and harmonized sales taxes applied in some Canadian provinces are often more than 10%.

[10] The OECD report Consumption Tax Trends (2020) contains several tables showing the evolution of VAT rates over time, the year of implementation of VAT, and the ratio of VAT revenues in OECD countries in 2018.

[11] Some countries have provided mechanisms to offset the negative effects of exemptions, such as targeted VAT refunds, full or partial right to deduct VAT on inputs or budgetary compensation, see OECD, Consumption Tax Trends 2020, for more details.

[12] To identify shifts in the composition of private consumption, the share of food and non-alcoholic beverages in consumption is used as a proxy of the share of necessity goods and services in the tax base (see e.g. (Sancak, Velloso and Xing, 2010[2]) and Simon and Harding (2020)).

[13] Changes in the pattern of private consumption could also be analysed by decomposing private consumption into the consumption of durable goods, semi-durable goods, non-durable goods and services (see e.g. (Cevik et al., 2019[13])). Given that a large part of the service sector (e.g. financial services) is exempt from VAT in almost all OECD countries, an increasing share of services in the economy can, for a given VAT rate, reduce the VRR. The average share of private expenditure on services in total

consumption followed a trend increase from 1995 to 2018, which was only interrupted during the GFC, when private consumption of both goods and services decreased slightly.

[14] Future studies could complement the present analysis by decomposing the VRR into compliance and policy gaps to further explore the extent to which changes in policy and compliance impact consumption tax revenues in OECD countries (see (Simon and Harding, 2020[1]) and (OECD, 2018[11]) for further details).

3 Tax Levels and Tax Structures, 1965-2019

Chapter 3 provides an overview of tax levels and tax structures in OECD countries.

In all of the following tables the symbol (..) indicates not available/or not applicable. The main series in this chapter cover a selection of years between 1990 and 2018. A complete series is, however, available on line. Data for 1955 and 1960 (for nineteen OECD countries) are provided in part V of the 1998 edition of this Report.

The Gross Domestic Product (GDP) figures are based on the 2008 System of National Accounts (SNA) for all OECD countries.

Box 3.1. Treatment of capital transfers

Footnotes to Tables 3.1 to 3.18 refer to the treatment of the capital transfers that some countries make to account for taxes that have been assessed but not collected. The capital transfer has been subtracted from the total tax revenue for Denmark, France, Lithuania, Luxembourg and Switzerland and this reduction has been allocated between tax headings in proportion to their tax revenues at the level of government against which these transfers were recorded. In the case of Belgium, the capital transfers were instead subtracted directly from the specific taxes to which they relate.

This applies to the following countries:

- Belgium from 1995.
- Denmark from 1971.
- France from 1992.
- Lithuania from 1999.
- Luxembourg from 2013.
- Switzerland from 1990.

Table 3.1. Total tax revenue as % of GDP

	1965	1990	2000	2007	2010	2013	2015	2017	2018	2019p
Australia	20.6	28.1	30.5	29.5	25.3	27.1	27.9	28.5	28.7	..
Austria	33.5	39.3	42.3	40.5	41.0	42.6	43.1	41.8	42.2	42.4
Belgium[1]	30.8	41.4	43.8	42.9	42.9	45.0	44.1	43.8	43.9	42.9
Canada	25.0	35.1	34.7	32.5	31.0	31.1	32.8	33.1	33.2	33.5
Chile	..	16.9	18.8	22.7	19.6	19.9	20.4	20.2	21.1	20.7
Colombia	..	11.3	15.7	19.3	18.1	20.0	19.9	19.0	19.3	19.7
Czech Republic	..	..	32.3	34.1	32.2	33.7	33.1	34.4	35.0	34.9
Denmark[1]	29.1	44.4	46.9	46.4	44.8	45.9	46.1	45.8	44.4	46.3
Estonia	..	..	31.0	31.0	32.9	31.5	33.1	32.5	32.9	33.1
Finland	30.0	42.9	45.8	41.4	40.6	43.4	43.5	42.9	42.4	42.2
France[1]	33.7	41.2	43.4	42.5	42.1	45.4	45.3	46.1	45.9	45.4
Germany	31.7	34.8	36.4	35.4	35.5	37.0	37.3	37.8	38.5	38.8
Greece	17.1	25.2	33.4	31.8	32.0	35.7	36.4	38.6	38.9	38.7
Hungary	..	..	38.6	39.4	37.2	38.6	38.9	38.3	37.5	35.8
Iceland	25.7	30.4	36.0	38.6	32.3	34.5	35.4	37.6	37.2	36.1
Ireland	24.5	32.4	30.8	30.8	27.7	28.9	23.4	22.8	22.7	22.7
Israel	..	..	34.8	34.2	30.7	30.8	31.2	32.5	30.9	30.5
Italy	24.6	36.3	40.5	41.6	41.7	43.8	43.0	41.9	41.9	42.4
Japan	17.6	28.2	25.8	27.5	26.5	28.9	30.7	31.4	32.0	..
Korea	..	18.4	20.9	23.7	22.4	23.1	23.7	25.4	26.8	27.4
Latvia	..	..	29.1	28.3	28.7	29.4	30.0	31.4	31.2	31.2
Lithuania[1]	..	..	30.8	30.0	28.4	26.8	28.7	29.5	30.2	30.3
Luxembourg[1]	26.4	33.5	36.9	36.2	37.5	38.2	37.0	37.6	39.7	39.2
Mexico	..	12.1	11.5	12.0	12.8	13.3	15.9	16.1	16.2	16.5
Netherlands	30.5	39.7	36.9	35.7	35.7	36.1	37.0	38.7	38.8	39.3
New Zealand	24.5	36.2	32.5	33.9	30.3	30.5	31.6	31.6	32.9	32.3
Norway	29.4	40.2	41.7	42.0	41.8	39.8	38.4	38.8	39.6	39.9
Poland	..	..	32.9	34.6	31.4	31.9	32.4	34.1	35.2	35.4
Portugal	15.7	26.5	31.1	31.8	30.5	34.0	34.4	34.1	34.8	34.8
Slovak Republic	..	..	33.6	29.2	28.1	31.0	32.7	34.2	34.3	34.7
Slovenia	..	..	37.7	38.1	37.8	37.2	37.3	37.1	37.4	37.7
Spain	14.3	31.5	33.1	36.4	31.3	33.1	33.8	33.9	34.6	34.6
Sweden	30.9	49.0	48.8	45.1	43.1	42.7	42.9	44.3	43.9	42.9
Switzerland[1]	16.5	23.7	27.6	26.2	26.6	27.0	27.6	28.4	28.0	28.5
Turkey	10.6	14.5	23.5	22.9	24.7	25.2	25.0	24.7	24.0	23.1
United Kingdom	30.1	32.9	32.8	32.8	32.1	32.1	32.4	32.8	32.9	33.0
United States	23.6	26.0	28.3	26.8	23.5	25.6	26.2	26.7	24.4	24.5
Unweighted average										
OECD Average[2]	**24.8**	**31.1**	**33.3**	**33.2**	**31.9**	**33.0**	**33.3**	**33.7**	**33.9**	**33.8**

.. Not available

Note: Full time series can be accessed at http://oe.cd/full-time-series.

1. The total tax revenue has been reduced by the amount of any capital transfer that represents uncollected taxes. The capital transfer has been allocated between tax headings in proportion to the reported tax revenue, except for Belgium, where the capital transfers were subtracted directly from the specific taxes to which they relate.
2. 2019: calculated by applying the unweighted average percentage change for 2019 in the 35 countries providing data for that year to the overall average tax to GDP ratio in 2018.

StatLink https://doi.org/10.1787/888934209856

Table 3.2. Total tax revenue in billions of US dollars at market exchange rates

	1965	1990	2000	2007	2010	2013	2015	2017	2018	2019p
Australia	5.6	90.9	124.4	290.8	328.3	418.1	348.2	404.0	417.2	..
Austria	..	68.6	83.2	157.6	160.5	183.3	164.7	174.3	192.2	189.4
Belgium[1]	..	89.4	103.6	201.9	206.2	234.9	204.0	220.2	238.3	227.3
Canada	14.2	209.2	262.8	477.2	501.4	574.9	511.1	546.2	570.0	580.8
Chile	..	5.8	14.6	39.4	42.8	55.3	49.7	55.9	62.8	58.3
Colombia	..	5.1	14.7	39.8	51.9	76.5	58.4	59.2	64.4	63.7
Czech Republic	..	..	20.0	64.9	67.4	71.4	62.3	75.3	87.1	87.6
Denmark[1]	3.0	61.4	76.9	148.3	144.2	157.6	139.5	151.1	157.8	160.8
Estonia	..	..	1.8	7.0	6.5	7.9	7.6	8.7	10.1	10.4
Finland	..	49.6	57.5	106.0	101.1	117.7	102.1	109.3	116.9	113.6
France[1]	..	550.7	591.8	1 130.7	1 113.7	1 275.1	1 104.3	1 193.0	1 279.5	1 232.8
Germany	..	577.4	706.9	1 210.4	1 206.8	1 379.1	1 250.9	1 388.8	1 526.8	1 498.5
Greece	..	14.6	43.5	101.3	95.9	85.7	71.6	78.5	84.8	81.2
Hungary	..	..	18.2	55.1	48.8	52.3	48.5	54.2	59.1	57.6
Iceland	0.1	2.0	3.2	8.3	4.4	5.5	6.2	9.2	9.6	8.7
Ireland	0.7	15.6	30.7	83.2	61.5	69.0	68.1	76.2	86.7	88.1
Israel	..	..	46.2	61.2	72.0	90.2	93.7	114.8	114.5	120.3
Italy	..	336.6	463.6	918.8	889.9	938.3	788.9	820.5	872.8	849.4
Japan	17.1	903.6	1 263.4	1 242.0	1 509.6	1 500.1	1 351.5	1 531.5	1 589.7	..
Korea	..	52.6	120.5	278.2	256.2	317.2	347.9	411.7	460.4	449.7
Latvia	..	..	1.8	8.8	6.8	8.9	8.1	9.5	10.7	10.6
Lithuania[1]	..	..	3.8	11.9	10.5	12.4	11.9	14.0	16.1	16.4
Luxembourg[1]	..	4.7	7.8	18.4	20.0	23.6	21.4	24.1	28.2	27.9
Mexico	..	35.9	81.2	126.5	135.9	169.6	186.1	186.9	198.0	..
Netherlands	..	132.6	153.7	302.5	301.9	316.6	283.3	322.0	354.4	356.7
New Zealand	1.4	16.4	18.0	47.1	44.9	59.2	56.8	65.8	69.1	65.6
Norway	2.4	48.2	71.4	168.5	179.3	208.1	148.2	154.5	171.8	161.1
Poland	..	..	56.6	148.7	150.4	167.1	154.9	179.6	206.4	209.5
Portugal	..	18.8	36.8	76.4	72.5	77.0	68.6	75.4	84.0	82.8
Slovak Republic	..	..	9.8	25.3	25.4	30.6	28.9	32.6	36.3	36.6
Slovenia	..	..	6.6	18.3	18.2	18.0	16.1	18.0	20.2	20.2
Spain	..	131.6	197.3	536.1	444.4	448.5	404.6	443.6	491.8	482.8
Sweden	7.8	128.3	128.2	221.6	213.6	250.6	216.6	239.8	244.0	227.9
Switzerland[1]	2.6	61.3	75.1	125.8	155.3	185.9	187.5	193.2	197.8	200.6
Turkey	1.3	30.2	64.5	156.2	192.0	240.8	215.5	212.0	186.3	175.6
United Kingdom	30.6	359.4	544.0	1 018.0	795.0	892.9	950.0	875.7	940.6	932.9
United States	167.0	1 552.4	2 900.5	3 868.6	3 517.1	4 291.8	4 774.2	5 225.9	5 031.7	5 243.8
Unweighted average										
OECD Average	**19.5**	**198.3**	**227.2**	**364.9**	**355.5**	**405.7**	**392.2**	**425.8**	**440.2**	..

.. Not available

Note: Full time series can be accessed at http://oe.cd/full-time-series.

1. The total tax revenue has been reduced by the amount of any capital transfer that represents uncollected taxes. The capital transfer has been allocated between tax headings in proportion to the reported tax revenue, except for Belgium, where the capital transfers were subtracted directly from the specific taxes to which they relate.

StatLink https://doi.org/10.1787/888934209875

Table 3.3. Tax revenue of main headings as % of GDP, 2018

	1000 Income & profits	2000 Social security	3000 Payroll	4000 Property	5000 Goods and services[2]	6000 Others	Memorandum item: supranational revenues
Australia	17.3	0.0	1.4	2.7	7.3	0.0	..
Austria	12.4	14.7	2.7	0.5	11.7	0.2	0.2
Belgium[1]	16.2	13.3	0.0	3.4	11.1	0.0	0.4
Canada	16.2	4.6	0.7	3.9	7.8	0.0	..
Chile	7.5	1.5	0.0	1.1	11.2	-0.2	..
Colombia	6.5	1.8	0.4	1.5	8.3	0.8	..
Czech Republic	7.9	15.3	0.0	0.5	11.3	0.0	0.2
Denmark[1]	27.6	0.0	0.3	1.8	14.6	0.0	0.1
Estonia	7.4	11.5	0.0	0.2	13.8	0.0	0.2
Finland	14.8	11.8	0.0	1.4	14.3	0.0	0.1
France[1]	11.5	16.0	1.5	4.1	12.2	0.5	0.2
Germany	12.6	14.5	0.0	1.1	10.3	0.0	0.2
Greece	8.9	11.6	0.0	3.0	15.4	0.0	0.2
Hungary	6.8	11.8	1.0	1.0	16.8	0.1	0.1
Iceland	18.4	3.5	0.3	2.0	12.4	0.6	..
Ireland	10.3	3.9	0.2	1.3	7.0	0.0	0.1
Israel	10.1	5.2	1.2	3.2	11.2	0.0	..
Italy	13.0	13.0	0.0	2.5	12.0	1.4	0.2
Japan	10.2	12.9	0.0	2.6	6.2	0.1	..
Korea	9.1	6.8	0.1	3.1	7.0	0.6	..
Latvia	7.1	9.1	0.0	0.9	14.1	0.0	0.2
Lithuania[1]	5.6	12.7	0.0	0.3	11.6	0.0	0.3
Luxembourg[1]	15.6	10.8	0.0	3.9	9.4	0.0	0.3
Mexico	7.1	2.2	0.4	0.3	5.9	0.3	..
Netherlands	11.5	14.0	0.0	1.6	11.7	0.1	0.4
New Zealand	18.5	0.0	0.0	1.9	12.5	0.0	..
Norway	16.5	10.1	0.1	1.2	11.7	0.0	..
Poland	7.4	13.1	0.2	1.3	13.1	0.1	0.2
Portugal	9.8	9.4	0.0	1.4	13.9	0.3	0.2
Slovak Republic	7.1	14.8	0.0	0.4	12.0	0.0	0.2
Slovenia	7.3	15.5	0.0	0.6	14.0	0.0	0.1
Spain	10.1	11.7	0.0	2.5	10.2	0.0	0.2
Sweden	15.8	9.6	5.1	0.9	12.4	0.0	0.3
Switzerland[1]	13.4	6.6	0.0	2.1	5.8	0.1	..
Turkey	5.8	7.2	0.0	1.0	9.7	0.3	..
United Kingdom	11.6	6.3	0.1	4.1	10.7	0.0	0.2
United States	11.0	6.1	0.0	3.0	4.3	0.0	..
Unweighted average							
OECD Average	**11.5**	**9.0**	**0.4**	**1.9**	**10.9**	**0.1**	**0.2**

.. Not available

1. The total tax revenue has been reduced by the amount of any capital transfer that represents uncollected taxes. The capital transfer has been allocated between tax headings in proportion to the reported tax revenue, except for Belgium, where the capital transfers were subtracted directly from the specific taxes to which they relate.
2. The figures in category 5000 include supranational revenues, which are also presented separately under the Supranational heading.

StatLink https://doi.org/10.1787/888934209894

Table 3.4. Tax revenue of main headings as % of total tax revenue, 2018

	1000 Income & profits	2000 Social security	3000 Payroll	4000 Property	5000 Goods and services[2]	6000 Others	Memorandum item: supranational revenues
Australia	60.2	0.0	4.8	9.5	25.5	0.0	..
Austria	29.3	34.8	6.4	1.3	27.7	0.5	0.4
Belgium[1]	36.8	30.2	0.0	7.8	25.2	0.0	0.9
Canada	48.8	14.0	2.0	11.6	23.5	0.1	..
Chile	35.8	6.9	0.0	5.2	53.3	-1.1	..
Colombia	33.7	9.6	1.8	8.0	42.8	4.2	..
Czech Republic	22.6	43.8	0.0	1.3	32.3	0.0	0.4
Denmark[1]	62.2	0.1	0.6	4.1	32.9	0.0	0.3
Estonia	22.6	34.9	0.0	0.7	41.8	0.0	0.6
Finland	34.8	27.9	0.0	3.4	33.8	0.0	0.2
France[1]	25.1	34.9	3.3	9.0	26.6	1.1	0.4
Germany	32.8	37.7	0.0	2.7	26.8	0.0	0.5
Greece	22.9	29.9	0.0	7.7	39.5	0.0	0.5
Hungary	18.2	31.6	2.6	2.6	44.7	0.2	0.4
Iceland	49.3	9.5	0.8	5.5	33.3	1.6	..
Ireland	45.3	17.3	0.8	5.8	30.8	0.0	0.6
Israel	32.8	16.8	3.8	10.3	36.3	0.0	..
Italy	31.0	31.0	0.0	6.1	28.7	3.2	0.5
Japan	31.9	40.2	0.0	8.1	19.5	0.3	..
Korea	34.1	25.4	0.3	11.6	26.3	2.3	..
Latvia	22.6	29.3	0.0	3.0	45.1	0.0	0.7
Lithuania[1]	18.5	42.1	0.0	1.0	38.4	0.0	0.9
Luxembourg[1]	39.4	27.1	0.0	9.7	23.7	0.1	0.6
Mexico	44.0	13.4	2.5	2.0	36.4	1.7	..
Netherlands	29.6	36.0	0.0	4.0	30.1	0.3	1.1
New Zealand	56.3	0.0	0.0	5.8	37.9	0.0	..
Norway	41.7	25.5	0.1	3.1	29.5	0.0	..
Poland	21.1	37.2	0.6	3.7	37.2	0.1	0.5
Portugal	28.3	26.9	0.0	4.0	39.8	1.0	0.5
Slovak Republic	20.7	43.0	0.0	1.2	35.0	0.0	0.5
Slovenia	19.5	41.4	0.1	1.6	37.4	0.0	0.4
Spain	29.3	33.9	0.0	7.3	29.5	0.0	0.6
Sweden	35.9	21.8	11.6	2.2	28.1	0.1	0.6
Switzerland[1]	47.7	23.6	0.0	7.3	20.8	0.5	..
Turkey	24.1	29.9	0.0	4.3	40.5	1.1	..
United Kingdom	35.3	19.1	0.4	12.5	32.6	0.0	0.5
United States	45.2	24.9	0.0	12.3	17.6	0.0	..
Unweighted average							
OECD Average	**34.3**	**25.7**	**1.2**	**5.6**	**32.7**	**0.5**	**0.6**

.. Not available

1. The total tax revenue has been reduced by the amount of any capital transfer that represents uncollected taxes. The capital transfer has been allocated between tax headings in proportion to the reported tax revenue, except for Belgium, where the capital transfers were subtracted directly from the specific taxes to which they relate.
2. The figures in category 5000 include supranational revenues, which are also presented separately under the Supranational heading.

StatLink https://doi.org/10.1787/888934209913

Table 3.5. Tax revenue of main headings as % of GDP, 2019p

	1000 Income & profits	2000 Social security	3000 Payroll	4000 Property	5000 Goods and services[2]	6000 Others	Memorandum item: supranational revenues
Australia	..	..	..	..	..	..	..
Austria	12.5	14.8	2.7	0.5	11.7	0.2	0.2
Belgium[1]	15.2	13.3	0.0	3.5	11.0	0.0	0.4
Canada	16.4	4.7	0.7	3.9	7.7	0.0	..
Chile	7.2	1.5	0.0	1.1	11.0	-0.1	..
Colombia	6.4	1.9	0.3	1.8	8.5	0.9	..
Czech Republic	7.9	15.5	0.0	0.4	11.2	0.0	0.2
Denmark[1]	30.0	0.0	0.3	1.9	14.1	0.0	0.1
Estonia	7.3	11.6	0.0	0.2	14.0	0.0	0.2
Finland	14.7	11.8	0.0	1.4	14.2	0.0	0.2
France[1]	11.8	14.9	1.8	4.0	12.3	0.5	0.2
Germany	12.7	14.7	0.0	1.1	10.4	0.0	0.2
Greece	8.3	11.9	0.0	3.1	15.3	0.0	0.2
Hungary	5.9	11.6	1.0	1.0	16.2	0.1	0.1
Iceland	17.9	3.3	0.3	2.1	11.8	0.6	..
Ireland	10.3	4.0	0.2	1.3	6.9	0.0	0.1
Israel	10.0	5.3	1.1	3.1	10.9	0.0	..
Italy	13.3	13.3	0.0	2.4	12.1	1.4	0.2
Japan	10.3	..	0.0	2.6	6.5	0.1	..
Korea	9.1	7.3	0.1	3.1	7.1	0.7	..
Latvia	6.6	9.6	0.0	0.9	14.1	0.0	0.2
Lithuania[1]	8.7	9.7	0.0	0.3	11.6	0.0	0.3
Luxembourg[1]	15.2	10.8	0.0	3.8	9.4	0.0	0.3
Mexico	7.0	2.3	..	..	..	..	..
Netherlands	12.2	13.5	0.0	1.5	12.1	0.1	0.4
New Zealand	17.8	0.0	0.0	2.0	12.6	0.0	..
Norway	16.2	10.6	0.1	1.3	11.8	0.0	..
Poland	7.6	13.3	0.2	1.3	8.5	4.5	0.2
Portugal	9.5	9.7	0.0	1.4	14.0	0.3	0.2
Slovak Republic	7.1	15.0	0.0	0.4	12.2	0.0	0.2
Slovenia	7.5	15.8	0.0	0.6	13.7	0.0	0.1
Spain	9.9	12.2	0.0	2.4	10.0	0.0	0.2
Sweden	15.1	9.2	5.3	0.9	12.1	0.0	0.3
Switzerland[1]	13.6	6.7	0.0	2.1	6.0	0.2	..
Turkey	5.6	7.2	0.0	1.0	9.0	0.3	..
United Kingdom	11.6	6.4	0.1	4.1	10.7	0.0	0.2
United States	11.1	6.1	0.0	3.0	4.3	0.0	..

.. Not available

1. The total tax revenue has been reduced by the amount of any capital transfer that represents uncollected taxes. The capital transfer has been allocated between tax headings in proportion to the reported tax revenue, except for Belgium, where the capital transfers were subtracted directly from the specific taxes to which they relate.

2. The figures in category 5000 include supranational revenues, which are also presented separately under the Supranational heading.

StatLink https://doi.org/10.1787/888934209932

Table 3.6. Tax revenue of main headings as % of total tax revenue, 2019p

	1000 Income & profits	2000 Social security	3000 Payroll	4000 Property	5000 Goods and services[2]	6000 Others	Memorandum item: supranational revenues
Australia	..	..	..	..	..	..	..
Austria	29.4	34.9	6.4	1.3	27.5	0.5	0.4
Belgium[1]	35.3	31.0	0.0	8.1	25.7	0.0	1.0
Canada	49.1	14.0	2.2	11.6	22.9	0.1	..
Chile	34.8	7.3	0.0	5.4	53.1	-0.6	..
Colombia	32.3	9.5	1.7	9.1	42.9	4.4	..
Czech Republic	22.5	44.3	0.0	1.2	32.0	0.0	0.4
Denmark[1]	64.7	0.1	0.6	4.1	30.5	0.0	0.3
Estonia	21.9	35.0	0.0	0.6	42.4	0.0	0.6
Finland	35.0	27.9	0.0	3.4	33.7	0.0	0.4
France[1]	26.1	32.8	4.0	8.9	27.1	1.2	0.4
Germany	32.6	37.9	0.0	2.8	26.7	0.0	0.5
Greece	21.6	30.8	0.0	8.1	39.6	0.0	0.5
Hungary	16.5	32.5	2.7	2.7	45.3	0.3	0.4
Iceland	49.5	9.2	0.8	5.9	32.7	1.8	..
Ireland	45.3	17.5	1.0	5.6	30.6	0.0	0.6
Israel	32.9	17.4	3.8	10.1	35.9	0.0	..
Italy	31.4	31.2	0.0	5.8	28.4	3.2	0.4
Japan	..	..	..	..	..	..	..
Korea	33.2	26.7	0.3	11.4	25.8	2.5	..
Latvia	21.3	30.6	0.0	3.0	45.1	0.0	0.5
Lithuania[1]	28.6	32.0	0.0	1.0	38.4	0.0	0.9
Luxembourg[1]	38.8	27.5	0.0	9.7	23.9	0.1	0.7
Mexico	..	..	..	..	..	..	..
Netherlands	31.0	34.3	0.0	3.7	30.7	0.3	1.1
New Zealand	55.0	0.0	0.0	6.2	38.9	0.0	..
Norway	40.5	26.6	0.1	3.2	29.5	0.0	..
Poland	21.4	37.6	0.6	3.6	24.1	12.7	0.5
Portugal	27.4	27.9	0.0	4.0	40.1	0.8	0.5
Slovak Republic	20.6	43.1	0.0	1.2	35.1	0.0	0.5
Slovenia	20.0	42.0	0.1	1.7	36.3	0.0	0.4
Spain	28.7	35.4	0.0	7.0	28.9	0.0	0.6
Sweden	35.2	21.5	12.4	2.2	28.3	0.1	0.6
Switzerland[1]	47.8	23.4	0.0	7.3	21.0	0.5	..
Turkey	24.2	31.4	0.0	4.2	39.0	1.2	..
United Kingdom	35.1	19.5	0.4	12.4	32.6	0.0	0.5
United States	45.4	24.9	0.0	12.1	17.6	0.0	..

.. Not available

1. The total tax revenue has been reduced by the amount of any capital transfer that represents uncollected taxes. The capital transfer has been allocated between tax headings in proportion to the reported tax revenue, except for Belgium, where the capital transfers were subtracted directly from the specific taxes to which they relate.
2. The figures in category 5000 include supranational revenues, which are also presented separately under the Supranational heading.

StatLink https://doi.org/10.1787/888934209951

Table 3.7. Taxes on income and profits (1000) as % of GDP and as % of total tax revenue

	% of GDP					% of total tax revenue				
	1990	2000	2010	2017	2018	1990	2000	2010	2017	2018
Australia	16.1	17.6	14.3	16.8	17.3	57.1	57.9	56.5	58.8	60.2
Austria	10.0	12.0	11.5	11.8	12.4	25.5	28.3	28.1	28.3	29.3
Belgium[1]	15.3	16.9	14.7	16.0	16.2	36.9	38.6	34.2	36.5	36.8
Canada	17.0	17.4	14.5	16.1	16.2	48.6	50.1	46.6	48.7	48.8
Chile	3.9	4.4	7.5	7.0	7.5	23.2	23.3	38.1	34.5	35.8
Colombia	3.4	3.6	4.8	6.3	6.5	29.9	23.2	26.6	33.0	33.7
Czech Republic	..	7.4	6.5	7.6	7.9	..	22.8	20.2	22.2	22.6
Denmark[1]	27.2	28.8	27.5	29.1	27.6	61.2	61.5	61.5	63.4	62.2
Estonia	..	7.7	6.5	7.2	7.4	..	24.8	19.8	22.0	22.6
Finland	16.8	19.7	14.4	15.2	14.8	39.2	43.1	35.5	35.5	34.8
France[1]	6.6	10.8	9.5	10.9	11.5	16.1	24.8	22.6	23.6	25.1
Germany	11.3	11.0	10.1	12.3	12.6	32.4	30.1	28.3	32.5	32.8
Greece	5.0	9.0	7.1	8.7	8.9	19.9	26.8	22.0	22.4	22.9
Hungary	..	9.4	7.7	7.4	6.8	..	24.3	20.6	19.3	18.2
Iceland	9.0	14.3	14.3	18.5	18.4	29.7	39.9	44.4	49.2	49.3
Ireland	12.3	13.4	11.1	10.0	10.3	38.0	43.6	40.1	43.8	45.3
Israel	..	13.8	8.9	11.6	10.1	..	39.6	29.1	35.6	32.8
Italy	13.2	13.4	13.6	13.3	13.0	36.5	33.2	32.7	31.7	31.0
Japan	14.2	9.0	8.0	9.6	10.2	50.2	34.8	30.2	30.7	31.9
Korea	6.0	6.0	6.3	8.1	9.1	32.8	28.8	28.0	32.1	34.1
Latvia	..	7.0	7.2	8.2	7.1	..	24.1	25.0	26.2	22.6
Lithuania[1]	..	8.3	4.6	5.3	5.6	..	27.0	16.2	18.1	18.5
Luxembourg[1]	13.5	13.5	13.6	14.0	15.6	40.2	36.5	36.3	37.2	39.4
Mexico	4.1	4.1	5.1	7.2	7.1	34.0	36.0	39.8	44.6	44.0
Netherlands	12.8	9.6	9.9	11.6	11.5	32.3	25.9	27.9	30.0	29.6
New Zealand	21.6	19.5	16.3	17.6	18.5	59.6	60.0	53.8	55.6	56.3
Norway	14.2	18.9	19.8	15.2	16.5	35.2	45.3	47.3	39.1	41.7
Poland	..	6.7	6.3	6.9	7.4	..	20.4	20.1	20.3	21.1
Portugal	6.8	9.1	8.2	9.6	9.8	25.7	29.3	26.8	28.2	28.3
Slovak Republic	..	6.9	5.3	7.1	7.1	..	20.5	18.8	20.6	20.7
Slovenia	..	6.8	7.4	6.9	7.3	..	18.0	19.6	18.5	19.5
Spain	9.7	9.3	8.7	9.6	10.1	30.6	28.1	28.0	28.4	29.3
Sweden	20.3	19.9	15.3	16.1	15.8	41.5	40.9	35.5	36.4	35.9
Switzerland[1]	11.2	12.2	12.1	13.4	13.4	47.0	44.1	45.5	47.3	47.7
Turkey	4.9	6.9	5.3	5.3	5.8	33.5	29.5	21.3	21.4	24.1
United Kingdom	12.9	13.0	12.0	11.6	11.6	39.3	39.6	37.4	35.3	35.3
United States	11.8	14.2	9.9	12.0	11.0	45.2	50.1	42.3	44.8	45.2
Unweighted average										
OECD Average	**11.8**	**11.7**	**10.4**	**11.4**	**11.5**	**37.2**	**34.5**	**32.6**	**33.9**	**34.3**

.. Not available

Note: Full time series can be accessed at http://oe.cd/full-time-series.

1. The total tax revenue has been reduced by the amount of any capital transfer that represents uncollected taxes. The capital transfer has been allocated between tax headings in proportion to the reported tax revenue, except for Belgium, where the capital transfers were subtracted directly from the specific taxes to which they relate.

StatLink https://doi.org/10.1787/888934209970

Table 3.8. Taxes on personal income (1100) as % of GDP and as % of total tax revenue

	% of GDP					% of total tax revenue				
	1990	2000	2010	2017	2018	1990	2000	2010	2017	2018
Australia	12.1	11.5	9.8	11.5	11.8	43.0	37.7	38.6	40.3	41.1
Austria	8.2	9.3	9.2	9.1	9.4	21.0	22.0	22.4	21.7	22.2
Belgium[1]	13.3	13.8	12.1	11.9	11.9	32.0	31.4	28.2	27.2	27.0
Canada	14.3	12.8	10.9	11.9	12.0	40.8	36.8	35.0	35.9	36.2
Chile	0.9	1.4	1.3	1.9	1.4	5.6	7.6	6.8	9.7	6.7
Colombia	0.2	0.8	1.0	1.1	1.2	1.8	4.9	5.3	5.9	6.4
Czech Republic	..	4.2	3.3	4.0	4.3	..	12.9	10.2	11.5	12.2
Denmark[1]	24.0	24.7	23.3	24.4	24.1	54.1	52.7	52.0	53.2	54.4
Estonia	..	6.8	5.2	5.6	5.4	..	22.0	15.9	17.3	16.5
Finland	14.9	14.0	12.0	12.5	12.2	34.7	30.6	29.5	29.2	28.9
France[1]	4.4	7.8	7.2	8.6	9.4	10.7	17.9	17.0	18.6	20.5
Germany	9.6	9.2	8.6	10.3	10.5	27.6	25.3	24.1	27.2	27.2
Greece	3.6	4.3	4.0	6.2	6.3	14.1	13.0	12.4	16.1	16.1
Hungary	..	7.2	6.5	5.4	5.5	..	18.6	17.4	14.1	14.6
Iceland	8.2	12.5	11.8	14.3	14.8	26.9	34.8	36.5	38.1	39.7
Ireland	10.7	9.8	8.7	7.2	7.1	33.1	31.9	31.6	31.6	31.2
Israel	..	10.1	5.5	6.7	6.4	..	29.1	18.0	20.7	20.6
Italy	9.5	10.1	11.2	10.8	10.7	26.3	24.8	26.9	25.7	25.6
Japan	7.8	5.4	4.9	5.9	6.1	27.8	21.1	18.6	18.8	19.1
Korea	3.7	3.1	3.2	4.5	4.9	20.0	14.6	14.2	17.9	18.4
Latvia	..	5.5	6.2	6.6	6.0	..	18.8	21.6	21.1	19.2
Lithuania[1]	..	7.6	3.6	3.8	4.1	..	24.8	12.7	13.0	13.5
Luxembourg[1]	8.1	6.8	7.9	8.9	9.3	24.1	18.5	20.9	23.7	23.5
Mexico	..	..	2.3	3.4	3.4	..	..	18.3	21.4	21.2
Netherlands	9.8	5.6	7.7	8.3	8.0	24.7	15.1	21.5	21.6	20.5
New Zealand	17.4	14.0	11.4	11.9	12.3	48.0	43.1	37.7	37.8	37.5
Norway	10.5	10.1	9.9	10.3	10.0	26.2	24.2	23.7	26.5	25.3
Poland	..	4.3	4.4	5.0	5.3	..	13.2	13.9	14.6	15.1
Portugal	4.2	5.4	5.4	6.4	6.5	15.9	17.4	17.6	18.9	18.7
Slovak Republic	..	3.3	2.6	3.4	3.6	..	9.9	9.3	9.9	10.5
Slovenia	..	5.5	5.6	5.1	5.3	..	14.6	14.7	13.7	14.3
Spain	6.9	6.4	6.9	7.4	7.7	21.7	19.3	22.1	21.8	22.2
Sweden	18.8	16.3	12.1	13.3	12.9	38.4	33.4	28.0	30.1	29.4
Switzerland[1]	7.7	8.2	8.4	8.6	8.6	32.5	29.6	31.7	30.2	30.7
Turkey	3.9	5.2	3.5	3.6	3.7	26.8	22.2	14.0	14.5	15.4
United Kingdom	9.7	9.5	9.2	9.0	9.0	29.4	29.0	28.6	27.3	27.3
United States	9.8	11.9	8.2	10.4	10.0	37.7	42.2	34.8	39.0	41.1
Unweighted average										
OECD Average	**9.3**	**8.5**	**7.4**	**8.1**	**8.1**	**27.6**	**24.0**	**22.5**	**23.4**	**23.5**

.. Not available

Note: Full time series can be accessed at http://oe.cd/full-time-series.

1. The total tax revenue has been reduced by the amount of any capital transfer that represents uncollected taxes. The capital transfer has been allocated between tax headings in proportion to the reported tax revenue, except for Belgium, where the capital transfers were subtracted directly from the specific taxes to which they relate.

StatLink https://doi.org/10.1787/888934209989

Table 3.9. Taxes on corporate income (1200) as % of GDP and as % of total tax revenue

	% of GDP					% of total tax revenue				
	1990	2000	2010	2017	2018	1990	2000	2010	2017	2018
Australia	4.0	6.2	4.5	5.3	5.5	14.1	20.2	17.9	18.5	19.1
Austria	1.4	1.9	1.9	2.5	2.7	3.6	4.6	4.6	5.9	6.4
Belgium[1]	2.0	3.1	2.5	4.1	4.3	4.8	7.2	5.9	9.3	9.8
Canada	2.5	4.2	3.2	3.9	3.8	7.0	12.2	10.5	11.7	11.3
Chile	2.1	2.1	4.0	4.3	4.7	12.4	11.2	20.4	21.1	22.1
Colombia	1.6	2.6	3.8	4.9	4.9	13.9	16.7	20.7	25.7	25.5
Czech Republic	..	3.2	3.2	3.7	3.6	..	9.9	10.0	10.7	10.4
Denmark[1]	1.7	3.2	2.3	3.2	2.9	3.8	6.8	5.0	7.1	6.5
Estonia	..	0.9	1.3	1.5	2.0	..	2.8	4.0	4.7	6.1
Finland	1.9	5.7	2.4	2.7	2.5	4.5	12.5	6.0	6.3	6.0
France[1]	2.2	3.0	2.3	2.3	2.1	5.3	6.9	5.5	5.0	4.6
Germany	1.7	1.8	1.5	2.0	2.1	4.8	4.8	4.2	5.4	5.6
Greece	1.4	4.0	2.5	1.9	2.2	5.5	11.9	7.9	5.0	5.6
Hungary	..	2.2	1.2	2.0	1.3	..	5.7	3.3	5.2	3.6
Iceland	0.8	1.2	0.9	3.1	2.4	2.8	3.3	2.7	8.1	6.5
Ireland	1.6	3.6	2.4	2.8	3.2	4.9	11.7	8.5	12.1	14.2
Israel	..	3.3	2.6	3.3	3.2	..	9.6	8.6	10.1	10.4
Italy	3.6	2.8	2.3	2.1	1.9	10.0	6.9	5.5	5.0	4.5
Japan	6.3	3.5	3.1	3.7	4.1	22.4	13.7	11.6	11.8	12.9
Korea	2.3	3.0	3.1	3.6	4.2	12.8	14.1	13.8	14.2	15.7
Latvia	..	1.5	1.0	1.6	1.1	..	5.3	3.4	5.1	3.4
Lithuania[1]	..	0.7	1.0	1.5	1.5	..	2.2	3.5	5.1	5.1
Luxembourg[1]	5.4	6.6	5.8	5.1	6.3	16.1	18.0	15.3	13.6	15.9
Mexico	..	..	1.8	3.5	3.4	..	..	14.4	21.8	21.3
Netherlands	3.0	4.0	2.3	3.3	3.5	7.5	10.9	6.4	8.5	9.0
New Zealand	2.3	4.0	3.7	4.6	5.1	6.5	12.4	12.2	14.7	15.6
Norway	3.6	8.8	9.9	4.9	6.5	9.0	21.0	23.6	12.6	16.4
Poland	..	2.4	1.9	1.9	2.1	..	7.3	6.2	5.7	5.9
Portugal	2.1	3.7	2.7	3.2	3.3	8.0	11.9	9.0	9.4	9.6
Slovak Republic	..	2.6	2.4	3.5	3.3	..	7.6	8.7	10.1	9.6
Slovenia	..	1.1	1.8	1.8	1.9	..	3.0	4.9	4.8	5.2
Spain	2.8	2.9	1.8	2.2	2.5	8.8	8.8	5.9	6.6	7.1
Sweden	1.5	3.6	3.2	2.8	2.8	3.1	7.5	7.5	6.3	6.5
Switzerland[1]	1.8	2.4	2.7	3.1	3.2	7.4	8.9	10.0	10.7	11.4
Turkey	1.0	1.7	1.8	1.7	2.1	6.7	7.3	7.3	6.8	8.7
United Kingdom	3.3	3.5	2.9	2.6	2.6	9.9	10.6	8.9	8.1	8.0
United States	2.0	2.2	1.8	1.6	1.0	7.5	7.9	7.5	5.9	4.1
Unweighted average										
OECD Average	**2.4**	**3.2**	**2.7**	**3.0**	**3.1**	**8.3**	**9.5**	**8.9**	**9.7**	**10.0**

.. Not available

Note: Full time series can be accessed at http://oe.cd/full-time-series.

1. The total tax revenue has been reduced by the amount of any capital transfer that represents uncollected taxes. The capital transfer has been allocated between tax headings in proportion to the reported tax revenue, except for Belgium, where the capital transfers were subtracted directly from the specific taxes to which they relate.

StatLink https://doi.org/10.1787/888934210008

Table 3.10. Social security contributions (2000) as % of GDP and as % of total tax revenue

	% of GDP					% of total tax revenue				
	1990	2000	2010	2017	2018	1990	2000	2010	2017	2018
Australia	0.0	0.0	0.0	0.0	0.0	0.0	0.0	0.0	0.0	0.0
Austria	12.9	14.3	14.0	14.6	14.7	32.9	33.8	34.2	34.9	34.8
Belgium[1]	13.7	13.5	13.9	13.4	13.3	33.2	30.8	32.4	30.6	30.2
Canada	4.3	4.7	4.6	4.6	4.6	12.1	13.6	14.9	14.0	14.0
Chile	1.5	1.4	1.3	1.5	1.5	9.0	7.3	6.8	7.3	6.9
Colombia	0.9	2.6	2.1	1.5	1.8	7.9	16.3	11.7	7.6	9.6
Czech Republic	..	14.3	14.4	14.8	15.3	..	44.3	44.8	43.0	43.8
Denmark[1]	0.0	0.6	0.1	0.0	0.0	0.0	1.4	0.2	0.1	0.1
Estonia	..	10.9	12.6	11.1	11.5	..	35.1	38.4	34.2	34.9
Finland	11.0	11.5	12.0	12.0	11.8	25.6	25.2	29.7	27.8	27.9
France[1]	18.1	15.6	16.1	16.7	16.0	44.1	35.8	38.2	36.3	34.9
Germany	13.0	14.2	13.8	14.3	14.5	37.5	39.0	38.9	37.9	37.7
Greece	7.6	10.1	10.9	11.5	11.6	30.2	30.3	34.2	29.8	29.9
Hungary	..	11.3	11.7	12.4	11.8	..	29.3	31.3	32.4	31.6
Iceland	1.0	2.8	3.8	3.4	3.5	3.1	7.7	11.8	9.1	9.5
Ireland	4.6	3.7	5.0	3.9	3.9	14.1	11.9	18.2	17.2	17.3
Israel	..	5.1	5.2	5.3	5.2	..	14.6	16.9	16.2	16.8
Italy	11.9	11.6	13.0	12.7	13.0	32.9	28.5	31.1	30.3	31.0
Japan	7.5	9.1	10.9	12.5	12.9	26.5	35.2	41.1	39.9	40.2
Korea	1.9	3.5	5.2	6.5	6.8	10.1	16.7	23.3	25.7	25.4
Latvia	..	9.8	8.6	8.4	9.1	..	33.5	30.1	26.9	29.3
Lithuania[1]	..	9.9	11.7	12.2	12.7	..	32.2	41.1	41.5	42.1
Luxembourg[1]	9.2	9.6	10.9	10.8	10.8	27.5	26.1	29.1	28.7	27.1
Mexico	2.0	2.1	2.1	2.1	2.2	16.8	18.0	16.2	13.3	13.4
Netherlands	14.9	14.3	12.9	13.8	14.0	37.4	38.7	36.3	35.7	36.0
New Zealand	0.0	0.0	0.0	0.0	0.0	0.0	0.0	0.0	0.0	0.0
Norway	10.6	8.8	9.4	10.3	10.1	26.3	21.0	22.4	26.6	25.5
Poland	..	12.9	10.8	12.8	13.1	..	39.2	34.4	37.6	37.2
Portugal	7.2	7.9	8.6	9.2	9.4	27.2	25.5	28.3	26.9	26.9
Slovak Republic	..	13.9	12.0	14.7	14.8	..	41.4	42.6	42.8	43.0
Slovenia	..	15.0	15.8	15.4	15.5	..	39.7	41.9	41.5	41.4
Spain	11.2	11.5	11.9	11.5	11.7	35.4	34.9	37.9	34.1	33.9
Sweden	13.3	12.7	10.8	9.6	9.6	27.1	26.1	25.0	21.6	21.8
Switzerland[1]	5.5	6.7	6.3	6.7	6.6	23.3	24.1	23.6	23.6	23.6
Turkey	2.9	4.4	6.1	7.2	7.2	19.7	18.7	24.9	29.3	29.9
United Kingdom	5.6	5.5	6.1	6.3	6.3	17.0	16.8	18.9	19.2	19.1
United States	6.7	6.7	6.1	6.2	6.1	25.6	23.6	26.1	23.1	24.9
Unweighted average										
OECD Average	**7.1**	**8.4**	**8.7**	**8.9**	**9.0**	**21.5**	**24.8**	**26.4**	**25.6**	**25.7**

.. Not available

Note: Full time series can be accessed at http://oe.cd/full-time-series.

1. The total tax revenue has been reduced by the amount of any capital transfer that represents uncollected taxes. The capital transfer has been allocated between tax headings in proportion to the reported tax revenue, except for Belgium, where the capital transfers were subtracted directly from the specific taxes to which they relate.

StatLink https://doi.org/10.1787/888934210027

Table 3.11. Taxes on payroll and workforce (3000) as % of GDP and as % of total tax revenue

	% of GDP					% of total tax revenue				
	1990	2000	2010	2017	2018	1990	2000	2010	2017	2018
Australia	1.7	1.4	1.3	1.4	1.4	6.1	4.5	5.2	4.8	4.8
Austria	2.4	2.7	2.8	2.8	2.7	6.0	6.4	6.9	6.6	6.4
Belgium[1]	0.0	0.0	0.0	0.0	0.0	0.0	0.0	0.0	0.0	0.0
Canada	0.8	0.7	0.6	0.7	0.7	2.3	2.1	2.1	2.0	2.0
Chile	0.0	0.0	0.0	0.0	0.0	0.0	0.0	0.0	0.0	0.0
Colombia	0.0	0.7	0.7	0.3	0.4	0.0	4.2	4.1	1.8	1.8
Czech Republic	..	0.0	0.0	0.0	0.0	..	0.0	0.0	0.0	0.0
Denmark[1]	0.3	0.2	0.2	0.3	0.3	0.7	0.4	0.5	0.5	0.6
Estonia	..	0.0	0.0	0.0	0.0	..	0.0	0.0	0.0	0.0
Finland	0.0	0.0	0.0	0.0	0.0	0.0	0.0	0.0	0.0	0.0
France[1]	0.8	1.0	1.3	1.5	1.5	1.9	2.3	3.2	3.4	3.3
Germany	0.0	0.0	0.0	0.0	0.0	0.0	0.0	0.0	0.0	0.0
Greece	0.2	0.0	0.0	0.0	0.0	0.7	0.0	0.0	0.0	0.0
Hungary	..	1.4	0.4	0.9	1.0	..	3.6	1.1	2.3	2.6
Iceland	1.1	0.0	0.2	0.3	0.3	3.5	0.1	0.5	0.8	0.8
Ireland	0.4	0.0	0.2	0.1	0.2	1.3	0.0	0.7	0.6	0.8
Israel	..	1.3	1.2	1.2	1.2	..	3.6	3.8	3.7	3.8
Italy	0.1	0.0	0.0	0.0	0.0	0.3	0.0	0.0	0.0	0.0
Japan	0.0	0.0	0.0	0.0	0.0	0.0	0.0	0.0	0.0	0.0
Korea	0.1	0.0	0.1	0.1	0.1	0.4	0.2	0.2	0.3	0.3
Latvia	..	0.0	0.0	0.0	0.0	..	0.0	0.1	0.0	0.0
Lithuania[1]	..	0.0	0.0	0.0	0.0	..	0.0	0.0	0.0	0.0
Luxembourg[1]	0.0	0.0	0.0	0.0	0.0	0.0	0.0	0.0	0.0	0.0
Mexico	0.2	0.2	0.3	0.4	0.4	1.8	1.5	2.2	2.4	2.5
Netherlands	0.0	0.0	0.0	0.0	0.0	0.0	0.0	0.0	0.0	0.0
New Zealand	0.0	0.0	0.0	0.0	0.0	0.0	0.0	0.0	0.0	0.0
Norway	0.0	0.0	0.0	0.1	0.1	0.0	0.0	0.0	0.1	0.1
Poland	..	0.2	0.3	0.2	0.2	..	0.7	0.8	0.7	0.6
Portugal	0.0	0.0	0.0	0.0	0.0	0.0	0.0	0.0	0.0	0.0
Slovak Republic	..	0.0	0.0	0.0	0.0	..	0.0	0.0	0.0	0.0
Slovenia	..	1.5	0.1	0.1	0.0	..	4.1	0.2	0.1	0.1
Spain	0.0	0.0	0.0	0.0	0.0	0.0	0.0	0.0	0.0	0.0
Sweden	1.2	2.1	3.0	5.0	5.1	2.5	4.3	7.0	11.4	11.6
Switzerland[1]	0.0	0.0	0.0	0.0	0.0	0.0	0.0	0.0	0.0	0.0
Turkey	0.0	0.0	0.0	0.0	0.0	0.0	0.0	0.0	0.0	0.0
United Kingdom	0.0	0.0	0.0	0.1	0.1	0.0	0.0	0.0	0.3	0.4
United States	0.0	0.0	0.0	0.0	0.0	0.0	0.0	0.1	0.0	0.0
Unweighted average										
OECD Average	**0.3**	**0.4**	**0.3**	**0.4**	**0.4**	**1.0**	**1.0**	**1.0**	**1.1**	**1.2**

.. Not available

Note: Full time series can be accessed at http://oe.cd/full-time-series.

1. The total tax revenue has been reduced by the amount of any capital transfer that represents uncollected taxes. The capital transfer has been allocated between tax headings in proportion to the reported tax revenue, except for Belgium, where the capital transfers were subtracted directly from the specific taxes to which they relate.

StatLink https://doi.org/10.1787/888934210046

Table 3.12. Taxes on property (4000) as % of GDP and as % of total tax revenue

	% of GDP					% of total tax revenue				
	1990	2000	2010	2017	2018	1990	2000	2010	2017	2018
Australia	2.5	2.7	2.4	2.9	2.7	9.0	8.8	9.4	10.0	9.5
Austria	1.1	0.6	0.5	0.5	0.5	2.7	1.3	1.3	1.3	1.3
Belgium[1]	1.6	2.1	3.1	3.5	3.4	3.8	4.7	7.2	7.9	7.8
Canada	3.5	3.3	3.8	3.9	3.9	10.0	9.5	12.3	11.9	11.6
Chile	1.0	1.3	0.8	1.1	1.1	6.2	7.0	4.1	5.4	5.2
Colombia	0.2	1.0	1.6	2.0	1.5	2.2	6.6	8.7	10.3	8.0
Czech Republic	..	0.5	0.4	0.5	0.5	..	1.4	1.3	1.4	1.3
Denmark[1]	1.9	1.6	1.8	1.8	1.8	4.3	3.3	4.1	3.9	4.1
Estonia	..	0.4	0.3	0.2	0.2	..	1.2	1.0	0.7	0.7
Finland	1.1	1.1	1.1	1.5	1.4	2.4	2.4	2.7	3.6	3.4
France[1]	2.6	3.1	3.7	4.4	4.1	6.3	7.2	8.7	9.5	9.0
Germany	1.2	0.8	0.8	1.0	1.1	3.4	2.3	2.3	2.7	2.7
Greece	1.2	2.6	1.7	3.1	3.0	4.6	7.7	5.2	8.0	7.7
Hungary	..	0.7	1.1	1.1	1.0	..	1.7	3.1	2.8	2.6
Iceland	2.6	2.8	2.3	2.1	2.0	8.4	7.9	7.0	5.5	5.5
Ireland	1.5	1.8	1.4	1.3	1.3	4.6	5.7	5.2	5.7	5.8
Israel	..	3.1	3.3	3.2	3.2	..	9.0	10.7	9.9	10.3
Italy	0.8	1.9	2.0	2.5	2.5	2.3	4.6	4.8	6.1	6.1
Japan	2.7	2.7	2.6	2.6	2.6	9.4	10.5	9.7	8.2	8.1
Korea	2.2	2.6	2.5	3.0	3.1	11.8	12.4	11.3	11.7	11.6
Latvia	..	1.1	0.9	1.0	0.9	..	3.8	3.0	3.3	3.0
Lithuania[1]	..	0.5	0.4	0.3	0.3	..	1.5	1.3	1.0	1.0
Luxembourg[1]	2.8	3.9	2.6	3.6	3.9	8.4	10.7	7.0	9.7	9.7
Mexico	0.2	0.2	0.3	0.3	0.3	1.9	1.8	2.3	1.9	2.0
Netherlands	1.5	1.9	1.4	1.6	1.6	3.7	5.3	3.8	4.0	4.0
New Zealand	2.5	1.7	2.0	1.9	1.9	6.8	5.3	6.6	6.0	5.8
Norway	1.2	1.0	1.1	1.3	1.2	2.9	2.3	2.6	3.3	3.1
Poland	..	1.4	1.3	1.4	1.3	..	4.3	4.2	4.0	3.7
Portugal	0.7	1.1	1.1	1.4	1.4	2.7	3.7	3.5	4.0	4.0
Slovak Republic	..	0.6	0.4	0.4	0.4	..	1.8	1.4	1.2	1.2
Slovenia	..	0.6	0.6	0.6	0.6	..	1.7	1.6	1.7	1.6
Spain	1.7	2.1	2.1	2.5	2.5	5.5	6.5	6.6	7.5	7.3
Sweden	1.7	1.7	1.0	1.0	0.9	3.5	3.4	2.4	2.2	2.2
Switzerland[1]	2.1	2.7	2.0	2.1	2.1	8.9	9.6	7.6	7.5	7.3
Turkey	0.3	0.7	1.0	1.1	1.0	2.3	3.2	4.1	4.5	4.3
United Kingdom	2.7	3.8	3.9	4.1	4.1	8.2	11.4	12.0	12.6	12.5
United States	3.1	2.9	3.2	4.4	3.0	11.8	10.3	13.5	16.3	12.3
Unweighted average										
OECD Average	**1.7**	**1.7**	**1.7**	**1.9**	**1.9**	**5.6**	**5.5**	**5.5**	**5.9**	**5.6**

.. Not available

Note: Full time series can be accessed at http://oe.cd/full-time-series.

1. The total tax revenue has been reduced by the amount of any capital transfer that represents uncollected taxes. The capital transfer has been allocated between tax headings in proportion to the reported tax revenue, except for Belgium, where the capital transfers were subtracted directly from the specific taxes to which they relate.

StatLink https://doi.org/10.1787/888934210065

Table 3.13. Taxes on goods and services (5000) as % of GDP and as % of total tax revenue

	% of GDP					% of total tax revenue				
	1990	2000	2010	2017	2018	1990	2000	2010	2017	2018
Australia	7.8	8.8	7.3	7.5	7.3	27.8	28.8	29.0	26.3	25.5
Austria	12.4	12.4	11.7	11.9	11.7	31.5	29.3	28.7	28.4	27.7
Belgium[1]	10.8	11.3	11.2	11.0	11.1	26.1	25.9	26.1	25.0	25.2
Canada	9.1	8.4	7.4	7.7	7.8	25.8	24.2	24.0	23.4	23.5
Chile	10.6	12.0	10.0	11.0	11.2	62.9	63.8	51.2	54.8	53.3
Colombia	6.1	7.3	8.2	8.2	8.3	53.8	46.3	45.1	43.1	42.8
Czech Republic	..	10.2	10.9	11.5	11.3	..	31.5	33.8	33.4	32.3
Denmark[1]	15.0	15.7	15.0	14.7	14.6	33.8	33.4	33.6	32.0	32.9
Estonia	..	12.1	13.4	14.0	13.8	..	38.8	40.7	43.0	41.8
Finland	14.0	13.4	13.0	14.2	14.3	32.6	29.2	32.0	33.1	33.8
France[1]	11.7	11.3	11.1	12.0	12.2	28.4	26.1	26.3	26.1	26.6
Germany	9.3	10.4	10.8	10.1	10.3	26.7	28.5	30.5	26.8	26.8
Greece	11.2	11.8	12.4	15.4	15.4	44.5	35.2	38.6	39.8	39.5
Hungary	..	15.6	16.1	16.4	16.8	..	40.5	43.2	43.0	44.7
Iceland	15.6	15.9	11.4	12.6	12.4	51.3	44.1	35.2	33.7	33.3
Ireland	13.6	11.9	9.9	7.4	7.0	41.9	38.8	35.8	32.6	30.8
Israel	..	11.5	12.1	11.3	11.2	..	33.1	39.4	34.7	36.3
Italy	10.2	11.4	11.1	12.1	12.0	28.0	28.2	26.6	28.8	28.7
Japan	3.9	5.0	5.0	6.6	6.2	13.7	19.3	18.7	21.0	19.5
Korea	8.1	8.0	7.5	7.0	7.0	44.3	38.4	33.7	27.7	26.3
Latvia	..	11.2	12.0	13.7	14.1	..	38.6	41.8	43.6	45.1
Lithuania[1]	..	12.1	11.7	11.6	11.6	..	39.4	41.4	39.4	38.4
Luxembourg[1]	7.9	9.8	10.3	9.1	9.4	23.6	26.6	27.4	24.3	23.7
Mexico	5.3	4.8	4.9	5.9	5.9	44.0	41.7	38.0	36.4	36.4
Netherlands	10.5	10.9	11.2	11.6	11.7	26.4	29.7	31.5	30.0	30.1
New Zealand	12.1	11.3	12.0	12.2	12.5	33.6	34.7	39.6	38.4	37.9
Norway	14.3	13.1	11.6	12.0	11.7	35.5	31.4	27.7	30.9	29.5
Poland	..	11.6	12.6	12.8	13.1	..	35.3	40.3	37.4	37.2
Portugal	11.7	12.7	12.3	13.7	13.9	44.2	40.8	40.5	40.1	39.8
Slovak Republic	..	12.2	10.5	12.1	12.0	..	36.3	37.2	35.3	35.0
Slovenia	..	13.8	13.9	14.1	14.0	..	36.6	36.7	38.1	37.4
Spain	9.0	10.1	8.6	10.2	10.2	28.4	30.6	27.5	30.0	29.5
Sweden	12.2	12.1	12.8	12.4	12.4	24.9	24.9	29.7	28.0	28.1
Switzerland[1]	4.9	6.1	6.1	6.0	5.8	20.6	21.9	22.9	21.1	20.8
Turkey	4.1	9.9	11.8	10.7	9.7	27.9	42.0	47.7	43.5	40.5
United Kingdom	10.2	10.6	10.2	10.7	10.7	31.0	32.2	31.7	32.6	32.6
United States	4.6	4.5	4.2	4.2	4.3	17.5	16.0	18.1	15.8	17.6
Unweighted average										
OECD Average	**9.9**	**10.8**	**10.6**	**11.0**	**10.9**	**33.2**	**33.6**	**33.8**	**33.0**	**32.7**

.. Not available

Note: Full time series can be accessed at http://oe.cd/full-time-series.

1. The total tax revenue has been reduced by the amount of any capital transfer that represents uncollected taxes. The capital transfer has been allocated between tax headings in proportion to the reported tax revenue, except for Belgium, where the capital transfers were subtracted directly from the specific taxes to which they relate.

StatLink https://doi.org/10.1787/888934210084

Table 3.14. Value added taxes (5111) as % of GDP and as % of total tax revenue

	% of GDP					% of total tax revenue				
	1990	2000	2010	2017	2018	1990	2000	2010	2017	2018
Australia	0.0	3.4	3.4	3.5	3.3	0.0	11.1	13.4	12.2	11.7
Austria	8.2	7.9	7.7	7.6	7.6	20.8	18.7	18.7	18.3	18.0
Belgium[1]	6.8	7.1	7.0	6.7	6.8	16.4	16.1	16.2	15.2	15.4
Canada	0.0	3.2	4.2	4.5	4.5	0.0	9.2	13.7	13.5	13.6
Chile	6.3	7.9	7.5	8.4	8.5	37.4	41.8	38.5	41.6	40.2
Colombia	2.6	4.3	5.3	5.5	5.7	22.6	27.6	29.3	29.0	29.4
Czech Republic	..	5.9	6.6	7.6	7.6	..	18.3	20.5	22.0	21.6
Denmark[1]	8.4	9.1	9.4	9.5	9.5	18.8	19.5	21.0	20.7	21.5
Estonia	..	8.4	8.5	9.0	9.0	..	27.1	25.7	27.7	27.3
Finland	8.3	8.0	8.3	9.0	9.1	19.3	17.4	20.4	21.0	21.6
France[1]	7.6	7.2	6.8	7.0	7.1	18.4	16.7	16.1	15.3	15.4
Germany	5.8	6.7	7.0	7.0	7.0	16.6	18.4	19.8	18.4	18.2
Greece	6.2	6.3	7.1	8.1	8.3	24.6	18.9	22.0	21.0	21.3
Hungary	..	8.7	8.5	9.3	9.7	..	22.4	22.9	24.4	25.8
Iceland	8.7	10.3	7.3	8.9	8.8	28.5	28.5	22.7	23.8	23.6
Ireland	6.6	7.1	6.0	4.4	4.4	20.4	22.9	21.7	19.3	19.3
Israel	..	7.4	7.5	7.4	7.5	..	21.1	24.4	22.9	24.2
Italy	5.3	6.2	6.1	6.2	6.2	14.7	15.4	14.5	14.8	14.8
Japan	1.2	2.3	2.5	4.1	4.1	4.4	9.1	9.6	13.0	12.8
Korea	3.4	3.6	3.9	4.1	4.1	18.7	17.0	17.5	16.0	15.3
Latvia	..	7.0	6.7	8.1	8.4	..	23.9	23.3	25.7	27.0
Lithuania[1]	..	7.5	7.8	7.8	7.8	..	24.4	27.5	26.6	25.8
Luxembourg[1]	4.0	4.9	6.4	5.9	6.1	12.1	13.2	17.0	15.8	15.4
Mexico	3.2	2.8	3.8	3.7	3.9	26.1	24.7	29.4	23.1	24.3
Netherlands	6.5	6.4	6.7	6.8	6.8	16.5	17.3	18.7	17.4	17.6
New Zealand	8.1	8.1	9.3	9.5	9.7	22.4	24.9	30.7	30.2	29.6
Norway	7.6	8.2	7.8	8.6	8.4	18.8	19.8	18.6	22.2	21.3
Poland	..	6.9	7.6	7.8	8.1	..	21.0	24.2	22.8	23.1
Portugal	5.2	7.6	7.5	8.6	8.7	19.6	24.4	24.7	25.1	25.1
Slovak Republic	..	6.8	6.1	7.0	7.1	..	20.4	21.8	20.5	20.5
Slovenia	..	8.5	8.1	8.1	8.2	..	22.6	21.3	21.8	22.0
Spain	5.0	5.8	5.2	6.5	6.6	15.7	17.6	16.5	19.2	19.0
Sweden	7.3	8.2	9.0	9.2	9.2	14.8	16.8	21.0	20.7	21.0
Switzerland[1]	2.8	3.6	3.4	3.4	3.3	11.6	13.1	12.7	12.0	11.7
Turkey	2.7	5.7	5.4	5.0	4.8	18.3	24.2	21.7	20.1	19.8
United Kingdom	5.5	5.9	6.1	6.9	7.0	16.9	18.1	19.0	20.9	21.1
United States	0.0	0.0	0.0	0.0	0.0	0.0	0.0	0.0	0.0	0.0
Unweighted average										
OECD Average	**5.1**	**6.3**	**6.4**	**6.8**	**6.8**	**16.9**	**19.6**	**20.5**	**20.4**	**20.4**

.. Not available

Note: Full time series can be accessed at http://oe.cd/full-time-series.

1. The total tax revenue has been reduced by the amount of any capital transfer that represents uncollected taxes. The capital transfer has been allocated between tax headings in proportion to the reported tax revenue, except for Belgium, where the capital transfers were subtracted directly from the specific taxes to which they relate.

StatLink https://doi.org/10.1787/888934210103

Table 3.15. Tax revenues of sub-sectors of general government as % of GDP

	Supranational			Central government			State or Regional government			Local government			Social Security Funds		
	1975	1995	2018	1975	1995	2018	1975	1995	2018	1975	1995	2018	1975	1995	2018
Federal countries															
Australia	..	..	..	20.3	21.9	23.3	4.0	5.4	4.4	1.1	1.0	1.0	0.0	0.0	0.0
Austria	..	0.2	0.2	18.8	26.7	27.8	3.9	0.7	0.7	4.5	1.7	1.3	9.2	12.0	12.3
Belgium[1]	0.6	0.4	0.4	25.4	25.8	23.1	..	0.8	4.5	1.7	2.0	2.0	11.2	13.8	13.9
Canada	..	..	..	14.8	13.5	13.8	10.1	12.8	13.1	3.1	3.4	3.3	3.1	4.8	3.0
Germany	0.4	0.2	0.2	11.5	11.4	11.4	7.6	7.9	9.1	3.1	2.7	3.3	11.7	14.1	14.5
Mexico	..	..	..	..	7.5	13.1	..	0.3	0.7	..	0.2	0.3	..	2.2	2.2
Switzerland[1]	..	..	..	6.9	8.0	10.1	6.1	6.2	7.0	4.6	4.5	4.3	4.9	6.8	6.6
United States	..	..	..	11.2	11.0	9.6	4.8	5.3	5.0	3.6	3.5	3.7	5.0	6.7	6.1
Unweighted average	0.5	0.3	0.3	15.6	15.7	16.5	6.1	4.9	5.6	3.1	2.4	2.4	6.5	7.6	7.3
Regional countries															
Colombia[2]	..	..	..	..	10.1	14.1	..	0.9	1.0	..	1.4	2.4	..	3.6	1.8
Spain[2]	..	0.2	0.2	8.6	16.0	14.4	..	1.6	5.3	0.8	2.7	3.2	8.5	10.8	11.4
Unitary countries															
Chile	..	..	..	..	16.5	18.2	..	..	..	..	1.2	1.7	..	0.7	1.2
Czech Republic	..	0.0	0.2	..	19.9	19.1	..	..	..	..	0.3	0.4	..	14.3	15.3
Denmark[1]	0.4	0.2	0.1	25.4	31.7	32.2	..	..	..	11.0	14.6	12.0	0.0	0.0	0.0
Estonia	..	0.0	0.2	..	29.6	27.0	..	..	..	..	0.3	0.3	..	5.2	5.4
Finland	..	0.2	0.1	20.3	20.7	20.8	..	..	..	8.5	9.9	9.6	7.4	13.7	11.8
France[1]	0.2	0.3	0.2	17.9	18.0	15.4	..	..	..	2.6	4.7	6.2	14.2	19.5	24.1
Greece	..	0.2	0.2	12.5	18.8	26.2	..	..	..	0.6	0.6	0.9	5.5	8.8	11.7
Hungary	..	0.0	0.1	..	26.0	23.1	..	..	..	..	1.0	2.2	..	13.7	12.0
Iceland	..	..	..	24.0	24.3	27.0	..	..	..	5.5	6.4	10.3	0.0	0.0	0.0
Ireland	0.6	0.5	0.1	21.6	26.4	18.8	..	..	..	2.0	0.8	0.5	3.6	4.0	3.3
Israel	..	..	..	..	28.1	23.3	..	..	..	..	2.3	2.4	..	4.9	5.2
Italy	..	0.1	0.2	13.0	24.1	23.8	..	..	..	0.2	2.1	4.9	11.2	12.1	13.0
Japan	..	..	..	9.2	10.6	11.7	..	..	..	5.1	6.5	7.4	5.8	8.7	12.9
Korea	..	..	..	12.9	12.9	15.5	..	..	..	1.5	3.5	4.5	0.1	2.3	6.8
Latvia	..	0.0	0.2	..	13.0	16.5	..	..	..	..	5.8	5.7	..	11.0	8.9
Lithuania[1]	..	0.0	0.3	..	19.8	16.9	..	..	..	..	0.6	0.4	..	7.2	12.7
Luxembourg[1]	0.2	0.2	0.3	20.0	23.1	27.2	..	..	..	2.1	2.3	1.8	9.1	9.3	10.5
Netherlands	0.6	0.5	0.4	22.2	20.9	23.1	..	..	..	0.4	1.2	1.4	14.5	14.7	14.0
New Zealand	..	..	..	27.7	33.7	30.7	..	..	..	2.3	1.9	2.2	0.0	0.0	0.0
Norway	..	..	..	19.7	22.7	33.5	..	..	..	8.7	7.9	6.1	10.5	8.8	0.0
Poland	..	0.0	0.2	..	22.4	17.4	..	..	..	..	3.1	4.5	..	11.1	13.1
Portugal	..	0.2	0.2	12.3	21.2	23.3	..	..	..	0.0	1.6	2.5	6.5	6.3	8.9
Slovak Republic	..	0.0	0.2	..	24.7	19.2	..	..	..	..	0.5	0.6	..	14.2	14.3
Slovenia	..	0.0	0.1	..	19.8	18.6	..	..	..	..	2.4	3.4	..	17.0	15.3
Sweden	..	0.3	0.3	19.7	21.2	22.9	..	..	..	11.2	13.9	15.4	7.5	9.8	5.3
Turkey	..	..	..	..	12.3	14.5	..	..	..	..	2.1	2.3	..	2.0	7.2
United Kingdom	0.3	0.3	0.2	24.1	22.7	24.8	..	..	..	3.8	1.1	1.7	6.0	5.2	6.3
Unweighted average	0.4	0.2	0.2	18.9	21.7	21.9	..	..	..	4.1	3.6	4.1	6.4	8.3	8.9

.. Not available

1. The total tax revenue has been reduced by the amount of any capital transfer that represents uncollected taxes.

2. Colombia and Spain are not constitutionally federal countries, but both have a highly decentralised political structure, with high autonomy of their territorial entities.

StatLink https://doi.org/10.1787/888934210122

Table 3.16. Main central government taxes as % of total tax revenues of central government, 2018

	1000 Income & profits	2000 Social security[3]	3000 Payroll	4000 Property	5000 Goods and services	6000 Others
Federal countries						
Australia	74.2	0.0	0.2	0.0	25.6	0.0
Austria	43.4	7.8	6.4	1.2	40.7	0.5
Belgium[1]	56.9	0.1	0.0	2.2	40.8	0.0
Canada	72.7	7.3	0.0	0.0	20.0	0.0
Germany	45.5	0.0	0.0	0.1	54.4	0.0
Mexico	54.4	0.0	0.0	0.0	44.1	1.5
Switzerland[1]	44.5	0.0	0.0	2.0	53.4	0.1
United States	90.7	0.0	0.0	1.2	8.1	0.0
Unweighted average	60.3	1.9	0.8	0.8	35.9	0.3
Regional countries						
Colombia[2]	46.0	0.0	2.5	5.2	45.9	0.4
Spain[2]	41.2	2.0	0.0	0.3	56.4	0.1
Unitary countries						
Chile	41.4	1.4	0.0	2.1	56.4	-1.3
Czech Republic	41.2	0.0	0.0	1.3	57.4	0.0
Denmark[1]	52.5	0.1	0.9	1.6	44.9	0.0
Estonia	27.5	22.4	0.0	0.0	50.0	0.0
Finland	28.5	0.0	0.0	3.2	68.3	0.1
France[1]	35.9	2.3	1.0	6.2	54.2	0.4
Greece	34.1	0.1	0.0	8.2	57.6	0.0
Hungary	28.2	2.0	4.1	2.6	62.9	0.3
Iceland	37.4	13.1	1.1	1.4	44.8	2.3
Ireland	54.7	3.1	0.9	4.7	36.5	0.0
Israel	43.5	0.0	5.1	3.7	47.7	0.0
Italy	50.5	0.0	0.0	6.1	43.3	0.0
Japan	55.1	0.0	0.0	5.3	39.6	0.0
Korea	53.1	0.0	0.0	6.8	38.6	1.5
Latvia	13.6	1.8	0.1	0.9	83.7	0.0
Lithuania[1]	33.1	0.0	0.0	0.0	66.8	0.0
Luxembourg[1]	51.4	1.0	0.0	13.7	33.6	0.2
Netherlands	49.8	0.0	0.0	3.7	46.1	0.5
New Zealand	60.2	0.0	0.0	0.1	39.7	0.0
Norway	33.6	30.1	0.2	1.4	34.7	0.0
Poland	25.8	0.0	1.3	0.0	72.9	0.0
Portugal	39.6	4.4	0.0	0.8	53.7	1.4
Slovak Republic	37.0	2.4	0.0	0.0	60.6	0.0
Slovenia	25.4	0.8	0.3	0.0	73.5	0.0
Sweden	3.1	18.7	22.1	2.5	53.4	0.2
Turkey	35.2	0.0	0.0	4.9	59.2	0.8
United Kingdom	46.9	0.0	0.5	9.9	42.7	0.0
Unweighted average	38.5	3.8	1.4	3.4	52.7	0.2

Note: Excluding social security contributions accruing to social security funds.

1. The total tax revenue has been reduced by the amount of any capital transfer that represents uncollected taxes. The capital transfer has been allocated between tax headings in proportion to the reported tax revenue, except for Belgium, where the capital transfers were subtracted directly from the specific taxes to which they relate.
2. Colombia and Spain are not constitutionally federal countries, but both have a highly decentralised political structure, with high autonomy of their territorial entities.
3. These comprise only social security contributions accruing to central government.

StatLink https://doi.org/10.1787/888934210141

Table 3.17. Main state government taxes as % of total tax revenues of state government, 2018

	1000 Income & profits	2000 Social security	3000 Payroll	4000 Property	5000 Goods and services	6000 Others
Federal countries						
Australia	0.0	0.0	29.9	39.6	30.4	0.0
Austria[1]	48.7	18.9	9.1	1.8	17.5	4.0
Belgium[1, 2]	45.8	1.2	0.0	38.3	14.6	0.0
Canada	47.0	5.2	5.1	4.7	38.0	0.0
Germany[1]	53.1	0.0	0.0	6.8	40.1	0.0
Mexico	0.0	0.0	60.7	18.7	15.8	4.8
Switzerland[2]	76.4	0.0	0.0	16.7	6.2	0.7
United States	42.1	0.0	0.2	3.4	54.3	0.0
Unweighted average	39.2	3.2	13.1	16.3	27.1	1.2
Regional countries						
Colombia[3]	0.0	0.0	0.0	0.0	72.3	27.7
Spain[1, 3]	68.0	0.0	0.0	19.9	12.1	0.0
Unitary countries						
Chile	..	..	..	..	..	..
Czech Republic	..	..	..	..	..	..
Denmark	..	..	..	..	..	..
Estonia	..	..	..	..	..	..
Finland	..	..	..	..	..	..
France	..	..	..	..	..	..
Greece	..	..	..	..	..	..
Hungary	..	..	..	..	..	..
Iceland	..	..	..	..	..	..
Ireland	..	..	..	..	..	..
Israel	..	..	..	..	..	..
Italy	..	..	..	..	..	..
Japan	..	..	..	..	..	..
Korea	..	..	..	..	..	..
Latvia	..	..	..	..	..	..
Lithuania	..	..	..	..	..	..
Luxembourg	..	..	..	..	..	..
Netherlands	..	..	..	..	..	..
New Zealand	..	..	..	..	..	..
Norway	..	..	..	..	..	..
Poland	..	..	..	..	..	..
Portugal	..	..	..	..	..	..
Slovak Republic	..	..	..	..	..	..
Slovenia	..	..	..	..	..	..
Sweden	..	..	..	..	..	..
Turkey	..	..	..	..	..	..
United Kingdom	..	..	..	..	..	..
Unweighted average	..	..	..	..	..	..

.. Not available

1. Payments to the European Union are excluded from these comparisons.
2. The total tax revenue has been reduced by the amount of any capital transfer that represents uncollected taxes. The capital transfer has been allocated between tax headings in proportion to the reported tax revenue, except for Belgium, where the capital transfers were subtracted directly from the specific taxes to which they relate.
3. Colombia and Spain are not constitutionally federal countries, but both have a highly decentralised political structure, with high autonomy of their territorial entities.

StatLink https://doi.org/10.1787/888934210160

Table 3.18. Main local government taxes as % of total tax revenues of local government, 2018

	1000 Income & profits	2000 Social security	3000 Payroll	4000 Property	5000 Goods and services	6000 Others
Federal countries						
Australia	0.0	0.0	0.0	100.0	0.0	0.0
Austria[1]	0.0	5.2	69.4	14.8	7.6	2.9
Belgium[1, 2]	35.1	0.1	0.0	57.3	7.5	0.0
Canada	0.0	0.0	0.0	97.3	1.7	1.0
Germany[1]	79.0	0.0	0.0	12.8	8.0	0.2
Mexico	0.0	0.0	0.0	78.5	2.8	18.7
Switzerland[2]	81.7	0.0	0.0	15.7	0.6	2.0
United States	5.5	0.0	0.0	73.1	21.3	0.0
Unweighted average	25.2	0.7	8.7	56.2	6.2	3.1
Regional countries						
Colombia[3]	0.0	0.0	0.0	34.0	45.6	20.4
Spain[1, 3]	17.9	0.0	0.0	44.4	37.6	0.1
Unitary countries						
Chile	0.0	0.0	0.0	42.4	57.6	0.0
Czech Republic[1]	0.0	0.0	0.0	56.9	43.1	0.0
Denmark[1, 2]	89.0	0.0	0.0	11.0	0.0	0.0
Estonia[1]	0.0	0.0	0.0	82.0	18.0	0.0
Finland[1]	91.9	0.0	0.0	8.1	0.0	0.0
France[1, 2]	0.0	0.0	7.2	50.9	34.9	6.9
Greece[1]	0.0	0.0	0.0	93.6	6.4	0.0
Hungary[1]	0.0	0.0	0.0	17.8	82.1	0.0
Iceland	80.7	0.0	0.0	16.2	3.1	0.0
Ireland[1]	0.0	9.9	0.0	90.1	0.0	0.0
Israel	0.0	0.0	0.0	95.1	4.9	0.0
Italy[1]	19.2	0.0	0.0	22.2	30.8	27.7
Japan	50.7	0.0	0.0	26.5	21.7	1.1
Korea	20.2	0.0	1.8	46.1	23.5	8.4
Latvia[1]	85.1	0.0	0.0	13.6	1.3	0.0
Lithuania[2]	0.0	0.0	0.0	85.1	14.9	0.0
Luxembourg[1, 2]	92.4	0.0	0.0	6.6	0.9	0.1
Netherlands[1]	0.0	0.0	0.0	52.4	47.6	0.0
New Zealand	0.0	0.0	0.0	86.9	13.1	0.0
Norway	86.5	0.0	0.0	12.8	0.8	0.0
Poland[1]	65.1	0.0	0.0	29.3	4.4	1.1
Portugal[1]	25.0	0.0	0.0	48.4	26.5	0.1
Slovak Republic[1]	0.0	0.0	0.0	65.7	34.3	0.0
Slovenia[1]	76.1	0.0	0.0	17.8	6.0	0.0
Sweden[1]	97.6	0.0	0.0	2.4	0.0	0.0
Turkey	30.0	0.0	0.0	14.4	48.9	6.7
United Kingdom[1]	0.0	0.0	0.0	100.0	0.0	0.0
Unweighted average	33.7	0.4	0.3	44.2	19.4	1.9

1. Payments to the European Union are excluded from these comparisons.
2. The total tax revenue has been reduced by the amount of any capital transfer that represents uncollected taxes. The capital transfer has been allocated between tax headings in proportion to the reported tax revenue, except for Belgium, where the capital transfers were subtracted directly from the specific taxes to which they relate.
3. Colombia and Spain are not constitutionally federal countries, but both have a highly decentralised political structure, with high autonomy of their territorial entities.

StatLink https://doi.org/10.1787/888934210179

Table 3.19. Gross domestic product for tax reporting years at market prices, in billions of national currency

		1965	1990	2000	2007	2010	2013	2015	2017	2018	2019p
Australia[1]	AUD	24.3	414.5	705.1	1 177.3	1 416.6	1 598.5	1 660.7	1 849.9	1 947.2	2 044.3
Austria	EUR	18.5	137.5	213.6	284.0	295.9	323.9	344.3	370.3	385.7	398.7
Belgium	EUR	20.9	170.1	256.4	343.6	363.1	392.9	416.7	446.0	459.5	473.1
Canada	CAD	61.3	696.1	1 125.5	1 577.7	1 666.0	1 902.2	1 990.4	2 141.1	2 223.9	2 303.9
Chile	CLP	..	10 522.7	42 005.2	90 702.9	111 508.6	137 876.2	159 553.3	179 756.1	191 266.0	198 440.7
Colombia	COP	..	22 731.4	195 108.6	428 506.0	544 060.0	714 093.0	804 692.0	920 471.0	985 931.0	1 062 342.5
Czech Republic	CZK	..	731.2	2 386.3	3 859.5	3 992.9	4 142.8	4 625.4	5 110.7	5 408.8	5 748.7
Denmark	DKK	71.5	855.6	1 326.9	1 738.8	1 810.9	1 929.7	2 036.4	2 175.1	2 246.0	2 314.5
Estonia	EUR	..	..	6.2	16.4	14.9	19.0	20.8	23.9	25.9	28.1
Finland	EUR	4.5	91.0	136.4	187.1	188.1	204.3	211.4	225.9	233.7	240.6
France	EUR	76.4	1 053.5	1 478.6	1 941.4	1 995.3	2 117.2	2 198.4	2 297.2	2 360.7	2 425.7
Germany	EUR	234.8	1 306.7	2 109.1	2 499.6	2 564.4	2 811.4	3 026.2	3 259.9	3 356.4	3 449.1
Greece	EUR	0.7	45.5	141.2	232.7	226.0	180.7	177.3	180.2	184.7	187.5
Hungary	HUF	..	..	13 324.1	25 701.4	27 268.9	30 290.3	34 785.2	38 835.2	42 661.8	46 786.7
Iceland	ISK	0.2	377.6	707.8	1 378.1	1 672.7	1 959.0	2 293.9	2 616.3	2 787.4	2 965.6
Ireland	EUR	1.3	37.9	108.4	197.2	167.7	179.7	262.8	297.1	324.0	347.2
Israel	ILS	..	119.4	541.1	735.6	874.9	1 056.8	1 166.5	1 269.4	1 330.1	1 406.7
Italy	EUR	22.4	730.9	1 241.5	1 614.8	1 611.3	1 612.8	1 655.4	1 736.6	1 766.2	1 787.7
Japan[1]	JPY	35 108.0	464 025.4	528 446.7	530 922.8	499 429.1	507 255.2	532 786.0	547 548.0	548 121.6	552 499.7
Korea	KRW	852.8	202 832.6	651 634.4	1 089 660.2	1 322 611.2	1 500 819.1	1 658 020.4	1 835 698.2	1 893 497.0	1 913 963.5
Latvia	EUR	..	..	6.8	22.6	18.0	22.8	24.4	26.8	29.1	30.5
Lithuania	EUR	..	..	13.4	29.0	28.0	35.0	37.3	42.3	45.3	48.4
Luxembourg	EUR	1.0	11.0	23.1	37.2	40.2	46.5	52.1	56.8	60.1	63.5
Mexico	MXN	..	843.6	6 693.7	11 504.1	13 366.4	16 277.2	18 551.5	21 911.9	23 491.5	24 239.1
Netherlands	EUR	35.6	263.0	452.0	619.2	639.2	660.5	690.0	738.1	774.0	810.2
New Zealand[1]	NZD	4.1	75.9	122.2	189.1	205.9	236.8	257.8	293.1	303.6	308.3
Norway	NOK	57.2	749.9	1 507.3	2 350.2	2 591.5	3 071.2	3 111.2	3 295.4	3 530.9	3 549.4
Poland	PLN	..	62.7	747.0	1 187.6	1 445.3	1 656.9	1 800.2	1 989.4	2 120.5	2 273.6
Portugal	EUR	0.6	56.0	128.4	175.5	179.6	170.5	179.7	195.9	204.3	212.3
Slovak Republic	EUR	..	10.0	31.7	63.2	68.1	74.4	79.8	84.5	89.6	94.2
Slovenia	EUR	..	0.9	18.9	35.1	36.4	36.5	38.9	43.0	45.8	48.0
Spain	EUR	8.7	328.7	647.9	1 075.5	1 072.7	1 020.3	1 077.6	1 161.9	1 204.2	1 244.8
Sweden	SEK	129.3	1 549.8	2 408.2	3 320.3	3 573.6	3 822.7	4 260.5	4 625.1	4 828.3	5 021.3
Switzerland	CHF	68.1	358.5	459.4	576.1	608.8	638.2	654.3	669.5	689.5	698.7
Turkey	TRY	0.0	0.5	171.5	887.7	1 167.7	1 823.4	2 350.9	3 133.7	3 758.3	4 320.2
United Kingdom	GBP	36.4	615.7	1 095.7	1 549.8	1 601.9	1 782.1	1 916.9	2 071.7	2 144.3	2 216.5
United States	USD	709.0	5 963.1	10 252.3	14 451.9	14 992.1	16 784.9	18 238.3	19 543.0	20 611.9	21 433.2

.. Not available

1. GDP is fiscal year. The year Y is calculated (at annual rate) as the average of: Q2(Y) to Q1(Y+1) for Japan; and Q3(Y) to Q2(Y+1) for Australia and New Zealand.

Source: OECD National Accounts.

StatLink https://doi.org/10.1787/888934210198

Table 3.20. Exchange rates used, national currency per US dollar at market exchange rates

		1965	1990	2000	2007	2010	2013	2015	2017	2018	2019p
Australia	AUD	0.9	1.3	1.7	1.2	1.1	1.0	1.3	1.3	1.3	1.4
Austria	EUR	..	0.8	1.1	0.7	0.8	0.8	0.9	0.9	0.8	0.9
Belgium	EUR	..	0.8	1.1	0.7	0.8	0.8	0.9	0.9	0.8	0.9
Canada	CAD	1.1	1.2	1.5	1.1	1.0	1.0	1.3	1.3	1.3	1.3
Chile	CLP	0.0	304.9	539.4	522.2	510.0	495.3	654.3	648.7	641.9	703.3
Colombia	COP	10.5	502.3	2 087.9	2 078.3	1 898.6	1 868.8	2 741.9	2 951.3	2 955.7	3 280.8
Czech Republic	CZK	..	..	38.6	20.3	19.1	19.6	24.6	23.4	21.7	22.9
Denmark	DKK	6.9	6.2	8.1	5.4	5.6	5.6	6.7	6.6	6.3	6.7
Estonia	EUR	..	0.8	1.1	0.7	0.8	0.8	0.9	0.9	0.8	0.9
Finland	EUR	..	0.8	1.1	0.7	0.8	0.8	0.9	0.9	0.8	0.9
France	EUR	..	0.8	1.1	0.7	0.8	0.8	0.9	0.9	0.8	0.9
Germany	EUR	..	0.8	1.1	0.7	0.8	0.8	0.9	0.9	0.8	0.9
Greece	EUR	..	0.8	1.1	0.7	0.8	0.8	0.9	0.9	0.8	0.9
Hungary	HUF	..	63.2	282.3	183.6	207.8	223.6	279.2	274.5	270.2	290.6
Iceland	ISK	0.4	58.4	78.8	64.1	122.2	122.2	131.9	106.8	108.3	122.6
Ireland	EUR	0.5	0.8	1.1	0.7	0.8	0.8	0.9	0.9	0.8	0.9
Israel	ILS	0.0	2.0	4.1	4.1	3.7	3.6	3.9	3.6	3.6	3.6
Italy	EUR	..	0.8	1.1	0.7	0.8	0.8	0.9	0.9	0.8	0.9
Japan	JPY	361.5	144.8	107.8	117.8	87.8	97.6	121.0	112.2	110.4	109.0
Korea	KRW	266.3	708.0	1 130.6	929.5	1 155.4	1 094.9	1 131.3	1 130.6	1 100.2	1 165.3
Latvia	EUR	..	0.8	1.1	0.7	0.8	0.8	0.9	0.9	0.8	0.9
Lithuania	EUR	..	0.8	1.1	0.7	0.8	0.8	0.9	0.9	0.8	0.9
Luxembourg	EUR	..	0.8	1.1	0.7	0.8	0.8	0.9	0.9	0.8	0.9
Mexico	MXN	0.0	2.8	9.5	10.9	12.6	12.8	15.9	18.9	19.2	19.2
Netherlands	EUR	..	0.8	1.1	0.7	0.8	0.8	0.9	0.9	0.8	0.9
New Zealand	NZD	0.7	1.7	2.2	1.4	1.4	1.2	1.4	1.4	1.4	1.5
Norway	NOK	7.2	6.3	8.8	5.9	6.0	5.9	8.1	8.3	8.1	8.8
Poland	PLN	0.0	1.0	4.3	2.8	3.0	3.2	3.8	3.8	3.6	3.8
Portugal	EUR	..	0.8	1.1	0.7	0.8	0.8	0.9	0.9	0.8	0.9
Slovak Republic	EUR	..	0.8	1.1	0.7	0.8	0.8	0.9	0.9	0.8	0.9
Slovenia	EUR	..	0.8	1.1	0.7	0.8	0.8	0.9	0.9	0.8	0.9
Spain	EUR	..	0.8	1.1	0.7	0.8	0.8	0.9	0.9	0.8	0.9
Sweden	SEK	5.2	5.9	9.2	6.8	7.2	6.5	8.4	8.5	8.7	9.5
Switzerland	CHF	4.3	1.4	1.7	1.2	1.0	0.9	1.0	1.0	1.0	1.0
Turkey	TRY	0.0	0.0	0.6	1.3	1.5	1.9	2.7	3.6	4.8	5.7
United Kingdom	GBP	0.4	0.6	0.7	0.5	0.6	0.6	0.7	0.8	0.7	0.8
United States	USD	1.0	1.0	1.0	1.0	1.0	1.0	1.0	1.0	1.0	1.0

.. Not available

Source: OECD Financial indicators data.

StatLink https://doi.org/10.1787/888934210217

4 Country tables, 1990-2018

Chapter 4 provides a summary of tax revenues by category and by level of government for each OECD country.

4.1. Tax revenue and % of GDP by selected tax category and by level of government

In all of the following tables the symbol (..) indicates not available/or not applicable. The main series in this chapter cover a selection of years between 1990 and 2018. A complete series is, however, available on line. Data for 1955 and 1960 (for nineteen OECD countries) are provided in part V of the 1998 edition of this Report.

The Gross Domestic Product (GDP) figures are based on the 2008 System of National Accounts (SNA) for all OECD countries.

Box 4.1. Treatment of capital transfers

Some tables refer to the treatment of the capital transfers that some countries make to account for taxes that have been assessed but not collected. The capital transfer has been subtracted from the total tax revenue for Denmark, France, Lithuania, Luxembourg and Switzerland and this reduction has been allocated between tax headings in proportion to their tax revenues at the level of government against which these transfers were recorded. In the case of Belgium, the capital transfers were instead subtracted directly from the specific taxes to which they relate.

This applies to the following countries:

- Belgium from 1995.
- Denmark from 1971.
- France from 1992.
- Lithuania from 1999.
- Luxembourg from 2013.
- Switzerland from 1990.

Table 4.1. Australia, tax revenue and % of GDP by selected tax category

	Billion AUD					% of GDP				
	1990	2000	2010	2017	2018	1990	2000	2010	2017	2018
Total tax revenue	**116.5**	**214.8**	**358.0**	**527.2**	**558.5**	**28.1**	**30.5**	**25.3**	**28.5**	**28.7**
1000 Taxes on income, profits and capital gains	**66.5**	**124.4**	**202.2**	**310.0**	**336.2**	**16.1**	**17.6**	**14.3**	**16.8**	**17.3**
1100 Of individuals	50.1	81.0	138.2	212.5	229.5	12.1	11.5	9.8	11.5	11.8
1200 Corporate	16.5	43.4	64.0	97.5	106.7	4.0	6.2	4.5	5.3	5.5
1300 Unallocable between 1100 and 1200	0.0	0.0	0.0	0.0	0.0	0.0	0.0	0.0	0.0	0.0
2000 Social security contributions	**0.0**	**0.0**	**0.0**	**0.0**	**0.0**	**0.0**	**0.0**	**0.0**	**0.0**	**0.0**
2100 Employees	0.0	0.0	0.0	0.0	0.0	0.0	0.0	0.0	0.0	0.0
2200 Employers	0.0	0.0	0.0	0.0	0.0	0.0	0.0	0.0	0.0	0.0
2300 Self-employed or non-employed	0.0	0.0	0.0	0.0	0.0	0.0	0.0	0.0	0.0	0.0
2400 Unallocable between 2100, 2200 and 2300	0.0	0.0	0.0	0.0	0.0	0.0	0.0	0.0	0.0	0.0
3000 Taxes on payroll and workforce	**7.1**	**9.6**	**18.5**	**25.5**	**26.9**	**1.7**	**1.4**	**1.3**	**1.4**	**1.4**
4000 Taxes on property	**10.4**	**18.8**	**33.5**	**53.0**	**53.1**	**2.5**	**2.7**	**2.4**	**2.9**	**2.7**
4100 Recurrent taxes on immovable property	6.1	9.1	19.9	30.3	32.7	1.5	1.3	1.4	1.6	1.7
4200 Recurrent taxes on net wealth	0.0	0.0	0.0	0.0	0.0	0.0	0.0	0.0	0.0	0.0
4300 Estate, inheritance and gift taxes	0.0	0.0	0.0	0.0	0.0	0.0	0.0	0.0	0.0	0.0
4400 Taxes on financial and capital transactions	4.3	9.8	13.6	22.7	20.4	1.0	1.4	1.0	1.2	1.1
4500 Non-recurrent taxes	0.0	0.0	0.0	0.0	0.0	0.0	0.0	0.0	0.0	0.0
4600 Other recurrent taxes on property	0.0	0.0	0.0	0.0	0.0	0.0	0.0	0.0	0.0	0.0
5000 Taxes on goods and services	**32.4**	**61.9**	**103.8**	**138.7**	**142.1**	**7.8**	**8.8**	**7.3**	**7.5**	**7.3**
5100 Taxes on production, sale, transfer, etc	27.2	56.2	92.0	118.9	122.1	6.6	8.0	6.5	6.4	6.3
5110 General taxes	9.4	25.8	49.3	65.7	66.8	2.3	3.7	3.5	3.6	3.4
5111 Value added taxes	0.0	23.9	48.1	64.1	65.1	0.0	3.4	3.4	3.5	3.3
5120 Taxes on specific goods and services	17.8	30.3	42.7	53.2	55.2	4.3	4.3	3.0	2.9	2.8
5121 Excises	12.0	19.8	26.7	23.7	24.5	2.9	2.8	1.9	1.3	1.3
5200 Taxes on use of goods and perform activities	5.2	5.7	11.7	19.8	20.1	1.3	0.8	0.8	1.1	1.0
5300 Unallocable between 5100 and 5200	0.0	0.0	0.0	0.0	0.0	0.0	0.0	0.0	0.0	0.0
6000 Other taxes	**0.0**	**0.0**	**0.0**	**0.0**	**0.0**	**0.0**	**0.0**	**0.0**	**0.0**	**0.0**
Non-wastable tax credits										
Non-wastable tax credits against 1000	..	0.2	6.7	9.5	9.8	..	0.0	0.5	0.5	0.5
Transfer component	..	0.0	4.4	7.0	7.4	..	0.0	0.3	0.4	0.4
Tax expenditure component	..	0.2	2.4	2.4	2.4	..	0.0	0.2	0.1	0.1

.. Not available

Note: More detailed country data and country notes are available in online chapter 5 "Detailed country tables": https://doi.org/10.1787/0bbc27da-en. Full time series can be accessed at http://oe.cd/full-time-series.

Source: Australian Bureau of Statistics.

StatLink https://doi.org/10.1787/888934210236

Table 4.2. Australia, tax revenue and % of GDP by level of government and main taxes

	Billion AUD					% of GDP				
	1990	2000	2010	2017	2018	1990	2000	2010	2017	2018
Federal or Central government										
Total tax revenue	**92.6**	**175.7**	**287.1**	**424.9**	**453.2**	**22.3**	**24.9**	**20.3**	**23.0**	**23.3**
1000 Taxes on income, profits and capital gains	66.5	124.4	202.2	310.0	336.2	16.1	17.6	14.3	16.8	17.3
2000 Social security contributions	0.0	0.0	0.0	0.0	0.0	0.0	0.0	0.0	0.0	0.0
3000 Taxes on payroll and workforce	1.3	0.1	0.5	1.1	1.1	0.3	0.0	0.0	0.1	0.1
4000 Taxes on property	0.2	0.0	0.0	0.0	0.0	0.1	0.0	0.0	0.0	0.0
5000 Taxes on goods and services	24.5	51.1	84.4	113.7	115.9	5.9	7.2	6.0	6.1	6.0
6000 Other taxes	0.0	0.0	0.0	0.0	0.0	0.0	0.0	0.0	0.0	0.0
State/Regional										
Total tax revenue	**19.7**	**32.7**	**58.4**	**84.2**	**86.3**	**4.7**	**4.6**	**4.1**	**4.6**	**4.4**
1000 Taxes on income, profits and capital gains	0.0	0.0	0.0	0.0	0.0	0.0	0.0	0.0	0.0	0.0
2000 Social security contributions	0.0	0.0	0.0	0.0	0.0	0.0	0.0	0.0	0.0	0.0
3000 Taxes on payroll and workforce	5.8	9.5	18.0	24.4	25.9	1.4	1.3	1.3	1.3	1.3
4000 Taxes on property	6.0	12.4	21.1	34.9	34.2	1.4	1.8	1.5	1.9	1.8
5000 Taxes on goods and services	7.9	10.8	19.3	25.0	26.3	1.9	1.5	1.4	1.3	1.3
6000 Other taxes	0.0	0.0	0.0	0.0	0.0	0.0	0.0	0.0	0.0	0.0
Local government										
Total tax revenue	**4.2**	**6.4**	**12.4**	**18.1**	**18.9**	**1.0**	**0.9**	**0.9**	**1.0**	**1.0**
1000 Taxes on income, profits and capital gains	0.0	0.0	0.0	0.0	0.0	0.0	0.0	0.0	0.0	0.0
2000 Social security contributions	0.0	0.0	0.0	0.0	0.0	0.0	0.0	0.0	0.0	0.0
3000 Taxes on payroll and workforce	0.0	0.0	0.0	0.0	0.0	0.0	0.0	0.0	0.0	0.0
4000 Taxes on property	4.2	6.4	12.4	18.1	18.9	1.0	0.9	0.9	1.0	1.0
5000 Taxes on goods and services	0.0	0.0	0.0	0.0	0.0	0.0	0.0	0.0	0.0	0.0
6000 Other taxes	0.0	0.0	0.0	0.0	0.0	0.0	0.0	0.0	0.0	0.0
Social Security Funds										
Total tax revenue	**0.0**	**0.0**	**0.0**	**0.0**	**0.0**	**0.0**	**0.0**	**0.0**	**0.0**	**0.0**
1000 Taxes on income, profits and capital gains	0.0	0.0	0.0	0.0	0.0	0.0	0.0	0.0	0.0	0.0
2000 Social security contributions	0.0	0.0	0.0	0.0	0.0	0.0	0.0	0.0	0.0	0.0
3000 Taxes on payroll and workforce	0.0	0.0	0.0	0.0	0.0	0.0	0.0	0.0	0.0	0.0
4000 Taxes on property	0.0	0.0	0.0	0.0	0.0	0.0	0.0	0.0	0.0	0.0
5000 Taxes on goods and services	0.0	0.0	0.0	0.0	0.0	0.0	0.0	0.0	0.0	0.0
6000 Other taxes	0.0	0.0	0.0	0.0	0.0	0.0	0.0	0.0	0.0	0.0

Note: More detailed country data and country notes are available in online chapter 6 "Tax revenues by sub-sectors of general government": https://doi.org/10.1787/0bbc27da-en. Full time series can be accessed at http://oe.cd/full-time-series.
Source: Australian Bureau of Statistics.

StatLink https://doi.org/10.1787/888934210255

Table 4.3. Austria, tax revenue and % of GDP by selected tax category

	Billion EUR					% of GDP				
	1990	2000	2010	2017	2018	1990	2000	2010	2017	2018
Total tax revenue	**54.0**	**90.3**	**121.2**	**154.6**	**162.8**	**39.3**	**42.3**	**41.0**	**41.8**	**42.2**
1000 Taxes on income, profits and capital gains	**13.8**	**25.6**	**34.0**	**43.7**	**47.8**	**10.0**	**12.0**	**11.5**	**11.8**	**12.4**
1100 Of individuals	11.3	19.9	27.1	33.5	36.2	8.2	9.3	9.2	9.1	9.4
1200 Corporate	1.9	4.2	5.5	9.1	10.4	1.4	1.9	1.9	2.5	2.7
1300 Unallocable between 1100 and 1200	0.5	1.5	1.4	1.1	1.1	0.4	0.7	0.5	0.3	0.3
2000 Social security contributions	**17.8**	**30.5**	**41.4**	**53.9**	**56.6**	**12.9**	**14.3**	**14.0**	**14.6**	**14.7**
2100 Employees	7.5	12.5	16.8	21.7	22.8	5.5	5.8	5.7	5.9	5.9
2200 Employers	8.8	14.7	19.4	25.3	26.7	6.4	6.9	6.6	6.8	6.9
2300 Self-employed or non-employed	1.5	3.4	5.2	6.9	7.2	1.1	1.6	1.7	1.9	1.9
2400 Unallocable between 2100, 2200 and 2300	0.0	0.0	0.0	0.0	0.0	0.0	0.0	0.0	0.0	0.0
3000 Taxes on payroll and workforce	**3.3**	**5.8**	**8.4**	**10.2**	**10.4**	**2.4**	**2.7**	**2.8**	**2.8**	**2.7**
4000 Taxes on property	**1.5**	**1.2**	**1.6**	**1.9**	**2.1**	**1.1**	**0.6**	**0.5**	**0.5**	**0.5**
4100 Recurrent taxes on immovable property	0.4	0.5	0.7	0.8	0.8	0.3	0.2	0.2	0.2	0.2
4200 Recurrent taxes on net wealth	0.6	0.0	0.0	0.0	0.0	0.5	0.0	0.0	0.0	0.0
4300 Estate, inheritance and gift taxes	0.1	0.1	0.0	0.0	0.0	0.1	0.1	0.0	0.0	0.0
4400 Taxes on financial and capital transactions	0.4	0.6	0.8	1.1	1.2	0.3	0.3	0.3	0.3	0.3
4500 Non-recurrent taxes	0.0	0.0	0.0	0.0	0.1	0.0	0.0	0.0	0.0	0.0
4600 Other recurrent taxes on property	0.0	0.0	0.0	0.0	0.0	0.0	0.0	0.0	0.0	0.0
5000 Taxes on goods and services	**17.0**	**26.5**	**34.7**	**44.0**	**45.1**	**12.4**	**12.4**	**11.7**	**11.9**	**11.7**
5100 Taxes on production, sale, transfer, etc	16.2	24.6	32.1	40.3	41.3	11.8	11.5	10.9	10.9	10.7
5110 General taxes	11.2	16.9	22.7	28.3	29.3	8.2	7.9	7.7	7.6	7.6
5111 Value added taxes	11.2	16.9	22.7	28.3	29.3	8.2	7.9	7.7	7.6	7.6
5120 Taxes on specific goods and services	4.9	7.7	9.4	11.9	11.9	3.5	3.6	3.2	3.2	3.1
5121 Excises	3.3	5.5	6.9	8.3	8.2	2.4	2.6	2.3	2.2	2.1
5200 Taxes on use of goods and perform activities	0.9	1.9	2.6	3.7	3.9	0.6	0.9	0.9	1.0	1.0
5300 Unallocable between 5100 and 5200	0.0	0.0	0.0	0.0	0.0	0.0	0.0	0.0	0.0	0.0
6000 Other taxes	**0.7**	**0.8**	**1.1**	**0.8**	**0.8**	**0.5**	**0.4**	**0.4**	**0.2**	**0.2**
Non-wastable tax credits										
Non-wastable tax credits against 1000	..	0.7	0.7	0.3	0.3	..	0.3	0.2	0.1	0.1
Transfer component	..	0.1	0.2	0.1	0.1	..	0.0	0.1	0.0	0.0
Tax expenditure component	..	0.6	0.4	0.2	0.2	..	0.3	0.1	0.1	0.1
Revenues collected on behalf of the EU										
Revenues collected on behalf of the EU, total	..	0.4	0.3	0.7	0.7	..	0.2	0.1	0.2	0.2
Customs duties	..	0.4	0.3	0.5	0.5	..	0.2	0.1	0.1	0.1
SRF contributions	..	..	..	0.2	0.2	..	..	..	0.1	0.1

.. Not available

Note: More detailed country data and country notes are available in online chapter 5 "Detailed country tables": https://doi.org/10.1787/0bbc27da-en. Full time series can be accessed at http://oe.cd/full-time-series.

Source: Statistics Austria.

StatLink https://doi.org/10.1787/888934210274

Table 4.4. Austria, tax revenue and % of GDP by level of government and main taxes

	Billion EUR					% of GDP				
	1990	2000	2010	2017	2018	1990	2000	2010	2017	2018
Federal or Central government										
Total tax revenue	**27.2**	**60.5**	**80.7**	**101.7**	**107.2**	**19.8**	**28.3**	**27.3**	**27.5**	**27.8**
1000 Taxes on income, profits and capital gains	8.6	24.9	33.1	42.6	46.5	6.3	11.7	11.2	11.5	12.1
2000 Social security contributions	2.4	5.1	6.3	8.0	8.3	1.7	2.4	2.1	2.2	2.2
3000 Taxes on payroll and workforce	2.6	3.9	5.8	6.8	6.8	1.9	1.8	1.9	1.8	1.8
4000 Taxes on property	0.9	0.7	0.9	1.2	1.3	0.6	0.3	0.3	0.3	0.3
5000 Taxes on goods and services	12.3	25.3	33.7	42.5	43.7	8.9	11.8	11.4	11.5	11.3
6000 Other taxes	0.5	0.6	0.9	0.6	0.5	0.4	0.3	0.3	0.1	0.1
State/Regional										
Total tax revenue	**5.8**	**1.4**	**2.0**	**2.5**	**2.5**	**4.2**	**0.7**	**0.7**	**0.7**	**0.7**
1000 Taxes on income, profits and capital gains	2.8	0.6	0.9	1.2	1.2	2.0	0.3	0.3	0.3	0.3
2000 Social security contributions	0.2	0.4	0.5	0.5	0.5	0.2	0.2	0.2	0.1	0.1
3000 Taxes on payroll and workforce	0.0	0.1	0.2	0.2	0.2	0.0	0.1	0.1	0.1	0.1
4000 Taxes on property	0.1	0.0	0.0	0.1	0.0	0.0	0.0	0.0	0.0	0.0
5000 Taxes on goods and services	2.7	0.2	0.3	0.4	0.4	2.0	0.1	0.1	0.1	0.1
6000 Other taxes	0.0	0.1	0.1	0.1	0.1	0.0	0.0	0.0	0.0	0.0
Local government										
Total tax revenue	**6.1**	**3.2**	**3.8**	**4.7**	**4.8**	**4.4**	**1.5**	**1.3**	**1.3**	**1.3**
1000 Taxes on income, profits and capital gains	2.4	0.0	0.0	0.0	0.0	1.8	0.0	0.0	0.0	0.0
2000 Social security contributions	0.2	0.3	0.3	0.3	0.3	0.1	0.1	0.1	0.1	0.1
3000 Taxes on payroll and workforce	0.7	1.8	2.4	3.2	3.4	0.5	0.8	0.8	0.9	0.9
4000 Taxes on property	0.5	0.5	0.6	0.7	0.7	0.4	0.2	0.2	0.2	0.2
5000 Taxes on goods and services	2.1	0.6	0.4	0.4	0.4	1.5	0.3	0.1	0.1	0.1
6000 Other taxes	0.2	0.1	0.1	0.1	0.1	0.1	0.0	0.0	0.0	0.0
Social Security Funds										
Total tax revenue	**15.0**	**24.8**	**34.4**	**45.1**	**47.6**	**10.9**	**11.6**	**11.6**	**12.2**	**12.3**
1000 Taxes on income, profits and capital gains	0.0	0.0	0.0	0.0	0.0	0.0	0.0	0.0	0.0	0.0
2000 Social security contributions	15.0	24.8	34.4	45.1	47.6	10.9	11.6	11.6	12.2	12.3
3000 Taxes on payroll and workforce	0.0	0.0	0.0	0.0	0.0	0.0	0.0	0.0	0.0	0.0
4000 Taxes on property	0.0	0.0	0.0	0.0	0.0	0.0	0.0	0.0	0.0	0.0
5000 Taxes on goods and services	0.0	0.0	0.0	0.0	0.0	0.0	0.0	0.0	0.0	0.0
6000 Other taxes	0.0	0.0	0.0	0.0	0.0	0.0	0.0	0.0	0.0	0.0

Note: More detailed country data and country notes are available in online chapter 6 "Tax revenues by sub-sectors of general government": https://doi.org/10.1787/0bbc27da-en. Full time series can be accessed at http://oe.cd/full-time-series.

Source: Statistics Austria.

StatLink https://doi.org/10.1787/888934210293

Table 4.5. Belgium, tax revenue and % of GDP by selected tax category

	Billion EUR					% of GDP				
	1990	2000	2010	2017	2018	1990	2000	2010	2017	2018
Total tax revenue	**70.4**	**112.4**	**155.7**	**195.3**	**202.0**	**41.4**	**43.8**	**42.9**	**43.8**	**43.9**
1000 Taxes on income, profits and capital gains	**26.0**	**43.4**	**53.2**	**71.3**	**74.3**	**15.3**	**16.9**	**14.7**	**16.0**	**16.2**
1100 Of individuals	22.5	35.3	44.0	53.2	54.5	13.3	13.8	12.1	11.9	11.9
1200 Corporate	3.4	8.1	9.2	18.1	19.7	2.0	3.1	2.5	4.1	4.3
1300 Unallocable between 1100 and 1200	0.0	0.1	0.0	0.1	0.1	0.0	0.0	0.0	0.0	0.0
2000 Social security contributions	**23.4**	**34.6**	**50.5**	**59.7**	**60.9**	**13.7**	**13.5**	**13.9**	**13.4**	**13.3**
2100 Employees	7.2	10.9	15.0	17.7	18.4	4.2	4.3	4.1	4.0	4.0
2200 Employers	14.7	20.8	30.9	36.0	36.4	8.6	8.1	8.5	8.1	7.9
2300 Self-employed or non-employed	1.5	2.9	4.6	5.9	6.1	0.9	1.1	1.3	1.3	1.3
2400 Unallocable between 2100, 2200 and 2300	0.0	0.0	0.0	0.0	0.0	0.0	0.0	0.0	0.0	0.0
3000 Taxes on payroll and workforce	**0.0**	**0.0**	**0.0**	**0.0**	**0.0**	**0.0**	**0.0**	**0.0**	**0.0**	**0.0**
4000 Taxes on property	**2.7**	**5.3**	**11.3**	**15.4**	**15.8**	**1.6**	**2.1**	**3.1**	**3.5**	**3.4**
4100 Recurrent taxes on immovable property	0.6	1.2	4.6	5.8	5.7	0.4	0.5	1.3	1.3	1.2
4200 Recurrent taxes on net wealth	0.0	0.1	0.2	0.9	1.0	0.0	0.0	0.1	0.2	0.2
4300 Estate, inheritance and gift taxes	0.5	1.1	2.3	3.1	3.3	0.3	0.4	0.6	0.7	0.7
4400 Taxes on financial and capital transactions	1.5	2.7	3.5	4.8	4.9	0.9	1.0	1.0	1.1	1.1
4500 Non-recurrent taxes	0.0	0.1	0.3	0.5	0.5	0.0	0.0	0.1	0.1	0.1
4600 Other recurrent taxes on property	0.1	0.2	0.3	0.3	0.5	0.1	0.1	0.1	0.1	0.1
5000 Taxes on goods and services	**18.4**	**29.1**	**40.7**	**48.9**	**50.9**	**10.8**	**11.3**	**11.2**	**11.0**	**11.1**
5100 Taxes on production, sale, transfer, etc	17.4	27.0	38.3	46.3	48.2	10.2	10.5	10.5	10.4	10.5
5110 General taxes	11.6	18.2	25.5	30.0	31.3	6.8	7.1	7.0	6.7	6.8
5111 Value added taxes	11.5	18.1	25.3	29.8	31.1	6.8	7.1	7.0	6.7	6.8
5120 Taxes on specific goods and services	5.8	8.7	12.8	16.4	17.0	3.4	3.4	3.5	3.7	3.7
5121 Excises	3.5	5.7	7.8	9.9	10.1	2.0	2.2	2.1	2.2	2.2
5200 Taxes on use of goods and perform activities	1.0	2.1	2.4	2.5	2.6	0.6	0.8	0.7	0.6	0.6
5300 Unallocable between 5100 and 5200	0.0	0.0	0.0	0.0	0.0	0.0	0.0	0.0	0.0	0.0
6000 Other taxes	**0.0**	**0.0**	**0.0**	**0.0**	**0.0**	**0.0**	**0.0**	**0.0**	**0.0**	**0.0**
Non-wastable tax credits										
Non-wastable tax credits against 1000	..	..	1.0	0.9	0.9	..	..	0.3	0.2	0.2
Transfer component	..	..	0.4	0.3	0.3	..	..	0.1	0.1	0.1
Tax expenditure component	..	..	0.6	0.6	0.6	..	..	0.2	0.1	0.1
Revenues collected on behalf of the EU										
Revenues collected on behalf of the EU, total	0.9	1.0	1.3	1.8	1.9	0.6	0.4	0.4	0.4	0.4
Customs duties	..	1.0	1.2	1.6	1.6	..	0.4	0.3	0.4	0.4
SRF contributions	..	..	..	0.3	0.3	..	..	..	0.1	0.1

.. Not available

Note: More detailed country data and country notes are available in online chapter 5 "Detailed country tables": https://doi.org/10.1787/0bbc27da-en. Full time series can be accessed at http://oe.cd/full-time-series.

The total tax revenue has been reduced by the amount of any capital transfer that represents uncollected taxes. The capital transfers were subtracted directly from the specific taxes to which they relate. Therefore, the tax revenue amounts are different to those reported in the detailed country data available in online chapter 5 "Detailed country tables".

Source: Federal Ministry of Finance.

StatLink https://doi.org/10.1787/888934210312

Table 4.6. Belgium, tax revenue and % of GDP by level of government and main taxes

	Billion EUR					% of GDP				
	1990	2000	2010	2017	2018	1990	2000	2010	2017	2018
Federal or Central government										
Total tax revenue	**42.5**	**69.4**	**87.8**	**100.3**	**106.1**	**25.0**	**27.1**	**24.2**	**22.5**	**23.1**
1000 Taxes on income, profits and capital gains	23.9	39.6	49.3	56.8	60.4	14.0	15.4	13.6	12.7	13.1
2000 Social security contributions	0.9	1.3	2.5	0.1	0.1	0.5	0.5	0.7	0.0	0.0
3000 Taxes on payroll and workforce	0.0	0.0	0.0	0.0	0.0	0.0	0.0	0.0	0.0	0.0
4000 Taxes on property	1.1	2.3	0.9	2.1	2.3	0.6	0.9	0.3	0.5	0.5
5000 Taxes on goods and services	16.7	26.3	35.0	41.4	43.3	9.8	10.2	9.7	9.3	9.4
6000 Other taxes	0.0	0.0	0.0	0.0	0.0	0.0	0.0	0.0	0.0	0.0
State/Regional										
Total tax revenue	**1.2**	**2.4**	**8.1**	**21.0**	**20.6**	**0.7**	**1.0**	**2.2**	**4.7**	**4.5**
1000 Taxes on income, profits and capital gains	0.0	0.1	0.0	9.9	9.5	0.0	0.0	0.0	2.2	2.1
2000 Social security contributions	0.0	0.0	0.0	0.2	0.3	0.0	0.0	0.0	0.1	0.1
3000 Taxes on payroll and workforce	0.0	0.0	0.0	0.0	0.0	0.0	0.0	0.0	0.0	0.0
4000 Taxes on property	0.9	1.9	5.6	7.6	7.9	0.5	0.7	1.6	1.7	1.7
5000 Taxes on goods and services	0.2	0.5	2.4	3.3	3.0	0.1	0.2	0.7	0.7	0.7
6000 Other taxes	0.0	0.0	0.0	0.0	0.0	0.0	0.0	0.0	0.0	0.0
Local government										
Total tax revenue	**3.1**	**4.6**	**7.9**	**9.5**	**9.2**	**1.8**	**1.8**	**2.2**	**2.1**	**2.0**
1000 Taxes on income, profits and capital gains	2.1	3.1	2.9	3.4	3.2	1.2	1.2	0.8	0.8	0.7
2000 Social security contributions	0.1	0.0	0.0	0.0	0.0	0.1	0.0	0.0	0.0	0.0
3000 Taxes on payroll and workforce	0.0	0.0	0.0	0.0	0.0	0.0	0.0	0.0	0.0	0.0
4000 Taxes on property	0.6	1.0	4.4	5.5	5.3	0.3	0.4	1.2	1.2	1.2
5000 Taxes on goods and services	0.3	0.4	0.6	0.6	0.7	0.2	0.2	0.2	0.1	0.2
6000 Other taxes	0.0	0.0	0.0	0.0	0.0	0.0	0.0	0.0	0.0	0.0
Social Security Funds										
Total tax revenue	**22.7**	**34.9**	**50.7**	**62.6**	**64.1**	**13.4**	**13.6**	**14.0**	**14.0**	**13.9**
1000 Taxes on income, profits and capital gains	0.0	0.6	1.0	1.2	1.3	0.0	0.2	0.3	0.3	0.3
2000 Social security contributions	22.4	33.3	48.0	59.4	60.6	13.2	13.0	13.2	13.3	13.2
3000 Taxes on payroll and workforce	0.0	0.0	0.0	0.0	0.0	0.0	0.0	0.0	0.0	0.0
4000 Taxes on property	0.1	0.2	0.3	0.3	0.3	0.1	0.1	0.1	0.1	0.1
5000 Taxes on goods and services	0.2	0.8	1.3	1.7	1.9	0.1	0.3	0.4	0.4	0.4
6000 Other taxes	0.0	0.0	0.0	0.0	0.0	0.0	0.0	0.0	0.0	0.0

Note: More detailed country data and country notes are available in online chapter 6 "Tax revenues by sub-sectors of general government": https://doi.org/10.1787/0bbc27da-en. Full time series can be accessed at http://oe.cd/full-time-series.

The total tax revenue has been reduced by the amount of any capital transfer that represents uncollected taxes. The capital transfers were subtracted directly from the specific taxes to which they relate. Therefore, the tax revenue amounts are different to those reported in the detailed country data available in online chapter 6 "Tax revenues by sub-sectors of general government".

Source: Federal Ministry of Finance.

StatLink https://doi.org/10.1787/888934210331

Table 4.7. Canada, tax revenue and % of GDP by selected tax category

	Billion CAD					% of GDP				
	1990	2000	2010	2017	2018	1990	2000	2010	2017	2018
Total tax revenue	**244.2**	**390.2**	**516.6**	**709.0**	**738.7**	**35.1**	**34.7**	**31.0**	**33.1**	**33.2**
1000 Taxes on income, profits and capital gains	**118.6**	**195.3**	**241.0**	**345.2**	**360.5**	**17.0**	**17.4**	**14.5**	**16.1**	**16.2**
1100 Of individuals	99.7	143.7	180.9	254.7	267.6	14.3	12.8	10.9	11.9	12.0
1200 Corporate	17.2	47.6	54.1	82.9	83.8	2.5	4.2	3.2	3.9	3.8
1300 Unallocable between 1100 and 1200	1.7	4.0	6.0	7.5	9.1	0.2	0.4	0.4	0.4	0.4
2000 Social security contributions	**29.7**	**53.1**	**76.8**	**99.0**	**103.2**	**4.3**	**4.7**	**4.6**	**4.6**	**4.6**
2100 Employees	10.6	21.4	30.6	39.9	41.5	1.5	1.9	1.8	1.9	1.9
2200 Employers	18.4	30.3	43.5	55.6	58.0	2.7	2.7	2.6	2.6	2.6
2300 Self-employed or non-employed	0.6	1.4	2.6	3.6	3.7	0.1	0.1	0.2	0.2	0.2
2400 Unallocable between 2100, 2200 and 2300	0.0	0.0	0.0	0.0	0.0	0.0	0.0	0.0	0.0	0.0
3000 Taxes on payroll and workforce	**5.5**	**8.0**	**10.8**	**14.2**	**14.9**	**0.8**	**0.7**	**0.6**	**0.7**	**0.7**
4000 Taxes on property	**24.5**	**37.2**	**63.7**	**84.1**	**85.9**	**3.5**	**3.3**	**3.8**	**3.9**	**3.9**
4100 Recurrent taxes on immovable property	20.2	30.2	51.7	66.7	69.8	2.9	2.7	3.1	3.1	3.1
4200 Recurrent taxes on net wealth	1.9	4.2	1.5	0.4	0.4	0.3	0.4	0.1	0.0	0.0
4300 Estate, inheritance and gift taxes	0.0	0.0	0.2	0.3	0.3	0.0	0.0	0.0	0.0	0.0
4400 Taxes on financial and capital transactions	0.0	0.0	3.1	7.2	6.3	0.0	0.0	0.2	0.3	0.3
4500 Non-recurrent taxes	2.4	2.7	7.3	9.5	9.0	0.3	0.2	0.4	0.4	0.4
4600 Other recurrent taxes on property	0.0	0.0	0.0	0.0	0.0	0.0	0.0	0.0	0.0	0.0
5000 Taxes on goods and services	**63.1**	**94.5**	**123.8**	**165.7**	**173.6**	**9.1**	**8.4**	**7.4**	**7.7**	**7.8**
5100 Taxes on production, sale, transfer, etc	59.6	88.9	116.2	153.9	161.6	8.6	7.9	7.0	7.2	7.3
5110 General taxes	34.5	55.3	72.1	99.9	105.0	5.0	4.9	4.3	4.7	4.7
5111 Value added taxes	0.0	35.9	70.7	96.0	100.6	0.0	3.2	4.2	4.5	4.5
5120 Taxes on specific goods and services	25.2	33.6	44.0	54.0	56.7	3.6	3.0	2.6	2.5	2.5
5121 Excises	14.5	18.4	23.3	27.3	28.0	2.1	1.6	1.4	1.3	1.3
5200 Taxes on use of goods and perform activities	3.5	5.6	7.6	11.8	11.9	0.5	0.5	0.5	0.6	0.5
5300 Unallocable between 5100 and 5200	0.0	0.0	0.0	0.0	0.0	0.0	0.0	0.0	0.0	0.0
6000 Other taxes	**2.9**	**2.2**	**0.6**	**0.7**	**0.8**	**0.4**	**0.2**	**0.0**	**0.0**	**0.0**
Non-wastable tax credits										
Non-wastable tax credits against 1000	..	3.4	11.1	11.7	13.8	..	0.3	0.7	0.5	0.6
Transfer component	..	3.1	10.2	10.6	11.4	..	0.3	0.6	0.5	0.5
Tax expenditure component	..	0.3	0.9	1.1	2.4	..	0.0	0.1	0.1	0.1

.. Not available

Note: More detailed country data and country notes are available in online chapter 5 "Detailed country tables": https://doi.org/10.1787/0bbc27da-en. Full time series can be accessed at http://oe.cd/full-time-series.

Source: Statistics Canada.

StatLink https://doi.org/10.1787/888934210350

Table 4.8. Canada, tax revenue and % of GDP by level of government and main taxes

	Billion CAD					% of GDP				
	1990	2000	2010	2017	2018	1990	2000	2010	2017	2018
Federal or Central government										
Total tax revenue	**101.7**	**184.4**	**212.8**	**291.8**	**306.9**	**14.6**	**16.4**	**12.8**	**13.6**	**13.8**
1000 Taxes on income, profits and capital gains	73.6	126.3	148.7	212.7	223.2	10.6	11.2	8.9	9.9	10.0
2000 Social security contributions	0.0	18.8	17.9	20.9	22.4	0.0	1.7	1.1	1.0	1.0
3000 Taxes on payroll and workforce	0.0	0.0	0.0	0.0	0.0	0.0	0.0	0.0	0.0	0.0
4000 Taxes on property	0.0	0.0	0.0	0.0	0.0	0.0	0.0	0.0	0.0	0.0
5000 Taxes on goods and services	28.1	39.4	46.2	58.3	61.4	4.0	3.5	2.8	2.7	2.8
6000 Other taxes	0.0	0.0	0.0	0.0	0.0	0.0	0.0	0.0	0.0	0.0
State/Regional										
Total tax revenue	**89.3**	**148.2**	**201.1**	**281.1**	**292.0**	**12.8**	**13.2**	**12.1**	**13.1**	**13.1**
1000 Taxes on income, profits and capital gains	44.9	69.0	92.2	132.5	137.3	6.5	6.1	5.5	6.2	6.2
2000 Social security contributions	0.0	8.3	11.7	14.6	15.2	0.0	0.7	0.7	0.7	0.7
3000 Taxes on payroll and workforce	5.5	8.0	10.8	14.2	14.9	0.8	0.7	0.6	0.7	0.7
4000 Taxes on property	4.2	8.4	9.8	13.5	13.6	0.6	0.7	0.6	0.6	0.6
5000 Taxes on goods and services	34.6	54.5	76.7	106.3	111.0	5.0	4.8	4.6	5.0	5.0
6000 Other taxes	0.0	0.0	0.0	0.0	0.0	0.0	0.0	0.0	0.0	0.0
Local government										
Total tax revenue	**23.5**	**31.5**	**55.4**	**72.5**	**74.2**	**3.4**	**2.8**	**3.3**	**3.4**	**3.3**
1000 Taxes on income, profits and capital gains	0.0	0.0	0.0	0.0	0.0	0.0	0.0	0.0	0.0	0.0
2000 Social security contributions	0.0	0.0	0.0	0.0	0.0	0.0	0.0	0.0	0.0	0.0
3000 Taxes on payroll and workforce	0.0	0.0	0.0	0.0	0.0	0.0	0.0	0.0	0.0	0.0
4000 Taxes on property	20.3	28.8	53.9	70.6	72.2	2.9	2.6	3.2	3.3	3.2
5000 Taxes on goods and services	0.4	0.6	0.9	1.2	1.2	0.1	0.1	0.1	0.1	0.1
6000 Other taxes	2.9	2.2	0.6	0.7	0.8	0.4	0.2	0.0	0.0	0.0
Social Security Funds										
Total tax revenue	**29.7**	**26.0**	**47.2**	**63.6**	**65.6**	**4.3**	**2.3**	**2.8**	**3.0**	**3.0**
1000 Taxes on income, profits and capital gains	0.0	0.0	0.0	0.0	0.0	0.0	0.0	0.0	0.0	0.0
2000 Social security contributions	29.7	26.0	47.2	63.6	65.6	4.3	2.3	2.8	3.0	3.0
3000 Taxes on payroll and workforce	0.0	0.0	0.0	0.0	0.0	0.0	0.0	0.0	0.0	0.0
4000 Taxes on property	0.0	0.0	0.0	0.0	0.0	0.0	0.0	0.0	0.0	0.0
5000 Taxes on goods and services	0.0	0.0	0.0	0.0	0.0	0.0	0.0	0.0	0.0	0.0
6000 Other taxes	0.0	0.0	0.0	0.0	0.0	0.0	0.0	0.0	0.0	0.0

Note: More detailed country data and country notes are available in online chapter 6 "Tax revenues by sub-sectors of general government": https://doi.org/10.1787/0bbc27da-en. Full time series can be accessed at http://oe.cd/full-time-series.

Source: Statistics Canada.

StatLink https://doi.org/10.1787/888934210369

Table 4.9. Chile, tax revenue and % of GDP by selected tax category

	Billion CLP					% of GDP				
	1990	2000	2010	2017	2018	1990	2000	2010	2017	2018
Total tax revenue	**1 777.2**	**7 902.0**	**21 845.7**	**36 238.6**	**40 314.7**	**16.9**	**18.8**	**19.6**	**20.2**	**21.1**
1000 Taxes on income, profits and capital gains	**413.0**	**1 841.6**	**8 329.1**	**12 516.2**	**14 418.9**	**3.9**	**4.4**	**7.5**	**7.0**	**7.5**
1100 Of individuals	99.2	604.1	1 492.8	3 500.0	2 701.4	0.9	1.4	1.3	1.9	1.4
1200 Corporate	219.6	882.9	4 448.7	7 658.4	8 920.5	2.1	2.1	4.0	4.3	4.7
1300 Unallocable between 1100 and 1200	94.2	354.6	2 387.5	1 357.7	2 796.9	0.9	0.8	2.1	0.8	1.5
2000 Social security contributions	**159.6**	**576.8**	**1 494.0**	**2 627.6**	**2 786.2**	**1.5**	**1.4**	**1.3**	**1.5**	**1.5**
2100 Employees	154.0	553.9	1 433.2	2 553.9	2 703.3	1.5	1.3	1.3	1.4	1.4
2200 Employers	5.5	22.8	60.8	73.6	82.9	0.1	0.1	0.1	0.0	0.0
2300 Self-employed or non-employed	0.0	0.0	0.0	0.0	0.0	0.0	0.0	0.0	0.0	0.0
2400 Unallocable between 2100, 2200 and 2300	0.0	0.0	0.0	0.0	0.0	0.0	0.0	0.0	0.0	0.0
3000 Taxes on payroll and workforce	**0.0**	**0.0**	**0.0**	**0.0**	**0.0**	**0.0**	**0.0**	**0.0**	**0.0**	**0.0**
4000 Taxes on property	**109.3**	**554.0**	**898.6**	**1 950.2**	**2 086.9**	**1.0**	**1.3**	**0.8**	**1.1**	**1.1**
4100 Recurrent taxes on immovable property	60.0	302.2	662.4	1 229.2	1 373.5	0.6	0.7	0.6	0.7	0.7
4200 Recurrent taxes on net wealth	0.0	0.0	0.0	0.0	0.0	0.0	0.0	0.0	0.0	0.0
4300 Estate, inheritance and gift taxes	3.4	10.9	39.3	202.4	125.6	0.0	0.0	0.0	0.1	0.1
4400 Taxes on financial and capital transactions	45.9	240.9	196.9	518.6	587.7	0.4	0.6	0.2	0.3	0.3
4500 Non-recurrent taxes	0.0	0.0	0.0	0.0	0.0	0.0	0.0	0.0	0.0	0.0
4600 Other recurrent taxes on property	0.0	0.0	0.0	0.0	0.0	0.0	0.0	0.0	0.0	0.0
5000 Taxes on goods and services	**1 118.7**	**5 041.8**	**11 185.2**	**19 858.9**	**21 470.5**	**10.6**	**12.0**	**10.0**	**11.0**	**11.2**
5100 Taxes on production, sale, transfer, etc	1 074.0	4 789.8	10 532.9	18 597.2	19 953.0	10.2	11.4	9.4	10.3	10.4
5110 General taxes	664.4	3 306.4	8 399.9	15 069.5	16 211.6	6.3	7.9	7.5	8.4	8.5
5111 Value added taxes	664.4	3 306.4	8 399.9	15 069.5	16 211.6	6.3	7.9	7.5	8.4	8.5
5120 Taxes on specific goods and services	409.6	1 483.5	2 133.0	3 527.6	3 741.4	3.9	3.5	1.9	2.0	2.0
5121 Excises	166.0	816.2	1 561.2	2 682.7	2 796.0	1.6	1.9	1.4	1.5	1.5
5200 Taxes on use of goods and perform activities	44.7	251.9	652.3	1 261.7	1 517.5	0.4	0.6	0.6	0.7	0.8
5300 Unallocable between 5100 and 5200	0.0	0.0	0.0	0.0	0.0	0.0	0.0	0.0	0.0	0.0
6000 Other taxes	**-23.4**	**-112.2**	**-61.1**	**-714.3**	**-447.7**	**-0.2**	**-0.3**	**-0.1**	**-0.4**	**-0.2**
Non-wastable tax credits										
Non-wastable tax credits against 1000	0.0	0.0	0.0	213.5	251.6	0.0	0.0	0.0	0.1	0.1
Transfer component	..	..	..	151.4	186.8	..	..	..	0.1	0.1
Tax expenditure component	..	..	..	62.1	64.8	..	..	..	0.0	0.0

.. Not available

Note: More detailed country data and country notes are available in online chapter 5 "Detailed country tables": https://doi.org/10.1787/0bbc27da-en. Full time series can be accessed at http://oe.cd/full-time-series.

Source: Servicio de Impuestos internos (Chile's Tax Service).

StatLink https://doi.org/10.1787/888934210388

Table 4.10. Chile, tax revenue and % of GDP by level of government and main taxes

	Billion CLP					% of GDP				
	1990	2000	2010	2017	2018	1990	2000	2010	2017	2018
Federal or Central government										
Total tax revenue	**1 579.7**	**6 936.8**	**19 214.8**	**31 274.2**	**34 816.0**	**15.0**	**16.5**	**17.2**	**17.4**	**18.2**
1000 Taxes on income, profits and capital gains	413.0	1 841.6	8 329.1	12 516.2	14 418.9	3.9	4.4	7.5	7.0	7.5
2000 Social security contributions	66.7	232.7	371.4	506.0	474.0	0.6	0.6	0.3	0.3	0.2
3000 Taxes on payroll and workforce	0.0	0.0	0.0	0.0	0.0	0.0	0.0	0.0	0.0	0.0
4000 Taxes on property	59.7	255.4	245.0	738.3	736.3	0.6	0.6	0.2	0.4	0.4
5000 Taxes on goods and services	1 063.7	4 719.3	10 330.4	18 228.0	19 634.6	10.1	11.2	9.3	10.1	10.3
6000 Other taxes	-23.4	-112.2	-61.1	-714.3	-447.7	-0.2	-0.3	-0.1	-0.4	-0.2
State/Regional										
Total tax revenue	..	..	..	..	..	..	..	..	..	..
1000 Taxes on income, profits and capital gains	..	..	..	..	..	..	..	..	..	..
2000 Social security contributions	..	..	..	..	..	..	..	..	..	..
3000 Taxes on payroll and workforce	..	..	..	..	..	..	..	..	..	..
4000 Taxes on property	..	..	..	..	..	..	..	..	..	..
5000 Taxes on goods and services	..	..	..	..	..	..	..	..	..	..
6000 Other taxes	..	..	..	..	..	..	..	..	..	..
Local government										
Total tax revenue	**104.7**	**621.2**	**1 508.3**	**2 842.8**	**3 186.5**	**1.0**	**1.5**	**1.4**	**1.6**	**1.7**
1000 Taxes on income, profits and capital gains	0.0	0.0	0.0	0.0	0.0	0.0	0.0	0.0	0.0	0.0
2000 Social security contributions	0.0	0.0	0.0	0.0	0.0	0.0	0.0	0.0	0.0	0.0
3000 Taxes on payroll and workforce	0.0	0.0	0.0	0.0	0.0	0.0	0.0	0.0	0.0	0.0
4000 Taxes on property	49.6	298.7	653.6	1 211.9	1 350.5	0.5	0.7	0.6	0.7	0.7
5000 Taxes on goods and services	55.0	322.5	854.8	1 630.9	1 835.9	0.5	0.8	0.8	0.9	1.0
6000 Other taxes	0.0	0.0	0.0	0.0	0.0	0.0	0.0	0.0	0.0	0.0
Social Security Funds										
Total tax revenue	**92.8**	**344.0**	**1 122.6**	**2 121.5**	**2 312.2**	**0.9**	**0.8**	**1.0**	**1.2**	**1.2**
1000 Taxes on income, profits and capital gains	0.0	0.0	0.0	0.0	0.0	0.0	0.0	0.0	0.0	0.0
2000 Social security contributions	92.8	344.0	1 122.6	2 121.5	2 312.2	0.9	0.8	1.0	1.2	1.2
3000 Taxes on payroll and workforce	0.0	0.0	0.0	0.0	0.0	0.0	0.0	0.0	0.0	0.0
4000 Taxes on property	0.0	0.0	0.0	0.0	0.0	0.0	0.0	0.0	0.0	0.0
5000 Taxes on goods and services	0.0	0.0	0.0	0.0	0.0	0.0	0.0	0.0	0.0	0.0
6000 Other taxes	0.0	0.0	0.0	0.0	0.0	0.0	0.0	0.0	0.0	0.0

.. Not available

Note: More detailed country data and country notes are available in online chapter 6 "Tax revenues by sub-sectors of general government": https://doi.org/10.1787/0bbc27da-en. Full time series can be accessed at http://oe.cd/full-time-series.

Source: Servicio de Impuestos internos (Chile's Tax Service).

StatLink https://doi.org/10.1787/888934210407

Table 4.11. Colombia, tax revenue and % of GDP by selected tax category

	Billion COP					% of GDP				
	1990	2000	2010	2017	2018	1990	2000	2010	2017	2018
Total tax revenue	**2 579.4**	**30 598.6**	**98 455.3**	**174 735.8**	**190 299.9**	**11.3**	**15.7**	**18.1**	**19.0**	**19.3**
1000 Taxes on income, profits and capital gains	**771.7**	**7 103.5**	**26 218.9**	**57 615.2**	**64 043.9**	**3.4**	**3.6**	**4.8**	**6.3**	**6.5**
1100 Of individuals	47.2	1 499.3	5 192.4	10 367.6	12 216.0	0.2	0.8	1.0	1.1	1.2
1200 Corporate	359.8	5 119.8	20 405.2	44 970.5	48 529.3	1.6	2.6	3.8	4.9	4.9
1300 Unallocable between 1100 and 1200	364.7	484.4	621.3	2 277.1	3 298.6	1.6	0.2	0.1	0.2	0.3
2000 Social security contributions	**203.6**	**4 989.0**	**11 478.1**	**13 351.7**	**18 192.0**	**0.9**	**2.6**	**2.1**	**1.5**	**1.8**
2100 Employees	..	..	..	..	..	..	..	..	..	..
2200 Employers	..	..	..	..	..	..	..	..	..	..
2300 Self-employed or non-employed	..	..	..	..	..	..	..	..	..	..
2400 Unallocable between 2100, 2200 and 2300	203.6	4 989.0	11 478.1	13 351.7	18 192.0	0.9	2.6	2.1	1.5	1.8
3000 Taxes on payroll and workforce	**0.0**	**1 286.8**	**4 022.5**	**3 200.2**	**3 461.4**	**0.0**	**0.7**	**0.7**	**0.3**	**0.4**
4000 Taxes on property	**56.2**	**2 027.7**	**8 535.2**	**17 950.5**	**15 265.5**	**0.2**	**1.0**	**1.6**	**2.0**	**1.5**
4100 Recurrent taxes on immovable property	56.2	991.1	3 338.9	7 310.2	7 982.0	0.2	0.5	0.6	0.8	0.8
4200 Recurrent taxes on net wealth	0.0	0.0	1 970.5	3 868.6	467.9	0.0	0.0	0.4	0.4	0.0
4300 Estate, inheritance and gift taxes	0.0	0.0	0.0	0.0	0.0	0.0	0.0	0.0	0.0	0.0
4400 Taxes on financial and capital transactions	0.0	1 036.6	3 225.8	6 771.7	6 815.6	0.0	0.5	0.6	0.7	0.7
4500 Non-recurrent taxes	0.0	0.0	0.0	0.0	0.0	0.0	0.0	0.0	0.0	0.0
4600 Other recurrent taxes on property	0.0	0.0	0.0	0.0	0.0	0.0	0.0	0.0	0.0	0.0
5000 Taxes on goods and services	**1 388.7**	**14 180.5**	**44 411.6**	**75 381.1**	**81 408.8**	**6.1**	**7.3**	**8.2**	**8.2**	**8.3**
5100 Taxes on production, sale, transfer, etc	1 388.7	14 048.7	44 038.1	74 003.6	79 935.3	6.1	7.2	8.1	8.0	8.1
5110 General taxes	672.4	9 585.9	33 333.8	58 565.8	64 316.0	3.0	4.9	6.1	6.4	6.5
5111 Value added taxes	583.1	8 445.8	28 811.7	50 619.8	55 879.1	2.6	4.3	5.3	5.5	5.7
5120 Taxes on specific goods and services	716.3	4 462.8	10 704.3	15 437.8	15 619.3	3.2	2.3	2.0	1.7	1.6
5121 Excises	404.7	2 718.7	6 052.3	11 616.8	12 061.1	1.8	1.4	1.1	1.3	1.2
5200 Taxes on use of goods and perform activities	0.0	131.8	373.6	1 377.6	1 473.5	0.0	0.1	0.1	0.2	0.1
5300 Unallocable between 5100 and 5200	0.0	0.0	0.0	0.0	0.0	0.0	0.0	0.0	0.0	0.0
6000 Other taxes	**159.3**	**1 011.2**	**3 789.0**	**7 237.0**	**7 928.3**	**0.7**	**0.5**	**0.7**	**0.8**	**0.8**
Non-wastable tax credits										
Non-wastable tax credits against 1000	..	..	..	..	..	..	..	..	..	..
Transfer component	..	..	..	..	..	..	..	..	..	..
Tax expenditure component	..	..	..	..	..	..	..	..	..	..

.. Not available

Note: More detailed country data and country notes are available in online chapter 5 "Detailed country tables": https://doi.org/10.1787/0bbc27da-en. Full time series can be accessed at http://oe.cd/full-time-series.

Source: Dirección de Impuestos y Aduanas Nacionales de Colombia, Ministerio de Hacienda y Crédito Público y Banco Central de Colombia. (National Tax and Customs Administration, Ministry of Finance and Public Credit and Central Bank of Colombia).

StatLink https://doi.org/10.1787/888934210426

Table 4.12. Colombia, tax revenue and % of GDP by level of government and main taxes

	Billion COP					% of GDP				
	1990	2000	2010	2017	2018	1990	2000	2010	2017	2018
Federal or Central government										
Total tax revenue	**1 885.9**	**21 016.3**	**71 304.3**	**130 704.4**	**139 228.1**	**8.3**	**10.8**	**13.1**	**14.2**	**14.1**
1000 Taxes on income, profits and capital gains	771.7	7 103.5	26 218.9	57 615.2	64 043.9	3.4	3.6	4.8	6.3	6.5
2000 Social security contributions	0.0	0.0	0.0	0.0	0.0	0.0	0.0	0.0	0.0	0.0
3000 Taxes on payroll and workforce	0.0	1 286.8	4 022.5	3 200.2	3 461.4	0.0	0.7	0.7	0.3	0.4
4000 Taxes on property	0.0	1 036.6	5 196.3	10 640.3	7 283.5	0.0	0.5	1.0	1.2	0.7
5000 Taxes on goods and services	1 035.9	11 108.6	35 382.9	58 769.7	63 898.3	4.6	5.7	6.5	6.4	6.5
6000 Other taxes	78.3	480.8	483.8	479.0	541.0	0.3	0.2	0.1	0.1	0.1
State/Regional										
Total tax revenue	**263.4**	**1 723.2**	**4 781.3**	**8 952.6**	**9 419.1**	**1.2**	**0.9**	**0.9**	**1.0**	**1.0**
1000 Taxes on income, profits and capital gains	0.0	0.0	0.0	0.0	0.0	0.0	0.0	0.0	0.0	0.0
2000 Social security contributions	0.0	0.0	0.0	0.0	0.0	0.0	0.0	0.0	0.0	0.0
3000 Taxes on payroll and workforce	0.0	0.0	0.0	0.0	0.0	0.0	0.0	0.0	0.0	0.0
4000 Taxes on property	0.0	0.0	0.0	0.0	0.0	0.0	0.0	0.0	0.0	0.0
5000 Taxes on goods and services	263.4	1 481.7	3 406.3	6 522.3	6 812.7	1.2	0.8	0.6	0.7	0.7
6000 Other taxes	0.0	241.5	1 375.0	2 430.3	2 606.4	0.0	0.1	0.3	0.3	0.3
Local government										
Total tax revenue	**226.5**	**2 870.1**	**10 891.7**	**21 727.1**	**23 460.7**	**1.0**	**1.5**	**2.0**	**2.4**	**2.4**
1000 Taxes on income, profits and capital gains	0.0	0.0	0.0	0.0	0.0	0.0	0.0	0.0	0.0	0.0
2000 Social security contributions	0.0	0.0	0.0	0.0	0.0	0.0	0.0	0.0	0.0	0.0
3000 Taxes on payroll and workforce	0.0	0.0	0.0	0.0	0.0	0.0	0.0	0.0	0.0	0.0
4000 Taxes on property	56.2	991.1	3 338.9	7 310.2	7 982.0	0.2	0.5	0.6	0.8	0.8
5000 Taxes on goods and services	89.3	1 590.1	5 622.5	10 089.1	10 697.8	0.4	0.8	1.0	1.1	1.1
6000 Other taxes	81.0	288.9	1 930.3	4 327.7	4 780.9	0.4	0.1	0.4	0.5	0.5
Social Security Funds										
Total tax revenue	**203.6**	**4 989.0**	**11 478.1**	**13 351.7**	**18 192.0**	**0.9**	**2.6**	**2.1**	**1.5**	**1.8**
1000 Taxes on income, profits and capital gains	0.0	0.0	0.0	0.0	0.0	0.0	0.0	0.0	0.0	0.0
2000 Social security contributions	203.6	4 989.0	11 478.1	13 351.7	18 192.0	0.9	2.6	2.1	1.5	1.8
3000 Taxes on payroll and workforce	0.0	0.0	0.0	0.0	0.0	0.0	0.0	0.0	0.0	0.0
4000 Taxes on property	0.0	0.0	0.0	0.0	0.0	0.0	0.0	0.0	0.0	0.0
5000 Taxes on goods and services	0.0	0.0	0.0	0.0	0.0	0.0	0.0	0.0	0.0	0.0
6000 Other taxes	0.0	0.0	0.0	0.0	0.0	0.0	0.0	0.0	0.0	0.0

Note: More detailed country data and country notes are available in online chapter 6 "Tax revenues by sub-sectors of general government": https://doi.org/10.1787/0bbc27da-en. Full time series can be accessed at http://oe.cd/full-time-series.

Source: Dirección de Impuestos y Aduanas Nacionales de Colombia, Ministerio de Hacienda y Crédito Público y Banco Central de Colombia. (National Tax and Customs Administration, Ministry of Finance and Public Credit and Central Bank of Colombia).

StatLink https://doi.org/10.1787/888934210445

Table 4.13. Czech Republic, tax revenue and % of GDP by selected tax category

	Billion CZK					% of GDP				
	1990	2000	2010	2017	2018	1990	2000	2010	2017	2018
Total tax revenue	..	**771.6**	**1 286.9**	**1 760.0**	**1 892.4**	..	**32.3**	**32.2**	**34.4**	**35.0**
1000 Taxes on income, profits and capital gains	..	**175.8**	**259.9**	**390.6**	**427.0**	..	**7.4**	**6.5**	**7.6**	**7.9**
1100 Of individuals	..	99.7	131.7	202.2	231.0	..	4.2	3.3	4.0	4.3
1200 Corporate	..	76.2	128.2	188.3	196.0	..	3.2	3.2	3.7	3.6
1300 Unallocable between 1100 and 1200	..	0.0	0.0	0.0	0.0	..	0.0	0.0	0.0	0.0
2000 Social security contributions	..	**341.5**	**576.0**	**757.2**	**829.7**	..	**14.3**	**14.4**	**14.8**	**15.3**
2100 Employees	..	77.3	116.8	155.8	171.8	..	3.2	2.9	3.0	3.2
2200 Employers	..	220.2	363.1	483.4	531.6	..	9.2	9.1	9.5	9.8
2300 Self-employed or non-employed	..	44.1	96.1	117.9	126.2	..	1.8	2.4	2.3	2.3
2400 Unallocable between 2100, 2200 and 2300	..	0.0	0.0	0.0	0.0	..	0.0	0.0	0.0	0.0
3000 Taxes on payroll and workforce	..	**0.0**	**0.0**	**0.0**	**0.0**	..	**0.0**	**0.0**	**0.0**	**0.0**
4000 Taxes on property	..	**10.9**	**16.4**	**23.8**	**24.6**	..	**0.5**	**0.4**	**0.5**	**0.5**
4100 Recurrent taxes on immovable property	..	4.5	8.8	10.8	10.9	..	0.2	0.2	0.2	0.2
4200 Recurrent taxes on net wealth	..	0.0	0.0	0.0	0.0	..	0.0	0.0	0.0	0.0
4300 Estate, inheritance and gift taxes	..	0.6	0.2	0.0	0.0	..	0.0	0.0	0.0	0.0
4400 Taxes on financial and capital transactions	..	5.8	7.4	13.1	13.8	..	0.2	0.2	0.3	0.3
4500 Non-recurrent taxes	..	0.0	0.0	0.0	0.0	..	0.0	0.0	0.0	0.0
4600 Other recurrent taxes on property	..	0.0	0.0	0.0	0.0	..	0.0	0.0	0.0	0.0
5000 Taxes on goods and services	..	**243.0**	**434.4**	**587.5**	**610.8**	..	**10.2**	**10.9**	**11.5**	**11.3**
5100 Taxes on production, sale, transfer, etc	..	226.4	408.6	560.3	582.8	..	9.5	10.2	11.0	10.8
5110 General taxes	..	141.2	263.5	387.5	408.5	..	5.9	6.6	7.6	7.6
5111 Value added taxes	..	141.2	263.5	387.5	408.5	..	5.9	6.6	7.6	7.6
5120 Taxes on specific goods and services	..	85.1	145.2	172.8	174.2	..	3.6	3.6	3.4	3.2
5121 Excises	..	71.4	138.4	164.1	165.4	..	3.0	3.5	3.2	3.1
5200 Taxes on use of goods and perform activities	..	16.6	25.7	27.2	28.1	..	0.7	0.6	0.5	0.5
5300 Unallocable between 5100 and 5200	..	0.0	0.0	0.0	0.0	..	0.0	0.0	0.0	0.0
6000 Other taxes	..	**0.4**	**0.1**	**0.9**	**0.3**	..	**0.0**	**0.0**	**0.0**	**0.0**
Non-wastable tax credits										
Non-wastable tax credits against 1000	..	0.0	25.7	35.7	39.1	..	0.0	0.6	0.7	0.7
Transfer component	..	..	7.8	8.9	8.7	..	..	0.2	0.2	0.2
Tax expenditure component	..	..	17.9	26.8	30.3	..	..	0.4	0.5	0.6
Revenues collected on behalf of the EU										
Revenues collected on behalf of the EU, total	..	..	6.6	8.3	8.3	..	..	0.2	0.2	0.2
Customs duties	..	..	6.6	8.3	8.3	..	..	0.2	0.2	0.2

.. Not available

Note: More detailed country data and country notes are available in online chapter 5 "Detailed country tables": https://doi.org/10.1787/0bbc27da-en. Full time series can be accessed at http://oe.cd/full-time-series.

Source: Ministry of Finance, Economic Department.

StatLink https://doi.org/10.1787/888934210464

Table 4.14. Czech Republic, tax revenue and % of GDP by level of government and main taxes

	Billion CZK					% of GDP				
	1990	2000	2010	2017	2018	1990	2000	2010	2017	2018
Federal or Central government										
Total tax revenue	**..**	**423.4**	**687.3**	**975.8**	**1 035.4**	**..**	**17.7**	**17.2**	**19.1**	**19.1**
1000 Taxes on income, profits and capital gains	..	175.8	259.9	390.6	427.0	..	7.4	6.5	7.6	7.9
2000 Social security contributions	..	0.0	0.0	0.0	0.0	..	0.0	0.0	0.0	0.0
3000 Taxes on payroll and workforce	..	0.0	0.0	0.0	0.0	..	0.0	0.0	0.0	0.0
4000 Taxes on property	..	6.4	7.6	13.1	13.8	..	0.3	0.2	0.3	0.3
5000 Taxes on goods and services	..	241.0	419.6	571.2	594.3	..	10.1	10.5	11.2	11.0
6000 Other taxes	..	0.1	0.1	0.9	0.3	..	0.0	0.0	0.0	0.0
State/Regional										
Total tax revenue	**..**	**..**	**..**	**..**	**..**	**..**	**..**	**..**	**..**	**..**
1000 Taxes on income, profits and capital gains	..	..	..	..	..	..	..	..	..	..
2000 Social security contributions	..	..	..	..	..	..	..	..	..	..
3000 Taxes on payroll and workforce	..	..	..	..	..	..	..	..	..	..
4000 Taxes on property	..	..	..	..	..	..	..	..	..	..
5000 Taxes on goods and services	..	..	..	..	..	..	..	..	..	..
6000 Other taxes	..	..	..	..	..	..	..	..	..	..
Local government										
Total tax revenue	**..**	**6.7**	**17.0**	**18.8**	**19.0**	**..**	**0.3**	**0.4**	**0.4**	**0.4**
1000 Taxes on income, profits and capital gains	..	0.0	0.0	0.0	0.0	..	0.0	0.0	0.0	0.0
2000 Social security contributions	..	0.0	0.0	0.0	0.0	..	0.0	0.0	0.0	0.0
3000 Taxes on payroll and workforce	..	0.0	0.0	0.0	0.0	..	0.0	0.0	0.0	0.0
4000 Taxes on property	..	4.5	8.7	10.8	10.8	..	0.2	0.2	0.2	0.2
5000 Taxes on goods and services	..	2.0	8.2	8.0	8.2	..	0.1	0.2	0.2	0.2
6000 Other taxes	..	0.3	0.0	0.0	0.0	..	0.0	0.0	0.0	0.0
Social Security Funds										
Total tax revenue	**..**	**341.5**	**576.0**	**757.2**	**829.7**	**..**	**14.3**	**14.4**	**14.8**	**15.3**
1000 Taxes on income, profits and capital gains	..	0.0	0.0	0.0	0.0	..	0.0	0.0	0.0	0.0
2000 Social security contributions	..	341.5	576.0	757.2	829.7	..	14.3	14.4	14.8	15.3
3000 Taxes on payroll and workforce	..	0.0	0.0	0.0	0.0	..	0.0	0.0	0.0	0.0
4000 Taxes on property	..	0.0	0.0	0.0	0.0	..	0.0	0.0	0.0	0.0
5000 Taxes on goods and services	..	0.0	0.0	0.0	0.0	..	0.0	0.0	0.0	0.0
6000 Other taxes	..	0.0	0.0	0.0	0.0	..	0.0	0.0	0.0	0.0

.. Not available

Note: More detailed country data and country notes are available in online chapter 6 "Tax revenues by sub-sectors of general government": https://doi.org/10.1787/0bbc27da-en. Full time series can be accessed at http://oe.cd/full-time-series.

Source: Ministry of Finance, Economic Department.

StatLink https://doi.org/10.1787/888934210483

Table 4.15. Denmark, tax revenue and % of GDP by selected tax category

	Billion DKK					% of GDP				
	1990	2000	2010	2017	2018	1990	2000	2010	2017	2018
Total tax revenue	**379.8**	**622.0**	**810.5**	**997.3**	**996.2**	**44.4**	**46.9**	**44.8**	**45.8**	**44.4**
1000 Taxes on income, profits and capital gains	**232.6**	**382.3**	**498.5**	**632.4**	**619.5**	**27.2**	**28.8**	**27.5**	**29.1**	**27.6**
1100 Of individuals	205.6	327.8	421.3	530.1	541.6	24.0	24.7	23.3	24.4	24.1
1200 Corporate	14.5	42.1	40.8	70.5	64.3	1.7	3.2	2.3	3.2	2.9
1300 Unallocable between 1100 and 1200	12.5	12.4	36.3	31.8	13.6	1.5	0.9	2.0	1.5	0.6
2000 Social security contributions	**0.1**	**8.4**	**1.8**	**1.1**	**1.1**	**0.0**	**0.6**	**0.1**	**0.0**	**0.0**
2100 Employees	0.1	8.2	0.9	0.7	0.7	0.0	0.6	0.0	0.0	0.0
2200 Employers	0.0	0.2	0.9	0.3	0.3	0.0	0.0	0.1	0.0	0.0
2300 Self-employed or non-employed	0.0	0.0	0.0	0.0	0.0	0.0	0.0	0.0	0.0	0.0
2400 Unallocable between 2100, 2200 and 2300	0.0	0.0	0.0	0.0	0.0	0.0	0.0	0.0	0.0	0.0
3000 Taxes on payroll and workforce	**2.5**	**2.2**	**4.1**	**5.4**	**6.2**	**0.3**	**0.2**	**0.2**	**0.3**	**0.3**
4000 Taxes on property	**16.2**	**20.7**	**33.5**	**39.1**	**41.1**	**1.9**	**1.6**	**1.8**	**1.8**	**1.8**
4100 Recurrent taxes on immovable property	8.9	13.6	24.2	28.5	29.6	1.0	1.0	1.3	1.3	1.3
4200 Recurrent taxes on net wealth	0.9	0.0	0.0	0.0	0.0	0.1	0.0	0.0	0.0	0.0
4300 Estate, inheritance and gift taxes	2.2	2.8	3.6	4.3	4.7	0.3	0.2	0.2	0.2	0.2
4400 Taxes on financial and capital transactions	4.1	4.2	5.7	6.4	6.7	0.5	0.3	0.3	0.3	0.3
4500 Non-recurrent taxes	0.1	0.1	0.0	0.0	0.0	0.0	0.0	0.0	0.0	0.0
4600 Other recurrent taxes on property	0.0	0.0	0.0	0.0	0.0	0.0	0.0	0.0	0.0	0.0
5000 Taxes on goods and services	**128.5**	**207.9**	**272.4**	**319.0**	**328.1**	**15.0**	**15.7**	**15.0**	**14.7**	**14.6**
5100 Taxes on production, sale, transfer, etc	122.5	197.1	252.8	294.5	302.1	14.3	14.9	14.0	13.5	13.5
5110 General taxes	79.9	121.4	170.6	206.2	214.1	9.3	9.1	9.4	9.5	9.5
5111 Value added taxes	71.5	121.4	170.6	206.2	214.1	8.4	9.1	9.4	9.5	9.5
5120 Taxes on specific goods and services	42.6	75.7	82.3	88.3	88.0	5.0	5.7	4.5	4.1	3.9
5121 Excises	38.0	68.7	73.6	80.5	79.9	4.4	5.2	4.1	3.7	3.6
5200 Taxes on use of goods and perform activities	4.4	7.4	14.6	16.1	17.2	0.5	0.6	0.8	0.7	0.8
5300 Unallocable between 5100 and 5200	1.6	3.4	4.9	8.4	8.8	0.2	0.3	0.3	0.4	0.4
6000 Other taxes	**0.0**	**0.4**	**0.2**	**0.3**	**0.3**	**0.0**	**0.0**	**0.0**	**0.0**	**0.0**
Non-wastable tax credits										
Non-wastable tax credits against 1000	..	..	5.0	4.2	3.7	..	..	0.3	0.2	0.2
Transfer component	..	..	0.2	0.2	0.2	..	..	0.0	0.0	0.0
Tax expenditure component	..	..	4.7	4.0	3.5	..	..	0.3	0.2	0.2
Revenues collected on behalf of the EU										
Revenues collected on behalf of the EU, total	2.7	2.6	3.3	3.2	3.2	0.3	0.2	0.2	0.1	0.1
Customs duties	1.8	2.3	3.2	3.1	3.2	0.2	0.2	0.2	0.1	0.1

.. Not available

Note: More detailed country data and country notes are available in online chapter 5 "Detailed country tables": https://doi.org/10.1787/0bbc27da-en. Full time series can be accessed at http://oe.cd/full-time-series.

The total tax revenue has been reduced by the amount of any capital transfer that represents uncollected taxes. The capital transfer has been allocated between tax headings in proportion to the reported tax revenue. Therefore, the tax revenue amounts are different to those reported in the detailed country data available in online chapter 5 "Detailed country tables".

Source: Danmarks Statistik.

StatLink https://doi.org/10.1787/888934210502

Table 4.16. Denmark, tax revenue and % of GDP by level of government and main taxes

	Billion DKK					% of GDP				
	1990	2000	2010	2017	2018	1990	2000	2010	2017	2018
Federal or Central government										
Total tax revenue	**259.5**	**420.6**	**589.0**	**728.4**	**723.9**	**30.3**	**31.7**	**32.5**	**33.5**	**32.2**
1000 Taxes on income, profits and capital gains	123.7	204.2	305.4	395.5	380.3	14.5	15.4	16.9	18.2	16.9
2000 Social security contributions	0.1	1.4	0.9	0.7	0.8	0.0	0.1	0.1	0.0	0.0
3000 Taxes on payroll and workforce	2.5	2.2	4.1	5.4	6.2	0.3	0.2	0.2	0.3	0.3
4000 Taxes on property	7.5	7.1	9.3	10.7	11.5	0.9	0.5	0.5	0.5	0.5
5000 Taxes on goods and services	125.8	205.3	269.1	315.8	324.9	14.7	15.5	14.9	14.5	14.5
6000 Other taxes	0.0	0.4	0.2	0.3	0.3	0.0	0.0	0.0	0.0	0.0
State/Regional										
Total tax revenue	..	..	..	..	..	..	..	..	..	..
1000 Taxes on income, profits and capital gains	..	..	..	..	..	..	..	..	..	..
2000 Social security contributions	..	..	..	..	..	..	..	..	..	..
3000 Taxes on payroll and workforce	..	..	..	..	..	..	..	..	..	..
4000 Taxes on property	..	..	..	..	..	..	..	..	..	..
5000 Taxes on goods and services	..	..	..	..	..	..	..	..	..	..
6000 Other taxes	..	..	..	..	..	..	..	..	..	..
Local government										
Total tax revenue	**117.6**	**191.7**	**217.3**	**265.4**	**268.8**	**13.8**	**14.4**	**12.0**	**12.2**	**12.0**
1000 Taxes on income, profits and capital gains	108.9	178.1	193.1	236.9	239.2	12.7	13.4	10.7	10.9	10.7
2000 Social security contributions	0.0	0.0	0.0	0.0	0.0	0.0	0.0	0.0	0.0	0.0
3000 Taxes on payroll and workforce	0.0	0.0	0.0	0.0	0.0	0.0	0.0	0.0	0.0	0.0
4000 Taxes on property	8.7	13.6	24.2	28.5	29.6	1.0	1.0	1.3	1.3	1.3
5000 Taxes on goods and services	0.0	0.0	0.0	0.0	0.0	0.0	0.0	0.0	0.0	0.0
6000 Other taxes	0.0	0.0	0.0	0.0	0.0	0.0	0.0	0.0	0.0	0.0
Social Security Funds										
Total tax revenue	**0.0**	**7.1**	**0.9**	**0.3**	**0.3**	**0.0**	**0.5**	**0.1**	**0.0**	**0.0**
1000 Taxes on income, profits and capital gains	0.0	0.0	0.0	0.0	0.0	0.0	0.0	0.0	0.0	0.0
2000 Social security contributions	0.0	7.1	0.9	0.3	0.3	0.0	0.5	0.1	0.0	0.0
3000 Taxes on payroll and workforce	0.0	0.0	0.0	0.0	0.0	0.0	0.0	0.0	0.0	0.0
4000 Taxes on property	0.0	0.0	0.0	0.0	0.0	0.0	0.0	0.0	0.0	0.0
5000 Taxes on goods and services	0.0	0.0	0.0	0.0	0.0	0.0	0.0	0.0	0.0	0.0
6000 Other taxes	0.0	0.0	0.0	0.0	0.0	0.0	0.0	0.0	0.0	0.0

.. Not available

Note: More detailed country data and country notes are available in online chapter 6 "Tax revenues by sub-sectors of general government": https://doi.org/10.1787/0bbc27da-en. Full time series can be accessed at http://oe.cd/full-time-series.

The total tax revenue has been reduced by the amount of any capital transfer that represents uncollected taxes. The capital transfer has been allocated between tax headings in proportion to the reported tax revenue. Therefore, the tax revenue amounts are different to those reported in the detailed country data available in online chapter 6 "Tax revenues by sub-sectors of general government".

Source: Danmarks Statistik.

StatLink https://doi.org/10.1787/888934210521

Table 4.17. Estonia, tax revenue and % of GDP by selected tax category

	Billion EUR					% of GDP				
	1990	2000	2010	2017	2018	1990	2000	2010	2017	2018
Total tax revenue	..	**1.9**	**4.9**	**7.8**	**8.5**	..	**31.0**	**32.9**	**32.5**	**32.9**
1000 Taxes on income, profits and capital gains	..	**0.5**	**1.0**	**1.7**	**1.9**	..	**7.7**	**6.5**	**7.2**	**7.4**
1100 Of individuals	..	0.4	0.8	1.3	1.4	..	6.8	5.2	5.6	5.4
1200 Corporate	..	0.1	0.2	0.4	0.5	..	0.9	1.3	1.5	2.0
1300 Unallocable between 1100 and 1200	..	0.0	0.0	0.0	0.0	..	0.0	0.0	0.0	0.0
2000 Social security contributions	..	**0.7**	**1.9**	**2.7**	**3.0**	..	**10.9**	**12.6**	**11.1**	**11.5**
2100 Employees	..	0.0	0.1	0.1	0.1	..	0.0	0.8	0.5	0.5
2200 Employers	..	0.7	1.7	2.5	2.8	..	10.7	11.7	10.6	10.9
2300 Self-employed or non-employed	..	0.0	0.0	0.0	0.0	..	0.2	0.1	0.1	0.1
2400 Unallocable between 2100, 2200 and 2300	..	0.0	0.0	0.0	0.0	..	0.0	0.0	0.0	0.0
3000 Taxes on payroll and workforce	..	**0.0**	**0.0**	**0.0**	**0.0**	..	**0.0**	**0.0**	**0.0**	**0.0**
4000 Taxes on property	..	**0.0**	**0.1**	**0.1**	**0.1**	..	**0.4**	**0.3**	**0.2**	**0.2**
4100 Recurrent taxes on immovable property	..	0.0	0.1	0.1	0.1	..	0.4	0.3	0.2	0.2
4200 Recurrent taxes on net wealth	..	0.0	0.0	0.0	0.0	..	0.0	0.0	0.0	0.0
4300 Estate, inheritance and gift taxes	..	0.0	0.0	0.0	0.0	..	0.0	0.0	0.0	0.0
4400 Taxes on financial and capital transactions	..	0.0	0.0	0.0	0.0	..	0.0	0.0	0.0	0.0
4500 Non-recurrent taxes	..	0.0	0.0	0.0	0.0	..	0.0	0.0	0.0	0.0
4600 Other recurrent taxes on property	..	0.0	0.0	0.0	0.0	..	0.0	0.0	0.0	0.0
5000 Taxes on goods and services	..	**0.7**	**2.0**	**3.3**	**3.6**	..	**12.1**	**13.4**	**14.0**	**13.8**
5100 Taxes on production, sale, transfer, etc	..	0.7	1.9	3.2	3.4	..	11.7	13.0	13.5	13.3
5110 General taxes	..	0.5	1.3	2.1	2.3	..	8.4	8.5	9.0	9.0
5111 Value added taxes	..	0.5	1.3	2.1	2.3	..	8.4	8.5	9.0	9.0
5120 Taxes on specific goods and services	..	0.2	0.7	1.1	1.1	..	3.3	4.5	4.5	4.3
5121 Excises	..	0.2	0.6	1.0	1.0	..	3.0	4.2	4.1	3.9
5200 Taxes on use of goods and perform activities	..	0.0	0.1	0.1	0.1	..	0.4	0.4	0.5	0.5
5300 Unallocable between 5100 and 5200	..	0.0	0.0	0.0	0.0	..	0.0	0.0	0.0	0.0
6000 Other taxes	..	**0.0**	**0.0**	**0.0**	**0.0**	..	**0.0**	**0.0**	**0.0**	**0.0**
Non-wastable tax credits										
Non-wastable tax credits against 1000	..	..	..	..	..	..	..	..	..	..
Transfer component	..	..	..	..	..	..	..	..	..	..
Tax expenditure component	..	..	..	..	..	..	..	..	..	..
Revenues collected on behalf of the EU										
Revenues collected on behalf of the EU, total	..	..	0.0	0.0	0.0	..	..	0.2	0.2	0.2
Customs duties	..	..	0.0	0.0	0.0	..	..	0.2	0.2	0.2
SRF contributions	..	..	..	0.0	0.0	..	..	..	0.0	0.0

.. Not available

Note: More detailed country data and country notes are available in online chapter 5 "Detailed country tables": https://doi.org/10.1787/0bbc27da-en. Full time series can be accessed at http://oe.cd/full-time-series.

Source: Statistics Estonia.

StatLink https://doi.org/10.1787/888934210540

Table 4.18. Estonia, tax revenue and % of GDP by level of government and main taxes

	Billion EUR					% of GDP				
	1990	2000	2010	2017	2018	1990	2000	2010	2017	2018
Federal or Central government										
Total tax revenue	**..**	**1.6**	**3.9**	**6.4**	**7.0**	**..**	**26.3**	**26.4**	**26.7**	**27.0**
1000 Taxes on income, profits and capital gains	..	0.5	1.0	1.7	1.9	..	7.7	6.5	7.2	7.4
2000 Social security contributions	..	0.4	1.0	1.4	1.6	..	6.6	6.8	5.7	6.1
3000 Taxes on payroll and workforce	..	0.0	0.0	0.0	0.0	..	0.0	0.0	0.0	0.0
4000 Taxes on property	..	0.0	0.0	0.0	0.0	..	0.0	0.0	0.0	0.0
5000 Taxes on goods and services	..	0.7	2.0	3.3	3.5	..	12.0	13.1	13.8	13.5
6000 Other taxes	..	0.0	0.0	0.0	0.0	..	0.0	0.0	0.0	0.0
State/Regional										
Total tax revenue	**..**	**..**	**..**	**..**	**..**	**..**	**..**	**..**	**..**	**..**
1000 Taxes on income, profits and capital gains	..	..	..	..	..	..	..	..	..	..
2000 Social security contributions	..	..	..	..	..	..	..	..	..	..
3000 Taxes on payroll and workforce	..	..	..	..	..	..	..	..	..	..
4000 Taxes on property	..	..	..	..	..	..	..	..	..	..
5000 Taxes on goods and services	..	..	..	..	..	..	..	..	..	..
6000 Other taxes	..	..	..	..	..	..	..	..	..	..
Local government										
Total tax revenue	**..**	**0.0**	**0.1**	**0.1**	**0.1**	**..**	**0.5**	**0.5**	**0.3**	**0.3**
1000 Taxes on income, profits and capital gains	..	0.0	0.0	0.0	0.0	..	0.0	0.0	0.0	0.0
2000 Social security contributions	..	0.0	0.0	0.0	0.0	..	0.0	0.0	0.0	0.0
3000 Taxes on payroll and workforce	..	0.0	0.0	0.0	0.0	..	0.0	0.0	0.0	0.0
4000 Taxes on property	..	0.0	0.1	0.1	0.1	..	0.4	0.3	0.2	0.2
5000 Taxes on goods and services	..	0.0	0.0	0.0	0.0	..	0.1	0.1	0.1	0.0
6000 Other taxes	..	0.0	0.0	0.0	0.0	..	0.0	0.0	0.0	0.0
Social Security Funds										
Total tax revenue	**..**	**0.3**	**0.9**	**1.3**	**1.4**	**..**	**4.3**	**5.9**	**5.4**	**5.4**
1000 Taxes on income, profits and capital gains	..	0.0	0.0	0.0	0.0	..	0.0	0.0	0.0	0.0
2000 Social security contributions	..	0.3	0.9	1.3	1.4	..	4.3	5.9	5.4	5.4
3000 Taxes on payroll and workforce	..	0.0	0.0	0.0	0.0	..	0.0	0.0	0.0	0.0
4000 Taxes on property	..	0.0	0.0	0.0	0.0	..	0.0	0.0	0.0	0.0
5000 Taxes on goods and services	..	0.0	0.0	0.0	0.0	..	0.0	0.0	0.0	0.0
6000 Other taxes	..	0.0	0.0	0.0	0.0	..	0.0	0.0	0.0	0.0

.. Not available

Note: More detailed country data and country notes are available in online chapter 6 "Tax revenues by sub-sectors of general government": https://doi.org/10.1787/0bbc27da-en. Full time series can be accessed at http://oe.cd/full-time-series.

Source: Statistics Estonia.

StatLink https://doi.org/10.1787/888934210559

Table 4.19. Finland, tax revenue and % of GDP by selected tax category

	Billion EUR					% of GDP				
	1990	2000	2010	2017	2018	1990	2000	2010	2017	2018
Total tax revenue	**39.1**	**62.4**	**76.3**	**97.0**	**99.0**	**42.9**	**45.8**	**40.6**	**42.9**	**42.4**
1000 Taxes on income, profits and capital gains	**15.3**	**26.9**	**27.1**	**34.4**	**34.5**	**16.8**	**19.7**	**14.4**	**15.2**	**14.8**
1100 Of individuals	13.6	19.1	22.5	28.3	28.6	14.9	14.0	12.0	12.5	12.2
1200 Corporate	1.8	7.8	4.6	6.1	5.9	1.9	5.7	2.4	2.7	2.5
1300 Unallocable between 1100 and 1200	0.0	0.0	0.0	0.0	0.0	0.0	0.0	0.0	0.0	0.0
2000 Social security contributions	**10.0**	**15.8**	**22.6**	**27.0**	**27.6**	**11.0**	**11.5**	**12.0**	**12.0**	**11.8**
2100 Employees	1.2	2.9	4.7	7.5	8.1	1.3	2.1	2.5	3.3	3.5
2200 Employers	8.1	11.6	16.0	17.6	17.6	8.9	8.5	8.5	7.8	7.5
2300 Self-employed or non-employed	0.7	1.3	1.9	1.9	1.9	0.8	0.9	1.0	0.9	0.8
2400 Unallocable between 2100, 2200 and 2300	0.0	0.0	0.0	0.0	0.0	0.0	0.0	0.0	0.0	0.0
3000 Taxes on payroll and workforce	**0.0**	**0.0**	**0.0**	**0.0**	**0.0**	**0.0**	**0.0**	**0.0**	**0.0**	**0.0**
4000 Taxes on property	**1.0**	**1.5**	**2.1**	**3.5**	**3.3**	**1.1**	**1.1**	**1.1**	**1.5**	**1.4**
4100 Recurrent taxes on immovable property	0.1	0.6	1.2	1.8	1.8	0.1	0.4	0.6	0.8	0.8
4200 Recurrent taxes on net wealth	0.0	0.2	0.0	0.0	0.0	0.0	0.1	0.0	0.0	0.0
4300 Estate, inheritance and gift taxes	0.1	0.4	0.4	0.9	0.7	0.2	0.3	0.2	0.4	0.3
4400 Taxes on financial and capital transactions	0.7	0.4	0.5	0.8	0.8	0.8	0.3	0.3	0.3	0.4
4500 Non-recurrent taxes	0.0	0.0	0.0	0.0	0.0	0.0	0.0	0.0	0.0	0.0
4600 Other recurrent taxes on property	0.0	0.0	0.0	0.0	0.0	0.0	0.0	0.0	0.0	0.0
5000 Taxes on goods and services	**12.7**	**18.2**	**24.4**	**32.1**	**33.5**	**14.0**	**13.4**	**13.0**	**14.2**	**14.3**
5100 Taxes on production, sale, transfer, etc	12.6	17.8	23.6	30.8	32.1	13.8	13.0	12.6	13.6	13.7
5110 General taxes	7.5	10.9	15.5	20.4	21.4	8.3	8.0	8.3	9.0	9.1
5111 Value added taxes	7.5	10.9	15.5	20.4	21.4	8.3	8.0	8.3	9.0	9.1
5120 Taxes on specific goods and services	5.0	6.9	8.1	10.3	10.7	5.5	5.1	4.3	4.6	4.6
5121 Excises	3.8	5.6	6.3	8.0	8.4	4.2	4.1	3.3	3.5	3.6
5200 Taxes on use of goods and perform activities	0.2	0.4	0.8	1.3	1.4	0.2	0.3	0.4	0.6	0.6
5300 Unallocable between 5100 and 5200	0.0	0.0	0.0	0.0	0.0	0.0	0.0	0.0	0.0	0.0
6000 Other taxes	**0.1**	**0.0**	**0.1**	**0.1**	**0.0**	**0.1**	**0.0**	**0.0**	**0.0**	**0.0**
Non-wastable tax credits										
Non-wastable tax credits against 1000	..	..	..	..	..	..	..	..	..	..
Transfer component	..	..	..	..	..	..	..	..	..	..
Tax expenditure component	..	..	..	..	..	..	..	..	..	..
Revenues collected on behalf of the EU										
Revenues collected on behalf of the EU, total	..	0.1	0.2	0.3	0.2	..	0.1	0.1	0.1	0.1
Customs duties	..	0.1	0.2	0.2	0.2	..	0.1	0.1	0.1	0.1
SRF contributions	..	..	..	0.1	0.1	..	..	..	0.1	0.0

.. Not available

Note: More detailed country data and country notes are available in online chapter 5 "Detailed country tables": https://doi.org/10.1787/0bbc27da-en. Full time series can be accessed at http://oe.cd/full-time-series.

Source: Bulletin of Statistics; Central Statistical Office (for Central Government revenues); the Annual report of the National Pension Institute and Official Statistics of Finland Series XXIIA published by the Ministry and Social Affairs (for the Social Security and private pension respectively); supplementary information from unpublished sources.

StatLink https://doi.org/10.1787/888934210578

Table 4.20. Finland, tax revenue and % of GDP by level of government and main taxes

	Billion EUR					% of GDP				
	1990	2000	2010	2017	2018	1990	2000	2010	2017	2018
Federal or Central government										
Total tax revenue	**20.7**	**33.1**	**35.0**	**46.9**	**48.7**	**22.7**	**24.2**	**18.6**	**20.8**	**20.8**
1000 Taxes on income, profits and capital gains	7.0	14.0	9.8	13.4	13.9	7.7	10.3	5.2	5.9	5.9
2000 Social security contributions	0.0	0.0	0.0	0.0	0.0	0.0	0.0	0.0	0.0	0.0
3000 Taxes on payroll and workforce	0.0	0.0	0.0	0.0	0.0	0.0	0.0	0.0	0.0	0.0
4000 Taxes on property	0.9	0.9	0.9	1.7	1.5	1.0	0.7	0.5	0.7	0.7
5000 Taxes on goods and services	12.7	18.1	24.3	31.8	33.2	14.0	13.2	12.9	14.1	14.2
6000 Other taxes	0.1	0.0	0.1	0.1	0.0	0.1	0.0	0.0	0.0	0.0
State/Regional										
Total tax revenue	..	..	..	..	..	..	..	..	..	..
1000 Taxes on income, profits and capital gains	..	..	..	..	..	..	..	..	..	..
2000 Social security contributions	..	..	..	..	..	..	..	..	..	..
3000 Taxes on payroll and workforce	..	..	..	..	..	..	..	..	..	..
4000 Taxes on property	..	..	..	..	..	..	..	..	..	..
5000 Taxes on goods and services	..	..	..	..	..	..	..	..	..	..
6000 Other taxes	..	..	..	..	..	..	..	..	..	..
Local government										
Total tax revenue	**8.4**	**13.5**	**18.5**	**22.8**	**22.5**	**9.2**	**9.9**	**9.8**	**10.1**	**9.6**
1000 Taxes on income, profits and capital gains	8.3	12.9	17.3	21.0	20.7	9.1	9.4	9.2	9.3	8.8
2000 Social security contributions	0.0	0.0	0.0	0.0	0.0	0.0	0.0	0.0	0.0	0.0
3000 Taxes on payroll and workforce	0.0	0.0	0.0	0.0	0.0	0.0	0.0	0.0	0.0	0.0
4000 Taxes on property	0.1	0.6	1.2	1.8	1.8	0.1	0.4	0.6	0.8	0.8
5000 Taxes on goods and services	0.0	0.0	0.0	0.0	0.0	0.0	0.0	0.0	0.0	0.0
6000 Other taxes	0.0	0.0	0.0	0.0	0.0	0.0	0.0	0.0	0.0	0.0
Social Security Funds										
Total tax revenue	**10.0**	**15.8**	**22.6**	**27.0**	**27.6**	**11.0**	**11.5**	**12.0**	**12.0**	**11.8**
1000 Taxes on income, profits and capital gains	0.0	0.0	0.0	0.0	0.0	0.0	0.0	0.0	0.0	0.0
2000 Social security contributions	10.0	15.8	22.6	27.0	27.6	11.0	11.5	12.0	12.0	11.8
3000 Taxes on payroll and workforce	0.0	0.0	0.0	0.0	0.0	0.0	0.0	0.0	0.0	0.0
4000 Taxes on property	0.0	0.0	0.0	0.0	0.0	0.0	0.0	0.0	0.0	0.0
5000 Taxes on goods and services	0.0	0.0	0.0	0.0	0.0	0.0	0.0	0.0	0.0	0.0
6000 Other taxes	0.0	0.0	0.0	0.0	0.0	0.0	0.0	0.0	0.0	0.0

.. Not available

Note: More detailed country data and country notes are available in online chapter 6 "Tax revenues by sub-sectors of general government": https://doi.org/10.1787/0bbc27da-en. Full time series can be accessed at http://oe.cd/full-time-series.

Source: Bulletin of Statistics; Central Statistical Office (for Central Government revenues); the Annual report of the National Pension Institute and Official Statistics of Finland Series XXIIA published by the Ministry and Social Affairs (for the Social Security and private pension respectively); supplementary information from unpublished sources.

StatLink https://doi.org/10.1787/888934210597

Table 4.21. France, tax revenue and % of GDP by selected tax category

	Billion EUR					% of GDP				
	1990	2000	2010	2017	2018	1990	2000	2010	2017	2018
Total tax revenue	**433.8**	**642.2**	**840.9**	**1 058.3**	**1 084.2**	**41.2**	**43.4**	**42.1**	**46.1**	**45.9**
1000 Taxes on income, profits and capital gains	**69.6**	**159.5**	**189.7**	**249.8**	**272.3**	**6.6**	**10.8**	**9.5**	**10.9**	**11.5**
1100 Of individuals	46.3	115.2	143.1	196.5	222.8	4.4	7.8	7.2	8.6	9.4
1200 Corporate	23.1	44.3	46.6	53.4	49.6	2.2	3.0	2.3	2.3	2.1
1300 Unallocable between 1100 and 1200	0.3	0.0	0.0	0.0	0.0	0.0	0.0	0.0	0.0	0.0
2000 Social security contributions	**191.1**	**230.2**	**321.3**	**384.4**	**378.5**	**18.1**	**15.6**	**16.1**	**16.7**	**16.0**
2100 Employees	57.3	57.3	77.7	100.1	88.5	5.4	3.9	3.9	4.4	3.8
2200 Employers	118.1	158.3	218.0	256.7	263.5	11.2	10.7	10.9	11.2	11.2
2300 Self-employed or non-employed	15.7	14.6	25.7	27.6	26.4	1.5	1.0	1.3	1.2	1.1
2400 Unallocable between 2100, 2200 and 2300	0.0	0.0	0.0	0.0	0.0	0.0	0.0	0.0	0.0	0.0
3000 Taxes on payroll and workforce	**8.3**	**14.9**	**26.8**	**35.6**	**35.7**	**0.8**	**1.0**	**1.3**	**1.5**	**1.5**
4000 Taxes on property	**27.4**	**46.1**	**73.0**	**100.8**	**97.4**	**2.6**	**3.1**	**3.7**	**4.4**	**4.1**
4100 Recurrent taxes on immovable property	14.8	29.4	50.0	64.1	62.8	1.4	2.0	2.5	2.8	2.7
4200 Recurrent taxes on net wealth	2.6	2.4	4.4	5.0	1.8	0.2	0.2	0.2	0.2	0.1
4300 Estate, inheritance and gift taxes	4.1	6.9	7.7	14.2	14.3	0.4	0.5	0.4	0.6	0.6
4400 Taxes on financial and capital transactions	5.9	7.4	10.8	17.4	18.5	0.6	0.5	0.5	0.8	0.8
4500 Non-recurrent taxes	0.0	0.0	0.0	0.0	0.0	0.0	0.0	0.0	0.0	0.0
4600 Other recurrent taxes on property	0.0	0.0	0.0	0.0	0.0	0.0	0.0	0.0	0.0	0.0
5000 Taxes on goods and services	**123.2**	**167.4**	**220.9**	**276.3**	**288.3**	**11.7**	**11.3**	**11.1**	**12.0**	**12.2**
5100 Taxes on production, sale, transfer, etc	119.2	162.8	214.6	268.8	280.1	11.3	11.0	10.8	11.7	11.9
5110 General taxes	81.3	109.8	150.6	178.7	185.3	7.7	7.4	7.5	7.8	7.9
5111 Value added taxes	80.0	107.1	135.2	161.6	167.4	7.6	7.2	6.8	7.0	7.1
5120 Taxes on specific goods and services	37.9	53.0	64.0	90.2	94.7	3.6	3.6	3.2	3.9	4.0
5121 Excises	26.8	39.7	45.6	61.5	64.6	2.5	2.7	2.3	2.7	2.7
5200 Taxes on use of goods and perform activities	4.0	4.6	6.3	7.5	8.2	0.4	0.3	0.3	0.3	0.3
5300 Unallocable between 5100 and 5200	0.0	0.0	0.0	0.0	0.0	0.0	0.0	0.0	0.0	0.0
6000 Other taxes	**14.1**	**24.1**	**9.2**	**11.3**	**12.1**	**1.3**	**1.6**	**0.5**	**0.5**	**0.5**
Non-wastable tax credits										
Non-wastable tax credits against 1000	..	0.5	17.4	29.0	35.8	..	0.0	0.9	1.3	1.5
Transfer component	..	..	7.9	14.6	19.7	..	..	0.4	0.6	0.8
Tax expenditure component	..	..	9.5	14.4	16.1	..	..	0.5	0.6	0.7
Revenues collected on behalf of the EU										
Revenues collected on behalf of the EU, total	2.6	1.9	2.0	4.0	4.6	0.2	0.1	0.1	0.2	0.2
Customs duties	..	1.5	1.8	1.9	2.1	..	0.1	0.1	0.1	0.1
SRF contributions	..	..	..	1.9	2.3	..	..	..	0.1	0.1

.. Not available

Note: More detailed country data and country notes are available in online chapter 5 "Detailed country tables": https://doi.org/10.1787/0bbc27da-en. Full time series can be accessed at http://oe.cd/full-time-series.

The total tax revenue has been reduced by the amount of any capital transfer that represents uncollected taxes. The capital transfer has been allocated between tax headings in proportion to the reported tax revenue. Therefore, the tax revenue amounts are different to those reported in the detailed country data available in online chapter 5 "Detailed country tables".

Source: General Account of the Administration of finances for the figures of fiscal receipts. OSCE for the figures of Social Security from 1965 to 1969, and ESA for the following years.

StatLink https://doi.org/10.1787/888934210616

Table 4.22. France, tax revenue and % of GDP by level of government and main taxes

	Billion EUR					% of GDP				
	1990	2000	2010	2017	2018	1990	2000	2010	2017	2018
Federal or Central government										
Total tax revenue	**200.1**	**270.3**	**299.6**	**361.5**	**364.0**	**19.0**	**18.3**	**15.0**	**15.7**	**15.4**
1000 Taxes on income, profits and capital gains	69.6	94.4	97.0	132.4	130.6	6.6	6.4	4.9	5.8	5.5
2000 Social security contributions	3.2	5.4	7.6	8.3	8.2	0.3	0.4	0.4	0.4	0.3
3000 Taxes on payroll and workforce	6.2	10.6	4.2	3.7	3.8	0.6	0.7	0.2	0.2	0.2
4000 Taxes on property	8.6	13.4	15.9	25.4	22.7	0.8	0.9	0.8	1.1	1.0
5000 Taxes on goods and services	112.1	143.4	167.5	190.6	197.2	10.6	9.7	8.4	8.3	8.4
6000 Other taxes	0.4	3.1	7.4	1.1	1.6	0.0	0.2	0.4	0.0	0.1
State/Regional										
Total tax revenue	..	..	..	..	..	..	..	..	..	..
1000 Taxes on income, profits and capital gains	..	..	..	..	..	..	..	..	..	..
2000 Social security contributions	..	..	..	..	..	..	..	..	..	..
3000 Taxes on payroll and workforce	..	..	..	..	..	..	..	..	..	..
4000 Taxes on property	..	..	..	..	..	..	..	..	..	..
5000 Taxes on goods and services	..	..	..	..	..	..	..	..	..	..
6000 Other taxes	..	..	..	..	..	..	..	..	..	..
Local government										
Total tax revenue	**40.2**	**64.7**	**89.3**	**141.6**	**146.8**	**3.8**	**4.4**	**4.5**	**6.2**	**6.2**
1000 Taxes on income, profits and capital gains	0.0	0.0	0.1	0.0	0.0	0.0	0.0	0.0	0.0	0.0
2000 Social security contributions	0.0	0.0	0.0	0.0	0.0	0.0	0.0	0.0	0.0	0.0
3000 Taxes on payroll and workforce	1.7	3.9	7.5	10.3	10.6	0.2	0.3	0.4	0.4	0.5
4000 Taxes on property	18.8	32.7	57.1	75.4	74.7	1.8	2.2	2.9	3.3	3.2
5000 Taxes on goods and services	6.0	7.3	23.0	46.0	51.3	0.6	0.5	1.2	2.0	2.2
6000 Other taxes	13.7	20.9	1.6	9.9	10.1	1.3	1.4	0.1	0.4	0.4
Social Security Funds										
Total tax revenue	**190.9**	**305.3**	**450.1**	**551.2**	**568.7**	**18.1**	**20.6**	**22.6**	**24.0**	**24.1**
1000 Taxes on income, profits and capital gains	0.0	65.0	92.7	117.4	141.7	0.0	4.4	4.6	5.1	6.0
2000 Social security contributions	187.9	224.8	313.7	376.2	370.2	17.8	15.2	15.7	16.4	15.7
3000 Taxes on payroll and workforce	0.4	0.4	15.1	21.6	21.2	0.0	0.0	0.8	0.9	0.9
4000 Taxes on property	0.0	0.0	0.0	0.0	0.0	0.0	0.0	0.0	0.0	0.0
5000 Taxes on goods and services	2.5	14.9	28.4	35.7	35.2	0.2	1.0	1.4	1.6	1.5
6000 Other taxes	0.0	0.1	0.2	0.4	0.4	0.0	0.0	0.0	0.0	0.0

.. Not available

Note: More detailed country data and country notes are available in online chapter 6 "Tax revenues by sub-sectors of general government": https://doi.org/10.1787/0bbc27da-en. Full time series can be accessed at http://oe.cd/full-time-series.

The total tax revenue has been reduced by the amount of any capital transfer that represents uncollected taxes. The capital transfer has been allocated between tax headings in proportion to the reported tax revenue. Therefore, the tax revenue amounts are different to those reported in the detailed country data available in online chapter 6 "Tax revenues by sub-sectors of general government".

Source: General Account of the Administration of finances for the figures of fiscal receipts. OSCE for the figures of Social Security from 1965 to 1969, and ESA for the following years.

StatLink https://doi.org/10.1787/888934210635

Table 4.23. Germany, tax revenue and % of GDP by selected tax category

	Billion EUR					% of GDP				
	1990	2000	2010	2017	2018	1990	2000	2010	2017	2018
Total tax revenue	**454.8**	**767.0**	**911.2**	**1 232.0**	**1 293.7**	**34.8**	**36.4**	**35.5**	**37.8**	**38.5**
1000 Taxes on income, profits and capital gains	**147.3**	**231.2**	**257.8**	**400.7**	**423.8**	**11.3**	**11.0**	**10.1**	**12.3**	**12.6**
1100 Of individuals	125.3	194.2	219.4	334.7	351.9	9.6	9.2	8.6	10.3	10.5
1200 Corporate	22.0	37.1	38.4	66.0	71.9	1.7	1.8	1.5	2.0	2.1
1300 Unallocable between 1100 and 1200	0.0	0.0	0.0	0.0	0.0	0.0	0.0	0.0	0.0	0.0
2000 Social security contributions	**170.4**	**299.4**	**354.3**	**467.2**	**487.8**	**13.0**	**14.2**	**13.8**	**14.3**	**14.5**
2100 Employees	73.6	131.6	152.8	206.8	216.7	5.6	6.2	6.0	6.3	6.5
2200 Employers	86.7	147.4	165.5	214.1	223.8	6.6	7.0	6.5	6.6	6.7
2300 Self-employed or non-employed	10.2	20.4	36.0	46.2	47.3	0.8	1.0	1.4	1.4	1.4
2400 Unallocable between 2100, 2200 and 2300	0.0	0.0	0.0	0.0	0.0	0.0	0.0	0.0	0.0	0.0
3000 Taxes on payroll and workforce	**0.0**	**0.0**	**0.0**	**0.0**	**0.0**	**0.0**	**0.0**	**0.0**	**0.0**	**0.0**
4000 Taxes on property	**15.3**	**17.5**	**21.0**	**33.6**	**35.5**	**1.2**	**0.8**	**0.8**	**1.0**	**1.1**
4100 Recurrent taxes on immovable property	4.5	8.8	11.3	14.0	14.2	0.3	0.4	0.4	0.4	0.4
4200 Recurrent taxes on net wealth	6.2	0.4	0.0	0.4	0.4	0.5	0.0	0.0	0.0	0.0
4300 Estate, inheritance and gift taxes	1.5	3.0	4.4	6.1	6.8	0.1	0.1	0.2	0.2	0.2
4400 Taxes on financial and capital transactions	3.1	5.2	5.3	13.1	14.1	0.2	0.2	0.2	0.4	0.4
4500 Non-recurrent taxes	0.0	0.0	0.0	0.0	0.0	0.0	0.0	0.0	0.0	0.0
4600 Other recurrent taxes on property	0.0	0.0	0.0	0.0	0.0	0.0	0.0	0.0	0.0	0.0
5000 Taxes on goods and services	**121.6**	**218.7**	**277.9**	**330.3**	**346.3**	**9.3**	**10.4**	**10.8**	**10.1**	**10.3**
5100 Taxes on production, sale, transfer, etc	117.2	211.4	261.2	318.4	327.4	9.0	10.0	10.2	9.8	9.8
5110 General taxes	75.5	140.9	180.5	226.9	235.4	5.8	6.7	7.0	7.0	7.0
5111 Value added taxes	75.5	140.9	180.5	226.9	235.4	5.8	6.7	7.0	7.0	7.0
5120 Taxes on specific goods and services	41.7	70.6	80.3	91.2	91.7	3.2	3.3	3.1	2.8	2.7
5121 Excises	31.2	57.2	63.4	66.5	66.1	2.4	2.7	2.5	2.0	2.0
5200 Taxes on use of goods and perform activities	4.4	7.2	16.8	11.9	18.9	0.3	0.3	0.7	0.4	0.6
5300 Unallocable between 5100 and 5200	0.0	0.0	0.0	0.0	0.0	0.0	0.0	0.0	0.0	0.0
6000 Other taxes	**0.2**	**0.2**	**0.1**	**0.3**	**0.3**	**0.0**	**0.0**	**0.0**	**0.0**	**0.0**
Non-wastable tax credits										
Non-wastable tax credits against 1000	..	39.3	46.3	43.5	43.9	..	1.9	1.8	1.3	1.3
Transfer component	..	..	17.7	15.3	14.7	..	..	0.7	0.5	0.4
Tax expenditure component	..	..	28.6	28.2	29.2	..	..	1.1	0.9	0.9
Revenues collected on behalf of the EU										
Revenues collected on behalf of the EU, total	4.1	3.7	4.3	6.8	7.0	0.3	0.2	0.2	0.2	0.2
Customs duties	3.7	3.4	4.2	5.0	5.0	0.3	0.2	0.2	0.2	0.2
SRF contributions	..	..	..	1.7	2.0	..	..	..	0.1	0.1

.. Not available

Note: More detailed country data and country notes are available in online chapter 5 "Detailed country tables": https://doi.org/10.1787/0bbc27da-en. Full time series can be accessed at http://oe.cd/full-time-series.

Source: Finanzbericht, Bonn; Tax Statistics. Unpublished estimates by the Ministry of Finance.

StatLink https://doi.org/10.1787/888934210654

Table 4.24. Germany, tax revenue and % of GDP by level of government and main taxes

	Billion EUR					% of GDP				
	1990	2000	2010	2017	2018	1990	2000	2010	2017	2018
Federal or Central government										
Total tax revenue	**143.9**	**234.8**	**283.2**	**363.6**	**382.1**	**11.0**	**11.1**	**11.0**	**11.2**	**11.4**
1000 Taxes on income, profits and capital gains	58.2	97.9	104.5	164.1	173.8	4.5	4.6	4.1	5.0	5.2
2000 Social security contributions	0.0	0.0	0.0	0.0	0.0	0.0	0.0	0.0	0.0	0.0
3000 Taxes on payroll and workforce	0.0	0.0	0.0	0.0	0.0	0.0	0.0	0.0	0.0	0.0
4000 Taxes on property	1.2	0.0	0.0	0.4	0.4	0.1	0.0	0.0	0.0	0.0
5000 Taxes on goods and services	84.6	136.9	178.6	199.1	207.9	6.5	6.5	7.0	6.1	6.2
6000 Other taxes	0.0	0.0	0.0	0.0	0.0	0.0	0.0	0.0	0.0	0.0
State/Regional										
Total tax revenue	**97.8**	**172.1**	**198.1**	**289.0**	**305.5**	**7.5**	**8.2**	**7.7**	**8.9**	**9.1**
1000 Taxes on income, profits and capital gains	58.2	88.9	97.6	152.9	162.1	4.5	4.2	3.8	4.7	4.8
2000 Social security contributions	0.0	0.0	0.0	0.0	0.0	0.0	0.0	0.0	0.0	0.0
3000 Taxes on payroll and workforce	0.0	0.0	0.0	0.0	0.0	0.0	0.0	0.0	0.0	0.0
4000 Taxes on property	7.0	8.5	9.7	19.3	20.9	0.5	0.4	0.4	0.6	0.6
5000 Taxes on goods and services	32.6	74.6	90.8	116.8	122.5	2.5	3.5	3.5	3.6	3.6
6000 Other taxes	0.0	0.0	0.0	0.0	0.0	0.0	0.0	0.0	0.0	0.0
Local government										
Total tax revenue	**38.4**	**57.0**	**71.4**	**105.4**	**111.3**	**2.9**	**2.7**	**2.8**	**3.2**	**3.3**
1000 Taxes on income, profits and capital gains	30.9	44.4	55.7	83.7	87.9	2.4	2.1	2.2	2.6	2.6
2000 Social security contributions	0.0	0.0	0.0	0.0	0.0	0.0	0.0	0.0	0.0	0.0
3000 Taxes on payroll and workforce	0.0	0.0	0.0	0.0	0.0	0.0	0.0	0.0	0.0	0.0
4000 Taxes on property	7.2	9.0	11.3	14.0	14.2	0.5	0.4	0.4	0.4	0.4
5000 Taxes on goods and services	0.3	3.4	4.3	7.5	9.0	0.0	0.2	0.2	0.2	0.3
6000 Other taxes	0.2	0.1	0.1	0.3	0.3	0.0	0.0	0.0	0.0	0.0
Social Security Funds										
Total tax revenue	**170.4**	**299.4**	**354.3**	**467.2**	**487.8**	**13.0**	**14.2**	**13.8**	**14.3**	**14.5**
1000 Taxes on income, profits and capital gains	0.0	0.0	0.0	0.0	0.0	0.0	0.0	0.0	0.0	0.0
2000 Social security contributions	170.4	299.4	354.3	467.2	487.8	13.0	14.2	13.8	14.3	14.5
3000 Taxes on payroll and workforce	0.0	0.0	0.0	0.0	0.0	0.0	0.0	0.0	0.0	0.0
4000 Taxes on property	0.0	0.0	0.0	0.0	0.0	0.0	0.0	0.0	0.0	0.0
5000 Taxes on goods and services	0.0	0.0	0.0	0.0	0.0	0.0	0.0	0.0	0.0	0.0
6000 Other taxes	0.0	0.0	0.0	0.0	0.0	0.0	0.0	0.0	0.0	0.0

Note: More detailed country data and country notes are available in online chapter 6 "Tax revenues by sub-sectors of general government": https://doi.org/10.1787/0bbc27da-en. Full time series can be accessed at http://oe.cd/full-time-series.

Source: Finanzbericht, Bonn; Tax Statistics. Unpublished estimates by the Ministry of Finance.

StatLink https://doi.org/10.1787/888934210673

Table 4.25. Greece, tax revenue and % of GDP by selected tax category

	Billion EUR					% of GDP				
	1990	2000	2010	2017	2018	1990	2000	2010	2017	2018
Total tax revenue	**11.5**	**47.2**	**72.4**	**69.6**	**71.9**	**25.2**	**33.4**	**32.0**	**38.6**	**38.9**
1000 Taxes on income, profits and capital gains	**2.3**	**12.7**	**16.0**	**15.6**	**16.5**	**5.0**	**9.0**	**7.1**	**8.7**	**8.9**
1100 Of individuals	1.6	6.1	9.0	11.2	11.6	3.6	4.3	4.0	6.2	6.3
1200 Corporate	0.6	5.6	5.7	3.5	4.0	1.4	4.0	2.5	1.9	2.2
1300 Unallocable between 1100 and 1200	0.0	0.9	1.2	0.9	0.9	0.1	0.6	0.5	0.5	0.5
2000 Social security contributions	**3.5**	**14.3**	**24.7**	**20.7**	**21.5**	**7.6**	**10.1**	**10.9**	**11.5**	**11.6**
2100 Employees	1.7	7.6	13.3	12.2	11.9	3.8	5.4	5.9	6.8	6.4
2200 Employers	1.7	6.7	11.5	8.5	9.6	3.8	4.7	5.1	4.7	5.2
2300 Self-employed or non-employed	0.0	0.0	0.0	0.0	0.0	0.0	0.0	0.0	0.0	0.0
2400 Unallocable between 2100, 2200 and 2300	0.0	0.0	0.0	0.0	0.0	0.0	0.0	0.0	0.0	0.0
3000 Taxes on payroll and workforce	**0.1**	**0.0**	**0.0**	**0.0**	**0.0**	**0.2**	**0.0**	**0.0**	**0.0**	**0.0**
4000 Taxes on property	**0.5**	**3.6**	**3.7**	**5.6**	**5.6**	**1.2**	**2.6**	**1.7**	**3.1**	**3.0**
4100 Recurrent taxes on immovable property	0.0	0.4	0.6	3.7	3.6	0.0	0.3	0.2	2.0	1.9
4200 Recurrent taxes on net wealth	0.0	0.7	1.3	1.2	1.2	0.0	0.5	0.6	0.6	0.6
4300 Estate, inheritance and gift taxes	0.1	0.4	0.2	0.2	0.1	0.3	0.3	0.1	0.1	0.1
4400 Taxes on financial and capital transactions	0.4	2.0	1.1	0.6	0.6	0.8	1.4	0.5	0.3	0.3
4500 Non-recurrent taxes	0.0	0.0	0.0	0.0	0.0	0.0	0.0	0.0	0.0	0.0
4600 Other recurrent taxes on property	0.0	0.1	0.6	0.0	0.0	0.0	0.1	0.3	0.0	0.0
5000 Taxes on goods and services	**5.1**	**16.6**	**28.0**	**27.7**	**28.4**	**11.2**	**11.8**	**12.4**	**15.4**	**15.4**
5100 Taxes on production, sale, transfer, etc	4.9	14.8	25.5	23.5	24.7	10.7	10.5	11.3	13.0	13.4
5110 General taxes	3.0	9.2	16.5	14.7	15.4	6.7	6.5	7.3	8.2	8.3
5111 Value added taxes	2.8	8.9	16.0	14.6	15.3	6.2	6.3	7.1	8.1	8.3
5120 Taxes on specific goods and services	1.8	5.5	8.9	8.6	9.1	3.9	3.9	3.9	4.8	5.0
5121 Excises	1.4	4.1	7.6	6.9	7.1	3.0	2.9	3.3	3.8	3.9
5200 Taxes on use of goods and perform activities	0.2	1.3	1.7	3.4	3.1	0.5	0.9	0.7	1.9	1.7
5300 Unallocable between 5100 and 5200	0.0	0.5	0.8	0.8	0.6	0.0	0.4	0.3	0.4	0.3
6000 Other taxes	**0.0**	**0.0**	**0.0**	**0.0**	**0.0**	**0.0**	**0.0**	**0.0**	**0.0**	**0.0**
Non-wastable tax credits										
Non-wastable tax credits against 1000	..	..	..	..	..	..	..	..	..	..
Transfer component	..	..	..	..	..	..	..	..	..	..
Tax expenditure component	..	..	..	..	..	..	..	..	..	..
Revenues collected on behalf of the EU										
Revenues collected on behalf of the EU, total	0.1	0.2	0.3	0.4	0.3	0.2	0.2	0.1	0.2	0.2
Customs duties	0.1	0.2	0.3	0.3	0.2	0.2	0.1	0.1	0.1	0.1
SRF contributions	..	..	..	0.1	0.1	..	..	..	0.0	0.1

.. Not available

Note: More detailed country data and country notes are available in online chapter 5 "Detailed country tables": https://doi.org/10.1787/0bbc27da-en. Full time series can be accessed at http://oe.cd/full-time-series.

Source: Ministry of Finance, General accounting Office, 20th Directorate of Budget except the heading 2000 provided by the National Statistics Bureau.

StatLink https://doi.org/10.1787/888934210692

Table 4.26. Greece, tax revenue and % of GDP by level of government and main taxes

	Billion EUR					% of GDP				
	1990	2000	2010	2017	2018	1990	2000	2010	2017	2018
Federal or Central government										
Total tax revenue	**7.8**	**31.9**	**46.5**	**46.8**	**48.3**	**17.1**	**22.6**	**20.6**	**26.0**	**26.2**
1000 Taxes on income, profits and capital gains	2.3	12.7	15.9	15.6	16.5	5.0	9.0	7.0	8.7	8.9
2000 Social security contributions	0.0	0.7	1.3	0.1	0.1	0.1	0.5	0.6	0.0	0.0
3000 Taxes on payroll and workforce	0.0	0.0	0.0	0.0	0.0	0.0	0.0	0.0	0.0	0.0
4000 Taxes on property	0.5	2.6	2.1	4.0	4.0	1.2	1.8	0.9	2.2	2.1
5000 Taxes on goods and services	4.9	16.0	27.1	27.1	27.8	10.9	11.3	12.0	15.1	15.1
6000 Other taxes	0.0	0.0	0.0	0.0	0.0	0.0	0.0	0.0	0.0	0.0
State/Regional										
Total tax revenue	..	..	..	..	..	..	..	..	..	..
1000 Taxes on income, profits and capital gains	..	..	..	..	..	..	..	..	..	..
2000 Social security contributions	..	..	..	..	..	..	..	..	..	..
3000 Taxes on payroll and workforce	..	..	..	..	..	..	..	..	..	..
4000 Taxes on property	..	..	..	..	..	..	..	..	..	..
5000 Taxes on goods and services	..	..	..	..	..	..	..	..	..	..
6000 Other taxes	..	..	..	..	..	..	..	..	..	..
Local government										
Total tax revenue	**0.1**	**1.0**	**1.7**	**1.7**	**1.7**	**0.3**	**0.7**	**0.8**	**0.9**	**0.9**
1000 Taxes on income, profits and capital gains	0.0	0.0	0.0	0.0	0.0	0.0	0.0	0.0	0.0	0.0
2000 Social security contributions	0.0	0.0	0.0	0.0	0.0	0.0	0.0	0.0	0.0	0.0
3000 Taxes on payroll and workforce	0.1	0.0	0.0	0.0	0.0	0.2	0.0	0.0	0.0	0.0
4000 Taxes on property	0.0	0.8	1.5	1.6	1.6	0.0	0.6	0.7	0.9	0.9
5000 Taxes on goods and services	0.1	0.2	0.2	0.1	0.1	0.1	0.1	0.1	0.1	0.1
6000 Other taxes	0.0	0.0	0.0	0.0	0.0	0.0	0.0	0.0	0.0	0.0
Social Security Funds										
Total tax revenue	**3.4**	**14.1**	**24.0**	**20.8**	**21.5**	**7.5**	**10.0**	**10.6**	**11.5**	**11.7**
1000 Taxes on income, profits and capital gains	0.0	0.0	0.0	0.0	0.0	0.0	0.0	0.0	0.0	0.0
2000 Social security contributions	3.4	13.6	23.4	20.7	21.4	7.5	9.6	10.4	11.5	11.6
3000 Taxes on payroll and workforce	0.0	0.0	0.0	0.0	0.0	0.0	0.0	0.0	0.0	0.0
4000 Taxes on property	0.0	0.2	0.1	0.0	0.0	0.0	0.1	0.1	0.0	0.0
5000 Taxes on goods and services	0.0	0.3	0.4	0.1	0.1	0.0	0.2	0.2	0.1	0.1
6000 Other taxes	0.0	0.0	0.0	0.0	0.0	0.0	0.0	0.0	0.0	0.0

.. Not available

Note: More detailed country data and country notes are available in online chapter 6 "Tax revenues by sub-sectors of general government": https://doi.org/10.1787/0bbc27da-en. Full time series can be accessed at http://oe.cd/full-time-series.

Source: Ministry of Finance, General accounting Office, 20th Directorate of Budget except the heading 2000 provided by the National Statistics Bureau.

StatLink https://doi.org/10.1787/888934210711

Table 4.27. Hungary, tax revenue and % of GDP by selected tax category

	Billion HUF					% of GDP				
	1990	2000	2010	2017	2018	1990	2000	2010	2017	2018
Total tax revenue	..	**5 140.9**	**10 142.3**	**14 867.3**	**15 976.9**	..	**38.6**	**37.2**	**38.3**	**37.5**
1000 Taxes on income, profits and capital gains	..	**1 247.4**	**2 093.8**	**2 862.6**	**2 912.2**	..	**9.4**	**7.7**	**7.4**	**6.8**
1100 Of individuals	..	954.7	1 764.1	2 088.8	2 340.3	..	7.2	6.5	5.4	5.5
1200 Corporate	..	292.7	329.7	773.8	571.9	..	2.2	1.2	2.0	1.3
1300 Unallocable between 1100 and 1200	..	0.0	0.0	0.0	0.0	..	0.0	0.0	0.0	0.0
2000 Social security contributions	..	**1 506.8**	**3 179.5**	**4 822.2**	**5 049.6**	..	**11.3**	**11.7**	**12.4**	**11.8**
2100 Employees	..	275.3	1 112.6	2 343.5	2 432.7	..	2.1	4.1	6.0	5.7
2200 Employers	..	1 213.2	2 043.8	2 452.5	2 590.1	..	9.1	7.5	6.3	6.1
2300 Self-employed or non-employed	..	0.9	0.0	0.0	0.0	..	0.0	0.0	0.0	0.0
2400 Unallocable between 2100, 2200 and 2300	..	17.4	23.2	26.1	26.8	..	0.1	0.1	0.1	0.1
3000 Taxes on payroll and workforce	..	**183.4**	**113.7**	**340.2**	**410.2**	..	**1.4**	**0.4**	**0.9**	**1.0**
4000 Taxes on property	..	**89.0**	**312.1**	**408.9**	**417.8**	..	**0.7**	**1.1**	**1.1**	**1.0**
4100 Recurrent taxes on immovable property	..	30.8	92.5	218.1	219.1	..	0.2	0.3	0.6	0.5
4200 Recurrent taxes on net wealth	..	0.0	135.7	51.6	42.6	..	0.0	0.5	0.1	0.1
4300 Estate, inheritance and gift taxes	..	5.5	6.3	9.4	8.5	..	0.0	0.0	0.0	0.0
4400 Taxes on financial and capital transactions	..	52.8	77.6	129.8	147.6	..	0.4	0.3	0.3	0.3
4500 Non-recurrent taxes	..	0.0	0.0	0.0	0.0	..	0.0	0.0	0.0	0.0
4600 Other recurrent taxes on property	..	0.0	0.0	0.0	0.0	..	0.0	0.0	0.0	0.0
5000 Taxes on goods and services	..	**2 081.4**	**4 383.9**	**6 385.9**	**7 148.8**	..	**15.6**	**16.1**	**16.4**	**16.8**
5100 Taxes on production, sale, transfer, etc	..	2 052.7	4 272.3	6 236.6	6 987.0	..	15.4	15.7	16.1	16.4
5110 General taxes	..	1 340.6	3 010.8	4 461.7	5 042.4	..	10.1	11.0	11.5	11.8
5111 Value added taxes	..	1 153.7	2 325.6	3 626.6	4 129.5	..	8.7	8.5	9.3	9.7
5120 Taxes on specific goods and services	..	712.1	1 261.5	1 774.9	1 944.6	..	5.3	4.6	4.6	4.6
5121 Excises	..	533.5	929.9	1 157.6	1 270.1	..	4.0	3.4	3.0	3.0
5200 Taxes on use of goods and perform activities	..	28.7	111.6	149.3	161.8	..	0.2	0.4	0.4	0.4
5300 Unallocable between 5100 and 5200	..	0.0	0.0	0.0	0.0	..	0.0	0.0	0.0	0.0
6000 Other taxes	..	**32.9**	**59.4**	**47.6**	**38.4**	..	**0.2**	**0.2**	**0.1**	**0.1**
Non-wastable tax credits										
Non-wastable tax credits against 1000	..	..	..	..	..	..	..	..	..	..
Transfer component	..	..	..	..	..	..	..	..	..	..
Tax expenditure component	..	..	..	..	..	..	..	..	..	..
Revenues collected on behalf of the EU										
Revenues collected on behalf of the EU, total	..	..	25.7	46.3	63.4	..	..	0.1	0.1	0.1
Customs duties	..	..	25.0	45.4	63.4	..	..	0.1	0.1	0.1

.. Not available

Note: More detailed country data and country notes are available in online chapter 5 "Detailed country tables": https://doi.org/10.1787/0bbc27da-en. Full time series can be accessed at http://oe.cd/full-time-series.

Source: Ministry of Finance, Economic Department.

StatLink https://doi.org/10.1787/888934210730

Table 4.28. Hungary, tax revenue and % of GDP by level of government and main taxes

	Billion HUF					% of GDP				
	1990	2000	2010	2017	2018	1990	2000	2010	2017	2018
Federal or Central government										
Total tax revenue	..	**3 316.3**	**6 400.0**	**9 228.2**	**9 850.0**	..	**24.9**	**23.5**	**23.8**	**23.1**
1000 Taxes on income, profits and capital gains	..	1 230.8	2 064.3	2 725.6	2 773.4	..	9.2	7.6	7.0	6.5
2000 Social security contributions	..	136.6	182.0	353.2	199.7	..	1.0	0.7	0.9	0.5
3000 Taxes on payroll and workforce	..	15.4	103.1	327.4	399.1	..	0.1	0.4	0.8	0.9
4000 Taxes on property	..	29.1	182.8	245.9	252.9	..	0.2	0.7	0.6	0.6
5000 Taxes on goods and services	..	1 878.6	3 808.5	5 538.5	6 193.3	..	14.1	14.0	14.3	14.5
6000 Other taxes	..	25.8	59.4	37.7	31.6	..	0.2	0.2	0.1	0.1
State/Regional										
Total tax revenue	..	..	..	..	..	..	..	..	..	..
1000 Taxes on income, profits and capital gains	..	..	..	..	..	..	..	..	..	..
2000 Social security contributions	..	..	..	..	..	..	..	..	..	..
3000 Taxes on payroll and workforce	..	..	..	..	..	..	..	..	..	..
4000 Taxes on property	..	..	..	..	..	..	..	..	..	..
5000 Taxes on goods and services	..	..	..	..	..	..	..	..	..	..
6000 Other taxes	..	..	..	..	..	..	..	..	..	..
Local government										
Total tax revenue	..	**266.0**	**652.2**	**846.2**	**923.8**	..	**2.0**	**2.4**	**2.2**	**2.2**
1000 Taxes on income, profits and capital gains	..	2.2	0.1	0.0	0.0	..	0.0	0.0	0.0	0.0
2000 Social security contributions	..	0.0	0.0	0.0	0.0	..	0.0	0.0	0.0	0.0
3000 Taxes on payroll and workforce	..	1.2	1.2	0.0	0.0	..	0.0	0.0	0.0	0.0
4000 Taxes on property	..	59.9	129.3	163.0	164.9	..	0.4	0.5	0.4	0.4
5000 Taxes on goods and services	..	202.8	521.6	683.2	758.9	..	1.5	1.9	1.8	1.8
6000 Other taxes	..	0.0	0.0	0.0	0.0	..	0.0	0.0	0.0	0.0
Social Security Funds										
Total tax revenue	..	**1 558.6**	**3 064.5**	**4 746.6**	**5 139.7**	..	**11.7**	**11.2**	**12.2**	**12.0**
1000 Taxes on income, profits and capital gains	..	14.5	29.4	136.9	138.7	..	0.1	0.1	0.4	0.3
2000 Social security contributions	..	1 370.2	2 997.5	4 469.0	4 849.9	..	10.3	11.0	11.5	11.4
3000 Taxes on payroll and workforce	..	166.9	9.4	12.8	11.1	..	1.3	0.0	0.0	0.0
4000 Taxes on property	..	0.0	0.0	0.0	0.0	..	0.0	0.0	0.0	0.0
5000 Taxes on goods and services	..	0.0	28.1	118.0	133.2	..	0.0	0.1	0.3	0.3
6000 Other taxes	..	7.0	0.0	9.9	6.8	..	0.1	0.0	0.0	0.0

.. Not available

Note: More detailed country data and country notes are available in online chapter 6 "Tax revenues by sub-sectors of general government": https://doi.org/10.1787/0bbc27da-en. Full time series can be accessed at http://oe.cd/full-time-series.

Source: Ministry of Finance, Economic Department.

StatLink https://doi.org/10.1787/888934210749

Table 4.29. Iceland, tax revenue and % of GDP by selected tax category

	Billion ISK					% of GDP				
	1990	2000	2010	2017	2018	1990	2000	2010	2017	2018
Total tax revenue	**114.9**	**254.6**	**540.3**	**982.8**	**1 037.6**	**30.4**	**36.0**	**32.3**	**37.6**	**37.2**
1000 Taxes on income, profits and capital gains	**34.1**	**101.5**	**239.7**	**484.0**	**511.7**	**9.0**	**14.3**	**14.3**	**18.5**	**18.4**
1100 Of individuals	30.9	88.5	197.3	374.4	412.4	8.2	12.5	11.8	14.3	14.8
1200 Corporate	3.2	8.4	14.6	80.0	67.7	0.8	1.2	0.9	3.1	2.4
1300 Unallocable between 1100 and 1200	0.0	4.6	27.7	29.6	31.6	0.0	0.7	1.7	1.1	1.1
2000 Social security contributions	**3.6**	**19.7**	**63.6**	**89.6**	**98.2**	**1.0**	**2.8**	**3.8**	**3.4**	**3.5**
2100 Employees	0.3	..	..	..	..	0.1	..	..	..	..
2200 Employers	3.3	..	..	..	..	0.9	..	..	..	..
2300 Self-employed or non-employed	0.0	..	..	..	..	0.0	..	..	..	..
2400 Unallocable between 2100, 2200 and 2300	0.0	19.7	63.6	89.6	98.2	0.0	2.8	3.8	3.4	3.5
3000 Taxes on payroll and workforce	**4.1**	**0.2**	**2.8**	**7.9**	**8.5**	**1.1**	**0.0**	**0.2**	**0.3**	**0.3**
4000 Taxes on property	**9.7**	**20.0**	**38.1**	**54.0**	**56.8**	**2.6**	**2.8**	**2.3**	**2.1**	**2.0**
4100 Recurrent taxes on immovable property	4.1	10.1	28.5	43.4	46.5	1.1	1.4	1.7	1.7	1.7
4200 Recurrent taxes on net wealth	2.4	5.2	3.8	0.3	0.1	0.6	0.7	0.2	0.0	0.0
4300 Estate, inheritance and gift taxes	0.2	0.8	2.6	4.3	4.7	0.1	0.1	0.2	0.2	0.2
4400 Taxes on financial and capital transactions	2.9	3.1	2.7	4.6	5.0	0.8	0.4	0.2	0.2	0.2
4500 Non-recurrent taxes	0.0	0.1	0.1	0.5	0.5	0.0	0.0	0.0	0.0	0.0
4600 Other recurrent taxes on property	0.0	0.7	0.3	0.9	0.1	0.0	0.1	0.0	0.0	0.0
5000 Taxes on goods and services	**58.9**	**112.2**	**190.1**	**330.8**	**345.3**	**15.6**	**15.9**	**11.4**	**12.6**	**12.4**
5100 Taxes on production, sale, transfer, etc	56.6	100.7	179.0	311.2	324.8	15.0	14.2	10.7	11.9	11.7
5110 General taxes	37.1	72.7	122.4	234.0	244.6	9.8	10.3	7.3	8.9	8.8
5111 Value added taxes	32.7	72.7	122.4	234.0	244.6	8.7	10.3	7.3	8.9	8.8
5120 Taxes on specific goods and services	19.5	28.0	56.6	77.2	80.1	5.2	4.0	3.4	3.0	2.9
5121 Excises	2.3	23.6	46.7	67.7	69.5	0.6	3.3	2.8	2.6	2.5
5200 Taxes on use of goods and perform activities	2.4	11.6	11.1	19.6	20.5	0.6	1.6	0.7	0.7	0.7
5300 Unallocable between 5100 and 5200	0.0	0.0	0.0	0.0	0.0	0.0	0.0	0.0	0.0	0.0
6000 Other taxes	**4.5**	**1.0**	**6.0**	**16.4**	**17.0**	**1.2**	**0.1**	**0.4**	**0.6**	**0.6**
Non-wastable tax credits										
Non-wastable tax credits against 1000	..	..	..	2.7	3.1	..	..	..	0.1	0.1
Transfer component	..	..	..	2.2	2.5	..	..	..	0.1	0.1
Tax expenditure component	..	..	..	0.5	0.6	..	..	..	0.0	0.0

.. Not available

Note: More detailed country data and country notes are available in online chapter 5 "Detailed country tables": https://doi.org/10.1787/0bbc27da-en. Full time series can be accessed at http://oe.cd/full-time-series.

Source: Ministry of Finance, Economic Department.

StatLink https://doi.org/10.1787/888934210768

Table 4.30. Iceland, tax revenue and % of GDP by level of government and main taxes

	Billion ISK					% of GDP				
	1990	2000	2010	2017	2018	1990	2000	2010	2017	2018
Federal or Central government										
Total tax revenue	**91.6**	**195.1**	**402.3**	**721.7**	**751.7**	**24.3**	**27.6**	**24.1**	**27.6**	**27.0**
1000 Taxes on income, profits and capital gains	19.9	55.5	132.9	274.6	281.0	5.3	7.8	7.9	10.5	10.1
2000 Social security contributions	3.6	19.7	63.6	89.6	98.2	1.0	2.8	3.8	3.4	3.5
3000 Taxes on payroll and workforce	4.1	0.2	2.8	7.9	8.5	1.1	0.0	0.2	0.3	0.3
4000 Taxes on property	6.0	9.9	9.7	10.8	10.5	1.6	1.4	0.6	0.4	0.4
5000 Taxes on goods and services	57.7	108.9	187.4	322.3	336.5	15.3	15.4	11.2	12.3	12.1
6000 Other taxes	0.4	1.0	6.0	16.4	17.0	0.1	0.1	0.4	0.6	0.6
State/Regional										
Total tax revenue	..	..	..	..	..	..	..	..	..	..
1000 Taxes on income, profits and capital gains	..	..	..	..	..	..	..	..	..	..
2000 Social security contributions	..	..	..	..	..	..	..	..	..	..
3000 Taxes on payroll and workforce	..	..	..	..	..	..	..	..	..	..
4000 Taxes on property	..	..	..	..	..	..	..	..	..	..
5000 Taxes on goods and services	..	..	..	..	..	..	..	..	..	..
6000 Other taxes	..	..	..	..	..	..	..	..	..	..
Local government										
Total tax revenue	**23.3**	**59.4**	**138.0**	**261.1**	**285.9**	**6.2**	**8.4**	**8.2**	**10.0**	**10.3**
1000 Taxes on income, profits and capital gains	14.2	46.0	106.8	209.4	230.8	3.8	6.5	6.4	8.0	8.3
2000 Social security contributions	0.0	0.0	0.0	0.0	0.0	0.0	0.0	0.0	0.0	0.0
3000 Taxes on payroll and workforce	0.0	0.0	0.0	0.0	0.0	0.0	0.0	0.0	0.0	0.0
4000 Taxes on property	3.7	10.1	28.4	43.2	46.3	1.0	1.4	1.7	1.7	1.7
5000 Taxes on goods and services	1.2	3.3	2.8	8.5	8.8	0.3	0.5	0.2	0.3	0.3
6000 Other taxes	4.1	0.0	0.0	0.0	0.0	1.1	0.0	0.0	0.0	0.0
Social Security Funds										
Total tax revenue	**0.0**	**0.0**	**0.0**	**0.0**	**0.0**	**0.0**	**0.0**	**0.0**	**0.0**	**0.0**
1000 Taxes on income, profits and capital gains	0.0	0.0	0.0	0.0	0.0	0.0	0.0	0.0	0.0	0.0
2000 Social security contributions	0.0	0.0	0.0	0.0	0.0	0.0	0.0	0.0	0.0	0.0
3000 Taxes on payroll and workforce	0.0	0.0	0.0	0.0	0.0	0.0	0.0	0.0	0.0	0.0
4000 Taxes on property	0.0	0.0	0.0	0.0	0.0	0.0	0.0	0.0	0.0	0.0
5000 Taxes on goods and services	0.0	0.0	0.0	0.0	0.0	0.0	0.0	0.0	0.0	0.0
6000 Other taxes	0.0	0.0	0.0	0.0	0.0	0.0	0.0	0.0	0.0	0.0

.. Not available

Note: More detailed country data and country notes are available in online chapter 5 "Detailed country tables": https://doi.org/10.1787/0bbc27da-en. Full time series can be accessed at http://oe.cd/full-time-series.

Source: Ministry of Finance, Economic Department.

StatLink https://doi.org/10.1787/888934210787

Table 4.31. Ireland, tax revenue and % of GDP by selected tax category

	Billion EUR					% of GDP				
	1990	2000	2010	2017	2018	1990	2000	2010	2017	2018
Total tax revenue	**12.3**	**33.4**	**46.4**	**67.6**	**73.5**	**32.4**	**30.8**	**27.7**	**22.8**	**22.7**
1000 Taxes on income, profits and capital gains	**4.7**	**14.6**	**18.6**	**29.6**	**33.3**	**12.3**	**13.4**	**11.1**	**10.0**	**10.3**
1100 Of individuals	4.1	10.6	14.7	21.4	22.9	10.7	9.8	8.7	7.2	7.1
1200 Corporate	0.6	3.9	3.9	8.2	10.4	1.6	3.6	2.4	2.8	3.2
1300 Unallocable between 1100 and 1200	0.0	0.0	0.0	0.0	0.0	0.0	0.0	0.0	0.0	0.0
2000 Social security contributions	**1.7**	**4.0**	**8.5**	**11.7**	**12.7**	**4.6**	**3.7**	**5.0**	**3.9**	**3.9**
2100 Employees	0.6	1.0	3.2	4.0	4.4	1.5	0.9	1.9	1.3	1.3
2200 Employers	1.1	2.8	4.9	7.2	7.7	2.9	2.6	2.9	2.4	2.4
2300 Self-employed or non-employed	0.1	0.2	0.3	0.5	0.6	0.2	0.2	0.2	0.2	0.2
2400 Unallocable between 2100, 2200 and 2300	0.0	0.0	0.0	0.0	0.0	0.0	0.0	0.0	0.0	0.0
3000 Taxes on payroll and workforce	**0.2**	**0.0**	**0.3**	**0.4**	**0.6**	**0.4**	**0.0**	**0.2**	**0.1**	**0.2**
4000 Taxes on property	**0.6**	**1.9**	**2.4**	**3.9**	**4.3**	**1.5**	**1.8**	**1.4**	**1.3**	**1.3**
4100 Recurrent taxes on immovable property	0.3	0.6	1.3	1.9	1.9	0.8	0.5	0.8	0.6	0.6
4200 Recurrent taxes on net wealth	0.0	0.0	0.0	0.0	0.0	0.0	0.0	0.0	0.0	0.0
4300 Estate, inheritance and gift taxes	0.0	0.2	0.2	0.4	0.5	0.1	0.2	0.1	0.2	0.2
4400 Taxes on financial and capital transactions	0.2	1.1	0.8	1.5	1.9	0.6	1.0	0.5	0.5	0.6
4500 Non-recurrent taxes	0.0	0.0	0.0	0.0	0.0	0.0	0.0	0.0	0.0	0.0
4600 Other recurrent taxes on property	0.0	0.0	0.0	0.0	0.0	0.0	0.0	0.0	0.0	0.0
5000 Taxes on goods and services	**5.1**	**12.9**	**16.6**	**22.1**	**22.6**	**13.6**	**11.9**	**9.9**	**7.4**	**7.0**
5100 Taxes on production, sale, transfer, etc	4.9	12.4	15.3	20.1	20.6	13.0	11.4	9.1	6.8	6.4
5110 General taxes	2.5	7.6	10.1	13.1	14.2	6.6	7.1	6.0	4.4	4.4
5111 Value added taxes	2.5	7.6	10.1	13.1	14.2	6.6	7.1	6.0	4.4	4.4
5120 Taxes on specific goods and services	2.4	4.7	5.3	7.0	6.5	6.4	4.4	3.1	2.4	2.0
5121 Excises	2.1	4.4	4.9	6.2	5.5	5.5	4.1	2.9	2.1	1.7
5200 Taxes on use of goods and perform activities	0.2	0.6	1.3	2.0	2.0	0.5	0.5	0.8	0.7	0.6
5300 Unallocable between 5100 and 5200	0.0	0.0	0.0	0.0	0.0	0.0	0.0	0.0	0.0	0.0
6000 Other taxes	**0.0**	**0.0**	**0.0**	**0.0**	**0.0**	**0.0**	**0.0**	**0.0**	**0.0**	**0.0**
Non-wastable tax credits										
Non-wastable tax credits against 1000	..	..	1.1	0.5	0.5	..	..	0.6	0.2	0.1
Transfer component	..	..	0.0	0.0	0.0	..	..	0.0	0.0	0.0
Tax expenditure component	..	..	1.1	0.5	0.5	..	..	0.6	0.2	0.1
Revenues collected on behalf of the EU										
Revenues collected on behalf of the EU, total	0.2	0.2	0.2	0.4	0.4	0.5	0.2	0.1	0.1	0.1
Customs duties	0.1	0.2	0.2	0.3	0.3	0.4	0.2	0.1	0.1	0.1
SRF contributions	..	..	..	0.1	0.1	..	..	..	0.0	0.0

.. Not available

Note: More detailed country data and country notes are available in online chapter 5 "Detailed country tables": https://doi.org/10.1787/0bbc27da-en. Full time series can be accessed at http://oe.cd/full-time-series.

Source: Annual Report of the Revenue Commissioners, Financial Accounts and National Income and Expenditure Accounts.

StatLink https://doi.org/10.1787/888934210806

Table 4.32. Ireland, tax revenue and % of GDP by level of government and main taxes

	Billion EUR					% of GDP				
	1990	2000	2010	2017	2018	1990	2000	2010	2017	2018
Federal or Central government										
Total tax revenue	**10.1**	**28.7**	**37.9**	**55.8**	**60.8**	**26.7**	**26.5**	**22.6**	**18.8**	**18.8**
1000 Taxes on income, profits and capital gains	4.7	14.6	18.6	29.6	33.3	12.3	13.4	11.1	10.0	10.3
2000 Social security contributions	0.1	0.1	1.5	1.7	1.9	0.2	0.1	0.9	0.6	0.6
3000 Taxes on payroll and workforce	0.2	0.0	0.3	0.4	0.6	0.4	0.0	0.2	0.1	0.2
4000 Taxes on property	0.3	1.3	1.1	2.5	2.9	0.7	1.2	0.6	0.8	0.9
5000 Taxes on goods and services	5.0	12.7	16.4	21.6	22.2	13.1	11.7	9.8	7.3	6.8
6000 Other taxes	0.0	0.0	0.0	0.0	0.0	0.0	0.0	0.0	0.0	0.0
State/Regional										
Total tax revenue	..	..	..	..	..	..	..	..	..	..
1000 Taxes on income, profits and capital gains	..	..	..	..	..	..	..	..	..	..
2000 Social security contributions	..	..	..	..	..	..	..	..	..	..
3000 Taxes on payroll and workforce	..	..	..	..	..	..	..	..	..	..
4000 Taxes on property	..	..	..	..	..	..	..	..	..	..
5000 Taxes on goods and services	..	..	..	..	..	..	..	..	..	..
6000 Other taxes	..	..	..	..	..	..	..	..	..	..
Local government										
Total tax revenue	**0.3**	**0.7**	**1.5**	**1.5**	**1.6**	**0.9**	**0.6**	**0.9**	**0.5**	**0.5**
1000 Taxes on income, profits and capital gains	0.0	0.0	0.0	0.0	0.0	0.0	0.0	0.0	0.0	0.0
2000 Social security contributions	0.0	0.1	0.2	0.1	0.2	0.1	0.1	0.1	0.0	0.0
3000 Taxes on payroll and workforce	0.0	0.0	0.0	0.0	0.0	0.0	0.0	0.0	0.0	0.0
4000 Taxes on property	0.3	0.6	1.3	1.4	1.4	0.8	0.5	0.8	0.5	0.4
5000 Taxes on goods and services	0.0	0.0	0.0	0.0	0.0	0.0	0.0	0.0	0.0	0.0
6000 Other taxes	0.0	0.0	0.0	0.0	0.0	0.0	0.0	0.0	0.0	0.0
Social Security Funds										
Total tax revenue	**1.6**	**3.8**	**6.7**	**9.8**	**10.6**	**4.3**	**3.5**	**4.0**	**3.3**	**3.3**
1000 Taxes on income, profits and capital gains	0.0	0.0	0.0	0.0	0.0	0.0	0.0	0.0	0.0	0.0
2000 Social security contributions	1.6	3.8	6.7	9.8	10.6	4.3	3.5	4.0	3.3	3.3
3000 Taxes on payroll and workforce	0.0	0.0	0.0	0.0	0.0	0.0	0.0	0.0	0.0	0.0
4000 Taxes on property	0.0	0.0	0.0	0.0	0.0	0.0	0.0	0.0	0.0	0.0
5000 Taxes on goods and services	0.0	0.0	0.0	0.0	0.0	0.0	0.0	0.0	0.0	0.0
6000 Other taxes	0.0	0.0	0.0	0.0	0.0	0.0	0.0	0.0	0.0	0.0

.. Not available

Note: More detailed country data and country notes are available in online chapter 6 "Tax revenues by sub-sectors of general government": https://doi.org/10.1787/0bbc27da-en. Full time series can be accessed at http://oe.cd/full-time-series.

Source: Annual Report of the Revenue Commissioners, Financial Accounts and National Income and Expenditure Accounts.

StatLink https://doi.org/10.1787/888934210825

Table 4.33. Israel, tax revenue and % of GDP by selected tax category

	Billion ILS					% of GDP				
	1990	2000	2010	2017	2018	1990	2000	2010	2017	2018
Total tax revenue	..	**188.3**	**268.6**	**413.1**	**411.6**	..	**34.8**	**30.7**	**32.5**	**30.9**
1000 Taxes on income, profits and capital gains	..	**74.6**	**78.3**	**146.9**	**135.0**	..	**13.8**	**8.9**	**11.6**	**10.1**
1100 Of individuals	..	54.8	48.2	85.4	84.9	..	10.1	5.5	6.7	6.4
1200 Corporate	..	18.0	23.1	41.9	42.9	..	3.3	2.6	3.3	3.2
1300 Unallocable between 1100 and 1200	..	1.8	6.9	19.6	7.1	..	0.3	0.8	1.5	0.5
2000 Social security contributions	..	**27.6**	**45.3**	**66.8**	**69.0**	..	**5.1**	**5.2**	**5.3**	**5.2**
2100 Employees	..	15.8	27.8	37.9	39.2	..	2.9	3.2	3.0	2.9
2200 Employers	..	8.2	11.4	20.6	21.0	..	1.5	1.3	1.6	1.6
2300 Self-employed or non-employed	..	3.6	6.1	8.3	8.8	..	0.7	0.7	0.7	0.7
2400 Unallocable between 2100, 2200 and 2300	..	0.0	0.0	0.0	0.0	..	0.0	0.0	0.0	0.0
3000 Taxes on payroll and workforce	..	**6.8**	**10.3**	**15.2**	**15.8**	..	**1.3**	**1.2**	**1.2**	**1.2**
4000 Taxes on property	..	**16.9**	**28.8**	**40.9**	**42.3**	..	**3.1**	**3.3**	**3.2**	**3.2**
4100 Recurrent taxes on immovable property	..	11.3	18.8	25.3	26.3	..	2.1	2.1	2.0	2.0
4200 Recurrent taxes on net wealth	..	0.0	0.0	0.0	0.0	..	0.0	0.0	0.0	0.0
4300 Estate, inheritance and gift taxes	..	0.0	0.0	0.0	0.0	..	0.0	0.0	0.0	0.0
4400 Taxes on financial and capital transactions	..	3.2	4.1	6.6	6.7	..	0.6	0.5	0.5	0.5
4500 Non-recurrent taxes	..	2.4	6.0	9.0	9.3	..	0.5	0.7	0.7	0.7
4600 Other recurrent taxes on property	..	0.0	0.0	0.0	0.0	..	0.0	0.0	0.0	0.0
5000 Taxes on goods and services	..	**62.4**	**105.9**	**143.2**	**149.5**	..	**11.5**	**12.1**	**11.3**	**11.2**
5100 Taxes on production, sale, transfer, etc	..	57.9	98.1	133.3	138.9	..	10.7	11.2	10.5	10.4
5110 General taxes	..	49.9	79.9	111.0	117.3	..	9.2	9.1	8.7	8.8
5111 Value added taxes	..	39.8	65.5	94.5	99.4	..	7.4	7.5	7.4	7.5
5120 Taxes on specific goods and services	..	8.0	18.1	22.3	21.7	..	1.5	2.1	1.8	1.6
5121 Excises	..	6.6	15.5	19.3	18.9	..	1.2	1.8	1.5	1.4
5200 Taxes on use of goods and perform activities	..	4.5	7.8	10.0	10.6	..	0.8	0.9	0.8	0.8
5300 Unallocable between 5100 and 5200	..	0.0	0.0	0.0	0.0	..	0.0	0.0	0.0	0.0
6000 Other taxes	..	**0.0**	**0.0**	**0.0**	**0.0**	..	**0.0**	**0.0**	**0.0**	**0.0**
Non-wastable tax credits										
Non-wastable tax credits against 1000	..	..	0.1	1.6	0.8	..	..	0.0	0.1	0.1
Transfer component	..	..	0.1	1.6	0.8	..	..	0.0	0.1	0.1
Tax expenditure component	..	..	0.0	0.0	0.0	..	..	0.0	0.0	0.0

.. Not available

Note: More detailed country data and country notes are available in online chapter 5 "Detailed country tables": https://doi.org/10.1787/0bbc27da-en. Full time series can be accessed at http://oe.cd/full-time-series.

Source: Israel Central Bureau of Statistics and Israel Ministry of Finance.

StatLink https://doi.org/10.1787/888934210844

Table 4.34. Israel, tax revenue and % of GDP by level of government and main taxes

	Billion ILS					% of GDP				
	1990	2000	2010	2017	2018	1990	2000	2010	2017	2018
Federal or Central government										
Total tax revenue	..	**148.0**	**199.9**	**315.1**	**310.1**	..	**27.4**	**22.8**	**24.8**	**23.3**
1000 Taxes on income, profits and capital gains	..	74.6	78.3	146.9	135.0	..	13.8	8.9	11.6	10.1
2000 Social security contributions	..	0.0	0.0	0.0	0.0	..	0.0	0.0	0.0	0.0
3000 Taxes on payroll and workforce	..	6.8	10.3	15.2	15.8	..	1.3	1.2	1.2	1.2
4000 Taxes on property	..	4.8	6.6	11.3	11.3	..	0.9	0.8	0.9	0.9
5000 Taxes on goods and services	..	61.8	104.7	141.7	147.9	..	11.4	12.0	11.2	11.1
6000 Other taxes	..	0.0	0.0	0.0	0.0	..	0.0	0.0	0.0	0.0
State/Regional										
Total tax revenue	..	..	..	..	..	..	..	..	..	..
1000 Taxes on income, profits and capital gains	..	..	..	..	..	..	..	..	..	..
2000 Social security contributions	..	..	..	..	..	..	..	..	..	..
3000 Taxes on payroll and workforce	..	..	..	..	..	..	..	..	..	..
4000 Taxes on property	..	..	..	..	..	..	..	..	..	..
5000 Taxes on goods and services	..	..	..	..	..	..	..	..	..	..
6000 Other taxes	..	..	..	..	..	..	..	..	..	..
Local government										
Total tax revenue	..	**12.7**	**23.4**	**31.2**	**32.6**	..	**2.3**	**2.7**	**2.5**	**2.4**
1000 Taxes on income, profits and capital gains	..	0.0	0.0	0.0	0.0	..	0.0	0.0	0.0	0.0
2000 Social security contributions	..	0.0	0.0	0.0	0.0	..	0.0	0.0	0.0	0.0
3000 Taxes on payroll and workforce	..	0.0	0.0	0.0	0.0	..	0.0	0.0	0.0	0.0
4000 Taxes on property	..	12.1	22.2	29.7	30.9	..	2.2	2.5	2.3	2.3
5000 Taxes on goods and services	..	0.6	1.1	1.5	1.6	..	0.1	0.1	0.1	0.1
6000 Other taxes	..	0.0	0.0	0.0	0.0	..	0.0	0.0	0.0	0.0
Social Security Funds										
Total tax revenue	..	**27.6**	**45.3**	**66.8**	**69.0**	..	**5.1**	**5.2**	**5.3**	**5.2**
1000 Taxes on income, profits and capital gains	..	0.0	0.0	0.0	0.0	..	0.0	0.0	0.0	0.0
2000 Social security contributions	..	27.6	45.3	66.8	69.0	..	5.1	5.2	5.3	5.2
3000 Taxes on payroll and workforce	..	0.0	0.0	0.0	0.0	..	0.0	0.0	0.0	0.0
4000 Taxes on property	..	0.0	0.0	0.0	0.0	..	0.0	0.0	0.0	0.0
5000 Taxes on goods and services	..	0.0	0.0	0.0	0.0	..	0.0	0.0	0.0	0.0
6000 Other taxes	..	0.0	0.0	0.0	0.0	..	0.0	0.0	0.0	0.0

.. Not available

Note: More detailed country data and country notes are available in online chapter 6 "Tax revenues by sub-sectors of general government": https://doi.org/10.1787/0bbc27da-en. Full time series can be accessed at http://oe.cd/full-time-series.

Source: Israel Central Bureau of Statistics and Israel Ministry of Finance.

StatLink https://doi.org/10.1787/888934210863

Table 4.35. Italy, tax revenue and % of GDP by selected tax category

	Billion EUR					% of GDP				
	1990	2000	2010	2017	2018	1990	2000	2010	2017	2018
Total tax revenue	**265.1**	**503.1**	**671.9**	**727.8**	**739.5**	**36.3**	**40.5**	**41.7**	**41.9**	**41.9**
1000 Taxes on income, profits and capital gains	**96.7**	**166.9**	**219.5**	**230.8**	**228.9**	**13.2**	**13.4**	**13.6**	**13.3**	**13.0**
1100 Of individuals	69.7	124.9	180.5	187.1	189.3	9.5	10.1	11.2	10.8	10.7
1200 Corporate	26.6	34.7	36.7	36.1	32.9	3.6	2.8	2.3	2.1	1.9
1300 Unallocable between 1100 and 1200	0.4	7.3	2.3	7.6	6.7	0.1	0.6	0.1	0.4	0.4
2000 Social security contributions	**87.3**	**143.6**	**209.1**	**220.6**	**229.6**	**11.9**	**11.6**	**13.0**	**12.7**	**13.0**
2100 Employees	16.8	27.3	37.6	40.9	42.7	2.3	2.2	2.3	2.4	2.4
2200 Employers	62.5	99.9	144.3	147.3	153.9	8.6	8.0	9.0	8.5	8.7
2300 Self-employed or non-employed	8.0	16.4	27.2	32.5	33.0	1.1	1.3	1.7	1.9	1.9
2400 Unallocable between 2100, 2200 and 2300	0.0	0.0	0.0	0.0	0.0	0.0	0.0	0.0	0.0	0.0
3000 Taxes on payroll and workforce	**0.9**	**0.0**	**0.0**	**0.0**	**0.0**	**0.1**	**0.0**	**0.0**	**0.0**	**0.0**
4000 Taxes on property	**6.0**	**23.4**	**32.4**	**44.2**	**44.9**	**0.8**	**1.9**	**2.0**	**2.5**	**2.5**
4100 Recurrent taxes on immovable property	0.0	9.4	9.7	21.9	22.0	0.0	0.8	0.6	1.3	1.2
4200 Recurrent taxes on net wealth	0.0	0.0	2.1	0.4	0.3	0.0	0.0	0.1	0.0	0.0
4300 Estate, inheritance and gift taxes	0.4	1.0	0.5	0.8	0.8	0.1	0.1	0.0	0.0	0.0
4400 Taxes on financial and capital transactions	5.6	12.3	17.4	17.7	18.8	0.8	1.0	1.1	1.0	1.1
4500 Non-recurrent taxes	0.0	0.1	0.9	1.2	0.4	0.0	0.0	0.1	0.1	0.0
4600 Other recurrent taxes on property	0.0	0.6	1.9	2.3	2.6	0.0	0.0	0.1	0.1	0.1
5000 Taxes on goods and services	**74.3**	**141.9**	**178.9**	**209.9**	**212.1**	**10.2**	**11.4**	**11.1**	**12.1**	**12.0**
5100 Taxes on production, sale, transfer, etc	67.1	127.3	160.8	184.3	184.7	9.2	10.3	10.0	10.6	10.5
5110 General taxes	38.9	77.5	97.6	107.6	109.3	5.3	6.2	6.1	6.2	6.2
5111 Value added taxes	38.9	77.5	97.6	107.6	109.3	5.3	6.2	6.1	6.2	6.2
5120 Taxes on specific goods and services	28.0	49.8	63.2	76.7	75.4	3.8	4.0	3.9	4.4	4.3
5121 Excises	20.3	31.5	36.4	47.6	47.1	2.8	2.5	2.3	2.7	2.7
5200 Taxes on use of goods and perform activities	4.5	8.5	10.5	13.1	14.5	0.6	0.7	0.7	0.8	0.8
5300 Unallocable between 5100 and 5200	2.7	6.1	7.6	12.4	12.9	0.4	0.5	0.5	0.7	0.7
6000 Other taxes	**0.0**	**27.3**	**31.9**	**22.2**	**23.9**	**0.0**	**2.2**	**2.0**	**1.3**	**1.4**
Non-wastable tax credits										
Non-wastable tax credits against 1000	..	..	0.0	16.2	11.8	..	..	0.0	0.9	0.7
Transfer component	..	..	0.1	7.1	2.6	..	..	0.0	0.4	0.1
Tax expenditure component	..	..	-0.1	9.1	9.1	..	..	0.0	0.5	0.5
Revenues collected on behalf of the EU										
Revenues collected on behalf of the EU, total	1.3	1.5	2.2	4.6	3.4	0.2	0.1	0.1	0.3	0.2
Customs duties	0.8	1.5	2.2	2.3	2.3	0.1	0.1	0.1	0.1	0.1
SRF contributions	..	..	..	2.3	1.1	..	..	..	0.1	0.1

.. Not available

Note: More detailed country data and country notes are available in online chapter 5 "Detailed country tables": https://doi.org/10.1787/0bbc27da-en. Full time series can be accessed at http://oe.cd/full-time-series.

Source: Ministero dell'economia e delle finanze; Istituto nazionale di statistica.

StatLink https://doi.org/10.1787/888934210882

Table 4.36. Italy, tax revenue and % of GDP by level of government and main taxes

	Billion EUR					% of GDP				
	1990	2000	2010	2017	2018	1990	2000	2010	2017	2018
Federal or Central government										
Total tax revenue	**168.9**	**280.8**	**357.3**	**419.6**	**420.2**	**23.1**	**22.6**	**22.2**	**24.2**	**23.8**
1000 Taxes on income, profits and capital gains	92.7	154.2	193.9	214.2	212.3	12.7	12.4	12.0	12.3	12.0
2000 Social security contributions	0.0	0.0	0.0	0.0	0.0	0.0	0.0	0.0	0.0	0.0
3000 Taxes on payroll and workforce	0.9	0.0	0.0	0.0	0.0	0.1	0.0	0.0	0.0	0.0
4000 Taxes on property	6.0	12.9	21.0	25.5	25.7	0.8	1.0	1.3	1.5	1.5
5000 Taxes on goods and services	69.3	113.6	142.5	179.8	182.1	9.5	9.2	8.8	10.4	10.3
6000 Other taxes	0.0	0.0	0.0	0.0	0.0	0.0	0.0	0.0	0.0	0.0
State/Regional										
Total tax revenue	..	..	..	..	..	..	..	..	..	..
1000 Taxes on income, profits and capital gains	..	..	..	..	..	..	..	..	..	..
2000 Social security contributions	..	..	..	..	..	..	..	..	..	..
3000 Taxes on payroll and workforce	..	..	..	..	..	..	..	..	..	..
4000 Taxes on property	..	..	..	..	..	..	..	..	..	..
5000 Taxes on goods and services	..	..	..	..	..	..	..	..	..	..
6000 Other taxes	..	..	..	..	..	..	..	..	..	..
Local government										
Total tax revenue	**7.7**	**77.2**	**103.2**	**83.1**	**86.3**	**1.1**	**6.2**	**6.4**	**4.8**	**4.9**
1000 Taxes on income, profits and capital gains	4.0	12.7	25.6	16.6	16.6	0.6	1.0	1.6	1.0	0.9
2000 Social security contributions	0.0	0.0	0.0	0.0	0.0	0.0	0.0	0.0	0.0	0.0
3000 Taxes on payroll and workforce	0.0	0.0	0.0	0.0	0.0	0.0	0.0	0.0	0.0	0.0
4000 Taxes on property	0.0	10.5	11.5	18.7	19.2	0.0	0.8	0.7	1.1	1.1
5000 Taxes on goods and services	3.7	26.7	34.2	25.5	26.6	0.5	2.2	2.1	1.5	1.5
6000 Other taxes	0.0	27.3	31.9	22.2	23.9	0.0	2.2	2.0	1.3	1.4
Social Security Funds										
Total tax revenue	**87.3**	**143.6**	**209.1**	**220.6**	**229.6**	**11.9**	**11.6**	**13.0**	**12.7**	**13.0**
1000 Taxes on income, profits and capital gains	0.0	0.0	0.0	0.0	0.0	0.0	0.0	0.0	0.0	0.0
2000 Social security contributions	87.3	143.6	209.1	220.6	229.6	11.9	11.6	13.0	12.7	13.0
3000 Taxes on payroll and workforce	0.0	0.0	0.0	0.0	0.0	0.0	0.0	0.0	0.0	0.0
4000 Taxes on property	0.0	0.0	0.0	0.0	0.0	0.0	0.0	0.0	0.0	0.0
5000 Taxes on goods and services	0.0	0.0	0.0	0.0	0.0	0.0	0.0	0.0	0.0	0.0
6000 Other taxes	0.0	0.0	0.0	0.0	0.0	0.0	0.0	0.0	0.0	0.0

.. Not available

Note: More detailed country data and country notes are available in online chapter 6 "Tax revenues by sub-sectors of general government": https://doi.org/10.1787/0bbc27da-en. Full time series can be accessed at http://oe.cd/full-time-series.

Source: Ministero dell'economia e delle finanze; Istituto nazionale di statistica.

StatLink https://doi.org/10.1787/888934210901

Table 4.37. Japan, tax revenue and % of GDP by selected tax category

	Billion JPY					% of GDP				
	1990	2000	2010	2017	2018	1990	2000	2010	2017	2018
Total tax revenue	**130 842.7**	**136 235.8**	**132 484.3**	**171 805.5**	**175 563.6**	**28.2**	**25.8**	**26.5**	**31.4**	**32.0**
1000 Taxes on income, profits and capital gains	**65 681.6**	**47 398.2**	**40 034.3**	**52 657.9**	**56 083.2**	**14.2**	**9.0**	**8.0**	**9.6**	**10.2**
1100 Of individuals	36 393.6	28 677.3	24 662.7	32 324.6	33 491.8	7.8	5.4	4.9	5.9	6.1
1200 Corporate	29 288.0	18 720.9	15 371.6	20 333.3	22 591.4	6.3	3.5	3.1	3.7	4.1
1300 Unallocable between 1100 and 1200	0.0	0.0	0.0	0.0	0.0	0.0	0.0	0.0	0.0	0.0
2000 Social security contributions	**34 612.6**	**47 968.3**	**54 460.6**	**68 615.8**	**70 588.1**	**7.5**	**9.1**	**10.9**	**12.5**	**12.9**
2100 Employees	13 895.0	19 829.9	23 592.6	32 577.8	33 656.3	3.0	3.8	4.7	6.0	6.1
2200 Employers	16 648.8	22 455.5	24 674.2	31 648.1	32 663.5	3.6	4.2	4.9	5.8	6.0
2300 Self-employed or non-employed	4 068.8	5 682.9	6 193.8	4 389.8	4 268.3	0.9	1.1	1.2	0.8	0.8
2400 Unallocable between 2100, 2200 and 2300	0.0	0.0	0.0	0.0	0.0	0.0	0.0	0.0	0.0	0.0
3000 Taxes on payroll and workforce	**0.0**	**0.0**	**0.0**	**0.0**	**0.0**	**0.0**	**0.0**	**0.0**	**0.0**	**0.0**
4000 Taxes on property	**12 296.3**	**14 294.4**	**12 878.3**	**14 073.1**	**14 195.5**	**2.7**	**2.7**	**2.6**	**2.6**	**2.6**
4100 Recurrent taxes on immovable property	7 098.5	10 413.7	10 225.0	10 323.1	10 385.7	1.5	2.0	2.0	1.9	1.9
4200 Recurrent taxes on net wealth	0.0	0.0	0.0	0.0	0.0	0.0	0.0	0.0	0.0	0.0
4300 Estate, inheritance and gift taxes	1 918.0	1 782.2	1 250.4	2 292.0	2 333.3	0.4	0.3	0.3	0.4	0.4
4400 Taxes on financial and capital transactions	3 279.8	2 098.5	1 402.9	1 458.0	1 476.5	0.7	0.4	0.3	0.3	0.3
4500 Non-recurrent taxes	0.0	0.0	0.0	0.0	0.0	0.0	0.0	0.0	0.0	0.0
4600 Other recurrent taxes on property	0.0	0.0	0.0	0.0	0.0	0.0	0.0	0.0	0.0	0.0
5000 Taxes on goods and services	**17 916.8**	**26 227.2**	**24 730.2**	**36 031.3**	**34 251.8**	**3.9**	**5.0**	**5.0**	**6.6**	**6.2**
5100 Taxes on production, sale, transfer, etc	15 646.5	23 180.2	22 160.4	33 581.7	31 754.0	3.4	4.4	4.4	6.1	5.8
5110 General taxes	5 778.3	12 350.3	12 675.2	22 249.2	22 496.4	1.2	2.3	2.5	4.1	4.1
5111 Value added taxes	5 778.3	12 350.3	12 675.2	22 249.2	22 496.4	1.2	2.3	2.5	4.1	4.1
5120 Taxes on specific goods and services	9 868.2	10 829.9	9 485.2	11 332.5	9 257.6	2.1	2.0	1.9	2.1	1.7
5121 Excises	8 637.2	9 837.0	8 622.4	10 241.0	8 120.8	1.9	1.9	1.7	1.9	1.5
5200 Taxes on use of goods and perform activities	2 270.3	3 047.0	2 569.8	2 449.6	2 497.8	0.5	0.6	0.5	0.4	0.5
5300 Unallocable between 5100 and 5200	0.0	0.0	0.0	0.0	0.0	0.0	0.0	0.0	0.0	0.0
6000 Other taxes	**335.4**	**347.7**	**381.1**	**427.4**	**445.0**	**0.1**	**0.1**	**0.1**	**0.1**	**0.1**
Non-wastable tax credits										
Non-wastable tax credits against 1000	..	..	..	..	..	..	..	..	..	..
Transfer component	..	..	..	..	..	..	..	..	..	..
Tax expenditure component	..	..	..	..	..	..	..	..	..	..

.. Not available

Note: More detailed country data and country notes are available in online chapter 5 "Detailed country tables": https://doi.org/10.1787/0bbc27da-en. Full time series can be accessed at http://oe.cd/full-time-series.

Source: Tax Bureau, Ministry of Finance.

StatLink https://doi.org/10.1787/888934210920

Table 4.38. Japan, tax revenue and % of GDP by level of government and main taxes

	Billion JPY					% of GDP				
	1990	2000	2010	2017	2018	1990	2000	2010	2017	2018
Federal or Central government										
Total tax revenue	**62 779.7**	**52 720.8**	**43 707.4**	**64 284.1**	**64 224.1**	**13.5**	**10.0**	**8.8**	**11.7**	**11.7**
1000 Taxes on income, profits and capital gains	44 379.1	30 536.2	23 372.1	33 782.5	35 402.6	9.6	5.8	4.7	6.2	6.5
2000 Social security contributions	0.0	0.0	0.0	0.0	0.0	0.0	0.0	0.0	0.0	0.0
3000 Taxes on payroll and workforce	0.0	0.0	0.0	0.0	0.0	0.0	0.0	0.0	0.0	0.0
4000 Taxes on property	4 601.6	3 314.9	2 274.5	3 343.5	3 406.2	1.0	0.6	0.5	0.6	0.6
5000 Taxes on goods and services	13 799.0	18 869.7	18 060.9	27 158.1	25 413.7	3.0	3.6	3.6	5.0	4.6
6000 Other taxes	0.0	0.0	0.0	0.0	1.6	0.0	0.0	0.0	0.0	0.0
State/Regional										
Total tax revenue	..	..	..	..	..	..	..	..	..	..
1000 Taxes on income, profits and capital gains	..	..	..	..	..	..	..	..	..	..
2000 Social security contributions	..	..	..	..	..	..	..	..	..	..
3000 Taxes on payroll and workforce	..	..	..	..	..	..	..	..	..	..
4000 Taxes on property	..	..	..	..	..	..	..	..	..	..
5000 Taxes on goods and services	..	..	..	..	..	..	..	..	..	..
6000 Other taxes	..	..	..	..	..	..	..	..	..	..
Local government										
Total tax revenue	**33 450.4**	**35 546.7**	**34 316.3**	**38 905.6**	**40 751.4**	**7.2**	**6.7**	**6.9**	**7.1**	**7.4**
1000 Taxes on income, profits and capital gains	21 302.5	16 862.0	16 662.3	18 875.4	20 680.6	4.6	3.2	3.3	3.4	3.8
2000 Social security contributions	0.0	0.0	0.0	0.0	0.0	0.0	0.0	0.0	0.0	0.0
3000 Taxes on payroll and workforce	0.0	0.0	0.0	0.0	0.0	0.0	0.0	0.0	0.0	0.0
4000 Taxes on property	7 694.7	10 979.5	10 603.8	10 729.6	10 789.3	1.7	2.1	2.1	2.0	2.0
5000 Taxes on goods and services	4 117.8	7 357.5	6 669.2	8 873.2	8 838.1	0.9	1.4	1.3	1.6	1.6
6000 Other taxes	335.4	347.7	381.1	427.4	443.4	0.1	0.1	0.1	0.1	0.1
Social Security Funds										
Total tax revenue	**34 612.6**	**47 968.3**	**54 460.6**	**68 615.8**	**70 588.1**	**7.5**	**9.1**	**10.9**	**12.5**	**12.9**
1000 Taxes on income, profits and capital gains	0.0	0.0	0.0	0.0	0.0	0.0	0.0	0.0	0.0	0.0
2000 Social security contributions	34 612.6	47 968.3	54 460.6	68 615.8	70 588.1	7.5	9.1	10.9	12.5	12.9
3000 Taxes on payroll and workforce	0.0	0.0	0.0	0.0	0.0	0.0	0.0	0.0	0.0	0.0
4000 Taxes on property	0.0	0.0	0.0	0.0	0.0	0.0	0.0	0.0	0.0	0.0
5000 Taxes on goods and services	0.0	0.0	0.0	0.0	0.0	0.0	0.0	0.0	0.0	0.0
6000 Other taxes	0.0	0.0	0.0	0.0	0.0	0.0	0.0	0.0	0.0	0.0

.. Not available

Note: More detailed country data and country notes are available in online chapter 6 "Tax revenues by sub-sectors of general government": https://doi.org/10.1787/0bbc27da-en. Full time series can be accessed at http://oe.cd/full-time-series.

Source: Tax Bureau, Ministry of Finance.

StatLink https://doi.org/10.1787/888934210939

Table 4.39. Korea, tax revenue and % of GDP by selected tax category

	Billion KRW					% of GDP				
	1990	2000	2010	2017	2018	1990	2000	2010	2017	2018
Total tax revenue	**37 261.7**	**136 295.0**	**295 968.0**	**465 470.0**	**506 548.0**	**18.4**	**20.9**	**22.4**	**25.4**	**26.8**
1000 Taxes on income, profits and capital gains	**12 203.5**	**39 254.0**	**82 905.0**	**149 420.0**	**172 976.0**	**6.0**	**6.0**	**6.3**	**8.1**	**9.1**
1100 Of individuals	7 440.4	19 950.0	42 098.0	83 121.0	93 274.0	3.7	3.1	3.2	4.5	4.9
1200 Corporate	4 756.6	19 271.0	40 807.0	66 299.0	79 702.0	2.3	3.0	3.1	3.6	4.2
1300 Unallocable between 1100 and 1200	6.5	33.0	0.0	0.0	0.0	0.0	0.0	0.0	0.0	0.0
2000 Social security contributions	**3 760.0**	**22 759.0**	**69 090.0**	**119 676.0**	**128 660.0**	**1.9**	**3.5**	**5.2**	**6.5**	**6.8**
2100 Employees	1 464.0	8 578.0	28 213.0	51 125.0	55 257.0	0.7	1.3	2.1	2.8	2.9
2200 Employers	1 694.0	9 409.0	30 856.0	54 063.0	58 712.0	0.8	1.4	2.3	2.9	3.1
2300 Self-employed or non-employed	602.0	4 772.0	10 021.0	14 488.0	14 691.0	0.3	0.7	0.8	0.8	0.8
2400 Unallocable between 2100, 2200 and 2300	0.0	0.0	0.0	0.0	0.0	0.0	0.0	0.0	0.0	0.0
3000 Taxes on payroll and workforce	**152.8**	**258.0**	**714.0**	**1 376.0**	**1 492.0**	**0.1**	**0.0**	**0.1**	**0.1**	**0.1**
4000 Taxes on property	**4 388.9**	**16 846.0**	**33 516.0**	**54 406.0**	**58 811.0**	**2.2**	**2.6**	**2.5**	**3.0**	**3.1**
4100 Recurrent taxes on immovable property	980.0	3 385.0	9 270.0	14 319.0	15 589.0	0.5	0.5	0.7	0.8	0.8
4200 Recurrent taxes on net wealth	0.0	0.0	0.0	0.0	0.0	0.0	0.0	0.0	0.0	0.0
4300 Estate, inheritance and gift taxes	353.9	989.0	3 076.0	6 785.0	7 359.0	0.2	0.2	0.2	0.4	0.4
4400 Taxes on financial and capital transactions	2 959.7	11 935.0	21 170.0	33 302.0	35 863.0	1.5	1.8	1.6	1.8	1.9
4500 Non-recurrent taxes	95.3	537.0	0.0	0.0	0.0	0.0	0.1	0.0	0.0	0.0
4600 Other recurrent taxes on property	0.0	0.0	0.0	0.0	0.0	0.0	0.0	0.0	0.0	0.0
5000 Taxes on goods and services	**16 497.5**	**52 271.0**	**99 769.0**	**129 065.0**	**133 095.0**	**8.1**	**8.0**	**7.5**	**7.0**	**7.0**
5100 Taxes on production, sale, transfer, etc	16 023.5	50 023.0	96 573.0	121 293.0	125 207.0	7.9	7.7	7.3	6.6	6.6
5110 General taxes	6 964.4	23 212.0	51 800.0	74 361.0	77 471.0	3.4	3.6	3.9	4.1	4.1
5111 Value added taxes	6 964.4	23 212.0	51 800.0	74 361.0	77 471.0	3.4	3.6	3.9	4.1	4.1
5120 Taxes on specific goods and services	9 059.1	26 811.0	44 773.0	46 932.0	47 736.0	4.5	4.1	3.4	2.6	2.5
5121 Excises	4 923.7	18 155.0	31 340.0	35 779.0	36 218.0	2.4	2.8	2.4	1.9	1.9
5200 Taxes on use of goods and perform activities	473.9	2 248.0	3 196.0	7 772.0	7 888.0	0.2	0.3	0.2	0.4	0.4
5300 Unallocable between 5100 and 5200	0.0	0.0	0.0	0.0	0.0	0.0	0.0	0.0	0.0	0.0
6000 Other taxes	**259.1**	**4 907.0**	**9 974.0**	**11 527.0**	**11 514.0**	**0.1**	**0.8**	**0.8**	**0.6**	**0.6**
Non-wastable tax credits										
Non-wastable tax credits against 1000	..	..	..	..	..	..	..	..	..	..
Transfer component	..	..	..	..	..	..	..	..	..	..
Tax expenditure component	..	..	..	..	..	..	..	..	..	..

.. Not available

Note: More detailed country data and country notes are available in online chapter 5 "Detailed country tables": https://doi.org/10.1787/0bbc27da-en. Full time series can be accessed at http://oe.cd/full-time-series.

Source: Ministry of Finance and Economy, Ministry of Home Affairs.

StatLink https://doi.org/10.1787/888934210958

Table 4.40. Korea, tax revenue and % of GDP by level of government and main taxes

	Billion KRW					% of GDP				
	1990	2000	2010	2017	2018	1990	2000	2010	2017	2018
Federal or Central government										
Total tax revenue	**27 140.8**	**92 935.0**	**177 718.0**	**265 385.0**	**293 570.0**	**13.4**	**14.3**	**13.4**	**14.5**	**15.5**
1000 Taxes on income, profits and capital gains	11 655.2	35 824.0	75 352.0	134 685.0	155 969.0	5.7	5.5	5.7	7.3	8.2
2000 Social security contributions	0.0	0.0	0.0	0.0	0.0	0.0	0.0	0.0	0.0	0.0
3000 Taxes on payroll and workforce	29.3	0.0	0.0	0.0	0.0	0.0	0.0	0.0	0.0	0.0
4000 Taxes on property	866.3	5 866.0	11 288.0	16 946.0	19 920.0	0.4	0.9	0.9	0.9	1.1
5000 Taxes on goods and services	14 377.5	46 812.0	86 629.0	109 365.0	113 251.0	7.1	7.2	6.6	6.0	6.0
6000 Other taxes	212.5	4 433.0	4 449.0	4 389.0	4 430.0	0.1	0.7	0.3	0.2	0.2
State/Regional										
Total tax revenue	..	..	..	..	..	..	..	..	..	..
1000 Taxes on income, profits and capital gains	..	..	..	..	..	..	..	..	..	..
2000 Social security contributions	..	..	..	..	..	..	..	..	..	..
3000 Taxes on payroll and workforce	..	..	..	..	..	..	..	..	..	..
4000 Taxes on property	..	..	..	..	..	..	..	..	..	..
5000 Taxes on goods and services	..	..	..	..	..	..	..	..	..	..
6000 Other taxes	..	..	..	..	..	..	..	..	..	..
Local government										
Total tax revenue	**6 360.9**	**20 601.0**	**49 160.0**	**80 409.0**	**84 318.0**	**3.1**	**3.2**	**3.7**	**4.4**	**4.5**
1000 Taxes on income, profits and capital gains	548.3	3 430.0	7 553.0	14 735.0	17 007.0	0.3	0.5	0.6	0.8	0.9
2000 Social security contributions	0.0	0.0	0.0	0.0	0.0	0.0	0.0	0.0	0.0	0.0
3000 Taxes on payroll and workforce	123.5	258.0	714.0	1 376.0	1 492.0	0.1	0.0	0.1	0.1	0.1
4000 Taxes on property	3 522.6	10 980.0	22 228.0	37 460.0	38 891.0	1.7	1.7	1.7	2.0	2.1
5000 Taxes on goods and services	2 120.0	5 459.0	13 140.0	19 700.0	19 844.0	1.0	0.8	1.0	1.1	1.0
6000 Other taxes	46.6	474.0	5 525.0	7 138.0	7 084.0	0.0	0.1	0.4	0.4	0.4
Social Security Funds										
Total tax revenue	**3 760.0**	**22 759.0**	**69 090.0**	**119 676.0**	**128 660.0**	**1.9**	**3.5**	**5.2**	**6.5**	**6.8**
1000 Taxes on income, profits and capital gains	0.0	0.0	0.0	0.0	0.0	0.0	0.0	0.0	0.0	0.0
2000 Social security contributions	3 760.0	22 759.0	69 090.0	119 676.0	128 660.0	1.9	3.5	5.2	6.5	6.8
3000 Taxes on payroll and workforce	0.0	0.0	0.0	0.0	0.0	0.0	0.0	0.0	0.0	0.0
4000 Taxes on property	0.0	0.0	0.0	0.0	0.0	0.0	0.0	0.0	0.0	0.0
5000 Taxes on goods and services	0.0	0.0	0.0	0.0	0.0	0.0	0.0	0.0	0.0	0.0
6000 Other taxes	0.0	0.0	0.0	0.0	0.0	0.0	0.0	0.0	0.0	0.0

.. Not available

Note: More detailed country data and country notes are available in online chapter 6 "Tax revenues by sub-sectors of general government": https://doi.org/10.1787/0bbc27da-en. Full time series can be accessed at http://oe.cd/full-time-series.

Source: Ministry of Finance and Economy, Ministry of Home Affairs.

StatLink https://doi.org/10.1787/888934210977

Table 4.41. Latvia, tax revenue and % of GDP by selected tax category

	Billion EUR					% of GDP				
	1990	2000	2010	2017	2018	1990	2000	2010	2017	2018
Total tax revenue	..	**2.0**	**5.2**	**8.4**	**9.1**	..	**29.1**	**28.7**	**31.4**	**31.2**
1000 Taxes on income, profits and capital gains	..	**0.5**	**1.3**	**2.2**	**2.0**	..	**7.0**	**7.2**	**8.2**	**7.1**
1100 Of individuals	..	0.4	1.1	1.8	1.7	..	5.5	6.2	6.6	6.0
1200 Corporate	..	0.1	0.2	0.4	0.3	..	1.5	1.0	1.6	1.1
1300 Unallocable between 1100 and 1200	..	0.0	0.0	0.0	0.0	..	0.0	0.0	0.0	0.0
2000 Social security contributions	..	**0.7**	**1.6**	**2.3**	**2.7**	..	**9.8**	**8.6**	**8.4**	**9.1**
2100 Employees	..	0.2	0.4	0.6	0.8	..	2.4	2.2	2.3	2.7
2200 Employers	..	0.5	1.2	1.6	1.9	..	7.3	6.4	6.0	6.4
2300 Self-employed or non-employed	..	0.0	0.0	0.0	0.0	..	0.0	0.1	0.1	0.1
2400 Unallocable between 2100, 2200 and 2300	..	0.0	0.0	0.0	0.0	..	0.0	0.0	0.0	0.0
3000 Taxes on payroll and workforce	..	**0.0**	**0.0**	**0.0**	**0.0**	..	**0.0**	**0.0**	**0.0**	**0.0**
4000 Taxes on property	..	**0.1**	**0.2**	**0.3**	**0.3**	..	**1.1**	**0.9**	**1.0**	**0.9**
4100 Recurrent taxes on immovable property	..	0.1	0.1	0.2	0.2	..	0.9	0.7	0.9	0.8
4200 Recurrent taxes on net wealth	..	0.0	0.0	0.0	0.0	..	0.0	0.0	0.0	0.0
4300 Estate, inheritance and gift taxes	..	0.0	0.0	0.0	0.0	..	0.0	0.0	0.0	0.0
4400 Taxes on financial and capital transactions	..	0.0	0.0	0.0	0.0	..	0.2	0.1	0.2	0.1
4500 Non-recurrent taxes	..	0.0	0.0	0.0	0.0	..	0.0	0.0	0.0	0.0
4600 Other recurrent taxes on property	..	0.0	0.0	0.0	0.0	..	0.0	0.0	0.0	0.0
5000 Taxes on goods and services	..	**0.8**	**2.2**	**3.7**	**4.1**	..	**11.2**	**12.0**	**13.7**	**14.1**
5100 Taxes on production, sale, transfer, etc	..	0.7	2.0	3.5	3.9	..	10.8	11.3	13.0	13.3
5110 General taxes	..	0.5	1.3	2.4	2.7	..	7.0	7.2	9.1	9.3
5111 Value added taxes	..	0.5	1.2	2.2	2.4	..	7.0	6.7	8.1	8.4
5120 Taxes on specific goods and services	..	0.3	0.7	1.0	1.2	..	3.8	4.1	3.9	4.1
5121 Excises	..	0.2	0.6	0.9	1.0	..	3.4	3.6	3.4	3.6
5200 Taxes on use of goods and perform activities	..	0.0	0.1	0.2	0.2	..	0.5	0.7	0.7	0.7
5300 Unallocable between 5100 and 5200	..	0.0	0.0	0.0	0.0	..	0.0	0.0	0.0	0.0
6000 Other taxes	..	**0.0**	**0.0**	**0.0**	**0.0**	..	**0.0**	**0.0**	**0.0**	**0.0**
Non-wastable tax credits										
Non-wastable tax credits against 1000	..	..	..	..	..	..	..	..	..	..
Transfer component	..	..	..	..	..	..	..	..	..	..
Tax expenditure component	..	..	..	..	..	..	..	..	..	..
Revenues collected on behalf of the EU										
Revenues collected on behalf of the EU, total	..	..	0.0	0.1	0.1	..	..	0.1	0.2	0.2
Customs duties	..	..	0.0	0.0	0.1	..	..	0.1	0.2	0.2
SRF contributions	..	..	..	0.0	0.0	..	..	..	0.0	0.0

.. Not available

Note: More detailed country data and country notes are available in online chapter 5 "Detailed country tables": https://doi.org/10.1787/0bbc27da-en. Full time series can be accessed at http://oe.cd/full-time-series.

Source: Ministry of Finance.

StatLink https://doi.org/10.1787/888934210996

Table 4.42. Latvia, tax revenue and % of GDP by level of government and main taxes

	Billion EUR					% of GDP				
	1990	2000	2010	2017	2018	1990	2000	2010	2017	2018
Federal or Central government										
Total tax revenue	..	**1.0**	**2.5**	**4.5**	**4.8**	..	**14.4**	**14.2**	**16.7**	**16.5**
1000 Taxes on income, profits and capital gains	..	0.2	0.4	0.8	0.6	..	3.1	2.2	3.1	2.2
2000 Social security contributions	..	0.0	0.0	0.0	0.1	..	0.0	0.0	0.0	0.3
3000 Taxes on payroll and workforce	..	0.0	0.0	0.0	0.0	..	0.0	0.0	0.0	0.0
4000 Taxes on property	..	0.0	0.0	0.0	0.0	..	0.2	0.2	0.2	0.2
5000 Taxes on goods and services	..	0.8	2.1	3.6	4.0	..	11.2	11.8	13.4	13.8
6000 Other taxes	..	0.0	0.0	0.0	0.0	..	0.0	0.0	0.0	0.0
State/Regional										
Total tax revenue	..	..	..	..	..	..	..	..	..	..
1000 Taxes on income, profits and capital gains	..	..	..	..	..	..	..	..	..	..
2000 Social security contributions	..	..	..	..	..	..	..	..	..	..
3000 Taxes on payroll and workforce	..	..	..	..	..	..	..	..	..	..
4000 Taxes on property	..	..	..	..	..	..	..	..	..	..
5000 Taxes on goods and services	..	..	..	..	..	..	..	..	..	..
6000 Other taxes	..	..	..	..	..	..	..	..	..	..
Local government										
Total tax revenue	..	**0.3**	**1.0**	**1.6**	**1.6**	..	**4.9**	**5.7**	**6.0**	**5.7**
1000 Taxes on income, profits and capital gains	..	0.3	0.9	1.4	1.4	..	3.9	5.0	5.1	4.8
2000 Social security contributions	..	0.0	0.0	0.0	0.0	..	0.0	0.0	0.0	0.0
3000 Taxes on payroll and workforce	..	0.0	0.0	0.0	0.0	..	0.0	0.0	0.0	0.0
4000 Taxes on property	..	0.1	0.1	0.2	0.2	..	0.9	0.7	0.9	0.8
5000 Taxes on goods and services	..	0.0	0.0	0.0	0.0	..	0.1	0.1	0.1	0.1
6000 Other taxes	..	0.0	0.0	0.0	0.0	..	0.0	0.0	0.0	0.0
Social Security Funds										
Total tax revenue	..	**0.7**	**1.6**	**2.3**	**2.6**	..	**9.8**	**8.7**	**8.5**	**8.9**
1000 Taxes on income, profits and capital gains	..	0.0	0.0	0.0	0.0	..	0.0	0.0	0.0	0.0
2000 Social security contributions	..	0.7	1.6	2.3	2.6	..	9.8	8.6	8.4	8.9
3000 Taxes on payroll and workforce	..	0.0	0.0	0.0	0.0	..	0.0	0.0	0.0	0.0
4000 Taxes on property	..	0.0	0.0	0.0	0.0	..	0.0	0.0	0.0	0.0
5000 Taxes on goods and services	..	0.0	0.0	0.0	0.0	..	0.0	0.0	0.0	0.0
6000 Other taxes	..	0.0	0.0	0.0	0.0	..	0.0	0.0	0.0	0.0

.. Not available

Note: More detailed country data and country notes are available in online chapter 6 "Tax revenues by sub-sectors of general government": https://doi.org/10.1787/0bbc27da-en. Full time series can be accessed at http://oe.cd/full-time-series.

Source: Ministry of Finance.

StatLink https://doi.org/10.1787/888934211015

Table 4.43. Lithuania, tax revenue and % of GDP by selected tax category

	Billion EUR					% of GDP				
	1990	2000	2010	2017	2018	1990	2000	2010	2017	2018
Total tax revenue	..	**4.1**	**7.9**	**12.5**	**13.7**	..	**30.8**	**28.4**	**29.5**	**30.2**
1000 Taxes on income, profits and capital gains	..	**1.1**	**1.3**	**2.3**	**2.5**	..	**8.3**	**4.6**	**5.3**	**5.6**
1100 Of individuals	..	1.0	1.0	1.6	1.8	..	7.6	3.6	3.8	4.1
1200 Corporate	..	0.1	0.3	0.6	0.7	..	0.7	1.0	1.5	1.5
1300 Unallocable between 1100 and 1200	..	0.0	0.0	0.0	0.0	..	0.0	0.0	0.0	0.0
2000 Social security contributions	..	**1.3**	**3.3**	**5.2**	**5.7**	..	**9.9**	**11.7**	**12.2**	**12.7**
2100 Employees	..	0.1	0.6	1.1	1.2	..	0.8	2.3	2.5	2.6
2200 Employers	..	1.1	2.1	3.5	3.9	..	8.1	7.5	8.3	8.6
2300 Self-employed or non-employed	..	0.1	0.5	0.6	0.7	..	1.0	1.9	1.4	1.5
2400 Unallocable between 2100, 2200 and 2300	..	0.0	0.0	0.0	0.0	..	0.0	0.0	0.0	0.0
3000 Taxes on payroll and workforce	..	**0.0**	**0.0**	**0.0**	**0.0**	..	**0.0**	**0.0**	**0.0**	**0.0**
4000 Taxes on property	..	**0.1**	**0.1**	**0.1**	**0.1**	..	**0.5**	**0.4**	**0.3**	**0.3**
4100 Recurrent taxes on immovable property	..	0.1	0.1	0.1	0.1	..	0.5	0.4	0.3	0.3
4200 Recurrent taxes on net wealth	..	0.0	0.0	0.0	0.0	..	0.0	0.0	0.0	0.0
4300 Estate, inheritance and gift taxes	..	0.0	0.0	0.0	0.0	..	0.0	0.0	0.0	0.0
4400 Taxes on financial and capital transactions	..	0.0	0.0	0.0	0.0	..	0.0	0.0	0.0	0.0
4500 Non-recurrent taxes	..	0.0	0.0	0.0	0.0	..	0.0	0.0	0.0	0.0
4600 Other recurrent taxes on property	..	0.0	0.0	0.0	0.0	..	0.0	0.0	0.0	0.0
5000 Taxes on goods and services	..	**1.6**	**3.3**	**4.9**	**5.2**	..	**12.1**	**11.7**	**11.6**	**11.6**
5100 Taxes on production, sale, transfer, etc	..	1.6	3.2	4.8	5.2	..	11.6	11.5	11.4	11.4
5110 General taxes	..	1.1	2.2	3.3	3.6	..	8.1	7.8	7.9	7.8
5111 Value added taxes	..	1.0	2.2	3.3	3.5	..	7.5	7.8	7.8	7.8
5120 Taxes on specific goods and services	..	0.5	1.0	1.5	1.6	..	3.5	3.6	3.5	3.5
5121 Excises	..	0.4	0.9	1.3	1.4	..	3.2	3.2	3.2	3.2
5200 Taxes on use of goods and perform activities	..	0.1	0.1	0.1	0.1	..	0.5	0.3	0.2	0.2
5300 Unallocable between 5100 and 5200	..	0.0	0.0	0.0	0.0	..	0.0	0.0	0.0	0.0
6000 Other taxes	..	**0.0**	**0.0**	**0.0**	**0.0**	..	**0.0**	**0.0**	**0.0**	**0.0**
Non-wastable tax credits										
Non-wastable tax credits against 1000	..	..	..	..	..	..	..	..	..	..
Transfer component	..	..	..	..	..	..	..	..	..	..
Tax expenditure component	..	..	..	..	..	..	..	..	..	..
Revenues collected on behalf of the EU										
Revenues collected on behalf of the EU, total	..	..	0.1	0.1	0.1	..	..	0.2	0.3	0.3
Customs duties	..	..	0.1	0.1	0.1	..	..	0.2	0.2	0.3
SRF contributions	..	..	..	0.0	0.0	..	..	..	0.0	0.0

.. Not available

Note: More detailed country data and country notes are available in online chapter 5 "Detailed country tables": https://doi.org/10.1787/0bbc27da-en. Full time series can be accessed at http://oe.cd/full-time-series.

The total tax revenue has been reduced by the amount of any capital transfer that represents uncollected taxes. The capital transfer has been allocated between tax headings in proportion to the reported tax revenue. Therefore, the tax revenue amounts are different to those reported in the detailed country data available in online chapter 5 "Detailed country tables".

Source: Ministry of Finance.

StatLink https://doi.org/10.1787/888934211034

Table 4.44. Lithuania, tax revenue and % of GDP by level of government and main taxes

	Billion EUR					% of GDP				
	1990	2000	2010	2017	2018	1990	2000	2010	2017	2018
Federal or Central government										
Total tax revenue	..	**2.7**	**4.5**	**7.0**	**7.6**	..	**20.3**	**16.0**	**16.6**	**16.9**
1000 Taxes on income, profits and capital gains	..	1.1	1.3	2.3	2.5	..	8.3	4.6	5.3	5.6
2000 Social security contributions	..	0.0	0.0	0.0	0.0	..	0.0	0.0	0.0	0.0
3000 Taxes on payroll and workforce	..	0.0	0.0	0.0	0.0	..	0.0	0.0	0.0	0.0
4000 Taxes on property	..	0.0	0.0	0.0	0.0	..	0.0	0.0	0.0	0.0
5000 Taxes on goods and services	..	1.6	3.2	4.8	5.1	..	12.0	11.4	11.3	11.3
6000 Other taxes	..	0.0	0.0	0.0	0.0	..	0.0	0.0	0.0	0.0
State/Regional										
Total tax revenue	..	..	..	..	..	..	..	..	..	..
1000 Taxes on income, profits and capital gains	..	..	..	..	..	..	..	..	..	..
2000 Social security contributions	..	..	..	..	..	..	..	..	..	..
3000 Taxes on payroll and workforce	..	..	..	..	..	..	..	..	..	..
4000 Taxes on property	..	..	..	..	..	..	..	..	..	..
5000 Taxes on goods and services	..	..	..	..	..	..	..	..	..	..
6000 Other taxes	..	..	..	..	..	..	..	..	..	..
Local government										
Total tax revenue	..	**0.1**	**0.1**	**0.1**	**0.2**	..	**0.6**	**0.5**	**0.3**	**0.4**
1000 Taxes on income, profits and capital gains	..	0.0	0.0	0.0	0.0	..	0.0	0.0	0.0	0.0
2000 Social security contributions	..	0.0	0.0	0.0	0.0	..	0.0	0.0	0.0	0.0
3000 Taxes on payroll and workforce	..	0.0	0.0	0.0	0.0	..	0.0	0.0	0.0	0.0
4000 Taxes on property	..	0.1	0.1	0.1	0.1	..	0.5	0.4	0.3	0.3
5000 Taxes on goods and services	..	0.0	0.0	0.0	0.0	..	0.1	0.1	0.0	0.1
6000 Other taxes	..	0.0	0.0	0.0	0.0	..	0.0	0.0	0.0	0.0
Social Security Funds										
Total tax revenue	..	**1.3**	**3.3**	**5.2**	**5.7**	..	**9.9**	**11.7**	**12.2**	**12.7**
1000 Taxes on income, profits and capital gains	..	0.0	0.0	0.0	0.0	..	0.0	0.0	0.0	0.0
2000 Social security contributions	..	1.3	3.3	5.2	5.7	..	9.9	11.7	12.2	12.7
3000 Taxes on payroll and workforce	..	0.0	0.0	0.0	0.0	..	0.0	0.0	0.0	0.0
4000 Taxes on property	..	0.0	0.0	0.0	0.0	..	0.0	0.0	0.0	0.0
5000 Taxes on goods and services	..	0.0	0.0	0.0	0.0	..	0.0	0.0	0.0	0.0
6000 Other taxes	..	0.0	0.0	0.0	0.0	..	0.0	0.0	0.0	0.0

.. Not available

Note: More detailed country data and country notes are available in online chapter 6 "Tax revenues by sub-sectors of general government": https://doi.org/10.1787/0bbc27da-en. Full time series can be accessed at http://oe.cd/full-time-series.

The total tax revenue has been reduced by the amount of any capital transfer that represents uncollected taxes. The capital transfer has been allocated between tax headings in proportion to the reported tax revenue. Therefore, the tax revenue amounts are different to those reported in the detailed country data available in online chapter 6 "Tax revenues by sub-sectors of general government".

Source: Ministry of Finance.

StatLink https://doi.org/10.1787/888934211053

Table 4.45. Luxembourg, tax revenue and % of GDP by selected tax category

	Billion EUR					% of GDP				
	1990	2000	2010	2017	2018	1990	2000	2010	2017	2018
Total tax revenue	**3.7**	**8.5**	**15.1**	**21.4**	**23.9**	**33.5**	**36.9**	**37.5**	**37.6**	**39.7**
1000 Taxes on income, profits and capital gains	**1.5**	**3.1**	**5.5**	**8.0**	**9.4**	**13.5**	**13.5**	**13.6**	**14.0**	**15.6**
1100 Of individuals	0.9	1.6	3.2	5.1	5.6	8.1	6.8	7.9	8.9	9.3
1200 Corporate	0.6	1.5	2.3	2.9	3.8	5.4	6.6	5.8	5.1	6.3
1300 Unallocable between 1100 and 1200	0.0	0.0	0.0	0.0	0.0	0.0	0.0	0.0	0.0	0.0
2000 Social security contributions	**1.0**	**2.2**	**4.4**	**6.1**	**6.5**	**9.2**	**9.6**	**10.9**	**10.8**	**10.8**
2100 Employees	0.4	1.0	2.0	2.8	3.0	3.5	4.3	5.0	4.9	4.9
2200 Employers	0.5	1.0	1.9	2.6	2.7	4.5	4.2	4.7	4.5	4.5
2300 Self-employed or non-employed	0.1	0.3	0.5	0.8	0.8	1.2	1.2	1.2	1.4	1.3
2400 Unallocable between 2100, 2200 and 2300	0.0	0.0	0.0	0.0	0.0	0.0	0.0	0.0	0.0	0.0
3000 Taxes on payroll and workforce	**0.0**	**0.0**	**0.0**	**0.0**	**0.0**	**0.0**	**0.0**	**0.0**	**0.0**	**0.0**
4000 Taxes on property	**0.3**	**0.9**	**1.1**	**2.1**	**2.3**	**2.8**	**3.9**	**2.6**	**3.6**	**3.9**
4100 Recurrent taxes on immovable property	0.0	0.0	0.0	0.0	0.0	0.1	0.1	0.1	0.1	0.1
4200 Recurrent taxes on net wealth	0.2	0.6	0.8	1.5	1.7	1.6	2.7	2.1	2.7	2.8
4300 Estate, inheritance and gift taxes	0.0	0.0	0.1	0.1	0.1	0.1	0.1	0.1	0.2	0.2
4400 Taxes on financial and capital transactions	0.1	0.2	0.2	0.4	0.5	1.0	1.0	0.4	0.7	0.8
4500 Non-recurrent taxes	0.0	0.0	0.0	0.0	0.0	0.0	0.0	0.0	0.0	0.0
4600 Other recurrent taxes on property	0.0	0.0	0.0	0.0	0.0	0.0	0.0	0.0	0.0	0.0
5000 Taxes on goods and services	**0.9**	**2.3**	**4.1**	**5.2**	**5.7**	**7.9**	**9.8**	**10.3**	**9.1**	**9.4**
5100 Taxes on production, sale, transfer, etc	0.8	2.2	4.1	5.1	5.6	7.7	9.7	10.1	9.0	9.3
5110 General taxes	0.4	1.1	2.6	3.4	3.7	4.0	4.9	6.4	5.9	6.1
5111 Value added taxes	0.4	1.1	2.6	3.4	3.7	4.0	4.9	6.4	5.9	6.1
5120 Taxes on specific goods and services	0.4	1.1	1.5	1.7	1.9	3.7	4.8	3.7	3.1	3.1
5121 Excises	0.4	1.0	1.4	1.4	1.6	3.3	4.5	3.5	2.6	2.6
5200 Taxes on use of goods and perform activities	0.0	0.0	0.1	0.1	0.1	0.2	0.1	0.2	0.2	0.2
5300 Unallocable between 5100 and 5200	0.0	0.0	0.0	0.0	0.0	0.0	0.0	0.0	0.0	0.0
6000 Other taxes	**0.0**	**0.0**	**0.0**	**0.0**	**0.0**	**0.1**	**0.0**	**0.1**	**0.0**	**0.0**
Non-wastable tax credits										
Non-wastable tax credits against 1000	..	..	..	0.2	0.2	..	..	..	0.3	0.3
Transfer component	..	..	..	..	..	..	..	..	..	..
Tax expenditure component	..	..	..	..	..	..	..	..	..	..
Revenues collected on behalf of the EU										
Revenues collected on behalf of the EU, total	0.0	0.0	0.0	0.1	0.2	0.2	0.1	0.0	0.2	0.3
Customs duties	0.0	0.0	0.0	0.0	0.0	0.1	0.1	0.0	0.0	0.0
SRF contributions	..	..	..	0.1	0.1	..	..	..	0.2	0.2

.. Not available

Note: More detailed country data and country notes are available in online chapter 5 "Detailed country tables": https://doi.org/10.1787/0bbc27da-en. Full time series can be accessed at http://oe.cd/full-time-series.

The total tax revenue has been reduced by the amount of any capital transfer that represents uncollected taxes. The capital transfer has been allocated between tax headings in proportion to the reported tax revenue. Therefore, the tax revenue amounts are different to those reported in the detailed country data available in online chapter 5 "Detailed country tables".

Source: General account of the State.

StatLink https://doi.org/10.1787/888934211072

Table 4.46. Luxembourg, tax revenue and % of GDP by level of government and main taxes

	Billion EUR					% of GDP				
	1990	2000	2010	2017	2018	1990	2000	2010	2017	2018
Federal or Central government										
Total tax revenue	**2.4**	**5.8**	**10.1**	**14.4**	**16.3**	**22.1**	**25.3**	**25.2**	**25.4**	**27.2**
1000 Taxes on income, profits and capital gains	1.3	2.6	4.9	7.2	8.4	11.6	11.5	12.1	12.6	14.0
2000 Social security contributions	0.0	0.1	0.1	0.2	0.2	0.1	0.3	0.3	0.3	0.3
3000 Taxes on payroll and workforce	0.0	0.0	0.0	0.0	0.0	0.0	0.0	0.0	0.0	0.0
4000 Taxes on property	0.3	0.9	1.0	2.0	2.2	2.6	3.8	2.5	3.5	3.7
5000 Taxes on goods and services	0.8	2.2	4.1	5.1	5.5	7.7	9.6	10.2	8.9	9.1
6000 Other taxes	0.0	0.0	0.0	0.0	0.0	0.1	0.0	0.0	0.0	0.0
State/Regional										
Total tax revenue	..	..	..	..	..	..	..	..	..	..
1000 Taxes on income, profits and capital gains	..	..	..	..	..	..	..	..	..	..
2000 Social security contributions	..	..	..	..	..	..	..	..	..	..
3000 Taxes on payroll and workforce	..	..	..	..	..	..	..	..	..	..
4000 Taxes on property	..	..	..	..	..	..	..	..	..	..
5000 Taxes on goods and services	..	..	..	..	..	..	..	..	..	..
6000 Other taxes	..	..	..	..	..	..	..	..	..	..
Local government										
Total tax revenue	**0.2**	**0.5**	**0.7**	**0.9**	**1.1**	**2.1**	**2.1**	**1.6**	**1.5**	**1.8**
1000 Taxes on income, profits and capital gains	0.2	0.5	0.6	0.8	1.0	1.9	2.0	1.5	1.4	1.7
2000 Social security contributions	0.0	0.0	0.0	0.0	0.0	0.0	0.0	0.0	0.0	0.0
3000 Taxes on payroll and workforce	0.0	0.0	0.0	0.0	0.0	0.0	0.0	0.0	0.0	0.0
4000 Taxes on property	0.0	0.0	0.0	0.1	0.1	0.2	0.1	0.1	0.1	0.1
5000 Taxes on goods and services	0.0	0.0	0.0	0.0	0.0	0.0	0.0	0.0	0.0	0.0
6000 Other taxes	0.0	0.0	0.0	0.0	0.0	0.0	0.0	0.0	0.0	0.0
Social Security Funds										
Total tax revenue	**1.0**	**2.2**	**4.3**	**6.0**	**6.3**	**9.1**	**9.4**	**10.6**	**10.5**	**10.5**
1000 Taxes on income, profits and capital gains	0.0	0.0	0.0	0.0	0.0	0.0	0.0	0.0	0.0	0.0
2000 Social security contributions	1.0	2.2	4.3	6.0	6.3	9.1	9.4	10.6	10.5	10.5
3000 Taxes on payroll and workforce	0.0	0.0	0.0	0.0	0.0	0.0	0.0	0.0	0.0	0.0
4000 Taxes on property	0.0	0.0	0.0	0.0	0.0	0.0	0.0	0.0	0.0	0.0
5000 Taxes on goods and services	0.0	0.0	0.0	0.0	0.0	0.0	0.0	0.0	0.0	0.0
6000 Other taxes	0.0	0.0	0.0	0.0	0.0	0.0	0.0	0.0	0.0	0.0

.. Not available

Note: More detailed country data and country notes are available in online chapter 6 "Tax revenues by sub-sectors of general government": https://doi.org/10.1787/0bbc27da-en. Full time series can be accessed at http://oe.cd/full-time-series.

The total tax revenue has been reduced by the amount of any capital transfer that represents uncollected taxes. The capital transfer has been allocated between tax headings in proportion to the reported tax revenue. Therefore, the tax revenue amounts are different to those reported in the detailed country data available in online chapter 6 "Tax revenues by sub-sectors of general government".

Source: General account of the State.

StatLink https://doi.org/10.1787/888934211091

Table 4.47. Mexico, tax revenue and % of GDP by selected tax category

	Billion MXN					% of GDP				
	1990	2000	2010	2017	2018	1990	2000	2010	2017	2018
Total tax revenue	**102.0**	**767.2**	**1 716.2**	**3 527.0**	**3 797.9**	**12.1**	**11.5**	**12.8**	**16.1**	**16.2**
1000 Taxes on income, profits and capital gains	**34.7**	**276.5**	**683.6**	**1 572.0**	**1 671.5**	**4.1**	**4.1**	**5.1**	**7.2**	**7.1**
1100 Of individuals	..	..	313.5	754.1	804.2	..	..	2.3	3.4	3.4
1200 Corporate	..	..	246.7	769.2	809.8	..	..	1.8	3.5	3.4
1300 Unallocable between 1100 and 1200	34.7	276.5	123.4	48.7	57.4	4.1	4.1	0.9	0.2	0.2
2000 Social security contributions	**17.2**	**138.2**	**277.5**	**467.6**	**509.1**	**2.0**	**2.1**	**2.1**	**2.1**	**2.2**
2100 Employees	..	..	..	..	..	..	..	..	..	..
2200 Employers	..	..	..	..	..	..	..	..	..	..
2300 Self-employed or non-employed	..	..	..	..	..	..	..	..	..	..
2400 Unallocable between 2100, 2200 and 2300	17.2	138.2	277.5	467.6	509.1	2.0	2.1	2.1	2.1	2.2
3000 Taxes on payroll and workforce	**1.8**	**11.2**	**36.9**	**84.1**	**93.3**	**0.2**	**0.2**	**0.3**	**0.4**	**0.4**
4000 Taxes on property	**1.9**	**14.0**	**39.0**	**67.8**	**77.1**	**0.2**	**0.2**	**0.3**	**0.3**	**0.3**
4100 Recurrent taxes on immovable property	1.0	9.9	25.7	44.7	49.4	0.1	0.1	0.2	0.2	0.2
4200 Recurrent taxes on net wealth	0.0	0.0	0.0	0.0	0.0	0.0	0.0	0.0	0.0	0.0
4300 Estate, inheritance and gift taxes	0.0	0.0	0.0	0.0	0.0	0.0	0.0	0.0	0.0	0.0
4400 Taxes on financial and capital transactions	0.9	4.0	13.2	23.2	27.7	0.1	0.1	0.1	0.1	0.1
4500 Non-recurrent taxes	0.0	0.0	0.0	0.0	0.0	0.0	0.0	0.0	0.0	0.0
4600 Other recurrent taxes on property	0.0	0.0	0.0	0.0	0.0	0.0	0.0	0.0	0.0	0.0
5000 Taxes on goods and services	**44.8**	**319.6**	**651.9**	**1 283.0**	**1 381.7**	**5.3**	**4.8**	**4.9**	**5.9**	**5.9**
5100 Taxes on production, sale, transfer, etc	44.2	310.3	630.1	1 262.8	1 364.2	5.2	4.6	4.7	5.8	5.8
5110 General taxes	26.6	189.6	504.5	816.0	922.2	3.2	2.8	3.8	3.7	3.9
5111 Value added taxes	26.6	189.6	504.5	816.0	922.2	3.2	2.8	3.8	3.7	3.9
5120 Taxes on specific goods and services	17.5	120.7	125.6	446.7	442.0	2.1	1.8	0.9	2.0	1.9
5121 Excises	10.1	86.2	86.1	378.5	358.6	1.2	1.3	0.6	1.7	1.5
5200 Taxes on use of goods and perform activities	0.7	9.3	21.8	20.3	17.5	0.1	0.1	0.2	0.1	0.1
5300 Unallocable between 5100 and 5200	0.0	0.0	0.0	0.0	0.0	0.0	0.0	0.0	0.0	0.0
6000 Other taxes	**1.6**	**7.7**	**27.4**	**52.5**	**65.2**	**0.2**	**0.1**	**0.2**	**0.2**	**0.3**
Non-wastable tax credits										
Non-wastable tax credits against 1000	..	..	40.3	46.8	49.1	..	..	0.3	0.2	0.2
Transfer component	..	..	9.7	1.0	1.2	..	..	0.1	0.0	0.0
Tax expenditure component	..	..	30.6	45.8	47.9	..	..	0.2	0.2	0.2

.. Not available

Note: More detailed country data and country notes are available in online chapter 5 "Detailed country tables": https://doi.org/10.1787/0bbc27da-en. Full time series can be accessed at http://oe.cd/full-time-series.

Source: Ministry of Finance, Economic Department.

StatLink https://doi.org/10.1787/888934211110

Table 4.48. Mexico, tax revenue and % of GDP by level of government and main taxes

	Billion MXN					% of GDP				
	1990	2000	2010	2017	2018	1990	2000	2010	2017	2018
Federal or Central government										
Total tax revenue	**81.4**	**600.5**	**1 351.5**	**2 859.3**	**3 073.4**	**9.7**	**9.0**	**10.1**	**13.0**	**13.1**
1000 Taxes on income, profits and capital gains	34.7	276.5	683.6	1 572.0	1 671.5	4.1	4.1	5.1	7.2	7.1
2000 Social security contributions	0.0	0.0	0.0	0.0	0.0	0.0	0.0	0.0	0.0	0.0
3000 Taxes on payroll and workforce	0.8	0.0	0.0	0.0	0.0	0.1	0.0	0.0	0.0	0.0
4000 Taxes on property	0.0	0.0	0.0	0.0	0.0	0.0	0.0	0.0	0.0	0.0
5000 Taxes on goods and services	44.6	318.1	645.6	1 254.9	1 355.6	5.3	4.8	4.8	5.7	5.8
6000 Other taxes	1.3	5.9	22.2	32.4	46.3	0.2	0.1	0.2	0.1	0.2
State/Regional										
Total tax revenue	**2.2**	**20.5**	**58.3**	**144.2**	**153.7**	**0.3**	**0.3**	**0.4**	**0.7**	**0.7**
1000 Taxes on income, profits and capital gains	0.0	0.0	0.0	0.0	0.0	0.0	0.0	0.0	0.0	0.0
2000 Social security contributions	0.0	0.0	0.0	0.0	0.0	0.0	0.0	0.0	0.0	0.0
3000 Taxes on payroll and workforce	1.0	11.2	36.8	84.1	93.3	0.1	0.2	0.3	0.4	0.4
4000 Taxes on property	0.9	7.0	13.1	26.1	28.7	0.1	0.1	0.1	0.1	0.1
5000 Taxes on goods and services	0.1	1.3	5.8	26.8	24.3	0.0	0.0	0.0	0.1	0.1
6000 Other taxes	0.2	0.9	2.5	7.2	7.4	0.0	0.0	0.0	0.0	0.0
Local government										
Total tax revenue	**1.3**	**8.0**	**29.0**	**56.0**	**61.7**	**0.1**	**0.1**	**0.2**	**0.3**	**0.3**
1000 Taxes on income, profits and capital gains	0.0	0.0	0.0	0.0	0.0	0.0	0.0	0.0	0.0	0.0
2000 Social security contributions	0.0	0.0	0.0	0.0	0.0	0.0	0.0	0.0	0.0	0.0
3000 Taxes on payroll and workforce	0.0	0.0	0.1	0.0	0.0	0.0	0.0	0.0	0.0	0.0
4000 Taxes on property	1.0	6.9	25.8	41.8	48.4	0.1	0.1	0.2	0.2	0.2
5000 Taxes on goods and services	0.1	0.2	0.5	1.4	1.7	0.0	0.0	0.0	0.0	0.0
6000 Other taxes	0.1	0.9	2.6	12.8	11.5	0.0	0.0	0.0	0.1	0.0
Social Security Funds										
Total tax revenue	**17.2**	**138.2**	**277.5**	**467.6**	**509.1**	**2.0**	**2.1**	**2.1**	**2.1**	**2.2**
1000 Taxes on income, profits and capital gains	0.0	0.0	0.0	0.0	0.0	0.0	0.0	0.0	0.0	0.0
2000 Social security contributions	17.2	138.2	277.5	467.6	509.1	2.0	2.1	2.1	2.1	2.2
3000 Taxes on payroll and workforce	0.0	0.0	0.0	0.0	0.0	0.0	0.0	0.0	0.0	0.0
4000 Taxes on property	0.0	0.0	0.0	0.0	0.0	0.0	0.0	0.0	0.0	0.0
5000 Taxes on goods and services	0.0	0.0	0.0	0.0	0.0	0.0	0.0	0.0	0.0	0.0
6000 Other taxes	0.0	0.0	0.0	0.0	0.0	0.0	0.0	0.0	0.0	0.0

Note: More detailed country data and country notes are available in online chapter 6 "Tax revenues by sub-sectors of general government": https://doi.org/10.1787/0bbc27da-en. Full time series can be accessed at http://oe.cd/full-time-series.

Source: Ministry of Finance, Economic Department.

StatLink https://doi.org/10.1787/888934211129

Table 4.49. Netherlands, tax revenue and % of GDP by selected tax category

	Billion EUR					% of GDP				
	1990	2000	2010	2017	2018	1990	2000	2010	2017	2018
Total tax revenue	**104.4**	**166.8**	**227.9**	**285.7**	**300.3**	**39.7**	**36.9**	**35.7**	**38.7**	**38.8**
1000 Taxes on income, profits and capital gains	**33.7**	**43.3**	**63.6**	**85.8**	**88.8**	**12.8**	**9.6**	**9.9**	**11.6**	**11.5**
1100 Of individuals	25.8	25.1	49.0	61.6	61.7	9.8	5.6	7.7	8.3	8.0
1200 Corporate	7.9	18.1	14.6	24.2	27.1	3.0	4.0	2.3	3.3	3.5
1300 Unallocable between 1100 and 1200	0.0	0.0	0.0	0.0	0.0	0.0	0.0	0.0	0.0	0.0
2000 Social security contributions	**39.1**	**64.5**	**82.7**	**101.9**	**108.0**	**14.9**	**14.3**	**12.9**	**13.8**	**14.0**
2100 Employees	24.1	35.3	41.6	39.9	41.8	9.2	7.8	6.5	5.4	5.4
2200 Employers	7.8	18.7	29.4	37.7	40.7	3.0	4.1	4.6	5.1	5.3
2300 Self-employed or non-employed	7.1	10.5	11.7	24.3	25.6	2.7	2.3	1.8	3.3	3.3
2400 Unallocable between 2100, 2200 and 2300	0.0	0.0	0.0	0.0	0.0	0.0	0.0	0.0	0.0	0.0
3000 Taxes on payroll and workforce	**0.0**	**0.0**	**0.0**	**0.0**	**0.0**	**0.0**	**0.0**	**0.0**	**0.0**	**0.0**
4000 Taxes on property	**3.8**	**8.8**	**8.8**	**11.5**	**12.1**	**1.5**	**1.9**	**1.4**	**1.6**	**1.6**
4100 Recurrent taxes on immovable property	1.7	3.1	4.2	6.9	7.4	0.7	0.7	0.7	0.9	1.0
4200 Recurrent taxes on net wealth	0.6	0.8	0.0	0.0	0.0	0.2	0.2	0.0	0.0	0.0
4300 Estate, inheritance and gift taxes	0.5	1.5	1.7	1.8	1.7	0.2	0.3	0.3	0.2	0.2
4400 Taxes on financial and capital transactions	1.0	3.4	2.8	2.7	3.0	0.4	0.8	0.4	0.4	0.4
4500 Non-recurrent taxes	0.0	0.0	0.0	0.0	0.0	0.0	0.0	0.0	0.0	0.0
4600 Other recurrent taxes on property	0.0	0.0	0.0	0.0	0.0	0.0	0.0	0.0	0.0	0.0
5000 Taxes on goods and services	**27.6**	**49.5**	**71.9**	**85.7**	**90.5**	**10.5**	**10.9**	**11.2**	**11.6**	**11.7**
5100 Taxes on production, sale, transfer, etc	25.1	44.9	64.2	76.8	81.5	9.5	9.9	10.1	10.4	10.5
5110 General taxes	17.2	28.9	42.7	49.9	52.8	6.5	6.4	6.7	6.8	6.8
5111 Value added taxes	17.2	28.8	42.7	49.8	52.7	6.5	6.4	6.7	6.8	6.8
5120 Taxes on specific goods and services	7.9	16.0	21.6	26.9	28.7	3.0	3.5	3.4	3.6	3.7
5121 Excises	6.0	13.8	18.4	19.7	21.0	2.3	3.0	2.9	2.7	2.7
5200 Taxes on use of goods and perform activities	2.5	4.6	7.6	8.8	9.1	1.0	1.0	1.2	1.2	1.2
5300 Unallocable between 5100 and 5200	0.0	0.0	0.0	0.0	0.0	0.0	0.0	0.0	0.0	0.0
6000 Other taxes	**0.3**	**0.8**	**1.0**	**0.9**	**0.8**	**0.1**	**0.2**	**0.2**	**0.1**	**0.1**
Non-wastable tax credits										
Non-wastable tax credits against 1000	..	..	..	..	..	..	..	..	..	..
Transfer component	..	..	..	..	..	..	..	..	..	..
Tax expenditure component	..	..	..	..	..	..	..	..	..	..
Revenues collected on behalf of the EU										
Revenues collected on behalf of the EU, total	1.5	1.6	2.0	3.2	3.4	0.6	0.4	0.3	0.4	0.4
Customs duties	..	1.3	1.7	2.4	2.5	..	0.3	0.3	0.3	0.3
SRF contributions	..	..	..	0.5	0.6	..	..	..	0.1	0.1

.. Not available

Note: More detailed country data and country notes are available in online chapter 5 "Detailed country tables": https://doi.org/10.1787/0bbc27da-en. Full time series can be accessed at http://oe.cd/full-time-series.

Source: Social security contributions and local taxes: Central Bureau of Statistics. Other taxes: Ministry of Finance.

StatLink https://doi.org/10.1787/888934211148

Table 4.50. Netherlands, tax revenue and % of GDP by level of government and main taxes

	Billion EUR					% of GDP				
	1990	2000	2010	2017	2018	1990	2000	2010	2017	2018
Federal or Central government										
Total tax revenue	**61.4**	**95.1**	**135.1**	**170.4**	**178.4**	**23.3**	**21.0**	**21.1**	**23.1**	**23.1**
1000 Taxes on income, profits and capital gains	33.7	43.3	63.6	85.8	88.8	12.8	9.6	9.9	11.6	11.5
2000 Social security contributions	0.0	0.0	0.0	0.0	0.0	0.0	0.0	0.0	0.0	0.0
3000 Taxes on payroll and workforce	0.0	0.0	0.0	0.0	0.0	0.0	0.0	0.0	0.0	0.0
4000 Taxes on property	2.1	5.7	4.6	6.2	6.7	0.8	1.3	0.7	0.8	0.9
5000 Taxes on goods and services	25.3	45.4	66.2	77.6	82.2	9.6	10.0	10.4	10.5	10.6
6000 Other taxes	0.3	0.8	0.8	0.9	0.8	0.1	0.2	0.1	0.1	0.1
State/Regional										
Total tax revenue	..	..	..	..	..	..	..	..	..	..
1000 Taxes on income, profits and capital gains	..	..	..	..	..	..	..	..	..	..
2000 Social security contributions	..	..	..	..	..	..	..	..	..	..
3000 Taxes on payroll and workforce	..	..	..	..	..	..	..	..	..	..
4000 Taxes on property	..	..	..	..	..	..	..	..	..	..
5000 Taxes on goods and services	..	..	..	..	..	..	..	..	..	..
6000 Other taxes	..	..	..	..	..	..	..	..	..	..
Local government										
Total tax revenue	**2.5**	**5.6**	**8.1**	**10.2**	**10.5**	**0.9**	**1.2**	**1.3**	**1.4**	**1.4**
1000 Taxes on income, profits and capital gains	0.0	0.0	0.0	0.0	0.0	0.0	0.0	0.0	0.0	0.0
2000 Social security contributions	0.0	0.0	0.0	0.0	0.0	0.0	0.0	0.0	0.0	0.0
3000 Taxes on payroll and workforce	0.0	0.0	0.0	0.0	0.0	0.0	0.0	0.0	0.0	0.0
4000 Taxes on property	1.7	3.1	4.2	5.3	5.5	0.7	0.7	0.7	0.7	0.7
5000 Taxes on goods and services	0.8	2.5	3.7	4.8	5.0	0.3	0.6	0.6	0.7	0.6
6000 Other taxes	0.0	0.0	0.2	0.0	0.0	0.0	0.0	0.0	0.0	0.0
Social Security Funds										
Total tax revenue	**39.1**	**64.5**	**82.7**	**101.9**	**108.0**	**14.9**	**14.3**	**12.9**	**13.8**	**14.0**
1000 Taxes on income, profits and capital gains	0.0	0.0	0.0	0.0	0.0	0.0	0.0	0.0	0.0	0.0
2000 Social security contributions	39.1	64.5	82.7	101.9	108.0	14.9	14.3	12.9	13.8	14.0
3000 Taxes on payroll and workforce	0.0	0.0	0.0	0.0	0.0	0.0	0.0	0.0	0.0	0.0
4000 Taxes on property	0.0	0.0	0.0	0.0	0.0	0.0	0.0	0.0	0.0	0.0
5000 Taxes on goods and services	0.0	0.0	0.0	0.0	0.0	0.0	0.0	0.0	0.0	0.0
6000 Other taxes	0.0	0.0	0.0	0.0	0.0	0.0	0.0	0.0	0.0	0.0

.. Not available

Note: More detailed country data and country notes are available in online chapter 6 "Tax revenues by sub-sectors of general government": https://doi.org/10.1787/0bbc27da-en. Full time series can be accessed at http://oe.cd/full-time-series.

Source: Social security contributions and local taxes: Central Bureau of Statistics. Other taxes: Ministry of Finance.

StatLink https://doi.org/10.1787/888934211167

Table 4.51. New Zealand, tax revenue and % of GDP by selected tax category

	Billion NZD					% of GDP				
	1990	2000	2010	2017	2018	1990	2000	2010	2017	2018
Total tax revenue	**27.5**	**39.8**	**62.3**	**92.6**	**99.8**	**36.2**	**32.5**	**30.3**	**31.6**	**32.9**
1000 Taxes on income, profits and capital gains	**16.4**	**23.9**	**33.5**	**51.5**	**56.2**	**21.6**	**19.5**	**16.3**	**17.6**	**18.5**
1100 Of individuals	13.2	17.1	23.5	35.0	37.5	17.4	14.0	11.4	11.9	12.3
1200 Corporate	1.8	4.9	7.6	13.6	15.6	2.3	4.0	3.7	4.6	5.1
1300 Unallocable between 1100 and 1200	1.4	1.8	2.4	2.9	3.1	1.9	1.5	1.1	1.0	1.0
2000 Social security contributions	**0.0**	**0.0**	**0.0**	**0.0**	**0.0**	**0.0**	**0.0**	**0.0**	**0.0**	**0.0**
2100 Employees	0.0	0.0	0.0	0.0	0.0	0.0	0.0	0.0	0.0	0.0
2200 Employers	0.0	0.0	0.0	0.0	0.0	0.0	0.0	0.0	0.0	0.0
2300 Self-employed or non-employed	0.0	0.0	0.0	0.0	0.0	0.0	0.0	0.0	0.0	0.0
2400 Unallocable between 2100, 2200 and 2300	0.0	0.0	0.0	0.0	0.0	0.0	0.0	0.0	0.0	0.0
3000 Taxes on payroll and workforce	**0.0**	**0.0**	**0.0**	**0.0**	**0.0**	**0.0**	**0.0**	**0.0**	**0.0**	**0.0**
4000 Taxes on property	**1.9**	**2.1**	**4.1**	**5.5**	**5.8**	**2.5**	**1.7**	**2.0**	**1.9**	**1.9**
4100 Recurrent taxes on immovable property	1.7	2.0	4.0	5.4	5.7	2.3	1.7	2.0	1.9	1.9
4200 Recurrent taxes on net wealth	0.0	0.0	0.0	0.0	0.0	0.0	0.0	0.0	0.0	0.0
4300 Estate, inheritance and gift taxes	0.1	0.0	0.0	0.0	0.0	0.1	0.0	0.0	0.0	0.0
4400 Taxes on financial and capital transactions	0.1	0.1	0.1	0.1	0.1	0.1	0.1	0.0	0.0	0.0
4500 Non-recurrent taxes	0.0	0.0	0.0	0.0	0.0	0.0	0.0	0.0	0.0	0.0
4600 Other recurrent taxes on property	0.0	0.0	0.0	0.0	0.0	0.0	0.0	0.0	0.0	0.0
5000 Taxes on goods and services	**9.2**	**13.8**	**24.7**	**35.6**	**37.8**	**12.1**	**11.3**	**12.0**	**12.2**	**12.5**
5100 Taxes on production, sale, transfer, etc	8.7	12.9	23.1	33.2	35.3	11.4	10.5	11.2	11.3	11.6
5110 General taxes	6.2	9.9	19.1	28.0	29.5	8.1	8.1	9.3	9.5	9.7
5111 Value added taxes	6.2	9.9	19.1	28.0	29.5	8.1	8.1	9.3	9.5	9.7
5120 Taxes on specific goods and services	2.5	3.0	4.0	5.3	5.8	3.3	2.5	1.9	1.8	1.9
5121 Excises	1.9	2.1	1.8	2.2	2.6	2.5	1.8	0.9	0.8	0.9
5200 Taxes on use of goods and perform activities	0.5	0.9	1.6	2.4	2.6	0.7	0.7	0.8	0.8	0.8
5300 Unallocable between 5100 and 5200	0.0	0.0	0.0	0.0	0.0	0.0	0.0	0.0	0.0	0.0
6000 Other taxes	**0.0**	**0.0**	**0.0**	**0.0**	**0.0**	**0.0**	**0.0**	**0.0**	**0.0**	**0.0**
Non-wastable tax credits										
Non-wastable tax credits against 1000	..	1.1	2.8	2.2	2.8	..	0.9	1.4	0.7	0.9
Transfer component	..	0.7	1.8	1.0	1.2	..	0.6	0.9	0.3	0.4
Tax expenditure component	..	0.3	1.0	1.2	1.5	..	0.3	0.5	0.4	0.5

.. Not available

Note: More detailed country data and country notes are available in online chapter 5 "Detailed country tables": https://doi.org/10.1787/0bbc27da-en. Full time series can be accessed at http://oe.cd/full-time-series.

Source: Local Authorities Statistics, Department of Statistics, Wellington.

StatLink https://doi.org/10.1787/888934211186

Table 4.52. New Zealand, tax revenue and % of GDP by level of government and main taxes

	Billion NZD					% of GDP				
	1990	2000	2010	2017	2018	1990	2000	2010	2017	2018
Federal or Central government										
Total tax revenue	**25.8**	**37.5**	**57.9**	**86.6**	**93.3**	**34.0**	**30.7**	**28.1**	**29.5**	**30.7**
1000 Taxes on income, profits and capital gains	16.4	23.9	33.5	51.5	56.2	21.6	19.5	16.3	17.6	18.5
2000 Social security contributions	0.0	0.0	0.0	0.0	0.0	0.0	0.0	0.0	0.0	0.0
3000 Taxes on payroll and workforce	0.0	0.0	0.0	0.0	0.0	0.0	0.0	0.0	0.0	0.0
4000 Taxes on property	0.3	0.1	0.1	0.1	0.1	0.4	0.1	0.0	0.0	0.0
5000 Taxes on goods and services	9.1	13.6	24.3	35.0	37.0	12.0	11.1	11.8	11.9	12.2
6000 Other taxes	0.0	0.0	0.0	0.0	0.0	0.0	0.0	0.0	0.0	0.0
State/Regional										
Total tax revenue	**..**	**..**	**..**	**..**	**..**	**..**	**..**	**..**	**..**	**..**
1000 Taxes on income, profits and capital gains	..	..	..	..	..	..	..	..	..	..
2000 Social security contributions	..	..	..	..	..	..	..	..	..	..
3000 Taxes on payroll and workforce	..	..	..	..	..	..	..	..	..	..
4000 Taxes on property	..	..	..	..	..	..	..	..	..	..
5000 Taxes on goods and services	..	..	..	..	..	..	..	..	..	..
6000 Other taxes	..	..	..	..	..	..	..	..	..	..
Local government										
Total tax revenue	**1.7**	**2.3**	**4.5**	**6.1**	**6.6**	**2.2**	**1.9**	**2.2**	**2.1**	**2.2**
1000 Taxes on income, profits and capital gains	0.0	0.0	0.0	0.0	0.0	0.0	0.0	0.0	0.0	0.0
2000 Social security contributions	0.0	0.0	0.0	0.0	0.0	0.0	0.0	0.0	0.0	0.0
3000 Taxes on payroll and workforce	0.0	0.0	0.0	0.0	0.0	0.0	0.0	0.0	0.0	0.0
4000 Taxes on property	1.6	2.0	4.0	5.4	5.7	2.0	1.7	2.0	1.9	1.9
5000 Taxes on goods and services	0.1	0.2	0.4	0.6	0.9	0.2	0.2	0.2	0.2	0.3
6000 Other taxes	0.0	0.0	0.0	0.0	0.0	0.0	0.0	0.0	0.0	0.0
Social Security Funds										
Total tax revenue	**0.0**	**0.0**	**0.0**	**0.0**	**0.0**	**0.0**	**0.0**	**0.0**	**0.0**	**0.0**
1000 Taxes on income, profits and capital gains	0.0	0.0	0.0	0.0	0.0	0.0	0.0	0.0	0.0	0.0
2000 Social security contributions	0.0	0.0	0.0	0.0	0.0	0.0	0.0	0.0	0.0	0.0
3000 Taxes on payroll and workforce	0.0	0.0	0.0	0.0	0.0	0.0	0.0	0.0	0.0	0.0
4000 Taxes on property	0.0	0.0	0.0	0.0	0.0	0.0	0.0	0.0	0.0	0.0
5000 Taxes on goods and services	0.0	0.0	0.0	0.0	0.0	0.0	0.0	0.0	0.0	0.0
6000 Other taxes	0.0	0.0	0.0	0.0	0.0	0.0	0.0	0.0	0.0	0.0

.. Not available

Note: More detailed country data and country notes are available in online chapter 6 "Tax revenues by sub-sectors of general government": https://doi.org/10.1787/0bbc27da-en. Full time series can be accessed at http://oe.cd/full-time-series.

Source: Local Authorities Statistics, Department of Statistics, Wellington.

StatLink https://doi.org/10.1787/888934211205

Table 4.53. Norway, tax revenue and % of GDP by selected tax category

	Billion NOK					% of GDP				
	1990	2000	2010	2017	2018	1990	2000	2010	2017	2018
Total tax revenue	**301.8**	**628.0**	**1 083.3**	**1 277.9**	**1 397.2**	**40.2**	**41.7**	**41.8**	**38.8**	**39.6**
1000 Taxes on income, profits and capital gains	**106.3**	**284.2**	**512.2**	**499.7**	**582.9**	**14.2**	**18.9**	**19.8**	**15.2**	**16.5**
1100 Of individuals	79.1	152.0	256.5	339.1	353.4	10.5	10.1	9.9	10.3	10.0
1200 Corporate	27.2	132.2	255.7	160.6	229.6	3.6	8.8	9.9	4.9	6.5
1300 Unallocable between 1100 and 1200	0.0	0.0	0.0	0.0	0.0	0.0	0.0	0.0	0.0	0.0
2000 Social security contributions	**79.4**	**132.2**	**243.0**	**339.8**	**356.6**	**10.6**	**8.8**	**9.4**	**10.3**	**10.1**
2100 Employees	25.3	45.2	81.0	119.0	124.5	3.4	3.0	3.1	3.6	3.5
2200 Employers	50.1	79.2	148.0	197.8	208.2	6.7	5.3	5.7	6.0	5.9
2300 Self-employed or non-employed	3.9	7.8	13.9	23.0	24.0	0.5	0.5	0.5	0.7	0.7
2400 Unallocable between 2100, 2200 and 2300	0.0	0.0	0.0	0.0	0.0	0.0	0.0	0.0	0.0	0.0
3000 Taxes on payroll and workforce	**0.0**	**0.0**	**0.0**	**1.9**	**2.0**	**0.0**	**0.0**	**0.0**	**0.1**	**0.1**
4000 Taxes on property	**8.9**	**14.4**	**28.5**	**41.9**	**43.9**	**1.2**	**1.0**	**1.1**	**1.3**	**1.2**
4100 Recurrent taxes on immovable property	2.2	2.7	7.1	13.6	14.2	0.3	0.2	0.3	0.4	0.4
4200 Recurrent taxes on net wealth	5.1	7.7	13.2	19.0	20.1	0.7	0.5	0.5	0.6	0.6
4300 Estate, inheritance and gift taxes	0.4	1.3	2.4	0.1	0.1	0.1	0.1	0.1	0.0	0.0
4400 Taxes on financial and capital transactions	1.1	2.7	5.9	9.2	9.6	0.1	0.2	0.2	0.3	0.3
4500 Non-recurrent taxes	0.0	0.0	0.0	0.0	0.0	0.0	0.0	0.0	0.0	0.0
4600 Other recurrent taxes on property	0.0	0.0	0.0	0.0	0.0	0.0	0.0	0.0	0.0	0.0
5000 Taxes on goods and services	**107.3**	**197.2**	**299.5**	**394.6**	**411.8**	**14.3**	**13.1**	**11.6**	**12.0**	**11.7**
5100 Taxes on production, sale, transfer, etc	102.9	185.9	284.6	376.3	392.8	13.7	12.3	11.0	11.4	11.1
5110 General taxes	56.7	125.0	201.8	284.5	297.9	7.6	8.3	7.8	8.6	8.4
5111 Value added taxes	56.7	124.2	201.2	283.5	296.9	7.6	8.2	7.8	8.6	8.4
5120 Taxes on specific goods and services	46.2	60.9	82.8	91.7	94.9	6.2	4.0	3.2	2.8	2.7
5121 Excises	37.5	54.9	76.3	81.3	84.0	5.0	3.6	2.9	2.5	2.4
5200 Taxes on use of goods and perform activities	4.4	11.3	14.9	18.3	19.0	0.6	0.7	0.6	0.6	0.5
5300 Unallocable between 5100 and 5200	0.0	0.0	0.0	0.0	0.0	0.0	0.0	0.0	0.0	0.0
6000 Other taxes	**0.0**	**0.0**	**0.0**	**0.0**	**0.0**	**0.0**	**0.0**	**0.0**	**0.0**	**0.0**
Non-wastable tax credits										
Non-wastable tax credits against 1000	..	..	1.2	4.0	4.0	..	..	0.0	0.1	0.1
Transfer component	..	..	1.2	3.2	3.2	..	..	0.0	0.1	0.1
Tax expenditure component	..	..	0.1	0.8	0.8	..	..	0.0	0.0	0.0

.. Not available

Note: More detailed country data and country notes are available in online chapter 5 "Detailed country tables": https://doi.org/10.1787/0bbc27da-en. Full time series can be accessed at http://oe.cd/full-time-series.

Source: Statistics Norway; National Accounts.

StatLink https://doi.org/10.1787/888934211224

Table 4.54. Norway, tax revenue and % of GDP by level of government and main taxes

	Billion NOK					% of GDP				
	1990	2000	2010	2017	2018	1990	2000	2010	2017	2018
Federal or Central government										
Total tax revenue	**165.4**	**532.5**	**935.7**	**1 075.0**	**1 183.5**	**22.1**	**35.3**	**36.1**	**32.6**	**33.5**
1000 Taxes on income, profits and capital gains	50.6	198.4	381.0	324.7	398.2	6.8	13.2	14.7	9.9	11.3
2000 Social security contributions	4.7	132.2	243.0	339.8	356.6	0.6	8.8	9.4	10.3	10.1
3000 Taxes on payroll and workforce	0.0	0.0	0.0	1.9	2.0	0.0	0.0	0.0	0.1	0.1
4000 Taxes on property	3.4	6.8	13.7	15.6	16.7	0.5	0.5	0.5	0.5	0.5
5000 Taxes on goods and services	106.7	195.1	298.0	393.0	410.1	14.2	12.9	11.5	11.9	11.6
6000 Other taxes	0.0	0.0	0.0	0.0	0.0	0.0	0.0	0.0	0.0	0.0
State/Regional										
Total tax revenue	..	..	..	..	..	..	..	..	..	..
1000 Taxes on income, profits and capital gains	..	..	..	..	..	..	..	..	..	..
2000 Social security contributions	..	..	..	..	..	..	..	..	..	..
3000 Taxes on payroll and workforce	..	..	..	..	..	..	..	..	..	..
4000 Taxes on property	..	..	..	..	..	..	..	..	..	..
5000 Taxes on goods and services	..	..	..	..	..	..	..	..	..	..
6000 Other taxes	..	..	..	..	..	..	..	..	..	..
Local government										
Total tax revenue	**61.6**	**95.5**	**147.7**	**202.9**	**213.7**	**8.2**	**6.3**	**5.7**	**6.2**	**6.1**
1000 Taxes on income, profits and capital gains	55.7	85.8	131.2	175.0	184.8	7.4	5.7	5.1	5.3	5.2
2000 Social security contributions	0.0	0.0	0.0	0.0	0.0	0.0	0.0	0.0	0.0	0.0
3000 Taxes on payroll and workforce	0.0	0.0	0.0	0.0	0.0	0.0	0.0	0.0	0.0	0.0
4000 Taxes on property	5.5	7.6	14.9	26.3	27.3	0.7	0.5	0.6	0.8	0.8
5000 Taxes on goods and services	0.4	2.1	1.6	1.6	1.7	0.1	0.1	0.1	0.1	0.0
6000 Other taxes	0.0	0.0	0.0	0.0	0.0	0.0	0.0	0.0	0.0	0.0
Social Security Funds										
Total tax revenue	**74.8**	**0.0**	**0.0**	**0.0**	**0.0**	**10.0**	**0.0**	**0.0**	**0.0**	**0.0**
1000 Taxes on income, profits and capital gains	0.0	0.0	0.0	0.0	0.0	0.0	0.0	0.0	0.0	0.0
2000 Social security contributions	74.6	0.0	0.0	0.0	0.0	10.0	0.0	0.0	0.0	0.0
3000 Taxes on payroll and workforce	0.0	0.0	0.0	0.0	0.0	0.0	0.0	0.0	0.0	0.0
4000 Taxes on property	0.0	0.0	0.0	0.0	0.0	0.0	0.0	0.0	0.0	0.0
5000 Taxes on goods and services	0.2	0.0	0.0	0.0	0.0	0.0	0.0	0.0	0.0	0.0
6000 Other taxes	0.0	0.0	0.0	0.0	0.0	0.0	0.0	0.0	0.0	0.0

.. Not available

Note: More detailed country data and country notes are available in online chapter 6 "Tax revenues by sub-sectors of general government": https://doi.org/10.1787/0bbc27da-en. Full time series can be accessed at http://oe.cd/full-time-series.

Source: Statistics Norway; National Accounts.

StatLink https://doi.org/10.1787/888934211243

Table 4.55. Poland, tax revenue and % of GDP by selected tax category

	Billion PLN					% of GDP				
	1990	2000	2010	2017	2018	1990	2000	2010	2017	2018
Total tax revenue	..	**246.0**	**453.3**	**678.9**	**745.5**	..	**32.9**	**31.4**	**34.1**	**35.2**
1000 Taxes on income, profits and capital gains	..	**50.3**	**91.0**	**137.5**	**157.0**	..	**6.7**	**6.3**	**6.9**	**7.4**
1100 Of individuals	..	32.4	62.9	99.1	112.7	..	4.3	4.4	5.0	5.3
1200 Corporate	..	17.9	28.1	38.4	44.3	..	2.4	1.9	1.9	2.1
1300 Unallocable between 1100 and 1200	..	0.0	0.0	0.0	0.0	..	0.0	0.0	0.0	0.0
2000 Social security contributions	..	**96.4**	**156.0**	**254.9**	**277.7**	..	**12.9**	**10.8**	**12.8**	**13.1**
2100 Employees	..	42.4	60.2	105.8	115.8	..	5.7	4.2	5.3	5.5
2200 Employers	..	41.1	65.4	100.9	108.7	..	5.5	4.5	5.1	5.1
2300 Self-employed or non-employed	..	12.9	30.4	48.2	53.2	..	1.7	2.1	2.4	2.5
2400 Unallocable between 2100, 2200 and 2300	..	0.0	0.0	0.0	0.0	..	0.0	0.0	0.0	0.0
3000 Taxes on payroll and workforce	..	**1.6**	**3.7**	**4.5**	**4.7**	..	**0.2**	**0.3**	**0.2**	**0.2**
4000 Taxes on property	..	**10.6**	**19.1**	**27.1**	**27.9**	..	**1.4**	**1.3**	**1.4**	**1.3**
4100 Recurrent taxes on immovable property	..	8.4	16.4	23.8	24.3	..	1.1	1.1	1.2	1.1
4200 Recurrent taxes on net wealth	..	0.0	0.0	0.0	0.0	..	0.0	0.0	0.0	0.0
4300 Estate, inheritance and gift taxes	..	0.2	0.3	0.3	0.3	..	0.0	0.0	0.0	0.0
4400 Taxes on financial and capital transactions	..	2.0	2.4	3.0	3.2	..	0.3	0.2	0.2	0.2
4500 Non-recurrent taxes	..	0.0	0.0	0.0	0.0	..	0.0	0.0	0.0	0.0
4600 Other recurrent taxes on property	..	0.0	0.0	0.0	0.0	..	0.0	0.0	0.0	0.0
5000 Taxes on goods and services	..	**86.9**	**182.8**	**253.9**	**277.2**	..	**11.6**	**12.6**	**12.8**	**13.1**
5100 Taxes on production, sale, transfer, etc	..	84.9	176.0	246.5	268.2	..	11.4	12.2	12.4	12.7
5110 General taxes	..	51.6	109.7	154.7	172.2	..	6.9	7.6	7.8	8.1
5111 Value added taxes	..	51.6	109.7	154.7	172.2	..	6.9	7.6	7.8	8.1
5120 Taxes on specific goods and services	..	33.3	66.3	91.9	96.0	..	4.5	4.6	4.6	4.5
5121 Excises	..	27.2	62.0	79.0	82.1	..	3.6	4.3	4.0	3.9
5200 Taxes on use of goods and perform activities	..	2.0	6.8	7.4	9.0	..	0.3	0.5	0.4	0.4
5300 Unallocable between 5100 and 5200	..	0.0	0.0	0.0	0.0	..	0.0	0.0	0.0	0.0
6000 Other taxes	..	**0.3**	**0.6**	**1.0**	**1.1**	..	**0.0**	**0.0**	**0.1**	**0.1**
Non-wastable tax credits										
Non-wastable tax credits against 1000	..	..	..	..	..	..	..	..	..	..
Transfer component	..	..	..	..	..	..	..	..	..	..
Tax expenditure component	..	..	..	..	..	..	..	..	..	..
Revenues collected on behalf of the EU										
Revenues collected on behalf of the EU, total	..	..	1.7	3.6	3.9	..	..	0.1	0.2	0.2
Customs duties	..	..	1.6	3.5	3.9	..	..	0.1	0.2	0.2

.. Not available

Note: More detailed country data and country notes are available in online chapter 5 "Detailed country tables": https://doi.org/10.1787/0bbc27da-en. Full time series can be accessed at http://oe.cd/full-time-series.

Source: Ministry of Finance, Economic Department.

StatLink https://doi.org/10.1787/888934211262

Table 4.56. Poland, tax revenue and % of GDP by level of government and main taxes

	Billion PLN					% of GDP				
	1990	2000	2010	2017	2018	1990	2000	2010	2017	2018
Federal or Central government										
Total tax revenue	..	**126.9**	**238.4**	**334.1**	**369.0**	..	**17.0**	**16.5**	**16.8**	**17.4**
1000 Taxes on income, profits and capital gains	..	40.0	57.7	83.4	95.2	..	5.3	4.0	4.2	4.5
2000 Social security contributions	..	0.0	0.0	0.0	0.0	..	0.0	0.0	0.0	0.0
3000 Taxes on payroll and workforce	..	1.6	3.7	4.5	4.7	..	0.2	0.3	0.2	0.2
4000 Taxes on property	..	0.0	0.0	0.0	0.0	..	0.0	0.0	0.0	0.0
5000 Taxes on goods and services	..	85.3	177.0	246.2	269.1	..	11.4	12.2	12.4	12.7
6000 Other taxes	..	0.0	0.0	0.0	0.0	..	0.0	0.0	0.0	0.0
State/Regional										
Total tax revenue	..	..	..	..	..	..	..	..	..	..
1000 Taxes on income, profits and capital gains	..	..	..	..	..	..	..	..	..	..
2000 Social security contributions	..	..	..	..	..	..	..	..	..	..
3000 Taxes on payroll and workforce	..	..	..	..	..	..	..	..	..	..
4000 Taxes on property	..	..	..	..	..	..	..	..	..	..
5000 Taxes on goods and services	..	..	..	..	..	..	..	..	..	..
6000 Other taxes	..	..	..	..	..	..	..	..	..	..
Local government										
Total tax revenue	..	**22.7**	**57.1**	**86.2**	**94.9**	..	**3.0**	**4.0**	**4.3**	**4.5**
1000 Taxes on income, profits and capital gains	..	10.3	33.3	54.1	61.8	..	1.4	2.3	2.7	2.9
2000 Social security contributions	..	0.0	0.0	0.0	0.0	..	0.0	0.0	0.0	0.0
3000 Taxes on payroll and workforce	..	0.0	0.0	0.0	0.0	..	0.0	0.0	0.0	0.0
4000 Taxes on property	..	10.6	19.1	27.1	27.9	..	1.4	1.3	1.4	1.3
5000 Taxes on goods and services	..	1.5	4.1	4.1	4.2	..	0.2	0.3	0.2	0.2
6000 Other taxes	..	0.3	0.6	1.0	1.1	..	0.0	0.0	0.1	0.1
Social Security Funds										
Total tax revenue	..	**96.4**	**156.0**	**254.9**	**277.7**	..	**12.9**	**10.8**	**12.8**	**13.1**
1000 Taxes on income, profits and capital gains	..	0.0	0.0	0.0	0.0	..	0.0	0.0	0.0	0.0
2000 Social security contributions	..	96.4	156.0	254.9	277.7	..	12.9	10.8	12.8	13.1
3000 Taxes on payroll and workforce	..	0.0	0.0	0.0	0.0	..	0.0	0.0	0.0	0.0
4000 Taxes on property	..	0.0	0.0	0.0	0.0	..	0.0	0.0	0.0	0.0
5000 Taxes on goods and services	..	0.0	0.0	0.0	0.0	..	0.0	0.0	0.0	0.0
6000 Other taxes	..	0.0	0.0	0.0	0.0	..	0.0	0.0	0.0	0.0

.. Not available

Note: More detailed country data and country notes are available in online chapter 6 "Tax revenues by sub-sectors of general government": https://doi.org/10.1787/0bbc27da-en. Full time series can be accessed at http://oe.cd/full-time-series.

Source: Ministry of Finance, Economic Department.

StatLink https://doi.org/10.1787/888934211281

Table 4.57. Portugal, tax revenue and % of GDP by selected tax category

	Billion EUR					% of GDP				
	1990	2000	2010	2017	2018	1990	2000	2010	2017	2018
Total tax revenue	**14.8**	**39.9**	**54.7**	**66.9**	**71.1**	**26.5**	**31.1**	**30.5**	**34.1**	**34.8**
1000 Taxes on income, profits and capital gains	**3.8**	**11.7**	**14.6**	**18.9**	**20.1**	**6.8**	**9.1**	**8.2**	**9.6**	**9.8**
1100 Of individuals	2.4	6.9	9.6	12.6	13.3	4.2	5.4	5.4	6.4	6.5
1200 Corporate	1.2	4.7	4.9	6.3	6.8	2.1	3.7	2.7	3.2	3.3
1300 Unallocable between 1100 and 1200	0.3	0.0	0.1	0.0	0.0	0.5	0.0	0.0	0.0	0.0
2000 Social security contributions	**4.0**	**10.2**	**15.5**	**18.0**	**19.1**	**7.2**	**7.9**	**8.6**	**9.2**	**9.4**
2100 Employees	1.5	4.3	6.7	7.6	7.7	2.6	3.3	3.7	3.9	3.8
2200 Employers	2.4	5.9	8.8	10.3	11.4	4.3	4.6	4.9	5.3	5.6
2300 Self-employed or non-employed	0.1	0.0	0.0	0.0	0.0	0.3	0.0	0.0	0.0	0.0
2400 Unallocable between 2100, 2200 and 2300	0.0	0.0	0.0	0.0	0.0	0.0	0.0	0.0	0.0	0.0
3000 Taxes on payroll and workforce	**0.0**	**0.0**	**0.0**	**0.0**	**0.0**	**0.0**	**0.0**	**0.0**	**0.0**	**0.0**
4000 Taxes on property	**0.4**	**1.5**	**1.9**	**2.7**	**2.9**	**0.7**	**1.1**	**1.1**	**1.4**	**1.4**
4100 Recurrent taxes on immovable property	0.1	0.5	1.1	1.6	1.6	0.2	0.4	0.6	0.8	0.8
4200 Recurrent taxes on net wealth	0.0	0.0	0.0	0.0	0.0	0.0	0.0	0.0	0.0	0.0
4300 Estate, inheritance and gift taxes	0.1	0.1	0.0	0.0	0.0	0.1	0.1	0.0	0.0	0.0
4400 Taxes on financial and capital transactions	0.2	0.9	0.8	1.1	1.2	0.3	0.7	0.5	0.6	0.6
4500 Non-recurrent taxes	0.0	0.0	0.0	0.0	0.0	0.0	0.0	0.0	0.0	0.0
4600 Other recurrent taxes on property	0.0	0.0	0.0	0.0	0.0	0.0	0.0	0.0	0.0	0.0
5000 Taxes on goods and services	**6.6**	**16.3**	**22.2**	**26.8**	**28.3**	**11.7**	**12.7**	**12.3**	**13.7**	**13.9**
5100 Taxes on production, sale, transfer, etc	6.4	15.8	21.4	25.8	27.1	11.5	12.3	11.9	13.2	13.3
5110 General taxes	2.9	9.7	13.5	16.8	17.9	5.2	7.6	7.5	8.6	8.7
5111 Value added taxes	2.9	9.7	13.5	16.8	17.9	5.2	7.6	7.5	8.6	8.7
5120 Taxes on specific goods and services	3.5	6.1	7.9	9.0	9.2	6.3	4.8	4.4	4.6	4.5
5121 Excises	2.1	4.5	5.7	6.1	6.2	3.7	3.5	3.2	3.1	3.1
5200 Taxes on use of goods and perform activities	0.1	0.4	0.7	1.0	1.2	0.2	0.3	0.4	0.5	0.6
5300 Unallocable between 5100 and 5200	0.0	0.1	0.0	0.0	0.0	0.0	0.0	0.0	0.0	0.0
6000 Other taxes	**0.0**	**0.3**	**0.5**	**0.6**	**0.7**	**0.1**	**0.2**	**0.3**	**0.3**	**0.3**
Non-wastable tax credits										
Non-wastable tax credits against 1000	..	..	..	..	..	..	..	..	..	..
Transfer component	..	..	..	..	..	..	..	..	..	..
Tax expenditure component	..	..	..	..	..	..	..	..	..	..
Revenues collected on behalf of the EU										
Revenues collected on behalf of the EU, total	0.2	0.2	0.2	0.3	0.4	0.3	0.2	0.1	0.2	0.2
Customs duties	..	0.2	0.2	0.2	0.2	..	0.2	0.1	0.1	0.1
SRF contributions	..	..	..	0.1	0.1	..	..	..	0.1	0.1

.. Not available

Note: More detailed country data and country notes are available in online chapter 5 "Detailed country tables": https://doi.org/10.1787/0bbc27da-en. Full time series can be accessed at http://oe.cd/full-time-series.

Source: Instituto Nacionale de Estatistica; Conta do Estado, Contas de Gerência dos Fundos e Serviços Autonomos da Administraçao Central; Estatisticas das Financas publicas; Relatorio do Instituto de Gestao Financeira da Seguranta Social, Contas de Gerência das Regioes Autonomas da Madeira e dos Atores.

StatLink https://doi.org/10.1787/888934211300

Table 4.58. Portugal, tax revenue and % of GDP by level of government and main taxes

	Billion EUR					% of GDP				
	1990	2000	2010	2017	2018	1990	2000	2010	2017	2018
Federal or Central government										
Total tax revenue	**9.8**	**27.8**	**36.5**	**44.9**	**47.5**	**17.6**	**21.6**	**20.3**	**22.9**	**23.3**
1000 Taxes on income, profits and capital gains	3.6	11.1	13.6	17.7	18.8	6.4	8.7	7.6	9.0	9.2
2000 Social security contributions	0.0	1.3	1.9	2.1	2.1	0.0	1.0	1.1	1.1	1.0
3000 Taxes on payroll and workforce	0.0	0.0	0.0	0.0	0.0	0.0	0.0	0.0	0.0	0.0
4000 Taxes on property	0.1	0.3	0.2	0.4	0.4	0.1	0.2	0.1	0.2	0.2
5000 Taxes on goods and services	6.1	14.8	20.3	24.2	25.6	10.9	11.5	11.3	12.4	12.5
6000 Other taxes	0.0	0.3	0.5	0.6	0.7	0.1	0.2	0.3	0.3	0.3
State/Regional										
Total tax revenue	**..**	**..**	**..**	**..**	**..**	**..**	**..**	**..**	**..**	**..**
1000 Taxes on income, profits and capital gains	..	..	..	..	..	..	..	..	..	..
2000 Social security contributions	..	..	..	..	..	..	..	..	..	..
3000 Taxes on payroll and workforce	..	..	..	..	..	..	..	..	..	..
4000 Taxes on property	..	..	..	..	..	..	..	..	..	..
5000 Taxes on goods and services	..	..	..	..	..	..	..	..	..	..
6000 Other taxes	..	..	..	..	..	..	..	..	..	..
Local government										
Total tax revenue	**0.8**	**2.5**	**3.6**	**4.7**	**5.1**	**1.5**	**2.0**	**2.0**	**2.4**	**2.5**
1000 Taxes on income, profits and capital gains	0.2	0.6	1.1	1.2	1.3	0.4	0.4	0.6	0.6	0.6
2000 Social security contributions	0.0	0.0	0.0	0.0	0.0	0.0	0.0	0.0	0.0	0.0
3000 Taxes on payroll and workforce	0.0	0.0	0.0	0.0	0.0	0.0	0.0	0.0	0.0	0.0
4000 Taxes on property	0.3	1.2	1.7	2.3	2.5	0.6	0.9	1.0	1.2	1.2
5000 Taxes on goods and services	0.3	0.7	0.8	1.2	1.4	0.5	0.6	0.5	0.6	0.7
6000 Other taxes	0.0	0.0	0.0	0.0	0.0	0.0	0.0	0.0	0.0	0.0
Social Security Funds										
Total tax revenue	**4.0**	**9.4**	**14.4**	**16.9**	**18.1**	**7.2**	**7.3**	**8.0**	**8.6**	**8.9**
1000 Taxes on income, profits and capital gains	0.0	0.0	0.0	0.0	0.0	0.0	0.0	0.0	0.0	0.0
2000 Social security contributions	4.0	8.8	13.5	15.8	17.0	7.2	6.9	7.5	8.1	8.3
3000 Taxes on payroll and workforce	0.0	0.0	0.0	0.0	0.0	0.0	0.0	0.0	0.0	0.0
4000 Taxes on property	0.0	0.0	0.0	0.0	0.0	0.0	0.0	0.0	0.0	0.0
5000 Taxes on goods and services	0.0	0.5	0.8	1.0	1.1	0.0	0.4	0.5	0.5	0.5
6000 Other taxes	0.0	0.0	0.0	0.0	0.0	0.0	0.0	0.0	0.0	0.0

.. Not available

Note: More detailed country data and country notes are available in online chapter 6 "Tax revenues by sub-sectors of general government": https://doi.org/10.1787/0bbc27da-en. Full time series can be accessed at http://oe.cd/full-time-series.

Source: Instituto Nacionale de Estatistica; Conta do Estado, Contas de Gerência dos Fundos e Serviços Autonomos da Administraçao Central; Estatisticas das Financas publicas; Relatorio do Instituto de Gestao Financeira da Seguranta Social, Contas de Gerência das Regioes Autonomas da Madeira e dos Atores.

StatLink https://doi.org/10.1787/888934211319

Table 4.59. Slovak Republic, tax revenue and % of GDP by selected tax category

	Billion EUR					% of GDP				
	1990	2000	2010	2017	2018	1990	2000	2010	2017	2018
Total tax revenue	..	**10.6**	**19.2**	**28.9**	**30.8**	..	**33.6**	**28.1**	**34.2**	**34.3**
1000 Taxes on income, profits and capital gains	..	**2.2**	**3.6**	**6.0**	**6.4**	..	**6.9**	**5.3**	**7.1**	**7.1**
1100 Of individuals	..	1.1	1.8	2.9	3.2	..	3.3	2.6	3.4	3.6
1200 Corporate	..	0.8	1.7	2.9	2.9	..	2.6	2.4	3.5	3.3
1300 Unallocable between 1100 and 1200	..	0.3	0.2	0.2	0.2	..	1.0	0.2	0.2	0.2
2000 Social security contributions	..	**4.4**	**8.2**	**12.4**	**13.2**	..	**13.9**	**12.0**	**14.7**	**14.8**
2100 Employees	..	0.9	2.1	2.9	3.3	..	2.8	3.1	3.5	3.6
2200 Employers	..	2.9	4.6	7.3	7.9	..	9.0	6.7	8.6	8.8
2300 Self-employed or non-employed	..	0.7	1.5	2.2	2.1	..	2.1	2.2	2.6	2.3
2400 Unallocable between 2100, 2200 and 2300	..	0.0	0.0	0.0	0.0	..	0.0	0.0	0.0	0.0
3000 Taxes on payroll and workforce	..	**0.0**	**0.0**	**0.0**	**0.0**	..	**0.0**	**0.0**	**0.0**	**0.0**
4000 Taxes on property	..	**0.2**	**0.3**	**0.4**	**0.4**	..	**0.6**	**0.4**	**0.4**	**0.4**
4100 Recurrent taxes on immovable property	..	0.1	0.3	0.4	0.4	..	0.5	0.4	0.4	0.4
4200 Recurrent taxes on net wealth	..	0.0	0.0	0.0	0.0	..	0.0	0.0	0.0	0.0
4300 Estate, inheritance and gift taxes	..	0.0	0.0	0.0	0.0	..	0.0	0.0	0.0	0.0
4400 Taxes on financial and capital transactions	..	0.0	0.0	0.0	0.0	..	0.1	0.0	0.0	0.0
4500 Non-recurrent taxes	..	0.0	0.0	0.0	0.0	..	0.0	0.0	0.0	0.0
4600 Other recurrent taxes on property	..	0.0	0.0	0.0	0.0	..	0.0	0.0	0.0	0.0
5000 Taxes on goods and services	..	**3.9**	**7.1**	**10.2**	**10.8**	..	**12.2**	**10.5**	**12.1**	**12.0**
5100 Taxes on production, sale, transfer, etc	..	3.6	6.6	9.5	10.0	..	11.5	9.7	11.2	11.2
5110 General taxes	..	2.2	4.2	5.9	6.3	..	6.8	6.1	7.0	7.1
5111 Value added taxes	..	2.2	4.2	5.9	6.3	..	6.8	6.1	7.0	7.1
5120 Taxes on specific goods and services	..	1.5	2.4	3.6	3.7	..	4.6	3.5	4.2	4.1
5121 Excises	..	1.0	2.1	2.8	2.9	..	3.1	3.1	3.3	3.3
5200 Taxes on use of goods and perform activities	..	0.2	0.4	0.6	0.6	..	0.7	0.6	0.7	0.7
5300 Unallocable between 5100 and 5200	..	0.0	0.1	0.2	0.2	..	0.0	0.2	0.2	0.2
6000 Other taxes	..	**0.0**	**0.0**	**0.0**	**0.0**	..	**0.0**	**0.0**	**0.0**	**0.0**
Non-wastable tax credits										
Non-wastable tax credits against 1000	..	..	0.3	0.3	0.3	..	..	0.4	0.3	0.3
Transfer component	..	..	..	..	..	..	..	..	..	..
Tax expenditure component	..	..	..	..	..	..	..	..	..	..
Revenues collected on behalf of the EU										
Revenues collected on behalf of the EU, total	..	..	0.1	0.2	0.2	..	..	0.2	0.2	0.2
Customs duties	..	..	0.1	0.1	0.1	..	..	0.2	0.2	0.2
SRF contributions	..	..	..	0.0	0.0	..	..	..	0.0	0.0

.. Not available

Note: More detailed country data and country notes are available in online chapter 5 "Detailed country tables": https://doi.org/10.1787/0bbc27da-en. Full time series can be accessed at http://oe.cd/full-time-series.

Source: Ministry of Finance.

StatLink https://doi.org/10.1787/888934211338

Table 4.60. Slovak Republic, tax revenue and % of GDP by level of government and main taxes

	Billion EUR					% of GDP				
	1990	2000	2010	2017	2018	1990	2000	2010	2017	2018
Federal or Central government										
Total tax revenue	**..**	**6.2**	**10.5**	**16.2**	**17.2**	**..**	**19.5**	**15.5**	**19.2**	**19.2**
1000 Taxes on income, profits and capital gains	..	2.2	3.6	6.0	6.4	..	6.9	5.3	7.1	7.1
2000 Social security contributions	..	0.1	0.2	0.4	0.4	..	0.3	0.3	0.5	0.5
3000 Taxes on payroll and workforce	..	0.0	0.0	0.0	0.0	..	0.0	0.0	0.0	0.0
4000 Taxes on property	..	0.1	0.0	0.0	0.0	..	0.2	0.0	0.0	0.0
5000 Taxes on goods and services	..	3.9	6.7	9.9	10.4	..	12.2	9.9	11.7	11.6
6000 Other taxes	..	0.0	0.0	0.0	0.0	..	0.0	0.0	0.0	0.0
State/Regional										
Total tax revenue	**..**	**..**	**..**	**..**	**..**	**..**	**..**	**..**	**..**	**..**
1000 Taxes on income, profits and capital gains	..	..	..	..	..	..	..	..	..	..
2000 Social security contributions	..	..	..	..	..	..	..	..	..	..
3000 Taxes on payroll and workforce	..	..	..	..	..	..	..	..	..	..
4000 Taxes on property	..	..	..	..	..	..	..	..	..	..
5000 Taxes on goods and services	..	..	..	..	..	..	..	..	..	..
6000 Other taxes	..	..	..	..	..	..	..	..	..	..
Local government										
Total tax revenue	**..**	**0.1**	**0.5**	**0.5**	**0.6**	**..**	**0.5**	**0.8**	**0.6**	**0.6**
1000 Taxes on income, profits and capital gains	..	0.0	0.0	0.0	0.0	..	0.0	0.0	0.0	0.0
2000 Social security contributions	..	0.0	0.0	0.0	0.0	..	0.0	0.0	0.0	0.0
3000 Taxes on payroll and workforce	..	0.0	0.0	0.0	0.0	..	0.0	0.0	0.0	0.0
4000 Taxes on property	..	0.1	0.3	0.4	0.4	..	0.4	0.4	0.4	0.4
5000 Taxes on goods and services	..	0.0	0.3	0.2	0.2	..	0.0	0.4	0.2	0.2
6000 Other taxes	..	0.0	0.0	0.0	0.0	..	0.0	0.0	0.0	0.0
Social Security Funds										
Total tax revenue	**..**	**4.3**	**7.9**	**12.0**	**12.8**	**..**	**13.6**	**11.7**	**14.2**	**14.3**
1000 Taxes on income, profits and capital gains	..	0.0	0.0	0.0	0.0	..	0.0	0.0	0.0	0.0
2000 Social security contributions	..	4.3	7.9	12.0	12.8	..	13.6	11.7	14.2	14.3
3000 Taxes on payroll and workforce	..	0.0	0.0	0.0	0.0	..	0.0	0.0	0.0	0.0
4000 Taxes on property	..	0.0	0.0	0.0	0.0	..	0.0	0.0	0.0	0.0
5000 Taxes on goods and services	..	0.0	0.0	0.0	0.0	..	0.0	0.0	0.0	0.0
6000 Other taxes	..	0.0	0.0	0.0	0.0	..	0.0	0.0	0.0	0.0

.. Not available

Note: More detailed country data and country notes are available in online chapter 6 "Tax revenues by sub-sectors of general government": https://doi.org/10.1787/0bbc27da-en. Full time series can be accessed at http://oe.cd/full-time-series.

Source: Ministry of Finance.

StatLink https://doi.org/10.1787/888934211357

Table 4.61. Slovenia, tax revenue and % of GDP by selected tax category

	Billion EUR					% of GDP				
	1990	2000	2010	2017	2018	1990	2000	2010	2017	2018
Total tax revenue	..	**7.1**	**13.8**	**16.0**	**17.1**	..	**37.7**	**37.8**	**37.1**	**37.4**
1000 Taxes on income, profits and capital gains	..	**1.3**	**2.7**	**3.0**	**3.3**	..	**6.8**	**7.4**	**6.9**	**7.3**
1100 Of individuals	..	1.0	2.0	2.2	2.4	..	5.5	5.6	5.1	5.3
1200 Corporate	..	0.2	0.7	0.8	0.9	..	1.1	1.8	1.8	1.9
1300 Unallocable between 1100 and 1200	..	0.0	0.0	0.0	0.0	..	0.1	0.0	0.0	0.0
2000 Social security contributions	..	**2.8**	**5.8**	**6.6**	**7.1**	..	**15.0**	**15.8**	**15.4**	**15.5**
2100 Employees	..	1.4	2.8	3.2	3.5	..	7.7	7.7	7.6	7.6
2200 Employers	..	1.0	2.1	2.4	2.6	..	5.4	5.7	5.6	5.7
2300 Self-employed or non-employed	..	0.4	0.9	1.0	1.0	..	1.9	2.5	2.3	2.2
2400 Unallocable between 2100, 2200 and 2300	..	0.0	0.0	0.0	0.0	..	0.0	0.0	0.0	0.0
3000 Taxes on payroll and workforce	..	**0.3**	**0.0**	**0.0**	**0.0**	..	**1.5**	**0.1**	**0.1**	**0.0**
4000 Taxes on property	..	**0.1**	**0.2**	**0.3**	**0.3**	..	**0.6**	**0.6**	**0.6**	**0.6**
4100 Recurrent taxes on immovable property	..	0.1	0.2	0.2	0.2	..	0.4	0.5	0.5	0.5
4200 Recurrent taxes on net wealth	..	0.0	0.0	0.0	0.0	..	0.0	0.0	0.0	0.0
4300 Estate, inheritance and gift taxes	..	0.0	0.0	0.0	0.0	..	0.0	0.0	0.0	0.0
4400 Taxes on financial and capital transactions	..	0.0	0.0	0.0	0.0	..	0.1	0.1	0.1	0.1
4500 Non-recurrent taxes	..	0.0	0.0	0.0	0.0	..	0.1	0.0	0.0	0.0
4600 Other recurrent taxes on property	..	0.0	0.0	0.0	0.0	..	0.0	0.0	0.0	0.0
5000 Taxes on goods and services	..	**2.6**	**5.1**	**6.1**	**6.4**	..	**13.8**	**13.9**	**14.1**	**14.0**
5100 Taxes on production, sale, transfer, etc	..	2.5	4.8	5.7	6.0	..	13.2	13.3	13.2	13.0
5110 General taxes	..	1.6	2.9	3.5	3.8	..	8.7	8.1	8.1	8.2
5111 Value added taxes	..	1.6	2.9	3.5	3.8	..	8.5	8.1	8.1	8.2
5120 Taxes on specific goods and services	..	0.8	1.9	2.2	2.2	..	4.5	5.3	5.1	4.8
5121 Excises	..	0.6	1.6	1.7	1.7	..	3.1	4.3	4.0	3.7
5200 Taxes on use of goods and perform activities	..	0.1	0.2	0.4	0.4	..	0.6	0.6	0.9	1.0
5300 Unallocable between 5100 and 5200	..	0.0	0.0	0.0	0.0	..	0.0	0.0	0.0	0.0
6000 Other taxes	..	**0.0**	**0.0**	**0.0**	**0.0**	..	**0.0**	**0.0**	**0.0**	**0.0**
Non-wastable tax credits										
Non-wastable tax credits against 1000	..	..	..	..	..	..	..	..	..	..
Transfer component	..	..	..	..	..	..	..	..	..	..
Tax expenditure component	..	..	..	..	..	..	..	..	..	..
Revenues collected on behalf of the EU										
Revenues collected on behalf of the EU, total	..	..	0.1	0.1	0.1	..	..	0.2	0.2	0.1
Customs duties	..	..	0.1	0.1	0.1	..	..	0.2	0.1	0.1
SRF contributions	..	..	..	0.0	0.0	..	..	..	0.0	0.0

.. Not available

Note: More detailed country data and country notes are available in online chapter 5 "Detailed country tables": https://doi.org/10.1787/0bbc27da-en. Full time series can be accessed at http://oe.cd/full-time-series.

Source: Statistical Office of the Republic of Slovenia.

StatLink https://doi.org/10.1787/888934211376

Table 4.62. Slovenia, tax revenue and % of GDP by level of government and main taxes

	Billion EUR					% of GDP				
	1990	2000	2010	2017	2018	1990	2000	2010	2017	2018
Federal or Central government										
Total tax revenue	..	**3.8**	**6.5**	**7.9**	**8.5**	..	**20.2**	**18.0**	**18.3**	**18.6**
1000 Taxes on income, profits and capital gains	..	0.9	1.6	1.9	2.2	..	4.8	4.3	4.3	4.7
2000 Social security contributions	..	0.0	0.1	0.1	0.1	..	0.1	0.2	0.2	0.2
3000 Taxes on payroll and workforce	..	0.3	0.0	0.0	0.0	..	1.5	0.1	0.1	0.0
4000 Taxes on property	..	0.0	0.0	0.0	0.0	..	0.1	0.0	0.0	0.0
5000 Taxes on goods and services	..	2.6	4.9	5.9	6.2	..	13.7	13.5	13.8	13.7
6000 Other taxes	..	0.0	0.0	0.0	0.0	..	0.0	0.0	0.0	0.0
State/Regional										
Total tax revenue	..	..	..	..	..	..	..	..	..	..
1000 Taxes on income, profits and capital gains	..	..	..	..	..	..	..	..	..	..
2000 Social security contributions	..	..	..	..	..	..	..	..	..	..
3000 Taxes on payroll and workforce	..	..	..	..	..	..	..	..	..	..
4000 Taxes on property	..	..	..	..	..	..	..	..	..	..
5000 Taxes on goods and services	..	..	..	..	..	..	..	..	..	..
6000 Other taxes	..	..	..	..	..	..	..	..	..	..
Local government										
Total tax revenue	..	**0.5**	**1.5**	**1.5**	**1.5**	..	**2.7**	**4.0**	**3.4**	**3.4**
1000 Taxes on income, profits and capital gains	..	0.4	1.1	1.1	1.2	..	2.0	3.1	2.6	2.6
2000 Social security contributions	..	0.0	0.0	0.0	0.0	..	0.0	0.0	0.0	0.0
3000 Taxes on payroll and workforce	..	0.0	0.0	0.0	0.0	..	0.0	0.0	0.0	0.0
4000 Taxes on property	..	0.1	0.2	0.3	0.3	..	0.6	0.6	0.6	0.6
5000 Taxes on goods and services	..	0.0	0.1	0.1	0.1	..	0.1	0.3	0.2	0.2
6000 Other taxes	..	0.0	0.0	0.0	0.0	..	0.0	0.0	0.0	0.0
Social Security Funds										
Total tax revenue	..	**2.8**	**5.7**	**6.6**	**7.0**	..	**14.8**	**15.7**	**15.3**	**15.3**
1000 Taxes on income, profits and capital gains	..	0.0	0.0	0.0	0.0	..	0.0	0.0	0.0	0.0
2000 Social security contributions	..	2.8	5.7	6.6	7.0	..	14.8	15.7	15.3	15.3
3000 Taxes on payroll and workforce	..	0.0	0.0	0.0	0.0	..	0.0	0.0	0.0	0.0
4000 Taxes on property	..	0.0	0.0	0.0	0.0	..	0.0	0.0	0.0	0.0
5000 Taxes on goods and services	..	0.0	0.0	0.0	0.0	..	0.0	0.0	0.0	0.0
6000 Other taxes	..	0.0	0.0	0.0	0.0	..	0.0	0.0	0.0	0.0

.. Not available

Note: More detailed country data and country notes are available in online chapter 6 "Tax revenues by sub-sectors of general government": https://doi.org/10.1787/0bbc27da-en. Full time series can be accessed at http://oe.cd/full-time-series.

Source: Statistical Office of the Republic of Slovenia.

StatLink https://doi.org/10.1787/888934211395

Table 4.63. Spain, tax revenue and % of GDP by selected tax category

	Billion EUR					% of GDP				
	1990	2000	2010	2017	2018	1990	2000	2010	2017	2018
Total tax revenue	**103.7**	**214.1**	**335.6**	**393.5**	**416.7**	**31.5**	**33.1**	**31.3**	**33.9**	**34.6**
1000 Taxes on income, profits and capital gains	**31.8**	**60.1**	**93.8**	**111.8**	**122.0**	**9.7**	**9.3**	**8.7**	**9.6**	**10.1**
1100 Of individuals	22.5	41.2	74.1	85.8	92.3	6.9	6.4	6.9	7.4	7.7
1200 Corporate	9.1	18.9	19.7	26.0	29.7	2.8	2.9	1.8	2.2	2.5
1300 Unallocable between 1100 and 1200	0.1	0.0	0.0	0.0	0.0	0.0	0.0	0.0	0.0	0.0
2000 Social security contributions	**36.7**	**74.7**	**127.2**	**134.1**	**141.2**	**11.2**	**11.5**	**11.9**	**11.5**	**11.7**
2100 Employees	6.0	11.7	19.4	20.6	21.6	1.8	1.8	1.8	1.8	1.8
2200 Employers	26.4	54.2	89.7	97.5	103.3	8.0	8.4	8.4	8.4	8.6
2300 Self-employed or non-employed	4.4	8.7	18.1	16.0	16.3	1.3	1.4	1.7	1.4	1.4
2400 Unallocable between 2100, 2200 and 2300	0.0	0.0	0.0	0.0	0.0	0.0	0.0	0.0	0.0	0.0
3000 Taxes on payroll and workforce	**0.0**	**0.0**	**0.0**	**0.0**	**0.0**	**0.0**	**0.0**	**0.0**	**0.0**	**0.0**
4000 Taxes on property	**5.7**	**13.8**	**22.2**	**29.5**	**30.3**	**1.7**	**2.1**	**2.1**	**2.5**	**2.5**
4100 Recurrent taxes on immovable property	1.5	4.0	9.7	13.2	13.2	0.5	0.6	0.9	1.1	1.1
4200 Recurrent taxes on net wealth	0.6	1.4	0.7	2.1	2.2	0.2	0.2	0.1	0.2	0.2
4300 Estate, inheritance and gift taxes	0.4	1.4	2.4	2.7	2.7	0.1	0.2	0.2	0.2	0.2
4400 Taxes on financial and capital transactions	2.5	5.9	7.6	8.5	9.3	0.8	0.9	0.7	0.7	0.8
4500 Non-recurrent taxes	0.6	1.1	1.8	3.0	2.9	0.2	0.2	0.2	0.3	0.2
4600 Other recurrent taxes on property	0.0	0.0	0.0	0.0	0.0	0.0	0.0	0.0	0.0	0.0
5000 Taxes on goods and services	**29.4**	**65.5**	**92.3**	**118.0**	**123.0**	**9.0**	**10.1**	**8.6**	**10.2**	**10.2**
5100 Taxes on production, sale, transfer, etc	26.7	59.4	85.0	109.4	113.8	8.1	9.2	7.9	9.4	9.5
5110 General taxes	16.6	37.8	55.6	75.8	79.5	5.1	5.8	5.2	6.5	6.6
5111 Value added taxes	16.3	37.8	55.3	75.6	79.3	5.0	5.8	5.2	6.5	6.6
5120 Taxes on specific goods and services	10.1	21.6	29.4	33.7	34.4	3.1	3.3	2.7	2.9	2.9
5121 Excises	6.0	18.0	24.4	26.5	26.8	1.8	2.8	2.3	2.3	2.2
5200 Taxes on use of goods and perform activities	2.6	6.1	7.4	8.6	9.1	0.8	0.9	0.7	0.7	0.8
5300 Unallocable between 5100 and 5200	0.1	0.0	0.0	0.0	0.0	0.0	0.0	0.0	0.0	0.0
6000 Other taxes	**0.0**	**0.0**	**0.0**	**0.1**	**0.2**	**0.0**	**0.0**	**0.0**	**0.0**	**0.0**
Non-wastable tax credits										
Non-wastable tax credits against 1000	..	..	1.9	2.5	3.1	..	..	0.2	0.2	0.3
Transfer component	..	..	1.2	1.5	2.2	..	..	0.1	0.1	0.2
Tax expenditure component	..	..	0.7	0.9	1.0	..	..	0.1	0.1	0.1
Revenues collected on behalf of the EU										
Revenues collected on behalf of the EU, total	0.5	1.0	1.5	2.6	2.7	0.2	0.2	0.1	0.2	0.2
Customs duties	..	1.0	1.5	1.9	1.9	..	0.2	0.1	0.2	0.2
SRF contributions	..	..	..	0.7	0.7	..	..	..	0.1	0.1

.. Not available

Note: More detailed country data and country notes are available in online chapter 5 "Detailed country tables": https://doi.org/10.1787/0bbc27da-en. Full time series can be accessed at http://oe.cd/full-time-series.

Source: Información Estadística del Ministerio de Hacienda (for national taxes). Cuentas de las Administraciones Públicas (for local taxes and social security) both published by Secretaría General Técnica del Ministerio de Hacienda.

StatLink https://doi.org/10.1787/888934211414

Table 4.64. Spain, tax revenue and % of GDP by level of government and main taxes

	Billion EUR					% of GDP				
	1990	2000	2010	2017	2018	1990	2000	2010	2017	2018
Federal or Central government										
Total tax revenue	**53.7**	**104.7**	**135.9**	**161.9**	**173.8**	**16.3**	**16.2**	**12.7**	**13.9**	**14.4**
1000 Taxes on income, profits and capital gains	29.5	51.0	60.6	63.8	71.7	9.0	7.9	5.6	5.5	6.0
2000 Social security contributions	0.4	2.3	3.5	3.4	3.5	0.1	0.4	0.3	0.3	0.3
3000 Taxes on payroll and workforce	0.0	0.0	0.0	0.0	0.0	0.0	0.0	0.0	0.0	0.0
4000 Taxes on property	0.4	0.4	0.1	0.4	0.4	0.1	0.1	0.0	0.0	0.0
5000 Taxes on goods and services	23.4	51.1	71.7	94.2	98.0	7.1	7.9	6.7	8.1	8.1
6000 Other taxes	0.0	0.0	0.0	0.1	0.2	0.0	0.0	0.0	0.0	0.0
State/Regional										
Total tax revenue	**5.0**	**16.9**	**44.1**	**60.9**	**63.8**	**1.5**	**2.6**	**4.1**	**5.2**	**5.3**
1000 Taxes on income, profits and capital gains	0.4	5.6	28.1	41.7	43.4	0.1	0.9	2.6	3.6	3.6
2000 Social security contributions	0.0	0.0	0.0	0.0	0.0	0.0	0.0	0.0	0.0	0.0
3000 Taxes on payroll and workforce	0.0	0.0	0.0	0.0	0.0	0.0	0.0	0.0	0.0	0.0
4000 Taxes on property	3.0	7.7	9.7	11.8	12.7	0.9	1.2	0.9	1.0	1.1
5000 Taxes on goods and services	1.6	3.6	6.3	7.4	7.7	0.5	0.6	0.6	0.6	0.6
6000 Other taxes	0.0	0.0	0.0	0.0	0.0	0.0	0.0	0.0	0.0	0.0
Local government										
Total tax revenue	**8.1**	**19.0**	**30.3**	**37.4**	**38.7**	**2.5**	**2.9**	**2.8**	**3.2**	**3.2**
1000 Taxes on income, profits and capital gains	1.9	3.5	5.2	6.3	6.9	0.6	0.5	0.5	0.5	0.6
2000 Social security contributions	0.0	0.0	0.0	0.0	0.0	0.0	0.0	0.0	0.0	0.0
3000 Taxes on payroll and workforce	0.0	0.0	0.0	0.0	0.0	0.0	0.0	0.0	0.0	0.0
4000 Taxes on property	2.3	5.8	12.4	17.2	17.2	0.7	0.9	1.2	1.5	1.4
5000 Taxes on goods and services	3.9	9.7	12.8	13.9	14.5	1.2	1.5	1.2	1.2	1.2
6000 Other taxes	0.0	0.0	0.0	0.0	0.0	0.0	0.0	0.0	0.0	0.0
Social Security Funds										
Total tax revenue	**36.4**	**72.4**	**123.7**	**130.7**	**137.8**	**11.1**	**11.2**	**11.5**	**11.2**	**11.4**
1000 Taxes on income, profits and capital gains	0.0	0.0	0.0	0.0	0.0	0.0	0.0	0.0	0.0	0.0
2000 Social security contributions	36.4	72.4	123.7	130.7	137.8	11.1	11.2	11.5	11.2	11.4
3000 Taxes on payroll and workforce	0.0	0.0	0.0	0.0	0.0	0.0	0.0	0.0	0.0	0.0
4000 Taxes on property	0.0	0.0	0.0	0.0	0.0	0.0	0.0	0.0	0.0	0.0
5000 Taxes on goods and services	0.0	0.0	0.0	0.0	0.0	0.0	0.0	0.0	0.0	0.0
6000 Other taxes	0.0	0.0	0.0	0.0	0.0	0.0	0.0	0.0	0.0	0.0

Note: More detailed country data and country notes are available in online chapter 6 "Tax revenues by sub-sectors of general government": https://doi.org/10.1787/0bbc27da-en. Full time series can be accessed at http://oe.cd/full-time-series.

Source: Información Estadística del Ministerio de Hacienda (for national taxes). Cuentas de las Administraciones Públicas (for local taxes and social security) both published by Secretaría General Técnica del Ministerio de Hacienda.

StatLink https://doi.org/10.1787/888934211433

Table 4.65. Sweden, tax revenue and % of GDP by selected tax category

	Billion SEK					% of GDP				
	1990	2000	2010	2017	2018	1990	2000	2010	2017	2018
Total tax revenue	**759.1**	**1 174.5**	**1 538.7**	**2 049.3**	**2 120.6**	**49.0**	**48.8**	**43.1**	**44.3**	**43.9**
1000 Taxes on income, profits and capital gains	**314.8**	**480.4**	**546.7**	**744.9**	**761.0**	**20.3**	**19.9**	**15.3**	**16.1**	**15.8**
1100 Of individuals	291.1	392.6	430.9	616.3	623.6	18.8	16.3	12.1	13.3	12.9
1200 Corporate	23.7	87.8	115.8	128.6	137.4	1.5	3.6	3.2	2.8	2.8
1300 Unallocable between 1100 and 1200	0.0	0.0	0.0	0.0	0.0	0.0	0.0	0.0	0.0	0.0
2000 Social security contributions	**205.9**	**307.0**	**384.7**	**443.1**	**463.3**	**13.3**	**12.7**	**10.8**	**9.6**	**9.6**
2100 Employees	0.8	63.1	89.2	118.7	123.7	0.1	2.6	2.5	2.6	2.6
2200 Employers	196.9	237.5	288.4	320.4	335.4	12.7	9.9	8.1	6.9	6.9
2300 Self-employed or non-employed	8.1	5.6	7.5	4.8	4.8	0.5	0.2	0.2	0.1	0.1
2400 Unallocable between 2100, 2200 and 2300	0.0	0.8	-0.4	-0.8	-0.5	0.0	0.0	0.0	0.0	0.0
3000 Taxes on payroll and workforce	**18.7**	**50.1**	**107.5**	**233.2**	**245.0**	**1.2**	**2.1**	**3.0**	**5.0**	**5.1**
4000 Taxes on property	**26.6**	**39.9**	**36.5**	**45.5**	**45.8**	**1.7**	**1.7**	**1.0**	**1.0**	**0.9**
4100 Recurrent taxes on immovable property	8.9	23.3	26.4	32.9	33.2	0.6	1.0	0.7	0.7	0.7
4200 Recurrent taxes on net wealth	3.2	8.2	0.0	0.0	0.0	0.2	0.3	0.0	0.0	0.0
4300 Estate, inheritance and gift taxes	1.4	2.5	0.0	0.0	0.0	0.1	0.1	0.0	0.0	0.0
4400 Taxes on financial and capital transactions	13.1	5.8	10.1	12.6	12.6	0.8	0.2	0.3	0.3	0.3
4500 Non-recurrent taxes	0.0	0.0	0.0	0.0	0.0	0.0	0.0	0.0	0.0	0.0
4600 Other recurrent taxes on property	0.0	0.0	0.0	0.0	0.0	0.0	0.0	0.0	0.0	0.0
5000 Taxes on goods and services	**188.7**	**292.3**	**456.5**	**574.1**	**596.9**	**12.2**	**12.1**	**12.8**	**12.4**	**12.4**
5100 Taxes on production, sale, transfer, etc	181.6	284.8	440.1	554.2	577.1	11.7	11.8	12.3	12.0	12.0
5110 General taxes	112.4	199.6	326.7	427.7	445.8	7.3	8.3	9.1	9.2	9.2
5111 Value added taxes	112.4	197.5	322.6	425.1	445.7	7.3	8.2	9.0	9.2	9.2
5120 Taxes on specific goods and services	69.2	85.2	113.4	126.4	131.3	4.5	3.5	3.2	2.7	2.7
5121 Excises	55.3	70.3	91.5	97.9	102.1	3.6	2.9	2.6	2.1	2.1
5200 Taxes on use of goods and perform activities	7.1	7.4	16.4	19.9	19.8	0.5	0.3	0.5	0.4	0.4
5300 Unallocable between 5100 and 5200	0.0	0.0	0.0	0.0	0.0	0.0	0.0	0.0	0.0	0.0
6000 Other taxes	**1.3**	**1.5**	**1.4**	**2.3**	**1.9**	**0.1**	**0.1**	**0.0**	**0.0**	**0.0**
Non-wastable tax credits										
Non-wastable tax credits against 1000	..	..	..	..	..	..	..	..	..	..
Transfer component	..	..	..	..	..	..	..	..	..	..
Tax expenditure component	..	..	..	..	..	..	..	..	..	..
Revenues collected on behalf of the EU										
Revenues collected on behalf of the EU, total	..	7.2	11.1	12.5	13.0	..	0.3	0.3	0.3	0.3
Customs duties	..	3.4	5.4	6.2	6.5	..	0.1	0.2	0.1	0.1

.. Not available

Note: More detailed country data and country notes are available in online chapter 5 "Detailed country tables": https://doi.org/10.1787/0bbc27da-en. Full time series can be accessed at http://oe.cd/full-time-series.

Source: Monthly reports of central Government Revenues (unpublished) National Audit Bureau, Stockholm. Local Government Finance (SOS), Tax assessment statistics (SOS), National Central Bureau of Statistics, Stockholm. National Accounts (Statistical Reports), National Bureau of Statistics, Stockholm.

StatLink https://doi.org/10.1787/888934211452

Table 4.66. Sweden, tax revenue and % of GDP by level of government and main taxes

	Billion SEK					% of GDP				
	1990	2000	2010	2017	2018	1990	2000	2010	2017	2018
Federal or Central government										
Total tax revenue	**387.0**	**704.1**	**807.2**	**1 074.7**	**1 106.6**	**25.0**	**29.2**	**22.6**	**23.2**	**22.9**
1000 Taxes on income, profits and capital gains	94.7	144.1	23.8	44.8	34.8	6.1	6.0	0.7	1.0	0.7
2000 Social security contributions	54.8	180.2	201.2	198.1	206.6	3.5	7.5	5.6	4.3	4.3
3000 Taxes on payroll and workforce	18.7	50.1	107.5	233.2	245.0	1.2	2.1	3.0	5.0	5.1
4000 Taxes on property	26.6	39.9	22.4	28.5	27.8	1.7	1.7	0.6	0.6	0.6
5000 Taxes on goods and services	187.8	288.5	450.8	567.8	590.4	12.1	12.0	12.6	12.3	12.2
6000 Other taxes	1.3	1.5	1.4	2.3	1.9	0.1	0.1	0.0	0.0	0.0
State/Regional										
Total tax revenue	..	..	..	..	..	..	..	..	..	..
1000 Taxes on income, profits and capital gains	..	..	..	..	..	..	..	..	..	..
2000 Social security contributions	..	..	..	..	..	..	..	..	..	..
3000 Taxes on payroll and workforce	..	..	..	..	..	..	..	..	..	..
4000 Taxes on property	..	..	..	..	..	..	..	..	..	..
5000 Taxes on goods and services	..	..	..	..	..	..	..	..	..	..
6000 Other taxes	..	..	..	..	..	..	..	..	..	..
Local government										
Total tax revenue	**221.0**	**336.3**	**537.0**	**717.0**	**744.3**	**14.3**	**14.0**	**15.0**	**15.5**	**15.4**
1000 Taxes on income, profits and capital gains	220.1	336.3	522.9	700.1	726.2	14.2	14.0	14.6	15.1	15.0
2000 Social security contributions	0.0	0.0	0.0	0.0	0.0	0.0	0.0	0.0	0.0	0.0
3000 Taxes on payroll and workforce	0.0	0.0	0.0	0.0	0.0	0.0	0.0	0.0	0.0	0.0
4000 Taxes on property	0.0	0.0	14.1	16.9	18.1	0.0	0.0	0.4	0.4	0.4
5000 Taxes on goods and services	0.9	0.0	0.0	0.0	0.0	0.1	0.0	0.0	0.0	0.0
6000 Other taxes	0.0	0.0	0.0	0.0	0.0	0.0	0.0	0.0	0.0	0.0
Social Security Funds										
Total tax revenue	**151.1**	**126.8**	**183.5**	**245.0**	**256.7**	**9.7**	**5.3**	**5.1**	**5.3**	**5.3**
1000 Taxes on income, profits and capital gains	0.0	0.0	0.0	0.0	0.0	0.0	0.0	0.0	0.0	0.0
2000 Social security contributions	151.1	126.8	183.5	245.0	256.7	9.7	5.3	5.1	5.3	5.3
3000 Taxes on payroll and workforce	0.0	0.0	0.0	0.0	0.0	0.0	0.0	0.0	0.0	0.0
4000 Taxes on property	0.0	0.0	0.0	0.0	0.0	0.0	0.0	0.0	0.0	0.0
5000 Taxes on goods and services	0.0	0.0	0.0	0.0	0.0	0.0	0.0	0.0	0.0	0.0
6000 Other taxes	0.0	0.0	0.0	0.0	0.0	0.0	0.0	0.0	0.0	0.0

.. Not available

Note: More detailed country data and country notes are available in online chapter 6 "Tax revenues by sub-sectors of general government": https://doi.org/10.1787/0bbc27da-en. Full time series can be accessed at http://oe.cd/full-time-series.

Source: Monthly reports of central Government Revenues (unpublished) National Audit Bureau, Stockholm. Local Government Finance (SOS), Tax assessment statistics (SOS), National Central Bureau of Statistics, Stockholm. National Accounts (Statistical Reports), National Bureau of Statistics, Stockholm.

StatLink https://doi.org/10.1787/888934211471

Table 4.67. Switzerland, tax revenue and % of GDP by selected tax category

	Billion CHF					% of GDP				
	1990	2000	2010	2017	2018	1990	2000	2010	2017	2018
Total tax revenue	**85.1**	**126.8**	**161.9**	**190.2**	**193.4**	**23.7**	**27.6**	**26.6**	**28.4**	**28.0**
1000 Taxes on income, profits and capital gains	**40.0**	**55.9**	**73.7**	**90.0**	**92.2**	**11.2**	**12.2**	**12.1**	**13.4**	**13.4**
1100 Of individuals	27.7	37.6	51.3	57.5	59.3	7.7	8.2	8.4	8.6	8.6
1200 Corporate	6.3	11.2	16.2	20.4	22.1	1.8	2.4	2.7	3.1	3.2
1300 Unallocable between 1100 and 1200	6.1	7.1	6.2	12.1	10.8	1.7	1.6	1.0	1.8	1.6
2000 Social security contributions	**19.9**	**30.6**	**38.3**	**44.9**	**45.7**	**5.5**	**6.7**	**6.3**	**6.7**	**6.6**
2100 Employees	9.3	14.3	17.5	20.8	21.3	2.6	3.1	2.9	3.1	3.1
2200 Employers	9.3	14.3	17.6	20.9	21.3	2.6	3.1	2.9	3.1	3.1
2300 Self-employed or non-employed	1.3	2.0	3.2	3.2	3.1	0.4	0.4	0.5	0.5	0.5
2400 Unallocable between 2100, 2200 and 2300	0.0	0.0	0.0	0.0	0.0	0.0	0.0	0.0	0.0	0.0
3000 Taxes on payroll and workforce	**0.0**	**0.0**	**0.0**	**0.0**	**0.0**	**0.0**	**0.0**	**0.0**	**0.0**	**0.0**
4000 Taxes on property	**7.6**	**12.2**	**12.3**	**14.2**	**14.2**	**2.1**	**2.7**	**2.0**	**2.1**	**2.1**
4100 Recurrent taxes on immovable property	0.4	0.7	1.0	1.2	1.2	0.1	0.2	0.2	0.2	0.2
4200 Recurrent taxes on net wealth	3.4	5.2	7.0	8.9	9.1	0.9	1.1	1.2	1.3	1.3
4300 Estate, inheritance and gift taxes	0.9	1.2	1.0	1.2	1.2	0.2	0.3	0.2	0.2	0.2
4400 Taxes on financial and capital transactions	2.2	4.3	2.4	2.0	1.7	0.6	0.9	0.4	0.3	0.2
4500 Non-recurrent taxes	0.0	0.0	0.0	0.0	0.0	0.0	0.0	0.0	0.0	0.0
4600 Other recurrent taxes on property	0.6	0.8	0.9	1.0	1.1	0.2	0.2	0.2	0.1	0.2
5000 Taxes on goods and services	**17.5**	**27.8**	**37.1**	**40.2**	**40.3**	**4.9**	**6.1**	**6.1**	**6.0**	**5.8**
5100 Taxes on production, sale, transfer, etc	16.0	25.3	32.2	34.3	34.4	4.5	5.5	5.3	5.1	5.0
5110 General taxes	9.9	16.9	21.0	23.3	23.0	2.8	3.7	3.4	3.5	3.3
5111 Value added taxes	9.9	16.6	20.6	22.9	22.6	2.8	3.6	3.4	3.4	3.3
5120 Taxes on specific goods and services	6.1	8.3	11.1	11.0	11.3	1.7	1.8	1.8	1.6	1.6
5121 Excises	4.6	6.8	8.3	8.1	8.4	1.3	1.5	1.4	1.2	1.2
5200 Taxes on use of goods and perform activities	1.6	2.5	4.9	5.8	5.9	0.4	0.6	0.8	0.9	0.9
5300 Unallocable between 5100 and 5200	0.0	0.0	0.0	0.0	0.0	0.0	0.0	0.0	0.0	0.0
6000 Other taxes	**0.1**	**0.2**	**0.6**	**1.0**	**1.0**	**0.0**	**0.0**	**0.1**	**0.1**	**0.1**
Non-wastable tax credits										
Non-wastable tax credits against 1000	..	..	..	..	..	..	..	..	..	..
Transfer component	..	..	..	..	..	..	..	..	..	..
Tax expenditure component	..	..	..	..	..	..	..	..	..	..

.. Not available

Note: More detailed country data and country notes are available in online chapter 5 "Detailed country tables": https://doi.org/10.1787/0bbc27da-en. Full time series can be accessed at http://oe.cd/full-time-series.

The total tax revenue has been reduced by the amount of any capital transfer that represents uncollected taxes. The capital transfer has been allocated between tax headings in proportion to the reported tax revenue. Therefore, the tax revenue amounts are different to those reported in the detailed country data available in online chapter 5 "Detailed country tables".

Source: Financial Statistics, Federal Finance Administration.

StatLink https://doi.org/10.1787/888934211490

Table 4.68. Switzerland, tax revenue and % of GDP by level of government and main taxes

	Billion CHF					% of GDP				
	1990	2000	2010	2017	2018	1990	2000	2010	2017	2018
Federal or Central government										
Total tax revenue	**29.0**	**46.9**	**59.2**	**69.6**	**69.5**	**8.1**	**10.2**	**9.7**	**10.4**	**10.1**
1000 Taxes on income, profits and capital gains	10.9	17.0	22.7	30.8	30.9	3.0	3.7	3.7	4.6	4.5
2000 Social security contributions	0.0	0.0	0.0	0.0	0.0	0.0	0.0	0.0	0.0	0.0
3000 Taxes on payroll and workforce	0.0	0.0	0.0	0.0	0.0	0.0	0.0	0.0	0.0	0.0
4000 Taxes on property	2.1	4.1	2.2	1.7	1.4	0.6	0.9	0.4	0.3	0.2
5000 Taxes on goods and services	16.0	25.7	34.3	37.1	37.1	4.5	5.6	5.6	5.5	5.4
6000 Other taxes	0.0	0.0	0.0	0.1	0.1	0.0	0.0	0.0	0.0	0.0
State/Regional										
Total tax revenue	**21.3**	**28.9**	**39.9**	**46.6**	**48.2**	**6.0**	**6.3**	**6.5**	**7.0**	**7.0**
1000 Taxes on income, profits and capital gains	16.4	21.8	30.9	35.5	36.8	4.6	4.7	5.1	5.3	5.3
2000 Social security contributions	0.0	0.0	0.0	0.0	0.0	0.0	0.0	0.0	0.0	0.0
3000 Taxes on payroll and workforce	0.0	0.0	0.0	0.0	0.0	0.0	0.0	0.0	0.0	0.0
4000 Taxes on property	3.5	5.0	6.3	7.9	8.0	1.0	1.1	1.0	1.2	1.2
5000 Taxes on goods and services	1.4	2.1	2.7	3.0	3.0	0.4	0.4	0.4	0.4	0.4
6000 Other taxes	0.0	0.0	0.0	0.3	0.4	0.0	0.0	0.0	0.0	0.1
Local government										
Total tax revenue	**14.9**	**20.5**	**24.6**	**29.1**	**30.0**	**4.2**	**4.5**	**4.0**	**4.4**	**4.3**
1000 Taxes on income, profits and capital gains	12.7	17.1	20.2	23.8	24.5	3.5	3.7	3.3	3.6	3.6
2000 Social security contributions	0.0	0.0	0.0	0.0	0.0	0.0	0.0	0.0	0.0	0.0
3000 Taxes on payroll and workforce	0.0	0.0	0.0	0.0	0.0	0.0	0.0	0.0	0.0	0.0
4000 Taxes on property	2.0	3.1	3.8	4.6	4.7	0.6	0.7	0.6	0.7	0.7
5000 Taxes on goods and services	0.1	0.1	0.1	0.2	0.2	0.0	0.0	0.0	0.0	0.0
6000 Other taxes	0.1	0.2	0.6	0.6	0.6	0.0	0.0	0.1	0.1	0.1
Social Security Funds										
Total tax revenue	**19.9**	**30.6**	**38.3**	**44.9**	**45.7**	**5.5**	**6.7**	**6.3**	**6.7**	**6.6**
1000 Taxes on income, profits and capital gains	0.0	0.0	0.0	0.0	0.0	0.0	0.0	0.0	0.0	0.0
2000 Social security contributions	19.9	30.6	38.3	44.9	45.7	5.5	6.7	6.3	6.7	6.6
3000 Taxes on payroll and workforce	0.0	0.0	0.0	0.0	0.0	0.0	0.0	0.0	0.0	0.0
4000 Taxes on property	0.0	0.0	0.0	0.0	0.0	0.0	0.0	0.0	0.0	0.0
5000 Taxes on goods and services	0.0	0.0	0.0	0.0	0.0	0.0	0.0	0.0	0.0	0.0
6000 Other taxes	0.0	0.0	0.0	0.0	0.0	0.0	0.0	0.0	0.0	0.0

Note: More detailed country data and country notes are available in online chapter 6 "Tax revenues by sub-sectors of general government": https://doi.org/10.1787/0bbc27da-en. Full time series can be accessed at http://oe.cd/full-time-series.

The total tax revenue has been reduced by the amount of any capital transfer that represents uncollected taxes. The capital transfer has been allocated between tax headings in proportion to the reported tax revenue. Therefore, the tax revenue amounts are different to those reported in the detailed country data available in online chapter 6 "Tax revenues by sub-sectors of general government".

Source: Financial Statistics, Federal Finance Administration.

StatLink https://doi.org/10.1787/888934211509

Table 4.69. Turkey, tax revenue and % of GDP by selected tax category

	Billion TRY					% of GDP				
	1990	2000	2010	2017	2018	1990	2000	2010	2017	2018
Total tax revenue	**0.1**	**40.3**	**287.9**	**773.4**	**901.5**	**14.5**	**23.5**	**24.7**	**24.7**	**24.0**
1000 Taxes on income, profits and capital gains	**0.0**	**11.9**	**61.3**	**165.3**	**217.7**	**4.9**	**6.9**	**5.3**	**5.3**	**5.8**
1100 Of individuals	0.0	9.0	40.4	112.4	139.0	3.9	5.2	3.5	3.6	3.7
1200 Corporate	0.0	2.9	20.9	52.9	78.7	1.0	1.7	1.8	1.7	2.1
1300 Unallocable between 1100 and 1200	0.0	0.0	0.0	0.0	0.0	0.0	0.0	0.0	0.0	0.0
2000 Social security contributions	**0.0**	**7.5**	**71.7**	**226.7**	**269.9**	**2.9**	**4.4**	**6.1**	**7.2**	**7.2**
2100 Employees	0.0	2.7	26.9	86.4	101.7	1.1	1.6	2.3	2.8	2.7
2200 Employers	0.0	3.6	39.4	128.3	151.4	1.6	2.1	3.4	4.1	4.0
2300 Self-employed or non-employed	0.0	1.2	5.4	12.0	16.9	0.2	0.7	0.5	0.4	0.4
2400 Unallocable between 2100, 2200 and 2300	0.0	0.0	0.0	0.0	0.0	0.0	0.0	0.0	0.0	0.0
3000 Taxes on payroll and workforce	**0.0**	**0.0**	**0.0**	**0.0**	**0.0**	**0.0**	**0.0**	**0.0**	**0.0**	**0.0**
4000 Taxes on property	**0.0**	**1.3**	**11.7**	**34.9**	**38.9**	**0.3**	**0.7**	**1.0**	**1.1**	**1.0**
4100 Recurrent taxes on immovable property	0.0	0.2	2.7	6.8	8.7	0.0	0.1	0.2	0.2	0.2
4200 Recurrent taxes on net wealth	0.0	0.0	0.0	0.0	0.0	0.0	0.0	0.0	0.0	0.0
4300 Estate, inheritance and gift taxes	0.0	0.0	0.2	0.7	0.9	0.0	0.0	0.0	0.0	0.0
4400 Taxes on financial and capital transactions	0.0	1.1	8.8	27.3	29.3	0.3	0.6	0.8	0.9	0.8
4500 Non-recurrent taxes	0.0	0.0	0.0	0.0	0.0	0.0	0.0	0.0	0.0	0.0
4600 Other recurrent taxes on property	0.0	0.0	0.0	0.0	0.0	0.0	0.0	0.0	0.0	0.0
5000 Taxes on goods and services	**0.0**	**16.9**	**137.3**	**336.3**	**365.0**	**4.1**	**9.9**	**11.8**	**10.7**	**9.7**
5100 Taxes on production, sale, transfer, etc	0.0	16.3	131.9	324.9	351.5	4.0	9.5	11.3	10.4	9.4
5110 General taxes	0.0	9.7	62.5	155.7	178.6	2.9	5.7	5.4	5.0	4.8
5111 Value added taxes	0.0	9.7	62.5	155.7	178.6	2.7	5.7	5.4	5.0	4.8
5120 Taxes on specific goods and services	0.0	6.6	69.3	169.3	172.8	1.1	3.8	5.9	5.4	4.6
5121 Excises	0.0	4.7	57.3	138.3	133.9	0.1	2.8	4.9	4.4	3.6
5200 Taxes on use of goods and perform activities	0.0	0.6	5.4	11.3	13.5	0.1	0.3	0.5	0.4	0.4
5300 Unallocable between 5100 and 5200	0.0	0.0	0.0	0.0	0.0	0.0	0.0	0.0	0.0	0.0
6000 Other taxes	**0.0**	**2.7**	**5.9**	**10.3**	**10.0**	**2.4**	**1.6**	**0.5**	**0.3**	**0.3**
Non-wastable tax credits										
Non-wastable tax credits against 1000	..	..	..	..	..	..	..	..	..	..
Transfer component	..	..	..	..	..	..	..	..	..	..
Tax expenditure component	..	..	..	..	..	..	..	..	..	..

.. Not available

Note: More detailed country data and country notes are available in online chapter 5 "Detailed country tables": https://doi.org/10.1787/0bbc27da-en. Full time series can be accessed at http://oe.cd/full-time-series.

Source: Bulletin of national accounts and the Budget revenue Bulletin.

StatLink https://doi.org/10.1787/888934211528

Table 4.70. Turkey, tax revenue and % of GDP by level of government and main taxes

	Billion TRY					% of GDP				
	1990	2000	2010	2017	2018	1990	2000	2010	2017	2018
Federal or Central government										
Total tax revenue	**0.1**	**29.1**	**189.4**	**473.2**	**545.0**	**10.4**	**17.0**	**16.2**	**15.1**	**14.5**
1000 Taxes on income, profits and capital gains	0.0	10.5	54.6	145.3	191.7	4.3	6.1	4.7	4.6	5.1
2000 Social security contributions	0.0	0.0	0.0	0.0	0.0	0.0	0.0	0.0	0.0	0.0
3000 Taxes on payroll and workforce	0.0	0.0	0.0	0.0	0.0	0.0	0.0	0.0	0.0	0.0
4000 Taxes on property	0.0	0.9	8.1	24.6	26.5	0.3	0.5	0.7	0.8	0.7
5000 Taxes on goods and services	0.0	15.2	124.0	299.4	322.7	3.6	8.9	10.6	9.6	8.6
6000 Other taxes	0.0	2.5	2.7	3.8	4.2	2.2	1.4	0.2	0.1	0.1
State/Regional										
Total tax revenue	..	..	..	..	..	..	..	..	..	..
1000 Taxes on income, profits and capital gains	..	..	..	..	..	..	..	..	..	..
2000 Social security contributions	..	..	..	..	..	..	..	..	..	..
3000 Taxes on payroll and workforce	..	..	..	..	..	..	..	..	..	..
4000 Taxes on property	..	..	..	..	..	..	..	..	..	..
5000 Taxes on goods and services	..	..	..	..	..	..	..	..	..	..
6000 Other taxes	..	..	..	..	..	..	..	..	..	..
Local government										
Total tax revenue	**0.0**	**3.6**	**26.8**	**73.5**	**86.5**	**1.3**	**2.1**	**2.3**	**2.3**	**2.3**
1000 Taxes on income, profits and capital gains	0.0	1.4	6.7	20.0	26.0	0.6	0.8	0.6	0.6	0.7
2000 Social security contributions	0.0	0.0	0.0	0.0	0.0	0.0	0.0	0.0	0.0	0.0
3000 Taxes on payroll and workforce	0.0	0.0	0.0	0.0	0.0	0.0	0.0	0.0	0.0	0.0
4000 Taxes on property	0.0	0.3	3.6	10.2	12.5	0.0	0.2	0.3	0.3	0.3
5000 Taxes on goods and services	0.0	1.7	13.3	36.8	42.3	0.5	1.0	1.1	1.2	1.1
6000 Other taxes	0.0	0.2	3.2	6.4	5.8	0.2	0.1	0.3	0.2	0.2
Social Security Funds										
Total tax revenue	**0.0**	**7.5**	**71.7**	**226.7**	**269.9**	**2.9**	**4.4**	**6.1**	**7.2**	**7.2**
1000 Taxes on income, profits and capital gains	0.0	0.0	0.0	0.0	0.0	0.0	0.0	0.0	0.0	0.0
2000 Social security contributions	0.0	7.5	71.7	226.7	269.9	2.9	4.4	6.1	7.2	7.2
3000 Taxes on payroll and workforce	0.0	0.0	0.0	0.0	0.0	0.0	0.0	0.0	0.0	0.0
4000 Taxes on property	0.0	0.0	0.0	0.0	0.0	0.0	0.0	0.0	0.0	0.0
5000 Taxes on goods and services	0.0	0.0	0.0	0.0	0.0	0.0	0.0	0.0	0.0	0.0
6000 Other taxes	0.0	0.0	0.0	0.0	0.0	0.0	0.0	0.0	0.0	0.0

.. Not available

Note: More detailed country data and country notes are available in online chapter 6 "Tax revenues by sub-sectors of general government": https://doi.org/10.1787/0bbc27da-en. Full time series can be accessed at http://oe.cd/full-time-series.

Source: Bulletin of national accounts and the Budget revenue Bulletin.

StatLink https://doi.org/10.1787/888934211547

Table 4.71. United Kingdom, tax revenue and % of GDP by selected tax category

	Billion GBP					% of GDP				
	1990	2000	2010	2017	2018	1990	2000	2010	2017	2018
Total tax revenue	**202.4**	**359.4**	**514.7**	**680.0**	**705.2**	**32.9**	**32.8**	**32.1**	**32.8**	**32.9**
1000 Taxes on income, profits and capital gains	**79.6**	**142.2**	**192.7**	**240.4**	**249.1**	**12.9**	**13.0**	**12.0**	**11.6**	**11.6**
1100 Of individuals	59.5	104.1	147.0	185.6	192.8	9.7	9.5	9.2	9.0	9.0
1200 Corporate	20.1	38.1	45.7	54.8	56.3	3.3	3.5	2.9	2.6	2.6
1300 Unallocable between 1100 and 1200	0.0	0.0	0.0	0.0	0.0	0.0	0.0	0.0	0.0	0.0
2000 Social security contributions	**34.5**	**60.3**	**97.3**	**130.4**	**135.0**	**5.6**	**5.5**	**6.1**	**6.3**	**6.3**
2100 Employees	13.3	24.2	38.7	50.4	52.1	2.2	2.2	2.4	2.4	2.4
2200 Employers	20.0	34.0	55.9	76.6	79.2	3.2	3.1	3.5	3.7	3.7
2300 Self-employed or non-employed	1.2	2.0	2.8	3.4	3.7	0.2	0.2	0.2	0.2	0.2
2400 Unallocable between 2100, 2200 and 2300	0.0	0.0	0.0	0.0	0.0	0.0	0.0	0.0	0.0	0.0
3000 Taxes on payroll and workforce	**0.0**	**0.0**	**0.0**	**1.8**	**2.6**	**0.0**	**0.0**	**0.0**	**0.1**	**0.1**
4000 Taxes on property	**16.5**	**41.1**	**61.8**	**85.6**	**88.4**	**2.7**	**3.8**	**3.9**	**4.1**	**4.1**
4100 Recurrent taxes on immovable property	13.5	30.6	50.0	62.9	66.2	2.2	2.8	3.1	3.0	3.1
4200 Recurrent taxes on net wealth	0.0	0.0	0.0	0.0	0.0	0.0	0.0	0.0	0.0	0.0
4300 Estate, inheritance and gift taxes	1.3	2.2	2.6	5.4	5.3	0.2	0.2	0.2	0.3	0.2
4400 Taxes on financial and capital transactions	1.8	8.4	9.1	17.1	16.7	0.3	0.8	0.6	0.8	0.8
4500 Non-recurrent taxes	0.0	0.0	0.0	0.3	0.3	0.0	0.0	0.0	0.0	0.0
4600 Other recurrent taxes on property	0.0	0.0	0.0	0.0	0.0	0.0	0.0	0.0	0.0	0.0
5000 Taxes on goods and services	**62.8**	**115.8**	**162.9**	**221.7**	**230.1**	**10.2**	**10.6**	**10.2**	**10.7**	**10.7**
5100 Taxes on production, sale, transfer, etc	59.4	110.8	155.5	214.0	222.0	9.6	10.1	9.7	10.3	10.4
5110 General taxes	34.1	65.0	97.6	142.4	149.1	5.5	5.9	6.1	6.9	7.0
5111 Value added taxes	34.1	65.0	97.6	142.4	149.1	5.5	5.9	6.1	6.9	7.0
5120 Taxes on specific goods and services	25.2	45.8	57.8	71.6	73.0	4.1	4.2	3.6	3.5	3.4
5121 Excises	19.7	37.3	45.5	48.7	49.1	3.2	3.4	2.8	2.4	2.3
5200 Taxes on use of goods and perform activities	3.4	5.0	7.4	7.8	8.1	0.6	0.5	0.5	0.4	0.4
5300 Unallocable between 5100 and 5200	0.0	0.0	0.0	0.0	0.0	0.0	0.0	0.0	0.0	0.0
6000 Other taxes	**9.0**	**0.0**	**0.0**	**0.0**	**0.0**	**1.5**	**0.0**	**0.0**	**0.0**	**0.0**
Non-wastable tax credits										
Non-wastable tax credits against 1000	7.5	4.7	30.2	31.3	29.0	1.2	0.4	1.9	1.5	1.4
Transfer component	0.5	3.4	23.7	27.3	25.0	0.1	0.3	1.5	1.3	1.2
Tax expenditure component	7.0	1.2	6.5	4.0	4.0	1.1	0.1	0.4	0.2	0.2
Revenues collected on behalf of the EU										
Revenues collected on behalf of the EU, total	1.8	2.1	2.9	3.4	3.6	0.3	0.2	0.2	0.2	0.2
Customs duties	..	1.8	2.9	3.4	3.3	..	0.2	0.2	0.2	0.2

.. Not available

Note: Please note that the non-wastable tax credit data for the United Kingdom is on a cash basis and includes estimates in some years. Please see the footnotes in the table for the United Kingdom in chapter 5 for more information.

Note: More detailed country data and country notes are available in online chapter 5 "Detailed country tables": https://doi.org/10.1787/0bbc27da-en. Full time series can be accessed at http://oe.cd/full-time-series.

Source: National Income and Expenditure; Central Statistical Office; Annual reports of Her Majesty's Revenue and Customs.

StatLink https://doi.org/10.1787/888934211566

Table 4.72. United Kingdom, tax revenue and % of GDP by level of government and main taxes

	Billion GBP					% of GDP				
	1990	2000	2010	2017	2018	1990	2000	2010	2017	2018
Federal or Central government										
Total tax revenue	**151.9**	**282.8**	**388.2**	**513.0**	**531.0**	**24.7**	**25.8**	**24.2**	**24.8**	**24.8**
1000 Taxes on income, profits and capital gains	79.6	142.2	192.7	240.4	249.1	12.9	13.0	12.0	11.6	11.6
2000 Social security contributions	0.0	0.0	0.0	0.0	0.0	0.0	0.0	0.0	0.0	0.0
3000 Taxes on payroll and workforce	0.0	0.0	0.0	1.8	2.6	0.0	0.0	0.0	0.1	0.1
4000 Taxes on property	11.4	26.9	35.5	52.5	52.8	1.9	2.5	2.2	2.5	2.5
5000 Taxes on goods and services	60.9	113.7	160.0	218.3	226.6	9.9	10.4	10.0	10.5	10.6
6000 Other taxes	0.0	0.0	0.0	0.0	0.0	0.0	0.0	0.0	0.0	0.0
State/Regional										
Total tax revenue	..	..	..	..	..	..	..	..	..	..
1000 Taxes on income, profits and capital gains	..	..	..	..	..	..	..	..	..	..
2000 Social security contributions	..	..	..	..	..	..	..	..	..	..
3000 Taxes on payroll and workforce	..	..	..	..	..	..	..	..	..	..
4000 Taxes on property	..	..	..	..	..	..	..	..	..	..
5000 Taxes on goods and services	..	..	..	..	..	..	..	..	..	..
6000 Other taxes	..	..	..	..	..	..	..	..	..	..
Local government										
Total tax revenue	**14.1**	**14.2**	**26.2**	**33.1**	**35.7**	**2.3**	**1.3**	**1.6**	**1.6**	**1.7**
1000 Taxes on income, profits and capital gains	0.0	0.0	0.0	0.0	0.0	0.0	0.0	0.0	0.0	0.0
2000 Social security contributions	0.0	0.0	0.0	0.0	0.0	0.0	0.0	0.0	0.0	0.0
3000 Taxes on payroll and workforce	0.0	0.0	0.0	0.0	0.0	0.0	0.0	0.0	0.0	0.0
4000 Taxes on property	5.1	14.2	26.2	33.1	35.7	0.8	1.3	1.6	1.6	1.7
5000 Taxes on goods and services	0.0	0.0	0.0	0.0	0.0	0.0	0.0	0.0	0.0	0.0
6000 Other taxes	9.0	0.0	0.0	0.0	0.0	1.5	0.0	0.0	0.0	0.0
Social Security Funds										
Total tax revenue	**34.5**	**60.3**	**97.3**	**130.4**	**135.0**	**5.6**	**5.5**	**6.1**	**6.3**	**6.3**
1000 Taxes on income, profits and capital gains	0.0	0.0	0.0	0.0	0.0	0.0	0.0	0.0	0.0	0.0
2000 Social security contributions	34.5	60.3	97.3	130.4	135.0	5.6	5.5	6.1	6.3	6.3
3000 Taxes on payroll and workforce	0.0	0.0	0.0	0.0	0.0	0.0	0.0	0.0	0.0	0.0
4000 Taxes on property	0.0	0.0	0.0	0.0	0.0	0.0	0.0	0.0	0.0	0.0
5000 Taxes on goods and services	0.0	0.0	0.0	0.0	0.0	0.0	0.0	0.0	0.0	0.0
6000 Other taxes	0.0	0.0	0.0	0.0	0.0	0.0	0.0	0.0	0.0	0.0

.. Not available

Note: More detailed country data and country notes are available in online chapter 5 "Detailed country tables": https://doi.org/10.1787/0bbc27da-en. Full time series can be accessed at http://oe.cd/full-time-series.

Source: National Income and Expenditure; Central Statistical Office; Annual reports of Her Majesty's Revenue and Customs.

StatLink https://doi.org/10.1787/888934211585

Table 4.73. United States, tax revenue and % of GDP by selected tax category

	Billion USD					% of GDP				
	1990	2000	2010	2017	2018	1990	2000	2010	2017	2018
Total tax revenue	**1 552.4**	**2 900.5**	**3 517.1**	**5 225.9**	**5 031.7**	**26.0**	**28.3**	**23.5**	**26.7**	**24.4**
1000 Taxes on income, profits and capital gains	**701.7**	**1 453.9**	**1 488.7**	**2 342.8**	**2 274.6**	**11.8**	**14.2**	**9.9**	**12.0**	**11.0**
1100 Of individuals	584.7	1 224.5	1 223.2	2 036.8	2 068.8	9.8	11.9	8.2	10.4	10.0
1200 Corporate	117.0	229.3	265.5	306.0	205.8	2.0	2.2	1.8	1.6	1.0
1300 Unallocable between 1100 and 1200	0.0	0.0	0.0	0.0	0.0	0.0	0.0	0.0	0.0	0.0
2000 Social security contributions	**397.0**	**683.1**	**917.4**	**1 205.3**	**1 250.4**	**6.7**	**6.7**	**6.1**	**6.2**	**6.1**
2100 Employees	173.9	305.6	406.4	543.3	568.3	2.9	3.0	2.7	2.8	2.8
2200 Employers	204.1	343.2	461.7	598.6	616.1	3.4	3.3	3.1	3.1	3.0
2300 Self-employed or non-employed	19.0	34.4	49.3	63.5	66.0	0.3	0.3	0.3	0.3	0.3
2400 Unallocable between 2100, 2200 and 2300	0.0	0.0	0.0	0.0	0.0	0.0	0.0	0.0	0.0	0.0
3000 Taxes on payroll and workforce	**0.0**	**0.0**	**2.3**	**2.0**	**2.2**	**0.0**	**0.0**	**0.0**	**0.0**	**0.0**
4000 Taxes on property	**182.4**	**299.5**	**473.4**	**850.5**	**617.7**	**3.1**	**2.9**	**3.2**	**4.4**	**3.0**
4100 Recurrent taxes on immovable property	161.5	254.7	438.6	545.8	562.0	2.7	2.5	2.9	2.8	2.7
4200 Recurrent taxes on net wealth	0.0	0.0	0.0	0.0	0.0	0.0	0.0	0.0	0.0	0.0
4300 Estate, inheritance and gift taxes	15.8	35.6	19.7	28.5	28.5	0.3	0.3	0.1	0.1	0.1
4400 Taxes on financial and capital transactions	2.1	4.4	7.5	16.5	17.1	0.0	0.0	0.1	0.1	0.1
4500 Non-recurrent taxes	0.0	0.0	0.0	250.0	0.0	0.0	0.0	0.0	1.3	0.0
4600 Other recurrent taxes on property	3.0	4.8	7.7	9.7	10.0	0.1	0.0	0.1	0.1	0.0
5000 Taxes on goods and services	**271.3**	**464.0**	**635.3**	**825.2**	**886.9**	**4.6**	**4.5**	**4.2**	**4.2**	**4.3**
5100 Taxes on production, sale, transfer, etc	235.2	404.1	546.7	722.0	777.1	3.9	3.9	3.6	3.7	3.8
5110 General taxes	125.6	221.4	295.1	394.7	411.9	2.1	2.2	2.0	2.0	2.0
5111 Value added taxes	0.0	0.0	0.0	0.0	0.0	0.0	0.0	0.0	0.0	0.0
5120 Taxes on specific goods and services	109.7	182.7	251.6	327.3	365.2	1.8	1.8	1.7	1.7	1.8
5121 Excises	65.0	108.6	146.6	162.2	164.4	1.1	1.1	1.0	0.8	0.8
5200 Taxes on use of goods and perform activities	36.1	59.9	88.6	103.2	109.8	0.6	0.6	0.6	0.5	0.5
5300 Unallocable between 5100 and 5200	0.0	0.0	0.0	0.0	0.0	0.0	0.0	0.0	0.0	0.0
6000 Other taxes	**0.0**	**0.0**	**0.0**	**0.0**	**0.0**	**0.0**	**0.0**	**0.0**	**0.0**	**0.0**
Non-wastable tax credits										
Non-wastable tax credits against 1000	6.2	36.5	171.9	177.0	194.7	0.1	0.4	1.1	0.9	0.9
Transfer component	4.4	26.9	101.8	127.6	137.0	0.1	0.3	0.7	0.7	0.7
Tax expenditure component	1.8	9.6	70.1	49.4	57.7	0.0	0.1	0.5	0.3	0.3

Note: More detailed country data and country notes are available in online chapter 5 "Detailed country tables": https://doi.org/10.1787/0bbc27da-en. Full time series can be accessed at http://oe.cd/full-time-series.

Source: Federal estimates are derived from the US Budget, the Final Monthly Treasury Statement and the Annual Report of the US Treasury Department. The State and Local estimates are derived from Government Finances, published by the Bureau of the Census.

StatLink https://doi.org/10.1787/888934211604

Table 4.74. United States, tax revenue and % of GDP by level of government and main taxes

	Billion USD					% of GDP				
	1990	2000	2010	2017	2018	1990	2000	2010	2017	2018
Federal or Central government										
Total tax revenue	**632.2**	**1 316.6**	**1 288.7**	**2 292.3**	**1 979.0**	**10.6**	**12.8**	**8.6**	**11.7**	**9.6**
1000 Taxes on income, profits and capital gains	569.7	1 201.3	1 176.8	1 890.5	1 795.3	9.6	11.7	7.9	9.7	8.7
2000 Social security contributions	0.0	0.0	0.0	0.0	0.0	0.0	0.0	0.0	0.0	0.0
3000 Taxes on payroll and workforce	0.0	0.0	0.0	0.0	0.0	0.0	0.0	0.0	0.0	0.0
4000 Taxes on property	11.6	28.1	15.1	273.2	22.9	0.2	0.3	0.1	1.4	0.1
5000 Taxes on goods and services	50.9	87.3	96.8	128.7	160.8	0.9	0.9	0.6	0.7	0.8
6000 Other taxes	0.0	0.0	0.0	0.0	0.0	0.0	0.0	0.0	0.0	0.0
State/Regional										
Total tax revenue	**309.7**	**547.6**	**723.9**	**983.5**	**1 036.8**	**5.2**	**5.3**	**4.8**	**5.0**	**5.0**
1000 Taxes on income, profits and capital gains	120.2	231.0	279.4	411.2	437.0	2.0	2.3	1.9	2.1	2.1
2000 Social security contributions	0.0	0.0	0.0	0.0	0.0	0.0	0.0	0.0	0.0	0.0
3000 Taxes on payroll and workforce	0.0	0.0	2.3	2.0	2.2	0.0	0.0	0.0	0.0	0.0
4000 Taxes on property	12.2	21.9	23.1	33.5	35.0	0.2	0.2	0.2	0.2	0.2
5000 Taxes on goods and services	177.3	294.7	419.1	536.8	562.7	3.0	2.9	2.8	2.7	2.7
6000 Other taxes	0.0	0.0	0.0	0.0	0.0	0.0	0.0	0.0	0.0	0.0
Local government										
Total tax revenue	**213.6**	**353.2**	**587.2**	**744.7**	**765.7**	**3.6**	**3.4**	**3.9**	**3.8**	**3.7**
1000 Taxes on income, profits and capital gains	11.9	21.6	32.5	41.2	42.4	0.2	0.2	0.2	0.2	0.2
2000 Social security contributions	0.0	0.0	0.0	0.0	0.0	0.0	0.0	0.0	0.0	0.0
3000 Taxes on payroll and workforce	0.0	0.0	0.0	0.0	0.0	0.0	0.0	0.0	0.0	0.0
4000 Taxes on property	158.6	249.5	435.3	543.9	559.8	2.7	2.4	2.9	2.8	2.7
5000 Taxes on goods and services	43.1	82.0	119.4	159.7	163.5	0.7	0.8	0.8	0.8	0.8
6000 Other taxes	0.0	0.0	0.0	0.0	0.0	0.0	0.0	0.0	0.0	0.0
Social Security Funds										
Total tax revenue	**397.0**	**683.1**	**917.4**	**1 205.3**	**1 250.4**	**6.7**	**6.7**	**6.1**	**6.2**	**6.1**
1000 Taxes on income, profits and capital gains	0.0	0.0	0.0	0.0	0.0	0.0	0.0	0.0	0.0	0.0
2000 Social security contributions	397.0	683.1	917.4	1 205.3	1 250.4	6.7	6.7	6.1	6.2	6.1
3000 Taxes on payroll and workforce	0.0	0.0	0.0	0.0	0.0	0.0	0.0	0.0	0.0	0.0
4000 Taxes on property	0.0	0.0	0.0	0.0	0.0	0.0	0.0	0.0	0.0	0.0
5000 Taxes on goods and services	0.0	0.0	0.0	0.0	0.0	0.0	0.0	0.0	0.0	0.0
6000 Other taxes	0.0	0.0	0.0	0.0	0.0	0.0	0.0	0.0	0.0	0.0

Note: More detailed country data and country notes are available in online chapter 6 "Tax revenues by sub-sectors of general government": https://doi.org/10.1787/0bbc27da-en. Full time series can be accessed at http://oe.cd/full-time-series.

Source: Federal estimates are derived from the US Budget, the Final Monthly Treasury Statement and the Annual Report of the US Treasury Department. The State and Local estimates are derived from Government Finances, published by the Bureau of the Census.

StatLink https://doi.org/10.1787/888934211623

4.2. Memorandum tables

Table 4.75 shows different sources for financing social benefits, beyond compulsory social security contributions reported in section 4.1. In addition, this table shows also data on other taxes, on voluntary contributions to government and on compulsory contributions to private sector.

Table 4.76 shows social security contributions and payroll taxes paid by government. During the revision of the Interpretative Guide in 1984, the question arose of how to treat taxes paid by government. The two most prominent examples of such taxes are social security contributions and payroll taxes paid by government in respect of its employees. After a long discussion it was decided that the data shown in this publication should continue to include taxes paid by government (see §7 of the Interpretative Guide in annex A).

Whilst it was recognised that for certain purposes (e.g. to show the cash flow to the government sector from the private sector) it would be appropriate to eliminate taxes paid by one sector of government to another or tax payments between different units of the same sector of government, the view was taken that to record tax flows in the context of the economy as a whole required that taxes paid by government should be included in the data. This treatment ensures that the different resource flows of an economy, including the calculation of the output of government, are measured consistently in after-tax units. Nevertheless, it was decided that data on identifiable taxes paid by government should be separately identified in a memorandum item and this is the purpose of the country tables which follow.

The data that are reproduced in the following tables refer to actual compulsory payments made by general government in respect of their employees. Fictive, voluntary and imputed contributions are excluded from these data. The definitions of social security contributions, payroll taxes and general government are those set out in §40 to §46, §47 and §3 to §4 of the Interpretative Guide. Information on the other taxes paid by government (namely property taxes and consumption taxes) is not available in most countries, although it is believed that in all countries taxes based upon payroll are the most important taxes paid by government. In many cases, the data are estimates and are not always constructed on a basis consistent with that used in the main tables.

Table 4.75. Financing of social security benefits

As % of GDP

	Total					2018				
	1990	2000	2010	2017	2018	Social security contributions	Other taxes	Voluntary contributions to government	Compulsory contributions to private sector	Total
Australia	0.0	0.0	0.0	0.0	0.0	..	..	..	..	0.0
Austria	13.0	14.4	14.1	14.6	14.8	14.7	0.0	0.1	0.0	14.8
Belgium	14.2	15.7	18.6	17.2	17.3	13.3	4.0	0.0	0.0	17.3
Canada	4.3	4.7	4.6	4.6	4.6	4.6	0.0	0.0	0.0	4.6
Chile	4.6	6.2	6.2	7.2	7.2	1.5	0.0	0.0	5.8	7.2
Colombia	0.9	2.6	7.1	5.4	5.9	1.8	0.0	0.0	4.0	5.9
Czech Republic	..	14.5	14.6	15.0	15.5	15.3	0.0	0.0	0.2	15.5
Denmark	1.1	2.0	1.3	0.9	0.8	0.0	0.0	0.7	0.1	0.8
Estonia	..	10.9	12.9	13.0	13.0	11.5	0.0	0.0	1.5	13.0
Finland	12.2	12.4	12.5	12.4	12.2	11.8	0.0	0.1	0.3	12.2
France	18.4	21.2	23.1	24.5	24.6	16.1	8.5	0.0	0.0	24.6
Germany	14.2	15.6	14.4	14.9	15.1	14.5	0.0	0.2	0.4	15.1
Greece	7.6	10.1	10.9	11.5	11.6	11.6	0.0	0.0	0.0	11.6
Hungary	..	13.2	13.0	13.2	12.6	11.8	0.8	0.0	0.0	12.6
Iceland	10.0	13.5	14.1	17.8	16.3	3.5	5.3	0.0	7.5	16.3
Ireland	4.6	3.7	5.0	3.9	3.9	3.9	0.0	0.0	0.0	3.9
Israel	..	5.1	6.2	7.9	7.9	5.2	0.0	0.0	2.7	7.9
Italy	11.9	11.6	13.0	12.7	13.0	13.0	0.0	0.0	0.0	13.0
Japan	7.5	9.1	10.9	12.5	12.9	12.9	0.0	0.0	0.0	12.9
Korea	1.9	3.5	5.2	6.5	6.8	6.8	0.0	0.0	0.0	6.8
Latvia	..	10.0	8.8	8.8	9.5	9.1	0.4	0.0	0.0	9.5
Lithuania	..	10.2	12.1	12.6	13.1	12.7	0.0	0.0	0.4	13.1
Luxembourg	9.3	9.7	11.0	10.9	10.9	10.8	0.0	0.1	0.0	10.9
Mexico	2.5	3.1	3.2	3.2	3.3	2.2	0.0	0.0	1.1	3.3
Netherlands	17.1	22.5	12.9	13.8	14.0	14.0	0.0	0.0	..	14.0
New Zealand	0.0	0.0	0.0	0.0	0.0	..	..	..	..	0.0
Norway	10.6	8.8	9.4	10.3	10.1	10.1	0.0	0.0	0.0	10.1
Poland	..	12.9	10.8	12.8	13.1	13.1	0.0	0.0	0.0	13.1
Portugal	7.2	8.3	9.0	9.6	9.8	9.4	0.4	0.0	0.0	9.8
Slovak Republic	..	13.9	13.1	15.3	15.5	14.8	0.0	0.0	0.7	15.5
Slovenia	..	15.0	15.8	15.4	15.5	15.5	0.0	0.0	0.0	15.5
Spain	11.2	11.6	12.0	11.6	11.8	11.7	0.0	0.1	0.0	11.8
Sweden	13.3	13.1	11.1	10.0	10.1	9.6	0.0	0.5	0.0	10.1
Switzerland	11.7	14.1	14.9	16.4	16.1	6.7	1.0	0.0	8.5	16.1
Turkey	2.9	4.4	6.1	7.2	7.2	7.2	0.0	0.0	0.0	7.2
United Kingdom	7.4	7.0	8.0	7.6	7.6	6.3	0.0	1.3	0.0	7.6
United States	6.9	6.9	6.5	6.6	6.6	6.1	0.0	0.5	0.0	6.6

.. Not available

StatLink https://doi.org/10.1787/888934211642

Table 4.76. Social security contributions and payroll taxes paid by government, totals

As % of GDP

	Total					2018				
	1990	2000	2010	2017	2018	Federal or Central government	State/Regional	Local government	Social security Funds	Total
Australia[1]	0.0	0.0	0.0	0.0	0.0	0.0	0.0	0.0	0.0	0.0
Austria	1.0	1.4	1.9	1.9	1.9	0.7	0.5	0.6	0.1	1.9
Belgium	1.0	1.2	1.5	1.8	1.8	0.2	0.6	0.9	0.1	1.8
Canada	..	0.6	0.6	0.6	0.6	0.1	0.3	0.2	0.0	0.6
Chile	..	0.1	0.2	0.2	0.2	0.1	..	0.0	0.0	0.2
Colombia	..	..	..	0.2	0.2	0.1	0.0	0.0	0.2	0.2
Czech Republic	..	1.4	1.4	1.8	1.9	0.9	..	1.0	0.0	1.9
Denmark	0.0	0.0	0.0	0.0	0.0	..	..	..	..	0.0
Estonia	..	2.9	3.6	3.5	3.5	2.0	..	1.2	0.3	3.5
Finland	2.1	2.8	3.0	2.4	2.3	0.4	..	1.8	0.1	2.3
France	2.2	2.5	2.7	2.7	2.6	0.7	..	1.0	1.0	2.6
Germany	1.0	0.8	0.8	0.8	0.8	0.1	0.3	0.4	0.1	0.8
Greece	0.3	1.2	1.6	0.9	1.1	0.9	..	0.0	0.2	1.1
Hungary	..	2.8	2.4	1.8	1.6	1.3	..	0.3	0.0	1.6
Iceland	..	..	..	..	..	..	..	..	..	..
Ireland	0.4	0.4	0.7	0.6	0.6	0.2	..	0.4	0.0	0.6
Israel	..	0.8	0.8	0.8	0.8	0.7	..	0.2	0.0	0.8
Italy	..	3.0	3.1	2.9	2.9	0.0	..	0.0	2.9	2.9
Japan	0.4	0.5	0.6	0.6	0.6	0.2	..	0.5	0.0	0.6
Korea	..	..	..	..	..	..	..	..	..	..
Latvia	..	0.6	1.0	0.9	1.2	..	..	..	..	1.2
Lithuania	..	2.7	2.5	2.2	2.2	1.2	..	1.0	0.0	2.2
Luxembourg	2.4	1.2	1.3	1.3	1.3	1.3	..	0.0	0.0	1.3
Mexico	0.3	0.7	0.8	0.7	0.7	0.7	0.0	0.0	0.0	0.7
Netherlands	0.1	0.4	0.0	0.0	0.0	..	..	..	..	0.0
New Zealand	0.0	0.0	0.0	0.0	0.0	..	..	..	..	0.0
Norway	2.4	2.4	2.9	3.4	3.3	1.4	..	1.9	0.0	3.3
Poland	..	1.6	1.3	1.4	1.4	0.6	..	0.8	0.0	1.4
Portugal	0.1	0.2	0.0	0.0	0.0	..	..	..	..	0.0
Slovak Republic	..	2.0	1.9	2.2	2.3	1.3	..	0.9	0.0	2.3
Slovenia	..	1.9	1.7	1.5	1.5	1.0	..	0.5	0.0	1.5
Spain	1.2	1.5	1.7	1.7	1.8	0.2	1.1	0.4	0.0	1.8
Sweden	4.5	4.2	3.8	4.1	4.0	0.9	..	3.1	0.0	4.0
Switzerland	0.4	0.4	0.5	0.5	0.5	0.1	0.3	0.1	0.0	0.5
Turkey	1.6	2.1	3.4	4.1	4.0	4.0	..	0.0	0.0	4.0
United Kingdom	0.7	0.6	0.7	0.7	0.7	0.4	..	0.2	0.0	0.7
United States	0.5	0.4	0.5	0.4	0.4	0.1	0.3	0.0	0.0	0.4

.. Not available

1. For Australia, the total differs from the sum of the four levels of government. The difference is due to a multi-jurisdictional (University) sector specific to this country. This sector contains units where jurisdiction is shared between two or more governments, or where classification of a unit to a jurisdiction is otherwise unclear. The main type of units currently falling into this category is public universities.

StatLink https://doi.org/10.1787/888934211661

5 Detailed country tables, 1965-2018

Chapter 5 provides detailed country information on tax revenues for each OECD country.

5.1. Tax revenues

In all of the following tables the symbol (..) indicates not available/or not applicable. The main series in this chapter cover a selection of years 1965 between 2018. A complete series is available on line. Data for 1955 and 1960 (for nineteen OECD countries) are provided in part V of the 1998 edition of this Report.

Table 5.1. Australia: Details of tax revenue, 1965-2018

Million AUD

	1965	1980	1990	2000	2007	2010	2013	2015	2017	2018
Total tax revenue	**5 024**	**39 878**	**116 500**	**214 752**	**347 545**	**357 958**	**433 342**	**463 350**	**527 181**	**558 453**
1000 Taxes on income, profits and capital gains	**2 547**	**22 383**	**66 542**	**124 427**	**206 134**	**202 184**	**246 073**	**262 357**	**310 041**	**336 239**
1100 Of individuals	1 729	17 532	50 062	80 991	127 587	138 163	169 972	191 747	212 520	229 499
1110 On income and profits	1 729	17 532	49 888	80 991	127 587	138 163	169 972	191 747	212 520	229 499
1120 On capital gains	0	0	174	0	0	0	0	0	0	0
1200 Corporate	818	4 851	16 480	43 436	78 547	64 021	76 101	70 610	97 521	106 740
1210 On profits	818	4 851	16 315	43 436	78 547	64 021	76 101	70 610	97 521	106 740
Income tax on companies	791	4 574	15 220	42 221	76 655	62 549	74 535	68 779	95 539	104 641
Dividend and interest taxes	17	161	899	846	1 892	1 472	1 566	1 831	1 982	2 099
Other withholding taxes	0	116	196	369	0	0	0	0	0	0
1220 On capital gains	0	0	165	0	0	0	0	0	0	0
1300 Unallocable between 1100 and 1200	0	0	0	0	0	0	0	0	0	0
2000 Social security contributions	**0**	**0**	**0**	**0**	**0**	**0**	**0**	**0**	**0**	**0**
2100 Employees	0	0	0	0	0	0	0	0	0	0
2110 On a payroll basis	..	..	..	..	..	..	..	..	..	..
2120 On an income tax basis	..	..	..	..	..	..	..	..	..	..
2200 Employers	0	0	0	0	0	0	0	0	0	0
2210 On a payroll basis	..	..	..	..	..	..	..	..	..	..
2220 On an income tax basis	..	..	..	..	..	..	..	..	..	..
2300 Self-employed or non-employed	0	0	0	0	0	0	0	0	0	0
2310 On a payroll basis	..	..	..	..	..	..	..	..	..	..
2320 On an income tax basis	..	..	..	..	..	..	..	..	..	..
2400 Unallocable between 2100, 2200 and 2300	0	0	0	0	0	0	0	0	0	0
2410 On a payroll basis	..	..	..	..	..	..	..	..	..	..
2420 On an income tax basis	..	..	..	..	..	..	..	..	..	..
3000 Taxes on payroll and workforce	**157**	**1 988**	**7 115**	**9 624**	**16 407**	**18 492**	**22 210**	**23 354**	**25 520**	**26 923**
4000 Taxes on property	**576**	**3 105**	**10 427**	**18 825**	**31 156**	**33 526**	**40 963**	**49 641**	**52 967**	**53 142**
4100 Recurrent taxes on immovable property	341	1 886	6 148	9 067	15 615	19 907	23 603	27 093	30 305	32 694
4110 Households	..	..	..	..	..	..	..	..	..	..
4120 Others	..	..	..	..	..	..	..	..	..	..
4200 Recurrent taxes on net wealth	0	0	0	0	0	0	0	0	0	0
4210 Individual	..	..	..	..	..	..	..	..	..	..
4220 Corporate	..	..	..	..	..	..	..	..	..	..
4300 Estate, inheritance and gift taxes	137	175	0	0	0	0	0	0	0	0
4310 Estate and inheritance taxes	131	174	..	..	..	..	..	..	..	..
Estate duty central government	36	17	..	..	..	..	..	..	..	..
St. and loc. estate probate and succession	95	157	..	..	..	..	..	..	..	..
4320 Gift taxes	7	1	..	..	..	..	..	..	..	..
4400 Taxes on financial and capital transactions	98	1 044	4 279	9 758	15 541	13 619	17 360	22 548	22 662	20 448
4500 Non-recurrent taxes	0	0	0	0	0	0	0	0	0	0
4510 On net wealth	..	..	..	..	..	..	..	..	..	..
4520 Other non-recurrent taxes	..	..	..	..	..	..	..	..	..	..
4600 Other recurrent taxes on property	0	0	0	0	0	0	0	0	0	0
5000 Taxes on goods and services	**1 744**	**12 402**	**32 416**	**61 876**	**93 848**	**103 756**	**124 096**	**127 998**	**138 653**	**142 149**
5100 Taxes on production, sale, transfer, etc.	1 508	11 097	27 213	56 178	84 851	92 007	103 419	110 185	118 867	122 064
5110 General taxes	370	2 102	9 365	25 830	45 486	49 329	56 819	61 815	65 700	66 829
5111 Value added taxes	0	0	0	23 854	44 381	48 093	55 517	60 312	64 062	65 147
5112 Sales tax	370	2 102	9 365	1 976	1 105	1 236	1 302	1 503	1 638	1 682
5113 Other	0	0	0	0	0	0	0	0	0	0
5120 Taxes on specific goods and services	1 138	8 995	17 848	30 348	39 365	42 678	46 600	48 370	53 167	55 235
5121 Excise duties	781	6 183	11 975	19 768	24 357	26 689	26 472	22 541	23 673	24 497
Excises central government	752	5 834	10 359	19 019	23 526	25 803	25 648	21 625	22 763	23 488
Statutory corporate payments	0	83	378	295	231	452	343	405	346	446
Primary production charges	29	266	1 238	454	600	434	481	511	564	563
5122 Profits of fiscal monopolies	0	0	0	0	0	0	0	0	0	0
5123 Customs and import duties	271	1 799	3 319	4 606	6 070	5 828	9 280	14 046	15 690	15 944
Customs duties central government	271	1 799	3 319	4 606	6 070	5 828	9 280	14 046	15 690	15 944
5124 Taxes on exports	1	117	57	0	10	11	10	11	0	0
Customs duties on coal exports	0	85	54	..	0	0	0	0	0	0
Other	1	32	3	..	10	11	10	11	..	..
5125 Taxes on investment goods	0	0	0	0	0	0	0	0	0	0
5126 Taxes on specific services	85	896	2 497	5 974	8 928	10 150	10 838	11 772	13 804	14 794
Taxes race meetings	31	240	651	300	358	366	318	257	265	411
Poker machines	16	140	295	2 074	3 009	3 125	3 238	3 684	3 881	3 986
Lotteries	7	122	325	890	1 118	1 147	1 257	1 369	1 330	1 632
Levies on fire insurance companies	16	157	363	574	937	1 232	740	786	812	806
Other	15	237	863	2 136	3 506	4 280	5 285	5 676	7 516	7 959
5127 Other taxes on internat. trade and transactions	0	0	0	0	0	0	0	0	0	0
5128 Other taxes	0	0	0	0	0	0	0	0	0	0

	1965	1980	1990	2000	2007	2010	2013	2015	2017	2018
5130 Unallocable between 5110 and 5120	0	0	0	0	0	0	0	0	0	0
5200 Taxes on use of goods and perform activities	236	1 305	5 203	5 698	8 997	11 749	20 677	17 813	19 786	20 085
5210 Recurrent taxes	197	1 260	5 109	5 698	8 997	11 749	20 677	17 813	19 786	20 085
5211 Paid by households: motor vehicles	65	448	1 373	3 908	6 196	7 229	8 591	9 586	7 781	7 990
5212 Paid by others: motor vehicles	65	351	937	125	189	232	301	318	3 005	2 996
Fees on motor vehicle registry	46	312	794	0	0	0	0	0	1 766	1 788
Drivers licences	12	30	111	0	0	0	0	0	0	0
Stamp duty on vehicle registry	6	9	32	125	189	232	301	318	1 239	1 208
5213 Paid in respect of other goods	67	461	2 799	1 665	2 611	4 288	11 786	7 910	9 000	9 099
Broadcasting tv licences	37	21	125	210	288	150	157	128	52	52
Business franchise lic. tobac. fuel	0	221	2 016	227	0	0	2	1	1	0
Other taxes	2	12	33	1 129	2 321	4 136	11 603	7 760	8 911	9 002
Liquor taxes	28	206	603	97	2	1	24	22	36	45
Dog licenses	0	1	22	0	0	0	0	0	0	0
5220 Non-recurrent taxes	39	45	94	0	0	0	0	0	0	0
5300 Unallocable between 5100 and 5200	0	0	0	0	0	0	0	0	0	0
6000 Other taxes	**0**	**0**	**0**	**0**	**0**	**0**	**0**	**0**	**0**	**0**
6100 Paid solely by business	..	..	..	..	..	..	..	..	..	..
6200 Other	..	..	..	..	..	..	..	..	..	..
Non-wastable tax credits										
Non-wastable tax credits against 1110	..	..	..	195	2 585	991	323	453	402	384
Tax expenditure component	..	..	..	175	178	110	215	307	267	250
Transfer component	..	..	..	20	2 407	881	108	146	135	134
Non-wastable tax credits against 1210	..	..	..	0	4 534	5 726	7 914	8 966	9 069	9 454
Tax expenditure component	..	..	..	..	1 922	2 253	2 147	2 453	2 166	2 178
Transfer component	..	..	..	..	2 642	3 473	5 767	6 513	6 903	7 276
Total tax revenue on cash basis	**5 024**	**39 878**	**116 500**	**..**	**..**	**..**	**..**	**..**	**..**	**..**
Total tax revenue on accrual basis	**..**	**..**	**..**	**214 752**	**347 545**	**357 958**	**433 342**	**463 350**	**527 181**	**558 453**
Conciliation with National Accounts										
Additional taxes included in National Accounts	..	..	..	0	0	0	0	0	0	0
Taxes excluded from National Accounts	..	..	..	0	0	0	0	0	0	0
Difference in treatment of tax credits	..	..	..	175	2 100	2 363	2 362	2 760	2 433	2 428
Capital transfer for uncollected revenue	..	..	..	0	0	0	0	0	0	0
Voluntary social security contributions	..	..	..	0	0	0	0	0	0	0
Miscellaneous differences	..	..	..	0	0	0	0	0	0	0
National Accounts: Taxes and actual social contributions	..	..	..	214 927	349 645	360 321	435 704	466 110	529 614	560 881
Imputed social contributions	..	..	..	0	0	0	0	0	0	0
National Accounts: Taxes and all social contributions	..	..	..	214 927	349 645	360 321	435 704	466 110	529 614	560 881

.. Not available

Note: Data are on a fiscal year basis beginning 1st July.

From 1998 taxes are recorded on an accrual basis; prior to that they were on a cash basis.

Direct taxes paid by public trading enterprises are excluded from receipts.

The figures for total tax revenue do not match the published totals in Taxation Revenue Australia. The latter is based on an accrual IMF GFS methodology and there are some differences between that and the OECD equivalent.

Heading 5213 includes radio and television licenses fees, though these are usually not regarded as a tax revenue in the OECD list.

Headings for non-wastable tax credits 1110 and 1210 include the private health insurance tax offset, family benefit, baby bonus tax offsets (paid during the 2003-04 budget year), film tax offset, and research and development tax offsets. The estimation of non-wastable credits into the expenditure and transfer components is in accordance with the OECD guidelines on the treatment and the data for this memorandum item has been provided by the Australian Taxation Office.

Source: Australian Bureau of Statistics.

StatLink https://doi.org/10.1787/888934211680

Table 5.2. Austria: Details of tax revenue, 1965-2018

Million EUR

	1965	1980	1990	2000	2007	2010	2013	2015	2017	2018
Total tax revenue	**6 210**	**29 759**	**54 040**	**90 324**	**115 146**	**121 192**	**138 099**	**148 469**	**154 624**	**162 818**
Total tax revenue exclusive of taxes collected for the EU	..	..	**54 040**	**89 897**	**114 728**	**120 843**	**137 741**	**147 841**	**153 964**	**162 161**
1000 Taxes on income, profits and capital gains	**1 584**	**7 959**	**13 797**	**25 553**	**34 319**	**34 021**	**39 792**	**44 796**	**43 735**	**47 758**
1100 Of individuals	1 240	6 899	11 326	19 890	25 741	27 098	31 474	35 841	33 523	36 194
1110 On income and profits	1 240	6 899	11 326	19 890	25 741	27 098	31 474	35 841	33 523	36 194
Income tax	415	1 576	2 501	3 202	3 253	3 358	3 737	4 274	4 502	5 014
Special income tax	0	0	0	0	0	0	0	0	0	0
Wage tax	417	4 626	7 823	15 630	20 607	21 783	25 669	28 429	26 459	28 344
Tax on industry and trade	196	402	454	7	0	0	0	0	0	0
Tax on capital yields	2	14	46	354	970	938	981	1 979	1 305	1 533
Contribution to chambers	60	279	501	697	910	1 018	1 087	1 159	1 256	1 302
Water supply fund	151	0	0	0	0	0	0	0	0	0
Contribution emergency fund	0	0	0	0	0	0	0	0	0	0
1120 On capital gains	0	0	0	0	0	0	0	0	0	0
1200 Corporate	334	1 049	1 930	4 157	6 622	5 519	6 963	7 659	9 121	10 440
1210 On profits	334	1 049	1 930	4 157	6 622	5 519	6 963	7 659	9 121	10 440
Corporation tax	195	698	998	3 865	6 094	4 978	6 377	6 752	8 438	9 676
Tax on industry and trade	83	254	624	10	0	1	0	0	0	0
Special tax on income	0	0	0	0	0	0	0	0	0	0
Tax on capital yields	5	33	108	118	346	347	370	684	447	513
Water supply fund	35	0	0	0	0	0	0	0	0	0
Contribution emergency fund	0	0	0	0	0	0	0	0	0	0
Contribution to chambers	14	58	200	164	182	193	216	224	237	251
Directors tax	2	6	0	0	0	0	0	0	0	0
1220 On capital gains	0	0	0	0	0	0	0	0	0	0
1300 Unallocable between 1100 and 1200	10	12	540	1 506	1 956	1 405	1 354	1 295	1 091	1 125
Fines related to tax offences	10	12	18	33	77	99	73	70	77	96
Tax on interest	0	0	522	1 473	1 879	1 305	1 282	1 225	1 014	1 028
2000 Social security contributions	**1 548**	**9 200**	**17 763**	**30 510**	**38 453**	**41 423**	**46 845**	**49 867**	**53 918**	**56 624**
2100 Employees	686	3 792	7 512	12 477	15 612	16 846	18 931	20 115	21 719	22 806
2110 On a payroll basis	..	..	..	12 477	15 612	16 846	18 931	20 115	21 719	22 806
Health insurance contributions	..	..	..	2 606	3 326	3 675	4 082	4 347	4 733	4 989
Pension insurance contributions	..	..	..	6 410	8 274	8 986	10 183	10 896	11 866	12 568
Pension contributions, civil servants	..	..	..	1 489	1 579	1 625	1 672	1 629	1 596	1 570
Unemployment insurance contributions	..	..	..	1 854	2 284	2 385	2 803	3 040	3 307	3 453
Health insurance contributions, local government employees	..	..	..	100	130	156	169	181	191	199
Special unemployment insurance contributions	..	..	..	17	19	20	22	23	25	27
2120 On an income tax basis	..	..	..	0	0	0	0	0	0	0
2200 Employers	721	4 563	8 768	14 651	18 091	19 421	21 922	23 281	25 286	26 662
2210 On a payroll basis	..	..	..	14 651	18 091	19 421	21 922	23 281	25 286	26 662
Health insurance contributions	..	..	..	2 667	3 395	3 669	4 075	4 339	4 724	4 980
Pension insurance contributions	..	..	..	7 888	10 214	11 144	12 642	13 549	14 764	15 630
Pension contributions, civil servants	..	..	..	438	376	361	297	298	276	268
Accident insurance contributions	..	..	..	952	1 157	1 254	1 409	1 394	1 498	1 573
Unemployment insurance contributions	..	..	..	1 854	2 284	2 385	2 803	3 040	3 307	3 453
Health insurance contributions, local government employees	..	..	..	101	141	157	170	181	192	199
Contributions to sickness benefit fund	..	..	..	341	0	0	0	0	0	0
Special pension contributions, nightshift workers	..	..	..	11	18	15	31	38	38	42
Contributions to insolvency fund	..	..	..	381	488	416	473	419	355	374
Special unemployment insurance contributions construction workers	..	..	..	17	19	20	22	23	132	143
2220 On an income tax basis	..	..	..	0	0	0	0	0	0	0
2300 Self-employed or non-employed	141	845	1 482	3 382	4 750	5 155	5 993	6 470	6 913	7 156
2310 On a payroll basis	..	..	..	3 382	4 750	5 155	5 993	6 470	6 913	7 156
Health insurance contributions	..	..	..	1 971	2 724	3 090	3 441	3 664	3 857	3 987
Pension insurance contributions	..	..	..	1 117	1 527	1 524	1 973	2 210	2 451	2 562
Pension contributions, civil servants (retired)	..	..	..	116	274	297	315	317	311	309
Accident insurance contributions	..	..	..	77	85	88	95	98	103	98
Health insurance contributions, local government employees	..	..	..	101	140	156	169	181	191	199
2320 On an income tax basis	..	..	..	0	0	0	0	0	0	0
2400 Unallocable between 2100, 2200 and 2300	0	0	0	0	0	0	0	0	0	0
2410 On a payroll basis	..	..	..	..	..	..	..	..	..	..
2420 On an income tax basis	..	..	..	..	..	..	..	..	..	..

	1965	1980	1990	2000	2007	2010	2013	2015	2017	2018
3000 Taxes on payroll and workforce	**472**	**2 097**	**3 259**	**5 788**	**7 266**	**8 359**	**9 489**	**10 040**	**10 245**	**10 416**
Emplr. contr. equaliz. of family.burdens	318	1 397	2 147	3 140	3 915	4 762	5 319	5 623	5 487	5 399
Tax on sum of wages	82	375	669	1 735	2 238	2 402	2 742	2 911	3 126	3 300
Promotion residential buildings	44	217	389	595	754	811	915	965	1 068	1 125
Tax on employment (Vienna undergr.)	0	20	21	21	22	22	67	65	66	67
Special levy for households allowances	26	80	0	0	0	0	0	0	0	0
Disabled persons equalization levy	2	8	34	54	83	91	138	148	154	155
Contributions to chambers	0	0	0	242	253	271	308	327	344	369
4000 Taxes on property	**246**	**858**	**1 473**	**1 206**	**1 572**	**1 555**	**2 341**	**1 965**	**1 942**	**2 100**
4100 Recurrent taxes on immovable property	92	231	355	526	626	682	736	761	805	807
4110 Households	47	66	84	87	92	93	105	107	125	110
Duty on farms	9	15	20	20	20	20	29	30	37	30
Farm contr. equaliz. of family burdens	5	6	6	6	6	6	6	6	8	7
Farm contribution to chambers	14	23	32	32	39	40	43	44	52	46
Contr. residential buildings reconstruction	4	0	0	0	0	0	0	0	0	0
Land tax A	16	22	25	28	26	26	26	26	28	28
4120 Others	45	165	271	440	534	589	631	654	681	697
Tax on vacant plots	1	4	5	5	5	6	6	6	6	6
Land tax B	44	161	266	435	529	583	625	649	675	691
4200 Recurrent taxes on net wealth	103	401	642	1	0	0	0	0	0	0
4210 Individual	37	140	189	1	..	..	..	..	..	..
Capital tax	25	109	189	1	..	..	..	..	..	..
Contribution emergency fund	0	0	0	0	..	..	..	..	..	..
Tax on industry and trade	10	26	0	0	..	..	..	..	..	..
Contribution to chambers	2	6	0	0	..	..	..	..	..	..
4220 Corporate	66	260	453	0	..	..	..	..	..	..
Capital tax	24	139	322	0	..	..	..	..	..	..
Capital death duty	20	53	131	0	..	..	..	..	..	..
Contribution emergency fund	0	0	0	0	..	..	..	..	..	..
Tax on industry and trade	19	56	0	0	..	..	..	..	..	..
Contribution to chambers	3	13	0	0	..	..	..	..	..	..
4300 Estate, inheritance and gift taxes	16	50	77	111	155	35	19	12	1	9
4310 Estate and inheritance taxes	..	..	..	..	..	..	..	..	..	..
4320 Gift taxes	..	..	..	..	..	..	..	..	..	..
4400 Taxes on financial and capital transactions	35	176	399	568	791	828	858	1 116	1 110	1 210
Land transfer tax	30	150	251	452	644	727	790	1 014	1 105	1 208
Capital transfer tax	5	27	148	115	147	102	67	102	5	2
4500 Non-recurrent taxes	0	0	0	0	0	10	728	76	27	75
4510 On net wealth	..	..	..	..	..	0	717	4	10	-1
Withholding tax	..	..	..	..	..	..	717	4	10	-1
4520 Other non-recurrent taxes	..	..	..	..	..	10	11	72	16	75
Foundation tax	..	..	..	..	..	10	11	72	16	75
4600 Other recurrent taxes on property	0	0	0	0	0	0	0	0	0	0
5000 Taxes on goods and services	**2 321**	**9 379**	**17 034**	**26 497**	**32 609**	**34 740**	**38 701**	**41 064**	**43 989**	**45 143**
5100 Taxes on production, sale, transfer, etc.	2 275	9 006	16 169	24 616	30 180	32 114	35 721	37 633	40 258	41 268
5110 General taxes	1 160	5 984	11 229	16 857	20 941	22 711	24 920	26 282	28 312	29 324
5111 Value added taxes	0	5 984	11 229	16 857	20 941	22 711	24 920	26 282	28 312	29 324
5112 Sales tax	0	0	0	0	0	0	0	0	0	0
5113 Other	1 160	0	0	0	0	0	0	0	0	0
Turnover tax	664	..	..	..	..	..	..	..	..	..
Additional federal levy-turnover	332	..	..	..	..	..	..	..	..	..
Additional lieu invoice stp.	164	..	..	..	..	..	..	..	..	..
5120 Taxes on specific goods and services	1 115	2 996	4 873	7 721	9 236	9 400	10 800	11 348	11 942	11 942

	1965	1980	1990	2000	2007	2010	2013	2015	2017	2018
5121 Excise duties	610	2 219	3 290	5 484	6 760	6 921	7 598	7 749	8 272	8 196
Tax on beer	39	44	56	161	200	198	193	189	192	200
Tax on wine	7	0	0	0	0	0	0	0	0	0
Tax on sparkling wine	1	7	25	25	1	1	1	19	23	23
Tax on tobacco	188	519	820	1 197	1 446	1 502	1 664	1 782	1 896	1 919
Tax on mineral oils	50	136	1 426	2 726	3 689	3 854	4 173	4 218	4 551	4 363
Additional federal levy mineral oils	202	876	0	0	0	0	0	0	0	0
Special duty alcoholic drinks	0	142	193	0	0	0	0	0	0	0
Special duty vehicles	0	0	0	0	0	0	0	0	0	0
Duty on starch products	0	4	13	0	0	0	0	0	0	0
Beverage tax	46	216	364	178	3	-1	-1	0	0	0
Other receipts-Market Organisation Act	26	35	9	0	1	0	0	0	0	0
Transport equality levy	0	5	1	0	0	0	0	0	0	0
Market Organisation Act - milk	35	177	192	0	0	0	0	0	0	0
Market Organisation Act - livestock	0	0	0	0	0	0	0	0	0	0
Market Organisation Act - grain	16	23	142	0	0	0	0	0	0	0
Duty promotion milk distrib.	0	34	13	0	0	0	0	0	0	0
Special tax on mineral oils	0	0	37	0	0	0	0	0	0	0
Duty on vehicles (fuel consumption)	0	0	0	433	457	453	455	395	473	532
Agricultural fund	0	0	0	23	16	18	18	17	17	18
Tax on energy	0	0	0	562	764	726	886	931	926	943
Social contributions to the artists' fund	0	0	0	0	11	6	7	13	7	7
Duty on exceeding milk-quota	0	0	0	36	24	6	26	11	0	0
Car registration taxes	0	0	0	143	148	158	175	174	188	191
5122 Profits of fiscal monopolies	37	57	52	130	122	129	324	328	384	403
Duty on spirits	5	14	17	130	122	129	130	120	142	154
Federal monopolies salt	1	0	0	0	0	0	0	0	0	0
Federal monopolies spirits	30	43	35	0	0	0	0	0	0	0
Federal monopolies gambling	0	0	0	0	0	0	194	208	242	248
5123 Customs and import duties	332	354	677	351	390	340	328	415	468	461
Customs duties	310	237	418	352	390	339	328	415	468	461
Other import duties	0	21	61	0	0	0	0	0	0	0
Contribution promote foreign trade	10	63	171	0	0	0	0	0	0	0
Import equalization duties	12	33	27	0	0	0	0	0	0	0
5124 Taxes on exports	8	36	1	0	0	0	0	0	0	0
Contribution to promote foreign trade	8	36	1	..	..	..	..	..	..	..
5125 Taxes on investment goods	0	33	0	0	0	0	0	0	0	0
5126 Taxes on specific services	129	297	854	1 720	1 967	2 005	2 545	2 852	2 814	2 886
Insurance tax	25	135	384	745	993	1 017	1 056	1 122	1 128	1 179
Transport tax	63	0	0	0	0	0	0	0	0	0
Duty on casinos	2	28	64	105	71	55	45	70	99	104
Fire protection tax	5	24	50	45	54	56	57	61	62	63
Advertisement tax	7	31	65	62	0	0	0	0	0	0
Entertainment tax	2	2	2	5	8	9	21	18	1	1
Tax on tourism	8	43	71	103	142	171	182	186	233	239
Amusement tax	13	17	51	73	94	107	84	30	18	16
Announcement tax	3	18	40	81	0	1	0	0	0	0
Tax on interest yields	0	0	0	0	0	0	0	0	0	0
Tax on gambling stakes - licences	0	0	116	197	202	221	251	254	250	292
Tax on advertisement	0	0	0	33	108	110	110	107	110	108
Levy on dangerous waste	0	0	10	71	72	51	53	56	62	79
Duty for airways security	0	0	0	28	56	30	0	0	0	0
Tax on gambling stakes - gains	0	0	0	171	166	176	0	0	0	0
Flight Charge	0	0	0	0	0	0	98	109	115	71
Financial Institutions Stability Fees	0	0	0	0	0	0	588	640	546	534
SRF Contributions	..	..	..	..	..	..	..	198	188	199
5127 Other taxes on internat. trade and transactions	0	0	0	0	0	0	0	0	0	0
5128 Other taxes	0	0	0	34	-3	4	4	4	4	-3
Levy on sugar	..	..	..	34	-3	4	4	4	4	-3
5130 Unallocable between 5110 and 5120	0	26	66	38	3	4	2	4	4	3
Fines related to tax offenses	..	26	66	38	3	4	2	4	4	3
5200 Taxes on use of goods and perform activities	46	373	865	1 881	2 429	2 626	2 980	3 431	3 731	3 875
5210 Recurrent taxes	38	335	757	1 733	2 253	2 416	2 715	3 124	3 412	3 469
5211 Paid by households: motor vehicles	22	156	366	811	1 173	1 293	1 482	1 814	1 986	2 033
5212 Paid by others: motor vehicles	13	41	97	298	370	334	352	421	460	471
5213 Paid in respect of other goods	3	138	294	624	710	789	881	890	966	965
Hunting and fishing duties	1	4	7	10	10	10	19	22	21	22
Dog tax	1	4	6	8	10	11	17	18	20	20
Contribution to promotion of arts	1	3	8	71	120	132	147	143	183	167
Tax on radio and tv - licenses	0	15	46	450	571	636	698	708	742	756
Road transport duty	0	112	226	84	0	0	0	0	0	0

	1965	1980	1990	2000	2007	2010	2013	2015	2017	2018
5220 Non-recurrent taxes	8	38	108	147	175	210	265	307	319	405
Certain user fees; taxes on emission of noxious gases	8	38	108	147	175	210	265	307	319	405
5300 Unallocable between 5100 and 5200	0	0	0	0	0	0	0	0	0	0
6000 Other taxes	**38**	**266**	**714**	**770**	**928**	**1 095**	**931**	**737**	**796**	**776**
Tax on financial institutions	0	0	123	-3	0	0	0	0	0	0
Administration duties	4	17	32	278	366	521	517	302	315	331
Stamp fees	7	46	76	135	92	84	27	32	37	33
Contributions of interested persons	0	0	130	0	0	0	0	0	0	0
Parking duty	0	0	6	0	0	0	0	0	0	0
Contrbutions to students' associations	0	0	0	4	8	11	12	11	12	14
Duty on contribution to political parties	0	0	0	0	-1	1	0	0	0	0
Other fees, taxes on production n.e.c.	0	0	0	272	346	353	227	252	279	248
Embossing fee	0	0	0	0	1	1	1	1	1	1
Other taxes	28	202	347	82	115	124	145	137	150	147
Compensation levy according to the Vienna Tree Protection Act	..	..	0	1	1	2	1	2	3	3
6100 Paid solely by business	..	..	..	..	..	..	..	..	..	..
6200 Other	..	..	..	..	..	..	..	..	..	..
Memorandum items										
Customs duties collected on behalf of the EU	..	..	..	352	390	339	328	415	468	461
SRF contributions collected on behalf of the EU	..	..	..	..	..	..	..	198	188	199
Non-wastable tax credits										
Non-wastable tax credits against 1110	..	..	..	650	650	650	570	540	330	330
Tax expenditure component	..	..	..	590	450	422	341	295	228	230
Transfer component	..	..	..	60	200	228	229	245	102	100
Non-wastable tax credits against 1210	..	..	..	0	0	0	0	0	0	0
Tax expenditure component	..	..	..	..	..	..	..	..	..	..
Transfer component	..	..	..	..	..	..	..	..	..	..
Total tax revenue on cash basis	**6 210**	**29 759**	**54 040**	**90 299**	**115 045**	**120 735**	**137 970**	**148 036**	**154 401**	**162 777**
Total tax revenue on accrual basis	**..**	**..**	**..**	**90 324**	**115 146**	**121 192**	**138 099**	**148 469**	**154 624**	**162 818**
Conciliation with National Accounts										
Additional taxes included in National Accounts	..	..	..	0	0	0	0	0	0	0
Taxes excluded from National Accounts	..	..	..	0	0	0	0	0	0	0
Difference in treatment of tax credits	..	..	..	590	450	422	341	295	228	230
Capital transfer for uncollected revenue	..	..	..	0	0	0	0	0	0	0
Voluntary social security contributions	..	..	..	206	256	339	299	321	317	321
Miscellaneous differences	..	..	..	0	0	0	0	0	0	0
National Accounts: Taxes and actual social contributions	..	..	..	91 120	115 853	121 953	138 739	149 085	155 170	163 369
Imputed social contributions	..	..	..	2 485	2 177	2 106	1 972	1 925	1 807	1 757
National Accounts: Taxes and all social contributions	..	..	..	93 605	118 030	124 060	140 711	151 010	156 976	165 126

.. Not available

Note: Year ending 31st December.

From 1995 data are on accrual basis.

Following national practice, one-third of the revenues from stamp fees (heading 6000) and fifty percent of the revenues from administration duties (heading 6000) are treated as tax revenues, the remainder being treated as non-tax revenue.

From 1988 onwards promoting residential building is being mainly financed by capital transfers from the Federal Government to the Länder. For the years 1985 to 1987 legally fixed shares of some taxes have been transmitted automatically from Federal Government to the Länder for this purpose and these funds have been classified as tax receipts of the Länder in those years. From 1988, they are classified as Federal Government tax revenues. This break in the time series (1987/1988) affects only the shares of the different subsectors and not total tax revenues.

From 1998 contributions of interested persons and parking duties are classified as non-tax revenues (sales) and no longer reported under heading 6000.

Source: Statistics Austria.

StatLink https://doi.org/10.1787/888934211699

Table 5.3. Belgium: Details of tax revenue, 1965-2018

Million EUR

	1965	1980	1990	2000	2007	2010	2013	2015	2017	2018
Total tax revenue	**6 421**	**37 443**	**70 408**	**112 710**	**147 861**	**156 317**	**177 665**	**184 429**	**195 930**	**202 645**
Total tax revenue exclusive of taxes collected for the EU	..	..	..	**111 675**	**146 411**	**155 042**	**176 488**	**182 812**	**194 093**	**200 728**
1000 Taxes on income, profits and capital gains	**1 774**	**15 379**	**25 983**	**43 461**	**52 854**	**53 313**	**62 762**	**65 572**	**71 379**	**74 373**
1100 Of individuals	1 317	13 626	22 538	35 318	41 020	44 027	50 518	51 877	53 218	54 566
1110 On income and profits	1 317	13 626	22 538	35 318	41 020	44 027	50 518	51 877	53 218	54 566
Immovable income withholding tax	148	532	1 053	1 857	0	0	0	0	0	0
Movable income withholding tax	119	1 062	3 014	1 755	2 351	2 426	4 314	4 104	3 769	3 693
Earned income withholding tax	740	9 119	15 422	27 778	36 022	39 829	44 686	45 658	46 889	47 575
Advance payments PIT	125	1 776	2 144	1 959	1 747	1 611	1 508	1 547	1 593	1 663
Non residents tax	0	-2	4	585	792	810	841	926	966	1 108
Assessments PIT	183	1 128	878	774	-915	-1 697	-1 988	-1 512	-1 252	-765
Special social contributions	0	0	19	602	957	1 032	1 117	1 106	1 209	1 253
Other income taxes	0	12	2	8	65	17	41	48	44	39
1120 On capital gains	0	0	0	0	0	0	0	0	0	0
1200 Corporate	397	1 744	3 405	8 065	11 749	9 249	12 192	13 644	18 098	19 736
1210 On profits	397	1 744	3 405	8 065	11 749	9 249	12 192	13 644	18 098	19 736
Immovable income withholding tax (corporate)	33	0	0	0	0	0	0	0	0	0
Movable income withholding tax (corporate)	41	367	1 206	527	686	315	477	466	290	303
Advance payments (corporate)	262	1 273	2 735	7 112	9 733	7 691	7 930	8 539	11 586	13 965
Assessments (corporate)	60	79	-553	404	1 270	1 196	3 662	4 466	5 936	5 276
Non residents tax (corporate)	0	-6	18	17	41	43	113	154	270	194
Other income taxes (corporate)	0	32	-2	5	19	4	10	19	15	-2
1220 On capital gains	0	0	0	0	0	0	0	0	0	0
1300 Unallocable between 1100 and 1200	61	9	40	77	85	38	52	51	63	71
Former income taxes	51	0	0	0	0	0	0	0	0	0
Penalties	3	0	0	0	0	0	0	0	0	0
Other	7	9	40	77	85	38	52	51	63	71
2000 Social security contributions	**2 018**	**10 798**	**23 386**	**34 865**	**45 929**	**50 674**	**56 527**	**58 812**	**59 779**	**61 070**
2100 Employees	569	3 130	7 152	10 932	13 847	14 996	16 476	17 036	17 744	18 419
2110 On a payroll basis	..	3 130	7 152	10 932	13 847	14 996	16 476	17 036	17 744	18 419
On gross wages	..	3 130	7 062	10 932	13 847	14 996	16 476	17 036	17 744	18 419
On social benefits	..	0	89	0	0	0	0	0	0	0
2120 On an income tax basis	..	0	0	0	0	0	0	0	0	0
2200 Employers	1 320	6 791	14 689	21 027	28 216	31 041	34 915	36 240	36 114	36 551
2210 On a payroll basis	..	6 791	14 689	21 027	28 216	31 041	34 915	36 240	36 114	36 551
Contributions by government	..	1 059	1 769	3 105	4 493	5 381	6 678	7 686	8 008	8 338
Contributions by other sectors	..	5 732	12 920	17 922	23 723	25 661	28 236	28 554	28 106	28 213
2220 On an income tax basis	..	0	0	0	0	0	0	0	0	0
2300 Self-employed or non-employed	129	877	1 546	2 906	3 866	4 637	5 136	5 537	5 921	6 100
Self-employed	..	803	1 230	2 053	2 678	3 342	3 703	3 975	4 153	4 238
Unemployed	..	0	0	0	0	0	0	0	0	0
Retired	..	29	198	709	1 012	1 134	1 324	1 449	1 658	1 743
Other	..	45	118	144	176	161	109	113	110	120
2310 On a payroll basis	..	877	1 546	2 906	3 866	4 637	5 136	5 537	5 921	6 100
2320 On an income tax basis	..	0	0	0	0	0	0	0	0	0
2400 Unallocable between 2100, 2200 and 2300	0	0	0	0	0	0	0	0	0	0
2410 On a payroll basis	..	..	..	..	..	..	..	..	..	..
2420 On an income tax basis	..	..	..	..	..	..	..	..	..	..
3000 Taxes on payroll and workforce	**0**	**0**	**0**	**0**	**6**	**7**	**8**	**8**	**8**	**7**
Levy on public mandates	..	..	..	..	6	7	8	8	8	7
4000 Taxes on property	**240**	**1 161**	**2 679**	**5 282**	**10 550**	**11 252**	**13 805**	**14 408**	**15 393**	**15 832**
4100 Recurrent taxes on immovable property	2	210	599	1 164	4 146	4 632	5 187	5 433	5 754	5 685
4110 Households	0	26	63	102	2 779	3 115	3 478	3 651	3 876	3 855
4120 Others	2	184	536	1 063	1 367	1 517	1 710	1 782	1 879	1 831
Tax on non profit institutions	2	7	17	41	32	33	38	41	45	47
Immovable income withholding tax (corporate)	0	177	519	929	1 269	1 416	1 584	1 651	1 746	1 686
Regional tax (Brussels)	0	0	0	94	66	68	88	90	89	98
4200 Recurrent taxes on net wealth	0	0	0	92	253	237	451	661	929	952
4210 Individual	..	..	..	0	0	0	0	0	0	0
4220 Corporate	..	..	..	92	253	237	451	661	929	952
4300 Estate, inheritance and gift taxes	75	309	504	1 101	2 053	2 269	3 096	3 004	3 131	3 250
4310 Estate and inheritance taxes	69	281	475	1 042	1 702	1 939	2 634	2 511	2 526	2 731
4320 Gift taxes	6	29	29	59	351	330	463	492	604	519

	1965	1980	1990	2000	2007	2010	2013	2015	2017	2018
4400 Taxes on financial and capital transactions	163	633	1 478	2 669	3 704	3 493	3 886	4 358	4 800	4 899
Registration duties	153	527	1 213	1 967	3 325	3 210	3 542	3 899	4 342	4 439
Mortgage duties	2	10	29	37	76	75	72	93	83	83
Court duties	2	8	29	38	31	34	37	41	40	31
Economic expansion fund	0	0	0	0	0	0	0	0	0	0
Tax on stock exchange transactions	4	31	92	386	234	134	193	287	296	307
Tax on stock exchange listings	2	4	21	0	0	0	0	0	0	0
Tax on bearer securities	0	0	0	79	3	0	6	0	0	0
Stamp duties	0	53	94	161	35	40	36	38	40	41
4500 Non-recurrent taxes	0	0	0	74	163	328	877	635	486	522
4510 On net wealth	..	..	..	0	0	0	0	0	0	0
4520 Other non-recurrent taxes	..	..	..	74	163	328	877	635	486	522
Tax on long term savings	..	..	..	74	163	194	207	413	369	361
Voluntary disclosure tax	..	..	..	0	0	0	0	0	0	0
Voluntary disclosure tax (Diamond)	..	..	..	0	0	0	0	0	0	0
Voluntary disclosure tax (bis)	..	..	..	0	0	134	614	145	12	12
Voluntary disclosure tax (ter)	..	..	..	0	0	0	54	78	105	148
Special contribution on credit associations	..	..	..	0	0	0	2	0	0	0
4600 Other recurrent taxes on property	0	8	99	182	232	294	309	318	293	524
Levy for fighting the non-use of an electric power production site by a producer	..	..	..	0	-16	0	0	0	0	0
Transfer to the Fund for Industrial Accidents of recognized private insurance corporations	..	..	..	182	249	294	309	318	293	297
Tax on securities accounts	..	..	..	0	0	0	0	0	0	226
5000 Taxes on goods and services	**2 386**	**10 105**	**18 360**	**29 103**	**38 462**	**41 035**	**44 517**	**45 589**	**49 371**	**51 364**
5100 Taxes on production, sale, transfer, etc.	2 187	9 606	17 387	27 000	36 091	38 646	42 087	43 098	46 816	48 731
5110 General taxes	1 355	6 321	11 570	18 258	24 411	25 882	27 979	28 170	30 449	31 775
5111 Value added taxes	0	6 321	11 547	18 132	24 140	25 628	27 738	27 952	30 255	31 545
VAT	..	6 293	11 491	18 132	24 140	25 628	27 738	27 952	30 255	31 545
Vehicle immatriculation tax	..	28	56	0	0	0	0	0	0	0
5112 Sales tax	0	0	23	126	271	253	241	219	194	230
5113 Other	1 355	0	0	0	0	0	0	0	0	0
Taxes assimilated to stamp duties	1 355	..	..	..	..	..	..	..	..	..
5120 Taxes on specific goods and services	832	3 285	5 818	8 742	11 680	12 764	14 109	14 927	16 368	16 955
5121 Excise duties	531	1 997	3 478	5 690	7 367	7 783	8 036	8 649	9 906	10 127
Mineral oil	278	1 109	2 017	3 392	3 891	4 148	4 072	4 556	5 195	5 543
Liquified gases and benzol	0	4	0	0	0	0	0	0	0	0
Tobacco	132	501	868	1 342	1 821	1 885	2 197	2 262	2 245	2 363
Spirits	23	123	191	206	225	235	272	318	320	314
Consumption tax on alcohol and spirits	26	54	0	0	0	0	0	0	0	0
Fermented sparkling beverages	1	7	11	24	39	57	77	92	103	102
Fermented fruit beverages	18	57	88	101	115	116	132	148	172	173
Beer	38	93	170	208	191	188	183	194	201	201
Non-alcoholic beverages	10	44	113	148	49	54	58	56	103	175
Coffee, sugar and syrup	5	5	22	13	12	13	15	14	15	14
Levy on energy	0	0	0	193	341	383	337	343	340	337
Intermediate alcoholic products	0	0	0	32	28	26	26	26	28	26
Inspection fee on domestic fuel oil	0	0	0	29	43	51	41	36	32	31
Ecotax	0	0	0	2	1	0	1	0	0	0
Levy on packaging	0	0	0	0	296	320	332	336	341	352
Federal contribution on electricity and natural gas	0	0	0	0	311	292	281	269	812	497
Environmental charge	0	0	0	0	5	15	14	1	0	0
5122 Profits of fiscal monopolies	0	0	0	0	0	0	0	0	0	0
5123 Customs and import duties	272	627	809	960	1 388	1 234	1 185	1 373	1 585	1 632
Import duties	206	0	0	0	0	0	0	0	0	0
Levies on agricultural products	63	0	0	0	0	0	0	0	0	0
ECSC levies	2	0	0	0	0	0	0	0	0	0
EU levies, import duties	0	383	716	932	1 365	1 210	1 149	1 368	1 585	1 632
EU levies on agricultural products	0	244	93	28	23	23	36	5	0	0
5124 Taxes on exports	0	1	0	0	0	0	0	0	0	0
5125 Taxes on investment goods	0	0	0	0	0	0	0	0	0	0
5126 Taxes on specific services	29	452	937	1 365	2 044	2 454	3 145	3 265	3 406	3 651
Gambling and betting tax	9	47	51	45	64	77	73	80	94	103
Insurance levy	19	404	885	1 282	1 930	2 123	2 285	2 307	2 382	2 469
Bill-posting tax	0	0	1	1	3	3	3	3	3	3
Deposit insurance	0	0	0	36	48	252	609	441	440	432
Resolution fund	0	0	0	0	0	0	167	380	250	285
Contracts art. 81 medicines	..	..	..	0	0	0	8	55	238	360
5127 Other taxes on internat. trade and transactions	0	0	0	0	0	0	0	0	0	0
5128 Other taxes	0	208	593	726	881	1 294	1 743	1 640	1 470	1 544
5130 Unallocable between 5110 and 5120	0	0	0	0	0	0	0	0	0	0
5200 Taxes on use of goods and perform activities	199	496	966	2 096	2 363	2 384	2 420	2 482	2 540	2 622

	1965	1980	1990	2000	2007	2010	2013	2015	2017	2018
5210 Recurrent taxes	199	496	966	1 887	2 032	2 005	2 023	2 032	1 993	1 955
Traffic tax	100	368	712	1 413	1 693	1 702	1 830	1 851	1 802	1 852
5211 Paid by households: motor vehicles	0	204	458	889	1 051	1 054	1 148	1 163	1 210	1 240
5212 Paid by others: motor vehicles	0	164	254	525	642	648	683	689	591	612
5213 Paid in respect of other goods	99	127	254	474	338	303	193	181	191	104
Tax on entertainment devices	6	20	20	71	56	58	74	56	54	52
Tax on pubs	1	5	24	18	0	0	0	0	0	0
Hunting tax	2	0	0	0	0	0	0	0	0	0
Local taxes	90	15	19	38	99	112	10	22	22	23
Radio and television licence fees	0	87	191	347	184	133	108	103	115	29
5220 Non-recurrent taxes	0	0	0	209	332	379	397	451	548	667
Vehicle registration tax	..	..	..	209	332	379	360	349	435	473
Vehicle registration tax (households)	..	..	..	139	221	252	240	233	290	315
Vehicle registration tax (others)	..	..	..	70	111	126	120	116	145	158
Emission permits	..	..	..	0	0	0	36	101	112	193
5300 Unallocable between 5100 and 5200	0	3	7	7	7	6	10	9	15	11
6000 Other taxes	**2**	**0**	**0**	**0**	**61**	**36**	**46**	**40**	**0**	**0**
6100 Paid solely by business	0	..	..	..	0	0	0	0	0	..
6200 Other	2	..	..	..	61	36	46	40	0	..
Fines and interest	2	..	..	..	0	0	0	0	0	..
Memorandum items										
Customs duties collected on behalf of the EU	..	..	..	960	1 388	1 234	1 185	1 373	1 585	1 632
SRF contributions collected on behalf of the EU	..	..	..	..	..	..	167	380	250	285
Other taxes collected on behalf of the EU	..	..	..	75	62	42	-7	9	2	..
Non-wastable tax credits										
Non-wastable tax credits against 1110	..	..	..	..	348	1 037	1 492	830	919	906
Tax expenditure component	..	..	..	..	78	588	1 077	537	600	616
Transfer component	..	..	..	..	270	449	415	293	319	291
Non-wastable tax credits against 1210	..	..	..	..	0	0	0	0	0	0
Tax expenditure component	..	..	..	..	..	..	..	..	..	..
Transfer component	..	..	..	..	..	..	..	..	..	..
Total tax revenue on cash basis	**6 421**	**37 438**	**70 268**	**..**	**..**	**..**	**..**	**..**	**..**	**..**
Total tax revenue on accrual basis	**..**	**37 443**	**70 408**	**112 710**	**147 861**	**156 317**	**177 665**	**184 429**	**195 930**	**202 645**
Conciliation with National Accounts										
Additional taxes included in National Accounts	..	107	447	1 300	1 740	2 458	3 354	3 616	3 863	4 099
National lottery profits	..	107	262	279	225	243	215	206	185	185
Water levies	..	0	66	378	119	137	122	104	119	140
Sanitel levy	..	0	0	14	13	15	14	6	12	14
Levy on industrial waste	..	0	27	74	68	54	46	55	79	88
Levy on manure	..	0	0	11	11	5	5	1	2	4
Levy on household waste	..	0	0	20	..	..	..	..	..	..
Earned income withholding tax (EU)	..	0	93	174	270	345	336	370	411	420
Social contributions (EU)	..	0	0	136	250	340	330	360	400	408
Imputed social contributions (EU)	..	0	0	213	431	508	511	554	615	627
Green certificates	..	..	..	..	354	812	1 777	1 959	2 041	2 213
Taxes excluded from National Accounts	..	0	0	0	0	0	0	0	0	0
Deposit insurance	..	..	..	..	..	..	..	..	..	..
Difference in treatment of tax credits	..	0	0	..	78	588	1 077	537	600	616
Capital transfer for uncollected revenue	..	0	0	-291	-381	-597	-730	-547	-624	-689
VAT on products assessed but unlikely to be collected	..	..	..	-18	-276	-367	-488	-357	-492	-492
Earned income withholding tax assessed but unlikely to be collected	..	..	..	-40	-53	-71	-47	-49	-50	-47
Employers' actual social contributions assessed but unlikely to be collected	..	..	..	-233	-52	-159	-194	-141	-81	-150
Voluntary social security contributions	..	41	52	58	57	59	77	70	75	85
Miscellaneous differences	..	0	0	0	0	0	0	0	0	0
Reallocation national levels of government	..	..	..	..	..	..	..	..	..	..
Reallocation EU	..	..	..	..	..	..	..	..	..	..
National Accounts: Taxes and actual social contributions	..	37 590	70 907	113 564	148 924	158 318	180 932	187 550	199 228	206 127
Imputed social contributions	..	1 497	2 886	5 377	7 568	8 713	10 071	9 812	10 550	10 820
National Accounts: Taxes and all social contributions	..	39 087	73 793	118 940	156 492	167 031	191 003	197 362	209 778	216 948

.. Not available

Note: Year ending 31st December. From 1970, data are on accrual basis

Source: Federal Ministry of Finance.

StatLink https://doi.org/10.1787/888934211718

Table 5.4. Canada: Details of tax revenue, 1965-2018

Million CAD

	1965	1980	1990	2000	2007	2010	2013	2015	2017	2018
Total tax revenue	**15 318**	**101 015**	**244 152**	**390 234**	**512 663**	**516 591**	**592 206**	**653 269**	**709 003**	**738 733**
1000 Taxes on income, profits and capital gains	**5 910**	**47 064**	**118 566**	**195 320**	**251 198**	**240 961**	**281 787**	**314 841**	**345 179**	**360 457**
1100 Of individuals	3 464	34 451	99 722	143 652	190 025	180 894	214 054	240 304	254 723	267 594
1110 On income and profits	3 464	34 451	99 722	143 652	190 025	180 894	214 054	240 304	254 723	267 594
Taxes federal government	2 635	21 231	60 252	90 694	116 395	109 341	127 655	143 315	154 267	162 295
Taxes on individuals - province	829	13 220	39 470	52 958	73 630	71 553	86 399	96 989	100 456	105 299
1120 On capital gains	0	0	0	0	0	0	0	0	0	0
1200 Corporate	2 276	11 741	17 190	47 643	54 272	54 101	62 359	67 894	82 936	83 763
1210 On profits	2 276	11 741	17 190	47 643	54 272	54 101	62 359	67 894	82 936	83 763
Taxes federal government	1 752	8 110	11 726	31 570	37 093	33 419	38 142	41 726	50 932	51 769
Taxes on corporations - province	524	3 631	5 464	16 073	17 179	20 682	24 217	26 168	32 004	31 994
1220 On capital gains	0	0	0	0	0	0	0	0	0	0
1300 Unallocable between 1100 and 1200	170	872	1 654	4 025	6 901	5 966	5 374	6 643	7 520	9 100
Non-resident withhold taxes - federal	170	872	1 654	4 025	6 901	5 966	5 374	6 643	7 520	9 100
2000 Social security contributions	**854**	**10 649**	**29 653**	**53 109**	**73 722**	**76 787**	**90 394**	**96 371**	**99 035**	**103 213**
2100 Employees	318	3 756	10 634	21 361	29 361	30 626	36 057	38 685	39 920	41 548
Canada pension plan	47	1 265	3 745	9 401	16 194	16 852	20 021	21 491	23 025	23 558
Quebec pension plan	15	431	1 108	2 897	4 124	5 450	5 815	6 293	6 991	7 413
Employment insurance	164	1 393	5 284	7 782	7 084	7 388	9 198	9 772	8 623	9 255
Hospital insurance premiums	92	667	496	1 281	1 959	937	1 023	1 128	1 281	1 322
2110 On a payroll basis	..	..	10 634	20 976	28 654	29 689	35 034	37 557	38 639	40 226
2120 On an income tax basis	..	..	0	385	707	937	1 023	1 128	1 281	1 322
2200 Employers	536	6 697	18 449	30 307	41 922	43 525	51 261	54 380	55 552	57 997
Canada pension plan	48	1 266	3 745	9 401	16 194	16 852	20 021	21 491	23 025	23 558
Quebec pension plan	15	432	1 108	2 897	4 124	5 450	5 815	6 293	6 991	7 413
Employment insurance	164	2 006	7 398	10 894	9 917	10 343	12 877	13 681	12 072	12 956
Hospital insurance premiums	92	1 270	496	897	1 252	0	0	0	0	0
Social insurance levies	217	1 723	5 702	6 218	10 434	10 881	12 548	12 914	13 464	14 070
2210 On a payroll basis	..	..	18 449	30 307	41 922	43 525	51 261	54 380	55 552	57 997
2220 On an income tax basis	..	..	0	0	0	0	0	0	0	0
2300 Self-employed or non-employed	0	196	570	1 442	2 440	2 636	3 076	3 307	3 563	3 667
Canada pension plan	..	153	478	1 200	2 096	2 181	2 591	2 781	2 979	3 049
Quebec pension plan	..	43	92	242	344	455	486	525	584	619
2310 On a payroll basis	..	196	570	1 442	2 440	2 636	3 076	3 307	3 563	3 667
2320 On an income tax basis	..	0	0	0	0	0	0	0	0	0
2400 Unallocable between 2100, 2200 and 2300	0	0	0	0	0	0	0	0	0	0
2410 On a payroll basis	..	..	..	..	..	..	..	..	..	..
2420 On an income tax basis	..	..	..	..	..	..	..	..	..	..
3000 Taxes on payroll and workforce	**0**	**0**	**5 499**	**8 013**	**10 038**	**10 760**	**12 482**	**13 256**	**14 223**	**14 871**
4000 Taxes on property	**2 186**	**9 195**	**24 467**	**37 157**	**54 507**	**63 735**	**70 451**	**77 778**	**84 081**	**85 859**
4100 Recurrent taxes on immovable property	1 830	8 315	20 189	30 242	44 567	51 702	57 769	62 651	66 699	69 750
On property provincial government	11	133	1 645	3 078	3 164	4 476	4 946	5 410	5 766	6 690
Personal property local government	17	0	18 544	27 165	41 403	47 226	52 823	57 241	60 933	63 060
Real property local government	1 802	8 182	0	0	0	0	0	0	0	0
4110 Households	..	..	..	..	..	..	..	..	..	..
4120 Others	..	..	..	..	..	..	..	..	..	..
4200 Recurrent taxes on net wealth	25	512	1 911	4 171	2 970	1 523	414	372	425	436
4210 Individual	0	0	0	0	0	0	0	0	0	0
4220 Corporate	25	512	1 911	4 171	2 970	1 523	414	372	425	436
4300 Estate, inheritance and gift taxes	223	75	3	2	0	178	221	268	304	331
4310 Estate and inheritance taxes	216	75	3	2	..	178	221	268	304	331
On inheritances federal government	108	0	0	0	..	0	0	0	0	0
Succession duties provincial government	108	75	3	2	..	178	221	268	304	331
4320 Gift taxes	7	0	0	0	..	0	0	0	0	0
On gifts federal government	7	..	..	..	..	..	..	..	..	..
4400 Taxes on financial and capital transactions	0	0	0	0	2 868	3 077	3 646	4 975	7 167	6 303
4500 Non-recurrent taxes	108	293	2 365	2 742	4 102	7 254	8 401	9 512	9 486	9 039
4510 On net wealth	0	0	0	0	0	0	0	0	0	0
4520 Other non-recurrent taxes	108	293	2 365	2 742	4 102	7 254	8 401	9 512	9 486	9 039
Special assessments and charges local govt.	108	293	2 365	2 742	4 102	7 254	8 401	9 512	9 486	9 039
4600 Other recurrent taxes on property	0	0	0	0	0	0	0	0	0	0
5000 Taxes on goods and services	**6 202**	**32 909**	**63 092**	**94 468**	**122 855**	**123 752**	**136 396**	**150 275**	**165 739**	**173 583**
5100 Taxes on production, sale, transfer, etc.	5 310	24 808	59 627	88 879	114 701	116 160	128 554	140 750	153 901	161 640
5110 General taxes	2 730	11 658	34 475	55 313	71 242	72 130	81 452	90 598	99 893	104 962
5111 Value added taxes	0	0	0	35 884	46 072	70 712	78 292	86 694	96 040	100 570
5112 Sales tax	2 730	11 658	34 475	19 429	25 170	1 418	3 160	3 904	3 853	4 392
Sales taxes federal government	813	5 429	16 866	0	0	0	0	0	0	0
Sales taxes provincial, local govt.	1 917	6 229	17 609	19 429	25 170	1 418	3 160	3 904	3 853	4 392
5113 Other	0	0	0	0	0	0	0	0	0	0

	1965	1980	1990	2000	2007	2010	2013	2015	2017	2018
5120 Taxes on specific goods and services	2 580	13 150	25 153	33 565	43 459	44 030	47 102	50 152	54 008	56 678
5121 Excise duties	1 499	6 805	14 473	18 417	22 759	23 281	24 470	25 284	27 342	28 040
Excises federal government	740	3 850	6 405	8 377	9 249	10 244	10 261	10 372	11 166	11 529
Liquor	..	..	926	1 103	1 224	1 554	1 488	1 521	1 700	1 811
Tobacco	..	..	2 247	2 176	2 466	3 025	3 019	2 875	3 115	3 406
Gasoline and motive fuel	..	..	2 472	4 807	5 272	5 306	5 460	5 678	6 040	6 015
Remitted gaming profits	..	..	45	0	0	0	0	0	0	0
Miscellaneous consumption taxes	..	..	715	291	287	358	294	297	311	297
Excises provincial government	759	2 955	8 067	10 039	13 510	13 037	14 209	14 912	16 176	16 511
Motor fuel	680	1 863	4 674	7 031	8 065	8 198	9 094	9 727	10 163	10 209
Tobacco	53	772	2 776	2 279	4 181	4 620	4 879	5 108	5 041	4 963
Other	26	320	617	730	1 264	219	236	77	972	1 339
5122 Profits of fiscal monopolies	294	1 406	3 758	8 756	11 565	11 565	12 059	13 016	13 915	14 316
Own enterprises contributions	294	1 406	3 758	8 756	11 565	11 565	12 059	13 016	13 915	14 316
5123 Customs and import duties	686	3 199	4 021	2 824	3 829	3 441	4 193	5 181	5 593	6 640
Customs and import duties federal govt.	686	3 199	4 021	2 824	3 829	3 441	4 193	5 181	5 593	6 640
5124 Taxes on exports	0	842	0	0	0	0	0	0	0	0
5125 Taxes on investment goods	0	0	0	0	0	0	0	0	0	0
5126 Taxes on specific services	84	575	2 385	2 524	4 088	4 489	5 087	5 213	5 983	6 536
Tax on insurance premiums, provincial govt.	45	261	1 141	1 740	2 796	3 305	3 901	3 962	4 544	5 014
Tax on insurance premiums, federal govt.	0	1	1	1	11	28	13	10	1	0
Amusement and admission taxes	4	25	126	538	537	322	280	291	333	320
Air transportation taxes	0	166	488	0	403	600	662	722	823	872
Racetrack betting	35	122	155	55	36	36	32	33	25	25
Tax on meals and hotels	0	0	473	191	305	198	199	195	257	305
5127 Other taxes on internat. trade and transactions	0	0	0	0	0	0	0	0	0	0
5128 Other taxes	17	323	517	1 045	1 217	1 255	1 292	1 458	1 176	1 146
Other taxes federal government	0	98	272	758	762	557	439	544	417	446
Other taxes provincial government	17	225	245	287	455	698	853	914	759	700
5130 Unallocable between 5110 and 5120	0	0	0	0	0	0	0	0	0	0
5200 Taxes on use of goods and perform activities	892	8 101	3 465	5 589	8 154	7 592	7 842	9 525	11 838	11 943
5210 Recurrent taxes	306	1 500	2 393	3 644	4 368	4 452	5 017	5 589	6 119	6 264
5211 Paid by households: motor vehicles	103	666	1 056	1 696	2 241	1 986	2 237	2 478	2 854	2 946
5212 Paid by others: motor vehicles	141	509	697	1 039	1 242	1 153	1 343	1 552	1 664	1 719
5213 Paid in respect of other goods	62	325	640	909	885	1 313	1 437	1 559	1 601	1 599
5220 Non-recurrent taxes	586	6 601	1 072	1 945	3 786	3 140	2 825	3 936	5 719	5 679
Licences and permits local govt.	36	132	317	499	889	807	952	1 023	1 035	1 036
Licences and permits provincial govt.	550	6 469	755	1 446	2 897	2 333	1 873	2 913	4 684	4 643
5300 Unallocable between 5100 and 5200	0	0	0	0	0	0	0	0	0	0
6000 Other taxes	**166**	**1 198**	**2 875**	**2 167**	**342**	**596**	**696**	**748**	**745**	**750**
6100 Paid solely by business	139	943	2 386	1 280	0	0	0	0	0	0
6200 Other	27	255	489	887	342	596	696	748	745	750
Poll tax local government	5	0	0	0	0	0	0	0	0	0
Miscellaneous local government	11	358	489	887	342	596	696	748	745	750
Other federal government	11	-103	0	0	0	0	0	0	0	0
Non-wastable tax credits										
Non-wastable tax credits against 1110	..	..	..	1 633	5 550	6 415	7 326	7 510	8 007	10 709
Tax expenditure component	..	..	..	276	824	875	965	968	1 057	2 395
Transfer component	..	..	..	1 357	4 726	5 540	6 361	6 542	6 950	8 314
Non-wastable tax credits against 1210	..	..	..	1 758	3 445	4 726	3 754	3 768	3 649	3 059
Tax expenditure component	..	..	..	20	12	19	17	15	16	12
Transfer component	..	..	..	1 738	3 433	4 707	3 737	3 753	3 633	3 047
Total tax revenue on cash basis	**15 318**	**101 015**	**244 152**	**388 833**	**527 734**	**..**	**..**	**..**	**..**	**..**
Total tax revenue on accrual basis	**..**	**..**	**..**	**390 234**	**512 663**	**516 591**	**592 206**	**653 269**	**709 003**	**738 733**
Conciliation with National Accounts										
Additional taxes included in National Accounts	..	..	..	0	0	0	0	0	0	0
Taxes excluded from National Accounts	..	..	..	0	0	0	0	0	0	0
Difference in treatment of tax credits	..	..	..	296	836	894	982	983	1 073	2 407
Capital transfer for uncollected revenue	..	..	..	0	0	0	0	0	0	0
Voluntary social security contributions	..	..	..	0	0	0	0	0	0	0
Miscellaneous differences	..	..	..	0	0	0	0	0	0	0
National Accounts: Taxes and actual social contributions	..	..	..	390 234	513 499	517 485	593 188	654 252	710 076	741 140
Imputed social contributions	..	..	..	0	0	0	0	0	0	0
National Accounts: Taxes and all social contributions	..	..	..	390 234	513 499	517 485	593 188	654 252	710 076	741 140

.. Not available

Note: From 2001, all data are for the year ending 31st December. For 2000 and earlier years, data for the Federal, Provincial and Territorial governments and Social security funds are on a fiscal year basis commencing 1st April. Data for local government are on a fiscal year basis commencing 1st January.
From 1999 data are on accrual basis except that personal income taxes are on a modified cash basis.
There are some minor differences between the data for the years 1965 to 1978 and those for subsequent years. These mostly relate to the inclusion of fines and penalities or late payment of taxes and deductions for the child tax credits in the data for the years 1979 to 1983.
Heading 1210 - Taxes federal government: Federal corporate taxes include capital taxes.
Heading 2000: Includes receipts from the Canadian Pension Plan, Quebec Pension Plan, Unemployement Insurance Fund and Provincial Health Insurance. Premiums, Medicare Premiums and Social Insurance levies but excludes that part of the taxes on income and sales taxes earmarked for old age security. The practice of earmarking these taxes was discontinued in June 1975.
Heading 4400: From 2002 onward includes land transfer taxes of the provincial, territorial and local governments. Prior to 2002 land transfer taxes of the local government were included in line 6000 and those provincial and territorial governments were included in line 4520.
Heading 5121: The large increase in this heading between 1980 and 1981 is due to the introduction of a 'special petroleum compensation charge', a 'Canadian ownership special charge' and to an increase in the natural gas tax of C$ 2399 millions.
Heading 5122: From 1988, profits on fiscal monopolies include lottery profits.
Heading 5128: From 1988, other taxes of Federal Government include the annual fees for managing the spectrum (airwaves) allocation to the cellular industry.
Heading 5211: Some Québec motor vehicle licence administrative fees are included in sales of goods and services for the period 1988-89 to 1997-98. From 1998-99 onward, these fees are included under other taxes - motor vehicle licences.
Source: Statistics Canada.

StatLink https://doi.org/10.1787/888934211737

Table 5.5. Chile: Details of tax revenue, 1965-2018

Million CLP

	1965	1980	1990	2000	2007	2010	2013	2015	2017	2018
Total tax revenue	..	..	**1 777 218**	**7 901 998**	**20 598 963**	**21 845 693**	**27 381 686**	**32 532 354**	**36 238 558**	**40 314 703**
1000 Taxes on income, profits and capital gains	..	..	**412 974**	**1 841 630**	**9 412 056**	**8 329 060**	**9 520 709**	**11 840 521**	**12 516 154**	**14 418 859**
1100 Of individuals	..	..	99 154	604 100	989 348	1 492 837	1 964 172	3 199 876	3 500 023	2 701 416
Second category tax	..	..	65 552	490 980	993 129	1 449 099	1 981 699	2 350 120	2 585 694	2 848 205
Global complementary tax	..	..	33 603	113 120	-3 781	43 738	-17 527	-36 757	50 495	-146 789
Other	..	..	0	0	0	0	0	886 513	863 834	0
1110 On income and profits	..	..	..	..	..	..	..	..	..	..
1120 On capital gains	..	..	..	..	..	..	..	..	..	..
1200 Corporate	..	..	219 586	882 896	6 054 487	4 448 745	6 041 089	6 839 133	7 658 420	8 920 497
First category tax	..	..	200 891	815 747	5 084 996	3 913 870	5 473 355	6 183 830	7 049 471	7 836 379
Surtax on state owned enterprises	..	..	16 074	47 634	113 334	194 203	124 220	132 352	193 058	184 442
Mining tax	..	..	0	0	835 452	298 558	324 577	323 507	101 970	184 382
Other	..	..	2 621	19 516	20 705	42 114	118 937	199 444	313 921	715 293
1210 On profits	..	..	..	..	..	..	..	..	..	..
1220 On capital gains	..	..	..	..	..	..	..	..	..	..
1300 Unallocable between 1100 and 1200	..	..	94 233	354 634	2 368 221	2 387 478	1 515 449	1 801 512	1 357 711	2 796 947
Additional tax	..	..	59 082	350 301	1 462 715	1 414 057	1 337 721	1 429 758	1 453 577	2 127 948
Other	..	..	35 151	4 332	905 507	973 421	177 727	371 755	-95 865	668 998
2000 Social security contributions	..	..	**159 559**	**576 758**	**1 148 647**	**1 493 987**	**1 968 973**	**2 252 489**	**2 627 558**	**2 786 173**
2100 Employees	..	..	154 021	553 937	1 098 620	1 433 159	1 906 340	2 188 575	2 553 916	2 703 261
2110 On a payroll basis	..	..	154 021	553 937	1 098 620	1 433 159	1 906 340	2 188 575	2 553 916	2 703 261
2120 On an income tax basis	..	..	0	0	0	0	0	0	0	0
2200 Employers	..	..	5 538	22 821	50 027	60 828	62 633	63 914	73 643	82 912
2210 On a payroll basis	..	..	5 538	22 821	50 027	60 828	62 633	63 914	73 643	82 912
2220 On an income tax basis	..	..	0	0	0	0	0	0	0	0
2300 Self-employed or non-employed	..	..	0	0	0	0	0	0	0	0
2310 On a payroll basis	..	..	..	..	..	..	..	..	..	..
2320 On an income tax basis	..	..	..	..	..	..	..	..	..	..
2400 Unallocable between 2100, 2200 and 2300	..	..	0	0	0	0	0	0	0	0
2410 On a payroll basis	..	..	..	..	..	..	..	..	..	..
2420 On an income tax basis	..	..	..	..	..	..	..	..	..	..
3000 Taxes on payroll and workforce	..	..	**0**	**0**	**0**	**0**	**0**	**0**	**0**	**0**
4000 Taxes on property	..	..	**109 319**	**554 037**	**1 013 571**	**898 607**	**1 133 765**	**1 421 274**	**1 950 217**	**2 086 866**
4100 Recurrent taxes on immovable property	..	..	59 968	302 244	496 311	662 368	840 842	1 056 920	1 229 195	1 373 495
4110 Households	..	..	..	..	..	..	..	..	..	..
4120 Others	..	..	..	..	..	..	..	..	..	..
4200 Recurrent taxes on net wealth	..	..	0	0	0	0	0	0	0	0
4210 Individual	..	..	..	..	..	..	..	..	..	..
4220 Corporate	..	..	..	..	..	..	..	..	..	..
4300 Estate, inheritance and gift taxes	..	..	3 444	10 906	28 501	39 338	45 550	92 236	202 376	125 649
4310 Estate and inheritance taxes	..	..	..	..	..	..	..	..	..	..
4320 Gift taxes	..	..	..	..	..	..	..	..	..	..
4400 Taxes on financial and capital transactions	..	..	45 907	240 886	488 759	196 901	247 373	272 118	518 645	587 721
4500 Non-recurrent taxes	..	..	0	0	0	0	0	0	0	0
4510 On net wealth	..	..	..	..	..	..	..	..	..	..
4520 Other non-recurrent taxes	..	..	..	..	..	..	..	..	..	..
4600 Other recurrent taxes on property	..	..	0	0	0	0	0	0	0	0
5000 Taxes on goods and services	..	..	**1 118 722**	**5 041 769**	**9 023 666**	**11 185 156**	**14 779 915**	**17 597 378**	**19 858 881**	**21 470 498**
5100 Taxes on production, sale, transfer, etc.	..	..	1 074 009	4 789 827	8 578 636	10 532 904	13 869 529	16 515 485	18 597 180	19 953 036
5110 General taxes	..	..	664 421	3 306 350	6 781 501	8 399 926	11 170 794	13 273 958	15 069 540	16 211 646
5111 Value added taxes	..	..	664 421	3 306 350	6 781 501	8 399 926	11 170 794	13 273 958	15 069 540	16 211 646
5112 Sales tax	..	..	0	0	0	0	0	0	0	0
5113 Other	..	..	0	0	0	0	0	0	0	0
5120 Taxes on specific goods and services	..	..	409 588	1 483 477	1 797 135	2 132 978	2 698 735	3 241 527	3 527 640	3 741 389
5121 Excise duties	..	..	166 050	816 160	1 299 844	1 561 205	1 987 475	2 412 773	2 682 659	2 796 033
Cigarettes and tobacco	..	..	60 604	283 275	455 595	647 637	815 991	981 422	978 696	981 456
Gasolene and diesel	..	..	105 445	532 885	844 249	913 568	1 171 483	1 388 218	1 629 561	1 727 392
Oil stabilisation fund	..	..	0	0	0	0	0	0	0	0
Fisheries Law Extraction Rights	..	..	0	0	0	0	0	8 558	11 749	19 623
Additional tax on new motor vehicles	..	..	0	0	0	0	0	34 575	62 654	67 561
5122 Profits of fiscal monopolies	..	..	0	0	0	0	0	0	0	0
5123 Customs and import duties	..	..	222 486	548 571	300 416	267 331	303 393	343 491	321 156	347 555
5124 Taxes on exports	..	..	0	0	0	0	0	0	0	0
5125 Taxes on investment goods	..	..	0	0	0	0	0	0	0	0
5126 Taxes on specific services	..	..	21 052	118 746	196 875	304 442	407 867	485 263	523 824	597 802
5127 Other taxes on internat. trade and transactions	..	..	0	0	0	0	0	0	0	0
5128 Other taxes	..	..	0	0	0	0	0	0	0	0
5130 Unallocable between 5110 and 5120	..	..	0	0	0	0	0	0	0	0
5200 Taxes on use of goods and perform activities	..	..	44 714	251 942	445 030	652 252	910 386	1 081 893	1 261 702	1 517 462

	1965	1980	1990	2000	2007	2010	2013	2015	2017	2018
5210 Recurrent taxes	..	..	44 714	251 942	445 030	652 252	910 386	1 081 893	1 261 702	1 402 110
Motor vehicles	..	..	24 469	93 880	155 158	218 219	330 754	397 608	482 009	539 918
5211 Paid by households: motor vehicles	..	..	0	0	0	0	0	0	0	0
5212 Paid by others: motor vehicles	..	..	0	0	0	0	0	0	0	0
5213 Paid in respect of other goods	..	..	20 245	158 062	289 872	434 033	579 632	684 285	779 693	862 192
Municipal permits	..	..	18 401	136 138	263 996	396 944	527 955	630 943	725 954	806 734
Mining patents	..	..	3 374	34 730	25 184	36 213	50 094	51 767	52 254	53 854
Other	..	..	-1 530	-12 806	692	876	1 583	1 575	1 485	1 604
5220 Non-recurrent taxes	..	..	0	0	0	0	0	0	0	115 352
Tax on Polluting Fixed Sources	..	..	..	..	..	..	..	..	..	115 352
5300 Unallocable between 5100 and 5200	..	..	0	0	0	0	0	0	0	0
6000 Other taxes	**..**	**..**	**-23 356**	**-112 195**	**1 023**	**-61 117**	**-21 676**	**-579 308**	**-714 253**	**-447 692**
6100 Paid solely by business	..	..	0	0	0	0	0	0	0	0
6200 Other	..	..	-23 356	-112 195	1 023	-61 117	-21 676	-579 308	-714 253	-447 692
Non-wastable tax credits										
Non-wastable tax credits against 1110	..	..	0	0	0	0	0	0	0	0
Tax expenditure component	..	..	..	..	..	..	..	..	..	..
Transfer component	..	..	..	..	..	..	..	..	..	..
Non-wastable tax credits against 1210	..	..	0	0	0	0	0	175 468	213 519	251 606
Tax expenditure component	..	..	..	..	..	..	..	45 774	62 076	64 837
Transfer component	..	..	..	..	..	..	..	129 694	151 443	186 769
Total tax revenue on cash basis	**..**	**..**	**1 777 218**	**7 901 998**	**20 598 963**	**21 845 693**	**27 381 686**	**32 532 354**	**36 238 558**	**40 314 703**
Total tax revenue on accrual basis	**..**	**..**	**..**	**..**	**..**	**..**	**..**	**..**	**..**	**..**
Conciliation with National Accounts										
Additional taxes included in National Accounts	..	..	..	..	..	..	..	..	..	..
Taxes excluded from National Accounts	..	..	..	..	..	..	..	..	..	..
Difference in treatment of tax credits	..	..	..	..	..	..	..	..	..	..
Capital transfer for uncollected revenue	..	..	..	..	..	..	..	..	..	..
Voluntary social security contributions	..	..	..	..	..	..	..	..	..	..
Miscellaneous differences	..	..	..	..	..	..	..	..	..	..
National Accounts: Taxes and actual social contributions	..	..	..	..	..	..	..	..	..	..
Imputed social contributions	..	..	..	..	..	..	..	..	..	..
National Accounts: Taxes and all social contributions	..	..	..	..	..	..	..	..	..	..

.. Not available

Note: Year ending 31st December.

The data are on a cash basis.

Source: Servicio de Impuestos internos (Chile's Tax Service).

StatLink https://doi.org/10.1787/888934211756

Table 5.6. Colombia: Details of tax revenue, 1965-2018

Million COP

	1965	1980	1990	2000	2007	2010	2013	2015	2017	2018
Total tax revenue	..	..	**2 579 426**	**30 598 630**	**82 697 457**	**98 455 335**	**142 976 023**	**160 157 693**	**174 735 823**	**190 299 911**
1000 Taxes on income, profits and capital gains	..	..	**771 694**	**7 103 525**	**24 010 404**	**26 218 852**	**47 743 096**	**52 656 876**	**57 615 236**	**64 043 928**
1100 Of individuals	..	..	47 210	1 499 345	4 751 580	5 192 384	7 787 050	9 210 448	10 367 606	12 215 963
1110 On income and profits	..	..	47 210	1 499 345	4 751 580	5 192 384	7 787 050	9 210 448	10 367 606	12 215 963
Income tax	..	..	47 210	1 499 345	4 751 580	5 192 384	7 787 050	9 210 448	10 367 606	12 215 963
Simple tax regime	..	..	0	0	0	0	0	0	0	0
1120 On capital gains	..	..	..	..	..	..	..	..	..	..
1200 Corporate	..	..	359 758	5 119 828	18 427 899	20 405 209	38 788 077	41 398 731	44 970 528	48 529 320
1210 On profits	..	..	359 758	5 119 828	18 427 899	20 405 209	38 788 077	41 398 731	44 970 528	48 529 320
Income tax	..	..	359 758	5 119 828	18 427 899	20 405 209	35 848 498	27 472 562	40 124 337	48 396 597
Pro Equity Income Tax - CREE	..	..	0	0	0	0	2 939 579	13 926 169	4 846 190	132 723
Simple tax regime	..	..	0	0	0	0	0	0	0	0
1220 On capital gains	..	..	..	..	..	..	..	..	..	..
1300 Unallocable between 1100 and 1200	..	..	364 726	484 352	830 925	621 258	1 167 968	2 047 697	2 277 102	3 298 645
Income tax	..	..	364 726	484 352	830 925	621 258	1 167 968	2 047 697	2 277 102	3 298 645
Pro Equity Income Tax - CREE	..	..	0	0	0	0	0	0	0	0
2000 Social security contributions	..	..	**203 596**	**4 989 000**	**9 694 000**	**11 478 085**	**16 644 445**	**13 585 138**	**13 351 711**	**18 192 049**
2100 Employees	..	..	..	..	..	..	..	..	..	..
2110 On a payroll basis	..	..	..	..	..	..	..	..	..	..
2120 On an income tax basis	..	..	..	..	..	..	..	..	..	..
2200 Employers	..	..	..	..	..	..	..	..	..	..
2210 On a payroll basis	..	..	..	..	..	..	..	..	..	..
2220 On an income tax basis	..	..	..	..	..	..	..	..	..	..
2300 Self-employed or non-employed	..	..	..	..	..	..	..	..	..	..
2310 On a payroll basis	..	..	..	..	..	..	..	..	..	..
2320 On an income tax basis	..	..	..	..	..	..	..	..	..	..
2400 Unallocable between 2100, 2200 and 2300	..	..	203 596	4 989 000	9 694 000	11 478 085	16 644 445	13 585 138	13 351 711	18 192 049
2410 On a payroll basis	..	..	203 596	4 989 000	9 694 000	11 478 085	16 644 445	13 585 138	13 351 711	18 192 049
2420 On an income tax basis	..	..	0	0	0	0	0	0	0	0
3000 Taxes on payroll and workforce	..	..	**0**	**1 286 803**	**2 798 906**	**4 022 503**	**3 527 459**	**2 797 308**	**3 200 238**	**3 461 352**
4000 Taxes on property	..	..	**56 160**	**2 027 654**	**6 459 259**	**8 535 238**	**14 907 909**	**18 156 105**	**17 950 494**	**15 265 472**
4100 Recurrent taxes on immovable property	..	..	56 160	991 070	2 298 829	3 338 935	4 735 321	6 061 965	7 310 244	7 981 989
4110 Households	..	..	0	0	0	0	0	0	0	0
4120 Others	..	..	56 160	991 070	2 298 829	3 338 935	4 735 321	6 061 965	7 310 244	7 981 989
4200 Recurrent taxes on net wealth	..	..	0	0	1 170 908	1 970 530	4 274 832	5 352 940	3 868 595	467 925
4210 Individual	..	..	..	..	1 170 908	1 970 530	4 274 832	5 352 940	3 868 595	467 925
4220 Corporate	..	..	..	..	0	0	0	0	0	0
4300 Estate, inheritance and gift taxes	..	..	0	0	0	0	0	0	0	0
4310 Estate and inheritance taxes	..	..	..	..	..	..	..	..	..	..
4320 Gift taxes	..	..	..	..	..	..	..	..	..	..
4400 Taxes on financial and capital transactions	..	..	0	1 036 584	2 989 522	3 225 773	5 897 755	6 741 200	6 771 655	6 815 558
4500 Non-recurrent taxes	..	..	0	0	0	0	0	0	0	0
4510 On net wealth	..	..	..	..	..	..	..	..	..	..
4520 Other non-recurrent taxes	..	..	..	..	..	..	..	..	..	..
4600 Other recurrent taxes on property	..	..	0	0	0	0	0	0	0	0
5000 Taxes on goods and services	..	..	**1 388 653**	**14 180 450**	**36 766 741**	**44 411 642**	**55 285 569**	**65 716 566**	**75 381 123**	**81 408 789**
5100 Taxes on production, sale, transfer, etc.	..	..	1 388 653	14 048 655	36 447 297	44 038 074	54 326 006	64 688 081	74 003 567	79 935 336
5110 General taxes	..	..	672 368	9 585 866	26 910 512	33 333 802	40 479 366	48 684 900	58 565 799	64 316 019
5111 Value added taxes	..	..	583 078	8 445 776	23 377 821	28 811 682	34 642 822	41 659 696	50 619 849	55 879 110
5112 Sales tax	..	..	89 290	1 140 090	3 532 691	4 522 121	5 836 544	7 025 204	7 945 950	8 436 909
Industry and commerce tax (State)	..	..	89 290	1 140 090	3 532 691	4 522 121	5 836 544	7 025 204	7 945 950	8 436 909
5113 Other	..	..	0	0	0	0	0	0	0	0
5120 Taxes on specific goods and services	..	..	716 285	4 462 789	9 536 785	10 704 271	13 846 640	16 003 181	15 437 768	15 619 317
5121 Excise duties	..	..	404 699	2 718 692	5 276 999	6 052 273	9 949 457	11 412 250	11 616 844	12 061 132
Petrol	..	..	141 270	833 004	1 211 511	1 418 766	2 883 410	3 297 392	1 352 793	1 517 546
Tobacco (State)	..	..	52 898	213 412	330 016	390 472	496 513	524 357	887 534	1 145 879
Beer (State)	..	..	85 722	471 135	1 203 838	1 432 453	2 031 349	2 305 895	2 572 771	2 637 674
Liquors (State)	..	..	124 808	520 394	834 390	929 328	1 292 743	1 253 466	1 907 802	1 800 605
Restaurant service, vehicle sale and mobile telephone service	..	..	0	0	0	0	1 181 998	1 684 179	1 948 718	2 047 419
Carbon	..	..	0	0	0	0	0	0	474 596	288 373
Plastic bags	..	..	0	0	0	0	0	0	6 546	28 099
Medicinal cannabis	..	..	0	0	0	0	0	0	10	3
Diesel surcharge	..	..	0	85 716	388 091	500 405	572 022	598 993	546 243	579 613
Petrol surcharge	..	..	0	595 031	1 309 154	1 380 848	1 491 423	1 747 969	1 919 830	2 015 922
5122 Profits of fiscal monopolies	..	..	0	0	0	0	0	0	0	0
5123 Customs and import duties	..	..	311 586	1 744 097	4 259 786	4 651 999	3 897 184	4 590 931	3 820 924	3 558 185
Custom duties	..	..	180 989	1 744 097	4 259 786	4 651 999	3 897 184	4 590 931	3 820 924	3 558 185
Imports surcharge	..	..	130 597	0	0	0	0	0	0	0

	1965	1980	1990	2000	2007	2010	2013	2015	2017	2018
5124 Taxes on exports	..	..	0	0	0	0	0	0	0	0
5125 Taxes on investment goods	..	..	0	0	0	0	0	0	0	0
5126 Taxes on specific services	..	..	0	0	0	0	0	0	0	0
5127 Other taxes on internat. trade and transactions	..	..	0	0	0	0	0	0	0	0
5128 Other taxes	..	..	0	0	0	0	0	0	0	0
5130 Unallocable between 5110 and 5120	..	..	0	0	0	0	0	0	0	0
5200 Taxes on use of goods and perform activities	..	..	0	131 795	319 444	373 568	959 563	1 028 485	1 377 556	1 473 453
5210 Recurrent taxes	..	..	..	131 795	319 444	373 568	959 563	1 028 485	1 377 556	1 473 453
5211 Paid by households: motor vehicles	..	..	..	131 795	319 444	373 568	959 563	1 028 485	1 377 556	1 473 453
Tax on motor vehicle ownership	..	..	..	131 795	319 444	373 568	959 563	1 028 485	1 377 556	1 473 453
5212 Paid by others: motor vehicles	..	..	..	..	..	..	..	..	..	..
5213 Paid in respect of other goods	..	..	..	..	..	..	..	..	..	..
5220 Non-recurrent taxes	..	..	..	..	..	..	..	..	..	..
5300 Unallocable between 5100 and 5200	..	..	0	0	0	0	0	0	0	0
6000 Other taxes	**..**	**..**	**159 323**	**1 011 197**	**2 968 147**	**3 789 014**	**4 867 545**	**7 245 701**	**7 237 021**	**7 928 320**
6100 Paid solely by business	..	..	0	0	0	0	0	0	0	0
6200 Other	..	..	159 323	1 011 197	2 968 147	3 789 014	4 867 545	7 245 701	7 237 021	7 928 320
Stamp tax	..	..	0	401 497	759 787	357 160	58 378	101 668	75 493	79 868
Other	..	..	78 306	79 287	86 297	126 602	200 465	318 271	403 473	461 160
Other (sub-national)	..	..	81 017	530 413	2 122 062	3 305 252	4 608 702	6 825 762	6 758 055	7 387 293
Total tax revenue on cash basis	**..**	**..**	**2 579 426**	**30 598 630**	**82 697 457**	**98 455 335**	**142 976 023**	**160 157 693**	**174 735 823**	**190 299 911**
Total tax revenue on accrual basis	**..**	**..**	..	..	..	..	..	..	..	..
Conciliation with National Accounts										
Additional taxes included in National Accounts	..	..	..	..	..	..	..	..	..	..
Taxes excluded from National Accounts	..	..	..	..	..	..	..	..	..	..
Difference in treatment of tax credits	..	..	..	..	..	..	..	..	..	..
Capital transfer for uncollected revenue	..	..	..	..	..	..	..	..	..	..
Voluntary social security contributions	..	..	..	..	..	..	..	..	..	..
Miscellaneous differences	..	..	..	..	..	..	..	..	..	..
National Accounts: Taxes and actual social contributions	..	..	..	..	..	..	..	..	..	..
Imputed social contributions	..	..	..	..	..	..	..	..	..	..
National Accounts: Taxes and all social contributions	..	..	..	..	..	..	..	..	..	..

.. Not available

Note: Year ending 31st December.

Data on an cash basis.

Includes the reported consolidated revenues of the territorial entities (departments and municipalities).

Heading 2000: Before 2013, social security contributions did not include all the contributions entering FOSYGA (Solidarity and Guarantee Fund). Only the portion of the contributions used to finance the subsidised regime (up to 1.5 pp of the 12.5% of the monthly wage paid by employers and employees as an obligatory health contribution) was included. The part of the contributions entering FOSYGA to finance the contributory regime was classified in the social security sector as "other incomes".

From 2013 onwards, all of the health contributions entering FOSYGA are classified as social security contributions. The portion of the contributions not entering FOSYGA that is both collected and spent by the health insurers – EPS - is not part of the fiscal accounts.

Headings 1100 and 1200: The data are estimated.

Source: Dirección de Impuestos y Aduanas Nacionales de Colombia, Ministerio de Hacienda y Crédito Público y Banco Central de Colombia.

(National Tax and Customs Administration, Ministry of Finance and Public Credit and Central Bank of Colombia).

StatLink https://doi.org/10.1787/888934211775

Table 5.7. Czech Republic: Details of tax revenue, 1965-2018

Million CZK

	1965	1980	1990	2000	2007	2010	2013	2015	2017	2018
Total tax revenue	..	..	..	**771 596**	**1 316 197**	**1 286 861**	**1 396 555**	**1 532 565**	**1 760 047**	**1 892 396**
Total tax revenue exclusive of taxes collected for the EU	..	..	..	**771 596**	**1 309 754**	**1 280 288**	**1 390 999**	**1 524 653**	**1 751 777**	**1 884 100**
1000 Taxes on income, profits and capital gains	..	..	..	**175 846**	**327 771**	**259 934**	**290 263**	**329 768**	**390 566**	**426 988**
1100 Of individuals	..	..	..	99 668	155 817	131 706	149 831	164 678	202 244	230 973
1110 On income and profits	..	..	..	99 668	155 817	131 706	149 831	164 678	202 244	230 973
Wages and salaries withholding	..	..	..	73 474	127 524	115 755	129 793	139 888	175 301	198 827
Of unincorporated individuals	..	..	..	17 254	19 568	5 747	7 437	9 100	10 974	13 632
Withheld on interest and dividends paid to individuals	..	..	..	8 940	8 725	10 204	12 602	15 691	15 969	18 513
1120 On capital gains	..	..	..	0	0	0	0	0	0	0
1200 Corporate	..	..	..	76 178	171 954	128 228	140 432	165 090	188 322	196 015
1210 On profits	..	..	..	76 178	171 954	128 228	140 432	165 090	188 322	196 015
Profit tax	..	..	..	68 945	164 016	118 248	124 820	147 157	167 120	179 022
Withheld on interest and dividends paid to corporations	..	..	..	7 233	7 162	9 156	7 736	9 415	8 760	7 892
Levy on lottery revenue	..	..	..	0	776	824	7 876	8 518	12 442	9 101
1220 On capital gains	..	..	..	0	0	0	0	0	0	0
1300 Unallocable between 1100 and 1200	..	..	..	0	0	0	0	0	0	0
2000 Social security contributions	..	..	..	**341 544**	**573 417**	**576 029**	**603 072**	**659 743**	**757 183**	**829 702**
2100 Employees	..	..	..	77 272	127 662	116 818	123 353	133 878	155 827	171 835
2110 On a payroll basis	..	..	..	77 272	127 662	116 818	123 353	133 878	155 827	171 835
Retirement	..	..	..	40 489	66 644	69 272	71 871	78 120	91 414	100 580
State employment policy	..	..	..	2 492	4 101	0	0	0	0	0
Sick leave	..	..	..	6 852	11 279	0	0	0	0	0
Health insurance	..	..	..	27 439	45 638	47 546	51 482	55 758	64 413	71 255
2120 On an income tax basis	..	..	..	0	0	0	0	0	0	0
2200 Employers	..	..	..	220 207	359 493	363 074	382 498	417 778	483 437	531 640
2210 On a payroll basis	..	..	..	220 207	359 493	363 074	382 498	417 778	483 437	531 640
Retirement	..	..	..	121 547	220 591	229 450	239 248	261 786	302 926	333 281
State employment policy	..	..	..	19 933	12 303	12 756	13 345	14 604	16 897	18 590
Sick leave	..	..	..	20 555	33 834	24 332	25 454	27 851	32 231	35 450
Health insurance	..	..	..	54 879	91 275	95 095	102 964	111 517	128 825	142 511
Penalties	..	..	..	3 293	1 490	1 441	1 487	2 020	2 558	1 808
2220 On an income tax basis	..	..	..	0	0	0	0	0	0	0
2300 Self-employed or non-employed	..	..	..	44 065	86 262	96 137	97 221	108 088	117 919	126 227
2310 On a payroll basis	..	..	..	44 065	86 262	96 137	97 221	108 088	117 919	126 227
Retirement	..	..	..	7 819	19 508	20 510	21 262	22 472	25 197	26 825
State employment policy	..	..	..	1 082	1 114	1 173	911	962	1 080	1 149
Sick leave	..	..	..	0	0	0	0	0	0	0
Health insurance	..	..	..	34 992	65 483	74 299	74 908	84 460	91 027	98 089
Self-employed	..	..	..	7 328	15 921	17 603	18 732	20 748	22 075	25 583
Non-employed	..	..	..	200	2 103	3 996	2 500	2 768	3 699	4 146
Government	..	..	..	27 464	47 459	52 700	53 676	60 944	65 253	68 360
Penalties	..	..	..	172	157	155	140	193	615	164
2320 On an income tax basis	..	..	..	0	0	0	0	0	0	0
2400 Unallocable between 2100, 2200 and 2300	..	..	..	0	0	0	0	0	0	0
2410 On a payroll basis	..	..	..	..	..	..	..	..	..	..
2420 On an income tax basis	..	..	..	..	..	..	..	..	..	..
3000 Taxes on payroll and workforce	..	..	..	**0**	**0**	**0**	**0**	**0**	**0**	**0**
4000 Taxes on property	..	..	..	**10 890**	**15 495**	**16 364**	**19 210**	**21 920**	**23 850**	**24 618**
4100 Recurrent taxes on immovable property	..	..	..	4 469	5 126	8 752	9 852	10 333	10 783	10 855
4110 Households	..	..	..	1 452	2 228	4 302	5 387	5 433	5 660	5 772
Real property tax	..	..	..	1 452	2 228	4 302	5 387	5 433	5 660	5 772
4120 Others	..	..	..	3 017	2 898	4 450	4 465	4 900	5 123	5 084
Levy collected by Winery Fund	..	..	..	0	2	5	5	20	25	26
Real property tax	..	..	..	3 017	2 895	4 445	4 461	4 880	5 098	5 057
4200 Recurrent taxes on net wealth	..	..	..	0	0	0	0	0	0	0
4210 Individual	..	..	..	..	..	..	..	..	..	..
4220 Corporate	..	..	..	..	..	..	..	..	..	..
4300 Estate, inheritance and gift taxes	..	..	..	587	460	218	215	20	13	3
4310 Estate and inheritance taxes	..	..	..	112	115	78	76	10	3	1
Inheritance tax	..	..	..	112	115	78	76	10	3	1
4320 Gift taxes	..	..	..	475	345	140	139	10	9	1
Gift tax	..	..	..	475	345	140	139	10	9	1
4400 Taxes on financial and capital transactions	..	..	..	5 834	9 909	7 394	9 143	11 566	13 054	13 760
Real property transfer tax	..	..	..	5 834	9 909	7 394	9 143	11 566	13 054	13 760
4500 Non-recurrent taxes	..	..	..	0	0	0	0	0	0	0
4510 On net wealth	..	..	..	..	..	..	..	..	..	..
4520 Other non-recurrent taxes	..	..	..	..	..	..	..	..	..	..

	1965	1980	1990	2000	2007	2010	2013	2015	2017	2018
4600 Other recurrent taxes on property	..	..	..	0	0	0	0	0	0	0
5000 Taxes on goods and services	**..**	**..**	**..**	**242 960**	**399 484**	**434 386**	**483 943**	**520 747**	**587 544**	**610 830**
5100 Taxes on production, sale, transfer, etc.	..	..	..	226 354	372 441	408 645	459 419	495 291	560 303	582 754
5110 General taxes	..	..	..	141 235	232 288	263 457	303 822	333 274	387 537	408 538
5111 Value added taxes	..	..	..	141 235	232 288	263 457	303 822	333 274	387 537	408 538
5112 Sales tax	..	..	..	0	0	0	0	0	0	0
5113 Other	..	..	..	0	0	0	0	0	0	0
Previous turnover tax	..	..	..	..	..	..	..	..	..	..
5120 Taxes on specific goods and services	..	..	..	85 119	140 153	145 188	155 597	162 017	172 766	174 216
5121 Excise duties	..	..	..	71 404	133 492	138 401	149 760	153 785	164 114	165 377
On mineral oils	..	..	..	46 998	81 661	80 508	77 160	83 460	88 878	89 990
On alcohol and liquor	..	..	..	5 629	7 201	5 820	6 658	7 203	7 354	8 075
On beer	..	..	..	3 410	3 564	4 396	4 545	4 648	4 657	4 756
On wine	..	..	..	350	342	317	288	332	368	423
On tobacco products	..	..	..	14 984	40 713	44 062	52 193	53 380	57 524	56 621
Duty on CFC	..	..	..	33	0	0	0	0	0	0
Levy collected by Winery Fund	..	..	..	0	11	24	21	0	5	5
On electricity	..	..	..	0	0	1 433	1 305	1 229	1 537	1 562
On natural gas	..	..	..	0	0	1 347	1 256	1 146	1 301	1 346
On solid fuels	..	..	..	0	0	495	469	415	452	401
Fee on electricity from solar radiation	..	..	..	0	0	0	5 866	1 972	2 038	2 198
5122 Profits of fiscal monopolies	..	..	..	0	0	0	0	0	0	0
5123 Customs and import duties	..	..	..	13 572	6 443	6 573	5 556	7 912	8 271	8 296
Customs duties	..	..	..	13 572	6 443	6 573	5 556	7 912	8 271	8 296
Previous import surcharge	..	..	..	0	0	0	0	0	0	0
5124 Taxes on exports	..	..	..	0	0	0	0	0	0	0
5125 Taxes on investment goods	..	..	..	0	0	0	0	0	0	0
5126 Taxes on specific services	..	..	..	143	218	214	281	320	382	543
Fees on entry tickets	..	..	..	65	61	53	56	53	69	70
Fees on recreational units (based on capacity)	..	..	..	69	144	147	213	240	279	288
Fees on advertising facilities	..	..	..	0	0	0	0	0	0	0
Restaurant sale alcoh. beverages and tobac. products	..	..	..	0	0	0	0	0	0	0
Fees collected by the cinematography EBF	..	..	..	9	13	14	12	27	34	0
Fees on advertisement	..	..	..	0	0	0	126	191	150	185
5127 Other taxes on internat. trade and transactions	..	..	..	0	0	0	0	0	0	0
5128 Other taxes	..	..	..	0	0	0	0	0	0	0
5130 Unallocable between 5110 and 5120	..	..	..	0	0	0	0	0	0	0
5200 Taxes on use of goods and perform activities	..	..	..	16 606	27 043	25 740	24 523	25 456	27 241	28 076
5210 Recurrent taxes	..	..	..	10 788	18 100	18 461	18 176	19 023	20 278	20 911
Highway fee	..	..	..	1 753	2 429	3 061	3 803	4 397	4 991	5 212
5211 Paid by households: motor vehicles	..	..	..	0	0	0	0	0	0	0
5212 Paid by others: motor vehicles	..	..	..	5 456	5 882	5 138	5 323	5 868	6 245	6 319
Road tax (commercial)	..	..	..	5 456	5 882	5 138	5 323	5 868	6 245	6 319
5213 Paid in respect of other goods	..	..	..	3 579	9 790	10 262	9 050	8 758	9 042	9 379
Resort and recreation fees on visitors	..	..	..	232	312	284	301	327	387	407
Dog fees	..	..	..	191	277	281	281	277	274	273
Motor vehicle entry fees	..	..	..	32	25	23	14	13	19	19
Water pollution fee	..	..	..	520	404	202	208	173	193	201
Air pollution fee	..	..	..	685	525	399	268	283	171	270
Waste deposit fee	..	..	..	454	5 728	5 948	6 162	6 218	6 361	6 443
Levy on temp. withdrawal of land from agriculture	..	..	..	94	40	34	52	39	59	86
Radioactive waste fee	..	..	..	642	1 310	1 430	1 563	1 393	1 547	1 646
Fees on operated gambling machines	..	..	..	722	1 145	927	131	0	0	0
Fees on registration and recording of packaging	..	..	..	0	17	17	16	18	17	17
Levy on temp. withdrawal of land from forestry	..	..	..	7	6	6	6	7	7	8
Other environmental fees	..	..	..	0	0	710	47	11	7	9
5220 Non-recurrent taxes	..	..	..	5 818	8 943	7 280	6 348	6 433	6 963	7 165
Levy on withdrawal of land from agriculture	..	..	..	532	361	306	469	348	534	776
Levy on withdrawal of land from forestry	..	..	..	40	57	57	55	59	60	72
Tax on use of public space	..	..	..	645	639	626	629	632	635	674
Misc. licence and permit fees	..	..	..	4 601	7 881	6 279	5 187	5 382	5 705	5 621
Land betterment fee	..	..	..	0	4	11	7	11	29	22
Licence for lorry transport	..	..	..	0	1	1	0	1	0	0
5300 Unallocable between 5100 and 5200	..	..	..	0	0	0	0	0	0	0
6000 Other taxes	**..**	**..**	**..**	**356**	**29**	**149**	**67**	**387**	**904**	**258**
Unallocated previous taxes and levies	..	..	..	0	0	0	0	0	0	0
6100 Paid solely by business	..	..	..	0	0	0	0	0	0	0
6200 Other	..	..	..	356	29	149	67	387	904	258
Other taxes, fees and related payments	..	..	..	356	29	149	67	387	904	258
Memorandum item										
Customs duties collected on behalf of the EU	..	..	..	..	6 443	6 573	5 556	7 912	8 271	8 296

	1965	1980	1990	2000	2007	2010	2013	2015	2017	2018
Non-wastable tax credits										
Non-wastable tax credits against 1110	..	..	..	0	13 093	25 727	28 696	31 415	35 673	39 057
Tax expenditure component	..	..	..	..	10 487	17 922	20 203	22 532	26 776	30 320
Transfer component	..	..	..	..	2 606	7 805	8 493	8 883	8 896	8 737
Total tax revenue on cash basis	**..**	**..**	**..**	**772 272**	**1 310 618**	**1 273 676**	**1 353 469**	**1 478 758**	**1 712 822**	**1 867 024**
Total tax revenue on accrual basis	**..**	**..**	**..**	**771 596**	**1 316 197**	**1 286 861**	**1 396 555**	**1 532 565**	**1 760 047**	**1 892 396**
Conciliation with National Accounts										
Additional taxes included in National Accounts	..	..	..	2 837	5 757	6 094	6 424	0	0	0
Compulsory injury insurance	..	..	..	2 837	5 757	6 094	6 424	0	0	0
Driving licence fees	..	..	..	0	0	0	0	0	0	0
Taxes excluded from National Accounts	..	..	..	-9 488	-17 797	-20 096	-18 893	-20 314	-23 258	-22 904
Tax on use of public space	..	..	..	-645	-639	-632	-629	-632	-635	-674
Waste deposit fee	..	..	..	-454	-5 728	-5 948	-6 162	-6 218	-6 361	-6 443
Misc. licence and permit fees	..	..	..	-2 301	-3 940	-3 139	-2 593	-2 691	-2 852	-2 810
Radioactive waste fee	..	..	..	-642	-1 310	-1 430	-1 563	-1 393	-1 547	-1 646
Health insurance: non-employed	..	..	..	-200	-2 103	-3 996	-2 500	-2 768	-3 699	-4 146
Health insurance: government	..	..	..	0	0	0	0	0	0	0
Soc. Security contr. employers: Penalties	..	..	..	-3 293	-1 490	-1 441	-1 487	-2 020	-2 558	-1 808
Soc. Security contr. Self-employed or non-employed: Penalties	..	..	..	-200	-157	-155	-140	-193	-615	-164
Licence for lorry transport	..	..	..	0	-1	-1	0	-1	0	0
Highway fee	..	..	..	-1 753	-2 429	-3 061	-3 803	-4 397	-4 991	-5 212
Other environmental fees	..	..	..	0	0	-105	-14	0	0	0
Levy on loterry revenue	..	..	..	0	0	-187	0	0	0	0
Value added taxes	..	..	..	0	0	0	0	0	0	0
Difference in treatment of tax credits	..	..	..	0	-127	451	-778	118	469	-28
Capital transfer for uncollected revenue	..	..	..	0	0	0	0	0	0	0
Voluntary social security contributions	..	..	..	1 099	974	661	337	386	463	523
Miscellaneous differences	..	..	..	2 162	0	0	0	0	0	0
National Accounts: Taxes and actual social contributions	..	..	..	768 206	1 305 004	1 273 971	1 383 645	1 512 755	1 737 721	1 869 988
Imputed social contributions	..	..	..	423	299	600	934	1 027	1 170	1 426
National Accounts: Taxes and all social contributions	..	..	..	768 629	1 305 303	1 274 571	1 384 579	1 513 782	1 738 891	1 871 414

.. Not available

Note: Year ending 31st December.

From 1995 data are on accrual basis.

Source: Ministry of Finance, Economic Department.

StatLink https://doi.org/10.1787/888934211794

Table 5.8. Denmark: Details of tax revenue, 1965-2018

Million DKK

	1965	1980	1990	2000	2007	2010	2013	2015	2017	2018
Total tax revenue	**20 821**	**166 358**	**382 232**	**623 911**	**809 988**	**813 972**	**901 001**	**957 281**	**1 005 914**	**1 005 957**
Total tax revenue exclusive of taxes collected for the EU	..	..	**379 547**	**621 274**	**806 337**	**810 697**	**898 126**	**953 963**	**1 002 745**	**1 002 772**
1000 Taxes on income, profits and capital gains	**9 712**	**92 404**	**233 739**	**383 244**	**486 845**	**500 276**	**564 937**	**605 698**	**637 102**	**624 641**
1100 Of individuals	8 758	86 958	206 478	328 532	427 412	422 685	490 887	525 144	533 557	545 670
1110 On income and profits	8 758	86 909	206 335	328 305	427 070	422 364	490 627	524 856	533 263	545 400
Central government income tax	5 020	33 351	91 638	77 491	155 540	124 943	141 399	169 059	180 081	185 679
County income tax	0	10 742	31 361	56 135	0	0	0	0	0	0
Municipality income tax	2 948	33 555	77 571	121 975	173 114	193 111	209 303	220 815	236 900	239 221
Seaman's income tax	66	457	0	0	0	0	0	0	0	0
Old-age pension fund contributions	592	2 163	0	0	0	0	0	0	0	0
Social pension fund contributions	0	3 340	0	0	0	0	0	0	0	0
Sickness benefit fund contributions	0	1 804	0	0	0	0	0	0	0	0
Pension schemes and annuity insurance	22	355	2 627	6 923	8 948	9 842	42 974	22 842	5 663	5 559
Special income tax	101	1 054	2 810	0	0	0	0	0	0	0
Duty on canceled pension schemes	9	82	0	0	0	0	0	0	0	0
Duty on feed rent increases	0	8	5	0	0	0	0	0	0	0
Duty on employees' remuneration compens. fund releases	0	0	325	654	1 144	982	1 129	11 177	2 198	2 360
Duty on interest on consumer loans	0	0	0	0	0	0	0	0	0	0
Labour market contributions	0	0	0	56 729	76 609	80 863	82 599	87 359	94 248	98 099
Imputed income from owner-occupied dwelling	0	0	0	8 399	11 716	12 623	13 223	13 604	14 172	14 481
1120 On capital gains	0	49	144	226	343	321	260	289	294	270
Tax on winnings from lotteries, pools, etc.	..	49	144	226	343	321	260	289	294	270
1200 Corporate	954	5 446	14 660	42 279	54 871	41 057	54 066	57 723	71 347	65 207
1210 On profits	954	5 446	14 660	42 279	54 871	41 057	54 066	57 723	71 347	65 207
1220 On capital gains	0	0	0	0	0	0	0	0	0	0
1300 Unallocable between 1100 and 1200	0	0	12 601	12 434	4 562	36 535	19 984	22 832	32 198	13 764
2000 Social security contributions	**690**	**710**	**101**	**8 453**	**1 286**	**1 815**	**1 618**	**1 378**	**1 060**	**1 061**
2100 Employees	567	1	98	8 209	1 057	900	879	826	729	751
Sickness benefit fund contributions	30	0	0	0	0	0	0	0	0	0
Sickday benefit contributions, ordinary	534	0	0	0	0	0	0	0	0	0
Sickday benefit contributions, special	3	0	0	0	0	0	0	0	0	0
Contribution to merchant marine's welf. board	0	1	1	0	0	0	0	0	0	0
Special pension scheme savings	0	0	0	6 846	0	0	0	0	0	0
Contr. to pension funds from officials in companies	0	0	0	879	555	450	476	438	377	410
Contr. to pension funds from officials in non-profit institutions	0	0	96	485	502	450	403	388	352	341
2110 On a payroll basis	..	..	..	..	..	..	..	..	..	..
2120 On an income tax basis	..	..	..	..	..	..	..	..	..	..
2200 Employers	123	709	3	244	229	914	739	552	331	311
Unemployment insurance contributions	41	598	0	0	0	0	0	0	0	0
Disablement insurance contributions	21	58	0	0	0	0	0	0	0	0
Sickness benefit fund contributions	61	0	0	0	0	0	0	0	0	0
Contribution to employee's wage guarantee fund	0	50	0	241	227	908	731	542	323	299
Contribution to merchant marine's welf. board	0	1	1	0	0	0	0	0	0	0
Shipping owners contr. sickness assist. seamen	0	1	2	3	2	6	8	10	8	12
2210 On a payroll basis	..	..	..	..	..	..	..	..	..	..
2220 On an income tax basis	..	..	..	..	..	..	..	..	..	..
2300 Self-employed or non-employed	0	0	0	0	0	0	0	0	0	0
2310 On a payroll basis	..	..	..	..	..	..	..	..	..	..
2320 On an income tax basis	..	..	..	..	..	..	..	..	..	..
2400 Unallocable between 2100, 2200 and 2300	0	0	0	0	0	0	0	0	0	0
2410 On a payroll basis	..	..	..	..	..	..	..	..	..	..
2420 On an income tax basis	..	..	..	..	..	..	..	..	..	..
3000 Taxes on payroll and workforce	**0**	**0**	**2 494**	**2 258**	**3 975**	**4 160**	**6 130**	**5 894**	**5 494**	**6 314**
4000 Taxes on property	**1 691**	**9 806**	**16 269**	**20 738**	**31 556**	**33 533**	**34 995**	**39 169**	**39 258**	**41 215**
4100 Recurrent taxes on immovable property	1 029	5 676	8 891	13 565	18 996	24 161	26 370	28 085	28 465	29 578
Central government land tax	130	264	0	0	0	0	0	0	0	0
County land tax	169	2 315	2 915	4 070	0	0	0	0	0	0
Municipal land tax	408	2 257	4 123	7 049	15 601	19 645	22 580	24 707	25 233	26 394
Centr. Govt. fixed tax on real property	32	11	0	0	0	0	0	0	0	0
County fixed tax on real property	45	0	0	0	0	0	0	0	0	0
Municipal fixed tax on real property	190	91	0	0	0	0	0	0	0	0
County duty on land (public property)	4	22	22	25	0	0	0	0	0	0
County duty on buildings (public property)	0	53	88	97	0	0	0	0	0	0
Municipal duty on land (public property)	26	103	244	383	393	434	359	364	374	339
Municipal duty on buildings (residential)	0	195	335	381	757	814	641	599	594	554
Municipal duty on buildings (business)	25	366	1 165	1 560	2 244	3 269	2 789	2 416	2 264	2 291
4110 Households	..	..	..	..	..	..	..	..	..	..

	1965	1980	1990	2000	2007	2010	2013	2015	2017	2018
4120 Others	..	..	..	..	..	..	..	..	..	..
4200 Recurrent taxes on net wealth	306	963	934	0	0	0	0	0	0	0
4210 Individual	306	963	934	..	..	..	..	..	..	..
4220 Corporate	0	0	0	..	..	..	..	..	..	..
4300 Estate, inheritance and gift taxes	137	738	2 197	2 863	3 896	3 646	3 940	5 177	4 368	4 810
4310 Estate and inheritance taxes	..	..	..	..	..	..	..	..	..	..
4320 Gift taxes	..	..	..	..	..	..	..	..	..	..
4400 Taxes on financial and capital transactions	219	2 313	4 166	4 171	8 659	5 726	4 685	5 907	6 426	6 828
Stamp duties	214	2 243	2 829	4 125	8 574	5 695	4 664	5 879	6 386	6 786
Duty on share capital creation	0	32	500	0	0	0	0	0	0	0
Duty to land registry office	5	38	28	46	85	30	21	28	40	41
Duty on transfers of shares	0	0	809	0	0	0	0	0	0	0
4500 Non-recurrent taxes	0	116	81	140	6	0	0	0	0	0
4510 On net wealth	..	0	0	0	0	0	..	..	..	..
4520 Other non-recurrent taxes	..	116	81	140	6	0	..	..	..	..
4600 Other recurrent taxes on property	0	0	0	0	0	0	0	0	0	0
5000 Taxes on goods and services	**8 727**	**63 437**	**129 630**	**208 826**	**286 136**	**273 982**	**293 170**	**304 823**	**322 729**	**332 461**
5100 Taxes on production, sale, transfer, etc.	8 239	60 545	123 645	197 991	267 325	254 303	270 493	281 109	297 925	306 191
5110 General taxes	2 139	37 727	80 650	121 955	174 639	171 583	181 378	191 479	208 643	217 046
5111 Value added taxes	2 139	37 727	72 120	121 955	174 639	171 583	181 378	191 479	208 643	217 046
5112 Sales tax	0	0	0	0	0	0	0	0	0	0
5113 Other	0	0	8 530	0	0	0	0	0	0	0
Labour market contrib. concerning imports	..	..	4 903	..	..	..	..	..	..	..
Labour market contrib. concerning value added	..	..	3 627	..	..	..	..	..	..	..
5120 Taxes on specific goods and services	6 100	22 817	42 995	76 036	92 686	82 720	89 116	89 630	89 282	89 145

	1965	1980	1990	2000	2007	2010	2013	2015	2017	2018
5121 Excise duties	5 466	20 473	38 339	68 977	82 861	74 032	81 894	81 893	81 482	81 021
Duty on petrol	1 016	3 713	5 637	10 005	9 154	8 029	7 286	7 348	7 499	7 521
Motor vehicle registration duty	818	2 989	7 917	13 858	24 289	13 586	15 218	17 988	19 976	20 602
Cigarettes and tobacco duties	1 469	4 472	6 516	7 489	7 201	8 283	8 417	7 658	7 547	7 045
Duties on cigars, cheroots and cigarillos	234	220	128	80	40	32	47	113	66	45
Sale of revenue labels	0	3	10	13	13	5	4	4	2	0
Sales duties on chocolate and sugar	254	331	801	1 205	1 289	1 470	2 020	2 156	2 184	2 168
Raw material duty on chocolate and sugar	11	14	54	60	93	144	180	187	169	132
Special tax on chocolate and sugar	0	2	13	76	46	51	68	103	126	104
Duty on ice-cream	33	58	135	168	180	201	297	297	308	354
Duty on coffee	5	249	224	266	250	243	271	280	254	280
Duty on mineral water	68	195	466	505	418	383	374	0	0	0
Duty on beer	622	1 983	3 100	1 510	1 080	895	977	916	918	943
Duty on wine	122	611	1 448	1 166	1 032	1 071	1 674	1 764	1 724	1 732
Duty on spirits	412	1 432	1 982	1 756	1 213	1 028	1 127	1 201	1 212	1 187
Duty on restaurant sales of alcoholic bev.	150	0	0	0	0	0	0	0	0	0
Duty on wireless sets	55	67	0	0	0	0	0	0	0	0
Duty on television sets	0	93	-18	0	0	0	0	0	0	0
Duty on video recorders	0	17	-15	0	0	0	0	0	0	0
Duty on major household appliances	0	199	-10	0	0	0	0	0	0	0
Duty on grammophone records	10	46	84	0	0	0	0	0	0	0
Duty on playing cards	1	2	0	0	0	0	0	0	0	0
Duty on matches	5	3	-1	0	0	0	0	0	0	0
Duty on lighters	1	8	-4	0	0	0	0	0	0	0
Duty on electric bulbs	36	67	152	176	211	117	95	86	65	54
Duty on perfumery and toilet articles	91	214	506	0	0	0	0	0	0	0
Duty on almanacs	3	0	0	0	0	0	0	0	0	0
Duty on salmon	0	1	0	0	0	0	0	0	0	0
Duty on paper and cardboard	45	0	0	0	0	0	0	0	0	0
Duty on sugar	0	174	-8	0	0	0	0	0	0	0
Duty on tea	0	12	10	8	8	8	8	8	5	0
Duty on electricity	0	1 222	4 317	7 430	8 665	10 195	10 013	11 501	12 164	12 119
Duty on certain oil products	0	1 719	2 938	6 757	8 549	8 623	9 306	9 347	9 804	10 012
Duty on certain retail containers	0	100	397	594	727	706	715	316	335	365
Duty on gas	0	56	47	0	0	0	0	0	0	0
Duty on extraction and import of raw materials	0	16	129	172	220	119	132	148	165	165
Duty on disposable tableware	0	0	72	65	126	120	121	138	141	148
Duty on insecticides, herbicides, etc.	0	0	13	366	449	466	656	598	532	568
Duty on videotapes	0	0	0	0	0	0	0	0	0	0
Duty on coal, etc.	0	0	849	1 217	1 450	2 587	2 991	2 255	1 916	1 852
Other duties on goods and services	5	186	20	53	147	189	-13	186	160	178
Duty on waste	0	0	404	1 025	1 225	51	167	130	161	154
Duty on CFC	0	0	27	0	53	56	82	65	58	55
Duty on CO2	0	0	0	4 883	5 108	5 822	5 762	3 652	3 632	3 627
Duty on cigarette paper	0	0	0	68	32	28	36	38	32	31
Duty on rechargeable Ni-Cd batteries	0	0	0	21	17	4	3	2	1	0
Duty on piped water	0	0	0	1 357	1 371	1 334	1 584	1 688	1 571	1 649
Duty on carrier bags made of paper, plastic, etc.	0	0	0	178	210	201	186	208	190	178
Duty on tires	0	0	0	29	45	62	50	57	54	53
Duty on sulphur	0	0	0	165	108	48	51	42	39	39
Duty on chlorinated solvents	0	0	0	2	0	0	0	0	0	0
Duty on natural gas	0	0	0	2 532	3 375	4 524	5 255	3 160	3 002	3 325
Duty on nitrogen	0	0	0	30	27	26	21	17	15	13
Duty on specific growth stimulants	0	0	0	0	0	0	0	0	0	0
Duty on PVC-film	0	0	0	7	12	11	10	11	11	11
Duty on PVC and phathalates	0	0	0	31	42	23	18	19	16	16
Duty on lead accumulators	0	0	0	14	0	0	0	0	0	0
Duty on mineral phosphorus	0	0	0	0	51	51	49	52	52	53
Surcharge on alcoholic soft drinks	0	0	0	0	17	26	33	33	33	0
Duty on nitrogen oxides	0	0	0	0	0	212	870	820	159	183
Duty on saturated fat	0	0	0	0	0	0	0	0	0	0
Duty on PSO (Public Service Obligations)	0	0	0	3 641	4 319	3 004	5 734	7 302	5 184	4 060
5122 Profits of fiscal monopolies	16	183	404	1 402	1 648	1 481	1 339	1 230	1 282	1 535
5123 Customs and import duties	556	1 113	1 849	2 325	3 282	3 242	2 824	3 285	3 136	3 186
Customs duties	0	1 032	1 779	2 325	3 282	3 242	2 824	3 285	3 136	3 186
Temporary import surcharge	556	0	0	0	0	0	0	0	0	0
Import duties on agricultural produce	0	81	70	0	0	0	0	0	0	0
5124 Taxes on exports	0	0	0	0	0	0	0	0	0	0
5125 Taxes on investment goods	0	0	0	0	0	0	0	0	0	0

	1965	1980	1990	2000	2007	2010	2013	2015	2017	2018
5126 Taxes on specific services	62	771	1 567	3 019	4 525	3 932	3 008	3 189	3 348	3 404
Sales tax on gambling stakes races	17	28	20	12	18	16	15	14	13	0
Tax on football pools	31	152	284	942	1 143	1 071	0	0	0	0
Tax on cinema tickets	14	0	0	0	0	0	0	0	0	0
Duty on motor vehicle compl. insurance	0	470	923	1 327	2 104	1 854	1 598	1 529	1 519	1 491
Duty on insurance on pleasure boats	0	13	57	66	100	122	127	126	124	119
Duty on charter flight	0	109	283	0	0	0	0	0	0	0
Turnover tax on 6-win horse race betting	0	0	0	0	0	0	0	0	0	0
Duty on casinos	0	0	0	180	261	173	192	200	216	202
Passenger duty	0	0	0	477	6	0	0	0	0	0
Duty on the Danish State Lottery	0	0	0	16	35	41	42	44	46	44
Duty on slot machines	0	0	0	0	858	656	545	618	627	592
Duty on gambling	0	0	0	0	0	0	288	397	450	511
Duty on online casinos	0	0	0	0	0	0	202	261	354	445
5127 Other taxes on internat. trade and transactions	0	0	0	0	0	0	0	0	0	0
5128 Other taxes	0	277	837	312	370	33	51	33	33	0
Duty paid to ECSC	..	4	5	0	0	0	0	0	0	..
Sugar storing duty	..	83	113	62	0	0	0	0	0	..
Duty on the production of sugar	..	81	145	249	-26	33	51	33	33	..
Duty on milk co-reponsibility levy	..	109	255	0	0	0	0	0	0	..
Grain co-reponsibility levy	..	0	319	0	0	0	0	0	0	..
Restructuring scheme for EU sugar system	..	0	0	0	397	0	0	0	0	..
5130 Unallocable between 5110 and 5120	0	0	0	0	0	0	0	0	0	0
5200 Taxes on use of goods and perform activities	488	2 893	4 410	7 468	14 088	14 731	16 180	16 537	16 268	17 383
5210 Recurrent taxes	488	2 893	4 410	7 468	14 088	14 731	15 966	16 171	15 735	15 968
5211 Paid by households: motor vehicles	199	1 874	2 922	5 485	7 105	7 614	8 094	8 136	7 549	7 773
Weight duty automobiles	199	1 874	2 922	5 318	6 954	7 467	7 936	7 859	7 280	7 526
Recycling fee on cars	0	0	0	167	151	147	158	277	270	247
5212 Paid by others: motor vehicles	287	1 014	1 441	1 919	3 125	2 980	3 336	3 483	3 659	3 605
Weight duty automobiles	287	1 014	1 441	1 612	2 652	2 611	2 952	3 088	3 188	3 116
Road charges	0	0	0	307	473	370	383	395	471	489
5213 Paid in respect of other goods	2	5	47	64	3 858	4 137	4 537	4 552	4 526	4 590
5220 Non-recurrent taxes	0	0	0	0	0	0	214	365	534	1 415
5300 Unallocable between 5100 and 5200	0	0	1 575	3 368	4 724	4 948	6 497	7 177	8 536	8 887
6000 Other taxes	**0**	**0**	**0**	**391**	**190**	**206**	**152**	**320**	**272**	**265**
6100 Paid solely by business	..	..	..	391	190	206	152	320	272	265
6200 Other	..	..	..	0	0	0	0	0	0	0
Memorandum item										
Customs duties collected on behalf of the EU	..	..	1 779	2 325	3 282	3 242	2 824	3 285	3 136	3 186
Non-wastable tax credits										
Non-wastable tax credits against 1110	..	..	..	..	..	4 960	5 515	4 228	4 229	3 736
Tax expenditure component	..	..	..	..	..	4 712	5 240	4 016	4 018	3 549
Transfer component	..	..	..	..	..	248	276	211	211	187
Non-wastable tax credits against 1210	..	..	..	..	..	0	0	0	0	0
Tax expenditure component	..	..	..	..	..	..	..	..	..	..
Transfer component	..	..	..	..	..	..	..	..	..	..
Total tax revenue on cash basis	**..**	**..**	**..**	**..**	**..**	**..**	**..**	**..**	**..**	**..**
Total tax revenue on accrual basis	**20 821**	**166 358**	**382 232**	**623 911**	**809 988**	**813 972**	**901 001**	**957 281**	**1 005 914**	**1 005 957**
Conciliation with National Accounts										
Additional taxes included in National Accounts	0	0	..	..	..	..	..	..	..	..
Taxes excluded from National Accounts	0	0	..	..	..	..	..	..	..	..
Difference in treatment of tax credits	0	0	0	0	0	4 712	5 240	4 016	4 018	3 549
Capital transfer for uncollected revenue	0	-1 374	-2 387	-1 917	-2 726	-3 475	-15 512	-19 396	-8 640	-9 791
Voluntary social security contributions	0	1 673	8 087	16 633	17 061	17 192	14 655	14 721	14 891	14 751
Miscellaneous differences	0	0	..	..	..	..	..	..	..	..
National Accounts: Taxes and actual social contributions	20 821	166 657	387 932	638 626	824 324	832 401	905 384	956 623	1 016 183	1 014 466
Imputed social contributions	0	5 958	4 592	6 223	5 693	5 356	4 520	4 067	3 507	3 158
National Accounts: Taxes and all social contributions	20 821	172 615	392 525	644 849	830 017	837 757	909 904	960 690	1 019 690	1 017 624

.. Not available

Note: Year ending 31st December.

The figures are on an accrual basis.

Heading 2300 includes a small amount of voluntary contributions which cannot be isolated.

Source: Danmarks Statistik.

StatLink https://doi.org/10.1787/888934211813

Table 5.9. Estonia: Details of tax revenue, 1965-2018

Million EUR

	1965	1980	1990	2000	2007	2010	2013	2015	2017	2018
Total tax revenue	..	..	..	**1 919**	**5 082**	**4 894**	**5 988**	**6 874**	**7 757**	**8 532**
Total tax revenue exclusive of taxes collected for the EU	..	..	..	**1 919**	**5 047**	**4 870**	**5 960**	**6 840**	**7 715**	**8 484**
1000 Taxes on income, profits and capital gains	..	..	..	**476**	**1 197**	**970**	**1 357**	**1 607**	**1 710**	**1 929**
1100 Of individuals	..	..	..	421	936	776	1 031	1 182	1 344	1 411
1110 On income and profits	..	..	..	421	936	776	1 031	1 182	1 344	1 411
1120 On capital gains	..	..	..	0	0	0	0	0	0	0
1200 Corporate	..	..	..	55	261	194	327	424	366	518
1210 On profits	..	..	..	55	65	35	62	38	40	71
1220 On capital gains	..	..	..	0	196	159	265	386	325	447
1300 Unallocable between 1100 and 1200	..	..	..	0	0	0	0	0	0	0
2000 Social security contributions	..	..	..	**674**	**1 683**	**1 879**	**2 077**	**2 300**	**2 653**	**2 978**
2100 Employees	..	..	..	0	28	116	109	99	112	123
2110 On a payroll basis	..	..	..	..	28	116	109	99	112	123
2120 On an income tax basis	..	..	..	..	0	0	0	0	0	0
2200 Employers	..	..	..	662	1 635	1 742	1 949	2 181	2 520	2 835
2210 On a payroll basis	..	..	..	662	1 635	1 742	1 949	2 181	2 520	2 835
2220 On an income tax basis	..	..	..	0	0	0	0	0	0	0
2300 Self-employed or non-employed	..	..	..	12	21	21	19	20	21	21
2310 On a payroll basis	..	..	..	12	21	21	19	20	21	21
2320 On an income tax basis	..	..	..	0	0	0	0	0	0	0
2400 Unallocable between 2100, 2200 and 2300	..	..	..	0	0	0	0	0	0	0
2410 On a payroll basis	..	..	..	..	..	..	..	..	..	..
2420 On an income tax basis	..	..	..	..	..	..	..	..	..	..
3000 Taxes on payroll and workforce	..	..	..	**0**	**0**	**0**	**0**	**0**	**0**	**0**
4000 Taxes on property	..	..	..	**24**	**35**	**51**	**57**	**58**	**58**	**58**
4100 Recurrent taxes on immovable property	..	..	..	24	35	51	57	58	58	58
Land tax	..	..	..	24	35	51	57	58	58	58
4110 Households	..	..	..	..	..	..	..	..	..	..
4120 Others	..	..	..	..	..	..	..	..	..	..
4200 Recurrent taxes on net wealth	..	..	..	0	0	0	0	0	0	0
4210 Individual	..	..	..	..	..	..	..	..	..	..
4220 Corporate	..	..	..	..	..	..	..	..	..	..
4300 Estate, inheritance and gift taxes	..	..	..	0	0	0	0	0	0	0
4310 Estate and inheritance taxes	..	..	..	..	..	..	..	..	..	..
4320 Gift taxes	..	..	..	..	..	..	..	..	..	..
4400 Taxes on financial and capital transactions	..	..	..	0	0	0	0	0	0	0
4500 Non-recurrent taxes	..	..	..	0	0	0	0	0	0	0
4510 On net wealth	..	..	..	..	..	..	..	..	..	..
4520 Other non-recurrent taxes	..	..	..	..	..	..	..	..	..	..
4600 Other recurrent taxes on property	..	..	..	0	0	0	0	0	0	0
5000 Taxes on goods and services	..	..	..	**745**	**2 166**	**1 993**	**2 496**	**2 909**	**3 337**	**3 566**
5100 Taxes on production, sale, transfer, etc.	..	..	..	723	2 099	1 938	2 431	2 829	3 227	3 437
5110 General taxes	..	..	..	521	1 423	1 263	1 558	1 873	2 149	2 331
5111 Value added taxes	..	..	..	520	1 423	1 257	1 558	1 873	2 149	2 331
5112 Sales tax	..	..	..	0	0	6	0	0	0	0
5113 Other	..	..	..	0	0	0	0	0	0	0
5120 Taxes on specific goods and services	..	..	..	202	675	675	873	956	1 078	1 106
5121 Excise duties	..	..	..	183	577	619	796	869	990	1 012
Alcohol	..	..	..	62	153	154	212	207	222	232
Tobacco	..	..	..	36	134	91	169	183	197	200
Fuel	..	..	..	76	290	343	383	444	535	543
Motor vehicle	..	..	..	9	0	0	0	0	0	0
Package	..	..	..	0	0	0	0	1	0	0
Fur	..	..	..	0	0	0	0	0	0	0
Electricity	..	..	..	0	0	31	33	34	36	37
5122 Profits of fiscal monopolies	..	..	..	0	0	0	0	0	0	0
5123 Customs and import duties	..	..	..	2	35	24	29	34	38	43
5124 Taxes on exports	..	..	..	0	0	0	0	0	0	0
5125 Taxes on investment goods	..	..	..	0	0	0	0	0	0	0
5126 Taxes on specific services	..	..	..	17	64	33	48	53	50	52
Gambling tax	..	..	..	7	30	21	22	23	27	27
Advertising tax	..	..	..	1	3	2	4	4	6	6
Postal service payment	..	..	..	0	0	0	0	0	0	0
Liquid fuel stockpiling fee	..	..	..	0	2	5	6	5	5	4
Contributions to the Guarantee Fund	..	..	..	9	29	5	17	20	13	14
5127 Other taxes on internat. trade and transactions	..	..	..	0	0	0	0	0	0	0
5128 Other taxes	..	..	..	0	0	0	0	0	0	0
5130 Unallocable between 5110 and 5120	..	..	..	0	0	0	0	0	0	0

	1965	1980	1990	2000	2007	2010	2013	2015	2017	2018
5200 Taxes on use of goods and perform activities	..	..	..	22	68	55	65	80	110	129
5210 Recurrent taxes	..	..	..	22	68	55	65	73	86	90
Car registration fee	..	..	..	2	5	4	7	7	8	8
Heavy vehicle tax	..	..	..	0	4	4	4	5	5	5
5211 Paid by households: motor vehicles	..	..	..	..	..	..	..	..	..	..
5212 Paid by others: motor vehicles	..	..	..	..	..	..	..	..	..	..
5213 Paid in respect of other goods	..	..	..	20	58	47	55	61	73	77
Business and professional licenses	..	..	..	3	2	1	1	1	3	3
Pollution fee	..	..	..	10	44	31	37	44	53	54
Specific use of water	..	..	..	4	9	13	14	13	15	16
Fees for closure of roads, streets and squares	..	..	..	0	1	1	1	2	1	2
Fishing fees	..	..	..	1	1	1	2	2	1	2
Tax on motor vehicle	..	..	..	2	0	0	0	0	0	0
Boat tax	..	..	..	0	0	0	0	0	0	0
Animal tax	..	..	..	0	0	0	0	0	0	0
5220 Non-recurrent taxes	..	..	..	0	0	0	0	7	24	39
Revenue from the sale of emission permits	..	..	..	..	..	..	..	7	24	39
5300 Unallocable between 5100 and 5200	..	..	..	0	0	0	0	0	0	0
6000 Other taxes	**..**	**..**	**..**	**0**	**0**	**0**	**0**	**0**	**0**	**0**
6100 Paid solely by business	..	..	..	..	..	..	..	..	..	..
6200 Other	..	..	..	..	..	..	..	..	..	..
Other taxes	..	..	..	..	..	..	..	..	..	..
Memorandum item										
Customs duties collected on behalf of the EU	..	..	..	..	35	24	29	34	38	43
SRF contributions collected on behalf of the EU	..	..	..	..	..	..	..	..	5	5
Total tax revenue on cash basis	**..**	**..**	**..**	**1 907**	**5 003**	**4 921**	**5 964**	**6 848**	**7 713**	**8 528**
Total tax revenue on accrual basis	**..**	**..**	**..**	**1 919**	**5 082**	**4 894**	**5 988**	**6 874**	**7 757**	**8 532**
Conciliation with National Accounts										
Additional taxes included in National Accounts	..	..	..	0	0	0	0	0	0	0
Taxes excluded from National Accounts	..	..	..	0	0	0	0	0	0	0
Difference in treatment of tax credits	..	..	..	0	0	0	0	0	0	0
Capital transfer for uncollected revenue	..	..	..	0	0	0	0	0	0	0
Voluntary social security contributions	..	..	..	0	0	0	0	0	0	0
Miscellaneous differences	..	..	..	0	0	0	0	0	0	0
National Accounts: Taxes and actual social contributions	..	..	..	1 919	5 082	4 894	5 988	6 874	7 757	8 532
Imputed social contributions	..	..	..	4	20	30	38	49	62	66
National Accounts: Taxes and all social contributions	..	..	..	1 922	5 102	4 924	6 026	6 923	7 819	8 597

.. Not available

Note: Year ending 31st December.

Data on an accrual basis.

Source: Statistics Estonia.

StatLink https://doi.org/10.1787/888934211832

Table 5.10. Finland: Details of tax revenue, 1965-2018

Million EUR

	1965	1980	1990	2000	2007	2010	2013	2015	2017	2018
Total tax revenue	**1 362**	**11 895**	**39 052**	**62 435**	**77 447**	**76 315**	**88 688**	**92 003**	**96 985**	**99 025**
Total tax revenue exclusive of taxes collected for the EU	..	..	**39 052**	**62 296**	**77 247**	**76 163**	**88 521**	**91 760**	**96 688**	**98 795**
1000 Taxes on income, profits and capital gains	**564**	**4 654**	**15 323**	**26 910**	**30 358**	**27 104**	**30 797**	**32 371**	**34 404**	**34 505**
1100 Of individuals	453	4 248	13 562	19 118	23 396	22 545	25 998	27 824	28 277	28 569
1110 On income and profits	453	4 234	13 520	19 118	23 396	22 545	25 998	27 824	28 277	28 569
Tax on income	125	1 827	5 917	9 036	9 086	6 465	7 903	9 138	9 109	9 734
The final withdrawal tax on interest income	0	0	0	92	254	205	207	110	66	44
Communal tax	279	2 376	7 603	9 990	14 056	15 875	17 888	18 576	19 102	18 791
Seaman's tax	3	31	0	0	0	0	0	0	0	0
National pension contributions	32	0	0	0	0	0	0	0	0	0
National health insurance contributions	15	0	0	0	0	0	0	0	0	0
1120 On capital gains	0	14	42	0	0	0	0	0	0	0
Tax on lottery prizes	..	14	42	..	..	..	..	..	..	..
1200 Corporate	111	405	1 761	7 792	6 962	4 559	4 799	4 547	6 127	5 936
1210 On profits	111	405	1 761	7 792	6 962	4 559	4 799	4 547	6 127	5 936
Tax on income	72	202	1 001	4 758	5 298	2 972	3 227	2 761	4 238	4 077
Communal tax	36	187	699	2 900	1 541	1 471	1 456	1 668	1 889	1 859
Church tax	3	16	61	134	123	116	116	118	0	0
1220 On capital gains	0	0	0	0	0	0	0	0	0	0
1300 Unallocable between 1100 and 1200	0	0	0	0	0	0	0	0	0	0
2000 Social security contributions	**93**	**2 776**	**10 012**	**15 756**	**21 384**	**22 648**	**25 632**	**26 639**	**27 000**	**27 647**
2100 Employees	1	394	1 152	2 926	4 050	4 710	5 811	6 364	7 467	8 102
For employment pension schemes	1	10	23	2 120	2 950	3 386	4 235	4 714	5 182	5 567
For unemployment schemes	0	0	0	435	369	267	457	489	1 242	1 519
2110 On a payroll basis	..	10	23	2 565	3 319	3 653	4 692	5 203	6 424	7 086
2120 On an income tax basis	..	384	1 129	361	731	1 057	1 119	1 161	1 043	1 016
National pension contributions	..	251	502	2	0	0	0	0	0	0
National health insurance contributions	..	133	627	359	731	1 057	1 119	1 161	1 043	1 016
2200 Employers	93	2 230	8 127	11 571	15 715	16 041	17 888	18 232	17 585	17 631
For national pension schemes	29	685	1 502	1 566	1 331	0	0	0	0	0
For national health insurance	10	244	792	839	1 142	1 590	1 612	1 662	914	748
For unemployment schemes	3	106	206	1 143	1 346	1 377	1 775	1 676	1 817	1 493
For employment pension schemes	50	1 195	5 627	8 023	11 896	13 074	14 501	14 894	14 854	15 390
For accident and group life insurance premiums	0	0	0	0	0	0	0	0	0	0
2210 On a payroll basis	..	2 230	8 127	11 571	15 715	16 041	17 888	18 232	17 585	17 631
2220 On an income tax basis	..	0	0	0	0	0	0	0	0	0
2300 Self-employed or non-employed	0	152	733	1 259	1 619	1 897	1 933	2 043	1 948	1 914
For employment pension schemes	..	84	394	576	817	932	1 187	1 269	1 252	1 237
2310 On a payroll basis	..	84	394	576	817	932	1 187	1 269	1 252	1 237
2320 On an income tax basis	..	68	339	683	802	965	746	774	696	677
National pension contributions	..	43	151	5	0	0	0	0	0	0
National health insurance contributions	..	25	188	678	802	965	746	774	696	677
2400 Unallocable between 2100, 2200 and 2300	0	0	0	0	0	0	0	0	0	0
2410 On a payroll basis	..	..	..	..	..	..	..	..	..	..
2420 On an income tax basis	..	..	..	..	..	..	..	..	..	..
3000 Taxes on payroll and workforce	**70**	**22**	**0**	**0**	**0**	**0**	**0**	**0**	**0**	**0**
Soc. Sec. contr. for children allowance	70	22	..	..	..	..	..	..	..	..
4000 Taxes on property	**54**	**221**	**956**	**1 518**	**2 012**	**2 087**	**2 599**	**3 017**	**3 459**	**3 349**
4100 Recurrent taxes on immovable property	0	0	76	570	855	1 169	1 363	1 603	1 774	1 813
4110 Households	..	..	46	273	405	576	623	733	811	834
4120 Others	..	..	30	297	450	593	740	870	963	979
4200 Recurrent taxes on net wealth	24	24	27	179	0	0	0	0	0	0
4210 Individual	11	23	25	175	..	..	..	..	..	..
4220 Corporate	13	2	2	4	..	..	..	..	..	..
4300 Estate, inheritance and gift taxes	3	26	146	368	459	387	646	631	909	692
4310 Estate and inheritance taxes	3	21	121	307	384	324	541	528	761	579
4320 Gift taxes	1	5	25	61	75	63	105	103	148	113
4400 Taxes on financial and capital transactions	27	170	707	401	698	531	590	783	776	844
Stamp duty excluded entertainment	27	170	688	-20	0	0	0	0	0	0
Credit tax	0	0	19	0	0	0	0	0	0	0
Transfer tax	0	0	0	421	698	531	590	783	776	844
4500 Non-recurrent taxes	0	0	0	0	0	0	0	0	0	0
4510 On net wealth	..	..	..	..	..	..	..	..	..	..
4520 Other non-recurrent taxes	..	..	..	..	..	..	..	..	..	..
4600 Other recurrent taxes on property	0	0	0	0	0	0	0	0	0	0
5000 Taxes on goods and services	**578**	**4 202**	**12 711**	**18 221**	**23 624**	**24 407**	**29 596**	**29 895**	**32 061**	**33 480**
5100 Taxes on production, sale, transfer, etc.	570	4 158	12 555	17 781	22 953	23 642	28 662	28 836	30 751	32 107
5110 General taxes	251	2 062	7 519	10 869	15 207	15 533	18 888	18 974	20 404	21 364

	1965	1980	1990	2000	2007	2010	2013	2015	2017	2018
5111 Value added taxes	251	2 062	7 519	10 869	15 207	15 533	18 888	18 974	20 404	21 364
Value added taxes	251	2 062	7 519	9 616	13 657	13 691	16 561	16 680	17 707	18 487
VAT repayments of local government	0	0	0	849	1 550	1 842	2 327	2 294	2 697	2 877
Social Insur. Institutions' part of VAT revenue	0	0	0	404	0	0	0	0	0	0
5112 Sales tax	0	0	0	0	0	0	0	0	0	0
5113 Other	0	0	0	0	0	0	0	0	0	0
Suppl. sales tax on consumer durables	..	..	..	..	..	..	..	..	..	..
5120 Taxes on specific goods and services	319	2 096	5 036	6 912	7 746	8 109	9 774	9 862	10 347	10 743
5121 Excise duties	183	1 615	3 813	5 613	6 013	6 286	7 511	7 678	8 002	8 390
Excise on tobacco products	52	206	473	561	622	655	852	885	962	1 115
Excise on sweetments	6	23	26	0	0	0	0	0	0	0
Excise on medium, strong beer	3	109	419	0	0	0	0	0	0	0
Excise on non-alcoholic beverages	2	17	22	32	35	37	204	250	151	154
Excise on certain foodstuffs	3	218	36	0	0	0	0	0	0	0
Excise on liquid fuels	58	504	986	2 583	2 907	3 167	3 925	4 054	4 324	4 395
Excise on motor cars	28	238	697	1 059	1 217	941	931	882	972	995
Tax on alcoholic beverages	29	353	813	1 239	1 016	1 279	1 355	1 356	1 340	1 475
Levies on pharmacy	2	16	46	85	113	122	153	165	182	180
Levies for price reduction on butter	0	3	0	0	0	0	0	0	0	0
Levies for marketing of milk	0	12	58	0	0	0	0	0	0	0
Excise on margarines	0	18	55	0	0	0	0	0	0	0
Stock-building levies on liquid fuels	0	15	44	46	50	48	45	43	43	45
Excise on sugar products	0	18	34	0	0	0	0	0	0	0
Excise on feeding stuffs	0	0	0	0	0	0	0	0	0	0
Excise on fertilizers	0	21	21	0	0	0	0	0	0	0
Excise on oil-based concentrated feed	0	1	0	0	0	0	0	0	0	0
Excise on protein feed	0	0	0	0	0	0	0	0	0	0
Equalization fee agricultural products	0	8	29	0	0	0	0	0	0	0
Excise on albumen	0	0	30	0	0	0	0	0	0	0
Tax on electricity	0	65	0	0	0	0	0	0	0	0
Oil damage levy	0	0	7	5	8	20	27	24	8	12
Oil waste levy	0	0	4	3	4	4	4	4	4	4
Price difference compensations	0	-231	0	0	0	0	0	0	0	0
The milk quota charge	0	0	6	0	0	0	0	0	0	0
Levies for marketing of special agric. prod.	0	0	0	0	0	0	0	0	0	0
Excise on phosphorous fertilizers	0	0	7	0	0	0	0	0	0	0
Excise on certain beverage packages	0	0	0	0	41	13	15	15	16	15
5122 Profits of fiscal monopolies	38	86	202	0	0	0	0	0	0	0
Excess profits on alcohol	38	86	202	..	..	..	..	..	..	..
5123 Customs and import duties	88	235	423	130	199	151	166	166	174	174
Import duties	62	126	232	0	0	0	0	0	0	0
Import levies on agricultural products	26	6	12	0	0	0	0	0	0	0
Local import duties (Town dues)	1	0	0	0	0	0	0	0	0	0
Import levies price stabilisation fund	0	3	0	0	0	0	0	0	0	0
Agricultural levies	0	0	0	0	0	0	0	0	0	0
Equalization tax	0	100	179	0	0	0	0	0	0	0
Custom duties	..	..	0	130	199	151	166	166	174	174
5124 Taxes on exports	0	0	0	0	0	0	0	0	0	0
Export duties	..	..	..	..	..	..	..	..	..	..
Levies on export	..	..	..	..	..	..	..	..	..	..
Counter-cyclical tax exports	..	..	..	..	..	..	..	..	..	..
5125 Taxes on investment goods	0	0	0	0	0	0	0	0	0	0
Investment tax on buildings	..	..	..	..	..	..	..	..	..	..
5126 Taxes on specific services	9	161	598	1 160	1 533	1 671	2 096	2 017	2 170	2 178
Net revenue of betting	8	94	328	704	807	874	948	967	1 060	1 109
Tax on motion pictures	0	0	0	0	0	0	0	0	0	0
Stamp duties on entertainment	2	5	0	0	0	0	0	0	0	0
Fire protection levy	0	3	7	6	8	9	10	11	11	11
Tax on waste	0	0	0	33	56	42	56	32	12	7
Rail tax	0	0	0	0	18	18	19	6	5	2
Tax on insurance premiums	0	58	263	337	509	584	712	777	768	772
Tax on lottery prizes	0	0	0	80	135	144	217	222	228	226
Tax on telecommunications	0	0	0	0	0	0	0	0	0	0
Bank tax	0	0	0	0	0	0	134	-74	-36	-4
Contributions to the Resolution Fund	..	..	..	..	..	..	..	76	122	55
5127 Other taxes on internat. trade and transactions	0	0	0	0	0	0	0	0	0	0
Tax on charter flights	..	..	..	..	..	..	..	..	..	..
5128 Other taxes	0	0	0	9	1	1	1	1	1	1
Sugar levy	..	..	..	9	1	1	1	1	1	1
Steel and coal levy	..	..	..	0	0	0	0	0	0	0
5130 Unallocable between 5110 and 5120	0	0	0	0	0	0	0	0	0	0
5200 Taxes on use of goods and perform activities	8	44	156	440	671	765	934	1 059	1 310	1 373

	1965	1980	1990	2000	2007	2010	2013	2015	2017	2018
5210 Recurrent taxes	8	44	156	423	637	725	897	960	1 204	1 233
5211 Paid by households: motor vehicles	0	2	5	165	486	541	696	748	960	979
5212 Paid by others: motor vehicles	7	32	135	235	126	150	170	182	209	215
5213 Paid in respect of other goods	1	10	16	23	25	34	31	30	35	39
Dog licenses	1	2	4	5	3	2	2	1	1	0
Hunting and fishing licenses	1	7	12	17	17	24	23	22	22	27
Seamens welfare and rescue levy	0	0	0	1	1	1	1	0	0	0
Nuclear energy research levy	0	0	0	0	4	7	5	7	12	12
5220 Non-recurrent taxes	0	0	0	17	34	40	37	99	106	140
Vehicle registration tax	..	..	..	17	34	40	37	36	31	27
Income from auction of emission allowances	..	..	..	0	0	0	0	63	75	113
5300 Unallocable between 5100 and 5200	0	0	0	0	0	0	0	0	0	0
6000 Other taxes	**2**	**21**	**50**	**30**	**69**	**69**	**64**	**81**	**61**	**44**
6100 Paid solely by business	0	0	0	0	0	0	0	0	0	0
6200 Other	2	21	50	30	69	69	64	81	61	44
Memorandum items										
Customs duties collected on behalf of the EU	..	..	..	130	199	151	166	166	174	174
SRF contributions collected on behalf of the EU	..	..	..	..	..	..	..	76	122	55
Total tax revenue on cash basis	**1 362**	**11 895**	**39 396**	**61 638**	**77 110**	**76 214**	**88 416**	**91 846**	**96 563**	**98 552**
Total tax revenue on accrual basis	**..**	**..**	**39 052**	**62 435**	**77 447**	**76 315**	**88 688**	**92 003**	**96 985**	**99 025**
Conciliation with National Accounts										
Additional taxes included in National Accounts	..	0	0	0	0	0	0	0	0	0
Taxes excluded from National Accounts	..	0	0	0	0	0	0	0	0	0
Difference in treatment of tax credits	..	0	0	0	0	0	0	0	0	0
Capital transfer for uncollected revenue	..	0	0	0	0	0	0	0	0	0
Voluntary social security contributions	..	262	632	236	228	254	270	303	300	269
Miscellaneous differences	..	0	0	0	0	0	0	0	0	0
National Accounts: Taxes and actual social contributions	..	12 157	39 684	62 671	77 675	76 569	88 958	92 306	97 285	99 294
Imputed social contributions	..	513	688	30	0	0	0	0	0	0
National Accounts: Taxes and all social contributions	..	12 670	40 372	62 701	77 675	76 569	88 958	92 306	97 285	99 294

.. Not available

Note: Year ending 31st December.

From 1988 data are on accrual basis.

Finland has an imputation system where the full credit is taken into account in shareholders taxation. According to estimates made by the National Board of Taxation, the credit given to shareholders was 193 million euros in 1991; the effects on personal income taxation are estimated.

Headings 2120 and 2320: The breakdown of contributions paid by employees and self-employed or non-employed is estimated.

Heading 4200: All figures in this subheading are estimated.

Heading 4400: Stamp duties include payment for some government services where the levy can be regarded as requited (the levy is linked to the cost of providing the service). However they are classified as taxes and recorded under this subheading as taxes on financial and capital transactions because the amounts involved cannot be identified.

Heading 5121: The negative item under the title 'Price difference compensations' refers to the subsidies paid out on agricultural products under the price compensation scheme which can be offset against any positive tax liability which arising under the same scheme. From 1983 this item has been offset against revenues from excises on certain foodstuffs, on medium and stronger beer and on non-alcoholic beverages.

Heading 5126: Prior to 1979, no figures are available for amounts paid under the Fire protection levy.

Heading 5212: Prior to 1990, a part of the tax is paid by 'households'.

Source: Bulletin of Statistics; Central Statistical Office (for Central Government revenues); the Annual report of the National Pension Institute and Official Statistics of Finland Series XXIIA published by the Ministry and Social Affairs (for the Social Security and private pension respectively); supplementary information from unpublished sources.

StatLink https://doi.org/10.1787/888934211851

Table 5.11. France: Details of tax revenue, 1965-2018

Million EUR

	1965	1980	1990	2000	2007	2010	2013	2015	2017	2018
Total tax revenue	**25 776**	**178 576**	**433 771**	**645 528**	**831 226**	**846 318**	**966 817**	**1 002 131**	**1 065 075**	**1 090 163**
Total tax revenue exclusive of taxes collected for the EU	..	..	..	**643 655**	**829 411**	**844 346**	**964 743**	**999 064**	**1 061 026**	**1 085 584**
1000 Taxes on income, profits and capital gains	**4 095**	**30 019**	**69 649**	**160 363**	**197 939**	**191 085**	**235 964**	**234 532**	**251 712**	**274 103**
1100 Of individuals	2 736	20 734	46 272	115 885	141 405	144 165	179 715	188 357	197 915	224 196
1110 On income and profits	2 723	20 674	46 252	115 884	141 405	144 165	179 715	188 357	197 915	224 196
Tax on individual income	..	18 207	39 237	49 548	48 597	49 575	70 098	72 750	76 744	77 573
Tax on non business profits	..	51	189	293	559	446	598	927	800	808
Tax on financial assets	..	2 333	3 971	0	0	0	0	0	0	0
CSG, CRDS, social security contributions for the benefit of the FSV, FNAL and / or the FS	..	0	0	65 953	92 204	93 972	108 247	113 065	115 449	140 372
Flat-rate tax on precious metals	..	70	58	47	37	52	69	71	72	78
Tax on multiple wages	..	7	20	38	0	0	0	0	0	0
Social solidarity contribution	..	0	2 207	5	0	82	381	0	2 633	2 746
Others	..	6	571	0	8	38	322	1 544	2 217	2 619
1120 On capital gains	14	59	20	1	0	0	0	0	0	0
On capital gains	..	0	0	0	..	..	..	..	..	..
Levies on construction profits	..	59	20	1	..	..	..	..	..	..
1200 Corporate	1 358	9 158	23 117	44 478	56 534	46 920	56 249	46 175	53 797	49 907
1210 On profits	1 358	9 158	23 117	44 478	56 534	46 920	56 249	46 175	53 797	49 907
Corporations' tax (excluding tax credits to reduce or remove the taxation)	..	8 524	20 804	39 755	51 063	39 095	46 474	39 579	47 832	44 834
3% tax on dividends	..	0	0	0	0	0	1 943	2 165	1 677	4
Tax on financial assets	..	487	1 333	1 460	3 492	5 952	5 894	3 325	3 063	3 814
Precount on distributed profits (exceptional levy of 25% since 2005)	..	36	247	1 135	88	28	-6	4	1	0
Exceptional levies on temporary work corporations	..	0	0	0	0	0	0	0	0	0
Social contribution on corporation profits	..	0	0	589	158	842	1 160	971	1 142	1 119
Annual flat-rate tax	..	111	658	1 484	1 656	599	680	4	2	1
Exceptionnal levies on insurances	..	0	61	55	64	94	104	127	80	135
Other	..	0	14	0	13	310	0	0	0	0
1220 On capital gains	0	0	0	0	0	0	0	0	0	0
1300 Unallocable between 1100 and 1200	0	127	260	0	0	0	0	0	0	0
2000 Social security contributions	**8 804**	**76 235**	**191 141**	**231 875**	**307 663**	**323 816**	**356 934**	**370 375**	**387 171**	**380 728**
2100 Employees	1 701	19 851	57 347	57 686	76 815	78 268	88 097	93 767	100 797	89 076
Actual cotisations	0	19 851	57 347	57 686	76 815	78 268	88 097	93 767	100 797	89 076
2110 On a payroll basis	0	0	0	57 686	76 815	78 268	88 097	93 767	100 797	89 076
2120 On an income tax basis	0	0	0	0	0	0	0	0	0	0
2200 Employers	6 525	50 742	118 079	159 476	208 688	219 687	240 672	248 173	258 532	265 116
Actual cotisations	0	50 742	118 079	159 476	208 688	219 687	240 672	248 173	258 532	265 116
2210 On a payroll basis	0	0	0	159 476	208 688	219 687	240 672	248 173	258 532	265 116
2220 On an income tax basis	0	0	0	0	0	0	0	0	0	0
2300 Self-employed or non-employed	578	5 642	15 714	14 713	22 160	25 861	28 165	28 435	27 842	26 536
Actual cotisations	..	5 642	15 714	14 713	22 160	25 861	28 165	28 435	27 842	26 536
2310 On a payroll basis	0	0	0	14 713	22 160	25 861	28 165	28 435	27 842	26 536
2320 On an income tax basis	0	0	0	0	0	0	0	0	0	0
2400 Unallocable between 2100, 2200 and 2300	0	0	0	0	0	0	0	0	0	0
2410 On a payroll basis	0	0	0	..	..	..	..	..	..	..
2420 On an income tax basis	0	0	0	..	..	..	..	..	..	..
3000 Taxes on payroll and workforce	**1 189**	**3 935**	**8 254**	**14 916**	**22 874**	**26 926**	**33 595**	**34 574**	**35 742**	**35 822**
Tax on wages	0	2 413	5 208	7 583	10 272	11 440	13 127	13 165	13 855	13 287
Corporate social contributions	0	0	0	0	0	657	4 654	5 019	5 497	5 715
Apprenticeship tax	0	172	101	102	964	1 130	1 317	1 436	1 602	1 938
Tax benefitting the wage garantee scheme (AGS): royalties for concessions, patents, licenses, trademarks, processes, rights and similar values	0	263	379	551	736	1 759	1 435	1 479	966	810
Tax on vocational training	0	236	30	97	19	13	17	17	21	20
Tax benefitting the FNAL: ACOSS (employer contributions)	0	120	754	1 506	2 412	2 465	3 123	2 929	2 683	2 692
Tax benefitting the transports union	0	731	1 600	3 786	5 738	6 344	7 326	7 842	8 699	8 953
Payment benefitting the UNEDIC	0	0	23	24	0	0	0	0	0	0
Tax on re-employed pensioners income	0	0	0	0	0	0	0	0	0	0
Providence contribution	0	0	0	415	773	1 120	496	415	397	343
Others	0	0	159	851	100	81	49	27	21	18
Taxes benefitting the national solidarity fund for autonomy (CNSA)	0	0	0	0	1 860	1 917	2 051	1 891	1 985	2 033
Employers' contribution to the early retirement of asbestos workers regime (FCAATA)	0	0	0	0	0	0	0	0	0	0
Exceptional levy on high wages	0	0	0	0	0	0	0	354	16	13
4000 Taxes on property	**1 105**	**8 591**	**27 434**	**46 169**	**67 573**	**73 085**	**84 209**	**92 323**	**100 989**	**97 559**
4100 Recurrent taxes on immovable property	506	5 358	14 808	29 439	42 130	50 061	57 411	60 443	64 153	62 811

	1965	1980	1990	2000	2007	2010	2013	2015	2017	2018
4110 Households	198	4 454	11 493	22 285	32 839	38 952	44 684	46 873	49 557	47 817
Council tax	0	2 306	5 100	8 366	12 433	15 254	17 470	18 424	19 311	16 892
Tax on real-estate properties	0	1 034	4 040	8 460	11 983	14 403	16 539	17 557	18 926	19 484
Waste collection tax	0	534	1 219	3 103	5 117	5 699	6 552	6 567	6 803	6 942
Contribution to public broadcasting	0	0	0	2 099	2 255	2 472	2 866	3 012	3 248	3 215
Tax on non-developped land	0	506	979	172	851	919	955	980	971	977
Chamber of Agriculture tax	0	0	0	53	59	61	62	61	61	55
Street-cleaning tax	0	0	0	68	74	75	109	109	113	114
Other taxes	0	74	156	-36	67	69	131	163	124	138
4120 Others	308	904	3 315	7 154	9 291	11 109	12 727	13 570	14 596	14 994
Tax on real-estate properties	0	759	3 032	6 256	9 054	10 865	12 477	13 246	14 278	14 698
Tax on non-developped land	0	127	245	688	0	0	0	0	0	0
Chamber of Agriculture tax	0	18	39	210	237	244	250	242	243	221
Other taxes	0	0	0	0	0	0	0	82	75	75
4200 Recurrent taxes on net wealth	0	0	2 615	2 440	4 390	4 461	4 372	5 224	5 068	1 847
4210 Individual	..	..	938	2 440	4 390	4 461	4 372	5 224	5 068	1 847
4220 Corporate	..	..	1 677	0	0	0	0	0	0	0
4300 Estate, inheritance and gift taxes	145	1 010	4 124	6 907	8 910	7 738	10 456	12 317	14 344	14 399
4310 Estate and inheritance taxes	140	875	3 490	5 508	7 853	6 862	9 368	10 690	11 898	11 982
Inheritance taxes	0	861	3 453	5 428	7 794	6 806	8 433	10 540	11 785	11 895
Various receipts and tax fines	0	14	37	80	59	56	935	150	113	87
4320 Gift taxes	5	135	634	1 399	1 057	876	1 088	1 627	2 446	2 417
Donations	0	113	568	1 399	1 057	876	1 088	1 627	2 446	2 417
Various receipts and tax fines	0	0	0	0	0	0	0	0	0	0
Other taxes	0	22	66	0	0	0	0	0	0	0
4400 Taxes on financial and capital transactions	447	2 224	5 886	7 383	12 143	10 825	11 970	14 339	17 424	18 502
Debts, annuities, offices	0	30	209	279	443	279	359	335	325	514
Business assets	0	253	518	199	268	154	135	132	153	146
Tangible movable assets	0	14	18	0	0	1	0	1	1	1
Properties and real property rights	0	63	4	2	2	3	1	1	1	0
Agreements and civil acts between companies	0	95	218	4	5	8	6	7	4	1
Various receipts and tax fines	0	35	60	367	179	253	4	6	10	15
Judicial and extra-judicial documents	0	6	10	0	0	0	0	0	0	0
Land registration tax	0	781	38	68	130	140	703	770	897	960
Various stamps and fees	0	94	242	0	0	0	0	0	0	0
Taxes on stock exchange transactions	0	168	525	407	271	0	0	0	0	0
Tax on financial transactions	0	0	0	0	0	0	697	917	964	1 047
Additional registration taxes	0	679	4 002	5 339	10 396	9 567	9 538	11 618	14 535	15 226
Other taxes and receipts	0	5	44	718	449	420	527	552	534	592
4500 Non-recurrent taxes	8	0	0	0	0	0	0	0	0	0
4510 On net wealth	8	..	..	..	..	..	..	..	..	..
4520 Other non-recurrent taxes	0	..	..	..	..	..	..	..	..	..
4600 Other recurrent taxes on property	0	0	0	0	0	0	0	0	0	0
5000 Taxes on goods and services	**9 902**	**54 317**	**123 235**	**168 121**	**207 950**	**222 165**	**245 423**	**258 741**	**278 119**	**289 869**
5100 Taxes on production, sale, transfer, etc.	9 676	52 719	119 201	163 520	202 109	215 844	238 774	251 793	270 606	281 681
5110 General taxes	5 994	37 760	81 341	110 296	142 033	151 565	163 103	169 913	179 964	186 522
5111 Value added taxes	5 173	37 282	79 972	107 511	137 137	136 129	145 264	152 550	162 877	168 526
VAT (general budget)	0	36 895	78 902	103 054	136 927	135 578	144 490	151 680	162 011	167 618
VAT (BAPSA)	0	62	101	4 111	0	0	0	0	0	0
Other VAT	0	325	969	0	0	0	0	0	0	0
Sub-compensations of agricultural VAT	0	0	0	346	138	330	462	381	369	397
Value added taxes on subsidies	0	0	0	0	72	221	312	489	497	511
5112 Sales tax	822	0	0	0	0	0	0	0	0	0
5113 Other	0	477	1 369	2 784	4 896	15 436	17 839	17 363	17 087	17 996
Social solidarity contribution	..	477	1 369	2 784	4 896	5 090	5 671	4 390	3 561	3 769
Contributions on the value added of the corporations	..	..	..	0	0	10 346	12 168	12 973	13 526	14 227
Tax on digital services	..	..	..	0	0	0	0	0	0	0
5120 Taxes on specific goods and services	3 682	14 960	37 860	53 225	60 076	64 279	75 671	81 880	90 642	95 159

	1965	1980	1990	2000	2007	2010	2013	2015	2017	2018
5121 Excise duties	2 775	11 013	26 834	39 850	44 013	45 770	52 343	56 660	61 864	64 894
Excise tax on energy products	0	7 136	17 476	23 493	24 318	23 577	23 693	26 238	29 589	31 898
Exceptional levies on oil product corporations	0	0	0	0	0	0	0	0	0	0
Taxes on wines, ciders and meads	0	97	174	0	121	121	486	501	495	534
Taxes on alcohol	0	1 238	1 593	3 025	484	2 482	2 950	2 956	2 974	2 945
Taxes on beer and mineral water	0	58	91	20	409	538	803	931	999	1 055
Other taxes and receipts	0	136	38	19	2 169	100	90	110	72	139
Taxes on tobaccos and matches	0	1 188	2 989	7 965	9 659	11 083	12 227	12 318	12 326	13 342
Fines and confiscations	0	2	1	0	0	0	0	0	0	0
Gold and silver warranty	0	6	19	29	2	0	0	0	0	0
ANDA taxes	0	84	147	89	0	0	0	0	0	0
Tax on health protection and the organisation of meat markets	0	0	0	48	46	43	41	43	42	43
Tax on cereals	0	147	275	19	19	24	18	14	8	8
Fees on tobacco stores	0	0	0	0	0	0	0	0	0	0
Fees on potash salt	0	0	0	0	0	0	0	0	0	0
Tax on flour	0	0	0	38	0	0	0	0	0	0
Fees included in fuel price	0	36	32	453	485	495	499	493	539	555
National Book Fund tax	0	7	17	0	0	0	0	0	0	0
Tax on logging products	0	11	0	0	0	0	0	0	0	0
Mining fees	0	16	59	43	23	25	22	16	15	18
Tax on electricity and heating	0	426	1 340	1 061	2 990	3 717	7 253	8 703	9 991	9 844
Surtax on appetizers	0	12	17	0	0	0	0	0	0	0
Pharmaceutical taxes	0	4	559	0	0	0	0	0	0	0
Tax on beet, sugar and alcohol	0	22	400	0	0	0	0	0	0	0
Solidarity tax on oil seeds	0	8	41	0	0	0	0	0	0	0
Tax on food fats	0	32	89	99	0	0	0	0	0	0
National Literature Fund tax	0	23	0	0	0	0	0	0	0	0
Tax on water consumption	0	34	51	74	5	11	1	2	2	0
Tax on meat	0	25	36	0	19	1	1	0	0	0
Tax on pollution, distribution, collection and extraction of water	0	217	609	1 624	1 821	1 763	2 175	2 268	2 364	2 340
Sugar market fund tax	0	0	0	0	0	0	0	0	0	0
Exceptional contribution on pharmacies and laboratories	0	16	0	522	0	0	0	0	0	0
Local tax	0	5	8	241	247	325	127	126	145	66
Contribution of low voltage electric energy suppliers	0	0	0	183	322	324	374	375	378	377
ADEME tax	0	0	0	80	212	489	499	449	449	0
Dock dues	0	0	0	449	544	581	386	422	439	453
General tax on polluting activities	0	0	0	6	16	16	205	117	81	316
Tax on oil products	0	0	0	0	0	0	367	379	377	386
Other taxes	0	30	772	78	102	55	126	199	579	575
Tax benefitting the French petrol institute (IFP)	0	0	0	193	0	0	0	0	0	0
5122 Profits of fiscal monopolies	0	0	0	0	0	0	0	0	0	0
5123 Customs and import duties	471	966	1 669	1 810	2 043	2 180	2 605	2 665	2 663	2 858
Import duties (State)	0	0	0	0	0	0	0	0	0	0
Import duties (UE)	0	873	1 623	0	0	0	0	0	0	0
Dock dues	0	0	0	267	327	361	627	678	707	741
Other taxes	0	94	46	30	59	67	136	55	48	48
5124 Taxes on exports	0	75	15	0	0	0	0	0	0	0
Agricultural levies (State part)	..	0	0	..	..	..	..	..	..	..
Agricultural levies (EU part)	..	75	15	..	..	..	..	..	..	..
5125 Taxes on investment goods	0	0	0	0	0	0	0	0	0	0

	1965	1980	1990	2000	2007	2010	2013	2015	2017	2018
5126 Taxes on specific services	431	2 690	8 373	11 204	14 007	16 274	20 656	22 501	26 061	27 353
Levies on horse-race bets	0	446	545	502	719	626	434	446	434	431
Levies on gambling casinos	0	0	0	727	1 022	748	708	691	741	746
Levies on the French national lottery	0	200	702	1 305	1 982	1 800	1 941	2 118	2 290	2 387
Exceptionnal levies on banks and lending institutions	0	0	0	0	0	0	0	0	0	0
Tax on insurance policies	0	1 292	4 782	5 097	6 571	7 099	9 973	10 386	10 618	11 001
Tax on leases	0	264	633	573	29	-5	-1	0	0	0
Taxes on funerals	0	11	32	14	11	12	12	12	13	13
Stamp taxes for transportation contracts	0	9	77	10	0	0	0	0	0	0
Tax on expertise and technical checks	0	0	0	0	0	0	0	0	0	0
ANAEM tax	0	0	0	33	58	129	145	146	150	115
Tax on the use of inland waterways	0	0	0	104	157	169	192	183	178	177
Other various taxes	0	98	272	273	449	1 007	547	798	1 913	2 484
Taxes on entertainment	0	75	195	274	372	425	799	785	867	1 086
Insurances contributions to the guarantee funds	0	32	135	223	274	323	387	450	755	757
Tax on automobile insurance	0	0	0	55	0	0	0	0	0	0
Additional contribution on insurance contracts to the FNGCA	0	0	0	261	96	101	120	125	60	60
National fund for housing improvement, 5% levy	0	114	258	678	604	604	726	932	1 145	977
Movie-making corporations contributions to the CNC	0	52	207	397	144	766	735	695	697	708
Agricultural insurances fund tax on food	0	0	0	0	0	0	0	0	0	0
National Sports Fund tax	0	3	0	0	0	0	0	0	0	0
Annuities and pensions upgrading fund tax	0	15	0	0	0	0	0	0	0	0
Annual tax on outstanding loans	0	0	0	0	0	0	0	0	0	0
Tax on advertisement	0	0	26	52	38	156	219	232	235	248
Levies on mortgage recording officers wages	0	67	188	0	0	0	0	0	0	0
Tax on safety and security	0	0	0	220	353	459	521	574	655	725
Tax on systemic risk	0	0	0	0	0	0	899	591	436	285
CMU tax on mutual insurances	0	0	0	247	560	1 637	1 851	1 909	2 370	2 305
Major natural disasters prevention fund (FPRNM) tax	0	0	0	0	0	0	197	205	211	129
SRF Contributions collected for the EU	..	..	..	..	..	..	..	916	1 922	2 291
Other taxes	0	10	320	159	568	218	251	307	371	428
5127 Other taxes on internat. trade and transactions	0	0	0	0	0	0	0	0	0	0
5128 Other taxes	5	215	970	360	13	55	67	54	54	54
Co-responsibility tax on milk	0	48	119	0	0	0	0	0	0	0
Co-responsibility tax on cereals	0	0	520	0	0	0	0	0	0	0
European Coal and Steel Community levy	0	14	0	0	0	0	0	0	0	0
Collector of customs	0	9	24	0	0	0	0	0	0	0
Various taxes (local government)	0	0	0	0	0	0	0	0	0	0
Contributions on sugar	0	68	185	270	0	42	54	41	41	41
Sugar market fund tax	0	76	120	76	0	0	0	0	0	0
Other taxes	0	0	2	14	13	13	13	13	13	13
5130 Unallocable between 5110 and 5120	0	0	0	0	0	0	0	0	0	0
5200 Taxes on use of goods and perform activities	226	1 598	4 034	4 601	5 841	6 321	6 649	6 948	7 513	8 188
5210 Recurrent taxes	178	1 226	3 024	2 810	3 009	2 866	2 849	2 669	2 859	3 072
5211 Paid by households: motor vehicles	27	545	1 236	126	0	0	0	0	0	0
Tax differential (central and local government)	0	545	1 236	126	..	..	..	..	..	..
5212 Paid by others: motor vehicles	79	545	1 086	1 280	1 559	1 269	1 181	1 028	780	896
Tax on corporation vehicles	0	197	345	644	891	992	876	753	638	751
Tax on vehicles (central and local government)	0	348	741	636	668	277	305	275	142	145
5213 Paid in respect of other goods	72	136	702	1 404	1 450	1 597	1 668	1 641	2 079	2 176
Special tax on use of roads	0	0	0	420	526	539	573	574	608	618
Weighing tax	0	17	14	0	0	0	0	0	0	0
Various taxes (local government)	0	7	33	0	0	0	0	0	0	0
Tax on video recorders	0	0	0	0	0	0	0	0	0	0
Fee on nuclear power plants monitoring	0	8	41	0	0	0	0	0	0	0
Tax on use of slaughterhouses	0	19	13	0	0	0	0	0	0	0
Corporation contributions on medicines preparation	0	0	20	238	0	379	213	255	296	284
Tax on electric pylons	0	1	66	128	183	213	244	231	251	258
Beverage licences	0	8	22	23	0	0	0	0	0	0
Gallicisation and navigation annual right (DAFN)	0	0	0	0	0	39	37	37	38	38
Fees on radio frequencies use	0	0	0	191	280	275	262	187	307	301
Other taxes	0	75	493	404	461	152	339	357	579	677
5220 Non-recurrent taxes	47	372	1 010	1 791	2 832	3 455	3 800	4 279	4 654	5 116
Entry into service receipt	0	75	0	0	0	0	0	0	0	0
Beverage taxes and licences	0	0	0	3	0	0	0	0	0	0
Fee for the right to build	0	79	53	72	0	18	18	0	0	0
Local tax on the equipement	0	146	263	305	848	1 252	1 381	1 839	2 073	2 231
Car registration tax	0	0	0	1 373	1 939	1 917	2 042	2 086	2 229	2 326
Tax on exceeding the density legal ceiling	0	38	270	38	45	82	82	52	0	0
Additional tax on car registration	0	0	0	0	0	186	277	302	352	559
Other taxes	0	35	423	0	0	0	0	0	0	0
5300 Unallocable between 5100 and 5200	0	0	0	0	0	0	0	0	0	0

	1965	1980	1990	2000	2007	2010	2013	2015	2017	2018
6000 Other taxes	**681**	**5 480**	**14 060**	**24 084**	**27 227**	**9 241**	**10 692**	**11 586**	**11 342**	**12 082**
6100 Paid solely by business	678	5 480	14 060	22 398	27 219	9 235	10 686	11 580	11 336	12 076
National Institute of intellectual property (INPI) tax on services	0	43	67	115	156	165	180	193	204	225
Tax on general charges	0	0	0	0	0	0	0	0	0	0
Tax on the use of fixed assets	0	5 152	13 381	19 641	22 035	0	0	0	0	0
Tax on union benefits (local government)	0	36	197	293	0	0	0	0	0	0
Various taxes (central government)	0	0	0	61	236	255	478	649	637	722
Annual tax on outstanding loans	0	110	0	0	0	0	0	0	0	0
Exceptionnal levies on insurance corporations	0	0	0	0	0	0	0	0	0	0
Fees of the chambers of commerce and industry	0	36	125	155	203	275	233	253	229	196
Payments of industrial enterprises to the benefit of the FNE	0	4	240	204	33	10	3	0	1	0
Other taxes	0	98	50	1 127	3 721	1 078	775	1 484	880	1 298
(ANDA) and (ADAR) tax	0	0	0	32	0	0	0	0	0	0
Property contributions of the corporations	..	..	..	0	0	10 346	12 168	12 973	13 526	14 227
Flat-rate tax on network corporations	0	0	0	0	0	1 223	1 206	1 297	1 329	1 346
Exit tax on insurance	0	0	0	0	0	0	0	0	0	0
Fees of the chambers of commerce and industry	0	0	0	770	835	1 103	1 323	458	871	720
Employers' contribution on stock options	0	0	0	0	0	185	380	490	300	287
Tax on railway companies profit	0	0	0	0	0	0	200	400	226	453
6200 Other	3	0	0	1 686	8	6	6	6	6	6
Other taxes	0	..	..	1 686	8	6	6	6	6	6
Sectors accounts differential	0	..	..	0	0	0	0	0	0	0
Memorandum items										
Customs duties collected on behalf of the EU	..	..	..	1 513	1 657	1 752	1 842	1 932	1 908	2 069
SRF contributions collected on behalf of the EU	..	..	..	..	..	..	..	916	1 922	2 291
Non-wastable tax credits										
Non-wastable tax credits against 1110	0	0	0	0	7 663	10 761	8 214	8 041	6 346	9 236
Tax component	0	0	0	0	0	8 234	6 755	5 669	3 721	5 448
Transfer component	0	0	0	0	0	2 527	1 459	2 372	2 625	3 788
Non-wastable tax credits against 1210	0	0	0	457	1 860	6 655	5 466	18 618	22 640	26 573
Tax component	0	0	0	0	0	1 277	3 572	10 560	10 663	10 663
Transfer component	0	0	0	0	0	5 378	1 894	8 058	11 977	15 910
Non-wastable tax credits against 3000	0	0	0	0	0	0	0	0	0	574
Tax expenditure component	0	0	0	0	0	0	0	0	0	574
Transfer component	0	0	0	0	0	0	0	0	0	0
Total tax revenue on cash basis	**25 776**	**178 576**	**433 771**	**642 156**	**825 954**	**840 905**	**960 513**	**995 462**	**1 058 287**	**1 084 161**
Total tax revenue on accrual basis	**0**	**0**	**0**	**645 528**	**831 226**	**846 318**	**966 817**	**1 002 131**	**1 065 075**	**1 090 163**
Conciliation with National Accounts										
Additional taxes included in national accounts	0	0	0	0	0	0	0	0	0	0
Tax excluded from national accounts	0	0	0	-3 171	-5 191	-5 774	-6 661	-6 676	-6 916	-7 056
Waste collection tax	..	..	..	-3 103	-5 117	-5 699	-6 552	-6 567	-6 803	-6 942
Tax on electric pylons	..	..	..	0	0	0	0	0	0	0
Street-cleaning tax	..	..	..	-68	-74	-75	-109	-109	-113	-114
Difference in treatment of tax credits	0	0	0	0	0	9 511	10 327	16 229	14 384	16 685
Capital transfer for uncollected revenue	0	0	0	-3 372	-5 272	-5 413	-6 304	-6 669	-6 788	-6 002
Voluntary social security contributions	0	0	0	0	0	0	0	0	0	0
Miscellaneous differences	0	0	0	0	0	0	0	0	0	0
National Accounts: taxes and actual social contributions	0	0	0	638 985	820 763	844 642	964 179	1 005 015	1 065 755	1 093 790
Imputed social contributions	0	0	0	25 875	33 510	38 028	41 947	42 655	43 041	43 660
National Accounts: taxes and all social contributions	0	0	0	664 860	854 273	882 670	1 006 126	1 047 670	1 108 796	1 137 450

.. Not available

Note: Calendar year ending on December 31st.

From 1992, the data are on an accrual basis.

From 1970, figures were calculated according to the new System of National Accounts and are not, therefore, comparable to those of the previous years.

The section 2000 includes certain voluntary contributions.

The section 4220 corresponds to the remuneration for the guarantee of the State given to savings banks.

Source: General Account of the Administration of finances for the figures of fiscal receipts. OSCE for the figures of Social Security from 1965 to 1969, and ESA for the following years.

StatLink https://doi.org/10.1787/888934211870

Table 5.12. Germany: Details of tax revenue, 1965-2018

Million EUR

	1965	1980	1990	2000	2007	2010	2013	2015	2017	2018
Total tax revenue	**74 359**	**287 373**	**454 764**	**767 045**	**884 216**	**911 161**	**1 038 902**	**1 127 631**	**1 232 001**	**1 293 678**
Total tax revenue exclusive of taxes collected for the EU	..	..	**450 620**	**763 300**	**880 273**	**906 897**	**1 034 587**	**1 120 820**	**1 225 214**	**1 286 710**
1000 Taxes on income, profits and capital gains	**25 059**	**100 821**	**147 257**	**231 249**	**273 596**	**257 817**	**319 926**	**351 473**	**400 672**	**423 781**
1100 Of individuals	19 254	85 134	125 296	194 173	218 848	219 387	270 179	299 379	334 667	351 896
1110 On income and profits	19 254	85 134	125 296	194 173	218 848	219 387	270 179	299 379	334 667	351 896
Taxes on wages and salaries	8 558	57 039	90 801	135 733	146 365	145 202	174 512	194 116	211 685	224 108
Assessed income tax	7 567	18 813	18 672	12 225	25 341	31 346	42 586	48 902	59 784	60 927
Withholding tax on dividends	691	2 135	5 538	13 515	13 572	12 982	17 258	17 944	20 918	23 196
Supplementary tax	0	0	0	10 347	10 907	10 706	13 085	14 555	16 141	17 041
Enterprise tax	2 438	7 147	10 285	16 486	14 630	13 709	17 305	18 570	21 294	22 518
Stabilisation tax	0	0	0	0	0	0	0	0	0	0
Withholding tax on interest	0	0	0	5 867	8 033	5 442	5 433	5 292	4 845	4 106
1120 On capital gains	0	0	0	0	0	0	0	0	0	0
1200 Corporate	5 806	15 686	21 961	37 076	54 748	38 430	49 747	52 094	66 005	71 885
1210 On profits	5 806	15 686	21 961	37 076	54 748	38 430	49 747	52 094	66 005	71 885
Corporation tax	4 177	10 902	15 385	23 575	23 386	12 516	19 762	20 224	29 832	34 216
Supplementary tax	0	20	1	1 494	1 550	982	1 337	1 409	1 902	1 975
Sacrifice for Berlin	3	0	0	0	0	0	0	0	0	0
Enterprise tax	1 625	4 765	6 576	10 540	25 486	22 002	25 722	27 613	31 663	33 484
Stabilisation tax	0	0	0	0	0	0	0	0	0	0
Withholding tax on interest	0	0	0	1 467	4 326	2 930	2 926	2 848	2 608	2 210
1220 On capital gains	0	0	0	0	0	0	0	0	0	0
1300 Unallocable between 1100 and 1200	0	0	0	0	0	0	0	0	0	0
2000 Social security contributions	**19 876**	**98 659**	**170 449**	**299 440**	**320 750**	**354 320**	**392 378**	**424 841**	**467 185**	**487 839**
2100 Employees	8 723	43 833	73 580	131 610	139 927	152 843	171 657	186 305	206 813	216 745
Payments by employees total	8 723	43 833	73 580	131 610	139 927	152 843	171 657	186 305	206 813	216 745
2110 On a payroll basis	..	..	..	131 610	139 927	152 843	171 657	186 305	206 813	216 745
2120 On an income tax basis	..	..	..	0	0	0	0	0	0	0
2200 Employers	10 693	52 985	86 659	147 410	151 094	165 476	181 782	196 679	214 134	223 806
Payments by employers total	10 693	52 985	86 659	147 410	151 094	165 476	181 782	196 679	214 134	223 806
2210 On a payroll basis	..	..	..	147 410	151 094	165 476	181 782	196 679	214 134	223 806
2220 On an income tax basis	..	..	..	0	0	0	0	0	0	0
2300 Self-employed or non-employed	460	1 841	10 210	20 420	29 729	36 001	38 939	41 857	46 238	47 288
Payments total	460	1 841	10 210	20 420	29 729	36 001	38 939	41 857	46 238	47 288
2310 On a payroll basis	..	..	..	20 420	29 729	36 001	38 939	41 857	46 238	47 288
2320 On an income tax basis	..	..	..	0	0	0	0	0	0	0
2400 Unallocable between 2100, 2200 and 2300	0	0	0	0	0	0	0	0	0	0
2410 On a payroll basis	..	..	..	..	..	..	..	..	..	..
2420 On an income tax basis	..	..	..	..	..	..	..	..	..	..
3000 Taxes on payroll and workforce	**477**	**445**	**0**	**0**	**0**	**0**	**0**	**0**	**0**	**0**
Payroll tax	477	445	..	..	..	..	..	..	..	..
4000 Taxes on property	**4 313**	**9 414**	**15 321**	**17 505**	**21 873**	**21 012**	**26 104**	**31 076**	**33 600**	**35 499**
4100 Recurrent taxes on immovable property	1 079	2 968	4 461	8 849	10 713	11 315	12 377	13 215	13 965	14 203
4110 Households	644	1 187	1 784	3 540	4 285	4 526	4 951	5 286	5 586	5 681
4120 Others	435	1 780	2 676	5 309	6 428	6 789	7 426	7 929	8 379	8 522
4200 Recurrent taxes on net wealth	2 530	4 362	6 213	433	5	2	700	322	382	399
4210 Individual	973	977	1 425	191	2	1	0	-1	0	0
General wealth tax	471	954	1 425	191	2	1	..	-1	..	..
Equalization of war burden	502	23	0	0	0	0	..	0	..	..
4220 Corporate	1 557	3 385	4 788	242	3	1	700	323	382	399
General wealth tax	490	1 431	1 813	242	3	1	0	-1	0	0
Equalization of war burden	350	15	0	0	0	0	0	0	0	0
Enterprise tax	717	1 939	2 975	0	0	0	0	0	0	0
Bank levy	0	0	0	0	0	0	520	0	10	11
Contribution to Deposit Protection Fund	0	0	0	0	0	0	180	324	372	388
4300 Estate, inheritance and gift taxes	162	520	1 545	2 982	4 203	4 405	4 633	6 290	6 114	6 814
4310 Estate and inheritance taxes	134	416	1 359	2 624	3 699	3 876	4 077	5 535	5 380	5 996
4320 Gift taxes	28	104	186	358	504	529	556	755	734	818
4400 Taxes on financial and capital transactions	542	1 564	3 103	5 241	6 952	5 290	8 394	11 249	13 139	14 083
Real property transfer tax	150	521	1 999	5 081	6 952	5 290	8 394	11 249	13 139	14 083
Additional real property transfer	198	680	148	160	0	0	0	0	0	0
Capital transfer tax	111	200	807	0	0	0	0	0	0	0
Bill of exchange tax	83	163	149	0	0	0	0	0	0	0
4500 Non-recurrent taxes	0	0	0	0	0	0	0	0	0	0
4510 On net wealth	..	..	..	..	..	..	..	..	..	..
4520 Other non-recurrent taxes	..	..	..	..	..	..	..	..	..	..
4600 Other recurrent taxes on property	0	0	0	0	0	0	0	0	0	0
5000 Taxes on goods and services	**24 462**	**77 863**	**121 577**	**218 686**	**267 901**	**277 912**	**300 366**	**320 025**	**330 292**	**346 289**

	1965	1980	1990	2000	2007	2010	2013	2015	2017	2018
5100 Taxes on production, sale, transfer, etc.	23 079	74 406	117 209	211 444	251 558	261 160	281 995	301 099	318 435	327 429
5110 General taxes	12 235	47 779	75 459	140 871	170 387	180 533	197 326	211 936	226 901	235 449
5111 Value added taxes	0	47 779	75 459	140 871	170 387	180 533	197 326	211 936	226 901	235 449
5112 Sales tax	0	0	0	0	0	0	0	0	0	0
5113 Other	12 235	0	0	0	0	0	0	0	0	0
Turnover tax old	11 028	..	..	..	..	..	..	..	..	..
Old turnover tax on import	1 208	..	..	..	..	..	..	..	..	..
5120 Taxes on specific goods and services	10 844	26 627	41 750	70 573	80 819	80 287	84 381	88 871	91 246	91 688
5121 Excise duties	8 213	20 566	31 158	57 224	63 780	63 438	64 621	65 330	66 507	66 137
Duty on mineral oils	3 798	10 917	17 701	37 826	38 877	39 601	39 260	39 605	40 998	40 834
Duty on power	0	0	0	3 356	6 439	6 167	6 987	6 560	7 003	6 848
Duty on tobacco	2 402	5 771	8 898	11 443	14 108	13 453	14 131	14 963	14 299	14 254
Duty on alcohol	771	1 986	2 162	2 151	2 169	2 049	2 098	2 073	2 090	2 116
Duty on beer	501	645	693	843	750	708	675	679	664	663
Duty on coffee	488	756	986	1 087	985	998	1 030	1 034	1 052	1 030
Duty on sugar	59	72	79	0	0	0	0	0	0	0
Duty on tea	16	32	31	0	0	0	0	0	0	0
Duty on salt	20	20	23	0	0	0	0	0	0	0
Duty on electric lamps	34	63	83	0	0	0	0	0	0	0
Duty on playing cards	2	4	0	0	0	0	0	0	0	0
Duty on beverages	46	22	8	6	1	0	0	0	0	0
Duty on acetic acid	3	2	0	0	0	0	0	0	0	0
Duty on champagne	69	274	494	512	451	462	440	416	401	392
Duty on matches	5	2	0	0	0	0	0	0	0	0
Duty on ice cream	1	0	0	0	0	0	0	0	0	0
5122 Profits of fiscal monopolies	8	2	0	0	0	0	0	0	0	0
5123 Customs and import duties	1 658	3 125	3 847	3 394	3 972	4 234	4 251	5 195	5 043	5 018
Monetary compensation accounts	0	368	1	0	0	0	0	0	0	0
Customs (mainly EU)	1 294	2 353	3 662	3 394	3 972	4 234	4 251	5 195	5 043	5 018
Agricultural levies EU	364	404	184	0	0	0	0	0	0	0
5124 Taxes on exports	0	0	0	0	0	0	0	0	0	0
5125 Taxes on investment goods	0	0	0	0	0	0	0	0	0	0
5126 Taxes on specific services	942	2 689	6 443	9 599	13 095	12 583	15 443	18 306	19 660	20 567
Duty transport goods on residents	0	0	0	0	0	0	0	0	0	0
Transport tax	452	0	0	0	0	0	0	0	0	0
Insurance tax	198	910	2 266	7 243	10 410	10 261	11 588	12 445	13 317	13 747
Fire insurance tax	33	124	200	288	319	326	392	413	451	467
Entertainment tax	55	44	140	267	210	376	708	881	1 048	1 072
Taxes on betting and gambling	204	655	1 046	1 801	1 702	1 412	1 635	1 711	1 834	1 893
Tax on electricity bills	0	956	2 792	0	0	0	0	0	0	0
Aviation tax	0	0	0	0	0	0	955	1 027	1 116	1 203
Gaming casinos levy	0	0	0	0	454	208	165	251	184	199
SRF Contributions	..	..	..	..	..	..	..	1 578	1 710	1 986
5127 Other taxes on internat. trade and transactions	0	0	4	5	1	2	2	2	2	2
5128 Other taxes	24	244	298	351	-29	30	64	38	34	-36
Levies CECA	24	56	36	0	0	0	0	0	0	0
Cotisation sugar EU	0	112	224	351	-29	30	64	38	34	-36
Levy on milk	0	75	38	0	0	0	0	0	0	0
5130 Unallocable between 5110 and 5120	0	0	0	0	352	340	288	292	288	292
Contributions to the German National Petroleum Stockpiling Agency	..	..	..	..	352	340	288	292	288	292
5200 Taxes on use of goods and perform activities	1 383	3 457	4 368	7 242	16 343	16 752	18 371	18 926	11 857	18 860
5210 Recurrent taxes	1 369	3 454	4 368	7 239	16 343	16 189	17 699	18 171	10 962	17 355
5211 Paid by households: motor vehicles	614	1 892	2 950	5 177	6 823	6 447	6 393	6 992	7 054	7 102
5212 Paid by others: motor vehicles	728	1 475	1 300	1 838	2 075	2 041	2 097	1 812	1 894	1 945
5213 Paid in respect of other goods	27	87	118	224	7 445	7 701	9 209	9 367	2 014	8 308
Dog taxes	24	75	101	198	240	258	299	322	349	359
Hunting and fishing taxes	4	13	17	26	23	19	10	10	9	9
Nuclear fuel tax	0	0	0	0	0	0	1 285	1 018	-6 284	0
Licence fee (private households)	0	0	0	0	6 464	6 681	6 914	7 280	7 210	7 210
Licence fee (companies)	0	0	0	0	718	743	701	737	730	730
5220 Non-recurrent taxes	14	3	1	3	0	563	672	755	895	1 505
Non-recurrent taxes	..	..	..	..	..	0	0	0	0	0
CO2 emission certificates	..	..	..	..	..	563	672	755	895	1 505
5300 Unallocable between 5100 and 5200	0	0	0	0	0	0	0	0	0	0
6000 Other taxes	**172**	**172**	**160**	**165**	**96**	**100**	**128**	**216**	**252**	**270**
6100 Paid solely by business	0	0	0	0	0	0	0	0	0	0
6200 Other	172	172	160	165	96	100	128	216	252	270
Memorandum items										
Customs duties collected on behalf of the EU	..	..	3 662	3 394	3 972	4 234	4 251	5 195	5 043	5 018
SRF contributions collected on behalf of the EU	..	..	..	..	..	..	..	1 578	1 710	1 986

	1965	1980	1990	2000	2007	2010	2013	2015	2017	2018
Non-wastable tax credits										
Non-wastable tax credits against 1110	..	..	..	38 356	43 602	45 475	41 890	41 951	43 440	43 913
Tax expenditure component	..	..	..	..	29 499	28 268	26 275	26 817	28 141	29 186
Transfer component	..	..	..	..	14 104	17 207	15 616	15 134	15 297	14 727
Non-wastable tax credits against 1210	..	..	..	962	804	802	426	200	24	12
Tax expenditure component	..	..	..	..	348	326	172	120	18	12
Transfer component	..	..	..	..	456	474	254	80	8	0
Total tax revenue on cash basis	**74 359**	**287 373**	**454 764**	**767 045**	**881 517**	**911 154**	**1 037 605**	**1 125 844**	**1 230 367**	**1 292 596**
Total tax revenue on accrual basis	**..**	**..**	**..**	**..**	**884 216**	**911 161**	**1 038 902**	**1 127 631**	**1 232 001**	**1 293 678**
Conciliation with National Accounts										
Additional taxes included in National Accounts	..	..	..	..	2 406	2 067	2 411	2 856	2 646	2 637
Several duties, administrative fees and other revenues	..	..	..	..	2 406	2 067	2 411	2 856	2 646	2 637
Taxes excluded from National Accounts	..	..	..	..	0	0	0	0	0	0
Difference in treatment of tax credits	..	..	..	..	12 623	9 230	6 358	5 619	5 654	6 266
Capital transfer for uncollected revenue	..	..	..	..	0	0	0	0	0	0
Voluntary social security contributions	..	..	..	..	21 409	5 102	5 352	6 068	7 069	7 415
Miscellaneous differences	..	..	..	..	33 134	34 234	34 083	35 690	44 520	39 264
National Accounts: Taxes and actual social contributions	..	..	..	..	953 788	961 794	1 087 106	1 177 864	1 291 890	1 349 260
Imputed social contributions	..	..	..	..	29 509	32 687	33 506	34 543	37 014	38 031
National Accounts: Taxes and all social contributions	..	..	..	..	983 297	994 481	1 120 612	1 212 407	1 328 904	1 387 291

.. Not available

Note: Year ending 31st December.

From 2002 data are on accrual basis.

The tax revenues for Germany refer to the old Länder until 1990 and to all Germany beginning in 1991.

Heading 1000: In the years up to 2000, the revenues shown take into account the whole amount of non-wastable tax credits including that part paid out by the tax authorities which should, under the OECD criteria, be treated as expenditure. From 2001, the data necessary to make the adjustment have become available and the revenue figures comply with the OECD criteria from that year. The impact of this change is shown in Table D in Part I of this Report.

Heading for non-wastable tax credits against 1110 comprise child tax credits (paid out of wage tax revenue), tax credits for owner occupied housing (paid out of assessed income tax revenue) and investment tax credits for unincorporated businesses (for investment in former East Germany; paid out of assessed income tax revenue).

Heading for non-wastable tax credits against 1210 are investment tax credits for incorporated businesses (for investment in former East Germany; paid out of corporate income tax revenue).

Source: Finanzbericht, Bonn; Tax Statistics. Unpublished estimates by the Ministry of Finance.

StatLink https://doi.org/10.1787/888934211889

Table 5.13. Greece: Details of tax revenue, 1965-2018

Million EUR

	1965	1980	1990	2000	2007	2010	2013	2015	2017	2018
Total tax revenue	**116**	**1 475**	**11 472**	**47 211**	**73 990**	**72 414**	**64 560**	**64 510**	**69 604**	**71 889**
Total tax revenue exclusive of taxes collected for the EU	..	..	**11 361**	**46 990**	**73 683**	**72 134**	**64 410**	**64 327**	**69 247**	**71 562**
1000 Taxes on income, profits and capital gains	**11**	**286**	**2 283**	**12 662**	**17 176**	**15 953**	**14 015**	**14 586**	**15 603**	**16 468**
1100 Of individuals	8	220	1 619	6 127	10 554	9 015	10 780	10 155	11 228	11 550
1110 On income and profits	8	220	1 619	6 102	10 500	8 948	10 698	10 047	11 149	11 427
Personal income tax	..	..	1 414	..	..	..	..	..	..	..
Receipts from previous years	..	..	62	..	..	..	..	..	..	..
Agricultural social security fund	..	..	143	..	..	..	..	..	..	..
1120 On capital gains	0	0	0	25	54	67	82	108	79	123
1200 Corporate	2	56	631	5 625	5 304	5 717	2 071	3 800	3 510	3 998
1210 On profits	2	56	631	5 625	5 304	5 717	2 071	3 800	3 510	3 998
Corporation income tax	2	39	553	..	..	..	..	..	..	..
Receipts from previous years	0	8	33	..	..	..	..	..	..	..
Agricultural social security fund	0	9	46	..	..	..	..	..	..	..
1220 On capital gains	0	0	0	0	0	0	0	0	0	0
1300 Unallocable between 1100 and 1200	1	10	32	910	1 318	1 221	1 164	631	865	920
Extraordinary taxes	0	10	32	..	..	..	..	..	..	..
Other taxes on income and profits	1	0	0	..	..	..	..	..	..	..
2000 Social security contributions	**37**	**485**	**3 466**	**14 284**	**24 940**	**24 748**	**19 354**	**18 807**	**20 743**	**21 473**
2100 Employees	15	214	1 735	7 629	13 417	13 292	10 881	11 095	12 200	11 887
2110 On a payroll basis	..	..	..	..	..	..	..	..	..	..
2120 On an income tax basis	..	..	..	..	..	..	..	..	..	..
2200 Employers	14	213	1 728	6 655	11 523	11 456	8 473	7 712	8 543	9 586
2210 On a payroll basis	..	..	..	..	..	..	..	..	..	..
2220 On an income tax basis	..	..	..	..	..	..	..	..	..	..
2300 Self-employed or non-employed	0	0	3	0	0	0	0	0	0	0
2310 On a payroll basis	..	..	..	..	..	..	..	..	..	..
2320 On an income tax basis	..	..	..	..	..	..	..	..	..	..
2400 Unallocable between 2100, 2200 and 2300	7	58	0	0	0	0	0	0	0	0
2410 On a payroll basis	..	..	..	..	..	..	..	..	..	..
2420 On an income tax basis	..	..	..	..	..	..	..	..	..	..
3000 Taxes on payroll and workforce	**1**	**27**	**79**	**0**	**0**	**0**	**0**	**0**	**0**	**0**
4000 Taxes on property	**11**	**68**	**532**	**3 631**	**4 908**	**3 741**	**5 698**	**5 418**	**5 561**	**5 554**
4100 Recurrent taxes on immovable property	0	4	22	372	709	553	2 619	3 592	3 654	3 594
4110 Households	0	3	22	..	..	..	..	..	..	..
4120 Others	0	1	0	..	..	..	..	..	..	..
Taxes on immovable property	0	0	..	..	..	..	..	..	..	..
4200 Recurrent taxes on net wealth	0	0	0	714	1 208	1 272	1 084	1 083	1 167	1 175
4210 Individual	..	..	..	..	..	..	..	..	..	..
4220 Corporate	..	..	..	..	..	..	..	..	..	..
4300 Estate, inheritance and gift taxes	1	18	141	372	208	165	99	134	154	135
4310 Estate and inheritance taxes	1	13	85	..	..	..	..	..	..	..
4320 Gift taxes	0	4	55	..	..	..	..	..	..	..
4400 Taxes on financial and capital transactions	10	44	368	2 035	2 556	1 146	615	547	577	640
Stamp and transaction taxes	10	41	368	2 035	2 556	1 146	615	547	577	640
Receipts from previous years	0	3	0	0	0	0	0	0	0	0
4500 Non-recurrent taxes	0	2	1	27	0	1	0	0	0	0
4510 On net wealth	0	0	0	..	..	..	..	..	..	..
4520 Other non-recurrent taxes	0	2	1	..	..	..	..	..	..	..
4600 Other recurrent taxes on property	0	0	0	111	227	604	1 281	62	9	10
5000 Taxes on goods and services	**57**	**608**	**5 109**	**16 634**	**26 966**	**27 972**	**25 493**	**25 699**	**27 697**	**28 394**
5100 Taxes on production, sale, transfer, etc.	51	564	4 881	14 797	24 541	25 505	21 536	21 388	23 461	24 670
5110 General taxes	12	194	3 040	9 234	17 020	16 504	13 100	13 077	14 743	15 385
5111 Value added taxes	0	0	2 821	8 927	16 511	15 958	12 593	12 885	14 642	15 288
5112 Sales tax	9	185	123	0	0	0	0	0	0	0
5113 Other	2	9	96	307	509	546	507	192	101	97
Other taxes on goods and services	1	9	34	307	509	546	507	192	101	97
Receipts from previous years	1	0	62	0	0	0	0	0	0	0
5120 Taxes on specific goods and services	39	370	1 789	5 526	7 407	8 922	8 327	8 210	8 582	9 143
5121 Excise duties	20	165	1 372	4 069	5 876	7 567	6 997	6 929	6 878	7 134
Duty on tobacco products	8	45	357	1 769	2 657	2 712	2 506	2 365	2 028	2 244
Duty on alcohol and spirits	1	7	50	262	334	501	417	393	535	530
Duty on mineral oil	7	75	637	2 016	2 878	4 242	3 894	3 971	4 052	4 052
Duty on sugar	3	6	0	0	0	0	0	0	0	0
Duty on coton and other products	0	30	328	22	7	112	180	200	263	308
5122 Profits of fiscal monopolies	2	6	0	0	0	0	0	0	0	0

	1965	1980	1990	2000	2007	2010	2013	2015	2017	2018
5123 Customs and import duties	12	94	112	220	314	279	153	181	266	232
Import duties	11	90	111	220	314	279	153	181	266	232
Agricultural social security fund	1	5	1	0	0	0	0	0	0	0
5124 Taxes on exports	0	1	1	0	0	0	0	0	0	0
5125 Taxes on investment goods	0	0	0	0	0	0	0	0	0	0
5126 Taxes on specific services	2	47	293	1 237	1 217	1 076	1 177	1 100	1 438	1 777
5127 Other taxes on internat. trade and transactions	0	0	0	0	0	0	0	0	0	0
5128 Other taxes	4	58	10	0	0	0	0	0	0	0
Agricultural social security fund	2	..	..	..	..	..	..	..	..	..
Other taxes	2	..	..	..	..	..	..	..	..	..
5130 Unallocable between 5110 and 5120	0	0	52	37	114	79	109	101	136	142
5200 Taxes on use of goods and perform activities	6	44	228	1 320	2 169	1 682	2 954	3 217	3 444	3 091
5210 Recurrent taxes	5	24	219	1 320	2 169	1 682	2 954	3 217	3 444	3 091
Motor vehicle tax	5	0	..	..	..	..	..	..	..	..
5211 Paid by households: motor vehicles	..	23	210	281	598	825	781	780	795	804
5212 Paid by others: motor vehicles	..	0	8	735	1 182	272	120	207	264	272
5213 Paid in respect of other goods	0	1	1	304	389	585	2 053	2 230	2 385	2 015
Taxes on boats/ships	0	0	1	..	..	..	..	..	..	..
5220 Non-recurrent taxes	1	20	9	0	0	0	0	0	0	0
Exceptional tax on construction of buildings	0	..	9	..	..	..	..	..	..	..
Building permits	0	..	0	..	..	..	..	..	..	..
5300 Unallocable between 5100 and 5200	0	0	0	517	256	785	1 003	1 094	792	633
6000 Other taxes	**0**	**1**	**3**	**0**	**0**	**0**	**0**	**0**	**0**	**0**
6100 Paid solely by business	..	0	0	..	..	..	..	..	..	..
6200 Other	..	1	3	..	..	..	..	..	..	..
Memorandum items										
Customs duties collected on behalf of the EU	..	..	100	210	307	278	148	181	266	225
SRF contributions collected on behalf of the EU	..	..	..	..	..	..	..	..	89	102
Total tax revenue on cash basis	**116**	**1 475**	**11 472**	**45 979**	**72 429**	**73 083**	**62 632**	**63 118**	**67 116**	**70 110**
Total tax revenue on accrual basis	**..**	**..**	**..**	**47 211**	**73 990**	**72 414**	**64 560**	**64 510**	**69 604**	**71 889**
Conciliation with National Accounts										
Additional taxes included in National Accounts	..	..	..	0	0	0	0	0	0	0
Taxes excluded from National Accounts	..	..	..	0	0	0	0	0	0	0
Difference in treatment of tax credits	..	..	..	0	0	0	0	0	0	0
Capital transfer for uncollected revenue	..	..	..	0	0	0	0	0	0	0
Tax (Employer's actual social contributions)	..	..	..	..	..	..	..	..	..	..
Tax (Employee's actual social contributions)	..	..	..	..	..	..	..	..	..	..
Voluntary social security contributions	..	..	..	0	0	0	0	0	0	0
Miscellaneous differences	..	..	..	0	0	0	0	0	0	0
National Accounts: Taxes and actual social contributions	..	..	..	47 211	73 990	72 414	64 560	64 510	69 604	71 889
Imputed social contributions	..	..	..	2 055	3 952	4 952	5 101	5 615	5 220	4 825
National Accounts: Taxes and all social contributions	..	..	..	49 266	77 942	77 366	69 661	70 125	74 824	76 714

.. Not available

Note: Year ending 31st December.

From 1998 data are on accrual basis.

Source: Ministry of Finance, General accounting Office, 20th Directorate of Budget except the heading 2000 provided by the National Statistics Bureau.

StatLink https://doi.org/10.1787/888934211908

Table 5.14. Hungary: Details of tax revenue, 1965-2018

Million HUF

	1965	1980	1990	2000	2007	2010	2013	2015	2017	2018
Total tax revenue	..	..	..	**5 140 924**	**10 115 072**	**10 142 330**	**11 687 770**	**13 531 760**	**14 867 258**	**15 976 928**
Total tax revenue exclusive of taxes collected for the EU	..	..	..	**5 140 924**	**10 071 432**	**10 116 676**	**11 660 552**	**13 492 035**	**14 821 001**	**15 913 497**
1000 Taxes on income, profits and capital gains	..	..	..	**1 247 420**	**2 539 389**	**2 093 830**	**2 009 010**	**2 425 958**	**2 862 551**	**2 912 179**
1100 Of individuals	..	..	..	954 698	1 838 563	1 764 082	1 604 686	1 824 671	2 088 801	2 340 282
1110 On income and profits	..	..	..	954 698	1 838 563	1 764 082	1 604 686	1 824 671	2 088 801	2 340 282
1120 On capital gains	..	..	..	0	0	0	0	0	0	0
1200 Corporate	..	..	..	292 722	700 826	329 748	404 324	601 287	773 750	571 897
Corporate income tax	..	..	..	292 722	510 781	323 370	322 467	539 777	710 069	506 674
Research and development fund levy	..	..	..	0	0	0	0	0	0	0
Financial institutions' special tax	..	..	..	0	10 890	21 618	27 686	19 902	10 557	5 566
Separate tax for companies	..	..	..	0	178 598	-32 390	0	0	0	0
Medicine tax	..	..	..	0	558	163	111	0	0	0
Energy corporations' special tax	..	..	..	0	0	16 987	54 060	41 608	53 124	59 657
1210 On profits	..	..	..	..	..	..	..	..	..	..
1220 On capital gains	..	..	..	..	..	..	..	..	..	..
1300 Unallocable between 1100 and 1200	..	..	..	0	0	0	0	0	0	0
Interest withholding	..	..	..	..	..	..	..	..	..	..
2000 Social security contributions	..	..	..	**1 506 755**	**3 402 194**	**3 179 509**	**3 899 154**	**4 433 464**	**4 822 165**	**5 049 592**
2100 Employees	..	..	..	275 323	941 682	1 112 583	1 592 995	1 770 923	2 343 539	2 432 664
Pensions	..	..	..	150 585	336 855	537 556	875 371	969 908	1 189 043	1 335 868
Health	..	..	..	81 874	513 633	467 208	591 224	656 147	802 505	898 485
Unemployment	..	..	..	42 864	91 194	107 819	126 400	144 868	351 991	198 311
2110 On a payroll basis	..	..	..	..	..	..	..	..	..	..
2120 On an income tax basis	..	..	..	..	..	..	..	..	..	..
2200 Employers	..	..	..	1 213 190	2 402 941	2 043 771	2 280 505	2 637 330	2 452 495	2 590 147
Pensions	..	..	..	734 456	1 508 490	1 800 864	2 254 959	2 235 536	1 889 638	2 037 421
Health	..	..	..	385 019	693 705	169 202	25 546	398 618	561 654	551 374
Unemployment	..	..	..	93 715	200 746	73 705	0	3 176	1 203	1 352
2210 On a payroll basis	..	..	..	..	..	..	..	..	..	..
2220 On an income tax basis	..	..	..	..	..	..	..	..	..	..
2300 Self-employed or non-employed	..	..	..	873	2 534	0	0	0	0	0
Pensions: of which	..	..	..	0	0	..	..	..	..	..
Self-employed	..	..	..	0	0	..	..	..	..	..
Unemployed	..	..	..	0	0	..	..	..	..	..
Retired	..	..	..	0	0	..	..	..	..	..
Other	..	..	..	0	0	..	..	..	..	..
Health: of which	..	..	..	873	2 534	..	..	..	..	..
Self-employed	..	..	..	873	2 534	..	..	..	..	..
Unemployed	..	..	..	0	0	..	..	..	..	..
Retired	..	..	..	0	0	..	..	..	..	..
Other	..	..	..	0	0	..	..	..	..	..
2310 On a payroll basis	..	..	..	..	..	..	..	..	..	..
2320 On an income tax basis	..	..	..	..	..	..	..	..	..	..
2400 Unallocable between 2100, 2200 and 2300	..	..	..	17 368	55 037	23 155	25 654	25 211	26 131	26 781
2410 On a payroll basis	..	..	..	..	..	..	..	..	..	..
2420 On an income tax basis	..	..	..	..	..	..	..	..	..	..
3000 Taxes on payroll and workforce	..	..	..	**183 430**	**82 068**	**113 689**	**206 426**	**241 750**	**340 175**	**410 179**
Rehabilitation contribution	..	..	..	2 184	13 559	56 004	64 400	67 460	80 661	92 654
Training levy	..	..	..	13 186	36 612	47 083	89 348	96 427	121 479	133 590
Wage guarantee contribution	..	..	..	0	0	0	0	0	0	0
Communal tax on enterprises	..	..	..	1 192	1 261	1 170	2	0	0	0
Health contribution	..	..	..	166 869	20 427	0	0	0	0	0
Medicine tax	..	..	..	0	10 209	9 431	9 547	10 283	12 757	11 113
Tax on home-workers	..	..	..	0	0	1	23	29	29	24
Lump sum tax for small taxpayers	..	..	..	0	0	0	31 241	55 409	100 972	127 779
Small business tax	..	..	..	0	0	0	11 865	12 142	24 277	45 019
4000 Taxes on property	..	..	..	**89 024**	**202 711**	**312 059**	**388 824**	**437 329**	**408 876**	**417 804**
4100 Recurrent taxes on immovable property	..	..	..	30 810	72 071	92 525	190 249	200 906	218 058	219 132
Land tax	..	..	..	0	0	0	0	0	0	0
Building tax	..	..	..	22 262	54 556	71 025	102 719	111 963	123 130	126 277
Development land tax	..	..	..	3 099	6 900	9 861	19 395	19 102	24 018	23 165
Communal tax on recreational howes	..	..	..	893	1 412	1 515	21	26	8	0
Communal tax on households	..	..	..	4 557	9 069	10 124	13 175	13 451	14 765	14 621
Luxury tax	..	..	..	0	134	0	0	0	0	0
Public utility tax	..	..	..	0	0	0	54 939	55 906	55 042	54 254
Community tax	..	..	..	0	0	0	0	458	1 095	815
4110 Households	..	..	..	..	..	..	..	..	..	..
4120 Others	..	..	..	..	..	..	..	..	..	..

	1965	1980	1990	2000	2007	2010	2013	2015	2017	2018
4200 Recurrent taxes on net wealth	..	..	..	0	0	135 652	128 560	135 661	51 594	42 591
Surtax payable by financial institutions	..	..	..	..	..	135 652	128 560	135 661	51 594	42 591
4210 Individual	..	..	..	..	..	..	..	..	..	..
4220 Corporate	..	..	..	..	..	..	..	..	..	..
4300 Estate, inheritance and gift taxes	..	..	..	5 460	13 175	6 264	5 307	7 373	9 393	8 519
4310 Estate and inheritance taxes	..	..	..	4 020	10 775	4 243	4 097	6 230	8 164	7 313
Inheritance tax-local	..	..	..	2 010	4 658	1 858	0	0	0	0
Inheritance tax-central	..	..	..	2 010	6 117	2 385	4 097	6 230	8 164	7 313
4320 Gift taxes	..	..	..	1 440	2 400	2 021	1 210	1 143	1 229	1 206
Gift tax-local	..	..	..	720	1 038	885	0	0	0	0
Gift tax-central	..	..	..	720	1 363	1 136	1 210	1 143	1 229	1 206
4400 Taxes on financial and capital transactions	..	..	..	52 754	117 465	77 618	64 708	93 389	129 831	147 562
Property transfer tax-local	..	..	..	26 349	50 783	33 990	0	0	0	0
Property transfer tax-central	..	..	..	26 405	66 682	43 628	64 708	93 389	129 831	147 562
4500 Non-recurrent taxes	..	..	..	0	0	0	0	0	0	0
4510 On net wealth	..	..	..	..	..	..	..	..	..	..
4520 Other non-recurrent taxes	..	..	..	..	..	..	..	..	..	..
4600 Other recurrent taxes on property	..	..	..	0	0	0	0	0	0	0
5000 Taxes on goods and services	**..**	**..**	**..**	**2 081 439**	**3 832 361**	**4 383 865**	**5 127 520**	**5 936 435**	**6 385 910**	**7 148 811**
5100 Taxes on production, sale, transfer, etc.	..	..	..	2 052 712	3 751 218	4 272 312	5 002 824	5 798 298	6 236 617	6 986 982
5110 General taxes	..	..	..	1 340 572	2 622 027	3 010 781	3 414 342	4 099 741	4 461 713	5 042 361
5111 Value added taxes	..	..	..	1 153 750	2 013 271	2 325 608	2 693 555	3 309 540	3 626 566	4 129 537
5112 Sales tax	..	..	..	0	0	37 795	47 927	50 635	65 133	73 573
Public health product tax	..	..	..	..	..	0	19 090	29 882	34 171	40 727
Hydrocarbons stockholding fee	..	..	..	..	..	37 795	28 837	20 753	30 962	32 846
5113 Other	..	..	..	186 823	608 756	647 378	672 860	739 566	770 014	839 251
Local tax on company sales	..	..	..	186 823	427 134	443 093	500 868	584 380	638 731	711 276
Simplified business tax	..	..	..	0	152 812	181 880	110 021	89 406	63 641	54 117
Research and development contribution	..	..	..	0	28 810	22 405	61 971	65 780	67 642	73 858
5120 Taxes on specific goods and services	..	..	..	712 140	1 129 192	1 261 531	1 588 482	1 698 557	1 774 904	1 944 621
5121 Excise duties	..	..	..	533 502	969 730	929 881	992 269	1 119 189	1 157 642	1 270 130
Road fund petrol tax	..	..	..	0	0	0	0	0	0	0
Alcohol production duty	..	..	..	3 848	5 621	3 021	196	8 007	6 803	8 078
Water fund tax	..	..	..	6 017	13 171	14 444	13 164	12 305	12 225	12 701
Forestry fund tax	..	..	..	2 858	3 353	284	0	0	0	0
Environment petrol tax	..	..	..	14 837	19 447	17 274	46 711	65 534	77 792	77 024
Budget excises (central budget)	..	..	..	505 942	916 869	877 778	915 546	1 015 555	1 041 979	1 153 070
Coffee	..	..	..	3 200	0	0	0	0	0	0
Alcohol	..	..	..	53 500	88 600	83 078	85 487	87 369	86 315	104 113
Tobacco	..	..	..	107 000	252 400	251 778	312 509	321 922	294 071	349 483
Petrol	..	..	..	156 000	218 200	216 728	189 755	206 220	221 662	230 138
Diesel	..	..	..	157 000	256 600	293 588	308 736	375 026	411 037	441 366
Other oil	..	..	..	6 000	2 200	2 567	3 451	3 608	3 873	2 617
Other budget excises	..	..	..	30 343	93 442	30 039	15 608	21 410	25 021	25 353
Energy tax	..	..	..	0	11 269	17 080	16 652	17 788	18 843	19 257
5122 Profits of fiscal monopolies	..	..	..	0	0	0	0	0	0	0
5123 Customs and import duties	..	..	..	137 730	37 174	33 446	35 307	52 395	57 423	79 130
Customs duties	..	..	..	137 730	37 174	33 446	35 307	52 395	57 423	79 130
5124 Taxes on exports	..	..	..	0	0	0	0	0	0	0
5125 Taxes on investment goods	..	..	..	0	0	0	0	0	0	0

	1965	1980	1990	2000	2007	2010	2013	2015	2017	2018
5126 Taxes on specific services	..	..	..	40 908	106 629	297 554	507 201	465 479	504 256	567 329
Gambling tax	..	..	..	27 935	71 804	62 718	41 316	44 972	38 066	39 265
Tourism tax	..	..	..	4 379	0	0	0	0	0	0
Communal tourism tax	..	..	..	2 943	4 935	5 798	8 411	10 475	13 602	14 863
Cultural contribution	..	..	..	4 387	8 432	1 096	105	127	93	152
Pork slaughterhouse tax	..	..	..	32	0	0	0	0	0	0
Breeding contribution	..	..	..	899	919	0	0	0	0	0
Medicine tax	..	..	..	0	19 789	28 104	40 496	45 529	45 939	48 676
Surtax payable by financial institutions	..	..	..	0	0	39 611	1 217	4 155	3 957	3 269
Specific sectors' surtax	..	..	..	0	0	151 693	9 815	285	1 112	669
Telecommunication services tax	..	..	..	0	0	0	50 176	54 516	53 609	53 732
Accident tax	..	..	..	0	0	0	23 313	27 694	37 904	43 801
Insurance tax	..	..	..	0	0	4 018	28 088	30 108	35 729	40 010
Financial transaction levy	..	..	..	0	0	0	289 321	205 616	216 337	234 364
Waste dumping contribution	..	..	..	0	0	0	6 639	11 123	12 036	14 648
Advertising tax	..	..	..	0	0	0	0	5 675	4 730	13 903
Protection Fund levies (BEVA)	..	..	..	0	0	1 036	1 000	2 600	10 221	7 545
Protection Fund levies (OBA)	..	..	..	0	0	2 435	7 299	14 391	15 613	15 347
Protection Fund levies (Resolution Fund)	..	..	..	0	0	0	0	7 290	8 712	10 553
Protection Fund levies (SZHTKA)	..	..	..	0	0	0	5	923	1 023	1 159
Protection Fund levies (KA)	..	..	..	0	0	0	0	0	5 573	4 285
Tourism development contribution	..	..	..	0	0	0	0	0	0	21 088
Protection Fund Levies (PGA)	..	..	..	332	750	1 045	0	0	0	0
5127 Other taxes on internat. trade and transactions	..	..	..	0	0	0	0	0	0	0
Previous differential producer's turnover tax	..	..	..	..	..	..	..	..	..	..
5128 Other taxes	..	..	..	0	15 659	650	53 705	61 494	55 583	28 032
Sugar duty	..	..	..	..	15 659	650	881	765	854	0
Payments by companies in the energy sector (MAVIR)	..	..	..	0	0	0	52 824	60 729	54 729	28 032
5130 Unallocable between 5110 and 5120	..	..	..	0	0	0	0	0	0	0
5200 Taxes on use of goods and perform activities	..	..	..	28 727	81 143	111 553	124 696	138 137	149 293	161 829
5210 Recurrent taxes	..	..	..	25 454	74 268	106 903	121 126	130 238	136 129	149 641
Tax on domestically registered vehicles-local	..	..	..	12 622	62 432	71 112	69 248	73 248	76 361	79 811
Tax on domestically registered vehicles-extra budget	..	..	..	0	0	0	0	0	0	0
Tax on domestically registered vehicles-central	..	..	..	8 250	0	79	0	0	0	0
Tax on foreign registered vehicles extra budget fund	..	..	..	0	0	0	0	0	0	0
Tax on foreign registered vehicles-central	..	..	..	3 078	1 655	1 397	0	0	0	0
Company car tax	..	..	..	0	0	25 867	32 935	31 570	33 339	35 676
5211 Paid by households: motor vehicles	..	..	..	0	0	0	0	0	0	0
5212 Paid by others: motor vehicles	..	..	..	0	0	0	0	0	0	0
5213 Paid in respect of other goods	..	..	..	1 504	10 181	8 448	18 943	25 420	26 429	34 154
Environmental protection charge	..	..	..	5	13	27	0	0	0	0
Fishing development contribution	..	..	..	40	104	0	0	0	0	0
Environmental pollution charge	..	..	..	0	8 785	7 653	7 861	6 680	5 109	6 303
Air pollution levy	..	..	..	751	610	53	0	0	0	0
Water pollution levy	..	..	..	225	186	0	0	0	0	0
Toxic waste levy	..	..	..	65	42	130	0	0	0	0
Noise abatement levy	..	..	..	13	8	19	0	0	0	0
Unidentified environmental protection levies paid to local governments	..	..	..	404	433	566	521	265	274	193
Sale of emission allowances	..	..	..	0	0	0	10 561	17 479	19 830	26 411
Concession fees (tobacco shops)	..	..	..	0	0	0	0	996	1 216	1 247
5220 Non-recurrent taxes	..	..	..	3 273	6 875	4 650	3 570	7 899	13 164	12 188
Land protection levy	..	..	..	1 640	3 777	2 488	1 881	3 610	8 770	7 555
Vehicle weight fee	..	..	..	805	1 288	820	624	0	0	0
Game protection contribution	..	..	..	178	176	1	0	0	0	0
Casino license fee	..	..	..	650	1 635	1 341	1 065	4 289	4 394	4 633
5300 Unallocable between 5100 and 5200	..	..	..	0	0	0	0	0	0	0
6000 Other taxes	**..**	**..**	**..**	**32 857**	**56 348**	**59 378**	**56 836**	**56 824**	**47 581**	**38 363**
Unallocable tax penalties	..	..	..	23 546	33 321	36 250	37 507	35 530	24 783	15 565
6100 Paid solely by business	..	..	..	9 311	23 028	23 128	19 329	21 294	22 798	22 798
Nuclear contribution	..	..	..	9 311	22 828	23 128	19 329	21 294	22 798	22 798
Medicine tax	..	..	..	0	200	0	0	0	0	0
6200 Other	..	..	..	0	0	0	0	0	0	0
Memorandum item										
Customs duties collected on behalf of the EU	..	..	..	..	27 981	25 004	26 337	38 960	45 403	63 431
Total tax revenue on cash basis	**..**	**..**	**..**	**5 140 924**	**10 020 734**	**10 137 257**	**11 479 816**	**13 218 609**	**14 412 430**	**15 345 821**
Total tax revenue on accrual basis	**..**	**..**	**..**	**..**	**10 115 072**	**10 142 330**	**11 687 770**	**13 531 760**	**14 867 258**	**15 976 928**

	1965	1980	1990	2000	2007	2010	2013	2015	2017	2018
Conciliation with National Accounts										
Additional taxes included in National Accounts	..	..	..	..	45 120	49 057	73 565	76 364	73 769	74 070
Social security contributions	..	..	..	..	0	11 675	36 063	40 688	39 324	39 096
Duty for state procedures	..	..	..	..	45 084	37 331	37 417	35 653	34 424	34 954
Other taxes	..	..	..	..	36	51	85	23	21	20
Taxes excluded from National Accounts	..	..	..	..	-49 439	-53 707	-51 838	-48 414	-37 311	-28 483
Water fund tax	..	..	..	..	-13 171	-14 444	-13 164	-12 305	-12 225	-12 701
Tax on foreign registered vehicles	..	..	..	..	-1 655	-1 397	0	0	0	0
Environmental protection fee	..	..	..	..	-446	-593	-520	-265	-274	-193
Air pollution levy	..	..	..	..	-610	-53	0	0	0	0
Water pollution levy	..	..	..	..	-186	0	0	0	0	0
Toxic waste levy	..	..	..	..	-42	-130	0	0	0	0
Noise abatement levy	..	..	..	..	-8	-19	0	0	0	0
Vehicle weight fee	..	..	..	..	0	-820	-624	0	0	0
Unallocable tax penalties	..	..	..	..	-33 320	-36 250	-37 507	-35 530	-24 783	-15 565
Tax on home-workers	..	..	..	..	0	-1	-23	-29	-29	-24
Specific sectors' surtax correction	..	..	..	..	0	0	0	-285	0	0
Difference in treatment of tax credits	..	..	..	..	0	0	0	0	0	0
Capital transfer for uncollected revenue	..	..	..	..	0	0	0	0	0	0
Voluntary social security contributions	..	..	..	..	1 762	1 693	1 523	1 229	1 163	1 090
Miscellaneous differences	..	..	..	..	-2 687	-28	2	-43	3 130	-866
Inheritance tax	..	..	..	..	0	0	0	0	0	0
Gift tax	..	..	..	..	0	0	0	0	0	0
Property transfer tax	..	..	..	..	0	0	0	0	0	0
Rounding	..	..	..	..	4	-2	2	0	2	0
Taxes on income and profits	..	..	..	..	-2 087	0	0	0	0	0
Corporate income tax	..	..	..	..	0	0	0	0	0	0
Customs duties	..	..	..	..	-603	-26	0	-43	3 128	-866
Vehicle weight fee	..	..	..	..	0	0	0	0	0	0
Environment petrol tax	..	..	..	..	0	0	0	0	0	0
Social security contributions	..	..	..	..	0	0	0	0	0	0
Credit institutions' special tax	..	..	..	..	0	0	0	0	0	0
National Accounts: Taxes and actual social contributions	..	..	..	..	10 109 828	10 139 345	11 711 022	13 560 896	14 908 009	16 022 739
Imputed social contributions	..	..	..	..	21 113	24 841	21 669	28 783	18 618	22 374
National Accounts: Taxes and all social contributions	..	..	..	..	10 130 941	10 164 186	11 732 691	13 589 679	14 926 627	16 045 113

.. Not available

Note: Year ending 31st December.

For 2002-2018, data are on accrual basis. Preliminary data for 2019 are on a cash basis.

Heading 5121: the aggregate figure for excise tax revenues is on a cash basis. Revenue from specific excises is in several cases reported on an accrual basis.

Tax base for "Environment petrol tax" is broader than petrol only.

Heading 5123: part of environmentally related payments is attributable to Local government. It is not possible to present a more detailed breakdown of these figures.

Source: Ministry of Finance, Economic Department.

StatLink https://doi.org/10.1787/888934211927

Table 5.15. Iceland: Details of tax revenue, 1965-2018

Million ISK

	1965	1980	1990	2000	2007	2010	2013	2015	2017	2018
Total tax revenue	**60**	**4 731**	**114 932**	**254 556**	**531 760**	**540 276**	**676 142**	**812 002**	**982 792**	**1 037 608**
1000 Taxes on income, profits and capital gains	**13**	**1 211**	**34 106**	**101 473**	**241 378**	**239 664**	**315 577**	**380 979**	**483 996**	**511 724**
1100 Of individuals	12	1 092	30 908	88 492	180 070	197 318	258 623	297 979	374 437	412 430
1110 On income and profits	..	..	30 908	88 492	180 070	197 318	258 623	297 979	374 437	412 430
1120 On capital gains	..	..	..	0	0	0	0	0	0	0
1200 Corporate	1	119	3 198	8 356	32 555	14 609	40 479	52 544	79 993	67 724
1210 On profits	..	..	3 198	8 356	32 555	14 609	40 479	52 544	79 993	67 724
1220 On capital gains	..	..	..	0	0	0	0	0	0	0
1300 Unallocable between 1100 and 1200	0	0	0	4 625	28 754	27 737	16 475	30 457	29 566	31 569
2000 Social security contributions	**5**	**102**	**3 607**	**19 680**	**39 594**	**63 599**	**69 899**	**79 707**	**89 649**	**98 230**
2100 Employees	0	0	315	..	..	..	..	..	..	..
2110 On a payroll basis	..	..	..	..	..	..	..	..	..	..
2120 On an income tax basis	..	..	..	..	..	..	..	..	..	..
2200 Employers	5	102	3 292	..	..	..	..	..	..	..
2210 On a payroll basis	..	..	..	..	..	..	..	..	..	..
2220 On an income tax basis	..	..	..	..	..	..	..	..	..	..
2300 Self-employed or non-employed	0	0	0	..	..	..	..	..	..	..
2310 On a payroll basis	..	..	..	..	..	..	..	..	..	..
2320 On an income tax basis	..	..	..	..	..	..	..	..	..	..
2400 Unallocable between 2100, 2200 and 2300	0	0	0	19 680	39 594	63 599	69 899	79 707	89 649	98 230
2410 On a payroll basis	..	..	..	19 680	39 594	63 599	69 899	79 707	89 649	98 230
2420 On an income tax basis	..	..	..	0	0	0	0	0	0	0
3000 Taxes on payroll and workforce	**1**	**180**	**4 071**	**184**	**1 519**	**2 827**	**6 534**	**6 638**	**7 946**	**8 542**
4000 Taxes on property	**2**	**297**	**9 689**	**19 983**	**32 523**	**38 068**	**46 493**	**43 487**	**53 958**	**56 798**
4100 Recurrent taxes on immovable property	1	138	4 131	10 107	20 567	28 542	30 664	34 879	43 364	46 497
4110 Households	0	50	1 862	..	..	..	..	..	..	..
4120 Others	1	88	2 269	..	..	..	..	..	..	..
4200 Recurrent taxes on net wealth	0	69	2 402	5 173	-8	3 849	8 886	657	346	100
4210 Individual	..	29	1 476	..	..	..	..	..	..	..
4220 Corporate	..	40	926	..	..	..	..	..	..	..
4300 Estate, inheritance and gift taxes	0	6	235	765	1 663	2 613	2 437	2 919	4 268	4 703
4310 Estate and inheritance taxes	0	6	235	765	1 663	2 613	2 437	2 919	4 268	4 703
4320 Gift taxes	0	0	0	0	0	0	0	0	0	0
4400 Taxes on financial and capital transactions	1	84	2 921	3 143	9 484	2 656	3 973	4 327	4 581	4 962
4500 Non-recurrent taxes	0	0	0	113	460	146	233	362	528	470
4510 On net wealth	..	..	..	0	0	0	0	0	0	0
4520 Other non-recurrent taxes	..	..	..	113	460	146	233	362	528	470
4600 Other recurrent taxes on property	0	0	0	681	356	263	299	343	871	65
5000 Taxes on goods and services	**37**	**2 834**	**58 943**	**112 245**	**214 988**	**190 131**	**226 619**	**262 828**	**330 795**	**345 295**
5100 Taxes on production, sale, transfer, etc.	37	2 778	56 564	100 669	191 957	178 995	215 271	250 095	311 200	324 763
5110 General taxes	10	1 368	37 084	72 667	137 593	122 393	149 828	183 674	233 951	244 624
5111 Value added taxes	0	0	32 698	72 667	137 593	122 393	149 828	183 674	233 951	244 624
5112 Sales tax	10	1 368	4 386	0	0	0	0	0	0	0
5113 Other	0	0	0	0	0	0	0	0	0	0
5120 Taxes on specific goods and services	27	1 410	19 480	28 002	54 364	56 603	65 444	66 421	77 249	80 138
5121 Excise duties	1	311	2 346	23 585	45 891	46 711	55 171	56 909	67 717	69 524
5122 Profits of fiscal monopolies	5	263	5 986	0	0	0	0	0	0	0
5123 Customs and import duties	20	715	9 181	2 702	5 446	5 950	5 815	4 989	3 912	4 118
5124 Taxes on exports	1	2	0	1	0	2	0	0	0	0
5125 Taxes on investment goods	0	0	0	0	0	0	0	0	0	0
5126 Taxes on specific services	1	69	1 404	1 715	3 026	3 940	4 457	4 523	5 620	6 497
5127 Other taxes on internat. trade and transactions	0	50	563	0	0	0	0	0	0	0
5128 Other taxes	0	0	0	0	0	0	0	0	0	0
5130 Unallocable between 5110 and 5120	0	0	0	0	0	0	0	0	0	0
5200 Taxes on use of goods and perform activities	1	56	2 379	11 576	23 032	11 135	11 347	12 733	19 595	20 533
5210 Recurrent taxes	1	56	2 379	..	..	..	..	..	..	..
5211 Paid by households: motor vehicles	0	10	970	..	..	..	..	..	..	..
5212 Paid by others: motor vehicles	0	41	1 331	..	..	..	..	..	..	..
5213 Paid in respect of other goods	0	5	78	..	..	..	..	..	..	..
5220 Non-recurrent taxes	0	0	0	..	..	..	..	..	..	..
5300 Unallocable between 5100 and 5200	0	0	0	0	0	0	0	0	0	0
6000 Other taxes	**2**	**107**	**4 516**	**991**	**1 758**	**5 988**	**11 020**	**38 364**	**16 448**	**17 019**
6100 Paid solely by business	2	107	4 145	418	628	763	5 255	32 477	10 331	10 414
6200 Other	0	0	371	573	1 130	5 225	5 766	5 887	6 117	6 605

	1965	1980	1990	2000	2007	2010	2013	2015	2017	2018
Non-wastable tax credits										
Non-wastable tax credits against 1110	..	..	..	..	..	..	0	0	0	0
Tax expenditure component	..	..	..	..	..	..	0	0	0	0
Transfer component	..	..	..	..	..	..	0	0	0	0
Non-wastable tax credits against 1210	..	..	..	..	..	..	1 085	1 304	2 659	3 079
Tax expenditure component	..	..	..	..	..	..	148	176	477	572
Transfer component	..	..	..	..	..	..	937	1 128	2 182	2 507
Total tax revenue on cash basis	**60**	**4 731**	**114 932**	**..**	**..**	**..**	**..**	**..**	**..**	**..**
Total tax revenue on accrual basis	**..**	**..**	**..**	**254 556**	**531 760**	**540 276**	**676 142**	**812 002**	**982 792**	**1 037 608**
Conciliation with National Accounts										
Additional taxes included in National Accounts	..	..	..	0	0	0	0	0	0	0
Taxes excluded from National Accounts	..	..	..	-765	-1 663	-2 613	-2 437	-2 919	-4 268	-4 703
Estate and inheritance taxes (4310)	..	..	..	-765	-1 663	-2 613	-2 437	-2 919	-4 268	-4 703
Difference in treatment of tax credits	..	..	..	0	0	0	0	0	0	0
Capital transfer for uncollected revenue	..	..	..	0	0	0	0	0	0	0
Voluntary social security contributions	..	..	..	0	0	0	0	0	0	0
Miscellaneous differences	..	..	..	0	0	0	0	0	0	0
National Accounts: Taxes and actual social contributions	..	..	..	253 791	530 097	537 662	673 704	809 084	978 524	1 032 904
Imputed social contributions	..	..	..	0	0	0	0	0	0	0
National Accounts: Taxes and all social contributions	..	..	..	253 791	530 097	537 662	673 704	809 084	978 524	1 032 904

.. Not available

Note: Year ending 31st December.

From 1998 data are on accrual basis.

Source: Ministry of Finance, Economic Department.

StatLink https://doi.org/10.1787/888934211946

Table 5.16. Ireland: Details of tax revenue, 1965-2018

Million EUR

	1965	1980	1990	2000	2007	2010	2013	2015	2017	2018
Total tax revenue	**317**	**4 046**	**12 260**	**33 363**	**60 790**	**46 399**	**51 947**	**61 424**	**67 630**	**73 468**
Total tax revenue exclusive of taxes collected for the EU	..	..	**12 075**	**33 155**	**60 517**	**46 170**	**51 700**	**61 097**	**67 197**	**73 035**
1000 Taxes on income, profits and capital gains	**82**	**1 478**	**4 662**	**14 551**	**25 364**	**18 617**	**21 298**	**26 599**	**29 601**	**33 291**
1100 Of individuals	53	1 294	4 059	10 650	18 970	14 665	17 020	19 722	21 399	22 889
1110 On income and profits	53	1 286	4 023	9 876	15 872	14 320	16 652	19 053	20 573	21 897
Income tax	66	1 286	4 023	9 876	15 872	14 320	16 652	19 053	20 573	21 897
Surtax	3	0	0	0	0	0	0	0	0	0
Income tax paid by corporations	-17	0	0	0	0	0	0	0	0	0
1120 On capital gains	0	8	36	774	3 097	345	369	669	826	992
1200 Corporate	29	184	603	3 900	6 395	3 945	4 273	6 873	8 198	10 402
1210 On profits	29	184	603	3 900	6 395	3 945	4 273	6 873	8 198	10 402
Corporation profits tax	12	2	0	0	0	0	0	0	0	0
Corporation tax	0	176	603	3 885	6 393	3 944	4 272	6 872	8 197	10 401
Income tax paid by corporation	17	0	0	0	0	0	0	0	0	0
Agricultural produce duty	0	6	0	14	1	1	1	1	1	1
1220 On capital gains	0	0	0	0	0	0	0	0	0	0
1300 Unallocable between 1100 and 1200	0	0	0	2	0	7	4	4	4	0
2000 Social security contributions	**21**	**578**	**1 729**	**3 966**	**8 143**	**8 458**	**9 359**	**10 524**	**11 661**	**12 707**
2100 Employees	10	190	570	962	1 926	3 195	3 630	3 853	3 963	4 368
2110 On a payroll basis	..	..	570	962	1 926	3 195	3 630	3 853	3 963	4 368
2120 On an income tax basis	..	..	0	0	0	0	0	0	0	0
2200 Employers	10	380	1 092	2 814	5 796	4 932	5 326	6 211	7 177	7 734
2210 On a payroll basis	..	..	1 092	2 814	5 796	4 932	5 326	6 211	7 177	7 734
2220 On an income tax basis	..	..	0	0	0	0	0	0	0	0
2300 Self-employed or non-employed	0	8	67	190	421	331	403	460	522	605
2310 On a payroll basis	..	..	67	190	421	331	403	460	522	605
2320 On an income tax basis	..	..	0	0	0	0	0	0	0	0
2400 Unallocable between 2100, 2200 and 2300	0	0	0	0	0	0	0	0	0	0
2410 On a payroll basis	..	..	..	..	..	..	..	..	..	..
2420 On an income tax basis	..	..	..	..	..	..	..	..	..	..
3000 Taxes on payroll and workforce	**0**	**9**	**159**	**15**	**411**	**310**	**314**	**357**	**431**	**565**
4000 Taxes on property	**48**	**213**	**569**	**1 902**	**4 789**	**2 389**	**3 632**	**3 918**	**3 852**	**4 278**
4100 Recurrent taxes on immovable property	39	139	312	587	1 233	1 322	1 724	1 864	1 856	1 880
4110 Households	..	..	..	..	..	..	..	..	..	..
4120 Others	..	..	..	..	..	..	..	..	..	..
4200 Recurrent taxes on net wealth	0	1	0	0	0	0	536	169	0	0
4210 Individual	..	..	..	..	..	..	0	0	0	0
4220 Corporate	..	..	..	..	..	..	536	169	0	0
4300 Estate, inheritance and gift taxes	6	14	48	225	405	235	278	401	448	518
4310 Estate and inheritance taxes	6	14	45	210	337	192	259	365	417	469
Estate duty	5	..	0	0	0	0	0	0	0	0
Legacy duty	1	..	0	0	0	0	0	0	0	0
Succession duty	0	..	0	0	0	0	0	0	0	0
4320 Gift taxes	0	0	3	15	68	43	20	36	31	50
4400 Taxes on financial and capital transactions	3	59	209	1 090	3 151	832	1 093	1 484	1 547	1 880
Stamp duty	3	59	209	1 090	3 151	832	1 093	1 484	1 547	1 880
4500 Non-recurrent taxes	0	0	0	0	0	0	0	0	0	0
4510 On net wealth	..	..	..	..	..	..	..	..	..	..
4520 Other non-recurrent taxes	..	..	..	..	..	..	..	..	..	..
4600 Other recurrent taxes on property	0	0	0	0	0	0	0	0	0	0
5000 Taxes on goods and services	**167**	**1 769**	**5 140**	**12 929**	**22 082**	**16 619**	**17 321**	**20 013**	**22 076**	**22 617**
5100 Taxes on production, sale, transfer, etc.	155	1 741	4 939	12 374	20 982	15 319	15 789	18 036	20 080	20 650
5110 General taxes	18	597	2 500	7 643	14 355	10 067	10 372	11 831	13 060	14 175
5111 Value added taxes	0	597	2 500	7 643	14 355	10 067	10 372	11 831	13 060	14 175
Value added tax	..	597	2 500	7 643	14 355	10 067	10 372	11 831	13 060	14 175
5112 Sales tax	18	0	0	0	0	0	0	0	0	0
Turnover tax	18	..	..	..	..	..	..	..	..	..
Wholesale tax	0	..	..	..	..	..	..	..	..	..
5113 Other	0	0	0	0	0	0	0	0	0	0
5120 Taxes on specific goods and services	137	1 143	2 439	4 731	6 627	5 252	5 417	6 205	7 020	6 475

	1965	1980	1990	2000	2007	2010	2013	2015	2017	2018
5121 Excise duties	124	1 045	2 084	4 402	6 125	4 859	5 013	5 474	6 163	5 487
Beer	19	192	356	475	459	316	363	418	419	433
Oils	31	330	745	1 491	2 204	2 099	2 035	2 120	2 233	2 154
Spirits	16	148	153	241	363	244	282	313	352	373
Table waters	0	11	23	0	0	0	0	0	0	0
Tobacco	50	187	419	1 035	1 192	1 160	1 064	1 055	1 397	748
Wine, cider, perry	1	18	46	154	297	266	354	414	446	431
Motor vehicle (incl. tyres)	7	148	331	985	1 554	395	459	702	850	872
Others	1	11	11	20	57	379	457	451	467	476
5122 Profits of fiscal monopolies	0	0	0	0	0	0	0	0	0	0
5123 Customs and import duties	10	62	147	208	273	229	247	327	334	325
5124 Taxes on exports	0	0	0	0	0	0	0	0	0	0
UE agriculture levies	..	..	0	..	..	..	..	..	..	..
5125 Taxes on investment goods	0	0	0	0	0	0	0	0	0	0
5126 Taxes on specific services	3	21	171	122	229	164	157	404	523	662
Duty on betting	2	19	37	59	36	30	26	37	52	51
Sweepstakes duty	1	1	0	0	0	0	0	0	0	0
Bank levy	0	0	46	61	66	-70	-23	190	249	422
Other	0	1	88	2	127	204	154	178	221	190
5127 Other taxes on internat. trade and transactions	0	0	0	0	0	0	0	0	0	0
5128 Other taxes	0	14	37	0	0	0	0	0	0	0
5130 Unallocable between 5110 and 5120	0	0	0	0	0	0	0	0	0	0
5200 Taxes on use of goods and perform activities	11	28	201	555	1 100	1 300	1 532	1 977	1 996	1 967
5210 Recurrent taxes	11	28	201	555	1 100	1 300	1 532	1 977	1 996	1 967
5211 Paid by households: motor vehicles	6	14	100	373	723	768	888	904	824	799
5212 Paid by others: motor vehicles	5	11	82	124	239	256	284	281	255	245
5213 Paid in respect of other goods	0	3	20	58	138	276	360	792	917	922
5220 Non-recurrent taxes	0	0	0	0	0	0	0	0	0	0
5300 Unallocable between 5100 and 5200	0	0	0	0	0	0	0	0	0	0
6000 Other taxes	**0**	**0**	**0**	**0**	**0**	**6**	**23**	**12**	**8**	**9**
6100 Paid solely by business	..	..	..	..	..	..	..	..	..	..
6200 Other	..	..	..	0	0	6	23	12	8	9
Memorandum items										
Customs duties collected on behalf of the EU	..	..	148	208	273	229	247	327	334	325
SRF contributions collected on behalf of the EU	..	..	..	..	..	..	..	..	98	107
Non-wastable tax credits										
Non-wastable tax credits against 1110	..	..	..	..	843	1 073	816	555	504	472
Tax expenditure component	..	..	0	0	843	1 073	816	555	504	472
Transfer component	..	..	0	0	0	0	0	0	0	0
Total tax revenue on cash basis	**317**	**4 046**	**12 260**	**32 997**	**60 836**	**46 609**	**51 979**	**61 393**	**67 835**	**73 466**
Total tax revenue on accrual basis	**..**	**..**	**..**	**33 363**	**60 790**	**46 399**	**51 947**	**61 424**	**67 630**	**73 468**
Conciliation with National Accounts										
Additional taxes included in National Accounts	..	..	..	0	0	178	178	177	178	182
Taxes excluded from National Accounts	..	..	..	0	0	0	0	0	0	0
Difference in treatment of tax credits	..	..	..	0	0	0	0	0	0	0
Capital transfer for uncollected revenue	..	..	..	0	0	0	0	0	0	0
Voluntary social security contributions	..	..	..	0	0	0	0	0	0	0
Miscellaneous differences	..	..	..	0	0	0	0	0	0	0
National Accounts: Taxes and actual social contributions	..	..	..	33 363	60 790	46 577	52 125	61 601	67 808	73 650
Imputed social contributions	..	..	..	1 366	2 579	1 053	1 669	1 797	2 247	2 244
National Accounts: Taxes and all social contributions	..	..	..	34 729	63 369	47 630	53 795	63 398	70 055	75 894

.. Not available

Note: The personal income tax data shown for the country table for Ireland is different to the ESA2010 presentation as the expenditure component of the payable tax credits are excluded in accordance with the OECD Interpretative Guide.

The data for years 1965 to 1973 are on fiscal year basis (commencing on 1st April) and are therefore not strictly comparable with the data for later years, which are on a calendar year basis.

From 1998, data are on accrual basis.

Heading 1200: Capital gains taxes paid by corporations are included in heading 1210.

Heading 2100: Includes contributions by self-employed and certain voluntary contributions.

Heading 2200: Since 1976 income tax paid by corporations and corporation profits tax have been replaced by corporation tax.

Heading 5111: Includes arrears of the wholesale and turnover taxes.

Tax receipts in 1988 were inflated by the success of the new arrangements for assessment and collection of tax. These arrangements included an amnesty for tax arrears paid by 30th September. This amnesty waived penalties and interest charge tax. It resulted in payments of 631 million of euros spread across the main tax headings.

Source: Annual Report of the Revenue Commissioners, Financial Accounts and National Income and Expenditure Accounts.

StatLink https://doi.org/10.1787/888934211965

Table 5.17. Israel: Details of tax revenue, 1965-2018

Million ILS

	1965	1980	1990	2000	2007	2010	2013	2015	2017	2018
Total tax revenue	..	..	..	**188 276**	**251 299**	**268 555**	**325 442**	**364 375**	**413 124**	**411 633**
1000 Taxes on income, profits and capital gains	..	..	..	**74 551**	**91 530**	**78 265**	**101 481**	**113 966**	**146 949**	**135 001**
1100 Of individuals	..	..	..	54 753	56 434	48 214	57 311	70 885	85 411	84 922
1110 On income and profits	..	..	..	53 698	55 213	47 550	55 881	68 405	79 411	82 022
On wages – deduction at source	..	..	..	45 278	45 515	40 159	46 458	54 087	62 431	65 249
On self employement income – deduction at source	..	..	..	2 655	3 676	3 135	3 891	4 880	5 243	5 772
On self employement income – other	..	..	..	5 764	6 022	4 256	5 532	9 438	11 737	11 001
1120 On capital gains	..	..	..	1 055	1 221	664	1 430	2 480	6 000	2 900
1200 Corporate	..	..	..	18 001	30 210	23 113	36 639	34 676	41 909	42 932
1210 On profits	..	..	..	16 109	27 582	22 291	33 939	33 476	40 049	40 962
Deduction at source	..	..	..	1 991	2 550	2 271	2 611	3 075	3 309	3 473
In lieu of VAT on the profits of Financial Institutions	..	..	..	1 290	2 200	1 920	2 440	1 910	2 070	2 150
Other	..	..	..	12 828	22 832	18 100	28 888	28 491	34 670	35 339
1220 On capital gains	..	..	..	1 892	2 628	822	2 700	1 200	1 860	1 970
1300 Unallocable between 1100 and 1200	..	..	..	1 797	4 886	6 938	7 531	8 405	19 629	7 147
Tax deducted at the source on the capital market	..	..	..	1 797	4 886	6 938	7 531	8 405	19 629	7 147
2000 Social security contributions	..	..	..	**27 565**	**37 909**	**45 343**	**53 364**	**59 561**	**66 783**	**69 016**
2100 Employees	..	..	..	15 771	23 093	27 788	31 537	34 692	37 884	39 232
2110 On a payroll basis	..	..	..	15 771	23 093	27 788	31 537	34 692	37 884	39 232
2120 On an income tax basis	..	..	..	0	0	0	0	0	0	0
2200 Employers	..	..	..	8 182	9 960	11 427	15 026	17 247	20 596	20 990
2210 On a payroll basis	..	..	..	8 182	9 960	11 427	15 026	17 247	20 596	20 990
2220 On an income tax basis	..	..	..	0	0	0	0	0	0	0
2300 Self-employed or non-employed	..	..	..	3 612	4 856	6 128	6 802	7 622	8 303	8 794
2310 On a payroll basis	..	..	..	3 612	4 856	6 128	6 802	7 622	8 303	8 794
2320 On an income tax basis	..	..	..	0	0	0	0	0	0	0
2400 Unallocable between 2100, 2200 and 2300	..	..	..	0	0	0	0	0	0	0
2410 On a payroll basis	..	..	..	..	..	..	..	..	..	..
2420 On an income tax basis	..	..	..	..	..	..	..	..	..	..
3000 Taxes on payroll and workforce	..	..	..	**6 850**	**9 920**	**10 280**	**12 780**	**13 770**	**15 196**	**15 828**
Employers tax on the the non-profit sector other than govt	..	..	..	1 250	1 500	320	390	410	404	502
In lieu of VAT on the wage-bill in the non-profit sector	..	..	..	4 260	6 580	7 650	9 540	10 320	11 203	11 948
In lieu VAT on the wage-bill in Financial Institutions	..	..	..	1 340	1 840	2 310	2 850	3 040	3 589	3 378
4000 Taxes on property	..	..	..	**16 935**	**24 282**	**28 817**	**32 680**	**38 804**	**40 949**	**42 285**
4100 Recurrent taxes on immovable property	..	..	..	11 311	16 156	18 768	21 541	23 765	25 296	26 311
Land tax	..	..	..	442	52	48	59	44	21	25
4110 Households	..	..	..	0	0	0	0	0	0	0
4120 Others	..	..	..	10 869	16 104	18 720	21 483	23 721	25 275	26 286
4200 Recurrent taxes on net wealth	..	..	..	0	0	0	0	0	0	0
4210 Individual	..	..	..	..	..	..	..	..	..	..
4220 Corporate	..	..	..	..	..	..	..	..	..	..
4300 Estate, inheritance and gift taxes	..	..	..	0	0	0	0	0	0	0
4310 Estate and inheritance taxes	..	..	..	..	..	..	..	..	..	..
4320 Gift taxes	..	..	..	..	..	..	..	..	..	..
4400 Taxes on financial and capital transactions	..	..	..	3 181	3 555	4 071	4 532	6 732	6 642	6 660
Transaction tax on the buyer of real estate	..	..	..	1 972	3 084	4 024	4 513	6 731	6 638	6 654
Transaction tax on the seller of real estate	..	..	..	206	404	27	19	1	4	6
Stamp tax	..	..	..	1 003	67	20	0	0	0	0
4500 Non-recurrent taxes	..	..	..	2 443	4 572	5 979	6 607	8 307	9 011	9 314
4510 On net wealth	..	..	..	0	0	0	0	0	0	0
4520 Other non-recurrent taxes	..	..	..	2 443	4 572	5 979	6 607	8 307	9 011	9 314
Capital gains tax on real estate	..	..	..	2 443	4 572	5 979	6 607	8 307	9 011	9 314
4600 Other recurrent taxes on property	..	..	..	0	0	0	0	0	0	0
5000 Taxes on goods and services	..	..	..	**62 375**	**87 658**	**105 850**	**125 137**	**138 274**	**143 247**	**149 503**
5100 Taxes on production, sale, transfer, etc.	..	..	..	57 887	81 107	98 092	116 335	128 277	133 293	138 931
5110 General taxes	..	..	..	49 876	67 569	79 945	97 357	107 765	110 971	117 251
5111 Value added taxes	..	..	..	39 805	53 982	65 508	81 524	90 824	94 531	99 442
5112 Sales tax	..	..	..	10 071	13 587	14 437	15 833	16 941	16 440	17 809
On domestic production	..	..	..	662	287	291	457	450	290	328
On imports	..	..	..	9 409	13 300	14 146	15 376	16 491	16 150	17 481
5113 Other	..	..	..	0	0	0	0	0	0	0
5120 Taxes on specific goods and services	..	..	..	8 012	13 538	18 147	18 978	20 512	22 322	21 680
5121 Excise duties	..	..	..	6 595	11 323	15 458	16 680	17 642	19 312	18 895
On domestically refined fuel	..	..	..	5 666	10 590	14 637	15 876	17 008	18 757	18 387
On domestically processed tobacco products	..	..	..	929	733	821	804	634	555	508
5122 Profits of fiscal monopolies	..	..	..	0	0	0	0	0	0	0
5123 Customs and import duties	..	..	..	1 417	2 215	2 689	2 298	2 870	3 010	2 785
5124 Taxes on exports	..	..	..	0	0	0	0	0	0	0

	1965	1980	1990	2000	2007	2010	2013	2015	2017	2018
5125 Taxes on investment goods	..	..	..	0	0	0	0	0	0	0
5126 Taxes on specific services	..	..	..	0	0	0	0	0	0	0
5127 Other taxes on internat. trade and transactions	..	..	..	0	0	0	0	0	0	0
5128 Other taxes	..	..	..	0	0	0	0	0	0	0
5130 Unallocable between 5110 and 5120	..	..	..	0	0	0	0	0	0	0
5200 Taxes on use of goods and perform activities	..	..	..	4 488	6 551	7 758	8 803	9 997	9 954	10 572
5210 Recurrent taxes	..	..	..	4 488	6 551	7 758	8 803	9 997	9 954	10 572
5211 Paid by households: motor vehicles	..	..	..	1 436	1 895	2 274	2 872	3 179	3 623	3 597
5212 Paid by others: motor vehicles	..	..	..	479	632	758	957	1 060	1 208	1 199
5213 Paid in respect of other goods	..	..	..	2 574	4 025	4 726	4 973	5 759	5 124	5 775
Licences collected by the Ministry of Transportation	..	..	..	257	535	350	132	196	61	128
Licences collected by the Ministry of Communication	..	..	..	151	0	274	299	338	199	338
Licences collected by other ministries	..	..	..	1 587	2 605	2 990	3 227	3 781	3 320	3 703
Business and professional licences paid locally	..	..	..	528	799	1 011	1 190	1 317	1 406	1 462
Other local authority fees	..	..	..	51	86	101	125	128	138	144
5220 Non-recurrent taxes	..	..	..	0	0	0	0	0	0	0
5300 Unallocable between 5100 and 5200	..	..	..	0	0	0	0	0	0	0
6000 Other taxes	**..**	**..**	**..**	**0**	**0**	**0**	**0**	**0**	**0**	**0**
6100 Paid solely by business	..	..	..	..	..	..	..	..	..	..
6200 Other	..	..	..	..	..	..	..	..	..	..
Non-wastable tax credits										
Non-wastable tax credits against 1110	..	..	..	..	..	87	911	1 415	1 589	807
Tax expenditure component	..	..	..	0	0	3	32	67	0	0
Transfer component	..	..	..	0	0	84	879	1 348	1 589	807
Non-wastable tax credits against 1210	..	..	..	0	0	0	0	0	0	0
Tax expenditure component	..	..	..	0	0	0	0	0	0	0
Transfer component	..	..	..	0	0	0	0	0	0	0
Total tax revenue on cash basis	**..**	**..**	**..**	**188 276**	**251 299**	**268 555**	**325 442**	**364 375**	**413 124**	**411 633**
Total tax revenue on accrual basis	**..**	**..**	**..**	**..**	**..**	**..**	**..**	**..**	**..**	**..**
Conciliation with National Accounts										
Additional taxes included in National Accounts	..	..	..	0	0	0	0	0	0	0
Taxes excluded from National Accounts	..	..	..	..	..	..	..	..	..	..
Difference in treatment of tax credits	..	..	..	..	..	..	..	..	..	..
Capital transfer for uncollected revenue	..	..	..	..	..	..	..	..	..	..
Voluntary social security contributions	..	..	..	..	..	..	..	..	..	..
Miscellaneous differences	..	..	..	..	..	..	..	..	..	..
National Accounts: Taxes and actual social contributions	..	..	..	188 276	251 299	268 555	325 442	364 375	413 124	411 633
Imputed social contributions	..	..	..	6 175	7 134	8 207	9 088	9 185	9 241	9 116
National Accounts: Taxes and all social contributions	..	..	..	194 451	258 433	276 762	334 530	373 560	422 364	420 749

.. Not available

Note: Year ending 31st December.

Data are on a cash basis.

Source: Israel Central Bureau of Statistics and Israel Ministry of Finance.

StatLink https://doi.org/10.1787/888934211984

Table 5.18. Italy: Details of tax revenue, 1965-2018

Million EUR

	1965	1980	1990	2000	2007	2010	2013	2015	2017	2018
Total tax revenue	**5 505**	**60 422**	**265 116**	**503 096**	**671 189**	**671 912**	**706 829**	**711 114**	**727 840**	**739 519**
Total tax revenue exclusive of taxes collected for the EU	..	..	**263 829**	**501 560**	**668 928**	**669 687**	**704 939**	**706 522**	**723 272**	**736 087**
1000 Taxes on income, profits and capital gains	**982**	**18 821**	**96 707**	**166 912**	**226 498**	**219 547**	**233 294**	**225 934**	**230 819**	**228 901**
1100 Of individuals	603	13 940	69 654	124 918	172 136	180 512	185 996	184 622	187 143	189 298
1110 On income and profits	603	13 796	68 786	124 233	172 122	180 505	185 991	184 619	187 143	189 298
Personal income tax	0	11 538	57 318	121 211	162 644	173 991	175 921	173 007	176 772	179 814
Local income tax paid by households	0	829	4 492	67	0	0	0	0	0	0
Tax on income from investments (60%)	319	55	15	0	0	0	11	80	54	52
10% Surcharge on income	94	37	5	0	0	0	0	0	0	0
10% proportional surcharge	1	0	0	0	0	0	0	0	0	0
Withholding tax on company dividends paid by households	23	51	496	110	542	393	564	875	1 144	1 158
Law 1177 proportional surcharge (60%)	39	0	1	0	0	0	0	0	0	0
Direct taxes 5% proportional surcharge (60%)	0	8	72	0	0	0	0	0	0	0
Additional Treasury increase (60%)	23	6	1	0	0	0	0	0	0	0
Decree 1132 revenues (60%)	0	0	0	0	0	0	0	0	0	0
Tax on households	65	7	0	0	0	0	0	0	0	0
Rental value tax	2	0	0	0	0	0	0	0	0	0
Driving licence tax	1	0	0	0	0	0	0	0	0	0
Municipal surcharge on buildings (40%)	37	5	0	22	0	0	0	0	0	0
Withholding tax on income from deposits paid by households	0	1 206	6 223	2 823	8 402	5 440	8 994	10 076	8 525	7 488
Direct taxes refund (60%)	0	0	41	0	0	0	0	0	0	0
Other	0	53	123	0	534	681	501	581	648	786
1120 On capital gains	0	144	867	685	14	7	5	3	0	0
Tax on capital gains on land	..	0	0	0	0	0	0	0	..	..
Municipal capital gains tax on buildings paid by households (60%)	..	144	867	685	14	7	5	3	..	..
1200 Corporate	379	4 710	26 605	34 699	50 529	36 740	41 194	33 530	36 103	32 937
1210 On profits	379	4 494	26 027	34 242	50 520	36 736	41 190	33 528	36 095	32 932
Corporation tax	0	1 245	9 042	28 877	47 192	34 841	39 160	31 927	34 578	31 107
Municipal surcharge on buildings (60%)	37	8	0	32	0	0	0	0	0	0
Tax on income from investments (40%)	213	37	10	0	0	0	8	54	36	35
Company franchise and liabilities tax	88	12	2	0	0	0	0	0	0	0
Law 1177 proportional surcharge (40%)	26	0	0	0	0	0	0	0	0	0
Direct taxes 5% proportional surcharge (40%)	0	20	48	0	0	0	0	0	0	0
Decree 1132 revenues (40%)	0	0	0	0	0	0	0	0	0	0
Additional Treasury increase (40%)	15	4	0	0	0	0	0	0	0	0
Withholding tax on company dividends paid by firms	0	77	745	166	0	0	0	0	0	0
Withholding tax on income from deposits paid by firms	0	1 810	9 334	4 235	2 370	605	1 464	759	378	393
Local income tax paid by firms	0	1 245	6 738	100	15	13	12	12	15	14
Direct taxes refund (40%)	0	0	27	0	0	0	0	0	0	0
Other	0	36	82	832	943	1 277	546	776	1 088	1 383
1220 On capital gains	0	216	578	457	9	4	4	2	8	5
Municipal capital gains tax on buildings paid by firms (40%)	..	216	578	457	9	4	4	2	8	5
1300 Unallocable between 1100 and 1200	0	171	448	7 295	3 833	2 295	6 104	7 782	7 573	6 667
Refunds tax on income	..	-240	-1 768	-5 175	0	0	0	0	0	0
Other	..	412	2 216	12 470	3 833	2 295	6 104	7 782	7 573	6 667
2000 Social security contributions	**1 881**	**22 976**	**87 256**	**143 629**	**200 772**	**209 122**	**210 462**	**214 376**	**220 624**	**229 607**
2100 Employees	..	4 171	16 753	27 333	35 715	37 598	39 284	39 805	40 860	42 708
2110 On a payroll basis	..	..	..	27 333	35 715	37 598	39 284	39 805	40 860	42 708
2120 On an income tax basis	..	..	..	0	0	0	0	0	0	0
2200 Employers	..	17 152	62 540	99 904	137 924	144 281	141 629	143 273	147 309	153 920
2210 On a payroll basis	..	..	..	99 904	137 924	144 281	141 629	143 273	147 309	153 920
2220 On an income tax basis	..	..	..	0	0	0	0	0	0	0
2300 Self-employed or non-employed	..	1 654	7 962	16 392	27 133	27 243	29 549	31 298	32 455	32 979
2310 On a payroll basis	..	..	..	16 392	27 133	27 243	29 549	31 298	32 455	32 979
2320 On an income tax basis	..	..	..	0	0	0	0	0	0	0
2400 Unallocable between 2100, 2200 and 2300	1 881	0	0	0	0	0	0	0	0	0
2410 On a payroll basis	..	..	..	..	..	..	..	..	..	..
2420 On an income tax basis	..	..	..	..	..	..	..	..	..	..
3000 Taxes on payroll and workforce	**0**	**387**	**890**	**0**	**0**	**0**	**0**	**0**	**0**	**0**
Contributions to GESCAL	..	387	890	..	..	..	..	..	..	..
4000 Taxes on property	**397**	**2 248**	**5 983**	**23 360**	**32 646**	**32 441**	**43 883**	**46 259**	**44 237**	**44 933**

	1965	1980	1990	2000	2007	2010	2013	2015	2017	2018
4100 Recurrent taxes on immovable property	96	7	1	9 354	12 778	9 663	20 748	25 558	21 887	21 955
Income tax on landowners	2	0	0	0	0	0	0	0	0	0
Income tax on buildings	12	2	1	0	0	0	0	0	0	0
Income tax on luxury buildings	1	0	0	0	0	0	0	0	0	0
Surcharge on land (provincial)	16	0	0	0	0	0	0	0	0	0
Surcharge on land (municipal)	18	0	0	0	0	0	0	0	0	0
Surcharge on buildings (provincial)	26	2	0	0	0	0	0	0	0	0
Surcharge on buildings (municipal)	21	3	0	0	0	0	0	0	0	0
Municipal real estate tax	0	0	0	9 354	12 778	9 663	20 748	20 798	20 755	20 817
Tax on indivisible services (TASI)	0	0	0	0	0	0	0	4 760	1 132	1 138
4110 Households	..	..	..	..	..	..	..	..	..	..
4120 Others	..	..	..	..	..	..	..	..	..	..
4200 Recurrent taxes on net wealth	0	0	0	14	1	2 118	2 547	231	355	311
4210 Individual	..	..	..	5	0	0	0	0	0	0
4220 Corporate	..	..	..	9	1	2 118	2 547	231	355	311
4300 Estate, inheritance and gift taxes	47	128	376	1 005	149	483	622	674	815	820
Inheritance and gift duty	33	119	376	1 005	149	483	622	674	815	820
Estate duty	11	9	0	0	0	0	0	0	0	0
Proportional surcharge and premium	3	0	0	0	0	0	0	0	0	0
4310 Estate and inheritance taxes	..	..	..	..	..	..	..	..	..	..
4320 Gift taxes	..	..	..	..	..	..	..	..	..	..
4400 Taxes on financial and capital transactions	255	2 113	5 606	12 320	18 256	17 365	17 092	17 245	17 686	18 847
Registration tax	120	1 048	2 421	6 794	9 410	9 019	7 353	7 625	8 542	9 359
Mortgage taxes and land registry duties	22	190	469	1 067	2 525	2 071	1 841	1 529	1 723	1 657
5% proportional surcharge	6	0	0	0	0	0	0	0	0	0
Additional surcharge	4	0	0	0	0	0	0	0	0	0
Stamp duties and surcharges accruing on cadastral acts	104	751	2 185	4 459	6 321	6 275	7 898	7 600	6 969	7 376
Other	0	123	530	0	0	0	0	491	452	455
4500 Non-recurrent taxes	0	0	0	98	151	916	985	309	1 155	442
4510 On net wealth	..	..	..	0	0	0	0	0	0	0
4520 Other non-recurrent taxes	..	..	..	98	151	916	985	309	1 155	442
4600 Other recurrent taxes on property	0	0	0	569	1 311	1 896	1 889	2 242	2 339	2 558
5000 Taxes on goods and services	**2 173**	**15 990**	**74 280**	**141 852**	**171 869**	**178 863**	**187 210**	**196 473**	**209 911**	**212 129**
5100 Taxes on production, sale, transfer, etc.	2 037	15 251	67 083	127 281	155 191	160 775	164 597	174 443	184 318	184 748
Direct taxes refund	0	-73	-86	0	0	0	0	0	0	0
5110 General taxes	710	9 438	38 940	77 473	95 623	97 586	93 921	100 692	107 576	109 333
5111 Value added taxes	0	9 438	38 940	77 473	95 623	97 586	93 921	100 692	107 576	109 333
VAT	..	9 438	38 940	77 473	95 623	97 586	93 921	100 692	107 576	109 333
5112 Sales tax	0	0	0	0	0	0	0	0	0	0
5113 Other	710	0	0	0	0	0	0	0	0	0
General tax on receipts	662	..	..	..	..	..	..	..	..	..
Compensation tax on imported products	48	..	..	..	..	..	..	..	..	..
5120 Taxes on specific goods and services	1 327	5 886	28 048	49 808	59 568	63 189	70 676	73 751	76 742	75 415
5121 Excise duties	816	4 088	20 304	31 479	32 904	36 414	45 720	46 238	47 610	47 088
Duty on mineral oils	465	3 462	15 928	22 172	23 252	22 884	26 332	25 759	26 160	25 947
Duty on spirits	27	87	206	486	595	570	571	600	649	679
Duty on beer	12	54	172	242	489	476	532	633	693	818
Duty on sugars	22	25	68	120	0	5	10	5	5	-8
Duty on electricity	20	51	2 018	3 079	3 034	7 152	13 542	15 246	15 558	15 069
Duty on bananas	9	53	97	0	0	0	0	0	0	0
Duty on coffee	31	60	74	0	0	0	0	0	0	0
Duty on cocoa	3	4	7	0	0	0	0	0	0	0
Duty on olive oil	0	0	0	0	0	0	0	0	0	0
Other duty	44	190	1 037	5 201	5 385	5 268	4 659	3 898	4 519	4 556
Alcohol, spirits, liquor	5	0	0	0	0	0	0	0	0	0
On matches and flints	13	22	47	0	0	0	0	0	0	0
Meat	26	0	0	0	0	0	0	0	0	0
In-bond surcharge	0	81	650	174	143	54	67	90	19	20
Combustible materials	39	0	0	0	0	0	0	0	0	0
Construction materials	30	0	0	0	0	0	0	0	0	0
Excise duty on sound and video	3	0	0	0	0	0	0	0	0	0
Tax on phonograph records	1	0	0	0	0	0	0	0	0	0
Stamp duty on playing cards	1	0	0	0	0	0	0	0	0	0
Other	66	0	0	5	6	5	7	7	7	7
5122 Profits of fiscal monopolies	303	1 033	3 248	7 718	10 440	10 983	10 683	10 711	10 524	10 601
Duty on tobacco	292	1 033	3 248	7 712	10 436	10 978	10 679	10 710	10 523	10 600
On salt	10	0	0	0	0	0	0	0	0	0
Duty on products of Monopoli di Stato	1	0	0	6	4	5	4	1	1	1

	1965	1980	1990	2000	2007	2010	2013	2015	2017	2018
5123 Customs and import duties	142	261	1 164	1 536	2 261	2 225	1 890	2 246	2 295	2 295
Common Customs tariff (CEE)	0	0	836	1 536	2 261	2 225	1 890	2 246	2 295	2 295
Customs and shipping duties	115	14	0	0	0	0	0	0	0	0
Administrative services duties	11	0	0	0	0	0	0	0	0	0
Tax on agriculture	15	228	207	0	0	0	0	0	0	0
Other duties	0	9	68	0	0	0	0	0	0	0
Compensatory amounts	0	9	53	0	0	0	0	0	0	0
5124 Taxes on exports	0	0	0	0	0	0	0	0	0	0
5125 Taxes on investment goods	0	0	0	0	0	0	0	0	0	0
5126 Taxes on specific services	67	483	3 141	9 029	13 932	13 567	12 383	14 556	16 313	15 431
Entertainment tax	20	59	167	118	68	58	42	40	42	34
Stamp duty	6	0	0	0	0	0	0	0	0	0
Tax on advertisements	6	56	168	389	392	384	424	405	452	456
Tax on lotto, lotteries, betting and Totocalcio game	3	123	617	4 164	7 144	7 983	7 088	7 488	9 240	9 350
Casino takings, special duties, etc.	0	0	0	158	152	192	130	112	125	114
Single tax on games of skill and betting-levied indirectly	9	74	476	487	405	242	85	116	123	143
Aerotaxi passengers tax	0	0	0	0	0	0	7	8	10	11
Local tax (including insurance)	23	171	1 714	3 713	5 771	4 708	4 607	3 835	4 048	4 186
Bank levy for the National Resolution Fund	..	..	..	..	..	..	..	2 552	2 273	1 137
5127 Other taxes on internat. trade and transactions	0	0	0	0	0	0	0	0	0	0
Special Duty on foreign payments and currency selling	..	..	..	..	..	..	..	..	..	..
5128 Other taxes	0	21	192	46	31	0	0	0	0	0
ECSC taxes and contributions on sugar and other levies	..	21	121	0	0	..	..	..	..	..
Other	..	0	70	46	31	..	..	..	..	..
Bank cont. to the unique European Resolution Fund	..	0	0	0	0	..	..	..	..	..
5130 Unallocable between 5110 and 5120	0	0	180	0	0	0	0	0	0	0
5200 Taxes on use of goods and perform activities	136	456	4 474	8 479	10 550	10 531	11 352	11 130	13 144	14 462
5210 Recurrent taxes	136	456	4 474	8 479	10 550	1 155	1 359	1 653	1 801	1 873
Public motor vehicle register tax	64	152	967	1 034	1 326	1 155	1 359	1 653	1 801	1 873
Tax on vehicles 5% proportional surcharge	3	13	450	0	0	0	0	0	0	0
Surcharge on diesel cars	0	66	683	0	0	0	0	0	0	0
Surcharge on gas cars	0	0	171	0	0	0	0	0	0	0
5211 Paid by households: motor vehicles	..	..	..	3 433	4 652	4 628	4 487	4 710	5 190	5 429
5212 Paid by others: motor vehicles	..	..	..	1 006	1 332	1 300	1 395	1 446	1 356	1 429
Motor vehicle duty paid by firms	..	..	..	1 006	1 332	1 300	1 395	1 446	1 356	1 429
5213 Paid in respect of other goods	67	225	2 203	3 006	3 240	3 448	4 111	3 321	4 797	5 731
Law 1177 proportional surcharge	22	0	0	0	0	0	0	0	0	0
Taxes on signs	2	4	0	0	0	0	0	0	0	0
Tax on dog tags	0	7	12	0	0	0	0	0	0	0
Tax on hunting and fishing	0	0	0	0	0	0	0	0	0	0
Duty on official franchises	43	215	2 191	3 006	3 240	3 448	4 111	3 321	2 855	3 809
Television tax (households)	0	0	0	0	0	0	0	0	1 942	1 922
5220 Non-recurrent taxes	0	0	0	0	0	0	0	0	0	0
Motor vehicles, airplanes	..	..	..	..	..	..	..	..	..	..
Pro-Friuli tax on vehicles	..	..	..	..	..	..	..	..	..	..
5300 Unallocable between 5100 and 5200	0	283	2 724	6 092	6 128	7 557	11 261	10 900	12 449	12 919
Indirect taxes refund	..	0	160	288	616	693	477	715	653	954
Other	..	283	2 564	5 804	5 512	6 864	10 784	10 185	11 796	11 965
6000 Other taxes	**72**	**0**	**0**	**27 343**	**39 404**	**31 939**	**31 980**	**28 072**	**22 249**	**23 949**
6100 Paid solely by business	0	..	..	27 343	39 404	31 939	31 980	28 072	22 249	23 949
6200 Other	72	..	..	0	0	0	0	0	0	0
Capital levies	2	..	..	..	..	..	..	..	..	..
Other taxes	71	..	..	..	..	..	..	..	..	..
Memorandum items										
Customs duties collected on behalf of the EU	..	..	836	1 536	2 261	2 225	1 890	2 246	2 295	2 295
SRF contributions collected on behalf of the EU	..	..	..	..	..	..	..	2 346	2 273	1 137
Non-wastable tax credits										
Non-wastable tax credits against 1110	..	..	..	..	0	0	357	9 793	10 276	10 303
Tax expenditure component	..	..	..	..	..	-109	206	8 615	9 075	9 142
Transfer component	..	..	..	..	..	109	151	1 178	1 201	1 162
Non-wastable tax credits against 1210	..	..	..	..	0	0	2 401	4 866	5 935	1 451
Tax expenditure component	..	..	..	..	..	0	0	0	0	0
Transfer component	..	..	..	..	..	0	2 401	4 866	5 935	1 451
Total tax revenue on cash basis	**5 505**	**60 422**	**265 116**	**488 738**	**653 836**	**659 704**	**689 299**	**711 837**	**722 719**	**734 307**
Total tax revenue on accrual basis	**..**	**..**	**..**	**503 096**	**671 189**	**671 912**	**706 829**	**711 114**	**727 840**	**739 519**

	1965	1980	1990	2000	2007	2010	2013	2015	2017	2018
Conciliation with National Accounts										
Additional taxes included in National Accounts	..	..	..	0	0	0	0	0	0	0
Taxes excluded from National Accounts	..	..	..	-5 416	-5 470	-6 538	-9 786	-9 801	-10 576	-10 740
The tax for the urban solid waste disposal (TARSU)	..	..	..	-4 387	-4 443	-5 519	-8 363	-8 519	-9 188	-9 296
Other	..	..	..	-1 029	-1 027	-1 019	-1 423	-1 282	-1 388	-1 444
Difference in treatment of tax credits	..	..	..	0	0	-109	206	8 615	9 075	9 142
Capital transfer for uncollected revenue	..	..	..	0	0	0	0	0	0	0
Voluntary social security contributions	..	..	..	464	567	561	738	750	769	790
Miscellaneous differences	..	..	..	0	0	0	0	0	0	0
National Accounts: Taxes and actual social contributions	..	..	..	498 144	666 286	665 826	697 987	710 678	727 108	738 711
Imputed social contributions	..	..	..	3 884	3 980	3 984	4 093	3 938	4 121	4 055
National Accounts: Taxes and all social contributions	..	..	..	502 028	670 266	669 810	702 080	714 616	731 229	742 766

.. Not available

Note: The tax year ends in December 31th.

As from 2000, revenues data are computed on accrual basis.

As from 1997, revenues data are based on data provided to the European Union as for the Treaty of Maastricht excessive deficit procedure.

Section 6000: Regional Tax on Productive Activities (IRAP); it is a tax on the value of production therefore its taxable base is different from other groups tax bases.

Regarding the section "Taxes excluded National Accounts" the item "Others" includes: tax on the public areas utilization and tax on the collection and disposal of waste water.

Source: Ministero dell'economia e delle finanze; Istituto nazionale di statistica.

StatLink https://doi.org/10.1787/888934212003

Table 5.19. Japan: Details of tax revenue, 1965-2018

Billion JPY

	1965	1980	1990	2000	2007	2010	2013	2015	2017	2018
Total tax revenue	**6 172**	**62 443**	**130 843**	**136 236**	**146 248**	**132 484**	**146 405**	**163 533**	**171 806**	**175 564**
1000 Taxes on income, profits and capital gains	**2 708**	**28 800**	**65 682**	**47 398**	**53 174**	**40 034**	**47 534**	**50 969**	**52 658**	**56 083**
1100 Of individuals	1 338	15 180	36 394	28 677	28 600	24 663	28 150	30 847	32 325	33 492
1110 On income and profits	1 338	15 180	36 394	28 677	28 600	24 663	28 150	30 847	32 325	33 492
Income tax	970	10 800	25 996	18 789	16 080	12 984	15 865	18 178	19 276	20 316
Prefectural inhabitants tax	123	1 415	3 675	3 621	5 008	4 699	5 090	5 252	5 376	4 863
Municipal inhabitants tax	220	2 890	6 475	6 044	7 294	6 795	7 015	7 224	7 471	8 106
Enterprise tax	25	75	249	223	218	184	181	194	203	207
1120 On capital gains	0	0	0	0	0	0	0	0	0	0
1200 Corporate	1 370	13 620	29 288	18 721	24 573	15 372	19 384	20 122	20 333	22 591
1210 On profits	1 370	13 620	29 288	18 721	24 573	15 372	19 384	20 122	20 333	22 591
Corporation tax	927	8 923	18 384	11 747	14 744	8 968	11 698	10 832	11 995	12 318
Prefectural inhabitants tax	53	557	1 414	879	1 206	777	854	859	762	835
Municipal inhabitants tax	85	1 297	3 198	2 176	3 015	1 954	2 157	2 324	2 224	2 427
Enterprise tax	305	2 843	6 293	3 918	5 608	2 253	2 674	3 510	3 991	4 243
Local special corporate tax	0	0	0	0	0	1 420	2 001	2 081	1 858	2 088
Local corporate tax	0	0	0	0	0	0	0	516	654	681
1220 On capital gains	0	0	0	0	0	0	0	0	0	0
1300 Unallocable between 1100 and 1200	0	0	0	0	0	0	0	0	0	0
2000 Social security contributions	**1 344**	**18 178**	**34 613**	**47 968**	**53 325**	**54 461**	**59 803**	**64 465**	**68 616**	**70 588**
2100 Employees	446	6 393	13 895	19 830	21 975	23 593	25 984	28 224	32 578	33 656
2110 On a payroll basis	..	..	13 895	19 830	21 975	23 593	25 984	28 224	32 578	33 656
2120 On an income tax basis	..	..	0	0	0	0	0	0	0	0
2200 Employers	588	9 267	16 649	22 456	24 243	24 674	27 143	29 479	31 648	32 664
2210 On a payroll basis	..	..	16 649	22 456	24 243	24 674	27 143	29 479	31 648	32 664
2220 On an income tax basis	..	..	0	0	0	0	0	0	0	0
2300 Self-employed or non-employed	107	2 518	4 069	5 683	7 108	6 194	6 676	6 763	4 390	4 268
2310 On a payroll basis	..	..	4 069	5 683	7 108	6 194	6 676	6 763	4 390	4 268
2320 On an income tax basis	..	..	0	0	0	0	0	0	0	0
2400 Unallocable between 2100, 2200 and 2300	203	0	0	0	0	0	0	0	0	0
2410 On a payroll basis	..	..	..	..	..	..	..	..	..	..
2420 On an income tax basis	..	..	..	..	..	..	..	..	..	..
3000 Taxes on payroll and workforce	**0**	**0**	**0**	**0**	**0**	**0**	**0**	**0**	**0**	**0**
4000 Taxes on property	**498**	**5 114**	**12 296**	**14 294**	**13 138**	**12 878**	**12 940**	**13 400**	**14 073**	**14 196**
4100 Recurrent taxes on immovable property	319	3 326	7 099	10 414	9 949	10 225	9 882	10 005	10 323	10 386
Prefectural property tax	4	8	15	11	14	5	2	2	4	11
Municipal property tax	296	2 784	6 023	9 041	8 729	8 961	8 653	8 755	9 025	9 083
City planning tax	19	469	942	1 318	1 202	1 256	1 227	1 244	1 277	1 291
Special landholding tax	0	65	118	43	4	3	1	3	1	0
Water and land utilization tax	0	0	0	0	0	0	0	0	0	0
Land value tax	0	0	0	1	0	0	0	0	0	0
4110 Households	..	..	..	..	..	..	..	..	..	..
4120 Others	..	..	..	..	..	..	..	..	..	..
4200 Recurrent taxes on net wealth	0	0	0	0	0	0	0	0	0	0
4210 Individual	..	..	..	..	..	..	..	..	..	..
4220 Corporate	..	..	..	..	..	..	..	..	..	..
4300 Estate, inheritance and gift taxes	44	441	1 918	1 782	1 503	1 250	1 574	1 968	2 292	2 333
4310 Estate and inheritance taxes	34	375	..	..	..	..	..	..	..	..
Inheritance tax	34	375	..	..	..	..	..	..	..	..
4320 Gift taxes	10	65	..	..	..	..	..	..	..	..
Tax on gifts	10	65	..	..	..	..	..	..	..	..
4400 Taxes on financial and capital transactions	135	1 347	3 280	2 099	1 686	1 403	1 483	1 426	1 458	1 477
Bourse tax	3	15	41	0	0	0	0	0	0	0
Securities transaction	8	209	748	0	0	0	0	0	0	0
Bank of Japan note issue tax	0	0	0	0	0	0	0	0	0	0
Stamp revenues	83	841	1 894	1 532	1 202	1 024	1 126	1 050	1 052	1 073
Real property acquisition tax	41	282	596	567	485	379	357	377	407	404
4500 Non-recurrent taxes	0	0	0	0	0	0	0	0	0	0
4510 On net wealth	..	..	..	..	..	..	..	..	..	..
4520 Other non-recurrent taxes	..	..	..	..	..	..	..	..	..	..
4600 Other recurrent taxes on property	0	0	0	0	0	0	0	0	0	0
5000 Taxes on goods and services	**1 620**	**10 200**	**17 917**	**26 227**	**26 256**	**24 730**	**25 744**	**34 286**	**36 031**	**34 252**
5100 Taxes on production, sale, transfer, etc.	1 544	8 822	15 647	23 180	23 241	22 160	23 313	31 871	33 582	31 754
5110 General taxes	0	0	5 778	12 350	12 841	12 675	13 479	22 400	22 249	22 496
5111 Value added taxes	..	..	5 778	12 350	12 841	12 675	13 479	22 400	22 249	22 496
5112 Sales tax	..	..	0	0	0	0	0	0	0	0
5113 Other	..	..	0	0	0	0	0	0	0	0
5120 Taxes on specific goods and services	1 544	8 822	9 868	10 830	10 400	9 485	9 834	9 470	11 333	9 258

	1965	1980	1990	2000	2007	2010	2013	2015	2017	2018
5121 Excise duties	1 062	6 674	8 637	9 837	9 374	8 622	8 728	8 351	10 241	8 121
Liquor tax	353	1 424	1 935	1 816	1 524	1 389	1 371	1 338	1 304	1 275
Sugar excises	29	43	0	0	0	0	0	0	0	0
Local gasoline tax	46	278	361	296	302	294	275	264	256	251
Gasoline tax	254	1 547	2 007	2 769	2 820	2 750	2 574	2 465	2 396	2 348
Liquefied petroleum gas tax	0	30	31	28	27	24	21	18	17	15
Aviation fuel tax	0	58	76	104	104	89	67	66	67	68
Commodity tax	138	1 038	5	0	0	0	0	0	0	0
Playing-card tax	1	1	0	0	0	0	0	0	0	0
Prefectural tobacco tax	44	229	361	282	278	256	173	153	141	139
Municipal tobacco tax	73	402	636	865	853	788	983	936	862	850
Timber delivery tax	3	3	0	0	0	0	0	0	0	0
Mineral product tax	2	5	3	2	2	2	2	2	2	2
Electricity and gas tax	54	386	0	0	0	0	0	0	0	0
Diesel oil tax	65	447	834	1 208	1 034	918	943	925	949	958
Vehicle acquisition tax	0	270	613	464	425	192	193	137	190	198
Promotion of power resources development tax	0	109	295	375	352	349	328	316	326	322
Petroleum and coal tax	0	404	487	489	513	502	600	630	691	701
Tobacco tax	0	0	996	876	925	908	1 038	954	864	861
Special tobacco tax	0	0	0	264	214	163	161	148	134	125
International tourist tax	..	..	0	0	0	0	0	0	0	7
5122 Profits of fiscal monopolies	179	808	0	0	0	0	0	0	0	0
Monopoly profits	179	808	..	..	..	..	..	..	..	..
5123 Customs and import duties	222	786	928	877	941	786	1 034	1 049	1 024	1 071
Customs duty	222	786	928	877	941	786	1 034	1 049	1 024	1 071
5124 Taxes on exports	0	0	0	0	0	0	0	0	0	0
5125 Taxes on investment goods	0	0	0	0	0	0	0	0	0	0
5126 Taxes on specific services	81	554	303	116	85	77	71	70	67	66
Travel tax	4	64	0	0	0	0	0	0	0	0
Admission tax	10	5	0	0	0	0	0	0	0	0
Local entertainment tax	10	74	0	0	0	0	0	0	0	0
Golf course utilization tax	0	0	90	81	60	55	49	48	45	43
Meal and lodging tax	56	398	0	0	0	0	0	0	0	0
Special local consumption tax	0	0	195	12	0	0	0	0	0	0
Bathing tax	1	13	18	23	25	22	22	23	23	22
5127 Other taxes on internat. trade and transactions	0	0	0	0	0	0	0	0	0	0
5128 Other taxes	0	0	0	0	0	0	0	0	0	0
5130 Unallocable between 5110 and 5120	0	0	0	0	0	0	0	0	0	0
5200 Taxes on use of goods and perform activities	76	1 378	2 270	3 047	3 015	2 570	2 431	2 416	2 450	2 498
5210 Recurrent taxes	69	1 358	2 250	3 027	2 993	2 548	2 409	2 393	2 427	2 475
Automobile tax	55	781	1 276	1 765	1 717	1 616	1 574	1 543	1 541	1 550
Light vehicle tax	13	43	88	125	164	178	189	200	249	258
Motor vehicle tonnage tax	0	527	881	1 134	1 110	753	643	649	637	665
Hunter licence tax	0	3	2	2	0	0	0	0	0	0
Hunting tax	0	3	2	1	2	2	2	1	1	1
Mine lot tax	1	1	1	1	0	0	0	0	0	0
5211 Paid by households: motor vehicles	..	..	..	..	..	..	..	..	..	..
5212 Paid by others: motor vehicles	..	..	..	..	..	..	..	..	..	..
5213 Paid in respect of other goods	..	..	..	..	..	..	..	..	..	..
5220 Non-recurrent taxes	7	20	20	20	22	21	22	22	22	23
5300 Unallocable between 5100 and 5200	0	0	0	0	0	0	0	0	0	0
6000 Other taxes	**2**	**151**	**335**	**348**	**356**	**381**	**384**	**413**	**427**	**445**
6100 Paid solely by business	0	139	288	324	313	330	348	361	371	378
Business office tax	..	139	288	324	313	330	348	361	371	378
6200 Other	2	12	47	24	43	52	36	52	56	67
Taxes not in local tax law	2	12	47	24	43	52	36	52	56	65
Other	0	0	0	0	0	0	0	0	0	2
Total tax revenue on cash basis	**6 172**	**62 443**	**..**	**..**	**..**	**..**	**..**	**..**	**..**	**..**
Total tax revenue on accrual basis	**..**	**..**	**130 843**	**136 236**	**146 248**	**132 484**	**146 405**	**163 533**	**171 806**	**175 564**
Conciliation with National Accounts										
Additional taxes included in National Accounts	..	..	..	..	..	..	..	..	..	..
Taxes excluded from National Accounts	..	..	..	..	..	..	..	..	..	..
Difference in treatment of tax credits	..	..	..	..	..	..	..	..	..	..
Capital transfer for uncollected revenue	..	..	..	..	..	..	..	..	..	..
Voluntary social security contributions	..	..	..	..	..	..	..	..	..	..
Miscellaneous differences	..	..	..	..	..	..	..	..	..	..
National Accounts: Taxes and actual social contributions	..	..	..	..	..	..	..	..	..	..
Imputed social contributions	..	..	..	..	..	..	..	..	..	..
National Accounts: Taxes and all social contributions	..	..	..	..	..	..	..	..	..	..

.. Not available

Note: Data are on a fiscal year basis beginning 1st April.

From 1990, data are on accrual basis.

The figures for different groups of taxes are reported on different reporting bases, namely: Social security contributions (heading 2000): in principle accrual basis, Central government taxes: accrual basis (revenues accrued during the fiscal year plus cash receipts collected before the end of May (the end of April until 1977), Local government taxes : accrual basis (due to be paid during the fiscal year and cash receipts collected before the end of May).

The Japanese authorities take the view that the Enterprise tax (classified in 1100 and 1200) and the Mineral product tax (classified in 5121) should be classified in heading 6000 since under articles 72 and 519 of the Local Tax Law these taxes are regarded as levies on the business or mining activity itself.

Heading 2000 includes some unidentifiable voluntary contributions.

Heading 2300: Includes contributions to the National pension, National Health Insurance and the Farmer's pension fund. Contributions to the Farmer's pension fund are not available for the years before 1999.

Heading 4100: Municipal property tax, includes Prefectural property tax from 1990 to 1994 because data is not available to provide a breakdown.

Heading 5121: Municipal tobacco tax, includes Prefectural tobacco tax from 1990 to 1994 because data is not available to provide a breakdown.

Heading 5121: In sub-item Petroleum and coal tax, the data before 2003 refer to petroleum tax.

Source: Tax Bureau, Ministry of Finance.

StatLink https://doi.org/10.1787/888934212022

Table 5.20. Korea: Details of tax revenue, 1965-2018

Billion KRW

	1965	1980	1990	2000	2007	2010	2013	2015	2017	2018
Total tax revenue	..	**6 687**	**37 262**	**136 295**	**258 571**	**295 968**	**347 332**	**393 559**	**465 470**	**506 548**
1000 Taxes on income, profits and capital gains	..	**1 704**	**12 203**	**39 254**	**82 239**	**82 905**	**101 792**	**119 151**	**149 420**	**172 976**
1100 Of individuals	..	766	7 440	19 950	43 276	42 098	53 311	67 600	83 121	93 274
1110 On income and profits	..	766	6 327	18 569	31 984	33 935	46 654	55 744	67 987	75 251
Income tax	..	0	0	0	0	0	0	0	0	0
Dividends and interest income tax	..	0	0	0	4 682	4 425	4 889	4 561	4 517	4 982
Wages and salaries income tax	..	0	0	0	14 124	15 517	21 931	27 055	34 034	38 000
Other income tax	..	0	0	0	2 607	2 986	3 432	4 467	5 333	5 975
Global income tax	..	661	4 723	16 128	6 151	6 369	10 901	12 784	16 049	17 483
Defence tax on income tax	..	105	938	0	0	0	0	0	0	0
Education tax on income tax	..	0	325	0	0	0	0	0	0	0
Rural dev. tax on interest, bus. Inc. & cap. gains relief	..	0	0	156	160	179	124	105	104	111
Inhabitant tax on income tax (local)	..	0	341	2 285	4 260	4 459	5 377	6 772	7 950	8 700
1120 On capital gains	..	0	1 113	1 381	11 292	8 163	6 657	11 856	15 134	18 023
Capital gains tax	..	..	1 113	1 381	11 292	8 163	6 657	11 856	15 134	18 023
1200 Corporate	..	738	4 757	19 271	38 963	40 807	48 481	51 551	66 299	79 702
1210 On profits	..	738	4 757	19 271	38 963	40 807	48 481	51 551	66 299	79 702
Corporation tax - withholding	..	..	677	8 577	8 360	9 095	12 176	12 317	11 990	13 174
Corporation tax - final returns	..	..	2 549	9 302	27 057	28 173	31 679	32 713	47 187	57 763
Defence tax on corporation tax	..	..	1 323	0	0	0	0	0	0	0
Inhabitant tax on corporation tax (local)	..	..	207	1 142	3 152	3 094	4 118	6 217	6 785	8 307
Rural development tax corporate income	..	..	0	251	394	445	508	304	337	458
Excess profit tax	..	0	0	0	0	0	0	0	0	0
1220 On capital gains	..	0	0	0	0	0	0	0	0	0
Capital gains tax	..	..	..	..	..	..	..	..	..	..
1300 Unallocable between 1100 and 1200	..	199	6	33	0	0	0	0	0	0
Business income tax	..	0	0	0	..	..	..	..	..	..
Real estate income tax	..	0	0	0	..	..	..	..	..	..
Defence tax on real estate & business income	..	0	0	0	..	..	..	..	..	..
Rural dev. tax on bus. inc. & cap. gains relief	..	0	0	30	..	..	..	..	..	..
Inhabitant tax before 1990 (local)	..	117	0	0	..	..	..	..	..	..
Farm land tax (local)	..	83	6	3	..	..	..	..	..	..
Inhabitant tax on farm land tax (local)	..	0	0	0	..	..	..	..	..	..
2000 Social security contributions	..	**73**	**3 760**	**22 759**	**53 588**	**69 090**	**91 596**	**104 693**	**119 676**	**128 660**
2100 Employees	..	0	1 464	8 578	21 773	28 213	38 396	44 281	51 125	55 257
Veterans' relief fund	..	0	0	0	0	0	0	0	0	0
Soldiers' annuity fund	..	0	0	0	0	0	0	0	0	0
Unemployment assurance	..	0	0	598	1 164	1 358	2 418	3 076	3 418	3 666
National welfare pension fund	..	0	429	4 325	9 338	11 004	13 890	15 821	17 864	19 090
Social benefit fund	..	0	0	0	0	0	0	0	0	0
Health Insurance	..	0	483	2 066	8 180	11 783	17 128	19 868	22 814	24 920
Teachers' pensions	..	0	86	279	581	868	1 077	1 125	1 507	1 595
Government employees pensions	..	0	406	1 144	2 202	2 878	3 435	3 876	4 934	5 371
Military personal pensions	..	0	60	166	308	322	448	515	588	615
2110 On a payroll basis	..	..	..	8 578	21 773	28 213	38 396	44 281	51 125	55 257
2120 On an income tax basis	..	..	..	0	0	0	0	0	0	0
2200 Employers	..	73	1 694	9 409	23 557	30 856	41 518	47 846	54 063	58 712
Ind. works' insurance fund	..	73	550	1 876	4 431	4 632	5 436	6 062	6 429	7 346
Soldiers' annuity fund	..	0	0	0	0	0	0	0	0	0
Pneumoconiosis fund	..	0	0	0	0	0	0	0	0	0
Unemployment insurance	..	0	0	1 449	2 474	2 860	4 545	5 499	6 082	6 517
Veterans' relief fund	..	0	0	0	0	0	0	0	0	0
National welfare pension fund	..	0	430	4 340	9 383	11 052	13 958	15 895	17 922	19 155
Social benefit fund	..	0	0	0	0	0	0	0	0	0
Health Insurance	..	0	658	1 547	6 844	11 718	16 826	19 493	22 397	24 346
Teachers' pensions	..	0	56	197	425	594	753	897	1 233	1 348
Government employees pensions	..	0	0	0	0	0	0	0	0	0
2210 On a payroll basis	..	..	..	9 409	23 557	30 856	41 518	47 846	54 063	58 712
2220 On an income tax basis	..	..	..	0	0	0	0	0	0	0
2300 Self-employed or non-employed	..	0	602	4 772	8 258	10 021	11 682	12 566	14 488	14 691
2310 On a payroll basis	..	..	0	0	0	0	0	0	0	0
2320 On an income tax basis	..	..	602	4 772	8 258	10 021	11 682	12 566	14 488	14 691
2400 Unallocable between 2100, 2200 and 2300	..	0	0	0	0	0	0	0	0	0
2410 On a payroll basis	..	..	..	..	..	..	..	..	..	..
2420 On an income tax basis	..	..	..	..	..	..	..	..	..	..
3000 Taxes on payroll and workforce	..	**34**	**153**	**258**	**619**	**714**	**981**	**1 122**	**1 376**	**1 492**
Workshop tax on workforce (local)	..	31	124	258	619	714	981	1 122	1 376	1 492
Vocational training promotion fund	..	3	29	0	0	0	0	0	0	0
4000 Taxes on property	..	**537**	**4 389**	**16 846**	**33 109**	**33 516**	**35 847**	**48 625**	**54 406**	**58 811**

	1965	1980	1990	2000	2007	2010	2013	2015	2017	2018
4100 Recurrent taxes on immovable property	..	183	980	3 385	9 196	9 270	10 809	12 486	14 319	15 589
Property tax (local)	..	119	227	728	3 755	4 817	8 267	9 294	10 662	11 532
City planning tax on urban real estate (local)	..	51	244	815	1 883	2 465	0	0	0	0
Community facilities tax (local)	..	13	86	341	543	650	912	1 351	1 513	1 626
Tax on excessive land holdings (local)	..	0	1	0	0	0	0	0	0	0
Tax on aggregate land holdings (local)	..	0	400	1 282	5	0	0	0	0	0
Rural dev. tax on local agg. land holdings tax	..	0	0	81	1	0	0	0	0	0
Tax on excessively increased land value	..	0	0	0	0	0	0	0	0	0
Comprehensive real estate tax	..	0	0	0	2 414	1 029	1 224	1 399	1 652	1 873
Rural dev. tax on comprehensive real estate tax	..	0	0	0	483	208	250	267	302	356
4110 Households	..	..	0	0	0	0	0	0	0	0
4120 Others	..	..	22	138	112	101	156	175	190	202
Workshop tax on property (local)	..	..	22	138	112	101	156	175	190	202
4200 Recurrent taxes on net wealth	..	0	0	0	0	0	0	0	0	0
4210 Individual	..	..	..	..	..	..	..	..	..	..
4220 Corporate	..	..	..	..	..	..	..	..	..	..
4300 Estate, inheritance and gift taxes	..	12	354	989	2 842	3 076	4 290	5 044	6 785	7 359
4310 Estate and inheritance taxes	..	5	85	449	1 059	1 203	1 587	1 944	2 342	2 832
Inheritance tax	..	3	71	449	1 059	1 203	1 587	1 944	2 342	2 832
Defence tax on inheritance tax	..	2	14	0	0	0	0	0	0	0
4320 Gift taxes	..	7	269	540	1 783	1 873	2 703	3 100	4 443	4 527
Gift tax	..	7	225	540	1 783	1 873	2 703	3 100	4 443	4 527
Defence tax on gift tax	..	0	44	0	0	0	0	0	0	0
4400 Taxes on financial and capital transactions	..	319	2 960	11 935	21 071	21 170	20 748	31 095	33 302	35 863
Registration tax (local)	..	122	1 378	4 528	7 254	7 370	1 312	1 831	1 608	1 718
Registration tax	..	0	0	0	0	0	0	0	0	0
Defence tax on registration tax	..	0	0	0	0	0	0	0	0	0
Rural dev. tax on local acquisition tax	..	0	0	246	627	632	874	969	1 028	993
Rural dev. tax on local registration tax	..	0	0	66	143	144	1	1	0	0
Securities transactions tax	..	0	224	2 736	3 469	3 667	3 077	4 670	4 508	6 241
Rural dev. tax on securities transaction tax	..	0	0	823	1 729	2 010	1 529	1 861	1 775	2 217
Acquisition tax (local)	..	163	1 165	3 148	7 261	6 825	13 318	20 810	23 487	23 813
Stamp tax	..	34	193	388	588	522	637	953	896	881
4500 Non-recurrent taxes	..	22	95	537	0	0	0	0	0	0
Asset revaluation tax	..	22	95	537	..	..	..	..	..	..
4510 On net wealth	..	..	..	..	..	..	..	..	..	..
4520 Other non-recurrent taxes	..	..	..	..	..	..	..	..	..	..
4600 Other recurrent taxes on property	..	0	0	0	0	0	0	0	0	0
5000 Taxes on goods and services	**..**	**4 190**	**16 497**	**52 271**	**80 861**	**99 769**	**106 717**	**110 326**	**129 065**	**133 095**
5100 Taxes on production, sale, transfer, etc.	..	4 114	16 024	50 023	78 414	96 573	99 970	103 254	121 293	125 207
5110 General taxes	..	1 471	6 964	23 212	40 942	51 800	59 105	60 162	74 361	77 471
5111 Value added taxes	..	1 471	6 964	23 212	40 942	51 800	59 105	60 162	74 361	77 471
Value added tax	..	1 471	6 964	23 212	40 942	51 800	59 105	60 162	74 361	77 471
5112 Sales tax	..	0	0	0	0	0	0	0	0	0
Business tax	..	..	..	..	..	..	..	..	..	..
5113 Other	..	0	0	0	0	0	0	0	0	0
5120 Taxes on specific goods and services	..	2 643	9 059	26 811	37 472	44 773	40 865	43 092	46 932	47 736
5121 Excise duties	..	1 029	4 924	18 155	27 880	31 340	27 661	31 857	35 779	36 218
Commodity tax	..	0	0	0	0	0	0	0	0	0
Defence tax on commodity tax	..	0	0	0	0	0	0	0	0	0
Liquor tax	..	298	1 022	1 963	2 268	2 878	2 947	3 228	3 035	3 261
Defence tax on liquor tax	..	78	0	0	0	0	0	0	0	0
Education tax on liquor tax	..	0	81	516	580	724	764	808	745	788
Textile tax	..	0	0	0	0	0	0	0	0	0
Petroleum tax	..	0	0	0	0	0	0	0	0	0
Transport tax on petrol products	..	0	0	8 404	11 464	13 970	13 248	14 055	15 553	15 335
Education tax on transport tax	..	0	0	1 247	1 715	2 133	1 895	2 154	2 320	2 304
Electricity and gas tax	..	0	0	0	0	0	0	0	0	0
Special excise tax	..	583	1 912	2 985	5 161	5 066	5 484	8 001	9 861	10 451
Defence tax on special excise tax	..	70	337	0	0	0	0	0	0	0
Education tax on special excise tax	..	0	0	498	607	501	485	515	602	545
Rural development on special excise tax	..	0	0	37	54	24	56	61	60	56
Tobacco sales tax (local)	..	0	0	0	0	0	0	0	0	0
Tobacco consumption tax (local)	..	0	1 572	2 251	2 761	2 875	2 782	3 035	3 603	3 478
Motor fuel tax (local)	..	0	0	254	3 270	3 169	0	0	0	0
5122 Profits of fiscal monopolies	..	510	0	0	0	0	0	0	0	0
Monopoly profit	..	510	..	..	..	..	..	..	..	..

	1965	1980	1990	2000	2007	2010	2013	2015	2017	2018
5123 Customs and import duties	..	1 014	3 692	5 936	7 690	11 046	11 012	8 907	8 938	9 213
Customs duties	..	762	2 765	5 800	7 411	10 666	10 562	8 495	8 529	8 815
Defence tax on customs duties	..	248	919	0	0	0	0	0	0	0
Special customs duties	..	0	0	0	0	0	0	0	0	0
Tonnage tax	..	0	0	0	0	0	0	0	0	0
Education tax on imports	..	0	7	99	234	336	429	390	382	370
Rural dev. tax on customs exemptions	..	0	0	37	45	44	21	22	27	28
Previous year receipts	..	4	0	0	0	0	0	0	0	0
5124 Taxes on exports	..	0	0	0	0	0	0	0	0	0
5125 Taxes on investment goods	..	0	0	0	0	0	0	0	0	0
5126 Taxes on specific services	..	90	444	2 720	1 902	2 387	2 192	2 328	2 215	2 305
Telephone tax	..	50	262	1 457	0	0	0	0	0	0
Defence tax on telephone tax	..	33	0	0	0	0	0	0	0	0
Entertainment tax	..	0	0	0	0	0	0	0	0	0
Defence tax on entertainment tax	..	0	0	0	0	0	0	0	0	0
Entertainment tax (local)	..	0	0	0	0	0	0	0	0	0
Travel tax	..	0	0	0	0	0	0	0	0	0
Admission tax	..	0	0	0	0	0	0	0	0	0
Defence tax on admission tax	..	0	0	0	0	0	0	0	0	0
Education tax on banking & insurance	..	0	108	473	721	951	938	1 004	959	1 092
Horse race tax (local)	..	3	56	566	864	1 068	1 042	1 089	1 051	1 016
Rural dev. tax on horse race tax	..	0	0	84	165	215	212	235	205	197
Butchery tax (local)	..	5	18	51	52	58	0	0	0	0
Regional development tax (local)	..	0	0	89	100	95	0	0	0	0
5127 Other taxes on internat. trade and transactions	..	0	0	0	0	0	0	0	0	0
5128 Other taxes	..	0	0	0	0	0	0	0	0	0
5130 Unallocable between 5110 and 5120	..	0	0	0	0	0	0	0	0	0
5200 Taxes on use of goods and perform activities	..	75	474	2 248	2 447	3 196	6 747	7 072	7 772	7 888
5210 Recurrent taxes	..	75	474	2 248	2 447	3 196	6 747	7 072	7 772	7 888
License tax (local)	..	18	48	241	77	76	0	0	0	0
Automobile tax (local)	..	57	426	2 007	2 370	3 120	6 747	7 072	7 772	7 888
5211 Paid by households: motor vehicles	..	..	..	..	..	..	..	..	..	..
5212 Paid by others: motor vehicles	..	..	..	..	..	..	..	..	..	..
5213 Paid in respect of other goods	..	..	..	..	..	..	..	..	..	..
5220 Non-recurrent taxes	..	0	0	0	0	0	0	0	0	0
5300 Unallocable between 5100 and 5200	..	0	0	0	0	0	0	0	0	0
6000 Other taxes	**..**	**150**	**259**	**4 907**	**8 155**	**9 974**	**10 399**	**9 642**	**11 527**	**11 514**
6100 Paid solely by business	..	0	0	0	0	0	0	0	0	0
6200 Other	..	150	259	4 907	8 155	9 974	10 399	9 642	11 527	11 514
Unallocable tax revenue	..	143	0	0	0	0	0	0	0	0
Previous year tax	..	0	213	1 474	2 965	4 449	4 774	3 435	4 389	4 430
Previous year tax (local)	..	6	47	474	672	654	601	392	715	540
Unallocable defence tax	..	0	0	-3	0	0	0	0	0	0
Education tax on local taxes	..	0	0	2 962	4 518	4 871	5 024	5 815	6 423	6 544
Total tax revenue on cash basis	**..**	**6 687**	**37 262**	**136 295**	**258 571**	**295 968**	**347 332**	**393 559**	**465 470**	**506 548**
Total tax revenue on accrual basis	**..**	**..**	**..**	**..**	**..**	**..**	**..**	**..**	**..**	**..**
Conciliation with National Accounts										
Additional taxes included in National Accounts	..	..	..	..	..	..	..	..	..	..
Taxes excluded from National Accounts	..	..	..	..	..	..	..	..	..	..
Difference in treatment of tax credits	..	..	..	..	..	..	..	..	..	..
Capital transfer for uncollected revenue	..	..	..	..	..	..	..	..	..	..
Voluntary social security contributions	..	..	..	..	..	..	..	..	..	..
Miscellaneous differences	..	..	..	..	..	..	..	..	..	..
National Accounts: Taxes and actual social contributions	..	..	..	..	..	..	..	..	..	..
Imputed social contributions	..	..	..	..	..	..	..	..	..	..
National Accounts: Taxes and all social contributions	..	..	..	..	..	..	..	..	..	..

.. Not available

Note: Year ending 31st December.

Data are on cash basis.

Heading 2000: From 1997 the contributions to the three funds (civil servant pension fund, private school teacher's pension fund and medical insurance fund) are classified as security social contributions. The reasons for the change are that the contributions either became mandatory or the fund started to be managed by public authorities in that year, thereby meeting the OECD definition of social security contributions.

Heading 2200: From 2007, this includes long-term care insurance.

Source: Ministry of Finance and Economy, Ministry of Home Affairs.

StatLink https://doi.org/10.1787/888934212041

Table 5.21. Latvia: Details of tax revenue, 1965-2018

Million EUR

	1965	1980	1990	2000	2007	2010	2013	2015	2017	2018
Total tax revenue	..	..	..	**1 995**	**6 401**	**5 162**	**6 695**	**7 334**	**8 412**	**9 076**
Total tax revenue exclusive of taxes collected for the EU	..	..	..	**1 995**	**6 362**	**5 137**	**6 667**	**7 286**	**8 359**	**9 016**
1000 Taxes on income, profits and capital gains	..	..	..	**480**	**1 857**	**1 292**	**1 690**	**1 833**	**2 204**	**2 049**
1100 Of individuals	..	..	..	376	1 287	1 116	1 320	1 445	1 777	1 742
1110 On income and profits	..	..	..	376	1 287	1 116	1 320	1 445	1 777	1 742
Personal income tax	..	..	..	376	1 287	1 116	1 320	1 445	1 712	1 740
Solidarity tax	..	..	..	0	0	0	0	0	65	2
1120 On capital gains	..	..	..	0	0	0	0	0	0	0
1200 Corporate	..	..	..	105	570	175	370	389	427	308
1210 On profits	..	..	..	105	570	175	370	389	427	308
1220 On capital gains	..	..	..	0	0	0	0	0	0	0
1300 Unallocable between 1100 and 1200	..	..	..	0	0	0	0	0	0	0
2000 Social security contributions	..	..	..	**669**	**1 774**	**1 554**	**1 933**	**2 030**	**2 259**	**2 658**
2100 Employees	..	..	..	167	479	389	531	585	627	779
2110 On a payroll basis	..	..	..	167	479	389	531	585	627	779
2120 On an income tax basis	..	..	..	0	0	0	0	0	0	0
2200 Employers	..	..	..	501	1 283	1 155	1 391	1 432	1 618	1 855
2210 On a payroll basis	..	..	..	501	1 283	1 155	1 391	1 432	1 618	1 855
2220 On an income tax basis	..	..	..	0	0	0	0	0	0	0
2300 Self-employed or non-employed	..	..	..	1	12	9	11	12	15	25
2310 On a payroll basis	..	..	..	1	12	9	11	12	15	25
2320 On an income tax basis	..	..	..	0	0	0	0	0	0	0
2400 Unallocable between 2100, 2200 and 2300	..	..	..	0	0	0	0	0	0	0
2410 On a payroll basis	..	..	..	..	..	..	..	..	..	..
2420 On an income tax basis	..	..	..	..	..	..	..	..	..	..
3000 Taxes on payroll and workforce	..	..	..	**0**	**4**	**3**	**3**	**3**	**3**	**3**
Risk duty of business	..	..	..	..	4	3	3	3	3	3
4000 Taxes on property	..	..	..	**76**	**195**	**157**	**221**	**246**	**278**	**275**
4100 Recurrent taxes on immovable property	..	..	..	63	106	128	173	197	228	223
4110 Households	..	..	..	0	0	0	22	24	35	37
4120 Others	..	..	..	63	106	128	151	173	193	186
Tax on property	..	..	..	63	106	128	151	173	193	186
Tax on land	..	..	..	0	0	0	0	0	0	0
4200 Recurrent taxes on net wealth	..	..	..	0	0	0	0	0	0	0
4210 Individual	..	..	..	..	..	..	..	..	..	..
4220 Corporate	..	..	..	..	..	..	..	..	..	..
4300 Estate, inheritance and gift taxes	..	..	..	0	3	3	5	7	9	10
4310 Estate and inheritance taxes	..	..	..	..	3	3	5	7	9	10
Duty for legacies and donations	..	..	..	..	0	2	3	4	6	8
Stamp duty for transactions made in Land Register in relation to legacies and donations	..	..	..	..	1	0	0	1	1	1
Duty for consolidation of ownership and legal cliens in Land Register anent legacies and donations	..	..	..	..	2	2	2	2	2	2
4320 Gift taxes	..	..	..	..	0	0	0	0	0	0
4400 Taxes on financial and capital transactions	..	..	..	13	86	26	43	42	41	42
Duties on transactions with privatization vouchers	..	..	..	0	0	0	0	0	0	0
Stamp duty for transactions made in Land Register, which have been collected from juridical persons, except legacies and donations	..	..	..	0	1	1	1	1	1	1
Duty for consolidation of ownership and legal liens in Land Register, which have been collected from juridical persons, except legacies and donations	..	..	..	4	27	13	17	18	17	18
Stamp duty for transactions made in Land Register, which have been collected from physical persons, except legacies and donations	..	..	..	1	8	1	2	2	2	2
Duty for consolidation of ownership and legal liens in Land Register, which have been collected from physical persons, except legacies and donations	..	..	..	7	51	11	23	20	21	21
4500 Non-recurrent taxes	..	..	..	0	0	0	0	0	0	0
4510 On net wealth	..	..	..	..	..	..	..	..	..	..
4520 Other non-recurrent taxes	..	..	..	..	..	..	..	..	..	..
4600 Other recurrent taxes on property	..	..	..	0	0	0	0	0	0	0
5000 Taxes on goods and services	..	..	..	**770**	**2 572**	**2 157**	**2 849**	**3 222**	**3 667**	**4 090**
5100 Taxes on production, sale, transfer, etc.	..	..	..	739	2 515	2 031	2 695	3 052	3 474	3 875
5110 General taxes	..	..	..	476	1 753	1 301	1 855	2 130	2 440	2 698
5111 Value added taxes	..	..	..	476	1 727	1 202	1 690	1 876	2 164	2 449
5112 Sales tax	..	..	..	0	0	0	0	31	31	0
Subsidised electricity tax	..	..	..	..	..	..	..	31	31	0
5113 Other	..	..	..	0	27	99	165	223	245	249
Mandatory procurement public service obligation fee	..	..	..	0	27	99	165	223	245	249

	1965	1980	1990	2000	2007	2010	2013	2015	2017	2018
5120 Taxes on specific goods and services	..	..	..	262	761	730	840	922	1 035	1 177
5121 Excise duties	..	..	..	232	626	645	742	807	913	1 041
Excise duty on alcoholic beverages	..	..	..	63	127	111	124	128	162	194
Excise duty on beer	..	..	..	4	15	25	24	27	37	53
Excise duty on oil products	..	..	..	124	359	360	388	428	484	536
Excise duty on tobacco	..	..	..	27	92	130	160	178	191	213
Excise duty on other products	..	..	..	14	32	18	24	25	15	16
Excise duty on coffee and non alcoholic beverages	..	..	..	6	8	13	14	14	15	16
Excise duty / Tax on cars and motorcycles	..	..	..	8	24	5	10	11	0	0
Excise duty on natural gas	..	..	..	0	0	1	22	20	19	23
Tax on electricity	..	..	..	0	1	1	1	2	5	5
5122 Profits of fiscal monopolies	..	..	..	0	0	0	0	0	0	0
5123 Customs and import duties	..	..	..	21	70	38	29	43	50	58
Customs duties	..	..	..	21	40	25	28	40	45	53
Levies on imported agricultural products	..	..	..	0	2	0	0	0	0	0
Excise duty of imported goods for omission for free turnover	..	..	..	0	28	14	2	3	4	5
5124 Taxes on exports	..	..	..	0	0	0	0	0	0	0
5125 Taxes on investment goods	..	..	..	0	0	0	0	0	0	0
5126 Taxes on specific services	..	..	..	10	66	47	68	72	72	78
Taxes on lotteries and gambling	..	..	..	7	42	22	29	32	36	44
Financial stability fee	..	..	..	0	0	0	5	4	11	10
Passenger departure duty	..	..	..	3	0	0	0	0	0	0
Contributions to the EU Single Resolution Fund	..	..	..	..	..	..	..	8	7	7
Contributions to the fund for the protection of the insured	..	..	..	0	1	1	1	1	0	0
Contributions to the deposit guarantee fund	..	..	..	0	22	24	32	28	17	17
5127 Other taxes on internat. trade and transactions	..	..	..	0	0	0	0	0	0	0
5128 Other taxes	..	..	..	0	0	0	0	0	0	0
5130 Unallocable between 5110 and 5120	..	..	..	0	0	0	0	0	0	0
5200 Taxes on use of goods and perform activities	..	..	..	32	57	126	154	170	193	215
5210 Recurrent taxes	..	..	..	32	57	73	140	142	156	168
5211 Paid by households: motor vehicles	..	..	..	12	16	34	48	54	61	62
Vehicle tax for vehicles which have been registered on physical persons	..	..	..	0	0	0	48	54	61	62
Annual vehicle duty for vehicles which have been registered on physical persons	..	..	..	12	16	34	0	0	0	0
5212 Paid by others: motor vehicles	..	..	..	0	20	22	45	46	52	53
Tax on cars belonging to enterprises	..	..	..	..	0	0	21	20	22	21
Vehicle tax for vehicles which have been registered on judical persons	..	..	..	..	0	0	24	26	30	32
Annual vehicle duty for vehicles which have been registered on judical persons	..	..	..	..	20	22	0	0	0	0
5213 Paid in respect of other goods	..	..	..	20	21	17	47	42	43	52
Duty for keeping animals	..	..	..	0	0	0	0	0	0	0
Income from lease of reservoirs and fishing rights and non-production use of fishing rights (fishing cards)	..	..	..	0	0	0	1	1	1	1
Business and professional licences	..	..	..	5	6	4	27	20	17	21
State duties and payments for issue of special permits (licences) and registration of documents that commensurate correspondence of professional qualification	..	..	..	1	0	0	0	0	0	0
Lottery and gambling state duty	..	..	..	1	4	2	2	2	3	4
Gambling equipment marking duty	..	..	..	0	1	1	0	0	0	0
Payment for rental of commercial fishing rights	..	..	..	0	0	0	0	1	1	1
Lottery of goods and services organization duty	..	..	..	2	0	0	0	0	0	0
State duty for using numerative rights	..	..	..	0	0	0	0	0	0	0
State duty for keeping oil products` security reserves	..	..	..	0	0	0	24	16	12	16
Tax on natural resources	..	..	..	15	15	12	19	22	26	30
5220 Non-recurrent taxes	..	..	..	0	0	53	14	28	37	47
Revenue from state-owned greenhouse gas emission unit trade	..	..	..	..	..	53	14	0	0	0
Payment for emission quota trading	..	..	..	..	..	0	0	11	12	20
The fee for the appeal of procurement	..	..	..	..	..	0	0	0	0	0
Toll for the use of motorways	..	..	..	..	..	0	0	17	25	27
5300 Unallocable between 5100 and 5200	..	..	..	0	0	0	0	0	0	0
6000 Other taxes	**..**	**..**	**..**	**0**	**0**	**0**	**0**	**0**	**0**	**0**
6100 Paid solely by business	..	..	..	..	..	..	..	..	..	..
6200 Other	..	..	..	..	..	..	..	..	..	..
Memorandum items										
Customs duties collected on behalf of the EU	..	..	..	..	37	25	28	40	46	53
SRF contributions collected on behalf of the EU	..	..	..	..	..	..	..	8	7	7
Total tax revenue on cash basis	**..**	**..**	**..**	**..**	**..**	**..**	**..**	**..**	**..**	**..**

	1965	1980	1990	2000	2007	2010	2013	2015	2017	2018
Total tax revenue on accrual basis	**..**	**..**	**..**	**1 995**	**6 401**	**5 162**	**6 695**	**7 334**	**8 412**	**9 076**
Conciliation with National Accounts										
Additional taxes included in National Accounts	..	..	..	14	1	1	0	0	0	0
Taxes excluded from National Accounts	..	..	..	0	0	0	0	0	0	0
Difference in treatment of tax credits	..	..	..	0	0	0	0	0	0	0
Capital transfer for uncollected revenue	..	..	..	0	0	0	0	0	0	0
Voluntary social security contributions	..	..	..	0	0	0	0	0	0	0
Miscellaneous differences	..	..	..	0	0	0	0	0	0	0
National Accounts: Taxes and actual social contributions	..	..	..	2 009	6 402	5 163	6 695	7 334	8 413	9 076
Imputed social contributions	..	..	..	12	51	36	59	80	97	108
National Accounts: Taxes and all social contributions	..	..	..	2 022	6 453	5 199	6 754	7 415	8 509	9 184

.. Not available

Note: Year ending 31st December.

Data on accrual basis.

Source: Ministry of Finance.

StatLink https://doi.org/10.1787/888934212060

Table 5.22. Lithuania: Details of tax revenue, 1965-2018

Million EUR

	1965	1980	1990	2000	2007	2010	2013	2015	2017	2018
Total tax revenue	..	..	..	**4 154**	**8 730**	**7 961**	**9 377**	**10 727**	**12 459**	**13 664**
Total tax revenue exclusive of taxes collected for the EU	..	..	..	**4 154**	**8 656**	**7 908**	**9 370**	**10 716**	**12 350**	**13 541**
1000 Taxes on income, profits and capital gains	..	..	..	**1 111**	**2 625**	**1 281**	**1 726**	**2 013**	**2 256**	**2 529**
1100 Of individuals	..	..	..	1 020	1 891	1 005	1 250	1 440	1 625	1 838
1110 On income and profits	..	..	..	1 020	1 810	972	1 226	1 390	1 556	1 751
Tax on payroll and workforce	..	..	..	950	1 628	793	1 008	1 148	1 233	1 408
Tax on income from individual activities	..	..	..	40	81	36	48	55	79	83
Tax on capital income	..	..	..	31	102	143	170	187	243	260
1120 On capital gains	..	..	..	0	81	33	24	50	69	86
1200 Corporate	..	..	..	90	734	276	477	574	631	691
1210 On profits	..	..	..	90	734	276	477	574	631	691
1220 On capital gains	..	..	..	0	0	0	0	0	0	0
1300 Unallocable between 1100 and 1200	..	..	..	0	0	0	0	0	0	0
2000 Social security contributions	..	..	..	**1 362**	**2 643**	**3 293**	**3 791**	**4 338**	**5 170**	**5 752**
2100 Employees	..	..	..	107	233	641	763	873	1 071	1 156
2110 On a payroll basis	..	..	..	107	233	641	763	873	1 071	1 156
2120 On an income tax basis	..	..	..	0	0	0	0	0	0	0
2200 Employers	..	..	..	1 119	2 180	2 109	2 526	2 916	3 512	3 894
2210 On a payroll basis	..	..	..	1 119	2 180	2 109	2 526	2 916	3 512	3 894
2220 On an income tax basis	..	..	..	0	0	0	0	0	0	0
2300 Self-employed or non-employed	..	..	..	135	230	544	502	549	587	702
2310 On a payroll basis	..	..	..	135	230	544	502	549	587	702
2320 On an income tax basis	..	..	..	0	0	0	0	0	0	0
2400 Unallocable between 2100, 2200 and 2300	..	..	..	0	0	0	0	0	0	0
2410 On a payroll basis	..	..	..	..	..	..	..	..	..	..
2420 On an income tax basis	..	..	..	..	..	..	..	..	..	..
3000 Taxes on payroll and workforce	..	..	..	**0**	**0**	**0**	**0**	**0**	**0**	**0**
4000 Taxes on property	..	..	..	**62**	**83**	**103**	**97**	**126**	**129**	**137**
4100 Recurrent taxes on immovable property	..	..	..	61	82	102	96	125	127	135
4110 Households	..	..	..	3	6	7	8	17	25	36
4120 Others	..	..	..	58	76	95	88	108	102	99
Tax on land from corporations	..	..	..	3	8	9	10	10	5	5
Tax on immovable property	..	..	..	55	69	86	77	98	97	94
4200 Recurrent taxes on net wealth	..	..	..	0	0	0	0	0	0	0
4210 Individual	..	..	..	..	..	..	..	..	..	..
4220 Corporate	..	..	..	..	..	..	..	..	..	..
4300 Estate, inheritance and gift taxes	..	..	..	1	2	1	1	1	2	2
4310 Estate and inheritance taxes	..	..	..	1	2	1	1	1	2	2
4320 Gift taxes	..	..	..	0	0	0	0	0	0	0
4400 Taxes on financial and capital transactions	..	..	..	0	0	0	0	0	0	0
4500 Non-recurrent taxes	..	..	..	0	0	0	0	0	0	0
4510 On net wealth	..	..	..	..	..	..	..	..	..	..
4520 Other non-recurrent taxes	..	..	..	..	..	..	..	..	..	..
4600 Other recurrent taxes on property	..	..	..	0	0	0	0	0	0	0
5000 Taxes on goods and services	..	..	..	**1 619**	**3 378**	**3 284**	**3 762**	**4 249**	**4 904**	**5 246**
5100 Taxes on production, sale, transfer, etc.	..	..	..	1 556	3 298	3 202	3 685	4 176	4 823	5 150
5110 General taxes	..	..	..	1 086	2 339	2 183	2 611	2 913	3 336	3 552
5111 Value added taxes	..	..	..	1 005	2 330	2 180	2 611	2 889	3 310	3 522
5112 Sales tax	..	..	..	0	0	0	0	0	0	0
5113 Other	..	..	..	81	8	3	0	24	26	30
Deductions from revenue according to the RoL on the financing of road maintence and development	..	..	..	81	0	0	..	0	0	0
Deductions from revenue according to the RoL Forestry Law	..	..	..	0	0	0	..	24	26	30
Turnover tax on goods	..	..	..	0	0	0	..	0	0	0
Deductions from Ignalina nuclear power plant income generated by sales of electricity	..	..	..	0	8	3	..	0	0	0
Turnover tax on publications of erotic and violent nature	..	..	..	0	0	0	..	0	0	0
Turnover tax on motor cars	..	..	..	0	0	0	..	0	0	0
Turnover tax on goods containing ethyl	..	..	..	0	0	0	..	0	0	0
5120 Taxes on specific goods and services	..	..	..	470	960	1 019	1 073	1 263	1 486	1 598

	1965	1980	1990	2000	2007	2010	2013	2015	2017	2018
5121 Excise duties	..	..	..	428	835	903	996	1 165	1 339	1 444
Alcoholic beverages	..	..	..	10	2	10	12	6	13	17
Manufactured tabacco	..	..	..	41	121	170	209	270	286	293
Oil and other oil products	..	..	..	230	451	487	534	619	730	807
Electricity	..	..	..	2	0	3	3	4	2	2
Luxury cars	..	..	..	1	0	0	0	0	0	0
Sugar	..	..	..	25	13	1	7	1	1	0
Other former minor excises	..	..	..	5	0	0	0	0	0	0
Wine and sparkling wine	..	..	..	6	23	30	31	36	41	43
Beer	..	..	..	24	38	44	38	50	79	86
Other alcoholic beverages	..	..	..	84	186	158	162	179	187	196
5122 Profits of fiscal monopolies	..	..	..	0	0	0	0	0	0	0
5123 Customs and import duties	..	..	..	41	61	53	0	0	101	116
Taxes on international trades and transactions	..	..	..	41	0	0	..	..	0	0
Imported sugar tax	..	..	..	0	0	0	..	..	0	0
Custom duties collected for the EU	..	..	..	..	61	53	68	99	101	116
5124 Taxes on exports	..	..	..	0	0	0	0	0	0	0
5125 Taxes on investment goods	..	..	..	0	0	0	0	0	0	0
5126 Taxes on specific services	..	..	..	0	64	63	77	98	47	37
Tax on lotteries and gambling	..	..	..	..	9	8	12	15	16	17
Contributions to the Guarantee Fund	..	..	..	..	11	5	12	16	0	0
Deposit and investment insurance tax	..	..	..	..	43	48	52	56	22	12
Resolution Fund	..	..	..	..	..	..	..	10	7	7
Other taxes on specific services	..	..	..	..	0	1	2	1	1	1
5127 Other taxes on internat. trade and transactions	..	..	..	0	0	0	0	0	0	0
5128 Other taxes	..	..	..	0	0	0	0	0	0	0
5130 Unallocable between 5110 and 5120	..	..	..	0	0	0	0	0	0	0
5200 Taxes on use of goods and perform activities	..	..	..	64	80	83	78	74	81	96
5210 Recurrent taxes	..	..	..	64	80	83	78	74	81	96
5211 Paid by households: motor vehicles	..	..	..	0	0	0	0	0	0	0
5212 Paid by others: motor vehicles	..	..	..	7	30	13	31	32	34	39
Car registration taxes	..	..	..	0	0	0	15	15	15	17
Conveyance taxes	..	..	..	7	30	13	16	17	19	21
5213 Paid in respect of other goods	..	..	..	57	50	70	47	42	47	57
Pollution taxes	..	..	..	6	18	7	19	13	15	22
Payments by households for licences (not for business purposes)	..	..	..	5	3	6	2	2	2	2
Tax on market place	..	..	..	2	0	0	0	0	0	0
State-imposed fees and charges	..	..	..	34	22	44	6	5	6	5
Other taxes on production	..	..	..	10	6	13	21	22	24	28
5220 Non-recurrent taxes	..	..	..	0	0	0	0	0	0	0
5300 Unallocable between 5100 and 5200	..	..	..	0	0	0	0	0	0	0
6000 Other taxes	**..**	**..**	**..**	**0**	**0**	**0**	**0**	**0**	**0**	**0**
6100 Paid solely by business	..	..	..	..	..	..	..	..	..	..
6200 Other	..	..	..	..	..	..	..	..	..	..
Memorandum items										
Customs duties collected on behalf of the EU	..	..	..	..	61	53	68	99	101	116
SRF contributions collected on behalf of the EU	..	..	..	..	..	..	..	10	7	7
Total tax revenue on cash basis	**..**	**..**	**..**	**..**	**..**	**..**	**..**	**..**	**..**	**..**
Total tax revenue on accrual basis	**..**	**..**	**..**	**4 154**	**8 730**	**7 961**	**9 377**	**10 727**	**12 459**	**13 664**
Conciliation with National Accounts										
Additional taxes included in National Accounts	..	..	..	0	0	0	0	0	0	0
Taxes excluded from National Accounts	..	..	..	0	0	0	0	0	0	0
Difference in treatment of tax credits	..	..	..	0	0	0	0	0	0	0
Capital transfer for uncollected revenue	..	..	..	-39	-9	-32	-17	-18	-3	-9
Voluntary social security contributions	..	..	..	0	2	2	3	2	2	2
Miscellaneous differences	..	..	..	0	0	0	0	0	0	0
National Accounts: Taxes and actual social contributions	..	..	..	4 115	8 723	7 932	9 362	10 712	12 458	13 657
Imputed social contributions	..	..	..	3	91	103	99	116	128	138
National Accounts: Taxes and all social contributions	..	..	..	4 118	8 814	8 035	9 461	10 828	12 586	13 795

.. Not available

Note: Year ending 31st December.

Data on an accrual basis.

Source: Ministry of Finance.

StatLink https://doi.org/10.1787/888934212079

Table 5.23. Luxembourg: Details of tax revenue, 1965-2018

Million EUR

	1965	1980	1990	2000	2007	2010	2013	2015	2017	2018
Total tax revenue	**266**	**1 543**	**3 671**	**8 511**	**13 455**	**15 069**	**17 756**	**19 257**	**21 371**	**23 872**
Total tax revenue exclusive of taxes collected for the EU	..	..	**3 654**	**8 482**	**13 431**	**15 051**	**17 740**	**19 205**	**21 244**	**23 719**
1000 Taxes on income, profits and capital gains	**95**	**667**	**1 476**	**3 106**	**4 654**	**5 467**	**6 274**	**7 011**	**7 958**	**9 391**
1100 Of individuals	66	417	884	1 573	2 677	3 156	4 061	4 716	5 056	5 599
1110 On income and profits	66	417	884	1 573	2 677	3 156	4 061	4 716	5 056	5 599
Personal income tax - fixed by assessment	27	106	184	258	389	540	666	721	822	751
Supplementary solidarity income tax	0	10	41	37	59	74	268	305	329	362
Tax on wages and salaries	36	287	601	1 177	1 909	2 136	2 797	3 227	3 424	3 904
Withholding tax on income from capital	2	11	52	88	188	315	223	313	385	488
Special tax on company directors fees	1	2	5	11	20	26	38	44	48	57
Tax on certain income of non-residents	0	1	1	2	1	1	1	1	1	1
Tax withheld on savings income (non-residents)	0	0	0	0	51	33	40	0	0	0
Withholding tax on interest	0	0	0	0	60	31	28	20	33	31
Crisis tax	0	0	0	0	0	0	0	0	0	0
Temporary budgetary balance tax	0	0	0	0	0	0	0	85	13	5
Tax withheld on contributions to a registered supplementary pension plan for self-employed persons	..	..	0	0	0	0	0	0	0	0
1120 On capital gains	0	0	0	0	0	0	0	0	0	0
Tax on betting gains	..	..	..	..	..	..	..	..	..	..
1200 Corporate	29	250	592	1 533	1 977	2 311	2 213	2 295	2 902	3 793
1210 On profits	29	250	592	1 533	1 977	2 311	2 213	2 295	2 902	3 793
Corporation tax	18	168	376	1 031	1 381	1 646	1 530	1 569	1 951	2 616
Supplementary solidarity corporation tax	0	2	8	43	58	61	113	120	149	177
Trade tax	0	80	209	460	538	603	569	606	802	1 000
1220 On capital gains	0	0	0	0	0	0	0	0	0	0
1300 Unallocable between 1100 and 1200	0	0	0	0	0	0	0	0	0	0
2000 Social security contributions	**86**	**443**	**1 011**	**2 224**	**3 710**	**4 387**	**5 131**	**5 547**	**6 126**	**6 483**
2100 Employees	32	175	388	993	1 691	2 017	2 308	2 498	2 786	2 972
2110 On a payroll basis	..	175	388	993	1 691	2 017	2 308	2 498	2 786	2 972
2120 On an income tax basis	..	0	0	0	0	0	0	0	0	0
2200 Employers	49	243	494	964	1 580	1 888	2 157	2 335	2 565	2 708
2210 On a payroll basis	..	243	494	964	1 580	1 888	2 157	2 335	2 565	2 708
2220 On an income tax basis	..	0	0	0	0	0	0	0	0	0
2300 Self-employed or non-employed	5	25	129	266	438	482	666	714	775	802
2310 On a payroll basis	..	25	129	266	438	482	666	714	775	802
2320 On an income tax basis	..	0	0	0	0	0	0	0	0	0
2400 Unallocable between 2100, 2200 and 2300	0	0	0	0	0	0	0	0	0	0
2410 On a payroll basis	..	..	..	..	..	..	..	..	..	..
2420 On an income tax basis	..	..	..	..	..	..	..	..	..	..
3000 Taxes on payroll and workforce	**2**	**10**	**0**	**0**	**0**	**0**	**0**	**0**	**0**	**0**
Payroll tax	2	10	..	..	..	..	..	..	..	..
4000 Taxes on property	**16**	**87**	**309**	**910**	**1 294**	**1 062**	**1 296**	**1 715**	**2 065**	**2 315**
4100 Recurrent taxes on immovable property	4	9	14	21	27	29	33	36	38	38
Taxes on ownership of lands and buildings	4	9	14	21	27	29	33	36	38	38
4110 Households	..	..	..	..	..	..	..	..	..	..
4120 Others	..	..	..	..	..	..	..	..	..	..
4200 Recurrent taxes on net wealth	7	44	172	633	878	831	980	1 318	1 513	1 692
4210 Individual	0	0	0	0	0	0	0	0	0	0
Wealth tax	..	..	..	..	..	..	..	..	..	..
4220 Corporate	7	44	172	633	878	831	980	1 318	1 513	1 692
Wealth tax	2	15	58	152	172	208	269	385	521	682
Holding tax	3	29	114	481	706	622	710	933	992	1 010
4300 Estate, inheritance and gift taxes	1	5	11	23	47	50	72	74	111	91
4310 Estate and inheritance taxes	1	5	11	23	47	50	72	74	111	91
4320 Gift taxes	0	0	0	0	0	0	0	0	0	0
4400 Taxes on financial and capital transactions	4	30	112	232	343	152	212	287	404	494
Registration taxes	4	26	94	208	288	116	164	221	319	385
Mortgage taxes	1	3	9	12	29	21	28	39	56	66
Stamp duties	0	2	2	5	7	5	7	8	8	8
Tax on contruction in dense sectors	0	0	0	0	1	1	1	2	1	2
Tax on sale of real estate	0	0	6	7	17	8	10	16	18	30
Mortgage tax on salaries	0	0	1	1	1	1	1	1	1	1
Building permits	0	0	0	0	0	0	0	0	0	0
Infrastructure tax	0	0	0	0	0	0	0	0	0	0
Authorisation taxes on oil tanks	0	0	0	0	0	0	0	0	0	0
Tax on secondary residence	0	0	0	0	0	1	0	0	0	0
4500 Non-recurrent taxes	0	0	0	0	0	0	0	0	0	0
4510 On net wealth	..	..	..	..	..	..	..	..	..	..

	1965	1980	1990	2000	2007	2010	2013	2015	2017	2018
4520 Other non-recurrent taxes	..	..	..	..	..	..	..	..	..	..
4600 Other recurrent taxes on property	0	0	0	0	0	0	0	0	0	0
5000 Taxes on goods and services	**66**	**336**	**868**	**2 260**	**3 783**	**4 132**	**5 033**	**4 957**	**5 195**	**5 655**
5100 Taxes on production, sale, transfer, etc.	62	327	848	2 230	3 708	4 057	4 950	4 871	5 110	5 558
5110 General taxes	33	179	443	1 127	2 230	2 568	3 380	3 375	3 367	3 669
5111 Value added taxes	0	179	443	1 127	2 230	2 568	3 380	3 375	3 367	3 669
VAT own resources	..	18	75	92	50	41	49	45	66	59
5112 Sales tax	0	0	0	0	0	0	0	0	0	0
5113 Other	33	0	0	0	0	0	0	0	0	0
Turnover tax	33	..	..	..	..	..	..	..	..	..
5120 Taxes on specific goods and services	30	148	404	1 103	1 478	1 489	1 570	1 496	1 743	1 888
5121 Excise duties	26	134	365	1 036	1 394	1 401	1 484	1 374	1 449	1 556
Excise duties on mineral oils	1	1	10	100	135	145	197	184	185	197
Excise duties on tobacco (part on national production)	..	0	8	24	66	70	85	81	95	146
Autonomous excise duties on mineral oils	..	76	173	414	559	536	530	495	497	532
Tax on the consumption of national alcoholic beverages and spirits	1	5	19	20	21	20	25	28	38	42
Excise duties on tobacco	..	40	141	407	418	422	445	394	440	430
Supplementary tax on fuel	..	0	0	59	145	132	126	117	119	128
Tax on control of domestic fuel	..	0	0	2	3	3	2	2	2	2
Excise duty on liquefied petroleum	..	0	0	0	0	0	0	0	0	0
Excise duty on benzol	..	0	0	1	1	1	1	1	1	1
Excise duties on imported alcoholic beverages	..	3	5	5	6	5	7	8	10	11
Excise duties on beers (national production)	..	4	2	3	4	4	4	5	4	4
Excise duty on fermented fruit beverages	..	2	3	0	0	0	0	0	0	0
Excise duties on fermented sparkling beverages	..	0	1	0	0	0	0	0	0	0
Excise duty on sugar	..	0	1	0	0	0	0	0	0	0
Excise UEBL	..	0	0	0	0	0	0	0	0	0
Excise duties on nationally produced alcoholic beverages	..	1	1	0	0	0	0	0	0	0
Excise duty on Kyoto	..	0	0	0	37	62	62	58	58	62
Excise duty on alcopops	..	0	0	0	0	0	0	0	0	0
5122 Profits of fiscal monopolies	0	0	0	0	0	0	0	0	0	0
5123 Customs and import duties	1	5	11	27	24	18	16	23	27	24
Levies on imported agricultural products	1	0	0	0	1	0	0	0	0	0
Customs duty	0	0	0	0	0	0	0	0	0	0
Customs duty + mobiles + C.E.C.A. + anti-dumping	0	4	11	27	23	18	15	23	27	24
Agricultural compensatory amounts	0	0	0	0	0	0	0	0	0	0
5124 Taxes on exports	0	0	0	0	0	0	0	0	0	0
5125 Taxes on investment goods	0	0	0	0	0	0	0	0	0	0
5126 Taxes on specific services	2	6	22	39	60	69	70	98	267	308
Tax on betting stakes	0	0	0	0	0	0	0	0	0	0
Tax on insurance	1	5	15	23	32	40	45	46	60	53
Tax on transport	1	0	0	0	0	0	0	0	0	0
Tourist tax	0	0	1	1	2	2	2	3	3	3
Tax on national lottery	0	0	3	4	3	3	0	0	0	0
Tax on casino gambling	0	0	3	9	21	23	21	19	19	20
Tax on bank notes	0	0	0	0	0	0	0	0	0	0
Entertainment tax	0	1	1	2	2	1	2	2	2	1
Contributions to FGDL	0	0	0	0	0	0	0	0	79	95
Contributions to FRL	..	..	..	..	..	..	..	29	100	129
Special tax for insurers in the interest of the rescue service	0	0	0	0	0	0	0	0	5	7
5127 Other taxes on internat. trade and transactions	0	0	0	0	0	0	0	0	0	0
5128 Other taxes	0	4	6	1	0	1	1	1	0	0
C.E.C.A.	..	3	4	0	0	0	0	0	0	0
Co-responsibility tax on milk	..	1	2	1	0	1	1	1	0	0
Co-responsibility tax on cereals	..	0	0	0	0	0	0	0	0	0
5130 Unallocable between 5110 and 5120	0	0	0	0	0	0	0	0	0	0
5200 Taxes on use of goods and perform activities	3	9	20	30	75	75	83	86	85	97
5210 Recurrent taxes	3	8	18	28	68	68	72	71	69	70
5211 Paid by households: motor vehicles	2	4	9	16	39	39	40	41	40	40
5212 Paid by others: motor vehicles	1	4	7	11	26	26	27	28	27	27
5213 Paid in respect of other goods	0	0	1	2	2	3	4	3	3	3
Tax on licenced premises	0	0	0	0	1	1	1	1	1	1
Ship registration tax	0	0	0	1	1	1	2	1	1	1
Dog tax	0	0	1	1	1	1	1	1	1	1
Tax on peddling	0	0	0	0	0	0	0	0	0	0
Tax on ships	0	0	0	0	0	0	0	0	0	0
5220 Non-recurrent taxes	0	0	2	2	7	7	11	15	16	27
Emission permits	..	..	0	0	0	0	5	7	7	18
Car registration taxes	..	..	2	2	7	7	6	8	9	9

	1965	1980	1990	2000	2007	2010	2013	2015	2017	2018
5300 Unallocable between 5100 and 5200	0	0	0	0	0	0	0	0	0	0
6000 Other taxes	**0**	**0**	**7**	**11**	**14**	**22**	**23**	**28**	**27**	**29**
6100 Paid solely by business	..	0	6	11	13	16	15	28	27	29
Supplementary tax on electricity	..	0	0	2	2	2	2	2	2	2
Tax on distribution of electricity	..	0	3	4	1	1	1	1	1	1
Tax on production of electricity	..	0	2	2	1	1	1	0	0	4
Tax on natural gas consumption	..	0	0	0	3	4	5	4	4	5
Tax on enterprise register	..	0	1	1	0	0	0	0	0	0
Tax concerning foreign affairs departments	..	0	0	0	2	5	5	4	7	5
Chancellery stamps	..	0	1	2	4	3	2	1	1	1
VAT reclassified as tax on production	..	0	0	1	1	1	1	1	1	1
Under-compensation of VAT (flat rate system)	..	0	2	0	0	0	0	0	0	0
Tax on water	..	0	2	0	0	0	0	0	0	0
6200 Other	..	0	0	0	0	0	0	0	0	0
Memorandum items										
Customs duties collected on behalf of the EU	..	..	11	27	23	18	15	23	27	24
SRF contributions collected on behalf of the EU	..	..	..	..	..	..	..	29	100	129
Non-wastable tax credits										
Non-wastable tax credits against 1110	..	..	..	..	..	..	..	198	196	194
Tax expenditure component	..	..	..	..	..	..	..	..	..	..
Transfer component	..	..	..	..	..	..	..	..	..	..
Total tax revenue on cash basis	**266**	**1 543**	**3 722**	**8 612**	**13 385**	**14 746**	**17 798**	**19 420**	**21 452**	**23 649**
Total tax revenue on accrual basis	**..**	**..**	**3 671**	**8 511**	**13 455**	**15 069**	**17 756**	**19 257**	**21 371**	**23 872**
Conciliation with National Accounts										
Additional taxes included in national accounts	..	..	0	0	0	0	0	0	0	0
Tax excluded from national accounts	..	..	0	0	0	0	0	0	0	0
Difference in treatment of tax credits	..	..	0	0	0	0	0	0	0	0
Capital transfer for uncollected revenue	..	..	0	0	0	0	-13	-1	-2	-6
Voluntary social security contributions	..	..	4	18	18	28	33	38	44	46
Miscellaneous differences	..	..	0	0	0	0	0	0	0	0
National Accounts: taxes and actual social contributions	..	..	3 675	8 528	13 474	15 098	17 776	19 295	21 413	23 913
Imputed social contributions	..	..	267	288	429	505	605	669	749	775
National Accounts: taxes and all social contributions	..	..	3 941	8 816	13 902	15 603	18 382	19 964	22 162	24 688

.. Not available

Note: The civil year ends December 31st.

From 1990 onwards, data are on an accrual basis.

Under the heading 2000, the difference between the total social security contributions and those collected by the social security parastatals corresponds to the levy for realignment of pensions operated on the remuneration and pensions of employees and former agents of P&T and BCEE; one of these establishments belonging to the "non-corporate and quasi-corporate sector" and the other to the "credit institutions sector".

Source: General account of the State.

StatLink https://doi.org/10.1787/888934212098

Table 5.24. Mexico: Details of tax revenue, 1965-2018

Million MXN

	1965	1980	1990	2000	2007	2010	2013	2015	2017	2018
Total tax revenue	..	**771**	**102 005**	**767 216**	**1 382 103**	**1 716 243**	**2 165 501**	**2 953 480**	**3 527 032**	**3 797 888**
1000 Taxes on income, profits and capital gains	..	**230**	**34 673**	**276 548**	**554 099**	**683 604**	**957 213**	**1 230 555**	**1 571 954**	**1 671 513**
1100 Of individuals	..	..	..	..	238 938	313 473	425 621	609 384	754 109	804 236
Tax on income of individuals	..	..	..	..	238 938	313 473	425 621	609 384	754 109	804 236
1110 On income and profits	..	..	..	..	..	..	..	..	..	..
1120 On capital gains	..	..	..	..	..	..	..	..	..	..
1200 Corporate	..	..	..	..	217 790	246 745	392 199	592 443	769 193	809 834
Tax on income of corporations	..	..	..	..	217 790	246 745	392 199	592 443	769 193	809 834
1210 On profits	..	..	..	..	..	..	..	..	..	..
1220 On capital gains	..	..	..	..	..	..	..	..	..	..
1300 Unallocable between 1100 and 1200	..	230	34 673	276 548	97 370	123 386	139 393	28 728	48 652	57 443
Tax on income	..	..	..	244 841	54 785	66 937	89 028	36 268	46 004	50 878
Tax on asset	..	..	..	13 913	15 670	-624	-1 325	-502	-1 069	-396
Credit on salary	..	..	..	17 794	23 177	9 708	1 274	993	1 036	1 172
Oil yields tax	..	..	..	0	3 738	2 296	3 210	0	0	0
IETU	..	..	..	0	0	45 069	47 205	-11 777	-1 648	319
Imposed by activity exploration and extraction of hydrocarbon	..	..	..	0	0	0	0	3 746	4 330	5 470
2000 Social security contributions	..	**109**	**17 165**	**138 223**	**236 727**	**277 459**	**351 993**	**409 249**	**467 619**	**509 087**
2100 Employees	..	..	..	..	..	..	..	..	..	..
2110 On a payroll basis	..	..	..	..	..	..	..	..	..	..
2120 On an income tax basis	..	..	..	..	..	..	..	..	..	..
2200 Employers	..	..	..	..	..	..	..	..	..	..
2210 On a payroll basis	..	..	..	..	..	..	..	..	..	..
2220 On an income tax basis	..	..	..	..	..	..	..	..	..	..
2300 Self-employed or non-employed	..	..	..	..	..	..	..	..	..	..
2310 On a payroll basis	..	..	..	..	..	..	..	..	..	..
2320 On an income tax basis	..	..	..	..	..	..	..	..	..	..
2400 Unallocable between 2100, 2200 and 2300	..	109	17 165	138 223	236 727	277 459	351 993	409 249	467 619	509 087
2410 On a payroll basis	..	..	..	138 223	236 727	277 459	351 993	409 249	467 619	509 087
2420 On an income tax basis	..	..	..	0	0	0	0	0	0	0
3000 Taxes on payroll and workforce	..	**8**	**1 797**	**11 217**	**28 071**	**36 911**	**53 042**	**70 221**	**84 099**	**93 303**
Substitute tax on salary	..	..	..	0	0	0	0	0	0	0
Payroll tax	..	..	..	11 101	20 277	27 813	41 184	69 866	83 608	92 833
Tax on remuneration to the personal work	..	..	..	65	7 578	8 841	11 645	152	246	270
Tax on professions and fees	..	..	..	36	68	71	50	106	103	111
Tax on operations by contract	..	..	..	15	148	186	163	96	141	90
4000 Taxes on property	..	**15**	**1 914**	**13 964**	**33 161**	**38 955**	**46 238**	**57 673**	**67 836**	**77 110**
4100 Recurrent taxes on immovable property	..	10	1 036	9 948	19 425	25 724	31 338	37 961	44 680	49 445
4110 Households	..	0	0	0	0	0	0	0	0	0
4120 Others	..	10	1 036	9 948	19 425	25 724	31 338	37 961	44 680	49 445
Property tax	..	..	..	9 948	19 425	25 724	31 338	37 961	44 680	49 445
4200 Recurrent taxes on net wealth	..	0	0	0	0	0	0	0	0	0
4210 Individual	..	..	..	..	..	..	..	..	..	..
4220 Corporate	..	..	..	..	..	..	..	..	..	..
4300 Estate, inheritance and gift taxes	..	0	8	0	0	0	0	0	0	0
4310 Estate and inheritance taxes	..	..	8	..	..	..	..	..	..	..
4320 Gift taxes	..	..	0	..	..	..	..	..	..	..
4400 Taxes on financial and capital transactions	..	5	870	4 017	13 736	13 231	14 900	19 712	23 156	27 665
Alienation of immovable property	..	..	..	1 763	1 076	1 122	1 271	1 595	1 623	1 823
Transfer of ownership of real estate	..	..	..	2 236	8 147	5 027	4 518	6 671	7 016	8 658
Purchasing property	..	..	..	18	4 513	7 082	9 110	11 447	14 516	17 184
4500 Non-recurrent taxes	..	0	0	0	0	0	0	0	0	0
4510 On net wealth	..	..	..	..	..	..	..	..	..	..
4520 Other non-recurrent taxes	..	..	..	..	..	..	..	..	..	..
4600 Other recurrent taxes on property	..	0	0	0	0	0	0	0	0	0
5000 Taxes on goods and services	..	**395**	**44 837**	**319 612**	**513 140**	**651 915**	**715 811**	**1 141 170**	**1 283 049**	**1 381 659**
5100 Taxes on production, sale, transfer, etc.	..	388	44 171	310 325	491 928	630 123	696 150	1 120 610	1 262 770	1 364 208
5110 General taxes	..	121	26 635	189 606	409 013	504 509	556 794	707 213	816 048	922 238
5111 Value added taxes	..	120	26 635	189 606	409 013	504 509	556 794	707 213	816 048	922 238
5112 Sales tax	..	0	0	0	0	0	0	0	0	0
5113 Other	..	1	0	0	0	0	0	0	0	0
5120 Taxes on specific goods and services	..	265	17 519	120 720	82 915	125 614	139 356	413 397	446 722	441 970
5121 Excise duties	..	45	10 072	86 163	47 008	86 098	104 111	361 538	378 537	358 577
Special tax on production and services	..	..	..	81 544	41 532	81 427	97 860	354 294	367 834	347 436
Tax on new automobiles	..	..	..	4 619	5 476	4 671	6 252	7 244	10 703	11 142
Tax on luxury goods and services	..	..	..	0	0	0	0	0	0	0
5122 Profits of fiscal monopolies	..	0	0	0	0	0	0	0	0	0

	1965	1980	1990	2000	2007	2010	2013	2015	2017	2018
5123 Customs and import duties	..	45	6 998	33 285	33 344	26 602	32 324	45 366	53 793	67 232
Step customs officer	..	..	..	423	1 156	2 071	3 065	1 270	1 463	1 690
Import taxes	..	..	..	32 861	32 188	24 531	29 260	44 096	52 330	65 543
5124 Taxes on exports	..	2	75	4	3	0	1	1	0	0
Tax on exports	..	..	..	4	3	0	1	1	0	0
5125 Taxes on investment goods	..	0	0	0	0	0	0	0	0	0
5126 Taxes on specific services	..	8	132	1 042	2 146	10 958	-967	1 763	7 778	8 692
IDE	..	8	..	0	0	8 022	-5 988	-3 323	-739	-629
Tax on lodging	..	0	..	504	1 059	1 384	1 890	2 561	3 598	3 945
Public entertainment tax	..	0	..	240	365	462	566	689	839	909
Tax on lotteries, raffles and gambling	..	0	..	267	705	923	1 213	1 416	2 717	2 947
Tax on commercials	..	0	..	4	17	166	203	210	1 082	1 231
Various indirect taxes	..	0	..	28	0	1	1 149	209	282	288
5127 Other taxes on internat. trade and transactions	..	0	0	0	0	0	0	0	0	0
5128 Other taxes	..	165	242	226	414	1 956	3 886	4 730	6 613	7 468
Mining fees	..	..	..	226	414	1 956	3 886	4 730	6 613	7 468
5130 Unallocable between 5110 and 5120	..	2	17	0	0	0	0	0	0	0
5200 Taxes on use of goods and perform activities	..	7	666	9 287	21 212	21 793	19 661	20 560	20 279	17 451
5210 Recurrent taxes	..	7	666	9 287	21 212	21 793	19 661	20 560	20 279	17 451
5211 Paid by households: motor vehicles	..	3	567	8 878	20 692	21 319	19 174	19 880	19 530	16 533
Tax on motor vehicules	..	..	..	8 878	20 692	21 319	19 174	19 880	19 530	16 533
5212 Paid by others: motor vehicles	..	0	0	301	275	281	357	439	554	640
Tax on federal auto transport	..	..	..	301	275	281	357	439	554	640
5213 Paid in respect of other goods	..	4	99	108	246	193	130	240	194	278
Sport fishing	..	..	..	40	98	59	50	62	71	73
Sport hunting	..	..	..	3	0	0	0	0	0	0
Tax on commercial activities	..	..	..	63	147	50	26	64	28	115
Trade in books and magazines	..	..	..	0	0	0	3	1	0	0
Tax on industrial activities	..	..	..	2	0	82	49	93	77	73
Mining	..	..	..	0	0	1	1	21	18	17
5220 Non-recurrent taxes	..	0	0	0	0	0	0	0	0	0
5300 Unallocable between 5100 and 5200	..	0	0	0	0	0	0	0	0	0
6000 Other taxes	**..**	**14**	**1 619**	**7 651**	**16 905**	**27 398**	**41 204**	**44 612**	**52 475**	**65 217**
6100 Paid solely by business	..	0	0	0	0	0	0	0	0	0
6200 Other	..	14	1 619	7 651	16 905	27 398	41 204	44 612	52 475	65 217
Accessories	..	..	..	5 504	12 403	22 206	25 301	23 211	32 153	45 864
Unallocable between 1000 and 5000 caused in exercices fiscal previous liquidation slopes or of payment	..	..	..	374	222	30	1 618	4 168	281	400
Additional state and local taxes	..	..	..	1 773	4 280	5 162	14 285	17 232	20 042	18 952
Non-wastable tax credits										
Non-wastable tax credits against 1000	..	..	..	..	59 065	40 344	41 800	43 806	46 793	49 101
Tax expenditure component	..	..	..	..	35 888	30 635	40 526	42 813	45 757	47 929
Transfer component	..	..	..	..	23 177	9 708	1 274	993	1 036	1 172
Total tax revenue on cash basis	**..**	**771**	**102 005**	**767 216**	**1 382 103**	**1 716 243**	**2 165 501**	**2 953 480**	**3 527 032**	**3 797 888**
Total tax revenue on accrual basis	**..**	**..**	**..**	**..**	**..**	**..**	**..**	**..**	**..**	**..**
Conciliation with National Accounts										
Additional taxes included in National Accounts	..	..	..	..	..	..	..	..	..	..
Taxes excluded from National Accounts	..	..	..	..	..	..	..	..	..	..
Difference in treatment of tax credits	..	..	..	..	..	..	..	..	..	..
Capital transfer for uncollected revenue	..	..	..	..	..	..	..	..	..	..
Voluntary social security contributions	..	..	..	..	..	..	..	..	..	..
Miscellaneous differences	..	..	..	..	..	..	..	..	..	..
National Accounts: Taxes and actual social contributions	..	..	..	..	..	..	..	..	..	..
Imputed social contributions	..	..	..	..	..	..	..	..	..	..
National Accounts: Taxes and all social contributions	..	..	..	..	..	..	..	..	..	..

.. Not available

Note: Year ending 31st December.

Data are on cash basis.

Source: Ministry of Finance, Economic Department.

StatLink https://doi.org/10.1787/888934212117

Table 5.25. Netherlands: Details of tax revenue, 1965-2018

Million EUR

	1965	1980	1990	2000	2007	2010	2013	2015	2017	2018
Total tax revenue	**10 860**	**69 982**	**104 419**	**166 824**	**220 950**	**227 911**	**238 488**	**255 348**	**285 671**	**300 298**
Total tax revenue exclusive of taxes collected for the EU	..	..	**102 926**	**165 227**	**218 926**	**225 943**	**236 479**	**252 272**	**282 463**	**296 931**
1000 Taxes on income, profits and capital gains	**3 884**	**22 998**	**33 689**	**43 256**	**62 463**	**63 581**	**59 085**	**70 849**	**85 761**	**88 769**
1100 Of individuals	3 008	18 383	25 806	25 116	41 414	48 992	44 830	52 405	61 571	61 660
1110 On income and profits	3 007	18 364	25 757	25 057	41 276	48 771	44 592	52 167	61 442	61 514
Income tax	1 359	2 895	2 455	-880	2 294	2 076	-1 337	-2 566	-1 183	-1 082
Wage tax	1 466	14 984	22 258	24 433	37 729	46 102	45 546	53 953	61 844	61 573
Dividend tax	123	486	1 044	1 504	1 253	593	383	780	781	1 023
Directors tax	14	0	0	0	0	0	0	0	0	0
Inhabited house tax	45	0	0	0	0	0	0	0	0	0
1120 On capital gains	1	18	50	59	138	221	238	238	129	146
Tax on games of chance	1	18	50	59	138	221	238	238	129	146
1200 Corporate	876	4 615	7 882	18 140	21 049	14 589	14 255	18 444	24 190	27 109
1210 On profits	876	4 615	7 882	18 140	21 049	14 589	14 255	18 444	24 190	27 109
Corporate income and dividend taxes	876	4 615	7 882	18 140	21 049	14 589	14 255	18 444	24 190	27 109
1220 On capital gains	0	0	0	0	0	0	0	0	0	0
1300 Unallocable between 1100 and 1200	0	0	0	0	0	0	0	0	0	0
2000 Social security contributions	**3 342**	**26 641**	**39 075**	**64 522**	**77 072**	**82 732**	**97 372**	**96 426**	**101 913**	**108 049**
2100 Employees	1 659	11 018	24 109	35 305	40 918	41 637	49 327	48 213	39 875	41 775
2110 On a payroll basis	..	..	..	35 305	40 918	41 637	49 327	48 213	39 875	41 775
2120 On an income tax basis	..	..	..	0	0	0	0	0	0	0
2200 Employers	1 371	12 465	7 837	18 671	25 925	29 351	31 603	34 614	37 720	40 702
2210 On a payroll basis	..	..	..	18 671	25 925	29 351	31 603	34 614	37 720	40 702
2220 On an income tax basis	..	..	..	0	0	0	0	0	0	0
2300 Self-employed or non-employed	311	3 158	7 129	10 546	10 229	11 744	16 442	13 599	24 318	25 572
2310 On a payroll basis	..	..	..	0	0	0	0	0	0	0
2320 On an income tax basis	..	..	..	10 546	10 229	11 744	16 442	13 599	24 318	25 572
2400 Unallocable between 2100, 2200 and 2300	0	0	0	0	0	0	0	0	0	0
2410 On a payroll basis	..	..	..	..	..	..	..	..	..	..
2420 On an income tax basis	..	..	..	..	..	..	..	..	..	..
3000 Taxes on payroll and workforce	**0**	**0**	**0**	**0**	**0**	**0**	**0**	**0**	**0**	**0**
4000 Taxes on property	**476**	**2 509**	**3 816**	**8 797**	**10 363**	**8 770**	**8 084**	**9 768**	**11 487**	**12 142**
4100 Recurrent taxes on immovable property	111	1 021	1 711	3 094	3 488	4 241	5 249	6 382	6 919	7 370
Municipal immovable property tax	-59	821	1 398	..	..	..	..	..	..	..
Other municipal taxes	66	5	18	..	..	..	..	..	..	..
Contributions polder boards	44	195	295	..	..	..	..	..	..	..
Tax on land	59	0	0	..	..	..	..	..	..	..
4110 Households	..	..	..	1 806	1 642	2 058	2 802	3 741	4 154	4 513
Municipal immovable property tax	..	..	..	1 651	1 368	1 553	1 754	1 882	1 975	2 032
Contributions polder boards	..	..	..	155	274	429	492	514	561	584
Levies on social housing corporations	..	..	..	0	0	76	556	1 345	1 618	1 897
4120 Others	..	..	..	1 288	1 846	2 183	2 447	2 641	2 765	2 857
Municipal immovable property tax	..	..	..	893	1 319	1 488	1 686	1 809	1 898	1 952
Contributions polder boards	..	..	..	395	527	695	761	832	867	905
4200 Recurrent taxes on net wealth	86	517	554	824	30	23	1	0	0	0
4210 Individual	86	517	554	824	30	23	1	..	..	..
Property tax of individuals	86	517	554	824	30	23	1	..	..	..
4220 Corporate	0	0	0	0	0	0	0	..	..	..
4300 Estate, inheritance and gift taxes	117	336	522	1 483	1 877	1 721	1 730	1 614	1 841	1 731
4310 Estate and inheritance taxes	..	304	472	1 303	1 877	1 721	1 730	1 614	1 841	1 731
Estate tax	..	0	0	0	0	0	0	0	0	0
Inheritance tax	..	304	472	1 303	1 877	1 721	1 730	1 614	1 841	1 731
4320 Gift taxes	..	32	50	180	0	0	0	0	0	0
4400 Taxes on financial and capital transactions	162	635	1 030	3 396	4 968	2 785	1 104	1 772	2 727	3 041
Stamp duties	44	0	0	0	0	0	0	0	0	0
Registration duties	118	0	0	0	0	0	0	0	0	0
Tax on legal transactions	0	635	1 030	0	0	0	0	0	0	0
Real estate transfer tax	0	0	0	2 804	4 925	2 785	1 104	1 772	2 727	3 041
Tax on capital formation	0	0	0	592	43	0	0	0	0	0
4500 Non-recurrent taxes	0	0	0	0	0	0	0	0	0	0
4510 On net wealth	..	..	..	..	..	..	..	..	..	..
4520 Other non-recurrent taxes	..	..	..	..	..	..	..	..	..	..
4600 Other recurrent taxes on property	0	0	0	0	0	0	0	0	0	0
5000 Taxes on goods and services	**3 110**	**17 675**	**27 585**	**49 472**	**70 084**	**71 866**	**72 824**	**77 889**	**85 653**	**90 531**
5100 Taxes on production, sale, transfer, etc.	2 943	16 204	25 067	44 871	63 673	64 247	65 030	69 315	76 819	81 470
5110 General taxes	1 344	11 081	17 216	28 857	42 884	42 674	42 459	44 922	49 893	52 782
5111 Value added taxes	0	11 081	17 216	28 849	42 873	42 654	42 424	44 879	49 833	52 712
5112 Sales tax	0	0	0	0	0	0	0	0	0	0

	1965	1980	1990	2000	2007	2010	2013	2015	2017	2018
5113 Other	1 344	0	0	8	11	20	35	43	60	70
Turnover tax	1 344	..	..	..	..	..	..	..	..	..
5120 Taxes on specific goods and services	1 600	5 123	7 850	16 014	20 789	21 573	22 571	24 393	26 926	28 688
5121 Excise duties	880	3 789	5 985	13 755	17 724	18 392	17 309	18 020	19 692	20 995
Excise on spirits	129	463	422	397	335	331	306	314	331	342
Excise on beer	34	123	259	263	310	389	413	451	447	457
Excise on sugar	45	9	27	0	0	0	0	0	0	0
Excise on tobacco	307	839	948	1 590	2 136	2 437	2 228	2 222	2 397	2 669
Excise on wine	14	82	91	173	257	304	348	354	346	347
Registration tax on motor vehicles	0	613	1 189	2 875	3 647	2 096	1 159	1 462	2 000	2 270
Excise on soft drinks	0	59	186	216	155	156	154	207	265	278
Levies for nuclear reactor	0	0	0	0	0	0	0	0	0	0
Excise on petrol	310	1 280	1 684	3 151	4 010	4 086	3 960	4 109	4 293	4 472
Excise on other mineral oils	41	295	808	2 139	2 965	3 573	3 630	3 757	3 875	3 919
Levies on air pollution	0	27	304	0	0	0	0	0	0	0
Taxes on pollution/resources	0	0	68	462	456	655	144	345	369	379
Levies on energy	0	0	0	2 387	3 333	4 250	4 856	4 679	5 213	5 724
Other excise duties and consumption taxes	0	0	0	0	0	0	0	0	0	0
Other environmental taxes	0	0	0	34	35	15	10	14	46	27
Strategic stockpile tax on mineral oils	0	0	0	68	85	100	101	106	110	111
5122 Profits of fiscal monopolies	0	0	0	0	0	0	0	0	0	0
5123 Customs and import duties	702	971	1 375	1 310	1 679	1 732	1 756	2 266	2 420	2 504
EU levies on food products	338	295	168	0	0	0	0	0	0	0
MCA levy	0	9	0	0	0	0	0	0	0	0
Remaining import duties	364	667	1 207	0	0	0	0	0	0	0
Custom duties collected for the EU	..	..	..	1 310	1 679	1 732	1 756	2 266	2 420	2 504
5124 Taxes on exports	0	0	0	0	0	0	0	0	0	0
5125 Taxes on investment goods	0	77	0	0	0	0	0	0	0	0
Selective investment regulation levy	..	77	..	..	..	..	..	..	..	..
5126 Taxes on specific services	16	222	372	662	1 041	1 213	3 253	3 751	4 571	4 946
Tax on fire insurance	2	0	0	0	0	0	0	0	0	0
Entertainment tax	14	0	0	0	0	0	0	0	0	0
Tax on insurances	0	209	340	512	807	861	2 343	2 375	2 486	2 715
Tourist tax	0	14	32	83	125	131	164	206	252	288
Tax on games of chance	0	0	0	67	109	221	239	238	340	384
Flight tax	0	0	0	0	0	0	0	0	0	0
Bank levies	0	0	0	0	0	0	507	478	948	939
Contribution to EU Single Resolution Fund	..	..	..	..	..	..	..	454	545	620
5127 Other taxes on internat. trade and transactions	0	0	0	0	0	0	0	0	0	0
5128 Other taxes	1	64	118	287	345	236	253	356	243	243
ESCC levy	1	5	0	0	0	0	0	0	0	0
Sugar contribution	0	23	36	0	0	0	0	0	0	0
Milk levy	0	36	82	0	0	0	0	0	0	0
EU levies on food products	0	0	0	273	345	236	253	356	243	243
Sugar storage duty	0	0	0	14	0	0	0	0	0	0
5130 Unallocable between 5110 and 5120	0	0	0	0	0	0	0	0	0	0
5200 Taxes on use of goods and perform activities	167	1 470	2 518	4 601	6 411	7 619	7 794	8 574	8 834	9 061
5210 Recurrent taxes	165	1 470	2 518	4 601	6 411	7 619	7 751	8 410	8 634	8 800
5211 Paid by households: motor vehicles	27	463	799	2 288	3 211	4 084	4 008	4 470	4 582	4 686
Motor vehicle tax	27	427	744	2 288	3 211	4 084	4 008	4 470	4 582	4 686
Motor vehicle licence	0	36	54	0	0	0	0	0	0	0
5212 Paid by others: motor vehicles	132	604	1 044	554	760	976	959	1 069	1 096	1 121
Motor vehicle tax	132	590	1 026	554	760	976	959	1 069	1 096	1 121
Motor vehicle licence	0	14	18	0	0	0	0	0	0	0
Heavy motor vehicle tax	0	0	0	0	0	0	0	0	0	0
5213 Paid in respect of other goods	6	404	676	1 759	2 440	2 559	2 784	2 871	2 956	2 993
Dog licences	3	23	27	40	54	59	67	65	61	56
Commuter tax	0	5	5	12	21	25	29	29	32	28
Levies on water pollution	1	372	644	1 003	1 220	1 127	1 182	1 212	1 257	1 284
Permission to sell spirits	2	5	0	0	0	0	0	0	1	0
Sewerage charges	0	0	0	650	1 094	1 304	1 463	1 531	1 597	1 619
Levies on manure surplus	0	0	0	18	-4	2	4	3	7	4
Noise nuisance tax civil aviation	0	0	0	36	55	42	39	31	1	2
5220 Non-recurrent taxes	2	0	0	0	0	0	43	164	200	261
Emission permits	..	..	..	..	..	..	43	164	200	261
5300 Unallocable between 5100 and 5200	0	0	0	0	0	0	0	0	0	0
6000 Other taxes	**48**	**159**	**254**	**777**	**968**	**962**	**1 123**	**416**	**857**	**807**
6100 Paid solely by business	48	159	254	410	322	326	139	0	0	0
Administrative levies	48	159	254	410	322	326	139	..	..	..

	1965	1980	1990	2000	2007	2010	2013	2015	2017	2018
6200 Other	0	0	0	367	646	636	984	416	857	807
Employers tax	..	..	..	331	497	609	804	208	569	563
Tax revenue from Caribbean Netherlands	..	..	..	0	0	13	100	128	153	152
Other taxes on wealth	..	..	..	36	149	14	80	80	135	92
Memorandum items										
Customs duties collected on behalf of the EU	..	..	..	1 310	1 679	1 732	1 756	2 266	2 420	2 504
SRF contributions collected on behalf of the EU	..	..	..	..	..	..	..	454	545	620
Total tax revenue on cash basis	**10 860**	**69 982**	**104 419**	**165 503**	**..**	**..**	**..**	**..**	**..**	**..**
Total tax revenue on accrual basis	**..**	**..**	**..**	**166 824**	**220 950**	**227 911**	**238 488**	**255 348**	**285 671**	**300 298**
Conciliation with National Accounts										
Additional taxes included in National Accounts	..	..	..	1 400	0	0	0	0	0	0
Wage Tax reductions	..	..	..	1 400	..	..	..	..	..	..
Taxes excluded from National Accounts	..	..	..	0	0	0	0	0	0	0
Difference in treatment of tax credits	..	..	..	0	0	0	0	0	0	0
Capital transfer for uncollected revenue	..	..	..	0	0	0	0	0	0	0
Voluntary social security contributions	..	..	..	0	0	0	0	0	0	0
Miscellaneous differences	..	..	..	-70	0	0	0	0	0	0
National Accounts: Taxes and actual social contributions	..	..	..	168 154	220 950	227 911	238 488	255 348	285 671	300 298
Imputed social contributions	..	..	..	3 808	3 509	3 545	3 414	3 160	3 622	3 685
National Accounts: Taxes and all social contributions	..	..	..	171 962	224 459	231 456	241 902	258 508	289 293	303 983

.. Not available

Note: Year ending 31st December.

From 1999 data are on accrual basis.

Heading 2000: From 1998 the figures include some voluntary contributions and the breakdown between premiums paid by employees (2100) and by self-employed / non-employed has been estimated. This is also the case for the breakdown between premiums paid on a payroll or on an income tax basis for those years where both apply.

Heading 4100: From 1992, there was a structural break in the data for the 'municipal immovable property tax'. The tax ceased to be collected by the central government at that time and the figures are presented on a different type of statistical registration (no longer cash basis).

Heading 5110: Includes 358 million of euros (1969) and 186 millions of euros (1970) in respect of deduction of turnover tax on stocks existing at 1st January 1969.

Heading 5213: Small amounts (less than 2.3 million euros) of hunting and fishing licence receipts which should be classified here have been omitted.

Source: Social security contributions and local taxes: Central Bureau of Statistics.

Other taxes: Ministry of Finance.

StatLink https://doi.org/10.1787/888934212136

Table 5.26. New Zealand: Details of tax revenue, 1965-2018

Million NZD

	1965	1980	1990	2000	2007	2010	2013	2015	2017	2018
Total tax revenue	**1 001**	**7 594**	**27 471**	**39 765**	**64 046**	**62 310**	**72 187**	**81 499**	**92 635**	**99 842**
1000 Taxes on income, profits and capital gains	**606**	**5 299**	**16 370**	**23 861**	**40 308**	**33 494**	**39 415**	**44 723**	**51 489**	**56 173**
1100 Of individuals	394	4 679	13 177	17 126	26 965	23 519	26 555	30 297	35 004	37 467
1110 On income and profits	394	4 679	13 177	17 126	26 965	23 519	26 555	30 297	35 004	37 467
1120 On capital gains	0	0	0	0	0	0	0	0	0	0
1200 Corporate	207	589	1 780	4 914	9 069	7 609	10 344	11 407	13 584	15 559
1210 On profits	207	589	1 780	4 914	9 069	7 609	10 344	11 407	13 584	15 559
1220 On capital gains	0	0	0	0	0	0	0	0	0	0
1300 Unallocable between 1100 and 1200	5	31	1 413	1 821	4 274	2 366	2 516	3 019	2 901	3 147
NRWT	5	24	277	760	1 506	467	427	733	619	651
Property speculation	0	0	0	0	0	0	0	0	0	0
Absentee income tax	0	7	0	0	0	0	0	0	0	0
Interest	0	0	1 028	990	2 699	1 704	1 643	1 660	1 530	1 659
Dividends	0	0	83	71	69	195	446	626	752	837
Other	0	0	25	0	0	0	0	0	0	0
2000 Social security contributions	**0**	**0**	**0**	**0**	**0**	**0**	**0**	**0**	**0**	**0**
2100 Employees	0	0	0	0	0	0	0	0	0	0
2110 On a payroll basis	..	..	..	..	..	..	..	..	..	..
2120 On an income tax basis	..	..	..	..	..	..	..	..	..	..
2200 Employers	0	0	0	0	0	0	0	0	0	0
2210 On a payroll basis	..	..	..	..	..	..	..	..	..	..
2220 On an income tax basis	..	..	..	..	..	..	..	..	..	..
2300 Self-employed or non-employed	0	0	0	0	0	0	0	0	0	0
2310 On a payroll basis	..	..	..	..	..	..	..	..	..	..
2320 On an income tax basis	..	..	..	..	..	..	..	..	..	..
2400 Unallocable between 2100, 2200 and 2300	0	0	0	0	0	0	0	0	0	0
2410 On a payroll basis	..	..	..	..	..	..	..	..	..	..
2420 On an income tax basis	..	..	..	..	..	..	..	..	..	..
3000 Taxes on payroll and workforce	**0**	**0**	**0**	**0**	**0**	**0**	**0**	**0**	**0**	**0**
4000 Taxes on property	**116**	**602**	**1 880**	**2 112**	**3 417**	**4 119**	**4 585**	**5 046**	**5 533**	**5 822**
4100 Recurrent taxes on immovable property	84	515	1 722	2 049	3 322	4 031	4 492	4 962	5 426	5 717
Local govt rates and services	81	503	1 550	2 049	3 322	4 031	4 492	4 962	5 426	5 717
Land tax	3	12	172	0	0	0	0	0	0	0
4110 Households	..	..	0	..	..	..	..	..	..	..
4120 Others	..	..	172	..	..	..	..	..	..	..
4200 Recurrent taxes on net wealth	0	0	0	0	0	0	0	0	0	0
4210 Individual	..	..	..	..	..	..	..	..	..	..
4220 Corporate	..	..	..	..	..	..	..	..	..	..
4300 Estate, inheritance and gift taxes	23	39	80	2	3	2	0	0	0	0
4310 Estate and inheritance taxes	21	37	74	0	0	0	..	..	..	..
4320 Gift taxes	2	2	6	2	3	2	..	..	..	..
4400 Taxes on financial and capital transactions	9	48	78	61	92	86	93	84	107	105
Instrument duty	7	40	62	51	85	82	91	84	107	105
Cheque duty	2	8	16	10	7	4	2	0	0	0
4500 Non-recurrent taxes	0	0	0	0	0	0	0	0	0	0
4510 On net wealth	..	..	..	..	..	..	..	..	..	..
4520 Other non-recurrent taxes	..	..	..	..	..	..	..	..	..	..
4600 Other recurrent taxes on property	0	0	0	0	0	0	0	0	0	0
5000 Taxes on goods and services	**280**	**1 693**	**9 220**	**13 792**	**20 290**	**24 692**	**28 184**	**31 728**	**35 612**	**37 845**
5100 Taxes on production, sale, transfer, etc.	262	1 624	8 680	12 887	18 832	23 107	26 344	29 584	33 220	35 271
5110 General taxes	77	776	6 163	9 885	15 046	19 143	22 063	24 587	27 951	29 521
5111 Value added taxes	0	0	6 163	9 885	15 046	19 143	22 063	24 587	27 951	29 521
5112 Sales tax	77	776	0	0	0	0	0	0	0	0
Motor vehicles	..	231	..	..	..	..	..	..	..	..
Other sales tax	..	544	..	..	..	..	..	..	..	..
5113 Other	0	0	0	0	0	0	0	0	0	0
5120 Taxes on specific goods and services	186	849	2 517	3 002	3 786	3 964	4 281	4 997	5 269	5 750

	1965	1980	1990	2000	2007	2010	2013	2015	2017	2018
5121 Excise duties	124	548	1 929	2 148	1 627	1 782	1 854	2 280	2 214	2 622
On alcoholic beverages	37	84	411	436	573	622	650	672	699	722
Beer	33	64	0	201	290	207	250	262	265	274
Wine	0	0	0	100	163	181	204	216	227	225
Spirits	4	20	0	135	120	234	196	194	207	223
Tobacco	33	99	568	764	159	220	273	362	399	483
Motor vehicles	0	0	7	0	0	0	0	0	0	0
Refined sugar	2	0	0	0	0	0	0	0	0	0
CA petroleum fuels	0	140	835	810	819	872	865	1 185	1 057	1 201
NRF fuel excise	49	121	0	0	0	0	0	0	0	0
Local petroleum fuels	0	18	21	27	30	32	31	33	33	190
CA mileage tax	0	0	0	0	0	0	0	0	0	0
NRF mileage tax	3	0	0	0	0	0	0	0	0	0
Road user charges	0	68	0	0	0	0	0	0	0	0
Energy resources levy	0	20	87	111	46	36	35	28	26	26
5122 Profits of fiscal monopolies	0	0	0	0	0	0	0	0	0	0
5123 Customs and import duties	49	231	505	648	1 857	1 916	2 160	2 442	2 738	2 814
5124 Taxes on exports	0	0	0	0	0	0	0	0	0	0
5125 Taxes on investment goods	0	0	0	0	0	0	0	0	0	0
5126 Taxes on specific services	13	57	83	206	302	266	267	275	317	314
Lottery (national)	1	6	26	167	290	253	254	260	301	299
Lottery (overseas)	0	0	0	0	0	0	0	0	0	0
Racing	12	46	57	39	12	13	13	15	16	15
Film hire tax	0	1	0	0	0	0	0	0	0	0
Domestic air travel tax	0	3	0	0	0	0	0	0	0	0
5127 Other taxes on internat. trade and transactions	0	12	0	0	0	0	0	0	0	0
Foreign fishing vessels tax	..	0	..	..	..	..	..	..	..	..
Foreign travel tax	..	0	..	..	..	..	..	..	..	..
International departure tax	..	12	..	..	..	..	..	..	..	..
5128 Other taxes	0	0	0	0	0	0	0	0	0	0
5130 Unallocable between 5110 and 5120	0	0	0	0	0	0	0	0	0	0
5200 Taxes on use of goods and perform activities	18	69	539	905	1 458	1 585	1 840	2 144	2 392	2 574
5210 Recurrent taxes	18	69	539	905	1 458	1 585	1 840	2 144	2 392	2 574
Motor vehicle registration	7	47	154	181	226	172	187	214	227	227
Heavy traffic fees	8	0	285	532	851	1 016	1 205	1 381	1 551	1 673
Accident compensation levies	0	0	0	0	0	0	0	0	0	0
5211 Paid by households: motor vehicles	0	0	0	0	0	0	0	0	0	0
5212 Paid by others: motor vehicles	0	0	0	0	0	0	0	0	0	0
5213 Paid in respect of other goods	3	23	100	192	381	397	448	549	614	674
Local authority fees and charges	3	23	100	192	381	397	448	549	614	674
5220 Non-recurrent taxes	0	0	0	0	0	0	0	0	0	0
5300 Unallocable between 5100 and 5200	0	0	0	0	0	0	0	0	0	0
6000 Other taxes	**0**	**0**	**1**	**0**	**31**	**5**	**3**	**2**	**1**	**2**
6100 Paid solely by business	..	..	0	..	0	0	0	0	0	0
6200 Other	..	..	1	..	31	5	3	2	1	2
Non-wastable tax credits										
Non-wastable tax credits against 1110	..	..	..	1 057	2 568	2 794	2 582	2 352	2 195	2 766
Tax expenditure component	..	..	..	311	873	950	1 349	1 254	1 205	1 518
Transfer component	..	..	..	746	1 695	1 844	1 233	1 098	990	1 248
Non-wastable tax credits against 1210	..	..	..	0	0	0	0	0	0	0
Tax expenditure component	..	..	..	..	..	..	..	..	..	..
Transfer component	..	..	..	..	..	..	..	..	..	..
Total tax revenue on cash basis	**1 001**	**7 594**	**27 471**	**39 276**	**64 273**	**62 053**	**73 172**	**82 481**	**93 901**	**98 594**
Total tax revenue on accrual basis	**..**	**..**	**..**	**39 765**	**64 046**	**62 310**	**72 187**	**81 499**	**92 635**	**99 842**
Conciliation with National Accounts										
Additional taxes included in National Accounts	..	..	..	..	0	0	2 490	2 818	4 559	4 781
Taxes excluded from National Accounts	..	..	..	..	0	0	-4 955	-5 769	-7 404	-7 787
Difference in treatment of tax credits	..	..	..	..	873	950	1 349	1 254	1 205	1 518
Capital transfer for uncollected revenue	..	..	..	..	0	0	0	0	0	0
Voluntary social security contributions	..	..	..	..	0	0	0	0	0	0
Miscellaneous differences	..	..	..	..	0	0	461	-1 602	-81	-3 325
National Accounts: Taxes and actual social contributions	..	..	..	..	64 919	63 260	71 532	78 200	90 914	95 029
Imputed social contributions	..	..	..	..	0	0	2 617	2 063	1 948	2 060
National Accounts: Taxes and all social contributions	..	..	..	..	64 919	63 260	74 149	80 263	92 862	97 089

.. Not available

Note: For the years before 1989 data are on a fiscal year basis ending 31st March. The figures provided for 1989 and onwards relate to the financial year ending 30th June of the following year.

From 1993, data are on accrual basis.

Heading 1000: Tax credits to exporters under the export incentives schemes are non-wastable, but that part of the excess of tax liability paid out to taxpayers is not identifiable.

Heading 1100: The figures up to 1969 include revenues collected by a social security income tax. The base of this tax was the same as the ordinary income tax base and the two have now been incorporated into a single income tax.

Heading 5121: From October 1986 incorporates that portion of the selective impost on wine, spirits, tobacco and motor vehicles which was formerly collected and reported as sales tax. The revenue collected on those imported goods which are subject to the equivalent of the domestic excise has been classified as excise duty. In this respect, there is a discontinuity between the excises recorded before and after October 1986.

Heading 5210: The other local authority licence fees include some small items which could be regarded as non-tax revenues.

Heading for non-wastable tax credits 1110 comprises four Family assistance tax credits. The total in item 1100 is net of the tax expenditure component but not net of the transfer component.

Source: Local Authorities Statistics, Department of Statistics, Wellington.

StatLink https://doi.org/10.1787/888934212155

Table 5.27. Norway: Details of tax revenue, 1965-2018

Million NOK

	1965	1980	1990	2000	2007	2010	2013	2015	2017	2018
Total tax revenue	**16 842**	**133 499**	**301 812**	**627 989**	**987 278**	**1 083 337**	**1 222 890**	**1 195 354**	**1 277 949**	**1 397 206**
1000 Taxes on income, profits and capital gains	**7 316**	**55 837**	**106 290**	**284 189**	**474 460**	**512 244**	**558 171**	**475 374**	**499 695**	**582 916**
1100 Of individuals	6 671	38 018	79 068	152 013	219 726	256 544	304 409	335 199	339 076	353 359
1110 On income and profits	6 671	38 018	79 068	152 013	219 726	256 544	304 409	335 199	339 076	353 359
Employee social security contributions	1 305	0	0	0	0	0	0	0	0	0
Income taxes	5 366	38 018	79 068	152 013	219 726	256 544	304 409	335 199	339 076	353 359
1120 On capital gains	0	0	0	0	0	0	0	0	0	0
1200 Corporate	645	17 819	27 222	132 176	254 734	255 700	253 762	140 175	160 619	229 557
1210 On profits	..	..	..	132 176	254 734	255 700	253 762	140 175	160 619	229 557
1220 On capital gains	..	..	..	0	0	0	0	0	0	0
1300 Unallocable between 1100 and 1200	0	0	0	0	0	0	0	0	0	0
2000 Social security contributions	**2 009**	**28 205**	**79 362**	**132 170**	**204 473**	**243 002**	**292 461**	**325 130**	**339 848**	**356 610**
2100 Employees	0	6 639	25 345	45 162	68 518	81 032	98 124	112 662	119 019	124 499
2110 On a payroll basis	..	..	..	45 162	68 518	81 032	98 124	112 662	119 019	124 499
2120 On an income tax basis	..	..	..	0	0	0	0	0	0	0
2200 Employers	1 716	20 454	50 116	79 242	124 178	148 047	177 458	190 923	197 813	208 153
2210 On a payroll basis	..	..	..	79 242	124 178	148 047	177 458	190 923	197 813	208 153
2220 On an income tax basis	..	..	..	0	0	0	0	0	0	0
2300 Self-employed or non-employed	293	1 112	3 901	7 766	11 777	13 923	16 879	21 545	23 016	23 958
2310 On a payroll basis	..	..	..	7 766	11 777	13 923	16 879	21 545	23 016	23 958
2320 On an income tax basis	..	..	..	0	0	0	0	0	0	0
2400 Unallocable between 2100, 2200 and 2300	0	0	0	0	0	0	0	0	0	0
2410 On a payroll basis	..	..	..	..	..	..	..	..	..	..
2420 On an income tax basis	..	..	..	..	..	..	..	..	..	..
3000 Taxes on payroll and workforce	**0**	**0**	**0**	**0**	**0**	**0**	**0**	**0**	**1 891**	**1 976**
4000 Taxes on property	**523**	**2 295**	**8 887**	**14 422**	**26 601**	**28 547**	**34 810**	**34 021**	**41 912**	**43 930**
4100 Recurrent taxes on immovable property	100	431	2 216	2 724	5 571	7 109	8 879	11 177	13 611	14 205
4110 Households	..	431	2 216	2 724	2 149	3 024	3 693	5 437	7 067	7 446
4120 Others	..	0	0	0	3 422	4 085	5 186	5 740	6 544	6 759
4200 Recurrent taxes on net wealth	341	1 450	5 118	7 703	12 900	13 193	16 376	14 123	18 965	20 083
4210 Individual	235	907	3 692	6 869	10 746	12 169	14 039	12 902	15 409	15 831
4220 Corporate	106	543	1 426	834	2 154	1 024	2 337	1 221	3 556	4 252
4300 Estate, inheritance and gift taxes	45	122	446	1 273	2 576	2 377	2 246	295	91	73
4310 Estate and inheritance taxes	..	122	446	1 273	2 576	2 377	2 246	295	91	73
4320 Gift taxes	..	0	0	0	0	0	0	0	0	0
4400 Taxes on financial and capital transactions	37	292	1 107	2 722	5 554	5 868	7 309	8 426	9 245	9 569
4500 Non-recurrent taxes	0	0	0	0	0	0	0	0	0	0
4510 On net wealth	..	..	..	..	..	..	..	..	..	..
4520 Other non-recurrent taxes	..	..	..	..	..	..	..	..	..	..
4600 Other recurrent taxes on property	0	0	0	0	0	0	0	0	0	0
5000 Taxes on goods and services	**6 928**	**47 154**	**107 262**	**197 208**	**281 744**	**299 544**	**337 448**	**360 829**	**394 603**	**411 774**
5100 Taxes on production, sale, transfer, etc.	6 720	45 882	102 901	185 921	266 456	284 646	321 557	342 410	376 280	392 783
5110 General taxes	3 622	24 350	56 656	124 985	189 424	201 802	235 771	256 029	284 534	297 918
5111 Value added taxes	0	24 350	56 656	124 166	188 705	201 184	234 941	255 182	283 518	296 900
Value added tax	..	24 350	56 656	124 166	188 705	201 184	234 941	255 182	283 518	296 900
5112 Sales tax	0	0	0	0	719	618	0	0	1 016	1 018
5113 Other	3 622	0	0	819	0	0	830	847	0	0
5120 Taxes on specific goods and services	3 098	21 532	46 245	60 936	77 032	82 844	85 786	86 381	91 746	94 865
5121 Excise duties	2 338	14 914	37 453	54 871	71 047	76 328	78 515	78 845	81 252	84 000
Stamp duty on tobacco	392	1 076	3 750	6 806	6 815	7 768	6 375	7 219	7 564	6 863
Taxes on spirits and wines	449	2 013	3 454	5 217	0	0	0	0	0	0
Excise on beer	162	605	2 195	3 650	0	0	0	0	0	0
Excise on petrol	480	2 310	7 057	9 756	8 132	7 373	6 417	5 711	5 597	5 535
Vehicles transfer tax	395	2 761	4 554	10 956	22 898	21 835	22 229	19 355	17 360	15 916
Chocolate and sweets	123	247	551	789	1 078	1 173	1 261	1 324	1 439	2 277
Sugar	0	0	217	230	192	196	201	206	206	186
Non-alcoholic beverages	38	120	487	1 113	1 024	1 739	1 803	1 972	2 111	2 964
Electric energy	89	1 515	3 414	5 091	7 079	8 110	8 656	9 233	11 575	12 000
Oil and gas products	0	3 703	8 729	88	92	98	108	103	109	114
Sales of radio and tv sets	0	163	220	920	0	0	0	0	0	0
Mineral oil	0	113	1 098	490	685	1 419	1 383	1 986	1 832	1 851
Cosmetics	0	0	0	159	0	0	0	0	0	0
Recording equipment	0	0	92	35	0	0	0	0	0	0
Others	210	288	1 635	1 249	1 821	1 965	2 060	2 535	2 737	3 015
Taxes on alcoholic beverages	0	0	0	0	10 338	11 317	12 602	12 969	13 638	14 103
Excise on diesel	0	0	0	4 802	6 424	8 653	10 507	10 267	9 924	10 432
Tax on Co2 emissions, petroleum sector excepted	0	0	0	3 520	4 469	4 682	4 913	5 965	7 160	8 744

	1965	1980	1990	2000	2007	2010	2013	2015	2017	2018
5122 Profits of fiscal monopolies	31	395	751	2 534	2 902	3 433	3 751	3 869	4 868	5 089
Profits state wine monopoly	31	30	67	41	32	44	36	0	0	0
Norsk tipping	0	365	684	2 493	2 870	3 389	3 715	3 869	4 868	5 089
5123 Customs and import duties	634	697	1 360	1 944	2 132	2 505	3 111	3 305	3 366	3 396
Customs revenue	615	689	1 305	1 944	2 132	2 505	3 111	3 305	3 366	3 396
Loading and lighthouse dues	11	0	0	0	0	0	0	0	0	0
Other import duties	8	8	55	0	0	0	0	0	0	0
5124 Taxes on exports	7	105	227	0	112	151	177	178	233	260
5125 Taxes on investment goods	0	4 274	4 454	0	0	0	0	0	0	0
5126 Taxes on specific services	88	195	1 233	1 386	131	114	140	138	1 972	2 060
Excise on race tracks	9	25	15	88	119	114	140	138	144	136
Taxes on specific services	34	49	150	1 298	0	0	0	0	1 828	1 924
Pengelotteriet (national lotteries)	45	121	462	0	0	0	0	0	0	0
Excise on lotto games	0	0	606	0	12	0	0	0	0	0
5127 Other taxes on internat. trade and transactions	0	0	0	0	0	0	0	0	0	0
5128 Other taxes	0	952	767	201	708	313	92	46	55	60
5130 Unallocable between 5110 and 5120	0	0	0	0	0	0	0	0	0	0
5200 Taxes on use of goods and perform activities	208	1 272	4 361	11 287	15 288	14 898	15 891	18 419	18 323	18 991
5210 Recurrent taxes	208	1 272	4 361	11 287	15 288	13 423	15 603	17 635	17 758	17 416
5211 Paid by households: motor vehicles	88	458	1 789	4 435	6 699	7 157	8 007	8 400	7 934	7 559
5212 Paid by others: motor vehicles	108	696	2 072	1 346	712	539	494	352	339	337
5213 Paid in respect of other goods	12	118	500	5 506	7 877	5 727	7 102	8 883	9 485	9 520
CO2 tax	0	0	0	3 047	3 385	2 166	3 293	4 906	5 223	5 296
Excise on pharmacies	6	32	59	105	153	80	78	99	94	61
Others	6	86	441	2 354	3 132	3 394	3 666	3 809	4 109	4 105
Tax on emissions of NOX	0	0	0	0	1 207	87	65	69	59	58
5220 Non-recurrent taxes	0	0	0	0	0	1 475	288	784	565	1 575
5300 Unallocable between 5100 and 5200	0	0	0	0	0	0	0	0	0	0
6000 Other taxes	**66**	**8**	**11**	**0**	**0**	**0**	**0**	**0**	**0**	**0**
6100 Paid solely by business	0	3	2	..	..	..	..	..	..	..
6200 Other	66	5	9	..	..	..	..	..	..	..
Non-wastable tax credits										
Non-wastable tax credits against 1210	..	..	..	..	994	1 229	1 576	2 959	3 990	4 029
Tax expenditure component	..	..	..	..	350	75	307	484	752	811
Transfer component	..	..	..	..	644	1 154	1 269	2 475	3 238	3 218
Total tax revenue on cash basis	**16 842**	**133 499**	**301 812**	**575 989**	**0**	**0**	**0**	**0**	**203 170**	**1 140 325**
Total tax revenue on accrual basis	**..**	**..**	**..**	**627 989**	**987 278**	**1 083 337**	**1 222 890**	**1 195 354**	**1 277 949**	**1 397 206**
Conciliation with National Accounts										
Additional taxes included in National Accounts	..	..	1 485	2 773	3 288	4 022	4 560	4 674	4 815	4 821
Taxes excluded from National Accounts	..	..	..	0	0	0	0	0	0	0
Difference in treatment of tax credits	..	..	..	0	350	75	307	484	752	811
Capital transfer for uncollected revenue	..	..	..	0	0	0	0	0	0	0
Voluntary social security contributions	..	..	..	0	0	0	0	0	0	0
Miscellaneous differences	..	..	..	0	0	0	0	0	0	0
National Accounts: Taxes and actual social contributions	..	..	..	630 762	990 916	1 087 434	1 227 757	1 200 512	1 283 516	1 402 838
Imputed social contributions	..	..	..	2 076	2 931	3 164	3 628	3 870	4 909	3 662
National Accounts: Taxes and all social contributions	..	..	..	632 838	993 847	1 090 598	1 231 385	1 204 382	1 288 425	1 406 500

.. Not available

Note: Year ending 31st December.

From 2000, data are on accrual basis.

Heading 5211: Up to 1971 this item contains motor vehicle licences paid by both households and enterprises.

Heading 5121: From 2005, taxes on alcoholic beverages include both 'taxes on spirits and wines' and 'excise on beer'.

Heading 5125: From 1998, revenue from taxes on investments goods is included in item 5121 "Others".

Source: Statistics Norway; National Accounts.

StatLink https://doi.org/10.1787/888934212174

Table 5.28. Poland: Details of tax revenue, 1965-2018

Million PLN

	1965	1980	1990	2000	2007	2010	2013	2015	2017	2018
Total tax revenue	..	..	..	**246 039**	**411 175**	**453 254**	**528 081**	**583 975**	**678 856**	**745 529**
Total tax revenue exclusive of taxes collected for the EU	..	..	..	**246 039**	**409 415**	**451 555**	**525 930**	**581 081**	**675 298**	**741 618**
1000 Taxes on income, profits and capital gains	..	..	..	**50 268**	**93 795**	**91 026**	**103 567**	**117 078**	**137 481**	**156 984**
1100 Of individuals	..	..	..	32 415	61 471	62 901	74 216	83 974	99 121	112 659
Individual income tax	..	..	..	32 415	61 403	62 818	74 124	83 861	98 969	112 503
Tax on winnings from lottery or gambling	..	..	..	0	68	83	92	113	152	156
1110 On income and profits	..	..	..	..	..	..	..	..	..	..
1120 On capital gains	..	..	..	..	..	..	..	..	..	..
1200 Corporate	..	..	..	17 853	32 324	28 125	29 351	33 104	38 360	44 325
1210 On profits	..	..	..	..	..	..	..	..	..	..
1220 On capital gains	..	..	..	..	..	..	..	..	..	..
1300 Unallocable between 1100 and 1200	..	..	..	0	0	0	0	0	0	0
2000 Social security contributions	..	..	..	**96 386**	**140 086**	**156 026**	**202 595**	**223 482**	**254 919**	**277 670**
2100 Employees	..	..	..	42 357	51 929	60 247	82 656	91 163	105 817	115 821
2110 On a payroll basis	..	..	..	..	..	..	..	..	..	..
2120 On an income tax basis	..	..	..	..	..	..	..	..	..	..
2200 Employers	..	..	..	41 130	54 331	65 353	79 524	87 616	100 873	108 672
2210 On a payroll basis	..	..	..	..	..	..	..	..	..	..
2220 On an income tax basis	..	..	..	..	..	..	..	..	..	..
2300 Self-employed or non-employed	..	..	..	12 899	33 826	30 426	40 415	44 703	48 229	53 177
2310 On a payroll basis	..	..	..	..	..	..	..	..	..	..
2320 On an income tax basis	..	..	..	..	..	..	..	..	..	..
2400 Unallocable between 2100, 2200 and 2300	..	..	..	0	0	0	0	0	0	0
2410 On a payroll basis	..	..	..	..	..	..	..	..	..	..
2420 On an income tax basis	..	..	..	..	..	..	..	..	..	..
3000 Taxes on payroll and workforce	..	..	..	**1 628**	**3 081**	**3 720**	**3 998**	**4 028**	**4 485**	**4 720**
Rehabilitation fund contribution	..	..	..	1 508	2 860	3 370	3 633	3 621	4 020	4 344
Wage guarantee fund contribution	..	..	..	120	221	350	365	407	465	376
4000 Taxes on property	..	..	..	**10 584**	**17 116**	**19 068**	**23 120**	**24 637**	**27 101**	**27 851**
4100 Recurrent taxes on immovable property	..	..	..	8 404	13 515	16 399	20 747	22 206	23 783	24 326
Agricultural tax-local	..	..	..	720	906	969	1 666	1 579	1 487	1 487
Forest tax-local	..	..	..	96	157	165	228	230	295	304
Real estate tax-local	..	..	..	7 588	12 452	15 265	18 853	20 397	22 001	22 535
4110 Households	..	..	..	2 348	3 613	4 555	6 289	6 549	6 945	7 157
4120 Others	..	..	..	6 056	9 902	11 844	14 458	15 657	16 838	17 168
4200 Recurrent taxes on net wealth	..	..	..	0	0	0	0	0	0	0
4210 Individual	..	..	..	..	..	..	..	..	..	..
4220 Corporate	..	..	..	..	..	..	..	..	..	..
4300 Estate, inheritance and gift taxes	..	..	..	172	328	290	252	246	295	299
Inheritance and gift tax-local	..	..	..	172	328	290	252	246	295	299
4310 Estate and inheritance taxes	..	..	..	..	..	..	..	..	..	..
4320 Gift taxes	..	..	..	..	..	..	..	..	..	..
4400 Taxes on financial and capital transactions	..	..	..	2 008	3 273	2 379	2 121	2 185	3 023	3 226
Tax on civil law transactions and stamp tax	..	..	..	2 008	3 273	2 379	2 121	2 185	3 023	3 226
4500 Non-recurrent taxes	..	..	..	0	0	0	0	0	0	0
4510 On net wealth	..	..	..	..	..	..	..	..	..	..
4520 Other non-recurrent taxes	..	..	..	..	..	..	..	..	..	..
4600 Other recurrent taxes on property	..	..	..	0	0	0	0	0	0	0
5000 Taxes on goods and services	..	..	..	**86 880**	**156 573**	**182 820**	**193 776**	**214 103**	**253 883**	**277 224**
5100 Taxes on production, sale, transfer, etc.	..	..	..	84 885	151 853	176 044	188 331	206 138	246 513	268 241
5110 General taxes	..	..	..	51 615	97 848	109 717	116 607	125 836	154 656	172 210
5111 Value added taxes	..	..	..	51 615	97 848	109 717	116 607	125 836	154 656	172 210
5112 Sales tax	..	..	..	0	0	0	0	0	0	0
5113 Other	..	..	..	0	0	0	0	0	0	0
Turnover tax, of which:	..	..	..	..	..	..	..	..	..	..
On spirits	..	..	..	..	..	..	..	..	..	..
On fuels	..	..	..	..	..	..	..	..	..	..
On tobacco	..	..	..	..	..	..	..	..	..	..
5120 Taxes on specific goods and services	..	..	..	33 270	54 005	66 327	71 724	80 302	91 857	96 031

	1965	1980	1990	2000	2007	2010	2013	2015	2017	2018
5121 Excise duties	..	..	..	27 170	49 376	62 016	66 310	70 632	78 957	82 140
On domestic excise products, of which:	..	..	..	24 213	45 752	58 935	60 774	62 442	73 764	77 377
On spirits	..	..	..	4 309	5 000	6 154	7 393	6 655	7 727	7 727
On fuels	..	..	..	11 056	22 128	26 545	28 184	29 874	38 169	38 169
On tobacco	..	..	..	6 143	11 973	17 348	18 126	17 788	18 752	18 752
On beer	..	..	..	1 758	2 975	3 303	3 473	3 547	3 398	3 398
On wine	..	..	..	459	378	315	219	246	227	227
On other products	..	..	..	488	3 298	5 270	3 379	4 332	5 491	9 104
On imported excise products, of which:	..	..	..	2 957	3 624	3 081	5 536	8 190	5 193	4 763
On spirits	..	..	..	90	253	311	279	267	323	323
On fuels	..	..	..	2 031	2 045	1 051	3 481	5 650	1 915	1 915
On tobacco	..	..	..	18	214	114	62	86	51	51
On beer	..	..	..	26	12	14	43	53	56	56
On wine	..	..	..	71	106	133	149	139	159	159
On other products	..	..	..	721	994	1 458	1 522	1 995	2 689	2 259
5122 Profits of fiscal monopolies	..	..	..	0	0	0	0	0	0	0
5123 Customs and import duties	..	..	..	5 038	1 760	1 627	1 977	2 823	3 485	3 911
5124 Taxes on exports	..	..	..	0	0	0	0	0	0	0
5125 Taxes on investment goods	..	..	..	0	0	0	0	0	0	0
5126 Taxes on specific services	..	..	..	1 062	1 297	1 974	2 534	5 795	8 364	8 915
Taxes and payments of financial institutions	..	..	..	443	189	375	1 077	4 472	2 383	2 491
Gambling tax	..	..	..	619	1 108	1 599	1 457	1 323	1 632	1 900
Tax from some financial institutions	..	..	..	0	0	0	0	0	4 349	4 524
5127 Other taxes on internat. trade and transactions	..	..	..	0	0	0	0	0	0	0
5128 Other taxes	..	..	..	0	1 572	710	903	1 052	1 051	1 065
5130 Unallocable between 5110 and 5120	..	..	..	0	0	0	0	0	0	0
5200 Taxes on use of goods and perform activities	..	..	..	1 995	4 720	6 776	5 445	7 965	7 370	8 983
5210 Recurrent taxes	..	..	..	433	2 224	3 667	3 432	4 317	4 084	4 013
5211 Paid by households: motor vehicles	..	..	..	0	0	0	0	0	0	0
5212 Paid by others: motor vehicles	..	..	..	0	0	0	0	0	0	0
5213 Paid in respect of other goods	..	..	..	433	2 224	3 667	3 432	4 317	4 084	4 013
5220 Non-recurrent taxes	..	..	..	1 562	2 496	3 109	2 013	3 648	3 286	4 970
5300 Unallocable between 5100 and 5200	..	..	..	0	0	0	0	0	0	0
6000 Other taxes	**..**	**..**	**..**	**293**	**524**	**594**	**1 025**	**647**	**987**	**1 080**
Abolished taxes	..	..	..	..	..	..	..	..	..	..
6100 Paid solely by business	..	..	..	0	0	0	0	0	0	0
6200 Other	..	..	..	293	524	594	1 025	647	987	1 080
Memorandum item										
Customs duties collected on behalf of the EU	..	..	..	..	1 760	1 627	1 977	2 823	3 485	3 911
Total tax revenue on cash basis	**..**	**..**	**..**	**..**	**..**	**..**	**..**	**..**	**..**	**..**
Total tax revenue on accrual basis	**..**	**..**	**..**	**246 039**	**411 175**	**453 254**	**528 081**	**583 975**	**678 856**	**745 529**
Conciliation with National Accounts										
Additional taxes included in National Accounts	..	..	..	..	..	..	..	..	..	..
Taxes excluded from National Accounts	..	..	..	..	..	..	..	..	..	..
Difference in treatment of tax credits	..	..	..	..	..	..	..	..	..	..
Capital transfer for uncollected revenue	..	..	..	..	..	..	..	..	..	..
Voluntary social security contributions	..	..	..	..	..	..	34	49	49	45
Miscellaneous differences	..	..	..	..	..	..	..	..	..	..
National Accounts: Taxes and actual social contributions	..	..	..	246 039	411 175	453 254	528 115	584 024	678 905	745 574
Imputed social contributions	..	..	..	777	10 848	13 841	16 603	17 423	18 098	18 322
National Accounts: Taxes and all social contributions	..	..	..	252 943	422 023	467 095	544 718	601 447	697 003	763 896

.. Not available

Note: Year ending 31st December.

From 2002, data are on accrual basis.

Source: Ministry of Finance, Economic Department.

StatLink https://doi.org/10.1787/888934212193

Table 5.29. Portugal: Details of tax revenue, 1965-2018

Million EUR

	1965	1980	1990	2000	2007	2010	2013	2015	2017	2018
Total tax revenue	**99**	**1 798**	**14 825**	**39 888**	**55 829**	**54 708**	**58 015**	**61 806**	**66 859**	**71 139**
Total tax revenue exclusive of taxes collected for the EU	..	..	**14 675**	**39 684**	**55 639**	**54 530**	**57 872**	**61 630**	**66 524**	**70 764**
1000 Taxes on income, profits and capital gains	**24**	**355**	**3 805**	**11 691**	**15 443**	**14 640**	**18 664**	**18 768**	**18 879**	**20 119**
1100 Of individuals	..	..	2 350	6 947	9 369	9 638	13 120	13 154	12 608	13 317
Individual income tax	..	..	2 350	6 947	9 369	9 638	13 120	13 154	12 608	13 317
1110 On income and profits	..	..	..	..	..	..	..	..	..	..
1120 On capital gains	..	..	..	..	..	..	..	..	..	..
1200 Corporate	..	..	1 182	4 744	6 073	4 919	5 545	5 614	6 271	6 802
Corporate income tax	..	..	1 088	4 457	5 760	4 653	5 327	5 405	5 956	6 493
Local corporate income tax ("Derrama")	..	..	84	287	313	266	217	208	315	308
Other	..	..	11	0	0	0	0	0	0	0
1210 On profits	..	..	..	..	..	..	..	..	..	..
1220 On capital gains	..	..	..	..	..	..	..	..	..	..
1300 Unallocable between 1100 and 1200	24	355	273	0	0	83	0	0	0	0
Tax on wages and professional income	2	93	9	..	..	0	..	..	..	..
Industrial tax	7	108	129	..	..	0	..	..	..	..
Tax on income from movable capital	2	71	1	..	..	0	..	..	..	..
Property income tax	3	23	17	..	..	0	..	..	..	..
Agricultural income tax	0	0	1	..	..	0	..	..	..	..
Complementary income ax	4	43	58	..	..	0	..	..	..	..
Tax on capital gains	0	3	1	..	..	83	..	..	..	..
Taxes abolished by DL 442-A/88 and DL 442-B/88	0	0	0	..	..	0	..	..	..	..
Other	6	15	58	..	..	0	..	..	..	..
2000 Social security contributions	**22**	**531**	**4 026**	**10 168**	**14 274**	**15 457**	**15 139**	**16 195**	**17 969**	**19 141**
2100 Employees	8	203	1 470	4 286	6 344	6 670	6 403	7 004	7 628	7 704
2110 On a payroll basis	8	203	1 470	4 286	6 344	6 670	6 403	7 004	7 628	7 704
Compulsory employee's social contributions	8	203	1 470	..	..	..	..	7 004	7 628	7 704
2120 On an income tax basis	0	0	0	0	0	0	0	0	0	0
2200 Employers	13	318	2 413	5 882	7 930	8 786	8 736	9 191	10 341	11 437
2210 On a payroll basis	13	318	2 413	5 882	7 930	8 786	8 736	9 191	10 341	11 437
Employers' social contributions	13	318	2 413	5 882	7 930	8 786	8 736	9 191	10 341	11 437
2220 On an income tax basis	0	0	0	0	0	0	0	0	0	0
2300 Self-employed or non-employed	0	10	143	0	0	0	0	0	0	0
Compulsory social contributions by self-employed	0	10	143	..	..	..	..	..	..	..
2310 On a payroll basis	..	..	..	..	..	..	..	..	..	..
2320 On an income tax basis	..	..	..	..	..	..	..	..	..	..
2400 Unallocable between 2100, 2200 and 2300	0	0	0	0	0	0	0	0	0	0
2410 On a payroll basis	..	..	..	..	..	..	..	..	..	..
2420 On an income tax basis	..	..	..	..	..	..	..	..	..	..
3000 Taxes on payroll and workforce	**1**	**47**	**0**	**0**	**0**	**0**	**0**	**0**	**0**	**0**
Contributions for Unemployment Fund	1	47	..	..	..	..	..	..	..	..
Stamp duty on wages and salaries	0	0	..	..	..	..	..	..	..	..
4000 Taxes on property	**5**	**26**	**402**	**1 468**	**2 284**	**1 935**	**1 906**	**2 307**	**2 656**	**2 862**
4100 Recurrent taxes on immovable property	0	0	133	508	1 008	1 101	1 337	1 535	1 556	1 645
Real estate tax	..	..	133	508	1 008	1 101	1 337	1 535	1 556	1 645
4110 Households	..	..	..	..	..	..	..	..	..	..
4120 Others	..	..	..	..	..	..	..	..	..	..
4200 Recurrent taxes on net wealth	0	0	0	0	0	0	0	0	0	0
4210 Individual	..	..	..	..	..	..	..	..	..	..
4220 Corporate	..	..	..	..	..	..	..	..	..	..
4300 Estate, inheritance and gift taxes	2	4	74	103	10	2	2	0	0	0
Inheritance and gift taxes	2	4	74	103	10	2	2	..	..	0
4310 Estate and inheritance taxes	..	..	..	..	..	..	..	..	..	0
4320 Gift taxes	..	..	..	..	..	..	..	..	..	0
4400 Taxes on financial and capital transactions	2	21	195	857	1 266	832	567	772	1 101	1 217
Real estate transfer tax	2	21	195	674	973	595	356	569	874	976
Stamp duty on registrations and mortgages	0	0	0	34	35	34	32	49	72	77
Stamp duty on the raising of capital	0	0	0	0	10	1	0	0	0	0
Stamp duty on real estate transactions	0	0	0	150	249	202	180	154	154	164
4500 Non-recurrent taxes	0	0	0	0	0	0	0	0	0	0
4510 On net wealth	..	..	..	..	..	..	..	..	..	..
4520 Other non-recurrent taxes	..	..	..	..	..	..	..	..	..	..
4600 Other recurrent taxes on property	0	0	0	0	0	0	0	0	0	0
5000 Taxes on goods and services	**47**	**837**	**6 555**	**16 274**	**23 410**	**22 181**	**21 827**	**23 957**	**26 793**	**28 336**
5100 Taxes on production, sale, transfer, etc.	44	810	6 440	15 839	22 735	21 424	20 614	23 094	25 774	27 109
5110 General taxes	0	290	2 906	9 733	14 333	13 527	13 710	15 368	16 809	17 865
5111 Value added taxes	0	0	2 899	9 733	14 333	13 527	13 710	15 368	16 809	17 865
VAT	..	..	2 899	9 733	14 333	13 527	13 710	15 368	16 809	17 865

	1965	1980	1990	2000	2007	2010	2013	2015	2017	2018
5112 Sales tax	0	290	7	0	0	0	0	0	0	0
General sales tax	..	290	7	..	..	..	..	..	..	..
5113 Other	0	0	0	0	0	0	0	0	0	0
5120 Taxes on specific goods and services	44	519	3 534	6 105	8 402	7 896	6 904	7 726	8 965	9 244
5121 Excise duties	15	295	2 052	4 501	5 940	5 665	4 675	5 211	6 125	6 230
Excise duties on tobacco	3	62	362	1 077	1 165	1 496	1 387	1 357	1 542	1 577
Excise duties on beer	1	0	55	90	100	82	76	75	90	90
Tax on motor vehicle sales	1	59	304	1 239	1 221	832	360	585	775	785
Tax on oil products	6	166	1 251	1 969	3 325	3 140	2 740	3 069	3 495	3 546
Excise duties on alcoholic beverages	0	0	23	126	128	114	109	115	135	137
Excise duties on alcohol	0	0	0	1	1	1	1	0	0	1
Tax on sugary soft drinks	0	0	0	0	0	0	0	0	71	74
Other	4	7	59	0	0	0	1	11	17	21
5122 Profits of fiscal monopolies	0	0	0	261	521	420	419	582	731	735
5123 Customs and import duties	21	96	511	205	186	178	144	158	187	224
Import levies	14	36	392	0	1	1	0	0	0	0
Import surtax	0	26	1	0	0	0	0	0	0	0
Other	6	34	119	0	0	0	0	0	0	0
Custom duties collected for the EU	..	..	..	204	185	177	144	158	187	224
5124 Taxes on exports	0	0	0	0	0	0	0	0	0	0
Taxes on Oporto wine exports	0	0	..	..	..	..	..	..	..	..
Other	0	0	..	..	..	..	..	..	..	..
5125 Taxes on investment goods	0	0	0	0	0	0	0	0	0	0
5126 Taxes on specific services	1	38	547	1 102	1 712	1 522	1 567	1 523	1 620	1 734
Tax on insurance premiums	0	6	47	131	170	215	200	218	244	254
Stamp duty on bank transactions	1	24	405	330	734	601	536	464	504	537
Stamp duty on debt related operations, interest and leasing of buildings	0	0	22	258	384	309	276	144	126	135
Stamp duty on insurance premiums	0	0	0	248	347	325	289	313	350	373
Bank levies	0	0	0	100	48	46	238	353	351	380
Other	2	8	73	34	29	25	29	30	45	57
5127 Other taxes on internat. trade and transactions	0	0	0	0	0	0	0	0	0	0
5128 Other taxes	6	91	424	36	43	111	99	251	301	321
Stamp taxes (miscellaneous)	6	91	424	36	43	111	99	251	301	321
Other	0	0	0	0	0	0	0	0	0	0
5130 Unallocable between 5110 and 5120	0	0	0	0	0	0	0	0	0	0
5200 Taxes on use of goods and perform activities	4	27	115	382	615	718	994	850	1 005	1 221
5210 Recurrent taxes	4	27	115	382	615	718	937	770	902	1 003
5211 Paid by households: motor vehicles	0	4	15	55	94	114	185	209	215	227
Local tax on vehicles	..	4	15	55	94	114	185	209	215	227
5212 Paid by others: motor vehicles	2	10	20	67	132	204	342	330	385	424
Local tax on vehicles	0	2	6	0	0	0	0	0	0	0
Road taxes	2	8	14	67	132	204	342	330	385	424
5213 Paid in respect of other goods	2	13	80	260	390	400	409	232	303	353
Gambling tax	0	3	72	110	140	143	107	108	145	198
Tax on the use, carrying and possession of weapons	0	0	1	3	6	4	7	5	11	9
Tax on motor vehicles - compensation	2	8	0	0	0	0	0	0	0	0
Hunting and fishery licenses	0	1	4	1	1	1	5	13	14	10
Fee for the use of water resources	0	0	0	0	2	13	13	19	20	22
Other	0	1	2	146	241	239	278	88	112	113
5220 Non-recurrent taxes	0	0	0	0	0	0	57	80	103	218
Special tax on motor vehicles	..	..	0	..	..	..	0	0	0	0
Emissions Permits	..	..	0	..	..	..	57	80	103	218
5300 Unallocable between 5100 and 5200	0	0	0	53	60	39	219	13	13	6
Miscellaneous taxes on production	..	..	..	53	60	39	219	13	13	6
6000 Other taxes	**0**	**3**	**37**	**288**	**417**	**495**	**479**	**580**	**561**	**681**
6100 Paid solely by business	0	2	17	107	217	225	234	341	281	411
General services and licenses granted to corporations	0	2	17	107	217	225	234	341	281	411
6200 Other	0	0	20	181	200	270	245	239	281	270
Fees collected by courts of justice	0	0	0	175	189	254	219	237	275	264
Miscellaneous taxes	0	0	20	5	11	17	25	1	6	5
Memorandum items										
Customs duties collected on behalf of the EU	..	..	..	204	185	177	144	158	187	224
SRF contributions collected on behalf of the EU	..	..	..	..	..	..	..	..	130	132
Total tax revenue on cash basis	**99**	**1 798**	**14 825**	**..**	**..**	**..**	**..**	**..**	**..**	**..**
Total tax revenue on accrual basis	**..**	**..**	**..**	**39 888**	**55 829**	**54 708**	**58 015**	**61 806**	**66 859**	**71 139**

	1965	1980	1990	2000	2007	2010	2013	2015	2017	2018
Conciliation with National Accounts										
Additional taxes included in National Accounts	..	..	..	0	0	0	0	0	0	0
Taxes excluded from National Accounts	..	..	..	0	0	0	0	0	0	0
Difference in treatment of tax credits	..	..	..	0	0	0	0	0	0	0
Capital transfer for uncollected revenue	..	..	..	0	0	0	0	0	0	0
Voluntary social security contributions	..	..	..	0	0	0	0	0	0	0
Miscellaneous differences	..	..	..	0	0	0	0	0	0	0
National Accounts: Taxes and actual social contributions	..	..	..	39 888	55 829	54 708	58 015	61 806	66 859	71 139
Imputed social contributions	..	..	..	3 292	5 592	5 906	5 310	4 602	4 738	4 708
National Accounts: Taxes and all social contributions	..	..	..	43 181	61 421	60 613	63 326	66 408	71 597	75 847

.. Not available

Note: Fiscal year ending 31 December.
From 1995, data are on accrual basis.

Source: Instituto Nacionale de Estatistica; Conta do Estado, Contas de Gerência dos Fundos e Serviços Autonomos da Administraçao Central; Estatisticas das Financas publicas; Relatorio do Instituto de Gestao Financeira da Seguranta Social, Contas de Gerência das Regioes Autonomas da Madeira e dos Atores.

StatLink https://doi.org/10.1787/888934212212

Table 5.30. Slovak Republic: Details of tax revenue, 1965-2018

Million EUR

	1965	1980	1990	2000	2007	2010	2013	2015	2017	2018
Total tax revenue	..	..	..	**10 648**	**18 456**	**19 159**	**23 082**	**26 049**	**28 927**	**30 754**
Total tax revenue exclusive of taxes collected for the EU	..	..	..	**10 648**	**18 321**	**19 016**	**22 967**	**25 930**	**28 773**	**30 598**
1000 Taxes on income, profits and capital gains	..	..	..	**2 181**	**3 844**	**3 601**	**4 471**	**5 542**	**5 959**	**6 370**
1100 Of individuals	..	..	..	1 055	1 820	1 790	2 175	2 464	2 855	3 218
1110 On income and profits	..	..	..	1 055	1 820	1 790	2 175	2 464	2 855	3 218
Wages and salaries withholding	..	..	..	..	..	..	..	..	..	..
Of unicorporated individuals	..	..	..	..	..	..	..	..	..	..
1120 On capital gains	..	..	..	0	0	0	0	0	0	0
1200 Corporate	..	..	..	813	1 835	1 659	2 118	2 917	2 925	2 943
1210 On profits	..	..	..	..	..	..	..	..	..	..
1220 On capital gains	..	..	..	..	..	..	..	..	..	..
1300 Unallocable between 1100 and 1200	..	..	..	314	189	152	178	162	178	209
2000 Social security contributions	..	..	..	**4 409**	**7 244**	**8 154**	**9 847**	**10 897**	**12 389**	**13 237**
2100 Employees	..	..	..	901	1 700	2 077	2 238	2 410	2 941	3 263
Retirement	..	..	..	..	..	..	..	..	..	..
State employment policy	..	..	..	..	..	..	..	..	..	..
Health insurance	..	..	..	..	..	..	..	..	..	..
Sick leave	..	..	..	..	..	..	..	..	..	..
2110 On a payroll basis	..	..	..	901	1 700	2 077	2 238	2 410	2 941	3 263
2120 On an income tax basis	..	..	..	0	0	0	0	0	0	0
2200 Employers	..	..	..	2 850	3 914	4 579	5 556	6 319	7 263	7 871
Retirement	..	..	..	..	..	..	..	..	..	..
State employment policy	..	..	..	..	..	..	..	..	..	..
Health insurance	..	..	..	..	..	..	..	..	..	..
Sick leave	..	..	..	..	..	..	..	..	..	..
2210 On a payroll basis	..	..	..	2 850	3 914	4 579	5 556	6 319	7 263	7 871
2220 On an income tax basis	..	..	..	0	0	0	0	0	0	0
2300 Self-employed or non-employed	..	..	..	658	1 631	1 498	2 054	2 168	2 186	2 104
Retirement	..	..	..	..	..	..	..	..	..	..
State employment policy	..	..	..	..	..	..	..	..	..	..
Health insurance	..	..	..	..	..	..	..	..	..	..
Sick leave	..	..	..	..	..	..	..	..	..	..
2310 On a payroll basis	..	..	..	658	1 631	1 498	2 054	2 168	2 186	2 104
2320 On an income tax basis	..	..	..	0	0	0	0	0	0	0
2400 Unallocable between 2100, 2200 and 2300	..	..	..	0	0	0	0	0	0	0
2410 On a payroll basis	..	..	..	..	..	..	..	..	..	..
2420 On an income tax basis	..	..	..	..	..	..	..	..	..	..
3000 Taxes on payroll and workforce	..	..	..	**0**	**0**	**0**	**0**	**0**	**0**	**0**
4000 Taxes on property	..	..	..	**194**	**245**	**277**	**327**	**335**	**361**	**369**
4100 Recurrent taxes on immovable property	..	..	..	143	243	277	327	335	361	369
4110 Households	..	..	..	28	22	25	28	29	31	31
4120 Others	..	..	..	114	222	252	299	306	330	338
4200 Recurrent taxes on net wealth	..	..	..	0	0	0	0	0	0	0
4210 Individual	..	..	..	..	..	..	..	..	..	..
4220 Corporate	..	..	..	..	..	..	..	..	..	..
4300 Estate, inheritance and gift taxes	..	..	..	8	0	0	0	0	0	0
4310 Estate and inheritance taxes	..	..	..	3	0	0	0	0	0	0
4320 Gift taxes	..	..	..	5	0	0	0	0	0	0
4400 Taxes on financial and capital transactions	..	..	..	43	1	0	0	0	0	0
Real property transfer tax	..	..	..	30	1	0	0	0	0	0
4500 Non-recurrent taxes	..	..	..	0	0	0	0	0	0	0
4510 On net wealth	..	..	..	..	..	..	..	..	..	..
4520 Other non-recurrent taxes	..	..	..	..	..	..	..	..	..	..
4600 Other recurrent taxes on property	..	..	..	0	0	0	0	0	0	0
5000 Taxes on goods and services	..	..	..	**3 864**	**7 123**	**7 127**	**8 436**	**9 275**	**10 217**	**10 778**
5100 Taxes on production, sale, transfer, etc.	..	..	..	3 631	6 580	6 573	7 780	8 573	9 472	10 019
5110 General taxes	..	..	..	2 168	4 147	4 182	4 696	5 423	5 919	6 319
5111 Value added taxes	..	..	..	2 168	4 147	4 182	4 696	5 423	5 919	6 319
5112 Sales tax	..	..	..	0	0	0	0	0	0	0
5113 Other	..	..	..	0	0	0	0	0	0	0
5120 Taxes on specific goods and services	..	..	..	1 464	2 433	2 391	3 084	3 151	3 553	3 700

	1965	1980	1990	2000	2007	2010	2013	2015	2017	2018
5121 Excise duties	..	..	..	971	2 171	2 081	2 462	2 567	2 819	2 916
On hydrocarbon fuels and lubricants	..	..	..	617	1 118	1 032	1 045	1 139	1 230	1 267
On alcohol and liquers	..	..	..	143	201	197	201	205	212	221
On beer	..	..	..	43	66	56	56	57	57	60
On wine	..	..	..	12	4	4	4	4	4	5
On tobacco products	..	..	..	156	783	602	636	665	711	728
On electricity	..	..	..	0	0	166	494	472	579	612
On coal	..	..	..	0	0	1	1	0	0	0
On natural gas	..	..	..	0	0	24	25	23	26	24
5122 Profits of fiscal monopolies	..	..	..	0	0	0	0	0	0	0
5123 Customs and import duties	..	..	..	437	136	143	115	119	136	137
Customs duties	..	..	..	122	136	143	115	119	136	137
Import surcharges	..	..	..	315	0	0	0	0	0	0
Other customs revenues	..	..	..	0	0	0	0	0	0	0
5124 Taxes on exports	..	..	..	0	0	0	0	0	0	0
5125 Taxes on investment goods	..	..	..	0	0	0	6	2	3	3
5126 Taxes on specific services	..	..	..	55	125	167	501	462	596	644
5127 Other taxes on internat. trade and transactions	..	..	..	0	0	0	0	0	0	0
5128 Other taxes	..	..	..	0	0	0	0	0	0	0
5130 Unallocable between 5110 and 5120	..	..	..	0	0	0	0	0	0	0
5200 Taxes on use of goods and perform activities	..	..	..	231	438	421	505	549	585	597
5210 Recurrent taxes	..	..	..	219	372	384	466	470	500	506
5211 Paid by households: motor vehicles	..	..	..	0	0	0	0	0	0	0
5212 Paid by others: motor vehicles	..	..	..	93	153	153	198	204	223	232
5213 Paid in respect of other goods	..	..	..	127	219	231	268	266	277	273
5220 Non-recurrent taxes	..	..	..	12	66	37	39	79	85	92
5300 Unallocable between 5100 and 5200	..	..	..	2	105	134	151	153	160	161
6000 Other taxes	**..**	**..**	**..**	**0**	**0**	**0**	**0**	**0**	**0**	**0**
6100 Paid solely by business	..	..	..	..	..	..	..	..	..	..
6200 Other	..	..	..	..	..	..	..	..	..	..
Memorandum items										
Customs duties collected on behalf of the EU	..	..	..	..	136	143	115	119	136	137
SRF contributions collected on behalf of the EU	..	..	..	..	..	..	..	..	18	19
Non-wastable tax credits										
Non-wastable tax credits against 1110	..	..	..	..	252	276	265	261	266	269
Tax expenditure component	..	..	..	..	..	..	..	..	..	..
Transfer component	..	..	..	..	..	..	..	..	..	..
Non-wastable tax credits against 1210	..	..	..	..	0	0	0	0	0	0
Tax expenditure component	..	..	..	..	..	..	..	..	..	..
Transfer component	..	..	..	..	..	..	..	..	..	..
Total tax revenue on cash basis	**..**	**..**	**..**	**10 843**	**18 033**	**18 509**	**22 559**	**26 216**	**28 275**	**30 338**
Total tax revenue on accrual basis	**..**	**..**	**..**	**10 648**	**18 456**	**19 159**	**23 082**	**26 049**	**28 927**	**30 754**
Conciliation with National Accounts										
Additional taxes included in National Accounts	..	..	..	53	33	47	0	43	3	..
Taxes excluded from National Accounts	..	..	..	0	-103	-131	-148	-149	-157	-158
Difference in treatment of tax credits	..	..	..	0	0	0	0	0	0	0
Capital transfer for uncollected revenue	..	..	..	0	0	0	0	0	0	0
Voluntary social security contributions	..	..	..	0	22	31	17	11	10	11
Miscellaneous differences	..	..	..	0	0	0	0	0	0	0
National Accounts: Taxes and actual social contributions	..	..	..	10 702	18 409	19 106	22 951	25 953	28 783	30 607
Imputed social contributions	..	..	..	19	80	139	142	171	189	188
National Accounts: Taxes and all social contributions	..	..	..	10 721	18 488	19 245	23 093	26 124	28 972	30 795

.. Not available

Note: Year ending 31st December.

Data are on accrual basis.

Source: Ministry of Finance.

StatLink https://doi.org/10.1787/888934212231

Table 5.31. Slovenia: Details of tax revenue, 1965-2018

Million EUR

	1965	1980	1990	2000	2007	2010	2013	2015	2017	2018
Total tax revenue	..	..	..	**7 117**	**13 352**	**13 756**	**13 576**	**14 496**	**15 963**	**17 118**
Total tax revenue exclusive of taxes collected for the EU	..	..	..	**7 117**	**13 267**	**13 696**	**13 524**	**14 428**	**15 898**	**17 050**
1000 Taxes on income, profits and capital gains	..	..	..	**1 280**	**3 041**	**2 692**	**2 285**	**2 547**	**2 957**	**3 331**
1100 Of individuals	..	..	..	1 041	1 919	2 020	1 849	1 977	2 190	2 442
1110 On income and profits	..	..	..	1 039	1 916	2 017	1 847	1 974	2 188	2 439
Personal income tax	..	..	..	1 039	1 916	2 017	1 847	1 974	2 188	2 439
Special contribution for the reconstruction of the Posocje region	..	..	..	0	0	0	0	0	0	0
1120 On capital gains	..	..	..	2	3	3	3	3	3	3
Taxes on winnings from lottery and gambling	..	..	..	2	3	3	3	3	3	3
1200 Corporate	..	..	..	216	1 116	668	433	568	764	886
1210 On profits	..	..	..	216	1 116	668	433	568	764	886
1220 On capital gains	..	..	..	0	0	0	0	0	0	0
1300 Unallocable between 1100 and 1200	..	..	..	24	5	4	3	2	3	2
Tax on income - copy rights, patents and trademarks	..	..	..	24	5	4	2	2	2	2
Tax on profits due to changes in land use	..	..	..	0	0	0	0	0	0	0
2000 Social security contributions	..	..	..	**2 824**	**5 046**	**5 761**	**5 647**	**5 983**	**6 626**	**7 081**
2100 Employees	..	..	..	1 447	2 490	2 785	2 637	2 910	3 247	3 490
2110 On a payroll basis	..	..	..	1 447	2 490	2 785	2 637	2 910	3 247	3 490
2120 On an income tax basis	..	..	..	0	0	0	0	0	0	0
2200 Employers	..	..	..	1 012	1 852	2 070	2 022	2 135	2 408	2 590
2210 On a payroll basis	..	..	..	1 012	1 852	2 070	2 022	2 135	2 408	2 590
2220 On an income tax basis	..	..	..	0	0	0	0	0	0	0
2300 Self-employed or non-employed	..	..	..	365	705	906	988	938	971	1 001
2310 On a payroll basis	..	..	..	365	705	906	988	938	971	1 001
2320 On an income tax basis	..	..	..	0	0	0	0	0	0	0
2400 Unallocable between 2100, 2200 and 2300	..	..	..	0	0	0	0	0	0	0
2410 On a payroll basis	..	..	..	..	..	..	..	..	..	..
2420 On an income tax basis	..	..	..	..	..	..	..	..	..	..
3000 Taxes on payroll and workforce	..	..	..	**289**	**418**	**28**	**23**	**20**	**21**	**22**
Payroll tax	..	..	..	272	391	0	0	0	0	0
Tax on work contracts	..	..	..	18	27	28	23	20	21	22
4000 Taxes on property	..	..	..	**120**	**206**	**222**	**232**	**241**	**277**	**276**
4100 Recurrent taxes on immovable property	..	..	..	81	140	173	199	199	221	223
4110 Households	..	..	..	17	38	46	61	56	64	65
Property tax on weekend cottages	..	..	..	1	1	1	1	1	1	0
Compensation on the use of building ground - paid by individuals	..	..	..	16	37	45	48	56	63	64
Tax on immovable property of higher value	..	..	..	0	0	0	13	0	0	0
4120 Others	..	..	..	65	102	127	138	142	158	158
Property tax on buildings	..	..	..	2	3	3	4	4	5	3
Compensation on the use of building ground - paid by legal entities	..	..	..	63	100	124	134	139	153	155
4200 Recurrent taxes on net wealth	..	..	..	4	0	0	0	0	0	0
4210 Individual	..	..	..	0	..	..	..	..	..	..
4220 Corporate	..	..	..	4	..	..	..	..	..	..
Tax on balance wealth paid by banks	..	..	..	4	..	..	..	..	..	..
4300 Estate, inheritance and gift taxes	..	..	..	2	9	14	8	8	11	10
4310 Estate and inheritance taxes	..	..	..	..	..	..	..	..	..	..
4320 Gift taxes	..	..	..	..	..	..	..	..	..	..
4400 Taxes on financial and capital transactions	..	..	..	23	57	32	23	29	41	40
Taxes on the sale of immovable property - from legal entities	..	..	..	11	19	7	5	7	5	7
Taxes on the sale of immovable property - from individuals	..	..	..	12	38	25	18	23	36	33
4500 Non-recurrent taxes	..	..	..	10	0	2	1	4	3	3
4510 On net wealth	..	..	..	0	..	0	0	0	0	0
4520 Other non-recurrent taxes	..	..	..	10	..	2	1	4	3	3
Payments for the change of use of agricultural and forest land	..	..	..	10	..	0	1	2	2	1
Granting of easements and the creation of building rights	..	..	..	0	..	2	1	3	2	2
4600 Other recurrent taxes on property	..	..	..	0	0	0	0	0	0	0
Property tax on boats	..	..	..	0	0	0	0	0	0	0
5000 Taxes on goods and services	..	..	..	**2 602**	**4 641**	**5 053**	**5 389**	**5 706**	**6 082**	**6 408**
5100 Taxes on production, sale, transfer, etc.	..	..	..	2 481	4 426	4 838	5 049	5 329	5 679	5 969
5110 General taxes	..	..	..	1 641	2 916	2 927	3 048	3 222	3 484	3 768
5111 Value added taxes	..	..	..	1 610	2 916	2 927	3 048	3 222	3 484	3 768
Value added tax	..	..	..	1 598	2 898	2 924	3 044	3 218	3 480	3 763
Negative compensation of farmers in a VAT flat rate	..	..	..	12	18	3	4	4	4	4

	1965	1980	1990	2000	2007	2010	2013	2015	2017	2018
system										
5112 Sales tax	..	..	..	8	0	0	0	0	0	0
Customs duties paid by individuals	..	..	..	1	..	..	..	..	..	..
Special import duties and customs charges	..	..	..	7	..	..	..	..	..	..
5113 Other	..	..	..	23	0	0	0	0	0	0
Turnover tax on goods	..	..	..	11	..	..	..	..	..	..
Turnover tax on services	..	..	..	12	..	..	..	..	..	..
Special turnover tax on alcohol	..	..	..	0	..	..	..	..	..	..
5120 Taxes on specific goods and services	..	..	..	841	1 510	1 911	2 001	2 107	2 195	2 202
5121 Excise duties	..	..	..	581	1 196	1 555	1 579	1 626	1 707	1 679
Alcohol and alcoholic drinks	..	..	..	39	71	89	96	108	113	119
Mineral oil and gas	..	..	..	405	758	1 016	998	1 033	1 099	1 066
Tobacco	..	..	..	97	301	391	425	419	428	420
Duty free shops - alcohol and alcoholic drinks	..	..	..	3	0	0	0	0	0	0
Duty free shops - tobacco	..	..	..	17	0	0	0	0	0	0
Electric power and coal	..	..	..	0	4	19	31	34	32	32
Tax on the sales of new motor vehicles	..	..	..	18	60	40	26	26	28	34
Tax on the sales of used motor vehicles	..	..	..	2	2	0	0	0	0	0
Additional tax on motor vehicles	..	..	..	0	0	0	3	6	7	8
5122 Profits of fiscal monopolies	..	..	..	0	0	0	0	0	0	0
5123 Customs and import duties	..	..	..	158	85	60	53	53	55	58
Import duties	..	..	..	151	0	0	0	0	0	0
Levies on imported agricultural products	..	..	..	7	0	0	0	0	0	0
Custom duties collected for the EU	..	..	..	0	85	60	53	53	55	58
5124 Taxes on exports	..	..	..	0	0	0	0	0	0	0
5125 Taxes on investment goods	..	..	..	0	0	0	0	0	0	0
5126 Taxes on specific services	..	..	..	102	230	296	369	428	432	464
Tax on special gambling (gambling in casinos)	..	..	..	25	64	53	41	48	45	45
Tax on classical gambling (lottery...)	..	..	..	1	3	3	3	3	3	3
Special tax on slot machines	..	..	..	4	0	0	0	0	0	0
Tax on insurance services	..	..	..	37	65	69	65	82	90	94
Sojourn tax	..	..	..	3	7	7	8	11	14	18
Concessions	..	..	..	1	29	40	90	79	69	67
Concessions duties on special gambling (in casinos)	..	..	..	26	55	47	38	37	38	38
Fire protection tax	..	..	..	4	6	7	8	8	8	8
Tax on lottery tickets	..	..	..	0	0	0	3	17	16	18
Tax on financial services	..	..	..	0	0	0	32	57	59	76
FIHO, FSO	..	..	..	0	0	25	26	27	22	25
SOS	..	..	..	0	0	23	10	11	11	12
Tax on balance wealth paid by banks	..	..	..	0	0	0	18	2	0	0
Commodity reserve fund	..	..	..	0	0	21	27	32	32	30
Deposit guarantee Fund, Single Resolution Fund	..	..	..	0	0	0	0	16	26	29
5127 Other taxes on internat. trade and transactions	..	..	..	0	0	0	0	0	0	0
5128 Other taxes	..	..	..	0	0	0	0	0	0	0
Sugar levy	..	..	..	..	0	..	..	..	..	..
5130 Unallocable between 5110 and 5120	..	..	..	0	0	0	0	0	0	0
5200 Taxes on use of goods and perform activities	..	..	..	121	215	215	340	377	403	439
5210 Recurrent taxes	..	..	..	121	215	215	321	353	369	373
5211 Paid by households: motor vehicles	..	..	..	49	87	86	109	118	122	125
Registration fees on motor vehicles, boats and airplanes paid by individuals	..	..	..	49	87	86	109	118	122	125
5212 Paid by others: motor vehicles	..	..	..	12	21	20	24	27	30	31
Registration fees on motor vehicles, boats and airplanes paid by legal entities	..	..	..	12	21	20	24	27	30	31
Registration fees on tractors	..	..	..	0	0	0	0	0	0	0
5213 Paid in respect of other goods	..	..	..	59	107	110	187	208	218	217
Charges on the use of water	..	..	..	4	22	23	29	32	30	31
Taxes on waste pollution	..	..	..	7	10	3	2	2	2	1
Taxes on air pollution - caused by gas and hard fuels	..	..	..	3	8	10	10	13	15	15
Cont. of nuclear power plant to finance its de-composition	..	..	..	16	8	8	8	8	9	8
Indemnity for the restricted use of area on the territory of nuclear power plant	..	..	..	0	7	10	11	12	12	12
Taxes on air pollution	..	..	..	29	21	23	98	114	126	126
Special water tax	..	..	..	0	30	33	29	27	24	23
5220 Non-recurrent taxes	..	..	..	0	0	0	19	24	34	67
Emission permits	..	..	..	..	..	..	19	24	34	67
5300 Unallocable between 5100 and 5200	..	..	..	0	0	0	0	0	0	0
6000 Other taxes	**..**	**..**	**..**	**0**	**0**	**0**	**0**	**0**	**0**	**0**
6100 Paid solely by business	..	..	..	..	..	..	..	..	..	..
Memorandum items										
Customs duties collected on behalf of the EU	..	..	..	..	85	60	53	53	55	58
SRF contributions collected on behalf of the EU	..	..	..	..	..	..	..	16	9	10

	1965	1980	1990	2000	2007	2010	2013	2015	2017	2018
Total tax revenue on cash basis	..	..	..	**7 135**	**13 140**	**13 605**	**13 485**	**14 560**	**16 034**	**17 164**
Total tax revenue on accrual basis	..	..	..	**7 117**	**13 352**	**13 756**	**13 576**	**14 496**	**15 963**	**17 118**
Conciliation with National Accounts										
Additional taxes included in National Accounts	..	..	..	0	0	87	90	94	94	95
Radio and television licence fee	..	..	..	..	..	87	90	94	94	95
Taxes excluded from National Accounts	..	..	..	0	0	0	0	0	0	0
Difference in treatment of tax credits	..	..	..	0	0	0	0	0	0	0
Capital transfer for uncollected revenue	..	..	..	0	0	0	0	0	0	0
Voluntary social security contributions	..	..	..	0	0	0	0	0	0	0
Miscellaneous differences	..	..	..	0	0	0	0	0	0	0
National Accounts: Taxes and actual social contributions	..	..	..	7 117	13 352	13 842	13 667	14 590	16 057	17 212
Imputed social contributions	..	..	..	39	81	100	117	118	121	126
National Accounts: Taxes and all social contributions	..	..	..	7 156	13 433	13 943	13 784	14 708	16 177	17 338

.. Not available

Note: Year ending 31st December.

Data are on accrual basis.

Source: Statistical Office of the Republic of Slovenia.

StatLink https://doi.org/10.1787/888934212250

Table 5.32. Spain: Details of tax revenue, 1965-2018

Million EUR

	1965	1980	1990	2000	2007	2010	2013	2015	2017	2018
Total tax revenue	**1 238**	**22 002**	**103 662**	**214 114**	**391 648**	**335 563**	**337 891**	**364 683**	**393 529**	**416 692**
Total tax revenue exclusive of taxes collected for the EU	..	..	..	**213 067**	**389 927**	**334 019**	**336 567**	**362 175**	**390 916**	**414 039**
1000 Taxes on income, profits and capital gains	**304**	**5 714**	**31 763**	**60 145**	**130 081**	**93 798**	**97 664**	**102 645**	**111 807**	**121 992**
1100 Of individuals	177	4 481	22 527	41 248	80 719	74 118	77 230	78 896	85 827	92 315
Personal income tax	..	..	22 527	40 366	79 973	73 534	76 690	78 586	85 378	91 796
Income tax of non-residents	..	..	0	882	746	584	540	310	449	519
1110 On income and profits	..	..	..	..	..	..	..	..	..	..
1120 On capital gains	..	..	..	..	..	..	..	..	..	..
1200 Corporate	114	1 119	9 146	18 897	49 362	19 680	20 434	23 749	25 980	29 677
Corporate income tax	..	..	9 146	18 597	47 499	17 567	19 516	22 471	24 123	27 501
Income tax of non-residents (legal persons)	..	..	0	300	1 863	2 113	918	1 278	1 857	2 176
1210 On profits	..	..	..	..	..	..	..	..	..	..
Tax on commercial activity	..	..	..	..	..	..	..	..	..	..
Special tax 4 percent	..	..	..	..	..	..	..	..	..	..
Taxes on profits	..	..	..	..	..	..	..	..	..	..
1220 On capital gains	..	..	..	..	..	..	..	..	..	..
1300 Unallocable between 1100 and 1200	13	114	91	0	0	0	0	0	0	0
Local taxes	13	114	0	..	..	..	..	..	..	..
Other taxes	..	..	..	..	..	..	..	..	..	..
2000 Social security contributions	**350**	**10 682**	**36 722**	**74 683**	**127 088**	**127 235**	**116 875**	**122 835**	**134 126**	**141 234**
2100 Employees	81	2 376	5 976	11 711	19 625	19 423	16 603	18 783	20 621	21 639
2110 On a payroll basis	..	..	5 976	11 711	19 625	19 423	16 603	18 783	20 621	21 639
2120 On an income tax basis	..	..	0	..	..	..	..	..	..	..
2200 Employers	269	8 306	26 385	54 226	93 234	89 666	82 224	87 988	97 529	103 317
2210 On a payroll basis	..	..	26 385	54 226	93 234	89 666	82 224	87 988	97 529	103 317
2220 On an income tax basis	..	..	0	..	..	..	..	..	..	..
2300 Self-employed or non-employed	0	0	4 361	8 746	14 229	18 146	18 048	16 064	15 976	16 278
Self-employment	..	..	2 492	6 788	10 120	10 119	10 244	10 872	11 498	11 714
Unemployment	..	..	1 869	1 958	4 109	8 027	7 804	5 192	4 478	4 564
2310 On a payroll basis	..	..	..	..	..	..	..	..	..	..
2320 On an income tax basis	..	..	..	..	..	..	..	..	..	..
2400 Unallocable between 2100, 2200 and 2300	0	0	0	0	0	0	0	0	0	0
2410 On a payroll basis	..	..	..	..	..	..	..	..	..	..
2420 On an income tax basis	..	..	..	..	..	..	..	..	..	..
3000 Taxes on payroll and workforce	**0**	**0**	**0**	**0**	**0**	**0**	**0**	**0**	**0**	**0**
4000 Taxes on property	**79**	**1 004**	**5 718**	**13 827**	**32 133**	**22 178**	**24 250**	**27 855**	**29 455**	**30 312**
4100 Recurrent taxes on immovable property	6	41	1 478	3 988	7 281	9 666	11 829	12 623	13 188	13 243
Real State tax (IBI)/Real State tax surcharge	..	41	1 478	3 982	7 267	9 657	11 755	12 581	13 162	13 199
Special Real State tax for non-residents	..	0	0	6	6	8	8	4	8	5
Other taxes on property, land or building use	..	0	0	0	3	0	1	1	0	0
4110 Households	..	..	..	..	..	..	..	..	..	..
4120 Others	..	..	..	0	5	1	65	37	18	39
Tax on large commercial establishments	..	..	..	..	5	1	65	37	18	39
4200 Recurrent taxes on net wealth	0	107	637	1 413	2 479	688	2 049	1 904	2 094	2 186
4210 Individual	..	107	637	1 413	2 479	688	2 049	1 904	2 094	2 186
Wealth tax	..	..	637	1 199	2 054	104	1 339	1 144	1 280	1 372
Real State tax (unoccupied dwellings) and others	..	..	0	214	425	584	710	760	814	814
4220 Corporate	..	0	0	0	0	0	0	0	0	0
4300 Estate, inheritance and gift taxes	13	90	440	1 379	2 901	2 412	2 492	2 790	2 710	2 687
Inheritance and gift tax	..	..	440	1 379	2 901	2 412	2 492	2 790	2 710	2 687
4310 Estate and inheritance taxes	..	..	..	..	..	..	..	..	..	..
4320 Gift taxes	..	..	..	..	..	..	..	..	..	..
4400 Taxes on financial and capital transactions	60	767	2 478	5 939	17 025	7 603	5 301	6 984	8 457	9 310
Taxes on property transactions	60	767	2 478	5 939	17 025	7 603	5 301	6 984	8 457	9 310
4500 Non-recurrent taxes	0	0	646	1 108	2 447	1 809	2 579	3 554	3 006	2 886
4510 On net wealth	..	..	467	0	495	192	325	1 006	331	353
Tax on land holding gains	..	..	467	..	..	..	..	0	0	0
Urban use tax	..	..	..	..	495	192	90	73	97	119
Extraordinary resource of FGD	..	..	..	..	0	0	235	933	234	234
4520 Other non-recurrent taxes	..	..	179	1 108	1 952	1 617	2 254	2 548	2 675	2 533
Special duties	..	..	179	180	168	129	84	70	72	74
Land development contributions	..	..	0	223	368	225	71	61	50	60
Tax on the increase in value of urban terrains	..	..	0	705	1 416	1 263	1 711	2 417	2 553	2 399
Others	..	..	0	0	0	0	2	0	0	0
Levy on "Revaluation of Reserve Account"	..	..	..	0	0	0	386	0	0	0
4600 Other recurrent taxes on property	0	0	38	0	0	0	0	0	0	0
5000 Taxes on goods and services	**506**	**4 553**	**29 437**	**65 456**	**102 334**	**92 344**	**99 026**	**111 159**	**118 018**	**122 950**
5100 Taxes on production, sale, transfer, etc.	503	4 552	26 732	59 383	93 814	84 985	91 122	102 912	109 448	113 814

	1965	1980	1990	2000	2007	2010	2013	2015	2017	2018
5110 General taxes	275	2 234	16 611	37 800	62 778	55 629	60 488	69 478	75 794	79 458
5111 Value added taxes	0	0	16 304	37 785	62 743	55 318	60 314	69 294	75 599	79 264
Value added tax (VAT)	..	..	16 304	37 045	61 472	54 509	59 207	67 913	73 970	77 561
Canary Islands general indirect tax	..	..	0	740	1 271	809	1 107	1 381	1 629	1 703
5112 Sales tax	0	0	0	15	35	311	174	184	195	194
Fees for RTVE (since 2010)	..	..	..	0	0	278	174	184	195	194
Fees from Nat. Commission of Telecomms. Market	..	..	..	15	35	33	0	0	0	0
5113 Other	275	2 234	307	0	0	0	0	0	0	0
Cascade tax	118	1 483	197	..	..	..	..	..	..	..
Excises on luxury expenditure	96	939	15	..	..	..	..	..	..	..
Other import duties	94	832	128	..	..	..	..	..	..	..
Refund of internal taxes	-33	-1 020	-33	..	..	..	..	..	..	..
5120 Taxes on specific goods and services	228	2 317	10 120	21 583	31 036	29 356	30 634	33 434	33 654	34 356
5121 Excise duties	69	1 239	6 048	17 952	25 581	24 384	24 550	25 908	26 476	26 790
Special excises	69	1 239	10	0	0	0	0	0	0	0
On beer	0	0	87	202	307	302	302	316	338	346
On wine	0	0	0	0	0	0	0	0	0	0
On alcohol	0	0	481	785	1 008	876	775	843	899	880
On hydrocarbon	0	0	4 222	9 977	11 787	10 907	11 949	12 465	13 116	13 408
On tobacco	0	0	1 123	4 507	7 258	7 976	7 114	7 213	7 265	7 174
On electricity bills	0	0	0	703	1 153	1 483	1 558	1 458	1 393	1 438
On carbon	0	0	0	0	0	0	148	308	312	271
Tax on retail sales of specific hydrocarbons	0	0	0	0	1 356	1 238	453	7	1	0
Tax on oil derived fuels	0	0	120	237	253	220	267	314	331	331
Petrol tax	0	0	0	6	5	5	13	22	25	25
Production and storage of electricity	0	0	0	0	0	0	1 261	1 576	1 513	1 585
Tax Greenhouse Effect Flourinated	0	0	0	0	0	0	0	99	120	110
Other taxes	0	0	5	17	21	18	17	22	21	21
Canary Islands taxes on national products	0	0	0	51	86	71	75	85	91	87
Taxes on national products in Ceuta and Melilla	0	0	0	108	110	105	103	115	114	114
Fees from the National Energy Commission	0	0	0	13	27	35	0	0	0	0
Contribution to the National Energy Efficiency Fund	0	0	0	0	0	366	150	207	206	208
Special tax on certain means of transport	0	0	0	1 317	2 158	735	325	358	482	609
Fee for use of continental waters for electricity production	0	0	0	0	0	0	0	453	197	110
Special duties and other taxes on imported products	0	0	0	29	52	47	40	47	29	31
Other taxes on products	0	0	0	0	0	0	0	0	23	42
5122 Profits of fiscal monopolies	66	132	546	0	0	0	0	0	0	0
Tobacco	21	77	0	..	..	..	..	..	..	..
Petroleum	45	55	546	..	..	..	..	..	..	..
5123 Customs and import duties	87	561	2 078	1 044	1 816	1 593	1 401	1 899	2 030	2 018
Import duties	87	561	1 394	0	0	0	0	0	0	0
Tax on Imports of Goods in the Canary Islands	0	0	137	33	51	44	45	53	57	54
Tax on Imports in Ceuta and Melilla	0	0	36	41	42	40	39	43	43	43
Customs duties collected for the EU	..	..	511	970	1 723	1 509	1 317	1 803	1 930	1 921
5124 Taxes on exports	0	0	0	0	0	0	0	0	0	0
5125 Taxes on investment goods	0	0	0	0	0	0	0	0	0	0
5126 Taxes on specific services	7	385	1 427	2 497	3 633	3 166	4 469	5 408	4 957	5 298
Taxes on betting and gambling	0	232	1 307	1 649	2 051	1 635	1 249	1 164	1 289	1 327
Taxes on other specific services	6	153	120	0	0	0	0	0	0	0
Taxes on insurance premiums	0	0	0	848	1 581	1 531	1 417	1 446	1 546	1 605
Tax on deposits of credit institution	0	0	0	0	1	0	227	421	414	377
Ordinary resource DGF	0	0	0	0	0	0	1 576	1 644	923	1 074
Tourist tax	0	0	0	0	0	0	0	43	109	180
EU SRF contribution	..	..	..	..	..	..	..	690	676	735
5127 Other taxes on internat. trade and transactions	0	0	0	0	0	0	0	0	0	0
5128 Other taxes	0	0	22	90	6	213	214	219	191	250
EU levies	..	..	22	77	-2	35	7	15	7	-3
Others	..	..	0	13	8	9	20	37	37	100
Resource CORES	..	..	0	0	0	169	187	167	147	153
5130 Unallocable between 5110 and 5120	0	0	0	0	0	0	0	0	0	0
5200 Taxes on use of goods and perform activities	3	1	2 633	6 073	8 520	7 359	7 904	8 247	8 570	9 136
5210 Recurrent taxes	3	1	1 616	4 306	5 311	5 782	6 493	6 420	6 667	6 740
Other taxes on luxury expenses	..	..	..	2	7	4	3	3	3	3
5211 Paid by households: motor vehicles	..	0	461	1 117	1 626	1 770	1 848	1 725	1 758	1 763
Car registration tax	..	..	461	1 117	1 626	1 770	1 848	1 725	1 758	1 763
5212 Paid by others: motor vehicles	..	0	117	298	502	498	503	470	486	487
Car registration tax	..	..	117	298	502	498	503	470	486	487

	1965	1980	1990	2000	2007	2010	2013	2015	2017	2018
5213 Paid in respect of other goods	..	1	1 038	2 889	3 176	3 510	4 139	4 222	4 420	4 487
Hunting and fishing taxes	..	..	0	28	28	34	34	30	32	30
Economic activity tax	..	..	925	1 934	1 633	1 785	1 701	1 794	1 844	1 893
Advertising	..	..	27	0	0	0	0	0	0	0
Taxes on environment and pollution	..	..	0	42	91	141	616	563	613	618
Tax on effluent, use of hydrocarbon and mines	..	..	0	51	83	67	158	184	184	194
Other fees paid by households for licences	..	..	0	179	264	228	206	245	323	331
Compensation for local taxes	..	..	86	140	176	165	129	118	137	133
Vehicle inspection duty	..	..	0	6	18	17	20	19	20	22
Municipal fees for private use of public space	..	..	0	509	883	1 073	1 275	1 269	1 267	1 266
5220 Non-recurrent taxes	0	0	1 017	1 767	3 209	1 577	1 411	1 827	1 903	2 396
Tax and building permits	..	..	327	1 117	2 227	859	519	575	759	960
Urban licenses	..	..	0	451	490	260	157	200	277	322
Greenhouse gas emission trading	..	..	0	0	0	0	138	412	452	723
Parafiscal taxes	..	..	690	199	492	458	597	640	415	391
5300 Unallocable between 5100 and 5200	0	0	72	0	0	0	0	0	0	0
6000 Other taxes	**0**	**49**	**22**	**3**	**12**	**8**	**76**	**189**	**123**	**204**
6100 Paid solely by business	..	49	0	0	0	0	0	0	0	0
6200 Other	..	0	22	3	12	8	76	189	123	204
Other taxes on production	..	..	..	3	12	8	76	189	123	204
Memorandum items										
Customs duties collected on behalf of the EU	..	..	..	970	1 723	1 509	1 317	1 803	1 930	1 921
SRF contributions collected on behalf of the EU	..	..	..	..	..	..	..	690	676	735
Non-wastable tax credits										
Non-wastable tax credits against 1110	..	..	..	0	1 323	1 897	774	1 093	1 803	1 852
Tax expenditure component	..	..	..	0	522	729	432	546	908	932
Transfer component	..	..	..	0	801	1 168	342	547	895	920
Non-wastable tax credits against 1210	..	..	..	0	0	0	0	46	658	1 265
Tax expenditure component	..	..	..	0	0	0	0	12	24	34
Transfer component	..	..	..	0	0	0	0	34	634	1 231
Total tax revenue on cash basis	**1 238**	**22 002**	**103 662**	**210 565**	**385 676**	**330 362**	**335 663**	**357 575**	**383 727**	**408 712**
Total tax revenue on accrual basis	..	..	..	**214 114**	**391 648**	**335 563**	**337 891**	**364 683**	**393 529**	**416 692**
Conciliation with National Accounts										
Additional taxes included in National Accounts	..	..	..	0	0	0	0	0	0	0
Taxes excluded from National Accounts	..	..	..	0	0	0	0	0	0	0
Difference in treatment of tax credits	..	..	..	0	522	729	432	558	932	966
Capital transfer for uncollected revenue	..	..	..	0	0	0	0	0	0	0
Voluntary social security contributions	..	..	..	447	937	1 155	2 209	1 170	1 133	1 038
Miscellaneous differences	..	..	..	0	0	0	0	0	0	0
National Accounts: Taxes and actual social contributions	..	..	..	214 561	393 107	337 447	340 532	366 411	395 594	418 696
Imputed social contributions	..	..	..	5 379	7 618	8 585	7 772	7 503	7 171	7 110
National Accounts: Taxes and all social contributions	..	..	..	219 940	400 725	346 032	348 304	373 914	402 765	425 806

.. Not available

Note: Year ending 31st December.

From 2000, data are on accrual basis.

From 1981 the figures take into account the classification procedures set out in the OECD Interpretative Guide. Consequently they are not completely comparable with the figures for earlier years though the amounts involved are quite small.

Heading 1000: Includes a tax on property 'Contribucion Rustica' which would be more appropriately classified in 4110, and the 'Licencia fiscal industrial and professionales' which, because it is a tax levied by reference to the size of the firm, energy input, etc., would be more appropriately classified in 6000. The data necessary to provide a breakdown is not available.

All subdivisions are estimated.

Heading 2300: Contributions paid by self-employed were shown under heading 2100 until 1982.

Heading 4100: Most of these receipts fall under 4110.

Heading 4400: In 1988 revenues from taxes on legal Acts issued by Autonomous Communities (Local) are included in 4400.

Heading 5121 comprises certain local levies which may include non-tax revenues.

Source: Informacion Estatistica del Ministerio de Hacienda (for national taxes).

Cuentas de las Administraciones Publicas (for local taxes and social security) both published by Secretaria General Tecnica del Ministerio de Hacienda.

StatLink https://doi.org/10.1787/888934212269

Table 5.33. Sweden: Details of tax revenue, 1965-2018

Million SEK

	1965	1980	1990	2000	2007	2010	2013	2015	2017	2018
Total tax revenue	**40 003**	**259 216**	**759 068**	**1 174 516**	**1 497 268**	**1 538 704**	**1 632 087**	**1 825 624**	**2 049 257**	**2 120 634**
Total tax revenue exclusive of taxes collected for the EU	..	..	**759 068**	**1 167 272**	**1 486 286**	**1 527 618**	**1 621 890**	**1 813 106**	**2 036 773**	**2 107 638**
1000 Taxes on income, profits and capital gains	**21 956**	**112 730**	**314 797**	**480 365**	**580 372**	**546 696**	**566 234**	**657 539**	**744 903**	**761 048**
1100 Of individuals	19 500	106 376	291 146	392 592	464 434	430 896	466 286	533 660	616 282	623 602
1110 On income and profits	19 390	105 866	289 598	358 167	414 728	396 353	433 985	464 596	535 892	554 257
Coupon tax	9	44	233	2 040	6 306	3 047	4 108	4 615	6 398	8 527
Duties on foreign artists	4	3	3	50	86	89	-1	2	0	0
National income tax individual	8 676	31 682	70 755	32 486	44 326	42 595	44 664	52 480	62 697	63 632
Local income tax individual	9 294	78 134	220 072	336 304	479 068	522 850	581 934	635 719	700 078	726 221
Tax reduction individual	0	-3 997	-1 465	-18 872	-122 029	-179 890	-204 632	-236 613	-241 976	-253 181
Public service tax	..	..	0	5 061	6 674	6 981	7 208	7 759	7 954	8 171
Other	1 407	0	0	1 098	296	681	704	635	741	886
1120 On capital gains	110	510	1 548	34 425	49 707	34 543	32 301	69 064	80 391	69 345
Lottery prize tax	110	510	1 548	60	0	0	0	0	0	0
1200 Corporate	2 456	6 354	23 651	87 772	115 937	115 800	99 948	123 878	128 621	137 447
1210 On profits	2 456	6 354	23 651	87 772	115 937	115 800	99 948	123 878	128 621	137 447
Tax on profits not distributed	1	10	3	0	0	0	0	0	0	0
National income tax b.c. list	1 425	2 078	19 774	74 501	103 150	103 944	93 097	115 507	124 419	132 089
Local income tax b.c. list	1 030	4 266	0	0	0	0	0	0	0	0
Special tax on profits	0	0	3 874	0	0	0	0	0	0	0
Taxes on pension insurance savings	0	0	0	13 271	12 787	11 856	6 850	8 371	4 202	5 358
1220 On capital gains	0	0	0	0	0	0	0	0	0	0
1300 Unallocable between 1100 and 1200	0	0	0	0	0	0	0	0	0	0
2000 Social security contributions	**4 851**	**74 647**	**205 867**	**306 974**	**388 505**	**384 668**	**376 684**	**404 851**	**443 110**	**463 338**
2100 Employees	743	254	823	63 074	81 088	89 175	100 861	108 356	118 740	123 661
Health insurance fees	743	9	5	0	0	0	0	0	0	0
Unemployment insurance fees	0	245	818	0	0	0	0	0	0	0
Pension fees	0	0	0	63 074	81 088	89 175	100 861	108 356	118 740	123 661
2110 On a payroll basis	..	..	..	63 074	81 088	89 175	100 861	108 356	118 740	123 661
2120 On an income tax basis	..	..	..	0	0	0	0	0	0	0
2200 Employers	3 568	71 602	196 905	237 527	300 010	288 426	271 449	291 646	320 387	335 354
Survivors pension fees	0	20 343	44 181	14 847	19 611	20 362	15 693	17 305	11 983	12 534
Health insurance fees	717	26 005	58 334	74 097	100 979	71 292	58 365	64 332	74 389	77 890
Unemployment insurance fees	0	0	0	0	0	0	0	0	0	0
Labour market fees	0	982	12 516	45 975	48 471	55 443	39 007	37 926	43 924	45 972
Industrial injury insurance fees	132	1 201	4 663	12 030	7 844	8 146	4 022	4 431	3 422	3 585
Seamen's pension fees	0	10	26	30	0	0	0	0	0	0
Part pension fees	0	1 119	2 897	0	0	0	0	0	0	0
Supplementary pension fees	2 719	21 458	73 129	71 335	97 748	106 828	119 508	129 204	142 220	148 819
Parent insurance fees	0	484	1 159	19 215	25 356	26 355	34 854	38 448	44 448	46 554
2210 On a payroll basis	..	..	..	237 527	300 010	288 426	271 449	291 646	320 387	335 354
2220 On an income tax basis	..	..	..	0	0	0	0	0	0	0
2300 Self-employed or non-employed	540	2 791	8 139	5 618	8 391	7 468	5 607	5 058	4 819	4 832
Survivors pension fees	0	943	1 580	451	662	687	442	443	256	256
Health insurance fees	260	992	1 702	1 988	3 297	2 082	550	256	273	291
Industrial injury insurance fees	0	64	191	365	264	275	113	84	58	59
Parent insurance fees	0	58	106	573	856	888	960	603	625	636
Supplementary pension fees	280	734	4 560	2 241	3 312	3 536	3 542	3 672	3 606	3 590
Reduction	0	0	0	0	0	0	0	0	0	0
2310 On a payroll basis	..	..	..	5 618	8 391	7 468	5 607	5 058	4 819	4 832
2320 On an income tax basis	..	..	..	0	0	0	0	0	0	0
2400 Unallocable between 2100, 2200 and 2300	0	0	0	756	-984	-401	-1 233	-209	-836	-509
2410 On a payroll basis	..	..	..	756	-984	-401	-1 233	-209	-836	-509
2420 On an income tax basis	..	..	..	0	0	0	0	0	0	0
3000 Taxes on payroll and workforce	**13**	**6 759**	**18 686**	**50 106**	**83 279**	**107 515**	**172 170**	**194 121**	**233 192**	**245 036**
Special wage tax	0	61	0	22 391	30 225	33 090	36 832	40 283	45 977	49 185
Child care fees	0	4 740	13 080	0	0	0	0	0	0	0
Adult education fees	0	614	1 555	0	0	0	0	0	0	0
Building research fees	13	105	0	0	0	0	0	0	0	0
Labour welfare fees	0	257	2 033	0	0	0	0	0	0	0
Labour education fees	0	982	0	0	0	0	0	0	0	0
Labour market fees	0	0	0	112	156	219	7	-1	1	1
General wage fees	0	0	2 018	27 603	52 898	74 207	135 331	153 839	187 213	195 849
4000 Taxes on property	**712**	**2 424**	**26 630**	**39 890**	**36 228**	**36 509**	**41 182**	**43 852**	**45 472**	**45 842**
4100 Recurrent taxes on immovable property	10	16	8 946	23 286	25 899	26 402	31 596	32 444	32 876	33 217
4110 Households	0	0	3 877	13 321	13 474	11 593	13 422	13 320	13 999	14 972
Special tax on real estate	..	..	3 877	13 321	13 474	11 593	13 422	13 320	13 999	14 972

	1965	1980	1990	2000	2007	2010	2013	2015	2017	2018
4120 Others	10	16	5 069	9 965	12 424	14 809	18 174	19 124	18 877	18 245
Forestry levy	10	16	423	22	34	18	37	19	15	10
Special tax on real estate	0	0	4 646	9 943	12 390	14 791	18 137	19 105	18 863	18 235
4200 Recurrent taxes on net wealth	366	717	3 200	8 223	0	0	0	0	0	0
4210 Individual	361	702	3 135	8 043	..	..	..	..	..	..
4220 Corporate	5	15	65	180	..	..	..	..	..	..
4300 Estate, inheritance and gift taxes	155	545	1 433	2 549	23	9	-4	0	0	0
4310 Estate and inheritance taxes	143	495	1 118	2 088	15	9	-4	0	..	..
4320 Gift taxes	12	50	315	460	8	0	0	0	..	..
4400 Taxes on financial and capital transactions	181	1 146	13 051	5 833	10 305	10 097	9 590	11 408	12 596	12 625
Taxes on financial and capital transactions	181	1 146	6 946	4 878	9 414	8 968	8 913	10 895	12 138	12 059
Turnover tax on securities	0	0	6 105	0	0	0	0	0	0	0
Tax on life group insurances	0	0	0	955	891	1 129	678	513	458	566
4500 Non-recurrent taxes	0	0	0	0	0	0	0	0	0	0
4510 On net wealth	..	..	..	..	..	..	..	..	..	..
4520 Other non-recurrent taxes	..	..	..	..	..	..	..	..	..	..
4600 Other recurrent taxes on property	0	0	0	0	0	0	0	0	0	0
5000 Taxes on goods and services	**12 471**	**62 234**	**188 709**	**292 252**	**402 018**	**456 483**	**469 034**	**517 663**	**574 098**	**596 947**
5100 Taxes on production, sale, transfer, etc.	11 808	58 474	181 587	284 820	388 936	440 083	452 532	498 910	554 174	577 112
5110 General taxes	4 147	34 643	112 399	199 606	286 211	326 685	341 952	382 712	427 738	445 799
5111 Value added taxes	0	34 643	112 399	197 483	282 586	322 603	337 822	378 830	425 053	445 671
5112 Sales tax	4 147	0	0	0	0	0	0	0	0	0
5113 Other	0	0	0	2 123	3 625	4 082	4 130	3 882	2 685	128
5120 Taxes on specific goods and services	7 661	23 831	69 188	85 214	102 725	113 398	110 580	116 198	126 436	131 313
5121 Excise duties	5 953	19 941	55 332	70 313	84 873	91 470	88 168	91 572	97 927	102 112
Taxes on petrol and fuel	1 420	4 229	17 171	39 011	44 501	47 426	43 869	44 906	47 145	48 198
Special sales tax	390	585	1 098	0	0	0	0	0	0	0
Sales tax on motor vehicles	325	553	1 983	195	3	0	0	0	0	0
Tobacco tax	1 150	3 087	5 636	7 747	9 742	10 588	11 136	11 825	11 872	12 374
Tax on spirits	1 548	4 431	6 205	4 902	4 249	4 324	4 001	4 208	4 327	4 466
Tax on wine	149	930	2 922	3 567	4 001	4 589	4 887	5 654	5 985	6 110
Tax on beer and soft drinks	242	964	2 532	2 355	2 773	3 219	3 329	3 895	4 122	4 344
Tax on energy consumption	729	5 162	16 352	11 451	18 994	21 035	20 827	20 787	23 557	25 009
Taxes on electricity from certain sources	0	0	1 018	0	0	0	0	0	0	0
Tax on wastes	0	0	0	1 085	609	289	119	297	185	234
Tax on cassette tapes	0	0	194	0	0	0	0	0	0	0
Tax on video recorders	0	0	221	0	0	0	0	0	0	0
Tax on chemicals	0	0	..	..	..	..	..	..	735	1 377
5122 Profits of fiscal monopolies	72	204	332	3 641	3 952	5 068	5 385	5 001	4 974	4 658
Alcohol monopoly wholesale	23	116	98	0	0	0	0	0	0	0
Alcohol monopoly retailing	49	88	234	80	296	302	116	198	282	180
Gaming monopoly retailing	0	0	0	3 561	3 657	4 766	5 269	4 803	4 691	4 478
5123 Customs and import duties	1 419	2 433	8 308	3 450	5 099	5 412	4 976	6 243	6 225	6 498
Customs	1 080	1 300	3 115	3 450	5 099	5 412	4 976	6 243	6 225	6 498
Agricultural levies	339	1 133	5 193	0	0	0	0	0	0	0
5124 Taxes on exports	0	0	0	0	0	0	0	0	0	0
5125 Taxes on investment goods	0	0	40	0	0	0	0	0	0	0
Investment tax	..	..	40	..	..	..	..	..	..	..
5126 Taxes on specific services	217	1 253	5 176	6 472	4 341	5 745	9 072	10 587	14 150	13 897
Betting tax	79	223	616	0	0	0	0	0	0	0
Advertisement tax	0	202	1 073	1 116	657	335	244	200	170	146
Tax on gambling	0	69	88	1 245	1 315	1 378	1 309	1 353	1 485	1 467
Other specific services	138	656	2 938	4 111	2 369	4 031	7 520	9 034	12 496	11 016
Tax on charter travelling	0	103	461	0	0	0	0	0	0	0
Tax on air travel	..	..	0	0	0	0	0	0	0	1 268
5127 Other taxes on internat. trade and transactions	0	0	0	0	0	0	0	0	0	0
5128 Other taxes	0	0	0	1 339	4 460	5 702	2 980	2 795	3 160	4 149
5130 Unallocable between 5110 and 5120	0	0	0	0	0	0	0	0	0	0
5200 Taxes on use of goods and perform activities	663	3 760	7 122	7 433	13 083	16 400	16 502	18 752	19 924	19 835
5210 Recurrent taxes	663	3 760	7 122	7 433	13 083	16 400	16 502	18 752	19 924	19 835
5211 Paid by households: motor vehicles	336	1 241	2 003	4 969	7 451	8 550	8 275	10 897	10 884	9 856
5212 Paid by others: motor vehicles	313	2 476	5 055	2 464	5 632	7 850	8 227	7 855	9 040	9 979
5213 Paid in respect of other goods	14	43	64	0	0	0	0	0	0	0
5220 Non-recurrent taxes	0	0	0	0	0	0	0	0	0	0
5300 Unallocable between 5100 and 5200	0	0	0	0	0	0	0	0	0	0
6000 Other taxes	**0**	**422**	**1 264**	**1 479**	**1 768**	**1 421**	**1 806**	**1 356**	**2 257**	**1 926**
6100 Paid solely by business	..	0	0	0	0	0	0	0	0	0
6200 Other	..	422	1 264	1 479	1 768	1 421	1 806	1 356	2 257	1 926
Memorandum item										
Customs duties collected on behalf of the EU	..	..	..	3 450	5 099	5 412	4 976	6 243	6 225	6 498
Total tax revenue on cash basis	**40 003**	**259 216**	**759 068**	**1 144 233**	**1 465 382**	**1 496 374**	**1 611 798**	**1 768 413**	**..**	**..**
Total tax revenue on accrual basis	**..**	**..**	**..**	**1 174 516**	**1 497 268**	**1 538 704**	**1 632 087**	**1 825 624**	**2 049 257**	**2 120 634**

	1965	1980	1990	2000	2007	2010	2013	2015	2017	2018
Conciliation with National Accounts										
Additional taxes included in National Accounts	..	..	..	0	0	0	0	0	0	0
Taxes excluded from National Accounts	..	..	..	0	0	0	0	0	0	0
Difference in treatment of tax credits	..	..	..	0	0	0	0	0	0	0
Capital transfer for uncollected revenue	..	..	..	0	0	0	0	0	0	0
Voluntary social security contributions	..	..	..	7 951	12 376	13 167	15 909	16 726	19 271	23 457
Miscellaneous differences	..	..	..	0	0	0	0	0	0	0
National Accounts: Taxes and actual social contributions	..	..	..	1 182 467	1 509 644	1 551 871	1 647 996	1 842 350	2 068 528	2 144 091
Imputed social contributions	..	..	..	0	0	0	0	0	0	0
National Accounts: Taxes and all social contributions	..	..	..	1 182 467	1 509 644	1 551 871	1 647 996	1 842 350	2 068 528	2 144 091

.. Not available

Note: Year ending 31st December.

From 2000 data are on accrual basis.

Figures prior to 1970 are not strictly comparable with those of later years, though the amounts involved are insignificant.

Heading 1000: Receipts are on accrual and not on a cash basis for all years.

Heading 2000 includes some voluntary contributions.

Source: Monthly reports of central Government Revenues (unpublished) National Audit Bureau, Stockholm. Local Government Finance (SOS), Tax assessment statistics (SOS) , National Central Bureau of Statistics, Stockholm.National Accounts (Statistical Reports), National Bureau of Statistics, Stockholm.

StatLink https://doi.org/10.1787/888934212288

Table 5.34. Switzerland: Details of tax revenue, 1965-2018

Million CHF

	1965	1980	1990	2000	2007	2010	2013	2015	2017	2018
Total tax revenue	**11 237**	**46 385**	**85 367**	**127 572**	**151 923**	**163 017**	**173 557**	**181 466**	**191 119**	**194 391**
1000 Taxes on income, profits and capital gains	**4 616**	**21 022**	**40 203**	**56 411**	**69 790**	**74 439**	**79 271**	**84 376**	**90 566**	**92 857**
1100 Of individuals	3 748	18 056	27 824	37 948	47 994	51 835	53 803	56 377	57 859	59 768
1110 On income and profits	3 547	17 622	27 824	37 948	47 994	51 835	53 803	56 377	57 859	59 768
Direct federal tax	245	2 525	4 432	5 713	8 589	9 880	9 655	10 394	10 397	11 171
Military service exemption tax	35	103	135	163	138	155	163	173	175	167
Cantonal tax individuals	1 473	7 510	12 856	17 592	23 094	24 957	26 273	27 185	28 070	28 821
Municipal tax individuals	1 322	6 235	10 402	14 481	16 174	16 844	17 712	18 625	19 217	19 609
Withholding tax	358	1 249	0	0	0	0	0	0	0	0
Coupons	114	0	0	0	0	0	0	0	0	0
1120 On capital gains	201	434	0	0	0	0	0	0	0	0
Cantonal tax individuals	84	229	..	..	..	..	..	..	..	..
Municipal tax individuals	112	190	..	..	..	..	..	..	..	..
Direct federal tax	5	15	..	..	..	..	..	..	..	..
1200 Corporate	868	2 966	6 300	11 323	16 161	16 378	17 815	19 443	20 535	22 217
1210 On profits	801	2 818	6 300	11 323	16 161	16 378	17 815	19 443	20 535	22 217
Direct federal tax	153	781	2 214	4 928	6 800	8 006	8 698	9 731	10 547	11 275
Corporate cantonal tax	363	1 230	2 576	3 989	6 098	5 445	5 985	6 294	6 454	7 008
Corporate municipal tax	285	807	1 510	2 406	3 263	2 927	3 132	3 418	3 535	3 933
Withholding tax	0	0	0	0	0	0	0	0	0	0
1220 On capital gains	67	148	..	..	..	..	..	..	..	..
Corporate tax on gains	2	7	..	..	..	..	..	..	..	..
Corporate cantonal tax	28	77	..	..	..	..	..	..	..	..
Corporate municipal tax	37	64	..	..	..	..	..	..	..	..
1300 Unallocable between 1100 and 1200	0	0	6 079	7 140	5 635	6 226	7 653	8 556	12 172	10 873
Withholding tax	..	..	4 044	6 202	4 211	4 723	5 619	6 543	9 710	8 347
Property gains tax	..	..	2 035	938	1 424	1 502	2 033	2 014	2 461	2 526
Other	..	..	..	..	..	..	..	..	..	..
2000 Social security contributions	**1 670**	**10 844**	**19 892**	**30 750**	**34 949**	**38 369**	**42 654**	**44 073**	**44 998**	**45 861**
2100 Employees	716	4 833	9 312	14 385	16 356	17 573	19 710	20 436	20 887	21 356
2110 On a payroll basis	716	4 833	9 312	14 385	16 356	17 573	19 710	20 436	20 887	21 356
2120 On an income tax basis	0	0	..	..	..	..	..	..	..	..
2200 Employers	747	4 897	9 320	14 398	16 371	17 600	19 742	20 468	20 922	21 394
2210 On a payroll basis	747	4 897	9 320	14 398	16 371	17 600	19 742	20 468	20 922	21 394
2220 On an income tax basis	0	0	..	..	..	..	..	..	..	..
2300 Self-employed or non-employed	208	1 046	1 261	1 967	2 222	3 197	3 202	3 169	3 189	3 111
2310 On a payroll basis	209	1 046	1 261	1 967	2 222	3 197	3 202	3 169	3 189	3 111
2320 On an income tax basis	0	0	..	..	..	..	..	..	..	..
2400 Unallocable between 2100, 2200 and 2300	0	68	0	0	0	0	0	0	0	0
2410 On a payroll basis	..	68	..	..	..	..	..	..	..	..
2420 On an income tax basis	..	0	..	..	..	..	..	..	..	..
3000 Taxes on payroll and workforce	**0**	**0**	**0**	**0**	**0**	**0**	**0**	**0**	**0**	**0**
4000 Taxes on property	**1 108**	**3 830**	**7 586**	**12 333**	**12 223**	**12 402**	**12 037**	**13 126**	**14 328**	**14 293**
4100 Recurrent taxes on immovable property	78	304	447	735	895	968	1 052	1 138	1 178	1 164
4110 Households	78	304	447	735	895	968	1 052	1 138	1 178	1 164
Cantonal tax on buildings	20	71	125	187	265	286	303	349	342	347
Municipal tax on buildings	58	233	322	548	630	682	748	789	836	817
4120 Others	0	0	..	..	..	..	..	..	..	..
4200 Recurrent taxes on net wealth	692	2 201	3 382	5 254	7 002	7 105	7 403	8 083	9 024	9 202
4210 Individual	420	1 383	2 194	3 972	5 309	5 576	5 785	6 604	7 324	7 409
Cantonal wealth tax	206	739	1 232	2 241	3 145	3 324	3 532	4 044	4 508	4 535
Municipal wealth tax	214	644	962	1 731	2 164	2 252	2 253	2 560	2 816	2 874
4220 Corporate	272	818	1 188	1 282	1 693	1 529	1 617	1 479	1 700	1 793
Direct federal tax on capital	21	92	0	0	0	0	0	0	0	0
Cantonal tax on capital	142	436	760	821	1 107	969	1 032	947	1 093	1 117
Municipal tax on capital	109	290	428	461	586	561	585	531	607	675
4300 Estate, inheritance and gift taxes	142	393	896	1 215	869	974	966	1 088	1 161	1 174
4310 Estate and inheritance taxes	142	393	896	1 215	869	974	966	1 088	1 161	1 174
Cantonal inheritance tax	128	361	820	1 118	774	886	854	964	1 042	1 058
Municipal inheritance tax	14	32	76	97	96	88	112	124	119	116
4320 Gift taxes	0	0	..	..	..	..	..	..	..	..
4400 Taxes on financial and capital transactions	196	932	2 245	4 342	2 562	2 428	1 671	1 902	1 970	1 681
Cantonal transfer tax	48	245	115	144	182	182	185	177	191	212
Municipal transfer tax	21	103	39	52	42	50	52	52	57	56
Securities issuance	99	175	0	0	405	779	182	360	407	248
Securities trading	19	409	0	0	1 933	1 417	1 253	1 314	1 315	1 166
Currency effects	9	0	0	0	0	0	0	0	0	0
Securities issuance and trading	0	0	2 091	4 146	0	0	0	0	0	0
4500 Non-recurrent taxes	0	0	0	0	0	0	0	0	0	0

	1965	1980	1990	2000	2007	2010	2013	2015	2017	2018
4510 On net wealth	..	..	..	..	..	..	..	..	..	..
4520 Other non-recurrent taxes	..	..	..	..	..	..	..	..	..	..
4600 Other recurrent taxes on property	0	0	616	786	895	927	946	915	994	1 072
5000 Taxes on goods and services	**3 843**	**10 689**	**17 546**	**27 864**	**34 711**	**37 216**	**38 930**	**39 092**	**40 261**	**40 350**
5100 Taxes on production, sale, transfer, etc.	3 582	9 863	15 975	25 302	30 669	32 264	33 861	33 760	34 397	34 461
5110 General taxes	1 191	4 772	9 871	16 917	19 962	21 035	22 870	22 791	23 298	23 042
5111 Value added taxes	0	0	9 871	16 594	19 604	20 662	22 501	22 397	22 902	22 644
5112 Sales tax	1 191	4 772	0	323	358	373	369	393	396	398
Automobile duty	..	..	..	323	358	373	369	393	396	398
Other sales taxes	..	..	..	0	0	0	0	0	0	0
5113 Other	0	0	..	..	..	..	..	..	..	..
5120 Taxes on specific goods and services	2 391	5 091	6 058	8 337	10 663	11 191	10 936	10 901	11 022	11 341
5121 Excise duties	1 016	3 427	4 604	6 810	7 805	8 295	8 099	8 056	8 105	8 457
Beer tax	26	33	0	0	107	112	113	114	112	115
Excises on tobacco	190	634	15	32	2 247	2 417	2 354	2 255	2 195	2 135
Other price supplements	104	542	1 503	1 783	3	0	0	3	3	3
Fuel tax	467	955	1 334	2 975	3 076	3 110	3 034	2 864	2 791	2 785
Additional fuel tax	229	1 263	1 753	2 020	2 071	2 082	2 025	1 905	1 855	1 847
Road tax	0	0	0	0	0	0	0	0	0	0
Mineral oil tax on combustibles	0	0	0	0	20	20	23	19	18	15
Automobile duty	0	0	0	0	0	0	0	0	0	0
Tax on distilled spirits	0	0	0	1	281	296	292	279	282	268
Electricity consumption tax	0	0	0	0	0	259	258	617	847	1 288
5122 Profits of fiscal monopolies	158	472	..	..	..	..	..	..	..	..
Alcohol monopoly	111	354	..	..	..	..	..	..	..	..
Salt monopoly	16	25	..	..	..	..	..	..	..	..
Water monopoly	30	90	..	..	..	..	..	..	..	..
Other	1	3	..	..	..	..	..	..	..	..
5123 Customs and import duties	1 104	953	1 201	1 096	1 040	1 079	1 059	1 056	1 103	1 103
Import duties	972	923	1 201	1 096	1 040	1 079	1 059	1 056	1 103	1 103
Tobacco duty	114	6	0	0	0	0	0	0	0	0
Additional duties	18	24	0	0	0	0	0	0	0	0
5124 Taxes on exports	0	0	0	0	0	0	0	0	0	0
5125 Taxes on investment goods	0	0	0	0	0	0	0	0	0	0
5126 Taxes on specific services	113	239	253	431	1 818	1 816	1 778	1 789	1 815	1 781
Games in B casinos Confederation	2	2	2	37	449	381	308	272	273	281
Cantonal entertainment tax	17	37	23	27	39	101	73	67	66	66
Municipal entertainment tax	11	19	46	26	18	17	15	15	15	17
Other cantonal expenditure taxes	24	63	0	0	0	0	0	0	0	0
Other municipal expenditure taxes	19	6	0	0	0	0	0	0	0	0
Premium stamp duty	40	112	0	0	645	659	700	715	713	703
Lottery taxes	0	0	181	320	474	459	466	517	546	512
Other	0	0	0	20	193	199	216	204	201	202
5127 Other taxes on internat. trade and transactions	0	0	0	0	0	0	0	0	0	0
5128 Other taxes	0	0	..	..	..	..	..	..	..	..
5130 Unallocable between 5110 and 5120	0	0	46	47	44	38	55	68	77	78
5200 Taxes on use of goods and perform activities	261	826	1 570	2 562	4 043	4 952	5 069	5 332	5 864	5 889
5210 Recurrent taxes	261	826	1 570	2 562	4 043	4 952	5 069	5 328	5 859	5 885
5211 Paid by households: motor vehicles	152	501	1 075	1 573	1 845	1 953	1 977	2 074	2 136	2 160
Paid by households in respect of motor vehicles	..	..	921	1 336	1 580	1 667	1 685	1 768	1 819	1 841
Paid by households in respect of motorway tax sticker	..	..	154	237	265	286	292	306	317	318
5212 Paid by others: motor vehicles	76	251	431	799	1 901	2 092	2 093	2 054	2 249	2 231
Paid by others in respect of motor vehicles	..	..	367	686	395	417	421	442	455	460
Paid by others in respect of motorway tax sticker	..	..	39	59	66	72	73	77	79	80
Paid by others in respect of heavy vehicle charge	..	..	25	54	1 440	1 604	1 599	1 536	1 715	1 691
5213 Paid in respect of other goods	33	74	64	190	296	907	999	1 199	1 475	1 494
Hunting and fishing	9	20	0	0	0	0	0	0	0	0
Cantonal dog license	3	9	6	9	8	8	10	9	10	10
Municipal dog license	2	8	14	21	25	30	33	35	40	44
Cantonal inns	12	24	0	0	0	0	0	0	0	0
Cantonal royalties	5	12	0	0	0	0	0	0	0	0
Other	2	1	0	33	33	30	31	24	13	13
Environmental incentive fees	0	0	3	73	166	755	833	1 036	1 294	1 294
Royalties and concessions	0	0	42	53	64	84	93	94	118	133
5220 Non-recurrent taxes	0	0	0	0	0	0	0	5	5	4
5300 Unallocable between 5100 and 5200	0	0	0	0	0	0	0	0	0	0
6000 Other taxes	**0**	**0**	**140**	**215**	**249**	**590**	**664**	**799**	**966**	**1 030**
6100 Paid solely by business	..	..	42	65	75	274	300	342	332	378
6200 Other	..	..	98	151	174	316	364	457	635	652
Exemption tax	..	..	98	151	174	187	191	190	198	203
Other	..	..	0	0	0	130	173	267	436	449
Total tax revenue on cash basis	**11 237**	**46 385**	..	..	..	..	..	..	..	..

	1965	1980	1990	2000	2007	2010	2013	2015	2017	2018
Total tax revenue on accrual basis	**..**	**..**	**85 367**	**127 572**	**151 923**	**163 017**	**173 557**	**181 466**	**191 119**	**194 391**
Conciliation with National Accounts										
Additional taxes included in national accounts	..	..	..	..	..	..	..	..	..	..
Tax excluded from national accounts	..	..	..	..	..	..	..	..	..	..
Difference in treatment of tax credits	..	..	..	..	..	..	..	..	..	..
Capital transfer for uncollected revenue	..	..	-242	-733	-964	-1 101	-1 265	-1 061	-870	-1 000
Voluntary social security contributions	..	..	..	..	..	..	..	..	..	..
Miscellaneous differences	..	..	..	..	..	..	..	..	..	..
National Accounts: taxes and actual social contributions	..	..	85 126	126 839	150 959	161 916	172 292	180 405	190 250	193 391
Imputed social contributions	..	..	362	501	468	399	482	334	380	343
National Accounts: taxes and all social contributions	..	..	85 488	127 340	151 427	162 315	172 774	180 739	190 630	193 734

.. Not available

Note: Calendar year ending on 31 December.

The data is on an accrual basis.

The pre-1970 figures are not strictly comparable with those from the following years which were revised slightly.

"Parish taxes" are not reported in these statistics from 1985 onward.

In section 1100: payments made in consideration for exemption from military service could be classed under nontax receipts.

Section 2000 (Social security contributions) has been revised from 1985 onward to take account of the sectoring of government units adopted when switching to the ESA 95 system of accounts (currently ESA 2010). Consequently, health insurance contributions and those to the Swiss National Accident Insurance Fund are now excluded from section 2000.

Source: Financial Statistics, Federal Finance Administration.

StatLink https://doi.org/10.1787/888934212307

Table 5.35. Turkey: Details of tax revenue, 1965-2018

Million TRY

	1965	1980	1990	2000	2007	2010	2013	2015	2017	2018
Total tax revenue	**0**	**1**	**79**	**40 263**	**203 053**	**287 873**	**458 698**	**586 722**	**773 406**	**901 485**
1000 Taxes on income, profits and capital gains	**0**	**0**	**26**	**11 890**	**48 197**	**61 317**	**92 749**	**119 144**	**165 306**	**217 666**
1100 Of individuals	0	0	21	8 954	34 447	40 392	63 761	85 756	112 401	138 992
1110 On income and profits	0	0	21	8 954	34 447	40 392	63 761	85 756	112 401	138 992
Income tax	0	0	21	8 954	34 447	40 392	63 761	85 756	112 401	138 992
1120 On capital gains	0	0	0	0	0	0	0	0	0	0
1200 Corporate	0	0	5	2 935	13 751	20 925	28 988	33 388	52 906	78 673
1210 On profits	0	0	5	2 935	13 751	20 925	28 988	33 388	52 906	78 673
Corporation tax	0	0	5	2 935	13 751	20 925	28 988	33 388	52 906	78 673
1220 On capital gains	0	0	0	0	0	0	0	0	0	0
1300 Unallocable between 1100 and 1200	0	0	0	0	0	0	0	0	0	0
Fiscal balance tax	..	0	..	..	..	..	..	..	..	..
Capital gains tax on real estate sales	..	0	..	..	..	..	..	..	..	..
2000 Social security contributions	**0**	**0**	**15**	**7 543**	**44 052**	**71 696**	**125 871**	**170 282**	**226 720**	**269 932**
2100 Employees	0	0	6	2 712	17 867	26 934	49 831	64 214	86 410	101 666
2110 On a payroll basis	..	..	..	2 712	17 867	26 934	49 831	64 214	86 410	101 666
2120 On an income tax basis	..	..	..	0	0	0	0	0	0	0
2200 Employers	0	0	9	3 619	20 442	39 363	71 184	95 067	128 331	151 373
2210 On a payroll basis	..	..	..	3 619	20 442	39 363	71 184	95 067	128 331	151 373
2220 On an income tax basis	..	..	..	0	0	0	0	0	0	0
2300 Self-employed or non-employed	0	0	1	1 211	5 743	5 399	4 856	11 001	11 979	16 893
2310 On a payroll basis	..	..	..	1 211	5 743	5 399	4 856	11 001	11 979	16 893
2320 On an income tax basis	..	..	..	0	0	0	0	0	0	0
2400 Unallocable between 2100, 2200 and 2300	0	0	0	0	0	0	0	0	0	0
2410 On a payroll basis	..	..	..	..	..	..	..	..	..	..
2420 On an income tax basis	..	..	..	..	..	..	..	..	..	..
3000 Taxes on payroll and workforce	**0**	**0**	**0**	**0**	**0**	**0**	**0**	**0**	**0**	**0**
4000 Taxes on property	**0**	**0**	**2**	**1 272**	**7 621**	**11 684**	**21 280**	**28 582**	**34 857**	**38 941**
4100 Recurrent taxes on immovable property	0	0	0	191	1 464	2 669	3 847	5 882	6 809	8 703
Real estate tax	0	0	..	191	1 464	2 669	3 847	5 882	6 809	8 703
4110 Households	..	..	..	..	..	..	..	..	..	..
4120 Others	..	..	..	..	..	..	..	..	..	..
4200 Recurrent taxes on net wealth	0	0	0	0	0	0	0	0	0	0
4210 Individual	..	..	..	..	..	..	..	..	..	..
4220 Corporate	..	..	..	..	..	..	..	..	..	..
4300 Estate, inheritance and gift taxes	0	0	0	15	125	215	340	435	718	921
Gift and inheritance tax	0	0	0	15	125	215	340	435	718	921
4310 Estate and inheritance taxes	..	..	..	..	..	..	..	..	..	..
4320 Gift taxes	..	..	..	..	..	..	..	..	..	..
4400 Taxes on financial and capital transactions	0	0	2	1 065	6 032	8 800	17 093	22 265	27 331	29 318
Stamp tax	0	0	2	818	3 642	5 083	9 416	12 045	15 596	16 961
Real estate purchase tax	0	0	0	0	0	0	0	0	0	0
Title deed fees	0	0	0	207	2 000	3 329	7 072	9 530	10 970	11 534
Notary fees	0	0	0	40	389	388	606	690	765	822
4500 Non-recurrent taxes	0	0	0	0	0	0	0	0	0	0
4510 On net wealth	..	..	..	..	..	..	..	..	..	..
4520 Other non-recurrent taxes	..	..	..	..	..	..	..	..	..	..
4600 Other recurrent taxes on property	0	0	0	0	0	0	0	0	0	0
5000 Taxes on goods and services	**0**	**0**	**22**	**16 901**	**96 766**	**137 252**	**211 257**	**259 964**	**336 256**	**364 982**
5100 Taxes on production, sale, transfer, etc.	0	0	22	16 328	92 605	131 878	203 364	250 261	324 935	351 455
5110 General taxes	0	0	16	9 735	43 285	62 533	100 723	121 070	155 680	178 616
5111 Value added taxes	..	..	14	9 735	43 285	62 533	100 723	121 070	155 680	178 616
5112 Sales tax	..	..	0	0	0	0	0	0	0	0
5113 Other	..	..	1	0	0	0	0	0	0	0
5120 Taxes on specific goods and services	0	0	6	6 593	49 320	69 345	102 641	129 191	169 256	172 839
5121 Excise duties	0	0	1	4 718	39 111	57 285	85 462	105 922	138 338	133 904
Sales taxes	0	0	0	0	0	0	0	0	0	0
Domestic production tax	0	0	0	0	0	0	0	0	0	0
Domestic production tax on petrol	0	0	0	0	0	0	0	0	0	0
Production tax on monopoly goods	0	0	0	0	0	0	0	0	0	0
Sugar consumption taxes	0	0	0	0	0	0	0	0	0	0
Motor vehicles purchase tax (Total)	0	0	1	916	4 293	6 193	10 565	17 027	22 017	17 328
Motor vehicles purchase tax	0	0	0	498	4 293	6 193	10 565	17 027	22 017	17 328
Additional motor vehicle purchase tax	0	0	0	418	0	0	0	0	0	0
Revenue from other excises	0	0	0	533	12 765	19 395	29 739	38 066	52 718	60 982
Petroleum consumption tax	0	0	0	3 269	22 052	31 697	45 158	50 830	63 603	55 593
5122 Profits of fiscal monopolies	0	0	0	0	0	0	0	0	0	0

	1965	1980	1990	2000	2007	2010	2013	2015	2017	2018
5123 Customs and import duties	0	0	4	462	2 478	3 319	5 542	8 521	12 837	15 959
Customs duty	0	0	1	449	2 441	3 240	5 409	8 280	12 329	15 276
Customs duty on petrol	0	0	0	0	0	0	0	0	0	0
Production tax on imports	0	0	0	0	0	0	0	0	0	0
Production tax on petrol imports	0	0	0	0	0	0	0	0	0	0
Stamp duty on imports	0	0	2	0	0	0	0	0	0	0
Wharf duty	0	0	1	0	0	0	0	0	0	0
Other	0	0	0	13	37	80	133	240	508	683
5124 Taxes on exports	0	0	0	0	0	0	0	0	0	0
5125 Taxes on investment goods	0	0	0	0	0	0	0	0	0	0
5126 Taxes on specific services	0	0	1	997	7 686	4 005	6 853	10 014	14 262	19 340
Bank, insurance transaction tax	0	0	1	997	3 149	3 571	6 160	9 172	13 270	18 184
Transportation tax	0	0	0	0	0	0	0	0	0	0
PTT service tax	0	0	0	0	4 211	0	0	0	0	0
Tax on football pool	0	0	0	0	0	0	0	0	0	0
Lottery tax	0	0	0	0	327	434	692	842	993	1 155
5127 Other taxes on internat. trade and transactions	0	0	0	0	0	0	0	0	0	0
Foreign travel expenditures tax	0	0	..	..	..	..	..	..	..	..
5128 Other taxes	0	0	0	416	46	4 736	4 785	4 734	3 818	3 637
5130 Unallocable between 5110 and 5120	0	0	0	0	0	0	0	0	0	0
5200 Taxes on use of goods and perform activities	0	0	0	572	4 161	5 374	7 894	9 703	11 321	13 527
5210 Recurrent taxes	0	0	0	359	4 161	5 374	7 894	9 703	11 321	13 527
Motor vehicles tax	0	0	0	359	0	5 374	7 894	9 703	11 321	13 527
5211 Paid by households: motor vehicles	..	..	..	0	0	0	0	0	0	0
5212 Paid by others: motor vehicles	..	..	..	359	4 161	5 374	7 894	9 703	11 321	13 527
Motor vehicles tax	..	..	..	302	3 521	5 033	7 353	8 949	10 825	12 844
Traffic fees	..	..	..	58	640	341	540	754	496	683
5213 Paid in respect of other goods	..	..	..	0	0	0	0	0	0	0
5220 Non-recurrent taxes	0	0	0	213	0	0	0	0	0	0
Building construction tax	..	0	..	0	..	..	..	..	..	..
5300 Unallocable between 5100 and 5200	0	0	0	0	0	0	0	0	0	0
6000 Other taxes	**0**	**0**	**13**	**2 658**	**6 417**	**5 924**	**7 541**	**8 750**	**10 266**	**9 963**
6100 Paid solely by business	..	0	0	0	0	0	0	0	0	0
6200 Other	..	0	13	2 658	6 417	5 924	7 541	8 750	10 266	9 963
Funds	..	..	..	1 938	0	0	0	0	0	0
Vocatial Train Pro.F.	..	..	..	67	0	0	0	0	0	0
Tax penalties and fines	..	..	..	548	4 191	2 689	3 175	3 779	3 838	4 159
Municipalities revenue	..	..	..	106	2 227	3 235	4 366	4 971	6 429	5 805
Total tax revenue on cash basis	**0**	**1**	**79**	**40 263**	**203 053**	**287 873**	**458 698**	**586 722**	**773 406**	**901 485**
Total tax revenue on accrual basis	**..**	**..**	**..**	**..**	**..**	**..**	**..**	**..**	**..**	**..**
Conciliation with National Accounts										
Additional taxes included in National Accounts	..	..	..	..	..	..	..	..	..	..
Taxes excluded from National Accounts	..	..	..	..	..	..	..	..	..	..
Difference in treatment of tax credits	..	..	..	..	..	..	..	..	..	..
Capital transfer for uncollected revenue	..	..	..	..	..	..	..	..	..	..
Voluntary social security contributions	..	..	..	..	..	..	..	..	..	..
Miscellaneous differences	..	..	..	..	..	..	..	..	..	..
National Accounts: Taxes and actual social contributions	..	..	..	..	..	..	..	..	..	..
Imputed social contributions	..	..	..	..	..	..	..	..	..	..
National Accounts: Taxes and all social contributions	..	..	..	..	..	..	..	..	..	..

.. Not available

Note: From 1982 the data are based on the fiscal year ending 31st December. Before that the data are on a fiscal year basis beginning 1st March.

Revenue is reported on a cash basis except for social security contributions which are reported on an assessment basis.

The figures under the local tax collections include taxes under "Municipalities Revenues Law" and Property tax. They also include transfers to the local authorities from central budget tax revenues under the revenue sharing system.

Heading 2000: Before 2003, contributions to some private social security schemes are included in this heading.

Source: Bulletin of national accounts and the Budget revenue Bulletin.

StatLink https://doi.org/10.1787/888934212326

Table 5.36. United Kingdom: Details of tax revenue, 1965-2018

Million GBP

	1965	1980	1990	2000	2007	2010	2013	2015	2017	2018
Total tax revenue	**10 945**	**81 153**	**202 368**	**359 370**	**508 720**	**514 729**	**571 259**	**621 767**	**680 029**	**705 206**
Total tax revenue exclusive of taxes collected for the EU	..	..	**200 520**	**357 240**	**506 305**	**511 784**	**568 333**	**618 680**	**676 602**	**701 634**
1000 Taxes on income, profits and capital gains	**4 050**	**30 651**	**79 576**	**142 197**	**201 312**	**192 703**	**202 235**	**223 355**	**240 387**	**249 059**
1100 Of individuals	3 618	23 868	59 506	104 136	151 157	147 019	156 570	168 873	185 560	192 765
1110 On income and profits	3 615	23 376	57 614	101 925	147 309	144 502	152 668	163 291	177 182	184 968
Income tax	..	23 370	57 614	101 925	147 309	144 502	152 668	163 291	177 182	184 968
Surtax	..	6	0	0	0	0	0	0	0	0
1120 On capital gains	3	492	1 892	2 211	3 848	2 517	3 902	5 582	8 378	7 797
1200 Corporate	484	6 783	20 070	38 061	50 155	45 684	45 665	54 482	54 827	56 294
1210 On profits	484	6 510	18 994	35 730	47 524	45 721	45 256	54 499	55 251	56 260
Petroleum revenue tax	..	1 799	941	1 540	1 387	1 349	1 296	-552	-634	-817
Supplementary petroleum duty	..	0	0	0	0	0	0	0	0	0
Corporation tax	..	4 712	18 053	34 190	45 423	43 729	43 293	54 431	55 146	56 385
Corporation tax overspill relief	..	-1	0	0	0	0	0	0	0	0
Profits tax	..	0	0	0	0	0	0	0	0	0
Windfall tax	..	0	0	0	0	0	0	0	0	0
Betting tax	..	0	0	0	590	568	605	595	737	692
Non fossil fuel obligation levy	..	0	0	0	124	75	62	25	2	0
1220 On capital gains	0	273	1 076	2 331	3 285	878	1 035	1 114	1 252	2 003
1300 Unallocable between 1100 and 1200	-52	0	0	0	0	0	0	0	0	0
2000 Social security contributions	**1 685**	**13 531**	**34 457**	**60 252**	**93 210**	**97 346**	**106 085**	**114 067**	**130 439**	**134 986**
2100 Employees	770	5 228	13 296	24 175	36 585	38 703	41 481	44 454	50 412	52 055
2110 On a payroll basis	..	..	13 296	24 175	36 585	38 703	41 481	44 454	50 412	52 055
2120 On an income tax basis	..	..	0	0	0	0	0	0	0	0
2200 Employers	831	8 210	19 984	34 028	53 765	55 887	62 019	66 491	76 591	79 240
2210 On a payroll basis	..	..	19 984	34 028	53 765	55 887	62 019	66 491	76 591	79 240
2220 On an income tax basis	..	..	0	0	0	0	0	0	0	0
2300 Self-employed or non-employed	75	317	1 177	2 049	2 860	2 756	2 585	3 122	3 436	3 691
2310 On a payroll basis	..	..	1 177	2 049	2 860	2 756	2 585	3 122	3 436	3 691
2320 On an income tax basis	..	..	0	0	0	0	0	0	0	0
2400 Unallocable between 2100, 2200 and 2300	9	-224	0	0	0	0	0	0	0	0
2410 On a payroll basis	..	..	..	..	..	..	..	..	..	..
2420 On an income tax basis	..	..	..	..	..	..	..	..	..	..
3000 Taxes on payroll and workforce	**0**	**3 498**	**0**	**0**	**0**	**0**	**0**	**0**	**1 842**	**2 604**
Selective employment tax	..	0	..	..	..	..	..	..	0	0
National insurance surcharge	..	3 498	..	..	..	..	..	..	0	0
Apprenticeship Levy	..	0	..	..	..	..	..	..	1 842	2 604
4000 Taxes on property	**1 591**	**9 774**	**16 538**	**41 134**	**63 392**	**61 768**	**70 094**	**76 565**	**85 614**	**88 416**
4100 Recurrent taxes on immovable property	1 228	8 665	13 462	30 552	44 891	50 028	55 139	58 185	62 856	66 159
4110 Households	539	3 687	2 373	14 205	23 609	25 919	27 640	29 356	32 270	34 733
Northern Ireland rates paid to CG	..	37	113	141	265	335	409	384	362	351
Council tax	..	0	0	13 991	23 217	25 438	27 061	28 777	31 690	34 153
Rates paid to LA	..	3 650	2 260	73	127	146	170	195	218	229
4120 Others	689	4 978	11 089	16 347	21 282	24 109	27 499	28 829	30 586	31 426
National non-domestic rates	..	0	7 542	14 966	19 358	21 602	24 611	25 834	27 401	28 166
Rates paid to LA	..	4 925	2 869	149	267	497	567	600	675	690
Northern Ireland rates paid to CG	..	53	115	207	353	361	373	398	420	431
London Regional Transport levy	..	0	47	0	0	0	0	0	0	0
LA payments of NNDR	..	0	469	889	1 111	1 236	1 389	1 389	1 389	1 389
NPISH payments of NNDR	..	0	47	136	193	245	342	384	430	474
Crossrail Business rates supplement	..	0	0	0	0	168	217	224	271	276
4200 Recurrent taxes on net wealth	0	0	0	0	0	0	0	0	0	0
4210 Individual	..	..	..	..	..	..	..	..	..	..
4220 Corporate	..	..	..	..	..	..	..	..	..	..
4300 Estate, inheritance and gift taxes	287	479	1 321	2 215	3 867	2 642	3 379	4 442	5 382	5 301
4310 Estate and inheritance taxes	287	479	1 321	2 215	3 867	2 642	3 379	4 442	5 382	5 301
Death duties	..	423	1 278	2 156	3 764	2 592	3 293	4 359	5 283	5 198
Development land tax	..	42	6	0	0	0	0	0	0	0
Taxes on other capital transfers	..	14	37	59	50	50	50	50	50	50
Special tax on bank deposits	..	0	0	0	0	0	0	0	0	0
Betterment duty	..	0	0	0	0	0	0	0	0	0
Special charges	..	0	0	0	0	0	0	0	0	0
Special contribution	..	0	0	0	0	0	0	0	0	0
Equal pay on capital transfers	..	0	0	0	53	0	36	33	49	53
4320 Gift taxes	0	0	0	0	0	0	0	0	0	0
4400 Taxes on financial and capital transactions	76	630	1 755	8 367	14 634	9 098	11 540	13 791	17 101	16 654
Stamp duties	..	630	1 755	8 367	14 634	9 098	11 540	13 791	17 101	16 654
4500 Non-recurrent taxes	0	0	0	0	0	0	36	147	275	302

	1965	1980	1990	2000	2007	2010	2013	2015	2017	2018
4510 On net wealth	..	..	..	..	..	..	0	0	0	0
4520 Other non-recurrent taxes	..	..	..	..	..	..	36	147	275	302
4600 Other recurrent taxes on property	0	0	0	0	0	0	0	0	0	0
5000 Taxes on goods and services	**3 619**	**23 699**	**62 780**	**115 787**	**150 806**	**162 912**	**192 845**	**207 780**	**221 747**	**230 141**
5100 Taxes on production, sale, transfer, etc.	3 406	22 677	59 379	110 804	144 752	155 471	185 262	200 337	213 965	222 044
5110 General taxes	647	11 897	34 136	65 018	93 374	97 646	121 460	133 064	142 401	149 078
5111 Value added taxes	0	11 897	34 136	65 018	93 374	97 646	121 460	133 064	142 401	149 078
Value added tax	..	11 893	33 620	64 918	93 348	97 565	121 650	132 948	142 655	149 228
Adj. to VAT contribution	..	4	516	100	26	81	-190	116	-254	-150
Purchase tax	..	0	0	0	0	0	0	0	0	0
5112 Sales tax	647	0	0	0	0	0	0	0	0	0
5113 Other	0	0	0	0	0	0	0	0	0	0
5120 Taxes on specific goods and services	2 759	10 780	25 243	45 786	51 378	57 825	63 802	67 273	71 564	72 966
5121 Excise duties	2 383	8 616	19 707	37 315	40 427	45 454	46 588	47 294	48 697	49 125
Beer	..	1 029	2 220	2 813	3 042	3 278	3 337	3 294	3 443	3 638
Wines, spirits, cider and perry	..	1 513	2 627	3 751	5 008	6 075	7 063	7 385	8 151	8 355
Tobacco	..	2 735	5 541	7 666	7 862	9 076	9 479	9 190	9 122	8 976
Hydrocarbon oil	..	3 327	9 302	23 041	24 512	27 013	26 697	27 415	27 973	27 919
Other excise duties	..	12	17	0	0	0	0	0	0	0
Sugar levy	..	12	0	44	3	12	12	10	8	0
Soft Drinks Levy	..	..	0	0	0	0	0	0	0	237
5122 Profits of fiscal monopolies	0	0	0	0	0	0	0	0	0	0
5123 Customs and import duties	343	1 109	1 837	2 086	2 522	3 058	3 042	3 219	3 564	3 480
Custom duties	..	..	..	1 800	2 074	2 933	2 914	3 077	3 419	3 335
Import duties	..	855	1 722	0	0	0	0	0	0	0
Agricultural levies	..	254	115	286	338	0	0	0	0	0
Temporary charges of import	..	0	0	0	0	0	0	0	0	0
British Transport Police	..	0	0	0	110	125	128	142	145	145
5124 Taxes on exports	0	-1	36	0	0	0	0	0	0	0
Levies on exports	..	-1	36	..	..	..	..	..	..	..
5125 Taxes on investment goods	0	0	0	0	0	0	0	0	0	0
5126 Taxes on specific services	33	456	1 022	5 826	6 523	7 292	11 601	13 626	15 663	16 320
Betting and gaming	..	456	1 022	1 522	959	1 092	1 538	2 053	2 235	2 202
National Lottery contributions to fund	..	0	0	1 590	1 310	1 625	1 644	1 713	1 713	1 713
Air passenger duty	..	0	0	940	1 883	2 094	2 960	3 119	3 398	3 513
Insurance premium tax	..	0	0	1 707	2 306	2 401	3 018	3 294	5 670	6 201
Bank Levy - Stability Fee Scheme	..	0	0	0	0	0	2 352	3 369	2 568	2 613
Light Dues	..	0	0	67	65	80	89	78	79	78
5127 Other taxes on internat. trade and transactions	0	0	0	0	0	0	0	0	0	0
5128 Other taxes	0	600	2 641	559	1 906	2 021	2 571	3 134	3 640	4 041
Fossil fuel levy	..	0	875	56	0	0	0	0	0	0
European coal and steel levy	..	21	11	0	0	0	0	0	0	0
Gas levy	..	12	291	0	0	0	0	0	0	0
Car tax	..	83	1 464	0	0	0	0	0	0	0
Landfill tax	..	484	0	461	877	1 065	1 191	1 028	904	853
Climate change levy	..	0	0	0	690	666	1 098	1 752	1 878	1 911
Aggregates levy	..	0	0	0	339	290	282	354	375	366
Hydro benefit	..	0	0	42	0	0	0	0	0	0
Renewable energy obligations	..	0	0	0	0	0	0	0	0	0
Channel 4 advertising formula	..	0	0	0	0	0	0	0	0	0
Milk super levy	..	0	0	0	0	0	0	0	0	0
Contracts for Difference	..	0	0	0	0	0	0	0	483	911
5130 Unallocable between 5110 and 5120	0	0	0	0	0	0	0	0	0	0
5200 Taxes on use of goods and perform activities	212	1 378	3 401	4 983	6 054	7 441	7 583	7 443	7 782	8 097
5210 Recurrent taxes	212	1 378	3 401	4 983	6 054	7 441	7 583	7 443	7 719	8 012
5211 Paid by households: motor vehicles	118	729	1 841	2 996	4 096	4 561	4 312	3 823	4 012	4 233
Motor vehicle duty	..	726	1 837	2 992	4 096	4 561	4 312	3 823	4 012	4 233
Boat licences	..	3	4	4	0	0	0	0	0	0
5212 Paid by others: motor vehicles	74	588	1 134	1 614	1 288	1 279	1 789	2 076	2 214	2 329
Motor vehicle levy	..	588	1 134	1 614	1 288	1 279	1 789	2 076	2 214	2 329
5213 Paid in respect of other goods	20	61	426	373	670	1 601	1 482	1 544	1 493	1 450
IBA levy	..	..	134	0	0	0	0	0	0	0
Telecommunications regulator fees	..	..	7	12	17	12	0	0	0	0
Gas regulator fees	..	..	2	0	0	0	0	0	0	0
Electricity regulator fees	..	..	5	0	0	0	0	0	0	0
Water regulator fees	..	..	6	11	11	12	24	27	24	33
Rail regulator fees	..	..	0	14	12	12	12	12	12	12
Company registration surplus fees	..	..	12	0	0	0	0	0	0	0
Consumer and credit act fees	..	..	163	119	281	480	480	480	480	480
Levy funded bodies	..	..	97	217	349	1 040	922	970	915	859
1936 Tithe Act payments	..	..	0	0	0	0	0	0	0	0
Recurrent taxes paid in respect of other goods	..	..	0	0	0	45	44	55	62	66

	1965	1980	1990	2000	2007	2010	2013	2015	2017	2018
5220 Non-recurrent taxes	0	0	0	0	0	0	0	0	63	85
Immigration Skills Charge	..	..	..	..	..	..	..	..	63	85
5300 Unallocable between 5100 and 5200	1	-356	0	0	0	0	0	0	0	0
6000 Other taxes	**0**	**0**	**9 017**	**0**	**0**	**0**	**0**	**0**	**0**	**0**
6100 Paid solely by business	..	..	0	..	..	..	..	..	..	..
6200 Other	..	..	9 017	..	..	..	..	..	..	..
Community charge	..	..	9 017	..	..	..	..	..	..	..
Memorandum item										
Customs duties collected on behalf of the EU	..	..	..	1 800	2 074	2 933	2 914	3 077	3 419	3 335
Non-wastable tax credits										
Non-wastable tax credits against 1110	..	..	7 454	4 651	20 030	28 879	29 710	28 539	25 940	22 877
Tax expenditure component	..	..	6 973	1 233	4 414	5 542	2 538	2 571	2 336	2 061
Transfer component	..	..	481	3 418	15 617	23 338	27 172	25 968	23 604	20 816
Non-wastable tax credits against 1210	..	..	0	0	918	1 313	1 156	3 245	5 356	6 152
Tax expenditure component	..	..	0	0	654	915	626	1 131	1 676	1 969
Transfer component	..	..	0	0	265	399	530	2 114	3 680	4 183
Total tax revenue on cash basis	**10 945**	**81 153**	**202 400**	**356 070**	**508 916**	**509 122**	**561 690**	**599 392**	**665 126**	**688 067**
Total tax revenue on accrual basis	**..**	**..**	**202 368**	**359 370**	**508 720**	**514 729**	**571 259**	**621 767**	**680 029**	**705 206**
Conciliation with National Accounts										
Additional taxes included in National Accounts	..	..	1 323	2 062	4 072	4 731	5 816	7 261	8 861	9 657
Taxes excluded from National Accounts	..	..	0	0	0	0	0	0	0	0
Difference in treatment of tax credits	..	..	6 973	1 233	5 068	6 457	3 164	3 702	4 012	4 030
Capital transfer for uncollected revenue	..	..	0	0	0	0	0	0	0	0
Voluntary social security contributions	..	..	3 288	8 103	18 629	21 217	22 438	25 025	26 678	27 546
Miscellaneous differences	..	..	0	0	0	0	0	0	0	0
National Accounts: Taxes and actual social contributions	..	..	213 952	370 768	536 489	547 134	602 677	657 755	719 580	746 439
Imputed social contributions	..	..	3 966	4 234	1 391	1 616	1 568	1 563	1 469	1 260
National Accounts: Taxes and all social contributions	..	..	217 918	375 002	537 880	548 750	604 245	659 318	721 049	747 699

.. Not available

Note: Year ending 31st December.

From 1990 data are on accrual basis.

Heading 1210: The corporate tax figures include company income tax from 1990 onwards.

Heading 2000: Includes some voluntary contributions which cannot be separately identified.

Heading 6200: The community charge replaced domestic rates in Scotland in April 1989 and was extended to England and Wales in April 1990. This tax has been classified in heading 6200 as it is a lump-sum tax levied on each adult in a household (domestic rates are classified in heading 4100). Headings for non-wastable tax credits 1110 and 1210 are consistent with the guidelines, and the figures in the data are treated accordingly. The following method is adopted separately for Working Families 'Tax Credit and Disabled Persons Tax Credit' paid from 1999 to 2003. For each calendar, a random sample of awards over-lapping the quarter is taken. Each recipient family's income tax liability for the fiscal year within which the quarter falls is calculated, based on the earned income reported for the award (uprated to the middle of the overlap period). And the result multiplied by the number of days in the overlap period divided by 365. The tax expenditure component is defined as the minimum of this amount and the total amount of award paid in the overlap period. The total amount of award paid and the tax expenditure component are each summed over the sample cases, and the ratio is taken as the tax expenditure ration for the quarter. From 2003, the equivalent breakdown for Child and Working tax credits is based on household survey data. Survey data is used to estimate the breakdown into the tax expenditure and the transfer components for the other smaller tax credits.

The United Kingdom Personal Tax Credit information presented in Revenue Statistics is on a cash basis (rather than an accrual basis as for the rest of the data). PTC information on a financial year basis has been used as a proxy for calendar year. Please note that since 2015-16 tax credits is no longer split into tax expenditure and transfer component. The split for years after 2014-15 is estimated by applying the 2014-15 split to total personal tax credits expenditure. The sum of tax expenditure and transfer components may not match the total due to rounding. Total values are consistent with published figures available here: https://www.gov.uk/government/statistics/hmrc-tax-and-nics-receipts-for-the-uk.

Please note that the sum of the corporate tax credit (CTC) components in the United Kingdom may not match total CTC's due to rounding. The CTC information presented in Revenue Statistics is on a cash basis (rather than an accrual basis as for the rest of the data). CTC information on a financial year basis has been used as a proxy for calendar year. Please note that the breakdown of total CTCs from 2002/03 to 2010/11 have been estimated using historic proportional splits applied to total published CTC information. Total values are consistent with published figures available here: https://www.gov.uk/government/statistics/hmrc-tax-and-nics-receipts-for-the-uk.

Source: National Income and Expenditure; Central Statistical Office; Annual reports of Her Majesty's Revenue and Customs.

StatLink https://doi.org/10.1787/888934212345

Table 5.37. United States: Details of tax revenue, 1965-2018

Million USD

	1965	1980	1990	2000	2007	2010	2013	2015	2017	2018
Total tax revenue	**167 022**	**730 672**	**1 552 413**	**2 900 519**	**3 868 612**	**3 517 144**	**4 291 752**	**4 774 203**	**5 225 865**	**5 031 748**
1000 Taxes on income, profits and capital gains	**80 284**	**364 137**	**701 731**	**1 453 865**	**1 865 205**	**1 488 699**	**2 016 390**	**2 313 247**	**2 342 790**	**2 274 596**
1100 Of individuals	52 894	285 513	584 733	1 224 538	1 479 085	1 223 218	1 664 074	1 927 952	2 036 811	2 068 821
1110 On income and profits	50 401	272 879	552 859	1 088 967	1 326 736	1 163 737	1 556 113	1 752 507	1 845 601	1 858 365
Individual income tax federal	46 492	233 269	449 239	895 677	1 062 755	910 874	1 235 275	1 412 239	1 485 100	1 480 259
Individual income tax state and local govt.	3 909	39 610	103 620	193 290	263 981	252 863	320 838	340 268	360 501	378 105
1120 On capital gains	2 493	12 634	31 874	135 571	152 349	59 481	107 961	175 446	191 210	210 457
Capital gains federal	2 300	10 800	25 900	111 507	122 036	46 557	85 702	141 381	153 861	167 637
Capital gains tax state and local govt.	193	1 834	5 974	24 064	30 313	12 924	22 259	34 065	37 349	42 820
1200 Corporate	27 390	78 624	116 998	229 327	386 119	265 481	352 316	385 295	305 979	205 774
1210 On profits	26 745	73 586	106 134	170 835	330 597	239 340	313 172	337 782	260 058	168 440
Corporate income tax federal	24 861	60 525	85 736	144 590	281 040	197 785	265 274	288 506	213 754	120 626
Corporate income tax state and local govt.	1 884	13 061	20 398	26 245	49 556	41 555	47 898	49 276	46 305	47 813
1220 On capital gains	645	5 038	10 864	58 492	55 523	26 141	39 144	47 513	45 920	37 335
Capital gains tax corp. federal	600	4 143	8 776	49 506	47 200	21 602	33 157	40 582	37 744	26 737
Capital gains tax corp. state and local govt.	45	895	2 088	8 986	8 323	4 539	5 987	6 931	8 176	10 598
1300 Unallocable between 1100 and 1200	0	0	0	0	0	0	0	0	0	0
2000 Social security contributions	**22 192**	**159 763**	**396 972**	**683 104**	**907 357**	**917 409**	**1 030 099**	**1 125 542**	**1 205 319**	**1 250 370**
2100 Employees	8 459	67 022	173 860	305 555	400 941	406 404	456 777	502 446	543 268	568 322
Federal insurance contribution Act tax	8 084	66 221	..	..	..	..	..	..	..	..
Less refund federal	-192	-507	..	..	..	..	..	..	..	..
Railroad retirement taxes federal	322	590	..	..	..	..	..	..	..	..
Fed. hosp. insur. recpts from railroad retir.	0	111	..	..	..	..	..	..	..	..
Unemployment state tax federal	20	127	..	..	..	..	..	..	..	..
Temp. disability insurance state and local	225	480	..	..	..	..	..	..	..	..
2110 On a payroll basis	..	..	..	..	..	..	..	..	..	..
2120 On an income tax basis	..	..	..	..	..	..	..	..	..	..
2200 Employers	12 703	87 019	204 102	343 184	456 602	461 702	519 064	561 881	598 598	616 078
Federal insurance contributions act tax	7 802	64 768	..	..	..	..	..	..	..	..
Railroad retirement taxes federal	314	1 722	..	..	..	..	..	..	..	..
Fed. hosp. insur. recpts from railroad retir.	0	111	..	..	..	..	..	..	..	..
Military service credit federal	14	652	..	..	..	..	..	..	..	..
Old-age dis. hosp. insur. fed. employer contr.	282	1 453	..	..	..	..	..	..	..	..
Unemployment state tax federal	3 032	11 788	..	..	..	..	..	..	..	..
Federal unemployment tax Act	615	3 246	..	..	..	..	..	..	..	..
Railroad unempl. insurance Act tax federal	152	175	..	..	..	..	..	..	..	..
Workmen's compensation state and local	484	3 039	..	..	..	..	..	..	..	..
Temp. disability insurance state and local	8	65	..	..	..	..	..	..	..	..
2210 On a payroll basis	..	..	..	..	..	..	..	..	..	..
2220 On an income tax basis	..	..	..	..	..	..	..	..	..	..
2300 Self-employed or non-employed	1 030	5 722	19 010	34 365	49 814	49 303	54 258	61 215	63 453	65 970
Federal old-age survivors trust	0	4 250	..	..	..	..	..	..	..	..
Federal disability insurance trust	1 030	733	..	..	..	..	..	..	..	..
Federal hospital insurance trust	0	739	..	..	..	..	..	..	..	..
2310 On a payroll basis	..	..	..	..	..	..	..	..	..	..
2320 On an income tax basis	..	..	..	..	..	..	..	..	..	..
2400 Unallocable between 2100, 2200 and 2300	0	0	0	0	0	0	0	0	0	0
2410 On a payroll basis	..	..	..	..	..	..	..	..	..	..
2420 On an income tax basis	..	..	..	..	..	..	..	..	..	..
3000 Taxes on payroll and workforce	**0**	**0**	**0**	**0**	**285**	**2 285**	**1 591**	**1 750**	**2 013**	**2 169**
4000 Taxes on property	**26 529**	**77 913**	**182 408**	**299 546**	**463 052**	**473 422**	**503 220**	**539 538**	**850 533**	**617 679**
4100 Recurrent taxes on immovable property	22 918	68 499	161 533	254 669	403 688	438 588	456 790	490 308	545 837	561 999
4110 Households	8 548	28 975	..	..	..	..	..	..	..	..
Property tax state and local	8 548	28 975	..	..	..	..	..	..	..	..
Other	0	0	..	..	..	..	..	..	..	..
4120 Others	14 370	39 524	..	..	..	..	..	..	..	..
Property tax state and local	14 370	39 524	..	..	..	..	..	..	..	..
Other	0	0	..	..	..	..	..	..	..	..
4200 Recurrent taxes on net wealth	0	0	0	0	0	0	0	0	0	0
4210 Individual	..	..	..	..	..	..	..	..	..	..
4220 Corporate	..	..	..	..	..	..	..	..	..	..
4300 Estate, inheritance and gift taxes	3 447	8 425	15 755	35 640	31 927	19 699	26 178	25 506	28 476	28 512
4310 Estate and inheritance taxes	3 080	8 149	..	..	..	..	..	..	..	..
Estate tax less refund federal	2 427	6 181	..	..	..	..	..	..	..	..
Estate tax state and local govt.	653	1 968	..	..	..	..	..	..	..	..
4320 Gift taxes	367	276	..	..	..	..	..	..	..	..
Gift tax less refund federal	289	209	..	..	..	..	..	..	..	..
Gift tax calculate state and local govt.	78	67	..	..	..	..	..	..	..	..

	1965	1980	1990	2000	2007	2010	2013	2015	2017	2018
4400 Taxes on financial and capital transactions	164	989	2 148	4 389	20 503	7 460	12 171	14 880	16 524	17 123
Interest equalisation tax federal	15	0	..	..	..	..	..	..	..	..
Document and stock transfer state and local	149	989	2 148	4 389	20 503	7 460	12 171	14 880	16 524	17 123
4500 Non-recurrent taxes	0	0	0	0	0	0	0	0	250 000	0
4510 On net wealth	..	..	..	..	..	..	..	..	250 000	0
4520 Other non-recurrent taxes	..	..	..	..	..	..	..	..	..	..
4600 Other recurrent taxes on property	0	0	2 972	4 848	6 934	7 675	8 081	8 844	9 696	10 045
5000 Taxes on goods and services	**38 017**	**128 844**	**271 301**	**464 004**	**632 713**	**635 329**	**740 452**	**794 126**	**825 210**	**886 934**
5100 Taxes on production, sale, transfer, etc.	33 300	111 810	235 233	404 093	540 291	546 710	640 249	696 737	722 021	777 138
5110 General taxes	8 016	51 328	125 575	221 358	301 403	295 123	343 853	375 466	394 718	411 905
5111 Value added taxes	0	0	0	0	0	0	0	0	0	0
5112 Sales tax	8 016	51 328	125 575	221 358	301 403	295 123	343 853	375 466	394 718	411 905
General sales - general receipts state and local	7 981	51 328	125 575	221 358	301 403	295 123	343 853	375 466	394 718	411 905
Other state and local	35	0	0	0	0	0	0	0	0	0
5113 Other	0	0	0	0	0	0	0	0	0	0
5120 Taxes on specific goods and services	25 284	60 482	109 658	182 735	238 888	251 587	296 396	321 271	327 303	365 233
5121 Excise duties	21 209	45 471	64 953	108 600	137 373	146 582	154 390	156 967	162 203	164 410
Alcohol taxes federal govt.	3 689	5 601	5 228	7 281	8 571	8 848	9 026	9 515	9 987	9 665
Tobacco taxes federal govt.	2 142	2 443	4 217	6 741	8 377	17 487	15 830	14 265	13 302	12 186
Airport, airway, highway federal	3 559	6 411	0	0	0	0	0	0	0	0
Manufacturer's excise taxes federal govt.	2 867	6 122	0	0	0	0	0	0	0	0
Sugar tax federal govt.	97	0	0	0	0	0	0	0	0	0
Other taxes excise federal govt.	889	2	0	0	0	0	0	0	0	0
Undistributed tax deposits federal government	-11	152	0	0	0	0	0	0	0	0
Other taxes excise and undist. fed.govt. -	0	0	13 316	32 005	31 747	26 913	33 746	35 287	36 125	36 599
Less special tax liquor occupations federal	-22	-21	0	0	0	0	0	0	0	0
Other federal (refunds)	-7	-32	0	0	0	0	0	0	0	0
Alcohol taxes state and local govt.	949	2 642	3 577	4 485	5 684	6 197	6 706	7 264	7 440	7 576
Tobacco taxes state and local govt.	1 386	3 874	6 009	8 726	16 433	18 611	18 464	17 997	19 579	19 614
Public utilities state and local govt.	871	5 888	11 814	17 989	27 879	28 892	28 544	27 911	27 600	27 989
Motor fuel taxes state and local govt.	4 331	9 822	20 792	31 373	38 682	39 634	42 074	44 728	48 170	50 782
Other state and local taxes	469	2 295	0	0	0	0	0	0	0	0
Coal tonnage tax federal govt.	0	272	0	0	0	0	0	0	0	0
Hazardous substances tax federal	0	0	0	0	0	0	0	0	0	0
Transportation fuels tax federal	0	0	0	0	0	0	0	0	0	0
Boat fuels and equipment tax federal	0	0	0	0	0	0	0	0	0	0
Waste site deposits tax federal	0	0	0	0	0	0	0	0	0	0
Leaking underground storage federal	0	0	0	0	0	0	0	0	0	0
Vaccine injury compens. federal	0	0	0	0	0	0	0	0	0	0
Ozone depletion tax federal	0	0	0	0	0	0	0	0	0	0
Oil spill liability federal	0	0	0	0	0	0	0	0	0	0
Luxury tax federal govt.	0	0	0	0	0	0	0	0	0	0
5122 Profits of fiscal monopolies	275	608	..	..	..	..	..	..	..	..
Liquor store revenue state and local govt.	1 447	3 200	..	..	..	..	..	..	..	..
Liquor store expend. state and local govt.	-1 172	-2 592	..	..	..	..	..	..	..	..
5123 Customs and import duties	1 442	7 436	17 490	21 123	28 793	28 603	35 468	38 123	38 513	53 284
Custom duties federal	1 442	7 436	17 490	21 123	28 793	28 603	35 468	38 123	38 513	53 284
Petroleum import fees federal govt.	0	0	0	0	0	0	0	0	0	0
5124 Taxes on exports	0	0	0	0	0	0	0	0	0	0
5125 Taxes on investment goods	0	0	0	0	0	0	0	0	0	0
5126 Taxes on specific services	2 358	6 967	8 895	13 857	23 639	23 642	26 899	30 227	33 872	34 730
Amusements state and local govt.	23	234	671	3 668	7 105	7 082	7 784	8 193	8 726	9 007
Parimutuels state and local govt.	386	731	659	326	328	206	193	190	192	198
Transportation of persons federal	126	1 601	0	0	0	0	0	0	0	0
Transport of property	0	92	0	0	0	0	0	0	0	0
General and toll telephone federal	1 079	1 118	0	0	0	0	0	0	0	0
Foreign insurance policies federal	0	75	0	0	0	0	0	0	0	0
Insurance state and local govt.	744	3 113	7 565	9 863	16 206	16 354	18 922	21 843	24 955	25 525
Employee pension plans federal	0	3	0	0	0	0	0	0	0	0
Inland waterway tax federal	0	0	0	0	0	0	0	0	0	0
Ship departure tax federal	0	0	0	0	0	0	0	0	0	0
5127 Other taxes on internat. trade and transactions	0	0	0	0	0	0	0	0	0	0
5128 Other taxes	0	0	18 320	39 155	49 083	52 760	79 639	95 955	92 715	112 808
5130 Unallocable between 5110 and 5120	0	0	0	0	0	0	0	0	0	0
5200 Taxes on use of goods and perform activities	4 717	17 034	36 068	59 910	92 422	88 619	100 203	97 389	103 189	109 796
5210 Recurrent taxes	3 490	9 501	21 262	37 114	68 547	66 440	70 557	74 713	78 598	81 264
5211 Paid by households: motor vehicles	1 211	3 370	8 104	11 409	14 996	16 294	17 781	18 800	19 975	20 948
Motor vehicle regis. license st. and loc.	1 056	2 981	..	..	..	..	..	..	..	..
Motor vehicle oper. license st. and loc.	152	389	..	..	..	..	..	..	..	..
Other motor vehicle	3	0	..	..	..	..	..	..	..	..

	1965	1980	1990	2000	2007	2010	2013	2015	2017	2018
5212 Paid by others: motor vehicles	937	2 343	3 564	6 688	8 484	9 108	10 071	10 677	11 457	12 032
Motor vehicle regis. license st. and loc.	937	2 343	..	..	..	..	..	..	..	..
Motor vehicle oper. license st. and loc.	0	0	..	..	..	..	..	..	..	..
5213 Paid in respect of other goods	1 342	3 788	9 594	19 017	45 067	41 038	42 705	45 236	47 166	48 284
Misc. fees permit license federal	19	0	0	0	0	0	0	0	0	0
Special tax liquor occupations federal	22	21	0	0	0	0	0	0	0	0
Use tax of certain vehicles federal	99	277	0	0	0	0	0	0	0	0
Use of internat. travel facilities federal	0	92	0	0	0	0	0	0	0	0
Use tax of aircraft federal	0	21	0	0	0	0	0	0	0	0
Corporation in general license st. and loc.	528	1 388	3 147	6 736	10 658	9 473	7 560	6 628	6 879	6 885
Alcoholic beverage license tax st. and loc.	133	179	264	308	608	596	899	822	933	944
Public utilities license tax st. and loc.	30	130	270	395	1 903	1 468	1 432	1 649	1 919	1 865
Amusements license taxes st. and loc.	7	69	202	196	966	638	604	753	736	870
Occupation and business license st. and loc.	349	1 113	3 512	7 651	16 484	17 812	19 284	20 589	21 261	21 686
Wagering occupation tax federal	7	12	0	0	0	0	0	0	0	0
Other license taxes st. and loc.	10	69	2 118	3 619	14 302	10 900	12 772	14 633	15 280	15 868
Hunting and fishing license taxes st. and loc.	138	417	82	112	146	151	155	162	159	165
Other	0	0	0	0	0	0	0	0	0	0
5220 Non-recurrent taxes	1 227	7 533	14 806	22 796	23 875	22 179	29 645	22 676	24 591	28 532
Severance state and local govt.	503	4 167	5 224	5 285	12 895	11 751	18 266	9 744	10 215	13 594
Poll taxes state and local govt.	9	0	0	0	0	0	0	0	0	0
Other taxes state and local govt.	715	3 366	9 582	17 511	10 980	10 428	11 379	12 932	14 376	14 938
5300 Unallocable between 5100 and 5200	0	0	0	0	0	0	0	0	0	0
6000 Other taxes	**0**	**15**	**0**	**0**	**0**	**0**	**0**	**0**	**0**	**0**
6100 Paid solely by business	..	0	..	..	..	..	..	..	..	..
6200 Other	..	15	..	..	..	..	..	..	..	..
Non-wastable tax credits										
Non-wastable tax credits against 1110	..	..	6 155	36 511	90 439	171 630	158 160	156 656	176 520	194 270
Tax expenditure component	..	..	1 800	9 602	35 910	69 870	41 560	42 826	48 950	57 340
Transfer component	..	..	4 355	26 909	54 529	101 760	116 600	113 830	127 570	136 930
Non-wastable tax credits against 1210	..	..	..	..	..	250	630	577	470	440
Tax expenditure component	..	..	..	..	..	240	610	527	410	380
Transfer component	..	..	..	..	..	10	20	50	60	60
Unallocable transfer component	..	..	..	..	..	2 420	4 280	4 890	4 740	4 795
Total tax revenue on cash basis	**167 022**	**730 672**	**..**	**..**	**..**	**..**	**..**	**..**	**..**	**..**
Total tax revenue on accrual basis	**..**	**..**	**..**	**..**	**..**	**..**	**..**	**..**	**..**	**..**
Conciliation with National Accounts										
Additional taxes included in National Accounts	..	..	..	..	..	..	..	..	..	..
Taxes excluded from National Accounts	..	..	..	..	..	..	..	..	..	..
Difference in treatment of tax credits	..	..	..	..	..	..	..	..	..	..
Capital transfer for uncollected revenue	..	..	..	..	..	..	..	..	..	..
Voluntary social security contributions	..	..	11 719	22 562	51 635	61 833	69 903	74 886	90 166	102 411
Miscellaneous differences	..	..	..	..	..	..	..	..	..	..
National Accounts: Taxes and actual social contributions	..	..	1 564 132	2 923 081	3 920 247	3 578 977	4 361 655	4 849 089	5 316 031	5 134 159
Imputed social contributions	..	..	3 384	3 727	7 134	9 428	9 438	9 557	9 121	8 853
National Accounts: Taxes and all social contributions	..	..	1 567 516	2 926 808	3 927 381	3 588 405	4 371 093	4 858 646	5 325 152	5 143 012

.. Not available

Note: From 1990, data are on a year ending 31st December basis. For years up to and including 1976 the dated covered fiscal years ending 30th June. Between 1977 and 1989, Federal government data covered fiscal years ending 30th September and State & Local government data covered fiscal years ending 30th June.

From 1990, data are on accrual basis. There are no separate estimates for the State and Local capital gains tax revenues.

Heading 5121: In 1994 through 1996, some Federal excise taxes formerly shown separately were included in 'Other taxes,excises and undistributed, Federal government'.

Source: Federal estimates are derived from the US Budget, the Final Monthly Treasury Statement and the Annual Report of the US Treasury Department. The State and Local estimates are derived from Government Finances, published by the Bureau of the Census.

StatLink https://doi.org/10.1787/888934212364

5.2. Memorandum tables

Table 5.38 shows different sources for financing social benefits, beyond compulsory social security contributions reported in section 5.1. In addition, this table shows also data on other taxes, on voluntary contributions to government and on compulsory contributions to private sector.

Table 5.39 shows social security contributions and payroll taxes paid by government. During the revision of the Interpretative Guide in 1984, the question arose of how to treat taxes paid by government. The two most prominent examples of such taxes are social security contributions and payroll taxes paid by government in respect of its employees. After a long discussion it was decided that the data shown in this publication should continue to include taxes paid by government (see §7 of the Interpretative Guide in annex A).

Whilst it was recognised that for certain purposes (e.g. to show the cash flow to the government sector from the private sector) it would be appropriate to eliminate taxes paid by one sector of government to another or tax payments between different units of the same sector of government, the view was taken that to record tax flows in the context of the economy as a whole required that taxes paid by government should be included in the data. This treatment ensures that the different resource flows of an economy, including the calculation of the output of government, are measured consistently in after-tax units. Nevertheless, it was decided that data on identifiable taxes paid by government should be separately identified in a memorandum item and this is the purpose of the country tables which follow.

The data that are reproduced in the following tables refer to actual compulsory payments made by general government in respect of their employees. Fictive, voluntary and imputed contributions are excluded from these data. The definitions of social security contributions, payroll taxes and general government are those set out in §40 to §46, §47 and §3 to §4 of the Interpretative Guide. Information on the other taxes paid by government (namely property taxes and consumption taxes) is not available in most countries, although it is believed that in all countries taxes based upon payroll are the most important taxes paid by government. In many cases, the data are estimates and are not always constructed on a basis consistent with that used in the main tables.

Table 5.38. Financing social benefits

	1965	1980	1990	2000	2007	2010	2013	2015	2017	2018
Australia, million AUD										
Contribution under 2000 heading	..	..	..	..	..	..	..	..	..	..
Other taxes	..	..	..	..	..	..	..	..	..	..
Voluntary contributions to government	..	..	..	..	..	..	..	..	..	..
Compulsory contributions to private sector	..	..	..	..	..	..	..	..	..	..
Total	**0**	**0**	**0**	**0**	**0**	**0**	**0**	**0**	**0**	**0**
Austria, million EUR										
Contribution under 2000 heading	1 548	9 200	17 763	30 510	38 453	41 423	46 845	49 867	53 918	56 624
Other taxes	0	0	0	0	0	0	0	0	0	0
Voluntary contributions to government	32	135	141	206	256	339	299	321	317	321
Compulsory contributions to private sector	0	0	0	0	0	0	0	0	0	0
Total	**1 580**	**9 335**	**17 904**	**30 716**	**38 709**	**41 762**	**47 144**	**50 188**	**54 235**	**56 945**
Belgium, million EUR										
Contribution under 2000 heading	2 018	10 798	23 386	34 865	45 929	50 674	56 527	58 812	59 779	61 070
Other taxes	0	171	644	5 375	13 659	16 772	18 390	12 347	16 920	18 320
Voluntary contributions to government	0	41	52	58	57	59	77	70	75	85
Compulsory contributions to private sector	0	0	0	0	0	0	0	0	0	0
Total	**2 018**	**11 009**	**24 082**	**40 298**	**59 644**	**67 505**	**74 994**	**71 228**	**76 773**	**79 474**
Canada, million CAD										
Contribution under 2000 heading	854	10 649	29 653	53 109	73 722	76 787	90 394	96 371	99 035	103 213
Other taxes	1 199	0	0	0	0	0	0	0	0	0
Voluntary contributions to government	0	0	0	0	0	0	0	0	0	0
Compulsory contributions to private sector	0	0	0	0	0	0	0	0	0	0
Total	**2 053**	**10 649**	**29 653**	**53 109**	**73 722**	**76 787**	**90 394**	**96 371**	**99 035**	**103 213**
Chile, million CLP										
Contribution under 2000 heading	..	..	159 559	576 758	1 148 647	1 493 987	1 968 973	2 252 489	2 627 558	2 786 173
Other taxes	..	..	0	0	0	0	0	0	0	0
Voluntary contributions to government	..	..	0	0	0	0	0	0	0	0
Compulsory contributions to private sector	..	..	328 102	2 021 631	3 808 658	5 408 703	7 583 251	8 914 415	10 263 722	11 077 114
Total	**..**	**..**	**487 661**	**2 598 389**	**4 957 305**	**6 902 690**	**9 552 224**	**11 166 904**	**12 891 280**	**13 863 286**
Colombia, million COP										
Contribution under 2000 heading	..	..	203 596	4 989 000	9 694 000	11 478 085	16 644 445	13 585 138	13 351 711	18 192 049
Other taxes	..	..	0	0	0	0	0	0	0	0
Voluntary contributions to government	..	..	0	0	0	0	0	0	0	0
Compulsory contributions to private sector	..	..	0	0	18 667 073	27 354 493	30 808 731	31 112 566	36 180 665	39 712 117
Total	**..**	**..**	**203 596**	**4 989 000**	**28 361 073**	**38 832 579**	**47 453 177**	**44 697 703**	**49 532 376**	**57 904 167**
Czech Republic, million CZK										
Contribution under 2000 heading	..	..	..	341 544	573 417	576 029	603 072	659 743	757 183	829 702
Other taxes	..	..	..	0	0	0	0	0	0	0
Voluntary contributions to government	..	..	..	1 099	974	661	337	386	463	523
Compulsory contributions to private sector	..	..	..	2 837	5 757	6 094	6 424	6 741	7 585	8 322
Total	**..**	**..**	**..**	**345 480**	**580 148**	**582 784**	**609 833**	**666 871**	**765 231**	**838 547**
Denmark, million DKK										
Contribution under 2000 heading	690	710	101	8 453	1 286	1 815	1 618	1 378	1 060	1 061
Other taxes	0	0	0	0	0	0	0	0	0	0
Voluntary contributions to government	0	1 673	8 087	16 633	17 061	17 192	14 655	14 721	14 891	14 751
Compulsory contributions to private sector	145	554	1 278	1 445	4 526	3 847	3 068	2 964	2 779	2 771
Total	**835**	**2 937**	**9 466**	**26 531**	**22 874**	**22 854**	**19 341**	**19 063**	**18 730**	**18 583**
Estonia, million EUR										
Contribution under 2000 heading	..	..	..	674	1 683	1 879	2 077	2 300	2 653	2 978
Other taxes	..	..	..	0	0	0	0	0	0	0
Voluntary contributions to government	..	..	..	0	0	0	0	0	0	0
Compulsory contributions to private sector	..	..	..	1	341	38	268	389	437	392
Total	**..**	**..**	**..**	**674**	**2 024**	**1 918**	**2 346**	**2 689**	**3 090**	**3 370**
Finland, million EUR										
Contribution under 2000 heading	93	2 776	10 012	15 756	21 384	22 648	25 632	26 639	27 000	27 647
Other taxes	47	22	0	404	0	0	0	0	0	0
Voluntary contributions to government	0	262	632	236	228	254	270	303	300	269
Compulsory contributions to private sector	0	123	431	532	653	619	694	673	626	645
Total	**140**	**3 183**	**11 075**	**16 928**	**22 265**	**23 521**	**26 596**	**27 615**	**27 926**	**28 561**

	1965	1980	1990	2000	2007	2010	2013	2015	2017	2018
France, million EUR										
Contribution under 2000 heading	8 804	76 235	191 141	231 875	307 663	323 816	356 934	370 375	387 171	380 728
Other taxes	0	895	2 950	81 001	127 511	137 383	162 838	170 210	176 209	199 702
Voluntary contributions to government	0	0	0	0	0	0	0	0	0	0
Compulsory contributions to private sector	0	0	0	0	0	0	0	0	0	0
Total	**8 804**	**77 130**	**194 091**	**312 876**	**435 174**	**461 199**	**519 772**	**540 585**	**563 380**	**580 430**
Germany, million EUR										
Contribution under 2000 heading	19 876	98 659	170 449	299 440	320 750	354 320	392 378	424 841	467 185	487 839
Other taxes	0	0	0	0	0	0	0	0	0	0
Voluntary contributions to government	1 946	8 441	13 002	23 329	21 409	5 102	5 352	6 068	7 069	7 415
Compulsory contributions to private sector	107	690	1 462	6 120	8 243	9 386	10 444	11 202	12 432	12 614
Total	**21 929**	**107 791**	**184 914**	**328 889**	**350 402**	**368 808**	**408 174**	**442 111**	**486 686**	**507 868**
Greece, million EUR										
Contribution under 2000 heading	37	485	3 466	14 284	24 940	24 748	19 354	18 807	20 743	21 473
Other taxes	8	0	0	0	0	0	0	0	0	0
Voluntary contributions to government	0	0	0	0	0	0	0	0	0	0
Compulsory contributions to private sector	0	0	0	0	0	0	0	0	0	0
Total	**44**	**485**	**3 466**	**14 284**	**24 940**	**24 748**	**19 354**	**18 807**	**20 743**	**21 473**
Hungary, million HUF										
Contribution under 2000 heading	..	..	..	1 506 755	3 402 194	3 179 509	3 899 154	4 433 464	4 822 165	5 049 592
Other taxes	..	..	..	188 413	85 058	78 629	246 574	294 313	316 915	328 876
Voluntary contributions to government	..	..	..	1 273	1 762	1 693	1 523	1 229	1 163	1 090
Compulsory contributions to private sector	..	..	..	62 836	190 331	279 814	0	0	0	0
Total	**..**	**..**	**..**	**1 759 277**	**3 679 344**	**3 539 645**	**4 147 251**	**4 729 006**	**5 140 243**	**5 379 558**
Iceland, million ISK										
Contribution under 2000 heading	5	102	3 607	19 680	39 594	63 599	69 899	79 707	89 649	98 230
Other taxes	0	1 047	20 571	26 732	52 444	77 472	90 895	97 987	133 273	146 820
Voluntary contributions to government	0	0	0	0	0	0	0	0	0	0
Compulsory contributions to private sector	0	459	13 454	48 847	118 117	95 438	117 903	139 792	243 733	209 341
Total	**5**	**1 608**	**37 632**	**95 260**	**210 155**	**236 509**	**278 697**	**317 486**	**466 655**	**454 391**
Ireland, million EUR										
Contribution under 2000 heading	21	578	1 729	3 966	8 143	8 458	9 359	10 524	11 661	12 707
Other taxes	0	0	0	0	0	0	0	0	0	0
Voluntary contributions to government	0	0	0	0	0	0	0	0	0	0
Compulsory contributions to private sector	0	0	0	0	0	0	0	0	0	0
Total	**21**	**578**	**1 729**	**3 966**	**8 143**	**8 458**	**9 359**	**10 524**	**11 661**	**12 707**
Israel, million ILS										
Contribution under 2000 heading	..	..	..	27 565	37 909	45 343	53 364	59 561	66 783	69 016
Other taxes	..	..	..	0	0	0	0	0	0	0
Voluntary contributions to government	..	..	..	0	0	0	0	0	0	0
Compulsory contributions to private sector	..	..	..	0	0	9 100	22 400	28 700	34 000	35 900
Total	**..**	**..**	**..**	**27 565**	**37 909**	**54 443**	**75 764**	**88 261**	**100 783**	**104 916**
Italy, million EUR										
Contribution under 2000 heading	1 881	22 976	87 256	143 629	200 772	209 122	210 462	214 376	220 624	229 607
Other taxes	0	0	0	0	0	0	0	0	0	0
Voluntary contributions to government	0	0	0	464	567	561	738	750	769	790
Compulsory contributions to private sector	0	0	0	0	0	0	0	0	0	0
Total	**1 881**	**22 976**	**87 256**	**144 093**	**201 339**	**209 683**	**211 200**	**215 126**	**221 393**	**230 397**
Japan, billion JPY										
Contribution under 2000 heading	1 344	18 178	34 613	47 968	53 325	54 461	59 803	64 465	68 616	70 588
Other taxes	0	0	0	0	0	0	0	0	0	0
Voluntary contributions to government	0	0	0	0	0	0	0	0	0	0
Compulsory contributions to private sector	0	0	0	0	0	0	0	0	0	0
Total	**1 344**	**18 178**	**34 613**	**47 968**	**53 325**	**54 461**	**59 803**	**64 465**	**68 616**	**70 588**
Korea, billion KRW										
Contribution under 2000 heading	..	73	3 760	22 759	53 588	69 090	91 596	104 693	119 676	128 660
Other taxes	..	0	0	0	0	0	0	0	0	0
Voluntary contributions to government	..	0	0	0	0	0	0	0	0	0
Compulsory contributions to private sector	..	0	0	0	0	0	0	0	0	0
Total	**..**	**73**	**3 760**	**22 759**	**53 588**	**69 090**	**91 596**	**104 693**	**119 676**	**128 660**

	1965	1980	1990	2000	2007	2010	2013	2015	2017	2018
Latvia, million EUR										
Contribution under 2000 heading	..	..	..	669	1 774	1 554	1 933	2 030	2 259	2 658
Other taxes	..	..	..	12	51	36	59	80	97	108
Voluntary contributions to government	..	..	..	0	0	0	0	0	0	0
Compulsory contributions to private sector	..	..	..	0	0	0	0	0	0	0
Total	**..**	**..**	**..**	**682**	**1 825**	**1 590**	**1 992**	**2 111**	**2 356**	**2 767**
Lithuania, million EUR										
Contribution under 2000 heading	..	..	..	1 362	2 643	3 293	3 791	4 338	5 170	5 752
Other taxes	..	..	..	0	0	0	0	0	0	0
Voluntary contributions to government	..	..	..	0	2	2	3	2	2	2
Compulsory contributions to private sector	..	..	..	0	247	95	149	140	173	192
Total	**..**	**..**	**..**	**1 362**	**2 892**	**3 391**	**3 943**	**4 480**	**5 345**	**5 947**
Luxembourg, million EUR										
Contribution under 2000 heading	86	443	1 011	2 224	3 710	4 387	5 131	5 547	6 126	6 483
Other taxes	0	0	0	0	0	0	0	0	0	0
Voluntary contributions to government	0	0	4	18	18	28	33	38	44	46
Compulsory contributions to private sector	0	0	0	0	0	0	0	0	0	0
Total	**86**	**443**	**1 015**	**2 241**	**3 728**	**4 415**	**5 164**	**5 585**	**6 170**	**6 529**
Mexico, million MXN										
Contribution under 2000 heading	..	109	17 165	138 223	236 727	277 459	351 993	409 249	467 619	509 087
Other taxes	..	0	0	0	0	0	0	0	0	0
Voluntary contributions to government	..	0	0	0	0	0	0	0	0	0
Compulsory contributions to private sector	..	25	3 840	67 352	144 331	146 110	168 111	206 824	243 726	269 500
Total	**..**	**134**	**21 005**	**205 575**	**381 057**	**423 569**	**520 104**	**616 073**	**711 345**	**778 587**
Netherlands, million EUR										
Contribution under 2000 heading	3 342	26 641	39 075	64 522	77 072	82 732	97 372	96 426	101 913	108 049
Other taxes	0	0	0	0	0	0	0	0	0	0
Voluntary contributions to government	168	1 139	163	0	0	0	0	0	0	0
Compulsory contributions to private sector	1 266	7 642	5 727	37 088	..	..	..	..	..	..
Total	**4 776**	**35 422**	**44 965**	**101 610**	**77 072**	**82 732**	**97 372**	**96 426**	**101 913**	**108 049**
New Zealand, million NZD										
Contribution under 2000 heading	..	..	..	..	..	..	..	..	..	..
Other taxes	..	..	..	..	..	..	..	..	..	..
Voluntary contributions to government	..	..	..	..	..	..	..	..	..	..
Compulsory contributions to private sector	..	..	..	..	..	..	..	..	..	..
Total	**0**	**0**	**0**	**0**	**0**	**0**	**0**	**0**	**0**	**0**
Norway, million NOK										
Contribution under 2000 heading	2 009	28 205	79 362	132 170	204 473	243 002	292 461	325 130	339 848	356 610
Other taxes	1 305	4 256	0	0	0	0	0	0	0	0
Voluntary contributions to government	0	0	0	0	0	0	0	0	0	0
Compulsory contributions to private sector	0	242	339	0	0	0	0	0	0	0
Total	**3 314**	**32 703**	**79 701**	**132 170**	**204 473**	**243 002**	**292 461**	**325 130**	**339 848**	**356 610**
Poland, million PLN										
Contribution under 2000 heading	..	..	..	96 386	140 086	156 026	202 595	223 482	254 919	277 670
Other taxes	..	..	..	0	0	0	0	0	0	0
Voluntary contributions to government	..	..	..	0	0	0	34	49	49	45
Compulsory contributions to private sector	..	..	..	0	0	0	0	0	0	0
Total	**..**	**..**	**..**	**96 386**	**140 086**	**156 026**	**202 629**	**223 531**	**254 968**	**277 715**
Portugal, million EUR										
Contribution under 2000 heading	22	531	4 026	10 168	14 274	15 457	15 139	16 195	17 969	19 141
Other taxes	0	1	29	434	658	698	970	994	797	824
Voluntary contributions to government	0	0	0	0	0	0	0	0	0	0
Compulsory contributions to private sector	0	0	0	0	0	0	0	0	0	0
Total	**22**	**532**	**4 055**	**10 602**	**14 932**	**16 154**	**16 109**	**17 189**	**18 766**	**19 965**
Slovak Republic, million EUR										
Contribution under 2000 heading	..	..	..	4 409	7 244	8 154	9 847	10 897	12 389	13 237
Other taxes	..	..	..	0	0	0	0	0	0	0
Voluntary contributions to government	..	..	..	0	22	31	17	11	10	11
Compulsory contributions to private sector	..	..	..	0	701	719	385	413	512	606
Total	**..**	**..**	**..**	**4 409**	**7 968**	**8 904**	**10 249**	**11 321**	**12 911**	**13 854**

	1965	1980	1990	2000	2007	2010	2013	2015	2017	2018
Slovenia, million EUR										
Contribution under 2000 heading	..	..	..	2 824	5 046	5 761	5 647	5 983	6 626	7 081
Other taxes	..	..	..	0	0	0	0	0	0	0
Voluntary contributions to government	..	..	..	0	0	0	0	0	0	0
Compulsory contributions to private sector	..	..	..	0	0	0	0	0	0	0
Total	**..**	**..**	**..**	**2 824**	**5 046**	**5 761**	**5 647**	**5 983**	**6 626**	**7 081**
Spain, million EUR										
Contribution under 2000 heading	350	10 682	36 722	74 683	127 088	127 235	116 875	122 835	134 126	141 234
Other taxes	0	49	0	0	0	0	0	0	0	0
Voluntary contributions to government	0	0	0	447	937	1 155	2 209	1 170	1 133	1 038
Compulsory contributions to private sector	0	0	0	0	0	0	0	0	0	0
Total	**350**	**10 731**	**36 722**	**75 130**	**128 025**	**128 390**	**119 084**	**124 005**	**135 259**	**142 272**
Sweden, million SEK										
Contribution under 2000 heading	4 851	74 647	205 867	306 974	388 505	384 668	376 684	404 851	443 110	463 338
Other taxes	1 407	0	0	0	0	0	0	0	0	0
Voluntary contributions to government	0	0	0	7 951	12 376	13 167	15 909	16 726	19 271	23 457
Compulsory contributions to private sector	0	0	0	0	0	0	0	0	0	0
Total	**6 258**	**74 647**	**205 867**	**314 925**	**400 881**	**397 835**	**392 593**	**421 577**	**462 381**	**486 795**
Switzerland, million CHF										
Contribution under 2000 heading	1 670	10 844	19 892	30 750	34 949	38 369	42 654	44 073	44 998	45 861
Other taxes	336	778	1 176	4 509	6 342	6 644	7 850	7 815	7 722	6 802
Voluntary contributions to government	95	431	0	0	0	0	0	0	0	0
Compulsory contributions to private sector	2 505	9 674	20 797	29 532	41 478	45 527	49 473	52 991	56 764	58 646
Total	**4 606**	**21 727**	**41 865**	**64 791**	**82 769**	**90 541**	**99 977**	**104 878**	**109 485**	**111 309**
Turkey, million TRY										
Contribution under 2000 heading	0	0	15	7 543	44 052	71 696	125 871	170 282	226 720	269 932
Other taxes	0	0	0	0	0	0	0	0	0	0
Voluntary contributions to government	0	0	0	0	0	0	0	0	0	0
Compulsory contributions to private sector	0	0	0	0	0	0	0	0	0	0
Total	**0**	**0**	**15**	**7 543**	**44 052**	**71 696**	**125 871**	**170 282**	**226 720**	**269 932**
United Kingdom, million GBP										
Contribution under 2000 heading	1 685	13 531	34 457	60 252	93 210	97 346	106 085	114 067	130 439	134 986
Other taxes	0	0	0	0	0	0	0	0	0	0
Voluntary contributions to government	0	11	3 288	8 103	18 629	21 217	22 438	25 025	26 678	27 546
Compulsory contributions to private sector	1 148	13 350	7 945	8 308	9 969	9 656	6 074	5 495	48	0
Total	**2 833**	**26 892**	**45 690**	**76 663**	**121 808**	**128 219**	**134 597**	**144 587**	**157 165**	**162 532**
United States, million USD										
Contribution under 2000 heading	22 192	159 763	396 972	683 104	907 357	917 409	1 030 099	1 125 542	1 205 319	1 250 370
Other taxes	0	0	0	0	0	0	0	0	0	0
Voluntary contributions to government	488	3 407	11 719	22 562	51 635	61 833	69 903	74 886	90 166	102 411
Compulsory contributions to private sector	0	0	0	0	0	0	0	0	0	0
Total	**22 680**	**163 170**	**408 691**	**705 666**	**958 992**	**979 242**	**1 100 002**	**1 200 428**	**1 295 485**	**1 352 781**

.. Not available

StatLink https://doi.org/10.1787/888934212383

Table 5.39. Social security contributions and payroll taxes paid by government, details

	1965	1980	1990	2000	2007	2010	2013	2015	2017	2018
Australia, million AUD										
2000 Social security contributions										
Federal or Central government	..	..	..	..	..	..	..	..	..	..
State/Regional	..	..	..	..	..	..	..	..	..	..
Local government	..	..	..	..	..	..	..	..	..	..
Social Security Funds	..	..	..	..	..	..	..	..	..	..
Total	**0**	**0**	**0**	**0**	**0**	**0**	**0**	**0**	**0**	**0**
3000 Taxes on payroll and workforce										
Federal or Central government	0	4	0	0	0	0	0	0	0	0
State/Regional	15	302	0	0	0	0	0	0	0	0
Local government	0	0	2	19	44	32	37	38	42	45
Social Security Funds	0	0	0	0	0	0	0	0	0	0
Multi-jurisdictional (University) sector[1]	..	..	..	..	..	..	..	..	..	..
Total	**15**	**306**	**92**	**301**	**499**	**580**	**702**	**765**	**840**	**936**
2000+3000 Total	**15**	**306**	**92**	**301**	**499**	**580**	**702**	**765**	**840**	**936**
Austria, million EUR[2]										
2000 Social security contributions										
Federal or Central government	48	230	337	620	1 244	1 532	1 664	1 825	2 050	2 120
State/Regional	13	166	337	692	988	1 179	1 255	1 376	1 535	1 631
Local government	17	145	292	699	1 036	1 277	1 379	1 515	1 620	1 690
Social Security Funds	11	79	48	176	203	226	250	264	279	284
Total	**88**	**619**	**1 015**	**2 186**	**3 471**	**4 213**	**4 547**	**4 980**	**5 484**	**5 725**
3000 Taxes on payroll and workforce										
Federal or Central government	0	49	134	186	337	533	558	624	618	633
State/Regional	0	48	74	232	351	458	485	492	494	490
Local government	1	29	79	301	262	359	396	428	424	464
Social Security Funds	0	0	39	44	51	55	61	65	67	68
Total	**1**	**125**	**326**	**763**	**1 000**	**1 405**	**1 500**	**1 609**	**1 603**	**1 655**
2000+3000 Total	**89**	**745**	**1 341**	**2 949**	**4 471**	**5 618**	**6 047**	**6 589**	**7 087**	**7 381**
Belgium, million EUR										
2000 Social security contributions										
Federal or Central government	..	536	211	259	434	493	532	859	876	912
State/Regional	..	0	614	1 218	1 600	1 873	2 089	2 440	2 528	2 632
Local government	..	434	768	1 376	2 151	2 655	3 641	3 973	4 183	4 356
Social Security Funds	..	89	176	252	308	360	416	415	421	438
Total	**..**	**1 059**	**1 769**	**3 105**	**4 493**	**5 381**	**6 678**	**7 686**	**8 008**	**8 338**
3000 Taxes on payroll and workforce										
Federal or Central government	..	..	..	..	..	..	..	..	..	..
State/Regional	..	..	..	..	..	..	..	..	..	..
Local government	..	..	..	..	..	..	..	..	..	..
Social Security Funds	..	..	..	..	..	..	..	..	..	..
Total	**..**	**0**	**0**	**0**	**0**	**0**	**0**	**0**	**0**	**0**
2000+3000 Total	**..**	**1 059**	**1 769**	**3 105**	**4 493**	**5 381**	**6 678**	**7 686**	**8 008**	**8 338**
Canada, million CAD										
2000 Social security contributions										
Federal or Central government	..	..	..	944	1 198	1 397	1 449	1 515	1 592	1 324
State/Regional	..	..	..	3 023	4 269	5 071	5 825	6 349	6 445	6 503
Local government	..	..	..	2 225	2 806	3 390	3 912	4 205	4 321	4 360
Social Security Funds	..	..	..	0	0	0	0	0	0	0
Total	**..**	**..**	**..**	**6 192**	**8 273**	**9 857**	**11 186**	**12 070**	**12 359**	**12 187**
3000 Taxes on payroll and workforce										
Federal or Central government	..	..	..	0	0	0	0	0	0	0
State/Regional	..	..	..	173	234	328	362	362	375	394
Local government	..	..	..	0	0	0	0	0	0	0
Social Security Funds	..	..	..	0	0	0	0	0	0	0
Total	**..**	**..**	**..**	**173**	**234**	**328**	**362**	**362**	**375**	**394**
2000+3000 Total	**..**	**..**	**..**	**6 365**	**8 507**	**10 185**	**11 548**	**12 432**	**12 734**	**12 581**

	1965	1980	1990	2000	2007	2010	2013	2015	2017	2018
Chile, million CLP										
2000 Social security contributions										
Federal or Central government	..	..	..	43 210	107 911	148 006	186 652	205 125	236 530	254 883
State/Regional	..	..	..	..	..	..	..	..	..	..
Local government	..	..	..	11 317	30 218	41 518	51 114	63 603	82 601	95 270
Social Security Funds	..	..	..	106	263	449	550	600	801	815
Total	**..**	**..**	**..**	**54 633**	**138 392**	**189 974**	**238 315**	**269 328**	**319 933**	**350 968**
3000 Taxes on payroll and workforce										
Federal or Central government	..	..	..	..	..	..	..	..	..	..
State/Regional	..	..	..	..	..	..	..	..	..	..
Local government	..	..	..	..	..	..	..	..	..	..
Social Security Funds	..	..	..	..	..	..	..	..	..	..
Total	**..**	**..**	**..**	**..**	**..**	**..**	**..**	**..**	**..**	**..**
2000+3000 Total	**..**	**..**	**..**	**54 633**	**138 392**	**189 974**	**238 315**	**269 328**	**319 933**	**350 968**
Colombia, million COP										
2000 Social security contributions										
Federal or Central government	..	..	..	..	..	..	0	0	0	0
State/Regional	..	..	..	..	..	..	0	0	0	0
Local government	..	..	..	..	..	..	0	0	0	0
Social Security Funds	..	..	..	..	..	..	1 007 283	1 255 666	1 596 055	1 778 257
Total	**..**	**..**	**..**	**..**	**..**	**..**	**1 007 283**	**1 255 666**	**1 596 055**	**1 778 257**
3000 Taxes on payroll and workforce										
Federal or Central government	..	..	..	..	..	..	372 476	436 646	513 161	563 148
State/Regional	..	..	..	..	..	..	0	0	0	0
Local government	..	..	..	..	..	..	0	0	0	0
Social Security Funds	..	..	..	..	..	..	0	0	0	0
Total	**..**	**..**	**..**	**..**	**..**	**..**	**372 476**	**436 646**	**513 161**	**563 148**
2000+3000 Total	**..**	**..**	**..**	**..**	**..**	**..**	**1 379 759**	**1 692 312**	**2 109 215**	**2 341 405**
Czech Republic, million CZK										
2000 Social security contributions										
Federal or Central government	..	..	..	28 050	44 437	45 439	46 360	37 553	43 564	48 579
State/Regional	..	..	..	..	..	..	..	..	..	..
Local government	..	..	..	5 660	8 253	9 394	9 448	41 954	47 919	54 940
Social Security Funds	..	..	..	510	791	938	881	975	1 056	1 148
Total	**..**	**..**	**..**	**34 220**	**53 481**	**55 771**	**56 689**	**80 482**	**92 538**	**104 666**
3000 Taxes on payroll and workforce										
Federal or Central government	..	..	..	..	..	..	..	..	..	..
State/Regional	..	..	..	..	..	..	..	..	..	..
Local government	..	..	..	..	..	..	..	..	..	..
Social Security Funds	..	..	..	..	..	..	..	..	..	..
Total	**..**	**..**	**..**	**0**	**0**	**0**	**0**	**0**	**0**	**0**
2000+3000 Total	**..**	**..**	**..**	**34 220**	**53 481**	**55 771**	**56 689**	**80 482**	**92 538**	**104 666**
Denmark, million DKK										
2000 Social security contributions										
Federal or Central government	..	179	..	..	..	..	..	..	..	..
State/Regional	..	..	..	..	..	..	..	..	..	..
Local government	..	0	..	..	..	..	..	..	..	..
Social Security Funds	..	0	..	..	..	..	..	..	..	..
Total	**..**	**179**	**0**	**0**	**0**	**0**	**0**	**0**	**0**	**0**
3000 Taxes on payroll and workforce										
Federal or Central government	..	..	..	..	..	..	..	..	..	..
State/Regional	..	..	..	..	..	..	..	..	..	..
Local government	..	..	..	..	..	..	..	..	..	..
Social Security Funds	..	..	..	..	..	..	..	..	..	..
Total	**..**	**0**	**0**	**0**	**0**	**0**	**0**	**0**	**0**	**0**
2000+3000 Total	**..**	**179**	**0**	**0**	**0**	**0**	**0**	**0**	**0**	**0**

	1965	1980	1990	2000	2007	2010	2013	2015	2017	2018
Estonia, million EUR										
2000 Social security contributions										
Federal or Central government	..	..	..	129	257	315	371	451	488	531
State/Regional	..	..	..	..	..	..	..	..	..	..
Local government	..	..	..	48	156	175	206	235	277	304
Social Security Funds	..	..	..	0	3	41	24	24	64	76
Total	**..**	**..**	**..**	**177**	**417**	**532**	**601**	**710**	**829**	**911**
3000 Taxes on payroll and workforce										
Federal or Central government	..	..	..	..	..	..	..	..	..	..
State/Regional	..	..	..	..	..	..	..	..	..	..
Local government	..	..	..	..	..	..	..	..	..	..
Social Security Funds	..	..	..	..	..	..	..	..	..	..
Total	**..**	**..**	**..**	**0**	**0**	**0**	**0**	**0**	**0**	**0**
2000+3000 Total	**..**	**..**	**..**	**177**	**417**	**532**	**601**	**710**	**829**	**911**
Finland, million EUR										
2000 Social security contributions										
Federal or Central government	..	61	196	908	1 057	1 138	1 227	1 229	1 003	1 050
State/Regional	..	..	..	..	..	..	..	..	..	..
Local government	..	170	1 709	2 786	4 061	4 352	4 881	4 868	4 327	4 231
Social Security Funds	..	9	34	75	88	89	101	109	117	121
Total	**..**	**239**	**1 939**	**3 769**	**5 206**	**5 579**	**6 209**	**6 206**	**5 447**	**5 402**
3000 Taxes on payroll and workforce										
Federal or Central government	..	1	..	..	..	..	..	..	..	..
State/Regional	..	..	..	..	..	..	..	..	..	..
Local government	..	4	..	..	..	..	..	..	..	..
Social Security Funds	..	0	..	..	..	..	..	..	..	..
Total	**..**	**5**	**0**	**0**	**0**	**0**	**0**	**0**	**0**	**0**
2000+3000 Total	**..**	**245**	**1 939**	**3 769**	**5 206**	**5 579**	**6 209**	**6 206**	**5 447**	**5 402**
France, million EUR										
2000 Social security contributions										
Federal or Central government	..	3 816	8 063	10 466	12 426	12 841	12 825	12 999	13 886	14 103
State/Regional	..	..	..	..	..	..	..	..	..	..
Local government	..	2 369	5 542	10 372	15 925	18 065	20 050	21 553	22 416	21 894
Social Security Funds	..	2 594	6 940	10 827	14 035	15 427	16 614	17 399	17 970	17 783
Total	**..**	**8 779**	**20 545**	**31 665**	**42 386**	**46 333**	**49 489**	**51 951**	**54 272**	**53 780**
3000 Taxes on payroll and workforce										
Federal or Central government	..	836	494	854	1 558	1 611	1 697	1 768	1 893	1 927
State/Regional	..	..	..	..	..	..	..	..	..	..
Local government	..	27	107	324	549	698	791	852	916	919
Social Security Funds	..	629	2 234	3 413	4 531	5 028	5 374	5 522	5 628	5 679
Total	**..**	**1 492**	**2 835**	**4 591**	**6 638**	**7 337**	**7 862**	**8 142**	**8 437**	**8 525**
2000+3000 Total	**..**	**10 271**	**23 380**	**36 256**	**49 024**	**53 670**	**57 351**	**60 093**	**62 709**	**62 305**
Germany, million EUR										
2000 Social security contributions										
Federal or Central government	775	1 324	2 376	1 553	1 377	1 649	1 631	1 766	1 982	2 078
State/Regional	293	2 611	4 647	5 660	6 044	6 781	7 231	7 749	8 436	8 718
Local government	325	3 140	5 791	6 917	8 294	9 499	9 967	10 767	12 046	12 717
Social Security Funds	1 495	456	767	1 805	2 130	2 446	2 614	2 840	3 027	3 155
Total	**2 887**	**7 531**	**13 581**	**15 936**	**17 845**	**20 374**	**21 443**	**23 122**	**25 492**	**26 668**
3000 Taxes on payroll and workforce										
Federal or Central government	..	..	..	..	..	..	..	..	..	..
State/Regional	..	..	..	..	..	..	..	..	..	..
Local government	..	..	..	..	..	..	..	..	..	..
Social Security Funds	..	..	..	..	..	..	..	..	..	..
Total	**0**	**0**	**0**	**0**	**0**	**0**	**0**	**0**	**0**	**0**
2000+3000 Total	**2 887**	**7 531**	**13 581**	**15 936**	**17 845**	**20 374**	**21 443**	**23 122**	**25 492**	**26 668**

	1965	1980	1990	2000	2007	2010	2013	2015	2017	2018
Greece, million EUR										
2000 Social security contributions										
Federal or Central government	..	..	124	1 542	2 888	3 217	2 372	2 337	1 282	1 594
State/Regional	..	..	..	..	..	..	..	..	..	..
Local government	..	..	0	0	0	0	0	0	0	0
Social Security Funds	..	..	0	200	440	387	350	265	355	391
Total	**..**	**..**	**124**	**1 742**	**3 328**	**3 604**	**2 722**	**2 602**	**1 637**	**1 985**
3000 Taxes on payroll and workforce										
Federal or Central government	..	..	..	..	..	..	..	..	..	..
State/Regional	..	..	..	..	..	..	..	..	..	..
Local government	..	..	..	..	..	..	..	..	..	..
Social Security Funds	..	..	..	..	..	..	..	..	..	..
Total	**..**	**..**	**0**	**0**	**0**	**0**	**0**	**0**	**0**	**0**
2000+3000 Total	**..**	**..**	**124**	**1 742**	**3 328**	**3 604**	**2 722**	**2 602**	**1 637**	**1 985**
Hungary, million HUF										
2000 Social security contributions										
Federal or Central government	..	..	..	148 251	293 684	352 354	449 428	539 106	535 993	521 151
State/Regional	..	..	..	..	..	..	..	..	..	..
Local government	..	..	..	173 475	343 306	291 375	124 111	152 189	149 461	142 851
Social Security Funds	..	..	..	4 936	8 052	6 763	2 781	2 977	1 922	730
Total	**..**	**..**	**..**	**326 661**	**645 042**	**650 492**	**576 320**	**694 272**	**687 375**	**664 732**
3000 Taxes on payroll and workforce										
Federal or Central government	..	..	..	13 901	7 287	5 419	12 435	12 876	16 067	18 145
State/Regional	..	..	..	..	..	..	..	..	..	..
Local government	..	..	..	25 990	11 928	9 275	4 224	3 357	3 770	4 134
Social Security Funds	..	..	..	406	162	194	101	110	96	38
Total	**..**	**..**	**..**	**40 297**	**19 377**	**14 888**	**16 760**	**16 342**	**19 933**	**22 317**
2000+3000 Total	**..**	**..**	**..**	**366 958**	**664 420**	**665 380**	**593 080**	**710 614**	**707 308**	**687 049**
Iceland, million ISK										
2000 Social security contributions										
Federal or Central government	..	..	..	..	..	..	..	..	..	..
State/Regional	..	..	..	..	..	..	..	..	..	..
Local government	..	..	..	..	..	..	..	..	..	..
Social Security Funds	..	..	..	..	..	..	..	..	..	..
Total	**..**	**..**	**..**	**..**	**..**	**..**	**..**	**..**	**..**	**..**
3000 Taxes on payroll and workforce										
Federal or Central government	..	..	..	..	..	..	..	..	..	..
State/Regional	..	..	..	..	..	..	..	..	..	..
Local government	..	..	..	..	..	..	..	..	..	..
Social Security Funds	..	..	..	..	..	..	..	..	..	..
Total	**..**	**..**	**..**	**..**	**..**	**..**	**..**	**..**	**..**	**..**
2000+3000 Total	**..**	**..**	**..**	**..**	**..**	**..**	**..**	**..**	**..**	**..**
Ireland, million EUR										
2000 Social security contributions										
Federal or Central government	..	21	65	166	460	395	426	497	574	619
State/Regional	..	..	..	..	..	..	..	..	..	..
Local government	..	25	83	277	862	740	799	932	1 077	1 160
Social Security Funds	..	0	1	4	6	6	6	6	6	6
Total	**..**	**46**	**149**	**447**	**1 328**	**1 140**	**1 231**	**1 435**	**1 657**	**1 785**
3000 Taxes on payroll and workforce										
Federal or Central government	..	..	..	..	..	..	..	..	..	..
State/Regional	..	..	..	..	..	..	..	..	..	..
Local government	..	..	..	..	..	..	..	..	..	..
Social Security Funds	..	..	..	..	..	..	..	..	..	..
Total	**..**	**0**	**0**	**0**	**0**	**0**	**0**	**0**	**0**	**0**
2000+3000 Total	**..**	**46**	**149**	**447**	**1 328**	**1 140**	**1 231**	**1 435**	**1 657**	**1 785**

	1965	1980	1990	2000	2007	2010	2013	2015	2017	2018
Israel, million ILS										
2000 Social security contributions										
Federal or Central government	..	..	..	840	1 030	1 180	1 550	1 780	2 120	2 160
State/Regional	..	..	..	..	..	..	..	..	..	..
Local government	..	..	..	280	340	390	510	590	700	710
Social Security Funds	..	..	..	0	0	0	0	0	0	0
Total	**..**	**..**	**..**	**1 120**	**1 370**	**1 570**	**2 060**	**2 370**	**2 820**	**2 870**
3000 Taxes on payroll and workforce										
Federal or Central government	..	..	..	2 330	3 600	4 180	5 220	5 650	6 130	6 540
State/Regional	..	..	..	..	..	..	..	..	..	..
Local government	..	..	..	660	880	960	1 190	1 290	1 400	1 490
Social Security Funds	..	..	..	0	0	0	0	0	0	0
Total	**..**	**..**	**..**	**2 990**	**4 480**	**5 140**	**6 410**	**6 940**	**7 530**	**8 030**
2000+3000 Total	**..**	**..**	**..**	**4 110**	**5 850**	**6 710**	**8 470**	**9 310**	**10 350**	**10 900**
Italy, million EUR										
2000 Social security contributions										
Federal or Central government	..	..	..	0	0	0	0	0	0	0
State/Regional	..	..	..	..	..	..	..	..	..	..
Local government	..	..	..	0	0	0	0	0	0	0
Social Security Funds	..	..	..	36 679	47 394	50 627	49 827	49 251	50 699	51 907
Total	**..**	**..**	**..**	**36 679**	**47 394**	**50 627**	**49 827**	**49 251**	**50 699**	**51 907**
3000 Taxes on payroll and workforce										
Federal or Central government	..	..	..	..	..	..	..	..	..	..
State/Regional	..	..	..	..	..	..	..	..	..	..
Local government	..	..	..	..	..	..	..	..	..	..
Social Security Funds	..	..	..	..	..	..	..	..	..	..
Total	**..**	**..**	**..**	**0**	**0**	**0**	**0**	**0**	**0**	**0**
2000+3000 Total	**..**	**..**	**..**	**36 679**	**47 394**	**50 627**	**49 827**	**49 251**	**50 699**	**51 907**
Japan, billion JPY										
2000 Social security contributions										
Federal or Central government	..	..	507	732	766	758	810	881	908	928
State/Regional	..	..	..	..	..	..	..	..	..	..
Local government	..	..	1 510	2 168	2 216	2 223	2 392	2 524	2 563	2 607
Social Security Funds	..	..	0	0	0	0	0	0	0	0
Total	**..**	**..**	**2 017**	**2 900**	**2 982**	**2 981**	**3 202**	**3 405**	**3 471**	**3 535**
3000 Taxes on payroll and workforce										
Federal or Central government	..	..	..	..	..	..	..	..	..	..
State/Regional	..	..	..	..	..	..	..	..	..	..
Local government	..	..	..	..	..	..	..	..	..	..
Social Security Funds	..	..	..	..	..	..	..	..	..	..
Total	**..**	**..**	**0**	**0**	**0**	**0**	**0**	**0**	**0**	**0**
2000+3000 Total	**..**	**..**	**2 017**	**2 900**	**2 982**	**2 981**	**3 202**	**3 405**	**3 471**	**3 535**
Korea, billion KRW										
2000 Social security contributions										
Federal or Central government	..	..	..	..	..	..	..	..	..	..
State/Regional	..	..	..	..	..	..	..	..	..	..
Local government	..	..	..	..	..	..	..	..	..	..
Social Security Funds	..	..	..	..	..	..	..	..	..	..
Total	**..**	**..**	**..**	**..**	**..**	**..**	**..**	**..**	**..**	**..**
3000 Taxes on payroll and workforce										
Federal or Central government	..	..	..	..	..	..	..	..	..	..
State/Regional	..	..	..	..	..	..	..	..	..	..
Local government	..	..	..	..	..	..	..	..	..	..
Social Security Funds	..	..	..	..	..	..	..	..	..	..
Total	**..**	**..**	**..**	**..**	**..**	**..**	**..**	**..**	**..**	**..**
2000+3000 Total	**..**	**..**	**..**	**..**	**..**	**..**	**..**	**..**	**..**	**..**

	1965	1980	1990	2000	2007	2010	2013	2015	2017	2018
Latvia, million EUR										
2000 Social security contributions										
Federal or Central government	..	..	..	..	..	..	..	..	..	..
State/Regional	..	..	..	..	..	..	..	..	..	..
Local government	..	..	..	..	..	..	..	..	..	..
Social Security Funds	..	..	..	..	..	..	..	..	..	..
Total	**..**	**..**	**..**	**40**	**156**	**174**	**228**	**262**	**252**	**339**
3000 Taxes on payroll and workforce										
Federal or Central government	..	..	..	..	..	..	..	..	..	..
State/Regional	..	..	..	..	..	..	..	..	..	..
Local government	..	..	..	..	..	..	..	..	..	..
Social Security Funds	..	..	..	..	..	..	..	..	..	..
Total	**..**	**..**	**..**	**0**	**0**	**0**	**0**	**0**	**0**	**0**
2000+3000 Total	**..**	**..**	**..**	**40**	**156**	**174**	**228**	**262**	**252**	**339**
Lithuania, million EUR										
2000 Social security contributions										
Federal or Central government	..	..	..	179	327	335	395	426	479	529
State/Regional	..	..	..	..	..	..	..	..	..	..
Local government	..	..	..	174	294	351	348	375	416	462
Social Security Funds	..	..	..	5	14	16	15	16	16	16
Total	**..**	**..**	**..**	**358**	**635**	**701**	**758**	**818**	**912**	**1 006**
3000 Taxes on payroll and workforce										
Federal or Central government	..	..	..	..	..	..	..	..	..	..
State/Regional	..	..	..	..	..	..	..	..	..	..
Local government	..	..	..	..	..	..	..	..	..	..
Social Security Funds	..	..	..	..	..	..	..	..	..	..
Total	**..**	**..**	**..**	**0**	**0**	**0**	**0**	**0**	**0**	**0**
2000+3000 Total	**..**	**..**	**..**	**358**	**635**	**701**	**758**	**818**	**912**	**1 006**
Luxembourg, million EUR										
2000 Social security contributions										
Federal or Central government	..	..	257	273	413	488	587	648	726	751
State/Regional	..	..	..	..	..	..	..	..	..	..
Local government	..	..	2	4	4	4	4	4	4	4
Social Security Funds	..	..	7	11	12	13	14	17	20	21
Total	**..**	**..**	**267**	**288**	**429**	**505**	**605**	**669**	**749**	**775**
3000 Taxes on payroll and workforce										
Federal or Central government	..	..	..	..	..	..	..	..	..	..
State/Regional	..	..	..	..	..	..	..	..	..	..
Local government	..	..	..	..	..	..	..	..	..	..
Social Security Funds	..	..	..	..	..	..	..	..	..	..
Total	**..**	**..**	**0**	**0**	**0**	**0**	**0**	**0**	**0**	**0**
2000+3000 Total	**..**	**..**	**267**	**288**	**429**	**505**	**605**	**669**	**749**	**775**
Mexico, million MXN										
2000 Social security contributions										
Federal or Central government	..	25	2 952	44 879	94 251	103 440	126 518	145 329	159 491	169 788
State/Regional	..	0	0	0	0	0	0	0	0	0
Local government	..	0	0	0	0	0	0	0	0	0
Social Security Funds	..	0	0	0	0	0	0	0	0	0
Total	**..**	**25**	**2 952**	**44 879**	**94 251**	**103 440**	**126 518**	**145 329**	**159 491**	**169 788**
3000 Taxes on payroll and workforce										
Federal or Central government	..	..	..	..	..	..	..	..	..	..
State/Regional	..	..	..	..	..	..	..	..	..	..
Local government	..	..	..	..	..	..	..	..	..	..
Social Security Funds	..	..	..	..	..	..	..	..	..	..
Total	**..**	**0**	**0**	**0**	**0**	**0**	**0**	**0**	**0**	**0**
2000+3000 Total	**..**	**25**	**2 952**	**44 879**	**94 251**	**103 440**	**126 518**	**145 329**	**159 491**	**169 788**

	1965	1980	1990	2000	2007	2010	2013	2015	2017	2018
Netherlands, million EUR										
2000 Social security contributions										
Federal or Central government	63	1 366	286	..	..	..	..	..	..	..
State/Regional	..	..	..	..	..	..	..	..	..	..
Local government	0	0	0	..	..	..	..	..	..	..
Social Security Funds	7	91	59	..	..	..	..	..	..	..
Total	**70**	**1 457**	**345**	**2 006**	**4 310**	**..**	**..**	**..**	**..**	**..**
3000 Taxes on payroll and workforce										
Federal or Central government	..	..	..	..	..	..	..	..	..	..
State/Regional	..	..	..	..	..	..	..	..	..	..
Local government	..	..	..	..	..	..	..	..	..	..
Social Security Funds	..	..	..	..	..	..	..	..	..	..
Total	**0**	**0**	**0**	**0**	**0**	**0**	**0**	**0**	**0**	**0**
2000+3000 Total	**70**	**1 457**	**345**	**2 006**	**4 310**	**0**	**0**	**0**	**0**	**0**
New Zealand, million NZD										
2000 Social security contributions										
Federal or Central government	..	..	..	..	..	..	..	..	..	..
State/Regional	..	..	..	..	..	..	..	..	..	..
Local government	..	..	..	..	..	..	..	..	..	..
Social Security Funds	..	..	..	..	..	..	..	..	..	..
Total	**0**	**0**	**0**	**0**	**0**	**0**	**0**	**0**	**0**	**0**
3000 Taxes on payroll and workforce										
Federal or Central government	..	..	..	..	..	..	..	..	..	..
State/Regional	..	..	..	..	..	..	..	..	..	..
Local government	..	..	..	..	..	..	..	..	..	..
Social Security Funds	..	..	..	..	..	..	..	..	..	..
Total	**0**	**0**	**0**	**0**	**0**	**0**	**0**	**0**	**0**	**0**
2000+3000 Total	**0**	**0**	**0**	**0**	**0**	**0**	**0**	**0**	**0**	**0**
Norway, million NOK										
2000 Social security contributions										
Federal or Central government	..	1 242	2 859	11 895	28 233	33 746	40 145	46 487	47 547	50 073
State/Regional	..	..	..	..	..	..	..	..	..	..
Local government	..	4 538	11 964	24 831	32 110	41 024	53 123	59 556	63 724	67 171
Social Security Funds	..	1 222	3 064	0	0	0	0	0	0	0
Total	**..**	**7 002**	**17 887**	**36 726**	**60 343**	**74 770**	**93 268**	**106 043**	**111 271**	**117 244**
3000 Taxes on payroll and workforce										
Federal or Central government	..	..	..	..	..	..	..	..	..	..
State/Regional	..	..	..	..	..	..	..	..	..	..
Local government	..	..	..	..	..	..	..	..	..	..
Social Security Funds	..	..	..	..	..	..	..	..	..	..
Total	**..**	**0**	**0**	**0**	**0**	**0**	**0**	**0**	**0**	**0**
2000+3000 Total	**..**	**7 002**	**17 887**	**36 726**	**60 343**	**74 770**	**93 268**	**106 043**	**111 271**	**117 244**
Poland, million PLN										
2000 Social security contributions										
Federal or Central government	..	..	..	4 566	6 023	6 643	8 231	9 839	10 993	11 683
State/Regional	..	..	..	..	..	..	..	..	..	..
Local government	..	..	..	6 756	9 856	11 411	13 638	14 797	16 330	17 283
Social Security Funds	..	..	..	279	426	499	514	517	589	593
Total	**..**	**..**	**..**	**11 601**	**16 305**	**18 553**	**22 383**	**25 153**	**27 912**	**29 559**
3000 Taxes on payroll and workforce										
Federal or Central government	..	..	..	..	..	..	..	..	..	..
State/Regional	..	..	..	..	..	..	..	..	..	..
Local government	..	..	..	..	..	..	..	..	..	..
Social Security Funds	..	..	..	..	..	..	..	..	..	..
Total	**..**	**..**	**..**	**0**	**0**	**0**	**0**	**0**	**0**	**0**
2000+3000 Total	**..**	**..**	**..**	**11 601**	**16 305**	**18 553**	**22 383**	**25 153**	**27 912**	**29 559**

	1965	1980	1990	2000	2007	2010	2013	2015	2017	2018
Portugal, million EUR										
2000 Social security contributions										
Federal or Central government	..	0	0	0	..	..	..	..	..	..
State/Regional	..	..	..	..	..	..	..	..	..	..
Local government	..	0	33	197	..	..	..	..	..	..
Social Security Funds	..	4	0	0	..	..	..	..	..	..
Total	**..**	**4**	**33**	**197**	**0**	**0**	**0**	**0**	**0**	**0**
3000 Taxes on payroll and workforce										
Federal or Central government	..	..	..	..	..	..	..	..	..	..
State/Regional	..	..	..	..	..	..	..	..	..	..
Local government	..	..	..	..	..	..	..	..	..	..
Social Security Funds	..	..	..	..	..	..	..	..	..	..
Total	**..**	**0**	**0**	**0**	**0**	**0**	**0**	**0**	**0**	**0**
2000+3000 Total	**..**	**4**	**33**	**197**	**0**	**0**	**0**	**0**	**0**	**0**
Slovak Republic, million EUR										
2000 Social security contributions										
Federal or Central government	..	..	..	489	602	785	936	1 033	1 120	1 186
State/Regional	..	..	..	..	..	..	..	..	..	..
Local government	..	..	..	130	427	493	562	650	739	795
Social Security Funds	..	..	..	22	26	44	32	36	40	43
Total	**..**	**..**	**..**	**642**	**1 055**	**1 322**	**1 530**	**1 719**	**1 899**	**2 024**
3000 Taxes on payroll and workforce										
Federal or Central government	..	..	..	..	..	..	..	..	..	..
State/Regional	..	..	..	..	..	..	..	..	..	..
Local government	..	..	..	..	..	..	..	..	..	..
Social Security Funds	..	..	..	..	..	..	..	..	..	..
Total	**..**	**..**	**..**	**0**	**0**	**0**	**0**	**0**	**0**	**0**
2000+3000 Total	**..**	**..**	**..**	**642**	**1 055**	**1 322**	**1 530**	**1 719**	**1 899**	**2 024**
Slovenia, million EUR										
2000 Social security contributions										
Federal or Central government	..	..	..	178	339	409	387	375	422	449
State/Regional	..	..	..	..	..	..	..	..	..	..
Local government	..	..	..	94	175	195	187	189	212	225
Social Security Funds	..	..	..	3	7	8	7	6	7	8
Total	**..**	**..**	**..**	**275**	**521**	**612**	**582**	**571**	**641**	**682**
3000 Taxes on payroll and workforce										
Federal or Central government	..	..	..	56	77	6	7	7	7	7
State/Regional	..	..	..	..	..	..	..	..	..	..
Local government	..	..	..	29	36	3	4	4	4	4
Social Security Funds	..	..	..	1	2	0	0	0	0	0
Total	**..**	**..**	**..**	**86**	**114**	**9**	**11**	**11**	**11**	**12**
2000+3000 Total	**..**	**..**	**..**	**361**	**636**	**621**	**593**	**582**	**652**	**693**
Spain, million EUR										
2000 Social security contributions										
Federal or Central government	..	387	989	1 408	1 966	2 201	2 014	2 234	2 366	2 472
State/Regional	..	2	0	4 411	9 426	10 996	10 212	11 245	12 341	13 080
Local government	..	252	1 819	2 524	4 098	4 781	4 617	4 797	5 001	5 042
Social Security Funds	..	396	1 202	1 284	484	527	498	496	491	494
Total	**..**	**1 037**	**4 010**	**9 627**	**15 974**	**18 505**	**17 341**	**18 772**	**20 199**	**21 088**
3000 Taxes on payroll and workforce										
Federal or Central government	..	..	..	..	..	..	..	..	..	..
State/Regional	..	..	..	..	..	..	..	..	..	..
Local government	..	..	..	..	..	..	..	..	..	..
Social Security Funds	..	..	..	..	..	..	..	..	..	..
Total	**..**	**0**	**0**	**0**	**0**	**0**	**0**	**0**	**0**	**0**
2000+3000 Total	**..**	**1 037**	**4 010**	**9 627**	**15 974**	**18 505**	**17 341**	**18 772**	**20 199**	**21 088**

	1965	1980	1990	2000	2007	2010	2013	2015	2017	2018
Sweden, million SEK										
2000 Social security contributions										
Federal or Central government	..	7 543	12 430	21 153	25 164	24 729	24 595	25 707	27 612	28 594
State/Regional	..	..	..	..	..	..	..	..	..	..
Local government	..	18 149	49 298	66 215	83 877	82 141	78 774	85 373	95 132	98 662
Social Security Funds	..	0	0	0	0	0	0	0	0	0
Total	**..**	**25 692**	**61 728**	**87 367**	**109 040**	**106 870**	**103 370**	**111 079**	**122 744**	**127 256**
3000 Taxes on payroll and workforce										
Federal or Central government	..	..	1 527	3 453	5 394	6 912	11 242	12 326	14 531	15 122
State/Regional	..	..	..	..	..	..	..	..	..	..
Local government	..	..	6 060	10 808	17 980	22 958	36 005	40 935	50 064	52 177
Social Security Funds	..	..	0	0	0	0	0	0	0	0
Total	**..**	**0**	**7 587**	**14 261**	**23 374**	**29 870**	**47 247**	**53 261**	**64 596**	**67 299**
2000+3000 Total	**..**	**25 692**	**69 315**	**101 628**	**132 414**	**136 740**	**150 616**	**164 340**	**187 340**	**194 555**
Switzerland, million CHF										
2000 Social security contributions										
Federal or Central government	13	91	224	293	375	439	485	489	548	554
State/Regional	34	380	770	971	1 296	1 524	1 699	1 767	1 858	1 901
Local government	22	270	460	595	745	823	867	911	955	958
Social Security Funds	2	21	4	14	18	23	25	26	26	27
Total	**71**	**762**	**1 458**	**1 873**	**2 434**	**2 809**	**3 075**	**3 193**	**3 387**	**3 440**
3000 Taxes on payroll and workforce										
Federal or Central government	..	..	..	..	..	..	..	..	..	..
State/Regional	..	..	..	..	..	..	..	..	..	..
Local government	..	..	..	..	..	..	..	..	..	..
Social Security Funds	..	..	..	..	..	..	..	..	..	..
Total	**0**	**0**	**0**	**0**	**0**	**0**	**0**	**0**	**0**	**0**
2000+3000 Total	**71**	**762**	**1 458**	**1 873**	**2 434**	**2 809**	**3 075**	**3 193**	**3 387**	**3 440**
Turkey, million TRY										
2000 Social security contributions										
Federal or Central government	..	..	9	3 619	20 442	39 363	71 184	95 067	128 331	151 373
State/Regional	..	..	..	..	..	..	..	..	..	..
Local government	..	..	0	0	0	0	0	0	0	0
Social Security Funds	..	..	0	0	0	0	0	0	0	0
Total	**..**	**..**	**9**	**3 619**	**20 442**	**39 363**	**71 184**	**95 067**	**128 331**	**151 373**
3000 Taxes on payroll and workforce										
Federal or Central government	..	..	..	..	..	..	..	..	..	..
State/Regional	..	..	..	..	..	..	..	..	..	..
Local government	..	..	..	..	..	..	..	..	..	..
Social Security Funds	..	..	..	..	..	..	..	..	..	..
Total	**..**	**..**	**0**	**0**	**0**	**0**	**0**	**0**	**0**	**0**
2000+3000 Total	**..**	**..**	**9**	**3 619**	**20 442**	**39 363**	**71 184**	**95 067**	**128 331**	**151 373**
United Kingdom, million GBP										
2000 Social security contributions										
Federal or Central government	87	920	2 134	3 146	5 865	6 475	7 074	7 830	9 250	9 595
State/Regional	..	..	..	..	..	..	..	..	..	..
Local government	83	926	1 957	2 924	4 866	5 343	4 668	4 538	4 763	4 723
Social Security Funds	0	0	0	0	0	0	0	0	0	0
Total	**170**	**1 846**	**4 091**	**6 070**	**10 731**	**11 818**	**11 742**	**12 368**	**14 013**	**14 318**
3000 Taxes on payroll and workforce										
Federal or Central government	..	360	..	..	..	..	..	..	..	..
State/Regional	..	..	..	..	..	..	..	..	..	..
Local government	..	410	..	..	..	..	..	..	..	..
Social Security Funds	..	0	..	..	..	..	..	..	..	..
Total	**0**	**770**	**0**	**0**	**0**	**0**	**0**	**0**	**0**	**0**
2000+3000 Total	**170**	**2 616**	**4 091**	**6 070**	**10 731**	**11 818**	**11 742**	**12 368**	**14 013**	**14 318**

	1965	1980	1990	2000	2007	2010	2013	2015	2017	2018
United States, million USD										
2000 Social security contributions										
Federal or Central government	301	2 053	9 059	11 323	19 628	25 434	25 938	26 696	27 236	27 974
State/Regional	699	7 585	19 802	32 814	44 061	45 936	46 832	49 361	52 233	53 585
Local government	0	0	0	0	0	0	0	0	0	0
Social Security Funds	0	0	0	0	0	0	0	0	0	0
Total	**1 000**	**9 638**	**28 861**	**44 137**	**63 689**	**71 370**	**72 770**	**76 057**	**79 469**	**81 559**
3000 Taxes on payroll and workforce										
Federal or Central government	..	..	..	..	..	..	..	..	..	..
State/Regional	..	..	..	..	..	..	..	..	..	..
Local government	..	..	..	..	..	..	..	..	..	..
Social Security Funds	..	..	..	..	..	..	..	..	..	..
Total	**0**	**0**	**0**	**0**	**0**	**0**	**0**	**0**	**0**	**0**
2000+3000 Total	**1 000**	**9 638**	**28 861**	**44 137**	**63 689**	**71 370**	**72 770**	**76 057**	**79 469**	**81 559**

.. Not available

1. The multi-jurisdictional sector contains units where jurisdiction is shared between two or more governments, or classification of a unit to a jurisdiction is otherwise unclear. The main type of units currently falling into this category is public universities.
2. There is a break in the series in 1990. The data are based on ESA 2010 from that year onwards.

StatLink https://doi.org/10.1787/888934212402

6 Tax revenues by subsectors of general government

Chapter 6 provides information on tax revenues by subsectors of general government for each OECD country.

6.1. Country tables 1975, 1985, 1995, 2005 and 2018

This chapter presents detailed country information on tax revenues by level of government. The data have been attributed to the sub-sectors of general government identified in section A.12 of the Interpretative Guide (see Annex A) and the attribution criteria used are those set out in that guide.

Table 6.1. Australia, tax revenues by sub-sectors of government

Million AUD

	Federal government					State/Regional				
	1975	1995	2005	2015	2018	1975	1995	2005	2015	2018
1000 Taxes on income, profits and capital gains	**11 831**	**82 615**	**175 695**	**262 357**	**336 239**	**0**	**0**	**0**	**0**	**0**
1100 Of individuals	9 213	60 602	118 239	191 747	229 499	..	..	..	..	..
1200 Corporate	2 618	22 013	57 456	70 610	106 740	..	..	..	..	..
1300 Unallocable between 1100 and 1200	0	0	0	0	0	0	0	0	0	0
2000 Social security contributions	**0**	**0**	**0**	**0**	**0**	**0**	**0**	**0**	**0**	**0**
2100 Employees	0	0	0	0	0	0	0	0	0	0
2200 Employers	0	0	0	0	0	0	0	0	0	0
2300 Self-employed or non-employed	0	0	0	0	0	0	0	0	0	0
2400 Unallocable between 2100, 2200 and 2300	0	0	0	0	0	0	0	0	0	0
3000 Taxes on payroll and workforce	**54**	**3 065**	**369**	**670**	**1 069**	**1 171**	**7 120**	**13 095**	**22 684**	**25 854**
4000 Taxes on property	**103**	**8**	**14**	**15**	**15**	**883**	**7 988**	**16 940**	**33 006**	**34 223**
4100 Recurrent taxes on immovable property	12	0	0	0	0	217	1 840	4 559	10 473	13 790
4200 Recurrent taxes on net wealth	0	0	0	0	0	0	0	0	0	0
4300 Estate, inheritance and gift taxes	87	0	0	0	0	227	0	0	0	0
4400 Taxes on financial and capital transactions	4	8	14	15	15	439	6 148	12 381	22 533	20 433
4500 Non-recurrent taxes	0	0	0	0	0	0	0	0	0	0
4600 Other recurrent taxes on property	0	0	0	0	0	0	0	0	0	0
5000 Taxes on goods and services	**4 932**	**30 004**	**69 360**	**104 590**	**115 891**	**1 262**	**13 295**	**14 479**	**23 408**	**26 258**
5100 Taxes on production, sale, transfer, etc	4 919	29 613	67 822	98 301	108 677	532	4 923	8 188	11 884	13 387
5110 General taxes	1 408	12 970	40 086	61 815	66 829	0	0	0	0	0
5120 Taxes on specific goods and services	3 511	16 643	27 736	36 486	41 848	532	4 923	8 188	11 884	13 387
5130 Unallocable between 5110 and 5120	0	0	0	0	0	0	0	0	0	0
5200 Taxes on use of goods and perform activities	13	391	1 538	6 289	7 214	730	8 372	6 291	11 524	12 871
5300 Unallocable between 5100 and 5200	0	0	0	0	0	0	0	0	0	0
6000 Other taxes	**0**	**0**	**0**	**0**	**0**	**0**	**0**	**0**	**0**	**0**
6100 Paid solely by business	..	..	..	..	..	..	..	..	..	..
6200 Other	..	..	..	..	..	..	..	..	..	..
Total tax revenue	**16 920**	**115 692**	**245 438**	**367 632**	**453 214**	**3 316**	**28 403**	**44 514**	**79 098**	**86 335**

	Local government					Social Security Funds				
	1975	1995	2005	2015	2018	1975	1995	2005	2015	2018
1000 Taxes on income, profits and capital gains	**0**	**0**	**0**	**0**	**0**	**0**	**0**	**0**	**0**	**0**
1100 Of individuals	..	..	..	..	..	..	..	..	..	..
1200 Corporate	..	..	..	..	..	..	..	..	..	..
1300 Unallocable between 1100 and 1200	0	0	0	0	0	0	0	0	0	0
2000 Social security contributions	**0**	**0**	**0**	**0**	**0**	**0**	**0**	**0**	**0**	**0**
2100 Employees	0	0	0	0	0	0	0	0	0	0
2200 Employers	0	0	0	0	0	0	0	0	0	0
2300 Self-employed or non-employed	0	0	0	0	0	0	0	0	0	0
2400 Unallocable between 2100, 2200 and 2300	0	0	0	0	0	0	0	0	0	0
3000 Taxes on payroll and workforce	**0**	**0**	**0**	**0**	**0**	**0**	**0**	**0**	**0**	**0**
4000 Taxes on property	**883**	**5 134**	**8 726**	**16 620**	**18 904**	**0**	**0**	**0**	**0**	**0**
4100 Recurrent taxes on immovable property	883	5 134	8 726	16 620	18 904	..	..	..	..	..
4200 Recurrent taxes on net wealth	0	0	0	0	0	..	..	..	..	..
4300 Estate, inheritance and gift taxes	0	0	0	0	0	..	..	..	..	..
4400 Taxes on financial and capital transactions	0	0	0	0	0	..	..	..	..	..
4500 Non-recurrent taxes	0	0	0	0	0	..	..	..	..	..
4600 Other recurrent taxes on property	0	0	0	0	0	..	..	..	..	..
5000 Taxes on goods and services	**0**	**0**	**0**	**0**	**0**	**0**	**0**	**0**	**0**	**0**
5100 Taxes on production, sale, transfer, etc	0	0	0	0	0	0	0	0	0	0
5110 General taxes	0	0	0	0	0	0	0	0	0	0
5120 Taxes on specific goods and services	0	0	0	0	0	0	0	0	0	0
5130 Unallocable between 5110 and 5120	0	0	0	0	0	0	0	0	0	0
5200 Taxes on use of goods and perform activities	0	0	0	0	0	0	0	0	0	0
5300 Unallocable between 5100 and 5200	0	0	0	0	0	0	0	0	0	0
6000 Other taxes	**0**	**0**	**0**	**0**	**0**	**0**	**0**	**0**	**0**	**0**
6100 Paid solely by business	..	..	..	..	..	..	..	..	..	..
6200 Other	..	..	..	..	..	..	..	..	..	..
Total tax revenue	**883**	**5 134**	**8 726**	**16 620**	**18 904**	**0**	**0**	**0**	**0**	**0**

.. Not available

StatLink https://doi.org/10.1787/888934212421

Table 6.2. Austria, tax revenues by sub-sectors of government

Million EUR

	Federal government					State/Regional				
	1975	1995	2005	2015	2018	1975	1995	2005	2015	2018
1000 Taxes on income, profits and capital gains	**3 064**	**18 452**	**28 781**	**43 714**	**46 528**	**865**	**547**	**742**	**1 081**	**1 230**
1100 Of individuals	2 381	14 649	22 126	34 901	35 122	834	459	637	941	1 071
1200 Corporate	655	2 267	5 341	7 519	10 282	31	88	104	141	159
1300 Unallocable between 1100 and 1200	27	1 536	1 313	1 295	1 125	0	0	0	0	0
2000 Social security contributions	**352**	**4 243**	**5 720**	**7 547**	**8 312**	**34**	**311**	**409**	**496**	**476**
2100 Employees	225	2 379	2 978	3 911	4 293	34	310	395	465	446
2200 Employers	127	1 830	2 498	3 350	3 740	0	0	0	0	0
2300 Self-employed or non-employed	0	34	243	286	279	0	1	14	31	30
2400 Unallocable between 2100, 2200 and 2300	0	0	0	0	0	0	0	0	0	0
3000 Taxes on payroll and workforce	**1 217**	**3 394**	**4 384**	**6 861**	**6 819**	**0**	**132**	**156**	**203**	**229**
4000 Taxes on property	**282**	**655**	**801**	**1 247**	**1 336**	**35**	**31**	**36**	**44**	**46**
4100 Recurrent taxes on immovable property	18	32	32	43	42	15	31	36	44	46
4200 Recurrent taxes on net wealth	226	58	0	0	0	10	0	0	0	0
4300 Estate, inheritance and gift taxes	24	82	140	12	9	10	0	0	0	0
4400 Taxes on financial and capital transactions	14	483	629	1 116	1 210	0	0	0	0	0
4500 Non-recurrent taxes	0	0	0	76	75	0	0	0	0	0
4600 Other recurrent taxes on property	0	0	0	0	0	0	0	0	0	0
5000 Taxes on goods and services	**4 554**	**19 894**	**29 646**	**39 720**	**43 678**	**1 013**	**222**	**234**	**362**	**442**
5100 Taxes on production, sale, transfer, etc	4 549	18 639	27 613	36 693	40 248	926	158	139	216	271
5110 General taxes	2 545	13 436	19 421	26 282	29 324	662	0	0	0	0
5120 Taxes on specific goods and services	1 991	5 159	8 148	10 408	10 922	264	158	139	216	271
5130 Unallocable between 5110 and 5120	14	44	45	4	3	0	0	0	0	0
5200 Taxes on use of goods and perform activities	5	1 255	2 033	3 027	3 429	87	64	95	146	171
5300 Unallocable between 5100 and 5200	0	0	0	0	0	0	0	0	0	0
6000 Other taxes	**52**	**486**	**699**	**517**	**532**	**8**	**50**	**61**	**91**	**102**
6100 Paid solely by business	..	..	..	..	..	..	..	..	..	..
6200 Other	..	..	..	..	..	..	..	..	..	..
Total tax revenue	**9 521**	**47 124**	**70 031**	**99 606**	**107 205**	**1 955**	**1 294**	**1 638**	**2 277**	**2 524**

	Local government					Social Security Funds				
	1975	1995	2005	2015	2018	1975	1995	2005	2015	2018
1000 Taxes on income, profits and capital gains	**887**	**46**	**0**	**0**	**0**	**0**	**0**	**0**	**0**	**0**
1100 Of individuals	771	19	0	0	0	..	..	..	..	..
1200 Corporate	115	26	0	0	0	..	..	..	..	..
1300 Unallocable between 1100 and 1200	0	0	0	0	0	..	..	..	..	..
2000 Social security contributions	**29**	**258**	**267**	**266**	**253**	**4 667**	**21 173**	**28 912**	**41 557**	**47 582**
2100 Employees	29	207	240	241	230	1 840	8 110	10 751	15 499	17 836
2200 Employers	0	50	27	26	23	2 375	10 912	14 037	19 906	22 899
2300 Self-employed or non-employed	0	0	0	0	0	453	2 151	4 125	6 153	6 847
2400 Unallocable between 2100, 2200 and 2300	0	0	0	0	0	0	0	0	0	0
3000 Taxes on payroll and workforce	**262**	**1 492**	**2 035**	**2 977**	**3 368**	**0**	**0**	**0**	**0**	**0**
4000 Taxes on property	**254**	**395**	**539**	**675**	**719**	**0**	**0**	**0**	**0**	**0**
4100 Recurrent taxes on immovable property	139	395	539	675	719	..	..	..	..	..
4200 Recurrent taxes on net wealth	35	0	0	0	0	..	..	..	..	..
4300 Estate, inheritance and gift taxes	0	0	0	0	0	..	..	..	..	..
4400 Taxes on financial and capital transactions	81	0	0	0	0	..	..	..	..	..
4500 Non-recurrent taxes	0	0	0	0	0	..	..	..	..	..
4600 Other recurrent taxes on property	0	0	0	0	0	..	..	..	..	..
5000 Taxes on goods and services	**792**	**738**	**302**	**353**	**367**	**0**	**0**	**0**	**0**	**0**
5100 Taxes on production, sale, transfer, etc	769	582	134	96	93	..	..	..	..	..
5110 General taxes	448	0	0	0	0	..	..	..	..	..
5120 Taxes on specific goods and services	321	582	134	96	93	..	..	..	..	..
5130 Unallocable between 5110 and 5120	0	0	0	0	0	..	..	..	..	..
5200 Taxes on use of goods and perform activities	24	155	168	258	275	..	..	..	..	..
5300 Unallocable between 5100 and 5200	0	0	0	0	0	..	..	..	..	..
6000 Other taxes	**55**	**60**	**103**	**129**	**142**	**0**	**0**	**0**	**0**	**0**
6100 Paid solely by business	..	..	..	..	..	..	..	..	..	..
6200 Other	..	..	..	..	..	..	..	..	..	..
Total tax revenue	**2 279**	**2 987**	**3 246**	**4 400**	**4 849**	**4 667**	**21 173**	**28 912**	**41 557**	**47 582**

.. Not available

Note: Including taxes collected on behalf of the European Union.

StatLink https://doi.org/10.1787/888934212440

Table 6.3. Belgium, tax revenues by sub-sectors of government

Million EUR

	Federal government					State/Regional				
	1975	1995	2005	2015	2018	1975	1995	2005	2015	2018
1000 Taxes on income, profits and capital gains	**8 534**	**30 905**	**45 859**	**57 131**	**60 428**	**..**	**79**	**0**	**4 283**	**9 458**
1100 Of individuals	6 929	25 997	36 007	43 436	40 621	..	79	..	4 283	9 458
1200 Corporate	1 596	4 867	9 811	13 644	19 736	..	0	..	0	0
1300 Unallocable between 1100 and 1200	10	41	42	51	71	..	0	..	0	0
2000 Social security contributions	**299**	**1 181**	**1 904**	**2 336**	**68**	**..**	**0**	**34**	**11**	**255**
2100 Employees	264	854	1 125	1 372	0	..	..	7	2	230
2200 Employers	36	228	608	715	68	..	..	27	9	25
2300 Self-employed or non-employed	0	99	171	249	0	..	..	0	0	0
2400 Unallocable between 2100, 2200 and 2300	0	0	0	0	0	..	..	0	0	0
3000 Taxes on payroll and workforce	**0**	**0**	**0**	**0**	**0**	**..**	**0**	**0**	**0**	**0**
4000 Taxes on property	**583**	**1 340**	**873**	**1 861**	**2 340**	**..**	**1 168**	**4 669**	**7 087**	**7 912**
4100 Recurrent taxes on immovable property	12	25	41	41	47	..	83	192	249	356
4200 Recurrent taxes on net wealth	0	8	189	661	952	..	0	0	0	0
4300 Estate, inheritance and gift taxes	178	42	0	0	0	..	647	1 749	3 004	3 250
4400 Taxes on financial and capital transactions	393	1 193	521	596	594	..	438	2 728	3 763	4 305
4500 Non-recurrent taxes	0	73	123	563	522	..	0	0	72	0
4600 Other recurrent taxes on property	0	0	0	0	226	..	0	0	0	0
5000 Taxes on goods and services	**5 813**	**20 951**	**29 984**	**39 004**	**43 816**	**..**	**412**	**2 044**	**2 678**	**3 016**
5100 Taxes on production, sale, transfer, etc	5 562	19 767	29 742	38 985	43 788	..	58	76	227	435
5110 General taxes	3 776	13 894	21 533	27 952	31 545	..	0	0	0	0
5120 Taxes on specific goods and services	1 785	5 872	8 208	11 034	12 242	..	58	76	227	435
5130 Unallocable between 5110 and 5120	0	0	0	0	0	..	0	0	0	0
5200 Taxes on use of goods and perform activities	249	1 178	234	10	18	..	355	1 968	2 451	2 582
5300 Unallocable between 5100 and 5200	3	6	8	9	11	..	0	0	0	0
6000 Other taxes	**0**	**0**	**0**	**0**	**0**	**..**	**0**	**68**	**40**	**0**
6100 Paid solely by business	..	..	..	..	..	..	..	0	0	..
6200 Other	..	..	..	..	..	..	..	68	40	..
Total tax revenue	**15 230**	**54 377**	**78 621**	**100 332**	**106 653**	**..**	**1 659**	**6 816**	**14 098**	**20 640**

	Local government					Social Security Funds				
	1975	1995	2005	2015	2018	1975	1995	2005	2015	2018
1000 Taxes on income, profits and capital gains	**683**	**3 058**	**2 249**	**3 052**	**3 234**	**0**	**335**	**825**	**1 106**	**1 253**
1100 Of individuals	675	3 058	2 249	3 052	3 234	..	335	825	1 106	1 253
1200 Corporate	8	0	0	0	0	..	0	0	0	0
1300 Unallocable between 1100 and 1200	0	0	0	0	0	..	0	0	0	0
2000 Social security contributions	**27**	**80**	**20**	**27**	**14**	**6 709**	**28 479**	**39 537**	**56 438**	**60 733**
2100 Employees	27	80	18	21	14	1 749	8 268	11 558	15 640	18 175
2200 Employers	0	0	3	6	0	4 347	17 746	24 613	35 510	36 458
2300 Self-employed or non-employed	0	0	0	0	0	612	2 465	3 366	5 289	6 100
2400 Unallocable between 2100, 2200 and 2300	0	0	0	0	0	0	0	0	0	0
3000 Taxes on payroll and workforce	**0**	**0**	**0**	**0**	**0**	**0**	**0**	**5**	**8**	**7**
4000 Taxes on property	**154**	**815**	**3 599**	**5 142**	**5 283**	**0**	**121**	**229**	**318**	**297**
4100 Recurrent taxes on immovable property	154	815	3 599	5 142	5 283	..	0	0	0	0
4200 Recurrent taxes on net wealth	0	0	0	0	0	..	0	0	0	0
4300 Estate, inheritance and gift taxes	0	0	0	0	0	..	0	0	0	0
4400 Taxes on financial and capital transactions	0	0	0	0	0	..	0	0	0	0
4500 Non-recurrent taxes	0	0	0	0	0	..	0	0	0	0
4600 Other recurrent taxes on property	0	0	0	0	0	..	121	229	318	297
5000 Taxes on goods and services	**166**	**332**	**523**	**715**	**696**	**14**	**330**	**1 237**	**1 575**	**1 918**
5100 Taxes on production, sale, transfer, etc	150	295	437	694	674	14	330	1 237	1 575	1 918
5110 General taxes	0	0	0	0	0	0	29	373	219	230
5120 Taxes on specific goods and services	150	295	437	694	674	14	301	865	1 356	1 687
5130 Unallocable between 5110 and 5120	0	0	0	0	0	0	0	0	0	0
5200 Taxes on use of goods and perform activities	16	37	87	22	23	0	0	0	0	0
5300 Unallocable between 5100 and 5200	0	0	0	0	0	0	0	0	0	0
6000 Other taxes	**0**	**0**	**0**	**0**	**0**	**0**	**0**	**0**	**0**	**0**
6100 Paid solely by business	..	..	..	..	..	..	..	..	..	..
6200 Other	..	..	..	..	..	..	..	..	..	..
Total tax revenue	**1 029**	**4 284**	**6 392**	**8 937**	**9 227**	**6 723**	**29 265**	**41 833**	**59 445**	**64 208**

.. Not available

Note: Including taxes collected on behalf of the European Union.

StatLink https://doi.org/10.1787/888934212459

Table 6.4. Canada, tax revenues by sub-sectors of government

Million CAD

	Federal government					State/Regional				
	1975	1995	2005	2015	2018	1975	1995	2005	2015	2018
1000 Taxes on income, profits and capital gains	**19 047**	**82 237**	**140 013**	**191 684**	**223 164**	**8 165**	**52 373**	**78 331**	**123 157**	**137 293**
1100 Of individuals	12 822	65 384	102 366	143 315	162 295	6 074	43 428	62 435	96 989	105 299
1200 Corporate	5 741	14 739	32 197	41 726	51 769	2 091	8 944	15 896	26 168	31 994
1300 Unallocable between 1100 and 1200	484	2 114	5 450	6 643	9 100	0	0	0	0	0
2000 Social security contributions	**0**	**0**	**17 936**	**23 603**	**22 374**	**0**	**0**	**11 759**	**13 892**	**15 229**
2100 Employees	..	..	7 429	9 772	9 255	..	..	1 858	1 128	1 322
2200 Employers	..	..	10 507	13 831	13 119	..	..	9 901	12 764	13 907
2300 Self-employed or non-employed	..	..	0	0	0	..	..	0	0	0
2400 Unallocable between 2100, 2200 and 2300	..	..	0	0	0	..	..	0	0	0
3000 Taxes on payroll and workforce	**0**	**0**	**0**	**0**	**0**	**0**	**6 498**	**9 230**	**13 256**	**14 871**
4000 Taxes on property	**13**	**0**	**0**	**0**	**0**	**428**	**6 492**	**9 298**	**11 809**	**13 616**
4100 Recurrent taxes on immovable property	0	..	..	..	..	85	2 960	2 934	5 410	6 690
4200 Recurrent taxes on net wealth	0	..	..	..	..	200	2 914	3 456	372	436
4300 Estate, inheritance and gift taxes	13	..	..	..	..	143	3	0	268	331
4400 Taxes on financial and capital transactions	0	..	..	..	..	0	0	1 965	3 912	4 957
4500 Non-recurrent taxes	0	..	..	..	..	0	615	943	1 847	1 202
4600 Other recurrent taxes on property	0	..	..	..	..	0	0	0	0	0
5000 Taxes on goods and services	**8 180**	**31 160**	**48 551**	**53 837**	**61 384**	**10 128**	**42 076**	**67 537**	**95 289**	**110 971**
5100 Taxes on production, sale, transfer, etc	8 180	31 136	48 506	53 797	61 349	6 800	37 961	61 316	86 827	100 099
5110 General taxes	3 504	19 167	35 069	36 958	41 852	3 664	21 328	33 353	53 577	63 038
5120 Taxes on specific goods and services	4 676	11 969	13 437	16 839	19 497	3 136	16 633	27 963	33 250	37 061
5130 Unallocable between 5110 and 5120	0	0	0	0	0	0	0	0	0	0
5200 Taxes on use of goods and perform activities	0	24	45	40	35	3 328	4 115	6 221	8 462	10 872
5300 Unallocable between 5100 and 5200	0	0	0	0	0	0	0	0	0	0
6000 Other taxes	**198**	**0**	**0**	**0**	**0**	**0**	**0**	**0**	**0**	**0**
6100 Paid solely by business	0	..	..	..	..	..	..	..	..	..
6200 Other	198	..	..	..	..	..	..	..	..	..
Total tax revenue	**27 438**	**113 397**	**206 500**	**269 124**	**306 922**	**18 721**	**107 439**	**176 156**	**257 403**	**291 980**

	Local government					Social Security Funds				
	1975	1995	2005	2015	2018	1975	1995	2005	2015	2018
1000 Taxes on income, profits and capital gains	**0**	**0**	**0**	**0**	**0**	**0**	**0**	**0**	**0**	**0**
1100 Of individuals	..	..	..	..	..	..	..	..	..	..
1200 Corporate	..	..	..	..	..	..	..	..	..	..
1300 Unallocable between 1100 and 1200	..	..	..	..	..	..	..	..	..	..
2000 Social security contributions	**0**	**0**	**0**	**0**	**0**	**5 787**	**40 559**	**38 834**	**58 876**	**65 610**
2100 Employees	..	..	..	..	..	2 142	15 028	18 328	27 785	30 971
2200 Employers	..	..	..	..	..	3 527	24 765	18 328	27 785	30 971
2300 Self-employed or non-employed	..	..	..	..	..	118	766	2 177	3 307	3 667
2400 Unallocable between 2100, 2200 and 2300	..	..	..	..	..	0	0	0	0	0
3000 Taxes on payroll and workforce	**0**	**0**	**0**	**0**	**0**	**0**	**0**	**0**	**0**	**0**
4000 Taxes on property	**5 018**	**24 415**	**40 495**	**65 969**	**72 243**	**0**	**0**	**0**	**0**	**0**
4100 Recurrent taxes on immovable property	4 770	23 150	37 409	57 241	63 060	..	..	..	..	..
4200 Recurrent taxes on net wealth	0	0	0	0	0	..	..	..	..	..
4300 Estate, inheritance and gift taxes	0	0	0	0	0	..	..	..	..	..
4400 Taxes on financial and capital transactions	0	0	375	1 063	1 346	..	..	..	..	..
4500 Non-recurrent taxes	248	1 265	2 711	7 665	7 837	..	..	..	..	..
4600 Other recurrent taxes on property	0	0	0	0	0	..	..	..	..	..
5000 Taxes on goods and services	**142**	**406**	**833**	**1 149**	**1 228**	**0**	**0**	**0**	**0**	**0**
5100 Taxes on production, sale, transfer, etc	22	51	104	126	192	..	..	..	..	..
5110 General taxes	10	40	88	63	72	..	..	..	..	..
5120 Taxes on specific goods and services	12	11	16	63	120	..	..	..	..	..
5130 Unallocable between 5110 and 5120	0	0	0	0	0	..	..	..	..	..
5200 Taxes on use of goods and perform activities	120	355	729	1 023	1 036	..	..	..	..	..
5300 Unallocable between 5100 and 5200	0	0	0	0	0	..	..	..	..	..
6000 Other taxes	**525**	**3 662**	**1 483**	**748**	**750**	**0**	**0**	**0**	**0**	**0**
6100 Paid solely by business	437	2 946	541	0	0	..	..	..	..	..
6200 Other	88	716	942	748	750	..	..	..	..	..
Total tax revenue	**5 685**	**28 483**	**42 811**	**67 866**	**74 221**	**5 787**	**40 559**	**38 834**	**58 876**	**65 610**

.. Not available

StatLink https://doi.org/10.1787/888934212478

Table 6.5. Chile, tax revenues by sub-sectors of government

Million CLP

	Central government					State/Regional				
	1975	1995	2005	2015	2018	1975	1995	2005	2015	2018
1000 Taxes on income, profits and capital gains	..	**1 359 694**	**5 171 293**	**11 840 521**	**14 418 859**	..	..	..	..	..
1100 Of individuals	..	281 293	738 620	3 199 876	2 701 416	..	..	..	..	..
1200 Corporate	..	836 725	3 155 480	6 839 133	8 920 497	..	..	..	..	..
1300 Unallocable between 1100 and 1200	..	241 676	1 277 193	1 801 512	2 796 947	..	..	..	..	..
2000 Social security contributions	..	**155 855**	**287 422**	**434 658**	**473 962**	..	..	..	..	..
2100 Employees	..	142 001	249 526	370 744	391 050	..	..	..	..	..
2200 Employers	..	13 854	37 896	63 914	82 912	..	..	..	..	..
2300 Self-employed or non-employed	..	0	0	0	0	..	..	..	..	..
2400 Unallocable between 2100, 2200 and 2300	..	0	0	0	0	..	..	..	..	..
3000 Taxes on payroll and workforce	..	**0**	**0**	**0**	**0**	..	..	..	..	..
4000 Taxes on property	..	**181 432**	**490 120**	**379 603**	**736 328**	..	..	..	..	..
4100 Recurrent taxes on immovable property	..	13 044	4 909	15 249	22 957	..	..	..	..	..
4200 Recurrent taxes on net wealth	..	0	0	0	0	..	..	..	..	..
4300 Estate, inheritance and gift taxes	..	13 245	23 184	92 236	125 649	..	..	..	..	..
4400 Taxes on financial and capital transactions	..	155 143	462 027	272 118	587 721	..	..	..	..	..
4500 Non-recurrent taxes	..	0	0	0	0	..	..	..	..	..
4600 Other recurrent taxes on property	..	0	0	0	0	..	..	..	..	..
5000 Taxes on goods and services	..	**3 179 304**	**6 831 482**	**16 181 720**	**19 634 567**	..	..	..	..	..
5100 Taxes on production, sale, transfer, etc	..	3 169 645	6 811 389	16 129 953	19 465 361	..	..	..	..	..
5110 General taxes	..	2 187 602	5 391 285	13 273 958	16 211 646	..	..	..	..	..
5120 Taxes on specific goods and services	..	982 043	1 420 104	2 855 995	3 253 715	..	..	..	..	..
5130 Unallocable between 5110 and 5120	..	0	0	0	0	..	..	..	..	..
5200 Taxes on use of goods and perform activities	..	9 659	20 094	51 767	169 206	..	..	..	..	..
5300 Unallocable between 5100 and 5200	..	0	0	0	0	..	..	..	..	..
6000 Other taxes	..	**-29 554**	**-85 954**	**-579 308**	**-447 692**	..	..	..	..	..
6100 Paid solely by business	..	0	0	0	0	..	..	..	..	..
6200 Other	..	-29 554	-85 954	-579 308	-447 692	..	..	..	..	..
Total tax revenue	..	**4 846 730**	**12 694 362**	**28 257 194**	**34 816 024**	..	..	..	..	..

	Local government					Social Security Funds				
	1975	1995	2005	2015	2018	1975	1995	2005	2015	2018
1000 Taxes on income, profits and capital gains	..	**0**	**0**	**0**	**0**	..	**0**	**0**	**0**	**0**
1100 Of individuals	..	0	0	0	0	..	0	0	0	0
1200 Corporate	..	0	0	0	0	..	0	0	0	0
1300 Unallocable between 1100 and 1200	..	0	0	0	0	..	0	0	0	0
2000 Social security contributions	..	**0**	**0**	**0**	**0**	..	**193 269**	**644 295**	**1 817 831**	**2 312 211**
2100 Employees	..	..	..	..	..	..	193 269	644 295	1 817 831	2 312 211
2200 Employers	..	..	..	..	..	..	0	0	0	0
2300 Self-employed or non-employed	..	..	..	..	..	..	0	0	0	0
2400 Unallocable between 2100, 2200 and 2300	..	..	..	..	..	..	0	0	0	0
3000 Taxes on payroll and workforce	..	**0**	**0**	**0**	**0**	..	**0**	**0**	**0**	**0**
4000 Taxes on property	..	**157 193**	**411 656**	**1 041 671**	**1 350 538**	..	**0**	**0**	**0**	**0**
4100 Recurrent taxes on immovable property	..	157 193	411 656	1 041 671	1 350 538	..	..	..	..	..
4200 Recurrent taxes on net wealth	..	0	0	0	0	..	..	..	..	..
4300 Estate, inheritance and gift taxes	..	0	0	0	0	..	..	..	..	..
4400 Taxes on financial and capital transactions	..	0	0	0	0	..	..	..	..	..
4500 Non-recurrent taxes	..	0	0	0	0	..	..	..	..	..
4600 Other recurrent taxes on property	..	0	0	0	0	..	..	..	..	..
5000 Taxes on goods and services	..	**192 325**	**514 952**	**1 415 658**	**1 835 931**	..	**0**	**0**	**0**	**0**
5100 Taxes on production, sale, transfer, etc	..	52 690	140 703	385 532	487 674	..	..	..	..	..
5110 General taxes	..	0	0	0	0	..	..	..	..	..
5120 Taxes on specific goods and services	..	52 690	140 703	385 532	487 674	..	..	..	..	..
5130 Unallocable between 5110 and 5120	..	0	0	0	0	..	..	..	..	..
5200 Taxes on use of goods and perform activities	..	139 635	374 249	1 030 126	1 348 256	..	..	..	..	..
5300 Unallocable between 5100 and 5200	..	0	0	0	0	..	..	..	..	..
6000 Other taxes	..	**0**	**0**	**0**	**0**	..	**0**	**0**	**0**	**0**
6100 Paid solely by business	..	..	..	..	..	..	..	..	..	..
6200 Other	..	..	..	..	..	..	..	..	..	..
Total tax revenue	..	**349 518**	**926 608**	**2 457 329**	**3 186 469**	..	**193 269**	**644 295**	**1 817 831**	**2 312 211**

.. Not available

StatLink https://doi.org/10.1787/888934212497

Table 6.6. Colombia, tax revenues by sub-sectors of government

Million COP

	Federal government					State/Regional				
	1975	1995	2005	2015	2018	1975	1995	2005	2015	2018
1000 Taxes on income, profits and capital gains	**..**	**3 393 700**	**17 348 618**	**52 656 876**	**64 043 928**	**..**	**0**	**0**	**0**	**0**
1100 Of individuals	..	131 405	3 594 441	9 210 448	12 215 963	..	..	..	..	..
1200 Corporate	..	988 082	13 044 361	41 398 731	48 529 320	..	..	..	..	..
1300 Unallocable between 1100 and 1200	..	2 274 213	709 816	2 047 697	3 298 645	..	..	..	..	..
2000 Social security contributions	**..**	**0**	**0**	**0**	**0**	**..**	**0**	**0**	**0**	**0**
2100 Employees	..	..	..	..	..	..	..	..	..	..
2200 Employers	..	..	..	..	..	..	..	..	..	..
2300 Self-employed or non-employed	..	..	..	..	..	..	..	..	..	..
2400 Unallocable between 2100, 2200 and 2300	..	..	..	..	..	..	..	..	..	..
3000 Taxes on payroll and workforce	**..**	**599 198**	**2 179 842**	**2 797 308**	**3 461 352**	**..**	**0**	**0**	**0**	**0**
4000 Taxes on property	**..**	**0**	**2 863 946**	**12 094 140**	**7 283 483**	**..**	**0**	**0**	**0**	**0**
4100 Recurrent taxes on immovable property	..	..	0	0	0	..	..	..	..	..
4200 Recurrent taxes on net wealth	..	..	462 720	5 352 940	467 925	..	..	..	..	..
4300 Estate, inheritance and gift taxes	..	..	0	0	0	..	..	..	..	..
4400 Taxes on financial and capital transactions	..	..	2 401 226	6 741 200	6 815 558	..	..	..	..	..
4500 Non-recurrent taxes	..	..	0	0	0	..	..	..	..	..
4600 Other recurrent taxes on property	..	..	0	0	0	..	..	..	..	..
5000 Taxes on goods and services	**..**	**4 773 500**	**21 645 318**	**51 831 190**	**63 898 347**	**..**	**771 560**	**2 507 423**	**4 986 314**	**6 812 676**
5100 Taxes on production, sale, transfer, etc	..	4 773 500	21 645 318	51 831 190	63 898 347	..	771 560	2 228 909	4 456 650	6 016 297
5110 General taxes	..	3 427 600	17 427 948	41 659 696	55 879 110	..	0	0	0	0
5120 Taxes on specific goods and services	..	1 345 900	4 217 370	10 171 494	8 019 237	..	771 560	2 228 909	4 456 650	6 016 297
5130 Unallocable between 5110 and 5120	..	0	0	0	0	..	0	0	0	0
5200 Taxes on use of goods and perform activities	..	0	0	0	0	..	0	278 514	529 665	796 379
5300 Unallocable between 5100 and 5200	..	0	0	0	0	..	0	0	0	0
6000 Other taxes	**..**	**17 900**	**682 084**	**419 939**	**541 027**	**..**	**0**	**575 919**	**2 624 769**	**2 606 397**
6100 Paid solely by business	..	0	0	0	0	..	..	0	0	0
6200 Other	..	17 900	682 084	419 939	541 027	..	..	575 919	2 624 769	2 606 397
Total tax revenue	**..**	**8 784 297**	**44 719 808**	**119 799 453**	**139 228 138**	**..**	**771 560**	**3 083 342**	**7 611 084**	**9 419 073**

	Local government					Social Security Funds				
	1975	1995	2005	2015	2018	1975	1995	2005	2015	2018
1000 Taxes on income, profits and capital gains	**..**	**0**	**0**	**0**	**0**	**..**	**0**	**0**	**0**	**0**
1100 Of individuals	..	..	..	..	..	..	..	..	..	..
1200 Corporate	..	..	..	..	..	..	..	..	..	..
1300 Unallocable between 1100 and 1200	..	..	..	..	..	..	..	..	..	..
2000 Social security contributions	**..**	**0**	**0**	**0**	**0**	**..**	**3 159 328**	**7 845 000**	**13 585 138**	**18 192 049**
2100 Employees	..	..	..	..	..	..	..	..	..	..
2200 Employers	..	..	..	..	..	..	..	..	..	..
2300 Self-employed or non-employed	..	..	..	..	..	..	..	..	..	..
2400 Unallocable between 2100, 2200 and 2300	..	..	..	..	..	..	3 159 328	7 845 000	13 585 138	18 192 049
3000 Taxes on payroll and workforce	**..**	**0**	**0**	**0**	**0**	**..**	**0**	**0**	**0**	**0**
4000 Taxes on property	**..**	**365 051**	**1 974 213**	**6 061 965**	**7 981 989**	**..**	**0**	**0**	**0**	**0**
4100 Recurrent taxes on immovable property	..	365 051	1 974 213	6 061 965	7 981 989	..	..	..	..	..
4200 Recurrent taxes on net wealth	..	0	0	0	0	..	..	..	..	..
4300 Estate, inheritance and gift taxes	..	0	0	0	0	..	..	..	..	..
4400 Taxes on financial and capital transactions	..	0	0	0	0	..	..	..	..	..
4500 Non-recurrent taxes	..	0	0	0	0	..	..	..	..	..
4600 Other recurrent taxes on property	..	0	0	0	0	..	..	..	..	..
5000 Taxes on goods and services	**..**	**471 710**	**3 496 411**	**8 899 062**	**10 697 766**	**..**	**0**	**0**	**0**	**0**
5100 Taxes on production, sale, transfer, etc	..	471 710	3 496 411	8 400 241	10 020 693	..	..	..	..	..
5110 General taxes	..	471 710	2 506 452	7 025 204	8 436 909	..	..	..	..	..
5120 Taxes on specific goods and services	..	0	989 959	1 375 037	1 583 783	..	..	..	..	..
5130 Unallocable between 5110 and 5120	..	0	0	0	0	..	..	..	..	..
5200 Taxes on use of goods and perform activities	..	0	0	498 821	677 073	..	..	..	..	..
5300 Unallocable between 5100 and 5200	..	0	0	0	0	..	..	..	..	..
6000 Other taxes	**..**	**355 943**	**588 614**	**4 200 992**	**4 780 896**	**..**	**0**	**0**	**0**	**0**
6100 Paid solely by business	..	0	0	0	0	..	..	..	..	..
6200 Other	..	355 943	588 614	4 200 992	4 780 896	..	..	..	..	..
Total tax revenue	**..**	**1 192 705**	**6 059 238**	**19 162 019**	**23 460 651**	**..**	**3 159 328**	**7 845 000**	**13 585 138**	**18 192 049**

.. Not available

StatLink https://doi.org/10.1787/888934212516

Table 6.7. Czech Republic, tax revenues by sub-sectors of government

Million CZK

	Central government[1]					State/Regional				
	1975	1995	2005	2015	2018	1975	1995	2005	2015	2018
1000 Taxes on income, profits and capital gains	..	**137 616**	**273 549**	**329 768**	**426 988**	..	..	..	..	..
1100 Of individuals	..	70 361	137 937	164 678	230 973	..	..	..	..	..
1200 Corporate	..	67 255	135 611	165 090	196 015	..	..	..	..	..
1300 Unallocable between 1100 and 1200	..	0	0	0	0	..	..	..	..	..
2000 Social security contributions	..	**0**	**0**	**0**	**0**	..	..	..	..	..
2100 Employees	..	..	..	..	..	..	..	..	..	..
2200 Employers	..	..	..	..	..	..	..	..	..	..
2300 Self-employed or non-employed	..	..	..	..	..	..	..	..	..	..
2400 Unallocable between 2100, 2200 and 2300	..	..	..	..	..	..	..	..	..	..
3000 Taxes on payroll and workforce	..	**0**	**0**	**0**	**0**	..	..	..	..	..
4000 Taxes on property	..	**3 857**	**8 050**	**11 607**	**13 789**	..	..	..	..	..
4100 Recurrent taxes on immovable property	..	0	5	20	26	..	..	..	..	..
4200 Recurrent taxes on net wealth	..	0	0	0	0	..	..	..	..	..
4300 Estate, inheritance and gift taxes	..	393	728	20	3	..	..	..	..	..
4400 Taxes on financial and capital transactions	..	3 464	7 317	11 566	13 760	..	..	..	..	..
4500 Non-recurrent taxes	..	0	0	0	0	..	..	..	..	..
4600 Other recurrent taxes on property	..	0	0	0	0	..	..	..	..	..
5000 Taxes on goods and services	..	**175 869**	**343 554**	**505 085**	**594 334**	..	..	..	..	..
5100 Taxes on production, sale, transfer, etc	..	162 913	325 662	487 086	574 100	..	..	..	..	..
5110 General taxes	..	91 673	215 118	333 274	408 538	..	..	..	..	..
5120 Taxes on specific goods and services	..	71 240	110 544	153 812	165 561	..	..	..	..	..
5130 Unallocable between 5110 and 5120	..	0	0	0	0	..	..	..	..	..
5200 Taxes on use of goods and perform activities	..	12 956	17 892	17 999	20 234	..	..	..	..	..
5300 Unallocable between 5100 and 5200	..	0	0	0	0	..	..	..	..	..
6000 Other taxes	..	**545**	**55**	**387**	**258**	..	..	..	..	..
6100 Paid solely by business	..	0	0	0	0	..	..	..	..	..
6200 Other	..	545	55	387	258	..	..	..	..	..
Total tax revenue	..	**317 887**	**625 207**	**846 847**	**1 035 369**	..	..	..	..	..

	Local government					Social Security Funds				
	1975	1995	2005	2015	2018	1975	1995	2005	2015	2018
1000 Taxes on income, profits and capital gains	..	**0**	**0**	**0**	**0**	..	**0**	**0**	**0**	**0**
1100 Of individuals	..	0	0	0	0	..	0	0	0	0
1200 Corporate	..	0	0	0	0	..	0	0	0	0
1300 Unallocable between 1100 and 1200	..	0	0	0	0	..	0	0	0	0
2000 Social security contributions	..	**0**	**0**	**0**	**0**	..	**227 871**	**481 626**	**659 743**	**829 702**
2100 Employees	..	..	..	..	..	..	54 536	108 316	133 878	171 835
2200 Employers	..	..	..	..	..	..	148 342	307 618	417 778	531 640
2300 Self-employed or non-employed	..	..	..	..	..	..	24 993	65 692	108 088	126 227
2400 Unallocable between 2100, 2200 and 2300	..	..	..	..	..	..	0	0	0	0
3000 Taxes on payroll and workforce	..	**0**	**0**	**0**	**0**	..	**0**	**0**	**0**	**0**
4000 Taxes on property	..	**3 778**	**4 987**	**10 313**	**10 829**	..	**0**	**0**	**0**	**0**
4100 Recurrent taxes on immovable property	..	3 778	4 987	10 313	10 829	..	..	..	..	..
4200 Recurrent taxes on net wealth	..	0	0	0	0	..	..	..	..	..
4300 Estate, inheritance and gift taxes	..	0	0	0	0	..	..	..	..	..
4400 Taxes on financial and capital transactions	..	0	0	0	0	..	..	..	..	..
4500 Non-recurrent taxes	..	0	0	0	0	..	..	..	..	..
4600 Other recurrent taxes on property	..	0	0	0	0	..	..	..	..	..
5000 Taxes on goods and services	..	**1 150**	**7 395**	**7 749**	**8 200**	..	**0**	**0**	**0**	**0**
5100 Taxes on production, sale, transfer, etc	..	124	199	292	358	..	..	..	..	..
5110 General taxes	..	0	0	0	0	..	..	..	..	..
5120 Taxes on specific goods and services	..	124	199	292	358	..	..	..	..	..
5130 Unallocable between 5110 and 5120	..	0	0	0	0	..	..	..	..	..
5200 Taxes on use of goods and perform activities	..	1 026	7 196	7 457	7 841	..	..	..	..	..
5300 Unallocable between 5100 and 5200	..	0	0	0	0	..	..	..	..	..
6000 Other taxes	..	**0**	**0**	**0**	**0**	..	**0**	**0**	**0**	**0**
6100 Paid solely by business	..	..	..	..	..	..	..	..	..	..
6200 Other	..	..	..	..	..	..	..	..	..	..
Total tax revenue	..	**4 928**	**12 382**	**18 063**	**19 029**	..	**227 871**	**481 626**	**659 743**	**829 702**

.. Not available

Note: Including taxes collected on behalf of the European Union.

1. Tax revenues of the regions are reported under the heading of central government up to and including 1995 and under local government thereafter.

StatLink https://doi.org/10.1787/888934212535

Table 6.8. Denmark, tax revenues by sub-sectors of government

Million DKK

	Central government					State/Regional				
	1975	1995	2005	2015	2018	1975	1995	2005	2015	2018
1000 Taxes on income, profits and capital gains	**28 694**	**164 962**	**258 922**	**384 883**	**385 420**	..	..	..	..	..
1100 Of individuals	25 904	124 613	167 082	304 329	306 449	..	..	..	..	..
1200 Corporate	2 790	23 803	54 597	57 723	65 207	..	..	..	..	..
1300 Unallocable between 1100 and 1200	0	16 546	37 244	22 832	13 764	..	..	..	..	..
2000 Social security contributions	**143**	**562**	**1 180**	**836**	**762**	..	..	..	..	..
2100 Employees	0	559	1 177	826	751	..	..	..	..	..
2200 Employers	142	3	3	10	12	..	..	..	..	..
2300 Self-employed or non-employed	0	0	0	0	0	..	..	..	..	..
2400 Unallocable between 2100, 2200 and 2300	0	0	0	0	0	..	..	..	..	..
3000 Taxes on payroll and workforce	**0**	**2 262**	**2 907**	**5 894**	**6 314**	..	..	..	..	..
4000 Taxes on property	**1 779**	**7 094**	**11 801**	**11 084**	**11 637**	..	..	..	..	..
4100 Recurrent taxes on immovable property	16	170	0	0	0	..	..	..	..	..
4200 Recurrent taxes on net wealth	414	930	0	0	0	..	..	..	..	..
4300 Estate, inheritance and gift taxes	336	2 372	3 154	5 177	4 810	..	..	..	..	..
4400 Taxes on financial and capital transactions	936	3 584	8 613	5 907	6 828	..	..	..	..	..
4500 Non-recurrent taxes	77	38	34	0	0	..	..	..	..	..
4600 Other recurrent taxes on property	0	0	0	0	0	..	..	..	..	..
5000 Taxes on goods and services	**29 014**	**156 578**	**253 352**	**301 504**	**329 275**	..	..	..	..	..
5100 Taxes on production, sale, transfer, etc	27 338	149 393	239 951	277 791	303 006	..	..	..	..	..
5110 General taxes	15 117	94 368	154 654	191 479	217 046	..	..	..	..	..
5120 Taxes on specific goods and services	12 221	55 026	85 298	86 312	85 960	..	..	..	..	..
5130 Unallocable between 5110 and 5120	0	0	0	0	0	..	..	..	..	..
5200 Taxes on use of goods and perform activities	1 676	4 739	9 379	16 537	17 383	..	..	..	..	..
5300 Unallocable between 5100 and 5200	0	2 446	4 021	7 177	8 887	..	..	..	..	..
6000 Other taxes	**0**	**0**	**203**	**320**	**265**	..	..	..	..	..
6100 Paid solely by business	..	..	203	320	265	..	..	..	..	..
6200 Other	..	..	0	0	0	..	..	..	..	..
Total tax revenue	**59 630**	**331 457**	**528 366**	**704 520**	**733 674**	..	..	..	..	..
	Local government					Social Security Funds				
	1975	1995	2005	2015	2018	1975	1995	2005	2015	2018
1000 Taxes on income, profits and capital gains	**22 171**	**140 762**	**214 581**	**220 815**	**239 221**	**0**	**0**	**0**	**0**	**0**
1100 Of individuals	22 170	140 758	214 581	220 815	239 221	..	..	..	..	..
1200 Corporate	1	5	0	0	0	..	..	..	..	..
1300 Unallocable between 1100 and 1200	0	0	0	0	0	..	..	..	..	..
2000 Social security contributions	**0**	**0**	**0**	**0**	**0**	**58**	**0**	**529**	**542**	**299**
2100 Employees	..	..	..	..	..	0	..	0	0	0
2200 Employers	..	..	..	..	..	58	..	529	542	299
2300 Self-employed or non-employed	..	..	..	..	..	0	..	0	0	0
2400 Unallocable between 2100, 2200 and 2300	..	..	..	..	..	0	..	0	0	0
3000 Taxes on payroll and workforce	**0**	**0**	**0**	**0**	**0**	**0**	**0**	**0**	**0**	**0**
4000 Taxes on property	**3 518**	**10 155**	**17 466**	**28 085**	**29 578**	**0**	**0**	**0**	**0**	**0**
4100 Recurrent taxes on immovable property	3 518	10 155	17 466	28 085	29 578	..	..	..	..	..
4200 Recurrent taxes on net wealth	0	0	0	0	0	..	..	..	..	..
4300 Estate, inheritance and gift taxes	0	0	0	0	0	..	..	..	..	..
4400 Taxes on financial and capital transactions	0	0	0	0	0	..	..	..	..	..
4500 Non-recurrent taxes	0	0	0	0	0	..	..	..	..	..
4600 Other recurrent taxes on property	0	0	0	0	0	..	..	..	..	..
5000 Taxes on goods and services	**0**	**0**	**0**	**0**	**0**	**0**	**0**	**0**	**0**	**0**
5100 Taxes on production, sale, transfer, etc	0	..	..	..	..	..	..	..	..	..
5110 General taxes	0	..	..	..	..	..	..	..	..	..
5120 Taxes on specific goods and services	0	..	..	..	..	..	..	..	..	..
5130 Unallocable between 5110 and 5120	0	0	0	0	0	..	..	..	..	..
5200 Taxes on use of goods and perform activities	..	..	..	..	..	..	..	..	..	..
5300 Unallocable between 5100 and 5200	0	0	0	0	0	..	..	..	..	..
6000 Other taxes	**0**	**0**	**0**	**0**	**0**	**0**	**0**	**0**	**0**	**0**
6100 Paid solely by business	..	..	..	..	..	..	..	..	..	..
6200 Other	..	..	..	..	..	..	..	..	..	..
Total tax revenue	**25 689**	**150 918**	**232 047**	**248 900**	**268 799**	**58**	**0**	**529**	**542**	**299**

.. Not available

Note: Including taxes collected on behalf of the European Union.

StatLink https://doi.org/10.1787/888934212554

Table 6.9. Estonia, tax revenues by sub-sectors of government

Million EUR

	Central government					State/Regional				
	1975	1995	2005	2015	2018	1975	1995	2005	2015	2018
1000 Taxes on income, profits and capital gains	..	**301**	**782**	**1 607**	**1 929**	..	..	..	..	..
1100 Of individuals	..	234	622	1 182	1 411	..	..	..	..	..
1200 Corporate	..	67	160	424	518	..	..	..	..	..
1300 Unallocable between 1100 and 1200	..	0	0	0	0	..	..	..	..	..
2000 Social security contributions	..	**191**	**636**	**1 191**	**1 571**	..	..	..	..	..
2100 Employees	..	0	0	0	0	..	..	..	..	..
2200 Employers	..	191	636	1 179	1 559	..	..	..	..	..
2300 Self-employed or non-employed	..	0	0	12	12	..	..	..	..	..
2400 Unallocable between 2100, 2200 and 2300	..	0	0	0	0	..	..	..	..	..
3000 Taxes on payroll and workforce	..	**0**	**0**	**0**	**0**	..	..	..	..	..
4000 Taxes on property	..	**3**	**0**	**0**	**0**	..	..	..	..	..
4100 Recurrent taxes on immovable property	..	3	..	..	..	..	..	..	..	..
4200 Recurrent taxes on net wealth	..	0	..	..	..	..	..	..	..	..
4300 Estate, inheritance and gift taxes	..	0	..	..	..	..	..	..	..	..
4400 Taxes on financial and capital transactions	..	0	..	..	..	..	..	..	..	..
4500 Non-recurrent taxes	..	0	..	..	..	..	..	..	..	..
4600 Other recurrent taxes on property	..	0	..	..	..	..	..	..	..	..
5000 Taxes on goods and services	..	**350**	**1 385**	**2 864**	**3 506**	..	..	..	..	..
5100 Taxes on production, sale, transfer, etc	..	345	1 348	2 790	3 383	..	..	..	..	..
5110 General taxes	..	266	908	1 873	2 331	..	..	..	..	..
5120 Taxes on specific goods and services	..	79	440	917	1 053	..	..	..	..	..
5130 Unallocable between 5110 and 5120	..	0	0	0	0	..	..	..	..	..
5200 Taxes on use of goods and perform activities	..	5	37	74	123	..	..	..	..	..
5300 Unallocable between 5100 and 5200	..	0	0	0	0	..	..	..	..	..
6000 Other taxes	..	**0**	**0**	**0**	**0**	..	..	..	..	..
6100 Paid solely by business	..	..	..	..	..	..	..	..	..	..
6200 Other	..	..	..	..	..	..	..	..	..	..
Total tax revenue	..	**845**	**2 803**	**5 662**	**7 006**	..	..	..	..	..
	Local government					Social Security Funds				
	1975	1995	2005	2015	2018	1975	1995	2005	2015	2018
1000 Taxes on income, profits and capital gains	..	**0**	**0**	**0**	**0**	..	**0**	**0**	**0**	**0**
1100 Of individuals	..	0	0	0	0	..	0	0	0	0
1200 Corporate	..	0	0	0	0	..	0	0	0	0
1300 Unallocable between 1100 and 1200	..	0	0	0	0	..	0	0	0	0
2000 Social security contributions	..	**0**	**0**	**0**	**0**	..	**149**	**511**	**1 110**	**1 407**
2100 Employees	..	..	..	..	..	..	0	31	99	123
2200 Employers	..	..	..	..	..	..	143	466	1 002	1 276
2300 Self-employed or non-employed	..	..	..	..	..	..	6	14	8	8
2400 Unallocable between 2100, 2200 and 2300	..	..	..	..	..	..	0	0	0	0
3000 Taxes on payroll and workforce	..	**0**	**0**	**0**	**0**	..	**0**	**0**	**0**	**0**
4000 Taxes on property	..	**7**	**32**	**58**	**58**	..	**0**	**0**	**0**	**0**
4100 Recurrent taxes on immovable property	..	7	32	58	58	..	..	..	..	..
4200 Recurrent taxes on net wealth	..	0	0	0	0	..	..	..	..	..
4300 Estate, inheritance and gift taxes	..	0	0	0	0	..	..	..	..	..
4400 Taxes on financial and capital transactions	..	0	0	0	0	..	..	..	..	..
4500 Non-recurrent taxes	..	0	0	0	0	..	..	..	..	..
4600 Other recurrent taxes on property	..	0	0	0	0	..	..	..	..	..
5000 Taxes on goods and services	..	**1**	**7**	**11**	**13**	..	**0**	**0**	**0**	**0**
5100 Taxes on production, sale, transfer, etc	..	0	2	4	6	..	..	..	..	..
5110 General taxes	..	0	0	0	0	..	..	..	..	..
5120 Taxes on specific goods and services	..	0	2	4	6	..	..	..	..	..
5130 Unallocable between 5110 and 5120	..	0	0	0	0	..	..	..	..	..
5200 Taxes on use of goods and perform activities	..	1	5	7	7	..	..	..	..	..
5300 Unallocable between 5100 and 5200	..	0	0	0	0	..	..	..	..	..
6000 Other taxes	..	**0**	**0**	**0**	**0**	..	**0**	**0**	**0**	**0**
6100 Paid solely by business	..	..	..	..	..	..	..	..	..	..
6200 Other	..	..	..	..	..	..	..	..	..	..
Total tax revenue	..	**8**	**40**	**69**	**71**	..	**149**	**511**	**1 110**	**1 407**

.. Not available

Note: Including taxes collected on behalf of the European Union.

StatLink https://doi.org/10.1787/888934212573

Table 6.10. Finland, tax revenues by sub-sectors of government

Million EUR

	Central government					State/Regional				
	1975	1995	2005	2015	2018	1975	1995	2005	2015	2018
1000 Taxes on income, profits and capital gains	**1 304**	**6 538**	**12 885**	**12 127**	**13 855**	..	..	..	..	..
1100 Of individuals	1 146	5 320	8 791	9 248	9 778	..	..	..	..	..
1200 Corporate	157	1 218	4 094	2 879	4 077	..	..	..	..	..
1300 Unallocable between 1100 and 1200	0	0	0	0	0	..	..	..	..	..
2000 Social security contributions	**0**	**25**	**0**	**0**	**0**	..	..	..	..	..
2100 Employees	..	0	..	..	..	..	..	..	..	..
2200 Employers	..	25	..	..	..	..	..	..	..	..
2300 Self-employed or non-employed	..	0	..	..	..	..	..	..	..	..
2400 Unallocable between 2100, 2200 and 2300	..	0	..	..	..	..	..	..	..	..
3000 Taxes on payroll and workforce	**153**	**0**	**0**	**0**	**0**	..	..	..	..	..
4000 Taxes on property	**127**	**533**	**1 169**	**1 414**	**1 536**	..	..	..	..	..
4100 Recurrent taxes on immovable property	0	0	0	0	0	..	..	..	..	..
4200 Recurrent taxes on net wealth	33	35	129	0	0	..	..	..	..	..
4300 Estate, inheritance and gift taxes	14	167	486	631	692	..	..	..	..	..
4400 Taxes on financial and capital transactions	80	331	554	783	844	..	..	..	..	..
4500 Non-recurrent taxes	0	0	0	0	0	..	..	..	..	..
4600 Other recurrent taxes on property	0	0	0	0	0	..	..	..	..	..
5000 Taxes on goods and services	**2 099**	**13 241**	**21 768**	**29 650**	**33 249**	..	..	..	..	..
5100 Taxes on production, sale, transfer, etc	2 082	12 937	21 178	28 592	31 876	..	..	..	..	..
5110 General taxes	1 030	7 621	13 748	18 974	21 364	..	..	..	..	..
5120 Taxes on specific goods and services	1 052	5 316	7 430	9 618	10 512	..	..	..	..	..
5130 Unallocable between 5110 and 5120	0	0	0	0	0	..	..	..	..	..
5200 Taxes on use of goods and perform activities	16	304	590	1 058	1 373	..	..	..	..	..
5300 Unallocable between 5100 and 5200	0	0	0	0	0	..	..	..	..	..
6000 Other taxes	**10**	**90**	**68**	**81**	**44**	..	..	..	..	..
6100 Paid solely by business	0	0	0	0	0	..	..	..	..	..
6200 Other	10	90	68	81	44	..	..	..	..	..
Total tax revenue	**3 693**	**20 427**	**35 890**	**43 272**	**48 684**	..	..	..	..	..

	Local government					Social Security Funds				
	1975	1995	2005	2015	2018	1975	1995	2005	2015	2018
1000 Taxes on income, profits and capital gains	**1 547**	**9 313**	**13 574**	**20 244**	**20 650**	**0**	**0**	**0**	**0**	**0**
1100 Of individuals	1 393	8 319	12 420	18 576	18 791	..	..	..	..	..
1200 Corporate	154	994	1 154	1 668	1 859	..	..	..	..	..
1300 Unallocable between 1100 and 1200	0	0	0	0	0	..	..	..	..	..
2000 Social security contributions	**0**	**0**	**0**	**0**	**0**	**1 347**	**13 493**	**18 879**	**26 639**	**27 647**
2100 Employees	..	..	..	..	..	278	2 537	3 464	6 364	8 102
2200 Employers	..	..	..	..	..	990	9 447	14 127	18 232	17 631
2300 Self-employed or non-employed	..	..	0	0	0	79	1 509	1 288	2 043	1 914
2400 Unallocable between 2100, 2200 and 2300	..	..	0	0	0	0	0	0	0	0
3000 Taxes on payroll and workforce	**0**	**0**	**0**	**0**	**0**	**0**	**0**	**0**	**0**	**0**
4000 Taxes on property	**0**	**441**	**725**	**1 603**	**1 813**	**0**	**0**	**0**	**0**	**0**
4100 Recurrent taxes on immovable property	0	441	725	1 603	1 813	..	..	..	..	..
4200 Recurrent taxes on net wealth	0	0	0	0	0	..	..	..	..	..
4300 Estate, inheritance and gift taxes	0	0	0	0	0	..	..	..	..	..
4400 Taxes on financial and capital transactions	0	0	0	0	0	..	..	..	..	..
4500 Non-recurrent taxes	0	0	0	0	0	..	..	..	..	..
4600 Other recurrent taxes on property	0	0	0	0	0	..	..	..	..	..
5000 Taxes on goods and services	**3**	**7**	**8**	**2**	**1**	**0**	**0**	**0**	**0**	**0**
5100 Taxes on production, sale, transfer, etc	1	1	4	1	1	..	..	..	..	..
5110 General taxes	0	0	0	0	0	..	..	..	..	..
5120 Taxes on specific goods and services	1	1	4	1	1	..	..	..	..	..
5130 Unallocable between 5110 and 5120	0	0	0	0	0	..	..	..	..	..
5200 Taxes on use of goods and perform activities	2	6	4	1	0	..	..	..	..	..
5300 Unallocable between 5100 and 5200	0	0	0	0	0	..	..	..	..	..
6000 Other taxes	**0**	**0**	**0**	**0**	**0**	**0**	**0**	**0**	**0**	**0**
6100 Paid solely by business	..	..	..	..	..	..	..	..	..	..
6200 Other	..	..	..	..	..	..	..	..	..	..
Total tax revenue	**1 550**	**9 761**	**14 307**	**21 849**	**22 464**	**1 347**	**13 493**	**18 879**	**26 639**	**27 647**

.. Not available

Note: Including taxes collected on behalf of the European Union.

StatLink https://doi.org/10.1787/888934212592

Table 6.11. France, tax revenues by sub-sectors of government

Million EUR

	Central government					State/Regional				
	1975	1995	2005	2015	2018	1975	1995	2005	2015	2018
1000 Taxes on income, profits and capital gains	**13 106**	**69 134**	**98 623**	**121 529**	**131 500**	**..**	**..**	**..**	**..**	**..**
1100 Of individuals	8 743	43 963	56 862	75 366	81 605	..	..	..	..	..
1200 Corporate	4 282	25 172	41 761	46 163	49 895	..	..	..	..	..
1300 Unallocable between 1100 and 1200	80	0	0	0	0	..	..	..	..	..
2000 Social security contributions	**419**	**3 733**	**5 796**	**7 941**	**8 297**	**..**	**..**	**..**	**..**	**..**
2100 Employees	419	3 733	4 812	6 048	6 847	..	..	..	..	..
2200 Employers	0	0	984	1 893	1 450	..	..	..	..	..
2300 Self-employed or non-employed	0	0	0	0	0	..	..	..	..	..
2400 Unallocable between 2100, 2200 and 2300	0	0	0	0	0	..	..	..	..	..
3000 Taxes on payroll and workforce	**1 194**	**10 299**	**13 117**	**4 796**	**3 807**	**..**	**..**	**..**	**..**	**..**
4000 Taxes on property	**1 372**	**9 196**	**16 021**	**23 374**	**22 815**	**..**	**..**	**..**	**..**	**..**
4100 Recurrent taxes on immovable property	26	1 849	2 106	3 112	3 293	..	..	..	..	..
4200 Recurrent taxes on net wealth	0	1 309	3 053	5 224	1 847	..	..	..	..	..
4300 Estate, inheritance and gift taxes	616	4 261	9 006	12 317	14 399	..	..	..	..	..
4400 Taxes on financial and capital transactions	731	1 777	1 856	2 721	3 276	..	..	..	..	..
4500 Non-recurrent taxes	0	0	0	0	0	..	..	..	..	..
4600 Other recurrent taxes on property	0	0	0	0	0	..	..	..	..	..
5000 Taxes on goods and services	**26 154**	**127 617**	**165 674**	**175 528**	**198 586**	**..**	**..**	**..**	**..**	**..**
5100 Taxes on production, sale, transfer, etc	25 618	126 699	163 729	173 782	196 342	..	..	..	..	..
5110 General taxes	19 077	89 768	127 096	141 371	155 202	..	..	..	..	..
5120 Taxes on specific goods and services	6 540	36 931	36 633	32 411	41 140	..	..	..	..	..
5130 Unallocable between 5110 and 5120	0	0	0	0	0	..	..	..	..	..
5200 Taxes on use of goods and perform activities	536	918	1 945	1 746	2 244	..	..	..	..	..
5300 Unallocable between 5100 and 5200	..	0	0	0	0	..	..	..	..	..
6000 Other taxes	**49**	**924**	**3 522**	**1 898**	**1 628**	**..**	**..**	**..**	**..**	**..**
6100 Paid solely by business	32	871	3 502	1 892	1 622	..	..	..	..	..
6200 Other	17	53	21	6	6	..	..	..	..	..
Total tax revenue	**42 294**	**220 903**	**302 753**	**335 066**	**366 633**	**..**	**..**	**..**	**..**	**..**

	Local government					Social Security Funds				
	1975	1995	2005	2015	2018	1975	1995	2005	2015	2018
1000 Taxes on income, profits and capital gains	**0**	**0**	**0**	**20**	**22**	**0**	**14 997**	**80 173**	**112 983**	**142 581**
1100 Of individuals	0	0	0	13	11	0	14 997	80 173	112 978	142 580
1200 Corporate	0	0	0	7	11	0	0	0	5	1
1300 Unallocable between 1100 and 1200	0	0	0	0	0	0	0	0	0	0
2000 Social security contributions	**0**	**0**	**0**	**0**	**0**	**33 089**	**217 995**	**275 433**	**362 434**	**372 431**
2100 Employees	..	..	..	..	..	6 683	65 964	65 369	87 719	82 229
2200 Employers	..	..	..	..	..	24 236	135 892	190 090	246 280	263 666
2300 Self-employed or non-employed	..	..	..	..	..	2 170	16 139	19 975	28 435	26 536
2400 Unallocable between 2100, 2200 and 2300	..	..	..	..	..	0	0	0	0	0
3000 Taxes on payroll and workforce	**299**	**2 529**	**5 437**	**9 278**	**10 641**	**107**	**36**	**1 767**	**20 500**	**21 374**
4000 Taxes on property	**2 876**	**27 105**	**44 534**	**68 949**	**74 744**	**0**	**0**	**0**	**0**	**0**
4100 Recurrent taxes on immovable property	2 626	23 117	35 989	57 331	59 518	..	..	..	..	..
4200 Recurrent taxes on net wealth	..	0	0	0	0	..	..	..	..	..
4300 Estate, inheritance and gift taxes	0	0	0	0	0	..	..	..	..	..
4400 Taxes on financial and capital transactions	250	3 988	8 545	11 618	15 226	..	..	..	..	..
4500 Non-recurrent taxes	0	0	0	0	0	..	..	..	..	..
4600 Other recurrent taxes on property	..	0	0	0	0	..	..	..	..	..
5000 Taxes on goods and services	**496**	**8 056**	**14 708**	**43 987**	**51 312**	**301**	**5 708**	**12 776**	**36 159**	**35 392**
5100 Taxes on production, sale, transfer, etc	297	4 168	12 233	39 742	46 454	301	5 429	12 393	35 202	34 306
5110 General taxes	0	0	0	12 973	18 425	248	1 810	4 271	15 569	12 895
5120 Taxes on specific goods and services	297	4 168	12 233	26 769	28 029	53	3 620	8 122	19 633	21 411
5130 Unallocable between 5110 and 5120	..	0	0	0	0	..	0	0	0	0
5200 Taxes on use of goods and perform activities	198	3 888	2 475	4 245	4 858	0	279	383	957	1 086
5300 Unallocable between 5100 and 5200	..	0	0	0	0	..	0	0	0	0
6000 Other taxes	**2 577**	**18 971**	**22 334**	**9 120**	**10 099**	**0**	**0**	**0**	**568**	**355**
6100 Paid solely by business	2 577	18 970	22 334	9 120	10 099	..	..	..	568	355
6200 Other	0	1	0	0	0	..	0	0	0	0
Total tax revenue	**6 248**	**56 661**	**87 013**	**131 354**	**146 818**	**33 497**	**238 737**	**370 149**	**532 644**	**572 133**

.. Not available

Note: Including taxes collected on behalf of the European Union.

StatLink https://doi.org/10.1787/888934212611

Table 6.12. Germany, tax revenues by sub-sectors of government

Million EUR

	Federal government					State/Regional				
	1975	1995	2005	2015	2018	1975	1995	2005	2015	2018
1000 Taxes on income, profits and capital gains	**26 782**	**90 688**	**89 383**	**143 677**	**173 776**	**26 428**	**77 258**	**83 503**	**133 880**	**162 139**
1100 Of individuals	23 469	83 710	77 468	129 731	152 354	23 267	71 598	70 916	118 873	139 717
1200 Corporate	3 314	6 978	11 915	13 946	21 422	3 160	5 659	12 587	15 007	22 422
1300 Unallocable between 1100 and 1200	0	0	0	0	0	0	0	0	0	0
2000 Social security contributions	**0**	**0**	**0**	**0**	**0**	**0**	**0**	**0**	**0**	**0**
2100 Employees	..	..	..	..	..	..	..	..	..	..
2200 Employers	..	..	..	..	..	..	..	..	..	..
2300 Self-employed or non-employed	..	..	..	..	..	..	..	..	..	..
2400 Unallocable between 2100, 2200 and 2300	..	..	..	..	..	..	..	..	..	..
3000 Taxes on payroll and workforce	**0**	**0**	**0**	**0**	**0**	**0**	**0**	**0**	**0**	**0**
4000 Taxes on property	**1 225**	**175**	**0**	**324**	**399**	**2 606**	**9 080**	**8 985**	**17 537**	**20 897**
4100 Recurrent taxes on immovable property	0	0	..	0	0	0	0	0	0	0
4200 Recurrent taxes on net wealth	920	147	..	324	399	1 993	4 163	97	-2	0
4300 Estate, inheritance and gift taxes	0	0	..	0	0	271	1 815	4 097	6 290	6 814
4400 Taxes on financial and capital transactions	305	28	..	0	0	342	3 102	4 791	11 249	14 083
4500 Non-recurrent taxes	0	0	..	0	0	0	0	0	0	0
4600 Other recurrent taxes on property	0	0	..	0	0	0	0	0	0	0
5000 Taxes on goods and services	**35 370**	**125 377**	**147 967**	**199 445**	**207 894**	**13 082**	**62 564**	**82 093**	**107 822**	**122 475**
5100 Taxes on production, sale, transfer, etc	35 370	125 377	147 967	188 868	197 342	10 371	55 506	66 406	99 805	114 535
5110 General taxes	18 458	67 178	74 361	110 451	116 624	9 194	52 783	62 851	96 751	111 313
5120 Taxes on specific goods and services	16 913	58 200	73 170	78 125	80 426	1 177	2 723	3 555	3 054	3 222
5130 Unallocable between 5110 and 5120	0	0	436	292	292	0	0	0	0	0
5200 Taxes on use of goods and perform activities	0	0	0	10 577	10 552	2 711	7 058	15 687	8 017	7 940
5300 Unallocable between 5100 and 5200	0	0	0	0	0	0	0	0	0	0
6000 Other taxes	**0**	**0**	**-1**	**0**	**0**	**0**	**0**	**0**	**0**	**0**
6100 Paid solely by business	..	..	0	..	..	..	..	..	..	..
6200 Other	..	..	-1	0	0	..	..	0	0	0
Total tax revenue	**63 378**	**216 240**	**237 349**	**343 446**	**382 069**	**42 116**	**148 902**	**174 581**	**259 239**	**305 511**

	Local government					Social Security Funds				
	1975	1995	2005	2015	2018	1975	1995	2005	2015	2018
1000 Taxes on income, profits and capital gains	**11 819**	**40 295**	**46 725**	**73 916**	**87 866**	**0**	**0**	**0**	**0**	**0**
1100 Of individuals	9 931	33 761	31 261	50 775	59 825	..	..	..	..	..
1200 Corporate	1 888	6 534	15 464	23 141	28 041	..	..	..	..	..
1300 Unallocable between 1100 and 1200	0	0	0	0	0	..	..	..	..	..
2000 Social security contributions	**0**	**0**	**0**	**0**	**0**	**64 290**	**268 052**	**311 530**	**424 841**	**487 839**
2100 Employees	..	..	..	..	..	28 106	117 916	134 939	186 305	216 745
2200 Employers	..	..	..	..	..	34 609	133 120	148 507	196 679	223 806
2300 Self-employed or non-employed	..	..	..	..	..	1 575	17 016	28 084	41 857	47 288
2400 Unallocable between 2100, 2200 and 2300	..	..	..	..	..	0	0	0	0	0
3000 Taxes on payroll and workforce	**1 533**	**0**	**0**	**0**	**0**	**0**	**0**	**0**	**0**	**0**
4000 Taxes on property	**3 461**	**9 794**	**10 247**	**13 215**	**14 203**	**0**	**0**	**0**	**0**	**0**
4100 Recurrent taxes on immovable property	2 122	7 027	10 247	13 215	14 203	..	..	..	..	..
4200 Recurrent taxes on net wealth	911	2 615	0	0	0	..	..	..	..	..
4300 Estate, inheritance and gift taxes	0	0	0	0	0	..	..	..	..	..
4400 Taxes on financial and capital transactions	428	151	0	0	0	..	..	..	..	..
4500 Non-recurrent taxes	0	0	0	0	0	..	..	..	..	..
4600 Other recurrent taxes on property	0	0	0	0	0	..	..	..	..	..
5000 Taxes on goods and services	**162**	**448**	**3 395**	**5 947**	**8 952**	**0**	**0**	**0**	**0**	**0**
5100 Taxes on production, sale, transfer, etc	94	271	3 136	5 615	8 584	..	..	..	..	..
5110 General taxes	0	0	2 909	4 734	7 512	..	..	..	..	..
5120 Taxes on specific goods and services	94	271	227	881	1 072	..	..	..	..	..
5130 Unallocable between 5110 and 5120	0	0	0	0	0	..	..	..	..	..
5200 Taxes on use of goods and perform activities	68	176	259	332	368	..	..	..	..	..
5300 Unallocable between 5100 and 5200	0	0	0	0	0	..	..	..	..	..
6000 Other taxes	**67**	**130**	**79**	**216**	**270**	**0**	**0**	**0**	**0**	**0**
6100 Paid solely by business	0	0	0	0	0	..	..	..	..	..
6200 Other	67	130	79	216	270	..	..	..	..	..
Total tax revenue	**17 042**	**50 666**	**60 446**	**93 294**	**111 291**	**64 290**	**268 052**	**311 530**	**424 841**	**487 839**

.. Not available

Note: Including taxes collected on behalf of the European Union.

StatLink https://doi.org/10.1787/888934212630

Table 6.13. Greece, tax revenues by sub-sectors of government

Million EUR

	Central government					State/Regional				
	1975	1995	2005	2015	2018	1975	1995	2005	2015	2018
1000 Taxes on income, profits and capital gains	**64**	**5 456**	**16 101**	**14 577**	**16 459**	**..**	**..**	**..**	**..**	**..**
1100 Of individuals	43	3 011	8 719	10 146	11 541	..	..	..	..	..
1200 Corporate	17	2 067	6 487	3 800	3 998	..	..	..	..	..
1300 Unallocable between 1100 and 1200	4	378	895	631	920	..	..	..	..	..
2000 Social security contributions	**0**	**380**	**1 048**	**745**	**68**	**..**	**..**	**..**	**..**	**..**
2100 Employees	..	380	1 031	744	68	..	..	..	..	..
2200 Employers	..	0	17	1	0	..	..	..	..	..
2300 Self-employed or non-employed	..	0	0	0	0	..	..	..	..	..
2400 Unallocable between 2100, 2200 and 2300	..	..	0	0	0	..	..	..	..	..
3000 Taxes on payroll and workforce	**1**	**0**	**0**	**0**	**0**	**..**	**..**	**..**	**..**	**..**
4000 Taxes on property	**47**	**1 060**	**2 263**	**3 931**	**3 958**	**..**	**..**	**..**	**..**	**..**
4100 Recurrent taxes on immovable property	1	0	0	3 046	2 992	..	..	..	..	..
4200 Recurrent taxes on net wealth	0	138	284	180	181	..	..	..	..	..
4300 Estate, inheritance and gift taxes	5	274	258	134	135	..	..	..	..	..
4400 Taxes on financial and capital transactions	41	641	1 469	509	640	..	..	..	..	..
4500 Non-recurrent taxes	0	0	73	0	0	..	..	..	..	..
4600 Other recurrent taxes on property	0	7	179	62	10	..	..	..	..	..
5000 Taxes on goods and services	**224**	**10 586**	**21 526**	**25 180**	**27 838**	**..**	**..**	**..**	**..**	**..**
5100 Taxes on production, sale, transfer, etc	205	9 953	19 454	20 899	24 132	..	..	..	..	..
5110 General taxes	90	5 504	13 605	12 904	15 299	..	..	..	..	..
5120 Taxes on specific goods and services	114	4 413	5 772	7 901	8 702	..	..	..	..	..
5130 Unallocable between 5110 and 5120	0	36	77	94	131	..	..	..	..	..
5200 Taxes on use of goods and perform activities	20	385	1 780	3 187	3 073	..	..	..	..	..
5300 Unallocable between 5100 and 5200	0	248	292	1 094	633	..	..	..	..	..
6000 Other taxes	**0**	**0**	**0**	**0**	**0**	**..**	**..**	**..**	**..**	**..**
6100 Paid solely by business	..	..	..	..	..	..	..	..	..	..
6200 Other	..	..	..	..	..	..	..	..	..	..
Total tax revenue	**337**	**17 482**	**40 938**	**44 433**	**48 323**	**..**	**..**	**..**	**..**	**..**

	Local government					Social Security Funds				
	1975	1995	2005	2015	2018	1975	1995	2005	2015	2018
1000 Taxes on income, profits and capital gains	**3**	**0**	**0**	**0**	**0**	**0**	**0**	**0**	**9**	**9**
1100 Of individuals	2	..	..	..	..	0	0	0	9	9
1200 Corporate	0	0	0	0	0	0	0	0	0	0
1300 Unallocable between 1100 and 1200	1	0	0	0	0	0	0	0	0	0
2000 Social security contributions	**0**	**0**	**0**	**0**	**0**	**148**	**7 991**	**20 288**	**18 062**	**21 405**
2100 Employees	..	..	..	..	..	62	4 181	10 206	10 351	11 819
2200 Employers	..	..	..	..	..	62	3 810	10 082	7 711	9 586
2300 Self-employed or non-employed	..	..	..	..	..	0	0	0	0	0
2400 Unallocable between 2100, 2200 and 2300	..	..	..	..	..	24	0	0	0	0
3000 Taxes on payroll and workforce	**0**	**0**	**0**	**0**	**0**	**0**	**0**	**0**	**0**	**0**
4000 Taxes on property	**1**	**447**	**1 208**	**1 449**	**1 596**	**0**	**66**	**361**	**38**	**0**
4100 Recurrent taxes on immovable property	0	180	420	546	602	..	32	83	0	0
4200 Recurrent taxes on net wealth	0	267	788	903	994	..	0	0	0	0
4300 Estate, inheritance and gift taxes	0	0	0	0	0	..	0	0	0	0
4400 Taxes on financial and capital transactions	0	0	0	0	0	..	34	278	38	0
4500 Non-recurrent taxes	0	0	0	0	0	..	0	0	0	0
4600 Other recurrent taxes on property	0	0	0	0	0	..	0	0	0	0
5000 Taxes on goods and services	**10**	**89**	**197**	**96**	**110**	**0**	**124**	**248**	**240**	**119**
5100 Taxes on production, sale, transfer, etc	7	87	185	82	96	..	102	195	224	115
5110 General taxes	2	32	26	3	2	..	86	85	170	84
5120 Taxes on specific goods and services	6	55	159	79	94	..	16	110	47	20
5130 Unallocable between 5110 and 5120	0	0	0	0	0	..	0	0	7	11
5200 Taxes on use of goods and perform activities	3	2	12	14	14	..	22	53	16	4
5300 Unallocable between 5100 and 5200	0	0	0	0	0	..	0	0	0	0
6000 Other taxes	**0**	**0**	**0**	**0**	**0**	**0**	**0**	**0**	**0**	**0**
6100 Paid solely by business	..	..	..	..	..	..	..	..	..	..
6200 Other	..	..	..	..	..	..	..	..	..	..
Total tax revenue	**17**	**536**	**1 405**	**1 545**	**1 706**	**148**	**8 181**	**20 897**	**18 349**	**21 533**

.. Not available

Note: Including taxes collected on behalf of the European Union.

StatLink https://doi.org/10.1787/888934212649

Table 6.14. Hungary, tax revenues by sub-sectors of government

Million HUF

	Central government					State/Regional				
	1975	1995	2005	2015	2018	1975	1995	2005	2015	2018
1000 Taxes on income, profits and capital gains	..	**498 608**	**1 915 178**	**2 299 697**	**2 773 438**	..	..	..	..	..
1100 Of individuals	..	383 744	1 449 552	1 698 410	2 201 541	..	..	..	..	..
1200 Corporate	..	106 259	465 626	601 287	571 897	..	..	..	..	..
1300 Unallocable between 1100 and 1200	..	8 605	0	0	0	..	..	..	..	..
2000 Social security contributions	..	**69 554**	**235 148**	**148 044**	**199 663**	..	..	..	..	..
2100 Employees	..	18 468	53 611	144 868	198 311	..	..	..	..	..
2200 Employers	..	51 086	175 013	3 176	1 352	..	..	..	..	..
2300 Self-employed or non-employed	..	0	0	0	0	..	..	..	..	..
2400 Unallocable between 2100, 2200 and 2300	..	0	6 524	0	0	..	..	..	..	..
3000 Taxes on payroll and workforce	..	**5 474**	**39 459**	**231 467**	**399 066**	..	..	..	..	..
4000 Taxes on property	..	**11 463**	**63 007**	**292 329**	**252 926**	..	..	..	..	..
4100 Recurrent taxes on immovable property	..	0	0	55 906	54 254	..	..	..	..	..
4200 Recurrent taxes on net wealth	..	0	0	135 661	42 591	..	..	..	..	..
4300 Estate, inheritance and gift taxes	..	1 364	7 678	7 373	8 519	..	..	..	..	..
4400 Taxes on financial and capital transactions	..	10 099	55 329	93 389	147 562	..	..	..	..	..
4500 Non-recurrent taxes	..	0	0	0	0	..	..	..	..	..
4600 Other recurrent taxes on property	..	0	0	0	0	..	..	..	..	..
5000 Taxes on goods and services	..	**924 906**	**2 870 189**	**5 168 034**	**6 193 250**	..	..	..	..	..
5100 Taxes on production, sale, transfer, etc	..	919 500	2 854 738	5 060 613	6 064 208	..	..	..	..	..
5110 General taxes	..	423 954	1 972 998	3 485 479	4 290 358	..	..	..	..	..
5120 Taxes on specific goods and services	..	495 546	881 740	1 575 134	1 773 850	..	..	..	..	..
5130 Unallocable between 5110 and 5120	..	0	0	0	0	..	..	..	..	..
5200 Taxes on use of goods and perform activities	..	5 406	15 451	107 421	129 042	..	..	..	..	..
5300 Unallocable between 5100 and 5200	..	0	0	0	0	..	..	..	..	..
6000 Other taxes	..	**8 901**	**44 873**	**42 803**	**31 608**	..	..	..	..	..
6100 Paid solely by business	..	..	23 710	21 294	22 798	..	..	..	..	..
6200 Other	..	..	0	0	0	..	..	..	..	..
Total tax revenue	..	**1 518 905**	**5 167 853**	**8 182 374**	**9 849 951**	..	..	..	..	..

	Local government					Social Security Funds				
	1975	1995	2005	2015	2018	1975	1995	2005	2015	2018
1000 Taxes on income, profits and capital gains	..	**0**	**173**	**45**	**33**	..	**0**	**26 307**	**126 216**	**138 708**
1100 Of individuals	..	0	173	45	33	..	0	26 307	126 216	138 708
1200 Corporate	..	0	0	0	0	..	0	0	0	0
1300 Unallocable between 1100 and 1200	..	0	0	0	0	..	0	0	0	0
2000 Social security contributions	..	**0**	**0**	**0**	**0**	..	**778 467**	**2 452 562**	**4 285 420**	**4 849 929**
2100 Employees	..	..	..	..	..	..	116 824	530 098	1 626 055	2 234 353
2200 Employers	..	..	..	..	..	..	632 478	1 894 306	2 634 154	2 588 795
2300 Self-employed or non-employed	..	..	..	..	..	..	27 466	2 080	0	0
2400 Unallocable between 2100, 2200 and 2300	..	..	..	..	..	..	1 699	26 078	25 211	26 781
3000 Taxes on payroll and workforce	..	**1 075**	**1 153**	**0**	**0**	..	**0**	**44 397**	**10 283**	**11 113**
4000 Taxes on property	..	**17 531**	**123 929**	**145 000**	**164 878**	..	**0**	**0**	**0**	**0**
4100 Recurrent taxes on immovable property	..	6 068	58 836	145 000	164 878	..	..	..	..	..
4200 Recurrent taxes on net wealth	..	0	0	0	0	..	..	..	..	..
4300 Estate, inheritance and gift taxes	..	1 364	7 932	0	0	..	..	..	..	..
4400 Taxes on financial and capital transactions	..	10 099	57 162	0	0	..	..	..	..	..
4500 Non-recurrent taxes	..	0	0	0	0	..	..	..	..	..
4600 Other recurrent taxes on property	..	0	0	0	0	..	..	..	..	..
5000 Taxes on goods and services	..	**41 970**	**388 385**	**625 571**	**758 926**	..	**0**	**0**	**103 105**	**133 204**
5100 Taxes on production, sale, transfer, etc	..	39 240	337 935	594 855	726 139	..	..	..	103 105	133 204
5110 General taxes	..	38 472	334 077	584 380	711 276	..	..	..	29 882	40 727
5120 Taxes on specific goods and services	..	768	3 858	10 475	14 863	..	..	..	73 223	92 477
5130 Unallocable between 5110 and 5120	..	0	0	0	0	..	..	..	0	0
5200 Taxes on use of goods and perform activities	..	2 730	50 450	30 716	32 787	..	..	..	0	0
5300 Unallocable between 5100 and 5200	..	0	0	0	0	..	..	..	0	0
6000 Other taxes	..	**0**	**0**	**0**	**0**	..	**21 605**	**9 616**	**14 021**	**6 755**
6100 Paid solely by business	..	..	..	..	..	..	..	..	..	..
6200 Other	..	..	..	..	..	..	..	..	..	..
Total tax revenue	..	**60 576**	**513 641**	**770 616**	**923 837**	..	**800 072**	**2 532 882**	**4 539 045**	**5 139 709**

.. Not available

Note: Including taxes collected on behalf of the European Union.

StatLink https://doi.org/10.1787/888934212668

Table 6.15. Iceland, tax revenues by sub-sectors of government

Million ISK

	Central government					State/Regional				
	1975	1995	2005	2015	2018	1975	1995	2005	2015	2018
1000 Taxes on income, profits and capital gains	**68**	**27 156**	**105 705**	**210 536**	**280 954**	..	..	..	..	..
1100 Of individuals	55	22 914	70 944	127 535	181 660	..	..	..	..	..
1200 Corporate	13	4 242	20 297	52 544	67 724	..	..	..	..	..
1300 Unallocable between 1100 and 1200	0	0	14 464	30 457	31 569	..	..	..	..	..
2000 Social security contributions	**17**	**11 452**	**32 777**	**79 707**	**98 230**	..	..	..	..	..
2100 Employees	0	460	..	..	..	..	..	..	..	..
2200 Employers	17	10 992	..	..	..	..	..	..	..	..
2300 Self-employed or non-employed	0	0	..	..	..	..	..	..	..	..
2400 Unallocable between 2100, 2200 and 2300	0	0	32 777	79 707	98 230	..	..	..	..	..
3000 Taxes on payroll and workforce	**27**	**0**	**324**	**6 638**	**8 542**	..	..	..	..	..
4000 Taxes on property	**15**	**7 198**	**13 340**	**8 786**	**10 519**	..	..	..	..	..
4100 Recurrent taxes on immovable property	0	47	0	178	219	..	..	..	..	..
4200 Recurrent taxes on net wealth	5	3 191	2 887	657	100	..	..	..	..	..
4300 Estate, inheritance and gift taxes	0	389	866	2 919	4 703	..	..	..	..	..
4400 Taxes on financial and capital transactions	9	3 571	9 073	4 327	4 962	..	..	..	..	..
4500 Non-recurrent taxes	0	0	248	362	470	..	..	..	..	..
4600 Other recurrent taxes on property	0	0	266	343	65	..	..	..	..	..
5000 Taxes on goods and services	**392**	**66 356**	**168 295**	**259 996**	**336 482**	..	..	..	..	..
5100 Taxes on production, sale, transfer, etc	387	62 140	157 941	250 095	324 763	..	..	..	..	..
5110 General taxes	182	42 358	113 897	183 674	244 624	..	..	..	..	..
5120 Taxes on specific goods and services	205	19 782	44 044	66 421	80 138	..	..	..	..	..
5130 Unallocable between 5110 and 5120	0	0	0	0	0	..	..	..	..	..
5200 Taxes on use of goods and perform activities	5	4 216	10 354	9 901	11 719	..	..	..	..	..
5300 Unallocable between 5100 and 5200	0	0	0	0	0	..	..	..	..	..
6000 Other taxes	**0**	**0**	**1 504**	**38 364**	**17 019**	..	..	..	..	..
6100 Paid solely by business	..	..	565	32 477	10 414	..	..	..	..	..
6200 Other	..	..	939	5 887	6 605	..	..	..	..	..
Total tax revenue	**519**	**112 162**	**321 944**	**604 026**	**751 747**	..	..	..	..	..

	Local government					Social Security Funds				
	1975	1995	2005	2015	2018	1975	1995	2005	2015	2018
1000 Taxes on income, profits and capital gains	**78**	**21 170**	**74 455**	**170 443**	**230 769**	**0**	**0**	**0**	**0**	**0**
1100 Of individuals	74	21 170	74 455	170 443	230 769	..	..	..	..	..
1200 Corporate	4	0	0	0	0	..	..	..	..	..
1300 Unallocable between 1100 and 1200	0	0	0	0	0	..	..	..	..	..
2000 Social security contributions	**0**	**0**	**0**	**0**	**0**	**0**	**0**	**0**	**0**	**0**
2100 Employees	..	..	..	..	..	..	..	..	..	..
2200 Employers	..	..	..	..	..	..	..	..	..	..
2300 Self-employed or non-employed	..	..	..	..	..	..	..	..	..	..
2400 Unallocable between 2100, 2200 and 2300	..	..	..	..	..	..	..	..	..	..
3000 Taxes on payroll and workforce	**0**	**0**	**0**	**0**	**0**	**0**	**0**	**0**	**0**	**0**
4000 Taxes on property	**18**	**5 674**	**13 931**	**34 701**	**46 278**	**0**	**0**	**0**	**0**	**0**
4100 Recurrent taxes on immovable property	18	5 674	13 931	34 701	46 278	..	..	..	..	..
4200 Recurrent taxes on net wealth	0	0	0	0	0	..	..	..	..	..
4300 Estate, inheritance and gift taxes	0	0	0	0	0	..	..	..	..	..
4400 Taxes on financial and capital transactions	0	0	0	0	0	..	..	..	..	..
4500 Non-recurrent taxes	0	0	0	0	0	..	..	..	..	..
4600 Other recurrent taxes on property	0	0	0	0	0	..	..	..	..	..
5000 Taxes on goods and services	**9**	**2 585**	**6 904**	**2 832**	**8 813**	**0**	**0**	**0**	**0**	**0**
5100 Taxes on production, sale, transfer, etc	9	2 585	0	0	0	..	..	..	..	..
5110 General taxes	0	2 585	0	0	0	..	..	..	..	..
5120 Taxes on specific goods and services	9	0	..	..	..	..	..	..	..	..
5130 Unallocable between 5110 and 5120	0	0	0	0	0	..	0	0	0	0
5200 Taxes on use of goods and perform activities	0	0	6 904	2 832	8 813	..	..	..	..	..
5300 Unallocable between 5100 and 5200	0	0	0	0	0	..	..	..	..	..
6000 Other taxes	**14**	**0**	**93**	**0**	**0**	**0**	**0**	**0**	**0**	**0**
6100 Paid solely by business	14	..	93	0	0	..	..	0	0	0
6200 Other	0	..	0	0	0	..	..	0	0	0
Total tax revenue	**119**	**29 429**	**95 383**	**207 976**	**285 861**	**0**	**0**	**0**	**0**	**0**

.. Not available

StatLink https://doi.org/10.1787/888934212687

Table 6.16. Ireland, tax revenues by sub-sectors of government

Million EUR

	Central government					State/Regional				
	1975	1995	2005	2015	2018	1975	1995	2005	2015	2018
1000 Taxes on income, profits and capital gains	**456**	**7 022**	**21 186**	**26 599**	**33 291**	..	..	..	..	..
1100 Of individuals	382	5 563	15 674	19 722	22 889	..	..	..	..	..
1200 Corporate	73	1 458	5 511	6 873	10 402	..	..	..	..	..
1300 Unallocable between 1100 and 1200	0	0	0	4	0	..	..	..	..	..
2000 Social security contributions	**11**	**87**	**217**	**1 834**	**1 904**	..	..	..	..	..
2100 Employees	10	87	217	1 834	1 904	..	..	..	..	..
2200 Employers	0	0	0	0	0	..	..	..	..	..
2300 Self-employed or non-employed	1	0	0	0	0	..	..	..	..	..
2400 Unallocable between 2100, 2200 and 2300	0	0	0	0	0	..	..	..	..	..
3000 Taxes on payroll and workforce	**0**	**209**	**332**	**357**	**565**	..	..	..	..	..
4000 Taxes on property	**37**	**370**	**2 741**	**2 530**	**2 880**	..	..	..	..	..
4100 Recurrent taxes on immovable property	0	15	0	475	482	..	..	..	..	..
4200 Recurrent taxes on net wealth	5	0	0	169	0	..	..	..	..	..
4300 Estate, inheritance and gift taxes	17	76	255	401	518	..	..	..	..	..
4400 Taxes on financial and capital transactions	15	279	2 486	1 484	1 880	..	..	..	..	..
4500 Non-recurrent taxes	0	0	0	0	0	..	..	..	..	..
4600 Other recurrent taxes on property	0	0	0	0	0	..	..	..	..	..
5000 Taxes on goods and services	**671**	**6 763**	**19 122**	**19 686**	**22 184**	..	..	..	..	..
5100 Taxes on production, sale, transfer, etc	639	6 419	18 106	17 709	20 217	..	..	..	..	..
5110 General taxes	223	3 666	12 373	11 831	14 175	..	..	..	..	..
5120 Taxes on specific goods and services	416	2 753	5 733	5 878	6 042	..	..	..	..	..
5130 Unallocable between 5110 and 5120	0	0	0	0	0	..	..	..	..	..
5200 Taxes on use of goods and perform activities	33	344	1 015	1 977	1 967	..	..	..	..	..
5300 Unallocable between 5100 and 5200	0	0	0	0	0	..	..	..	..	..
6000 Other taxes	**0**	**0**	**0**	**12**	**9**	..	..	..	..	..
6100 Paid solely by business	..	..	..	..	..	..	..	..	..	..
6200 Other	..	..	0	12	9	..	..	..	..	..
Total tax revenue	**1 175**	**14 451**	**43 598**	**51 018**	**60 834**	..	..	..	..	..

	Local government					Social Security Funds				
	1975	1995	2005	2015	2018	1975	1995	2005	2015	2018
1000 Taxes on income, profits and capital gains	**0**	**0**	**0**	**0**	**0**	**0**	**0**	**0**	**0**	**0**
1100 Of individuals	..	..	..	..	..	..	..	..	..	..
1200 Corporate	..	..	..	..	..	..	..	..	..	..
1300 Unallocable between 1100 and 1200	0	..	..	..	..	0	..	..	..	..
2000 Social security contributions	**0**	**56**	**90**	**164**	**154**	**198**	**2 215**	**6 230**	**8 527**	**10 649**
2100 Employees	..	56	90	164	154	73	576	1 415	1 856	2 310
2200 Employers	..	0	0	0	0	125	1 528	4 427	6 211	7 734
2300 Self-employed or non-employed	..	0	0	0	0	0	111	388	460	605
2400 Unallocable between 2100, 2200 and 2300	..	0	0	0	0	0	0	0	0	0
3000 Taxes on payroll and workforce	**0**	**0**	**0**	**0**	**0**	**0**	**0**	**0**	**0**	**0**
4000 Taxes on property	**110**	**408**	**1 020**	**1 389**	**1 398**	..	**0**	**0**	**0**	**0**
4100 Recurrent taxes on immovable property	110	408	1 020	1 389	1 398	..	..	..	..	..
4200 Recurrent taxes on net wealth	0	0	0	0	0	..	..	..	..	..
4300 Estate, inheritance and gift taxes	0	0	0	0	0	..	..	..	..	..
4400 Taxes on financial and capital transactions	0	0	0	0	0	..	..	..	..	..
4500 Non-recurrent taxes	0	0	0	0	0	..	..	..	..	..
4600 Other recurrent taxes on property	0	0	0	0	0	..	..	..	..	..
5000 Taxes on goods and services	**0**	**0**	**0**	**0**	**0**	**0**	**0**	**0**	**0**	**0**
5100 Taxes on production, sale, transfer, etc	..	..	..	..	..	..	..	..	..	..
5110 General taxes	..	..	..	..	..	..	..	..	..	..
5120 Taxes on specific goods and services	..	..	..	..	..	..	..	..	..	..
5130 Unallocable between 5110 and 5120	0	..	..	..	..	0	..	..	..	..
5200 Taxes on use of goods and perform activities	..	..	..	..	..	0	0	0	0	0
5300 Unallocable between 5100 and 5200	0	..	..	..	..	0	..	..	..	..
6000 Other taxes	**0**	**0**	**0**	**0**	**0**	**0**	**0**	**0**	**0**	**0**
6100 Paid solely by business	..	..	..	..	..	..	..	..	..	..
6200 Other	..	..	..	..	..	..	..	..	..	..
Total tax revenue	**110**	**464**	**1 110**	**1 552**	**1 552**	**198**	**2 215**	**6 230**	**8 527**	**10 649**

.. Not available

Note: Including taxes collected on behalf of the European Union. The personal income tax data shown for the country table for Ireland is different to the ESA2010 presentation as the expenditure component of the payable tax credits are excluded in accordance with the OECD Interpretative Guide.

StatLink https://doi.org/10.1787/888934212706

Table 6.17. Israel, tax revenues by sub-sectors of government

Million ILS

	Central government					State/Regional				
	1975	1995	2005	2015	2018	1975	1995	2005	2015	2018
1000 Taxes on income, profits and capital gains	..	**37 422**	**73 082**	**113 966**	**135 001**	..	..	..	..	..
1100 Of individuals	..	28 399	47 062	70 885	84 922	..	..	..	..	..
1200 Corporate	..	8 514	21 909	34 676	42 932	..	..	..	..	..
1300 Unallocable between 1100 and 1200	..	509	4 111	8 405	7 147	..	..	..	..	..
2000 Social security contributions	..	**0**	**0**	**0**	**0**	..	..	..	..	..
2100 Employees	..	..	..	..	..	..	..	..	..	..
2200 Employers	..	..	..	..	..	..	..	..	..	..
2300 Self-employed or non-employed	..	..	..	..	..	..	..	..	..	..
2400 Unallocable between 2100, 2200 and 2300	..	..	..	..	..	..	..	..	..	..
3000 Taxes on payroll and workforce	..	**5 007**	**9 920**	**13 770**	**15 828**	..	..	..	..	..
4000 Taxes on property	..	**4 122**	**5 547**	**10 593**	**11 337**	..	..	..	..	..
4100 Recurrent taxes on immovable property	..	786	322	44	25	..	..	..	..	..
4200 Recurrent taxes on net wealth	..	0	0	0	0	..	..	..	..	..
4300 Estate, inheritance and gift taxes	..	0	0	0	0	..	..	..	..	..
4400 Taxes on financial and capital transactions	..	2 049	3 591	6 732	6 660	..	..	..	..	..
4500 Non-recurrent taxes	..	1 287	1 634	3 817	4 652	..	..	..	..	..
4600 Other recurrent taxes on property	..	0	0	0	0	..	..	..	..	..
5000 Taxes on goods and services	..	**38 673**	**75 932**	**136 829**	**147 897**	..	..	..	..	..
5100 Taxes on production, sale, transfer, etc	..	36 637	70 741	128 277	138 931	..	..	..	..	..
5110 General taxes	..	31 975	59 374	107 765	117 251	..	..	..	..	..
5120 Taxes on specific goods and services	..	4 662	11 367	20 512	21 680	..	..	..	..	..
5130 Unallocable between 5110 and 5120	..	0	0	0	0	..	..	..	..	..
5200 Taxes on use of goods and perform activities	..	2 036	5 191	8 552	8 966	..	..	..	..	..
5300 Unallocable between 5100 and 5200	..	0	0	0	0	..	..	..	..	..
6000 Other taxes	..	**0**	**0**	**0**	**0**	..	..	..	..	..
6100 Paid solely by business	..	..	..	..	..	..	..	..	..	..
6200 Other	..	..	..	..	..	..	..	..	..	..
Total tax revenue	..	**85 224**	**164 481**	**275 158**	**310 063**	..	..	..	..	..

	Local government					Social Security Funds				
	1975	1995	2005	2015	2018	1975	1995	2005	2015	2018
1000 Taxes on income, profits and capital gains	..	**0**	**0**	**0**	**0**	..	**0**	**0**	**0**	**0**
1100 Of individuals	..	0	0	0	0	..	0	0	0	0
1200 Corporate	..	..	..	..	..	..	..	..	..	..
1300 Unallocable between 1100 and 1200	..	0	0	0	0	..	0	0	0	0
2000 Social security contributions	..	**0**	**0**	**0**	**0**	..	**14 958**	**34 597**	**59 561**	**69 016**
2100 Employees	..	..	..	..	..	..	7 953	19 720	34 692	39 232
2200 Employers	..	..	..	..	..	..	4 672	10 679	17 247	20 990
2300 Self-employed or non-employed	..	..	..	..	..	..	2 334	4 198	7 622	8 794
2400 Unallocable between 2100, 2200 and 2300	..	..	..	..	..	..	0	0	0	0
3000 Taxes on payroll and workforce	..	**0**	**0**	**0**	**0**	..	**0**	**0**	**0**	**0**
4000 Taxes on property	..	**6 445**	**15 689**	**28 210**	**30 948**	..	**0**	**0**	**0**	**0**
4100 Recurrent taxes on immovable property	..	5 489	13 962	23 721	26 286	..	..	..	..	..
4200 Recurrent taxes on net wealth	..	0	0	0	0	..	..	..	..	..
4300 Estate, inheritance and gift taxes	..	0	0	0	0	..	..	..	..	..
4400 Taxes on financial and capital transactions	..	0	0	0	0	..	..	..	..	..
4500 Non-recurrent taxes	..	956	1 727	4 490	4 662	..	..	..	..	..
4600 Other recurrent taxes on property	..	0	0	0	0	..	..	..	..	..
5000 Taxes on goods and services	..	**401**	**763**	**1 445**	**1 605**	..	**0**	**0**	**0**	**0**
5100 Taxes on production, sale, transfer, etc	..	0	0	0	0	..	..	..	..	..
5110 General taxes	..	0	0	0	0	..	..	..	..	..
5120 Taxes on specific goods and services	..	0	0	0	0	..	..	..	..	..
5130 Unallocable between 5110 and 5120	..	0	0	0	0	..	..	..	..	..
5200 Taxes on use of goods and perform activities	..	401	763	1 445	1 605	..	..	..	..	..
5300 Unallocable between 5100 and 5200	..	0	0	0	0	..	..	..	..	..
6000 Other taxes	..	**0**	**0**	**0**	**0**	..	**0**	**0**	**0**	**0**
6100 Paid solely by business	..	..	..	..	..	..	..	..	..	..
6200 Other	..	..	..	..	..	..	..	..	..	..
Total tax revenue	..	**6 846**	**16 452**	**29 656**	**32 554**	..	**14 958**	**34 597**	**59 561**	**69 016**

.. Not available

StatLink https://doi.org/10.1787/888934212725

Table 6.18. Italy, tax revenues by sub-sectors of government

Million EUR

	Central government					State/Regional				
	1975	1995	2005	2015	2018	1975	1995	2005	2015	2018
1000 Taxes on income, profits and capital gains	**3 897**	**128 458**	**165 580**	**195 451**	**212 301**	..	..	..	..	..
1100 Of individuals	2 767	98 695	131 047	156 320	172 698	..	..	..	..	..
1200 Corporate	1 131	32 890	31 969	31 421	32 937	..	..	..	..	..
1300 Unallocable between 1100 and 1200	0	-3 127	2 564	7 710	6 667	..	..	..	..	..
2000 Social security contributions	**0**	**0**	**0**	**0**	**0**	..	..	..	..	..
2100 Employees	..	..	..	..	..	..	..	..	..	..
2200 Employers	..	..	..	..	..	..	..	..	..	..
2300 Self-employed or non-employed	..	..	..	..	..	..	..	..	..	..
2400 Unallocable between 2100, 2200 and 2300	..	..	..	..	..	..	..	..	..	..
3000 Taxes on payroll and workforce	**0**	**1 136**	**0**	**0**	**0**	..	..	..	..	..
4000 Taxes on property	**587**	**13 546**	**15 717**	**22 226**	**25 747**	..	..	..	..	..
4100 Recurrent taxes on immovable property	4	0	0	3 892	3 815	..	..	..	..	..
4200 Recurrent taxes on net wealth	0	4 494	0	231	311	..	..	..	..	..
4300 Estate, inheritance and gift taxes	39	587	56	638	820	..	..	..	..	..
4400 Taxes on financial and capital transactions	544	8 464	13 794	16 310	18 847	..	..	..	..	..
4500 Non-recurrent taxes	0	0	1 322	303	362	..	..	..	..	..
4600 Other recurrent taxes on property	0	0	545	852	1 592	..	..	..	..	..
5000 Taxes on goods and services	**5 506**	**95 323**	**123 870**	**157 330**	**182 121**	..	..	..	..	..
5100 Taxes on production, sale, transfer, etc	5 306	92 042	121 824	154 713	175 726	..	..	..	..	..
5110 General taxes	2 685	52 531	80 619	93 282	109 333	..	..	..	..	..
5120 Taxes on specific goods and services	2 621	39 245	41 205	61 431	66 393	..	..	..	..	..
5130 Unallocable between 5110 and 5120	0	323	0	0	0	..	..	..	..	..
5200 Taxes on use of goods and perform activities	200	2 802	1 535	2 191	5 201	..	..	..	..	..
5300 Unallocable between 5100 and 5200	0	479	511	426	1 194	..	..	..	..	..
6000 Other taxes	**1**	**0**	**0**	**0**	**0**	..	..	..	..	..
6100 Paid solely by business	0	..	..	..	..	..	..	..	..	..
6200 Other	1	..	..	..	..	..	..	..	..	..
Total tax revenue	**9 991**	**238 462**	**305 167**	**375 007**	**420 169**	..	..	..	..	..

	Local government					Social Security Funds				
	1975	1995	2005	2015	2018	1975	1995	2005	2015	2018
1000 Taxes on income, profits and capital gains	**134**	**5 658**	**18 494**	**30 483**	**16 600**	**0**	**0**	**0**	**0**	**0**
1100 Of individuals	81	145	16 995	28 302	16 600	..	..	..	..	..
1200 Corporate	54	97	1 491	2 109	0	..	..	..	..	..
1300 Unallocable between 1100 and 1200	0	5 416	8	72	0	..	..	..	..	..
2000 Social security contributions	**0**	**0**	**0**	**0**	**0**	**8 607**	**119 612**	**179 362**	**214 376**	**229 607**
2100 Employees	..	..	..	..	..	1 692	23 036	31 998	39 805	42 708
2200 Employers	..	..	..	..	..	6 915	79 716	125 099	143 273	153 920
2300 Self-employed or non-employed	..	..	..	..	..	0	16 860	22 265	31 298	32 979
2400 Unallocable between 2100, 2200 and 2300	..	..	..	..	..	0	0	0	0	0
3000 Taxes on payroll and workforce	**0**	**0**	**0**	**0**	**0**	**0**	**0**	**0**	**0**	**0**
4000 Taxes on property	**29**	**7 915**	**13 484**	**24 033**	**19 186**	**0**	**0**	**0**	**0**	**0**
4100 Recurrent taxes on immovable property	29	7 449	11 736	21 666	18 140	..	..	..	..	..
4200 Recurrent taxes on net wealth	0	0	0	0	0	..	..	..	..	..
4300 Estate, inheritance and gift taxes	0	0	5	36	0	..	..	..	..	..
4400 Taxes on financial and capital transactions	0	466	904	935	0	..	..	..	..	..
4500 Non-recurrent taxes	0	0	481	6	80	..	..	..	..	..
4600 Other recurrent taxes on property	0	0	358	1 390	966	..	..	..	..	..
5000 Taxes on goods and services	**4**	**6 941**	**30 231**	**34 551**	**26 576**	**0**	**0**	**0**	**0**	**0**
5100 Taxes on production, sale, transfer, etc	0	1 505	17 114	15 138	5 590	..	..	..	..	..
5110 General taxes	..	0	4 698	7 410	0	..	..	..	..	..
5120 Taxes on specific goods and services	..	1 505	12 416	7 728	5 590	..	..	..	..	..
5130 Unallocable between 5110 and 5120	..	0	0	0	0	..	..	..	..	..
5200 Taxes on use of goods and perform activities	4	2 838	7 512	8 939	9 261	..	..	..	..	..
5300 Unallocable between 5100 and 5200	0	2 597	5 605	10 474	11 725	..	..	..	..	..
6000 Other taxes	**0**	**0**	**34 690**	**28 072**	**23 949**	**0**	**0**	**0**	**0**	**0**
6100 Paid solely by business	..	..	34 690	28 072	23 949	..	..	..	..	..
6200 Other	..	..	0	0	0	..	..	..	..	..
Total tax revenue	**168**	**20 514**	**96 899**	**117 139**	**86 311**	**8 607**	**119 612**	**179 362**	**214 376**	**229 607**

.. Not available

Note: Including taxes collected on behalf of the European Union.

StatLink https://doi.org/10.1787/888934212744

Table 6.19. Japan, tax revenues by sub-sectors of government

Billion JPY

	Central government					State/Regional				
	1975	1995	2005	2015	2018	1975	1995	2005	2015	2018
1000 Taxes on income, profits and capital gains	**9 747**	**33 255**	**29 975**	**31 607**	**35 403**	..	..	..	..	..
1100 Of individuals	5 482	19 515	16 702	18 178	20 316	..	..	..	..	..
1200 Corporate	4 265	13 740	13 274	13 429	15 087	..	..	..	..	..
1300 Unallocable between 1100 and 1200	0	0	0	0	0	..	..	..	..	..
2000 Social security contributions	**0**	**0**	**0**	**0**	**0**	..	..	..	..	..
2100 Employees	..	..	..	..	..	..	..	..	..	..
2200 Employers	..	..	..	..	..	..	..	..	..	..
2300 Self-employed or non-employed	..	..	..	..	..	..	..	..	..	..
2400 Unallocable between 2100, 2200 and 2300	..	..	..	..	..	..	..	..	..	..
3000 Taxes on payroll and workforce	**0**	**0**	**0**	**0**	**0**	..	..	..	..	..
4000 Taxes on property	**871**	**5 561**	**2 735**	**3 018**	**3 406**	..	..	..	..	..
4100 Recurrent taxes on immovable property	0	406	0	0	0	..	..	..	..	..
4200 Recurrent taxes on net wealth	0	0	0	0	0	..	..	..	..	..
4300 Estate, inheritance and gift taxes	310	2 690	1 566	1 968	2 333	..	..	..	..	..
4400 Taxes on financial and capital transactions	561	2 464	1 169	1 050	1 073	..	..	..	..	..
4500 Non-recurrent taxes	0	0	0	0	0	..	..	..	..	..
4600 Other recurrent taxes on property	0	0	0	0	0	..	..	..	..	..
5000 Taxes on goods and services	**3 888**	**16 147**	**19 580**	**25 345**	**25 414**	..	..	..	..	..
5100 Taxes on production, sale, transfer, etc	3 579	15 083	18 424	24 673	24 725	..	..	..	..	..
5110 General taxes	0	7 238	10 583	17 426	17 681	..	..	..	..	..
5120 Taxes on specific goods and services	3 579	7 845	7 840	7 247	7 045	..	..	..	..	..
5130 Unallocable between 5110 and 5120	0	0	0	0	0	..	..	..	..	..
5200 Taxes on use of goods and perform activities	309	1 065	1 157	671	688	..	..	..	..	..
5300 Unallocable between 5100 and 5200	0	0	0	0	0	..	..	..	..	..
6000 Other taxes	**0**	**0**	**0**	**0**	**2**	..	..	..	..	..
6100 Paid solely by business	..	..	..	..	0	..	..	..	..	..
6200 Other	..	..	..	..	2	..	..	..	..	..
Total tax revenue	**14 506**	**54 963**	**52 290**	**59 969**	**64 224**	..	..	..	..	..

	Local government					Social Security Funds				
	1975	1995	2005	2015	2018	1975	1995	2005	2015	2018
1000 Taxes on income, profits and capital gains	**4 472**	**17 752**	**16 655**	**19 362**	**20 681**	**0**	**0**	**0**	**0**	**0**
1100 Of individuals	2 147	10 283	8 520	12 669	13 176	..	..	..	..	..
1200 Corporate	2 325	7 470	8 135	6 693	7 505	..	..	..	..	..
1300 Unallocable between 1100 and 1200	0	0	0	0	0	..	..	..	..	..
2000 Social security contributions	**0**	**0**	**0**	**0**	**0**	**9 253**	**44 794**	**50 848**	**64 465**	**70 588**
2100 Employees	..	..	..	..	..	3 436	18 404	20 982	28 224	33 656
2200 Employers	..	..	..	..	..	4 825	21 432	23 154	29 479	32 664
2300 Self-employed or non-employed	..	..	..	..	..	992	4 958	6 712	6 763	4 268
2400 Unallocable between 2100, 2200 and 2300	..	..	..	..	..	0	0	0	0	0
3000 Taxes on payroll and workforce	**0**	**0**	**0**	**0**	**0**	**0**	**0**	**0**	**0**	**0**
4000 Taxes on property	**2 029**	**10 653**	**10 593**	**10 382**	**10 789**	**0**	**0**	**0**	**0**	**0**
4100 Recurrent taxes on immovable property	1 848	9 865	10 116	10 005	10 386	..	..	..	..	..
4200 Recurrent taxes on net wealth	0	0	0	0	0	..	..	..	..	..
4300 Estate, inheritance and gift taxes	0	0	0	0	0	..	..	..	..	..
4400 Taxes on financial and capital transactions	181	788	477	377	404	..	..	..	..	..
4500 Non-recurrent taxes	0	0	0	0	0	..	..	..	..	..
4600 Other recurrent taxes on property	0	0	0	0	0	..	..	..	..	..
5000 Taxes on goods and services	**1 636**	**4 941**	**7 206**	**8 942**	**8 838**	**0**	**0**	**0**	**0**	**0**
5100 Taxes on production, sale, transfer, etc	1 234	3 245	5 299	7 198	7 029	..	..	..	..	..
5110 General taxes	0	0	2 551	4 974	4 816	..	..	..	..	..
5120 Taxes on specific goods and services	1 234	3 245	2 747	2 223	2 213	..	..	..	..	..
5130 Unallocable between 5110 and 5120	0	0	0	0	0	..	..	..	..	..
5200 Taxes on use of goods and perform activities	402	1 697	1 907	1 744	1 810	..	..	..	..	..
5300 Unallocable between 5100 and 5200	0	0	0	0	0	..	..	..	..	..
6000 Other taxes	**20**	**329**	**351**	**413**	**443**	**0**	**0**	**0**	**0**	**0**
6100 Paid solely by business	15	307	297	361	378	..	..	..	..	..
6200 Other	5	22	54	52	65	..	..	..	..	..
Total tax revenue	**8 157**	**33 675**	**34 805**	**39 099**	**40 751**	**9 253**	**44 794**	**50 848**	**64 465**	**70 588**

.. Not available

StatLink https://doi.org/10.1787/888934212763

Table 6.20. Korea, tax revenues by sub-sectors of government

Billion KRW

	Central government					State/Regional				
	1975	1995	2005	2015	2018	1975	1995	2005	2015	2018
1000 Taxes on income, profits and capital gains	**344**	**23 000**	**55 109**	**106 162**	**155 969**	..	..	..	..	..
1100 Of individuals	134	13 713	24 766	60 828	84 574	..	..	..	..	..
1200 Corporate	139	8 988	30 343	45 334	71 395	..	..	..	..	..
1300 Unallocable between 1100 and 1200	71	300	0	0	0	..	..	..	..	..
2000 Social security contributions	**0**	**0**	**0**	**0**	**0**	..	..	..	..	..
2100 Employees	..	..	..	..	..	..	..	..	..	..
2200 Employers	..	..	..	..	..	..	..	..	..	..
2300 Self-employed or non-employed	..	..	..	..	..	..	..	..	..	..
2400 Unallocable between 2100, 2200 and 2300	..	..	..	..	..	..	..	..	..	..
3000 Taxes on payroll and workforce	**0**	**0**	**0**	**0**	**0**	..	..	..	..	..
4000 Taxes on property	**65**	**2 482**	**6 769**	**15 164**	**19 920**	..	..	..	..	..
4100 Recurrent taxes on immovable property	0	106	535	1 666	2 229	..	..	..	..	..
4200 Recurrent taxes on net wealth	0	0	0	0	0	..	..	..	..	..
4300 Estate, inheritance and gift taxes	11	1 029	1 873	5 044	7 359	..	..	..	..	..
4400 Taxes on financial and capital transactions	49	1 258	4 363	8 454	10 332	..	..	..	..	..
4500 Non-recurrent taxes	5	89	-2	0	0	..	..	..	..	..
4600 Other recurrent taxes on property	0	0	0	0	..	..	..	..	..	..
5000 Taxes on goods and services	**920**	**29 170**	**63 480**	**93 127**	**113 251**	..	..	..	..	..
5100 Taxes on production, sale, transfer, etc	920	29 170	63 480	93 127	113 251	..	..	..	..	..
5110 General taxes	198	14 637	36 118	54 159	70 009	..	..	..	..	..
5120 Taxes on specific goods and services	722	14 533	27 362	38 968	43 242	..	..	..	..	..
5130 Unallocable between 5110 and 5120	0	0	0	0	..	..	..	..	..	..
5200 Taxes on use of goods and perform activities	0	0	0	0	0	..	..	..	..	..
5300 Unallocable between 5100 and 5200	0	0	0	0	..	..	..	..	..	..
6000 Other taxes	**64**	**2 121**	**2 108**	**3 435**	**4 430**	..	..	..	..	..
6100 Paid solely by business	0	0	0	0	..	..	..	..	..	..
6200 Other	64	2 121	2 108	3 435	4 430	..	..	..	..	..
Total tax revenue	**1 393**	**56 774**	**127 466**	**217 888**	**293 570**	..	..	..	..	..

	Local government					Social Security Funds				
	1975	1995	2005	2015	2018	1975	1995	2005	2015	2018
1000 Taxes on income, profits and capital gains	**36**	**1 704**	**5 500**	**12 989**	**17 007**	**0**	**0**	**0**	**0**	**0**
1100 Of individuals	0	1 137	2 804	6 772	8 700	..	..	..	..	..
1200 Corporate	0	565	2 696	6 217	8 307	..	..	..	..	..
1300 Unallocable between 1100 and 1200	36	3	0	0	0	..	..	..	..	..
2000 Social security contributions	**0**	**0**	**0**	**0**	**0**	**13**	**9 913**	**43 902**	**104 693**	**128 660**
2100 Employees	..	..	..	..	..	0	4 539	17 632	44 281	55 257
2200 Employers	..	..	..	..	..	13	3 918	18 486	47 846	58 712
2300 Self-employed or non-employed	..	..	..	..	..	0	1 456	7 784	12 566	14 691
2400 Unallocable between 2100, 2200 and 2300	..	..	..	..	..	0	0	0	0	..
3000 Taxes on payroll and workforce	**0**	**237**	**514**	**1 122**	**1 492**	**0**	**0**	**0**	**0**	**0**
4000 Taxes on property	**87**	**8 960**	**17 928**	**33 461**	**38 891**	**0**	**0**	**0**	**0**	**0**
4100 Recurrent taxes on immovable property	45	2 636	4 495	10 820	13 360	..	..	..	..	..
4200 Recurrent taxes on net wealth	0	0	0	0	0	..	..	..	..	..
4300 Estate, inheritance and gift taxes	0	0	0	0	0	..	..	..	..	..
4400 Taxes on financial and capital transactions	42	6 324	13 433	22 641	25 531	..	..	..	..	..
4500 Non-recurrent taxes	0	0	0	0	0	..	..	..	..	..
4600 Other recurrent taxes on property	0	0	0	0	..	..	..	..	..	..
5000 Taxes on goods and services	**36**	**4 218**	**7 561**	**17 199**	**19 844**	**0**	**0**	**0**	**0**	**0**
5100 Taxes on production, sale, transfer, etc	19	2 464	5 589	10 127	11 956	..	..	..	..	..
5110 General taxes	0	0	0	6 003	7 462	..	..	..	..	..
5120 Taxes on specific goods and services	19	2 464	5 589	4 124	4 494	..	..	..	..	..
5130 Unallocable between 5110 and 5120	0	0	0	0	..	..	..	..	..	..
5200 Taxes on use of goods and perform activities	17	1 754	1 972	7 072	7 888	..	..	..	..	..
5300 Unallocable between 5100 and 5200	0	0	0	0	..	..	..	..	..	..
6000 Other taxes	**0**	**198**	**4 474**	**6 207**	**7 084**	**0**	**0**	**0**	**0**	**0**
6100 Paid solely by business	..	0	0	0	..	..	..	..	..	..
6200 Other	..	198	4 474	6 207	7 084	..	..	..	..	..
Total tax revenue	**159**	**15 316**	**35 977**	**70 978**	**84 318**	**13**	**9 913**	**43 902**	**104 693**	**128 660**

.. Not available

StatLink https://doi.org/10.1787/888934212782

Table 6.21. Latvia, tax revenues by sub-sectors of government

Million EUR

	Central government					State/Regional				
	1975	1995	2005	2015	2018	1975	1995	2005	2015	2018
1000 Taxes on income, profits and capital gains	..	**68**	**453**	**677**	**650**	..	..	..	..	..
1100 Of individuals	..	0	195	289	342	..	..	..	..	..
1200 Corporate	..	68	258	389	308	..	..	..	..	..
1300 Unallocable between 1100 and 1200	..	0	0	0	..	..	..	..	..	..
2000 Social security contributions	..	**0**	**0**	**0**	**86**	..	..	..	..	..
2100 Employees	..	..	..	..	86	..	..	..	..	..
2200 Employers	..	..	..	..	..	..	..	..	..	..
2300 Self-employed or non-employed	..	..	..	..	..	..	..	..	..	..
2400 Unallocable between 2100, 2200 and 2300	..	..	..	..	..	..	..	..	..	..
3000 Taxes on payroll and workforce	..	**0**	**4**	**3**	**3**	..	..	..	..	..
4000 Taxes on property	..	**4**	**48**	**44**	**44**	..	..	..	..	..
4100 Recurrent taxes on immovable property	..	0	0	0	0	..	..	..	..	..
4200 Recurrent taxes on net wealth	..	0	0	0	0	..	..	..	..	..
4300 Estate, inheritance and gift taxes	..	0	0	3	3	..	..	..	..	..
4400 Taxes on financial and capital transactions	..	4	48	42	42	..	..	..	..	..
4500 Non-recurrent taxes	..	0	0	0	0	..	..	..	..	..
4600 Other recurrent taxes on property	..	0	0	0	0	..	..	..	..	..
5000 Taxes on goods and services	..	**453**	**1 553**	**3 156**	**4 009**	..	..	..	..	..
5100 Taxes on production, sale, transfer, etc	..	453	1 510	2 997	3 806	..	..	..	..	..
5110 General taxes	..	343	1 002	2 130	2 698	..	..	..	..	..
5120 Taxes on specific goods and services	..	110	508	867	1 108	..	..	..	..	..
5130 Unallocable between 5110 and 5120	..	0	0	0	0	..	..	..	..	..
5200 Taxes on use of goods and perform activities	..	1	43	159	203	..	..	..	..	..
5300 Unallocable between 5100 and 5200	..	0	0	0	0	..	..	..	..	..
6000 Other taxes	..	**0**	**0**	**0**	**0**	..	..	..	..	..
6100 Paid solely by business	..	..	..	..	..	..	..	..	..	..
6200 Other	..	..	..	..	..	..	..	..	..	..
Total tax revenue	..	**525**	**2 058**	**3 881**	**4 792**	..	..	..	..	..

	Local government					Social Security Funds				
	1975	1995	2005	2015	2018	1975	1995	2005	2015	2018
1000 Taxes on income, profits and capital gains	..	**197**	**538**	**1 156**	**1 399**	..	**0**	**0**	**0**	**0**
1100 Of individuals	..	197	538	1 156	1 399	..	..	..	..	..
1200 Corporate	..	0	0	0	0	..	..	..	..	..
1300 Unallocable between 1100 and 1200	..	0	0	0	0	..	..	..	..	..
2000 Social security contributions	..	**0**	**0**	**0**	**0**	..	**445**	**1 079**	**2 030**	**2 573**
2100 Employees	..	..	..	..	..	..	12	292	585	693
2200 Employers	..	..	..	..	..	..	433	781	1 432	1 855
2300 Self-employed or non-employed	..	..	..	..	..	..	1	7	12	25
2400 Unallocable between 2100, 2200 and 2300	..	..	..	..	..	..	0	0	0	0
3000 Taxes on payroll and workforce	..	**0**	**0**	**0**	**0**	..	**0**	**0**	**0**	**0**
4000 Taxes on property	..	**37**	**88**	**197**	**223**	..	**0**	**0**	**4**	**8**
4100 Recurrent taxes on immovable property	..	37	88	197	223	..	..	..	..	..
4200 Recurrent taxes on net wealth	..	0	0	0	0	..	..	..	..	..
4300 Estate, inheritance and gift taxes	..	0	0	0	0	..	..	0	4	8
4400 Taxes on financial and capital transactions	..	0	0	0	0	..	..	..	..	0
4500 Non-recurrent taxes	..	0	0	0	0	..	..	..	..	..
4600 Other recurrent taxes on property	..	0	0	0	0	..	..	..	..	..
5000 Taxes on goods and services	..	**2**	**8**	**18**	**21**	..	**0**	**0**	**0**	**0**
5100 Taxes on production, sale, transfer, etc	..	0	5	7	9	..	..	..	..	..
5110 General taxes	..	0	0	0	0	..	..	..	..	..
5120 Taxes on specific goods and services	..	0	5	7	9	..	..	..	..	..
5130 Unallocable between 5110 and 5120	..	0	0	0	0	..	..	..	..	..
5200 Taxes on use of goods and perform activities	..	2	3	11	12	..	..	..	..	..
5300 Unallocable between 5100 and 5200	..	0	0	0	0	..	..	..	..	..
6000 Other taxes	..	**0**	**0**	**0**	**0**	..	**0**	**0**	**0**	**0**
6100 Paid solely by business	..	..	..	..	..	..	..	..	..	..
6200 Other	..	..	..	..	..	..	..	..	..	..
Total tax revenue	..	**236**	**634**	**1 371**	**1 644**	..	**445**	**1 079**	**2 034**	**2 581**

.. Not available

Note: Including taxes collected on behalf of the European Union.

StatLink https://doi.org/10.1787/888934212801

Table 6.22. Lithuania, tax revenues by sub-sectors of government

Million EUR

	Central government					State/Regional				
	1975	1995	2005	2015	2018	1975	1995	2005	2015	2018
1000 Taxes on income, profits and capital gains	**..**	**646**	**1 871**	**2 013**	**2 529**	**..**	**..**	**..**	**..**	**..**
1100 Of individuals	..	487	1 435	1 440	1 838	..	..	..	..	..
1200 Corporate	..	160	437	574	691	..	..	..	..	..
1300 Unallocable between 1100 and 1200	..	0	0	0	0	..	..	..	..	..
2000 Social security contributions	**..**	**0**	**0**	**0**	**0**	**..**	**..**	**..**	**..**	**..**
2100 Employees	..	..	..	..	..	..	..	..	..	..
2200 Employers	..	..	..	..	..	..	..	..	..	..
2300 Self-employed or non-employed	..	..	..	..	..	..	..	..	..	..
2400 Unallocable between 2100, 2200 and 2300	..	..	..	..	..	..	..	..	..	..
3000 Taxes on payroll and workforce	**..**	**0**	**0**	**0**	**0**	**..**	**..**	**..**	**..**	**..**
4000 Taxes on property	**..**	**0**	**0**	**1**	**2**	**..**	**..**	**..**	**..**	**..**
4100 Recurrent taxes on immovable property	..	..	..	1	2	..	..	..	..	..
4200 Recurrent taxes on net wealth	..	..	..	0	0	..	..	..	..	..
4300 Estate, inheritance and gift taxes	..	..	..	0	0	..	..	..	..	..
4400 Taxes on financial and capital transactions	..	..	..	0	0	..	..	..	..	..
4500 Non-recurrent taxes	..	..	..	0	0	..	..	..	..	..
4600 Other recurrent taxes on property	..	..	..	0	0	..	..	..	..	..
5000 Taxes on goods and services	**..**	**892**	**2 273**	**4 220**	**5 099**	**..**	**..**	**..**	**..**	**..**
5100 Taxes on production, sale, transfer, etc	..	869	2 235	4 164	5 027	..	..	..	..	..
5110 General taxes	..	635	1 584	2 913	3 552	..	..	..	..	..
5120 Taxes on specific goods and services	..	234	651	1 252	1 475	..	..	..	..	..
5130 Unallocable between 5110 and 5120	..	0	0	0	0	..	..	..	..	..
5200 Taxes on use of goods and perform activities	..	24	38	56	72	..	..	..	..	..
5300 Unallocable between 5100 and 5200	..	0	0	0	0	..	..	..	..	..
6000 Other taxes	**..**	**0**	**0**	**0**	**0**	**..**	**..**	**..**	**..**	**..**
6100 Paid solely by business	..	..	..	..	..	..	..	..	..	..
6200 Other	..	..	..	..	..	..	..	..	..	..
Total tax revenue	**..**	**1 539**	**4 145**	**6 235**	**7 630**	**..**	**..**	**..**	**..**	**..**

	Local government					Social Security Funds				
	1975	1995	2005	2015	2018	1975	1995	2005	2015	2018
1000 Taxes on income, profits and capital gains	**..**	**0**	**0**	**0**	**0**	**..**	**0**	**0**	**0**	**0**
1100 Of individuals	..	..	..	..	..	..	..	..	..	..
1200 Corporate	..	..	..	..	..	..	..	..	..	..
1300 Unallocable between 1100 and 1200	..	..	..	..	..	..	..	..	..	..
2000 Social security contributions	**..**	**0**	**0**	**0**	**0**	**..**	**559**	**1 864**	**4 338**	**5 752**
2100 Employees	..	..	..	..	..	..	17	154	873	1 156
2200 Employers	..	..	..	..	..	..	537	1 522	2 916	3 894
2300 Self-employed or non-employed	..	..	..	..	..	..	4	188	549	702
2400 Unallocable between 2100, 2200 and 2300	..	..	..	..	..	..	0	0	0	0
3000 Taxes on payroll and workforce	**..**	**0**	**0**	**0**	**0**	**..**	**0**	**0**	**0**	**0**
4000 Taxes on property	**..**	**25**	**72**	**125**	**135**	**..**	**0**	**0**	**0**	**0**
4100 Recurrent taxes on immovable property	..	25	71	124	133	..	..	..	..	..
4200 Recurrent taxes on net wealth	..	0	0	0	0	..	..	..	..	..
4300 Estate, inheritance and gift taxes	..	0	1	1	2	..	..	..	..	..
4400 Taxes on financial and capital transactions	..	0	0	0	0	..	..	..	..	..
4500 Non-recurrent taxes	..	0	0	0	0	..	..	..	..	..
4600 Other recurrent taxes on property	..	0	0	0	0	..	..	..	..	..
5000 Taxes on goods and services	**..**	**23**	**17**	**18**	**24**	**..**	**0**	**0**	**0**	**0**
5100 Taxes on production, sale, transfer, etc	..	0	0	0	0	..	..	..	..	..
5110 General taxes	..	..	..	..	..	..	..	..	..	..
5120 Taxes on specific goods and services	..	..	..	..	..	..	..	..	..	..
5130 Unallocable between 5110 and 5120	..	..	..	..	..	..	..	..	..	..
5200 Taxes on use of goods and perform activities	..	23	17	18	24	..	..	..	..	..
5300 Unallocable between 5100 and 5200	..	0	0	0	0	..	..	..	..	..
6000 Other taxes	**..**	**0**	**0**	**0**	**0**	**..**	**0**	**0**	**0**	**0**
6100 Paid solely by business	..	..	..	..	..	..	..	..	..	..
6200 Other	..	..	..	..	..	..	..	..	..	..
Total tax revenue	**..**	**48**	**89**	**143**	**159**	**..**	**559**	**1 864**	**4 338**	**5 752**

.. Not available

Note: Including taxes collected on behalf of the European Union.

StatLink https://doi.org/10.1787/888934212820

Table 6.23. Luxembourg, tax revenues by sub-sectors of government

Million EUR

	Central government					State/Regional				
	1975	1995	2005	2015	2018	1975	1995	2005	2015	2018
1000 Taxes on income, profits and capital gains	**353**	**1 873**	**3 454**	**6 405**	**8 392**	..	..	..	..	..
1100 Of individuals	254	1 214	2 161	4 716	5 599	..	..	..	..	..
1200 Corporate	99	659	1 293	1 689	2 793	..	..	..	..	..
1300 Unallocable between 1100 and 1200	0	0	0	0	0	..	..	..	..	..
2000 Social security contributions	**4**	**20**	**89**	**150**	**169**	..	..	..	..	..
2100 Employees	3	15	89	150	169	..	..	..	..	..
2200 Employers	0	0	0	0	0	..	..	..	..	..
2300 Self-employed or non-employed	1	5	0	0	0	..	..	..	..	..
2400 Unallocable between 2100, 2200 and 2300	0	0	0	0	0	..	..	..	..	..
3000 Taxes on payroll and workforce	**0**	**0**	**0**	**0**	**0**	..	..	..	..	..
4000 Taxes on property	**42**	**371**	**928**	**1 661**	**2 244**	..	..	..	..	..
4100 Recurrent taxes on immovable property	0	0	0	0	0	..	..	..	..	..
4200 Recurrent taxes on net wealth	21	268	698	1 318	1 692	..	..	..	..	..
4300 Estate, inheritance and gift taxes	3	15	44	74	91	..	..	..	..	..
4400 Taxes on financial and capital transactions	18	88	186	269	460	..	..	..	..	..
4500 Non-recurrent taxes	0	0	0	0	0	..	..	..	..	..
4600 Other recurrent taxes on property	0	0	0	0	0	..	..	..	..	..
5000 Taxes on goods and services	**189**	**1 374**	**3 241**	**4 895**	**5 492**	..	..	..	..	..
5100 Taxes on production, sale, transfer, etc	182	1 350	3 202	4 810	5 396	..	..	..	..	..
5110 General taxes	112	670	1 812	3 375	3 669	..	..	..	..	..
5120 Taxes on specific goods and services	70	680	1 390	1 435	1 727	..	..	..	..	..
5130 Unallocable between 5110 and 5120	0	0	0	0	0	..	..	..	..	..
5200 Taxes on use of goods and perform activities	7	23	39	85	96	..	..	..	..	..
5300 Unallocable between 5100 and 5200	0	0	0	0	0	..	..	..	..	..
6000 Other taxes	**0**	**6**	**11**	**27**	**27**	..	..	..	..	..
6100 Paid solely by business	..	6	10	27	27	..	..	..	..	..
6200 Other	..	0	0	0	0	..	..	..	..	..
Total tax revenue	**588**	**3 644**	**7 723**	**13 137**	**16 324**	..	..	..	..	..

	Local government					Social Security Funds				
	1975	1995	2005	2015	2018	1975	1995	2005	2015	2018
1000 Taxes on income, profits and capital gains	**46**	**331**	**460**	**606**	**1 000**	**0**	**0**	**0**	**0**	**0**
1100 Of individuals	0	0	0	0	0	..	..	..	..	..
1200 Corporate	46	331	460	606	1 000	..	..	..	..	..
1300 Unallocable between 1100 and 1200	0	0	0	0	0	..	0	0	0	0
2000 Social security contributions	**0**	**0**	**0**	**0**	**0**	**268**	**1 460**	**3 086**	**5 397**	**6 313**
2100 Employees	..	..	..	..	..	102	577	1 321	2 348	2 803
2200 Employers	..	..	..	..	..	150	684	1 378	2 335	2 708
2300 Self-employed or non-employed	..	..	..	..	..	16	200	387	714	802
2400 Unallocable between 2100, 2200 and 2300	..	..	..	..	..	0	0	0	0	0
3000 Taxes on payroll and workforce	**9**	**0**	**0**	**0**	**0**	**0**	**0**	**0**	**0**	**0**
4000 Taxes on property	**6**	**21**	**35**	**54**	**71**	**0**	**0**	**0**	**0**	**0**
4100 Recurrent taxes on immovable property	6	17	26	36	38	..	..	..	..	..
4200 Recurrent taxes on net wealth	0	0	0	0	0	..	..	..	..	..
4300 Estate, inheritance and gift taxes	0	0	0	0	0	..	..	..	..	..
4400 Taxes on financial and capital transactions	0	4	10	18	33	..	..	..	..	..
4500 Non-recurrent taxes	0	0	0	0	0	..	..	..	..	..
4600 Other recurrent taxes on property	0	0	0	0	0	..	0	0	0	0
5000 Taxes on goods and services	**1**	**4**	**8**	**10**	**10**	**0**	**0**	**0**	**0**	**0**
5100 Taxes on production, sale, transfer, etc	1	3	7	8	8	..	..	..	..	..
5110 General taxes	0	0	0	0	0	..	..	..	..	..
5120 Taxes on specific goods and services	1	3	7	8	8	..	..	..	..	..
5130 Unallocable between 5110 and 5120	0	0	0	0	0	..	0	0	0	0
5200 Taxes on use of goods and perform activities	0	1	1	1	1	..	..	..	..	..
5300 Unallocable between 5100 and 5200	0	0	0	0	0	..	0	0	0	0
6000 Other taxes	**0**	**1**	**2**	**1**	**1**	**0**	**0**	**0**	**0**	**0**
6100 Paid solely by business	..	1	2	1	1	..	..	..	..	..
6200 Other	..	0	0	0	0	..	0	0	0	0
Total tax revenue	**62**	**357**	**505**	**671**	**1 082**	**268**	**1 460**	**3 086**	**5 397**	**6 313**

.. Not available

Note: Including taxes collected on behalf of the European Union.

StatLink https://doi.org/10.1787/888934212839

Table 6.24. Mexico, tax revenues by sub-sectors of government

Million MXN

	Federal government					State/Regional				
	1975	1995	2005	2015	2018	1975	1995	2005	2015	2018
1000 Taxes on income, profits and capital gains	..	76 148	402 036	1 230 555	1 671 513	..	1	0	0	0
1100 Of individuals	..	..	195 869	609 384	804 236	..	..	..	..	..
1200 Corporate	..	..	135 840	592 443	809 834	..	..	..	..	..
1300 Unallocable between 1100 and 1200	..	76 148	70 327	28 728	57 443	..	1	..	..	..
2000 Social security contributions	..	0	0	0	0	..	0	0	0	0
2100 Employees	..	..	..	..	..	..	..	..	..	..
2200 Employers	..	..	..	..	..	..	..	..	..	..
2300 Self-employed or non-employed	..	..	..	..	..	..	..	..	..	..
2400 Unallocable between 2100, 2200 and 2300	..	..	..	..	..	..	..	..	..	..
3000 Taxes on payroll and workforce	..	0	0	0	0	..	2 976	20 429	70 221	93 303
4000 Taxes on property	..	0	0	0	0	..	2 927	10 905	22 481	28 676
4100 Recurrent taxes on immovable property	..	..	..	..	..	..	2 198	6 544	14 245	17 812
4200 Recurrent taxes on net wealth	..	..	..	..	..	..	0	0	0	0
4300 Estate, inheritance and gift taxes	..	..	..	..	..	..	2	0	0	0
4400 Taxes on financial and capital transactions	..	..	..	..	..	..	727	4 361	8 235	10 864
4500 Non-recurrent taxes	..	..	..	..	..	..	0	0	0	0
4600 Other recurrent taxes on property	..	..	..	..	..	..	0	0	0	0
5000 Taxes on goods and services	..	91 452	416 533	1 116 026	1 355 600	..	441	2 124	24 355	24 335
5100 Taxes on production, sale, transfer, etc	..	88 372	401 580	1 115 525	1 354 887	..	22	1 364	4 357	7 691
5110 General taxes	..	51 785	318 432	707 213	922 238	..	0	0	0	0
5120 Taxes on specific goods and services	..	36 587	83 148	408 312	432 649	..	22	1 364	4 357	7 691
5130 Unallocable between 5110 and 5120	..	0	0	0	0	..	0	0	0	0
5200 Taxes on use of goods and perform activities	..	3 080	14 954	501	713	..	419	760	19 998	16 645
5300 Unallocable between 5100 and 5200	..	0	0	0	0	..	0	0	0	0
6000 Other taxes	..	5 149	8 616	27 379	46 264	..	228	1 537	6 489	7 404
6100 Paid solely by business	..	0	0	0	0	..	0	0	0	0
6200 Other	..	5 149	8 616	27 379	46 264	..	228	1 537	6 489	7 404
Total tax revenue (collecting government)	..	172 749	827 186	2 373 960	3 073 377	..	6 573	34 995	123 545	153 719
Adjustment[1]	..	-49 115	-278 892	-629 130	0	..	39 225	218 291	494 239	669 105
Total tax revenue (beneficiary government)	..	123 634	548 294	1 744 830	3 073 377	..	45 798	253 286	617 784	822 825

	Local government					Social Security Funds				
	1975	1995	2005	2015	2018	1975	1995	2005	2015	2018
1000 Taxes on income, profits and capital gains	..	16	0	0	0	..	0	0	0	0
1100 Of individuals	..	..	..	..	..	..	..	..	..	..
1200 Corporate	..	..	..	..	..	..	..	..	..	..
1300 Unallocable between 1100 and 1200	..	16	..	..	..	..	..	..	..	..
2000 Social security contributions	..	0	0	0	0	..	50 871	206 551	409 249	509 087
2100 Employees	..	..	..	..	..	..	..	..	..	..
2200 Employers	..	..	..	..	..	..	..	..	..	..
2300 Self-employed or non-employed	..	..	..	..	..	..	..	..	..	..
2400 Unallocable between 2100, 2200 and 2300	..	..	..	..	..	..	50 871	206 551	409 249	509 087
3000 Taxes on payroll and workforce	..	6	32	1	0	..	0	0	0	0
4000 Taxes on property	..	2 702	15 891	35 193	48 433	..	0	0	0	0
4100 Recurrent taxes on immovable property	..	1 854	10 098	23 715	31 632	..	..	..	..	..
4200 Recurrent taxes on net wealth	..	0	0	0	0	..	..	..	..	..
4300 Estate, inheritance and gift taxes	..	0	0	0	0	..	..	..	..	..
4400 Taxes on financial and capital transactions	..	848	5 793	11 477	16 801	..	..	..	..	..
4500 Non-recurrent taxes	..	0	0	0	0	..	..	..	..	..
4600 Other recurrent taxes on property	..	0	0	0	0	..	..	..	..	..
5000 Taxes on goods and services	..	582	288	789	1 723	..	0	0	0	0
5100 Taxes on production, sale, transfer, etc	..	575	214	728	1 630	..	..	..	..	..
5110 General taxes	..	0	0	0	0	..	..	..	..	..
5120 Taxes on specific goods and services	..	572	214	728	1 630	..	..	..	..	..
5130 Unallocable between 5110 and 5120	..	3	0	0	0	..	..	..	..	..
5200 Taxes on use of goods and perform activities	..	7	74	61	94	..	..	..	..	..
5300 Unallocable between 5100 and 5200	..	0	0	0	0	..	..	..	..	..
6000 Other taxes	..	179	1 539	10 743	11 548	..	0	0	0	0
6100 Paid solely by business	..	0	0	0	0	..	..	..	..	..
6200 Other	..	179	1 539	10 743	11 548	..	..	..	..	..
Total tax revenue (collecting government)	..	3 485	17 750	46 726	61 705	..	50 871	206 551	409 249	509 087
Adjustment[1]	..	9 890	60 601	134 892	174 940	..	0	0	0	0
Total tax revenue (beneficiary government)	..	13 375	78 351	181 617	236 645	..	50 871	206 551	409 249	509 087

.. Not available

1. This adjustment is for taxes collected by Federal government in which States and Local governments have a share. Sub-central government's shares cannot be identified by type of tax.

StatLink https://doi.org/10.1787/888934212858

Table 6.25. Netherlands, tax revenues by sub-sectors of government

Million EUR

	Central government					State/Regional				
	1975	1995	2005	2015	2018	1975	1995	2005	2015	2018
1000 Taxes on income, profits and capital gains	**15 075**	**33 520**	**52 640**	**70 849**	**88 769**	..	..	..	..	..
1100 Of individuals	11 713	23 557	33 905	52 405	61 660	..	..	..	..	..
1200 Corporate	3 361	9 963	18 735	18 444	27 109	..	..	..	..	..
1300 Unallocable between 1100 and 1200	0	0	0	0	0	..	..	..	..	..
2000 Social security contributions	**0**	**0**	**0**	**0**	**0**	..	..	..	..	..
2100 Employees	..	..	..	..	..	..	..	..	..	..
2200 Employers	..	..	..	..	..	..	..	..	..	..
2300 Self-employed or non-employed	..	..	..	..	..	..	..	..	..	..
2400 Unallocable between 2100, 2200 and 2300	..	..	..	..	..	..	..	..	..	..
3000 Taxes on payroll and workforce	**0**	**0**	**0**	**0**	**0**	..	..	..	..	..
4000 Taxes on property	**767**	**2 880**	**6 235**	**4 731**	**6 669**	..	..	..	..	..
4100 Recurrent taxes on immovable property	50	0	0	1 345	1 897	..	..	..	..	..
4200 Recurrent taxes on net wealth	231	671	60	0	0	..	..	..	..	..
4300 Estate, inheritance and gift taxes	163	773	1 709	1 614	1 731	..	..	..	..	..
4400 Taxes on financial and capital transactions	323	1 436	4 466	1 772	3 041	..	..	..	..	..
4500 Non-recurrent taxes	0	0	0	0	0	..	..	..	..	..
4600 Other recurrent taxes on property	0	0	0	0	0	..	..	..	..	..
5000 Taxes on goods and services	**9 716**	**31 892**	**57 116**	**70 161**	**82 185**	..	..	..	..	..
5100 Taxes on production, sale, transfer, etc	9 113	29 728	54 658	65 990	77 745	..	..	..	..	..
5110 General taxes	6 257	19 832	36 950	44 879	52 712	..	..	..	..	..
5120 Taxes on specific goods and services	2 856	9 896	17 708	21 111	25 033	..	..	..	..	..
5130 Unallocable between 5110 and 5120	0	0	0	0	0	..	..	..	..	..
5200 Taxes on use of goods and perform activities	604	2 164	2 458	4 171	4 440	..	..	..	..	..
5300 Unallocable between 5100 and 5200	0	0	0	0	0	..	..	..	..	..
6000 Other taxes	**109**	**491**	**989**	**416**	**807**	..	..	..	..	..
6100 Paid solely by business	109	448	372	0	0	..	..	..	..	..
6200 Other	0	43	617	416	807	..	..	..	..	..
Total tax revenue	**25 667**	**68 783**	**116 980**	**146 157**	**178 430**	..	..	..	..	..

	Local government					Social Security Funds				
	1975	1995	2005	2015	2018	1975	1995	2005	2015	2018
1000 Taxes on income, profits and capital gains	**77**	**0**	**0**	**0**	**0**	**0**	**0**	**0**	**0**	**0**
1100 Of individuals	77	0	0	0	0	0	0	0	0	0
1200 Corporate	0	0	0	0	0	0	0	0	0	0
1300 Unallocable between 1100 and 1200	0	0	0	0	0	0	0	0	0	0
2000 Social security contributions	**0**	**0**	**0**	**0**	**0**	**16 732**	**48 532**	**66 547**	**96 426**	**108 049**
2100 Employees	..	..	..	..	..	7 139	32 795	35 383	48 213	41 775
2200 Employers	..	..	..	..	..	7 687	5 941	20 595	34 614	40 702
2300 Self-employed or non-employed	..	..	..	..	..	1 905	9 796	10 569	13 599	25 572
2400 Unallocable between 2100, 2200 and 2300	..	..	..	..	..	0	0	0	0	0
3000 Taxes on payroll and workforce	**0**	**0**	**0**	**0**	**0**	**0**	**0**	**0**	**0**	**0**
4000 Taxes on property	**272**	**2 287**	**4 341**	**5 037**	**5 473**	**0**	**0**	**0**	**0**	**0**
4100 Recurrent taxes on immovable property	272	2 287	4 341	5 037	5 473	..	..	..	..	..
4200 Recurrent taxes on net wealth	0	0	0	0	0	..	..	..	..	..
4300 Estate, inheritance and gift taxes	0	0	0	0	0	..	..	..	..	..
4400 Taxes on financial and capital transactions	0	0	0	0	0	..	..	..	..	..
4500 Non-recurrent taxes	0	0	0	0	0	..	..	..	..	..
4600 Other recurrent taxes on property	0	0	0	0	0	..	..	..	..	..
5000 Taxes on goods and services	**153**	**1 533**	**3 330**	**4 652**	**4 979**	**0**	**0**	**0**	**0**	**0**
5100 Taxes on production, sale, transfer, etc	14	59	118	249	358	..	..	..	..	..
5110 General taxes	0	6	10	43	70	..	..	..	..	..
5120 Taxes on specific goods and services	14	53	108	206	288	..	..	..	..	..
5130 Unallocable between 5110 and 5120	0	0	0	0	0	..	..	..	..	..
5200 Taxes on use of goods and perform activities	139	1 474	3 212	4 403	4 621	..	..	..	..	..
5300 Unallocable between 5100 and 5200	0	0	0	0	0	..	..	..	..	..
6000 Other taxes	**0**	**0**	**0**	**0**	**0**	**0**	**0**	**0**	**0**	**0**
6100 Paid solely by business	..	..	..	..	..	..	..	..	..	..
6200 Other	..	..	..	..	..	..	..	..	..	..
Total tax revenue	**502**	**3 820**	**7 671**	**9 689**	**10 452**	**16 732**	**48 532**	**66 547**	**96 426**	**108 049**

.. Not available

Note: Including taxes collected on behalf of the European Union.

StatLink https://doi.org/10.1787/888934212877

Table 6.26. New Zealand, tax revenues by sub-sectors of government

Million NZD

	Central government					State/Regional				
	1975	1995	2005	2015	2018	1975	1995	2005	2015	2018
1000 Taxes on income, profits and capital gains	**2 296**	**21 253**	**37 379**	**44 723**	**56 173**	..	..	..	..	..
1100 Of individuals	1 874	15 626	24 373	30 297	37 467	..	..	..	..	..
1200 Corporate	407	4 122	9 957	11 407	15 559	..	..	..	..	..
1300 Unallocable between 1100 and 1200	16	1 505	3 049	3 019	3 147	..	..	..	..	..
2000 Social security contributions	**0**	**0**	**0**	**0**	**0**	..	..	..	..	..
2100 Employees	..	..	..	..	..	..	..	..	..	..
2200 Employers	..	..	..	..	..	..	..	..	..	..
2300 Self-employed or non-employed	..	..	..	..	..	..	..	..	..	..
2400 Unallocable between 2100, 2200 and 2300	..	..	..	..	..	..	..	..	..	..
3000 Taxes on payroll and workforce	**0**	**0**	**0**	**0**	**0**	..	..	..	..	..
4000 Taxes on property	**83**	**218**	**86**	**84**	**105**	..	..	..	..	..
4100 Recurrent taxes on immovable property	3	-1	0	0	0	..	..	..	..	..
4200 Recurrent taxes on net wealth	0	0	0	0	0	..	..	..	..	..
4300 Estate, inheritance and gift taxes	54	3	3	0	0	..	..	..	..	..
4400 Taxes on financial and capital transactions	25	216	83	84	105	..	..	..	..	..
4500 Non-recurrent taxes	0	0	0	0	0	..	..	..	..	..
4600 Other recurrent taxes on property	0	0	0	0	0	..	..	..	..	..
5000 Taxes on goods and services	**807**	**11 395**	**18 744**	**31 146**	**36 981**	..	..	..	..	..
5100 Taxes on production, sale, transfer, etc	770	10 833	17 792	29 551	35 081	..	..	..	..	..
5110 General taxes	311	7 895	14 133	24 587	29 521	..	..	..	..	..
5120 Taxes on specific goods and services	459	2 938	3 659	4 964	5 560	..	..	..	..	..
5130 Unallocable between 5110 and 5120	0	0	0	0	0	..	..	..	..	..
5200 Taxes on use of goods and perform activities	37	562	952	1 595	1 900	..	..	..	..	..
5300 Unallocable between 5100 and 5200	0	0	0	0	0	..	..	..	..	..
6000 Other taxes	**0**	**0**	**14**	**2**	**2**	..	..	..	..	..
6100 Paid solely by business	..	..	0	0	0	..	..	..	..	..
6200 Other	..	..	14	2	2	..	..	..	..	..
Total tax revenue	**3 186**	**32 866**	**56 223**	**75 955**	**93 261**	..	..	..	..	..

	Local government					Social Security Funds				
	1975	1995	2005	2015	2018	1975	1995	2005	2015	2018
1000 Taxes on income, profits and capital gains	**0**	**0**	**0**	**0**	**0**	**0**	**0**	**0**	**0**	**0**
1100 Of individuals	0	0	0	0	0	0	0	0	0	0
1200 Corporate	0	0	0	0	0	0	0	0	0	0
1300 Unallocable between 1100 and 1200	0	0	0	0	0	0	0	0	0	0
2000 Social security contributions	**0**	**0**	**0**	**0**	**0**	**0**	**0**	**0**	**0**	**0**
2100 Employees	..	..	..	..	..	..	..	..	..	..
2200 Employers	..	..	..	..	..	..	..	..	..	..
2300 Self-employed or non-employed	..	..	..	..	..	..	..	..	..	..
2400 Unallocable between 2100, 2200 and 2300	..	..	..	..	..	..	..	..	..	..
3000 Taxes on payroll and workforce	**0**	**0**	**0**	**0**	**0**	**0**	**0**	**0**	**0**	**0**
4000 Taxes on property	**237**	**1 646**	**2 825**	**4 962**	**5 717**	**0**	**0**	**0**	**0**	**0**
4100 Recurrent taxes on immovable property	237	1 646	2 825	4 962	5 717	..	..	..	..	..
4200 Recurrent taxes on net wealth	0	0	0	0	0	..	..	..	..	..
4300 Estate, inheritance and gift taxes	0	0	0	0	0	..	..	..	..	..
4400 Taxes on financial and capital transactions	0	0	0	0	0	..	..	..	..	..
4500 Non-recurrent taxes	0	0	0	0	0	..	..	..	..	..
4600 Other recurrent taxes on property	0	0	0	0	0	..	..	..	..	0
5000 Taxes on goods and services	**29**	**184**	**310**	**582**	**864**	**0**	**0**	**0**	**0**	**0**
5100 Taxes on production, sale, transfer, etc	18	33	30	33	190	..	..	..	..	..
5110 General taxes	0	0	0	0	0	..	..	..	..	..
5120 Taxes on specific goods and services	18	33	30	33	190	..	..	..	..	..
5130 Unallocable between 5110 and 5120	0	0	0	0	0	..	..	..	..	0
5200 Taxes on use of goods and perform activities	11	151	280	549	674	..	..	..	..	..
5300 Unallocable between 5100 and 5200	0	0	0	0	0	..	..	..	..	0
6000 Other taxes	**0**	**0**	**0**	**0**	**0**	**0**	**0**	**0**	**0**	**0**
6100 Paid solely by business	..	..	..	0	0	..	..	..	0	0
6200 Other	..	..	..	0	0	..	..	..	0	0
Total tax revenue	**266**	**1 830**	**3 135**	**5 544**	**6 581**	**0**	**0**	**0**	**0**	**0**

.. Not available

StatLink https://doi.org/10.1787/888934212896

Table 6.27. Norway, tax revenues by sub-sectors of government

Million NOK

	Central government[1]					State/Regional				
	1975	1995	2005	2015	2018	1975	1995	2005	2015	2018
1000 Taxes on income, profits and capital gains	**6 495**	**67 402**	**316 851**	**314 792**	**398 158**	..	..	..	..	..
1100 Of individuals	5 424	38 059	87 503	174 617	168 601	..	..	..	..	..
1200 Corporate	1 071	29 343	229 348	140 175	229 557	..	..	..	..	..
1300 Unallocable between 1100 and 1200	0	0	0	0	0	..	..	..	..	..
2000 Social security contributions	**1 341**	**6 013**	**173 151**	**325 130**	**356 610**	..	..	..	..	..
2100 Employees	331	1 233	58 320	112 662	124 499	..	..	..	..	..
2200 Employers	1 010	4 780	104 794	190 923	208 153	..	..	..	..	..
2300 Self-employed or non-employed	0	0	10 037	21 545	23 958	..	..	..	..	..
2400 Unallocable between 2100, 2200 and 2300	0	0	0	0	0	..	..	..	..	..
3000 Taxes on payroll and workforce	**0**	**0**	**0**	**0**	**1 976**	..	..	..	..	..
4000 Taxes on property	**771**	**3 497**	**11 178**	**12 209**	**16 652**	..	..	..	..	..
4100 Recurrent taxes on immovable property	0	0	0	0	0	..	..	..	..	..
4200 Recurrent taxes on net wealth	490	1 172	4 741	3 488	7 010	..	..	..	..	..
4300 Estate, inheritance and gift taxes	146	975	1 768	295	73	..	..	..	..	..
4400 Taxes on financial and capital transactions	135	1 350	4 669	8 426	9 569	..	..	..	..	..
4500 Non-recurrent taxes	0	0	0	0	0	..	..	..	..	..
4600 Other recurrent taxes on property	0	0	0	0	0	..	..	..	..	..
5000 Taxes on goods and services	**25 056**	**141 645**	**232 462**	**359 255**	**410 098**	..	..	..	..	..
5100 Taxes on production, sale, transfer, etc	24 367	134 965	220 898	342 410	392 783	..	..	..	..	..
5110 General taxes	13 670	81 772	153 820	256 029	297 918	..	..	..	..	..
5120 Taxes on specific goods and services	10 697	53 193	67 078	86 381	94 865	..	..	..	..	..
5130 Unallocable between 5110 and 5120	0	0	0	0	0	..	..	..	..	..
5200 Taxes on use of goods and perform activities	689	6 680	11 564	16 845	17 315	..	..	..	..	..
5300 Unallocable between 5100 and 5200	0	0	0	0	0	..	..	..	..	..
6000 Other taxes	**130**	**15**	**0**	**0**	**0**	..	..	..	..	..
6100 Paid solely by business	124	1	..	..	..	..	..	..	..	..
6200 Other	6	14	..	..	..	..	..	..	..	..
Total tax revenue	**33 793**	**218 572**	**733 642**	**1 011 386**	**1 183 494**	..	..	..	..	..

	Local government					Social Security Funds				
	1975	1995	2005	2015	2018	1975	1995	2005	2015	2018
1000 Taxes on income, profits and capital gains	**13 725**	**67 978**	**100 512**	**160 582**	**184 758**	**2 728**	**0**	**0**	**0**	**0**
1100 Of individuals	12 877	61 784	100 512	160 582	184 758	2 728	..	..	..	..
1200 Corporate	848	6 194	0	0	0	0	..	..	..	..
1300 Unallocable between 1100 and 1200	0	0	0	0	0	0	..	..	..	..
2000 Social security contributions	**0**	**0**	**0**	**0**	**0**	**15 224**	**84 563**	**0**	**0**	**0**
2100 Employees	..	..	..	..	..	2 949	30 417	..	..	..
2200 Employers	..	..	..	..	..	11 315	48 396	..	..	..
2300 Self-employed or non-employed	..	..	..	..	..	960	5 750	..	..	..
2400 Unallocable between 2100, 2200 and 2300	..	..	..	..	..	0	0	..	..	..
3000 Taxes on payroll and workforce	**0**	**0**	**0**	**0**	**0**	**0**	**0**	**0**	**0**	**0**
4000 Taxes on property	**772**	**7 352**	**10 283**	**21 812**	**27 278**	**0**	**0**	**0**	**0**	**0**
4100 Recurrent taxes on immovable property	278	2 792	4 324	11 177	14 205	..	..	..	..	..
4200 Recurrent taxes on net wealth	494	4 560	5 959	10 635	13 073	..	..	..	..	..
4300 Estate, inheritance and gift taxes	0	0	0	0	0	..	..	..	..	..
4400 Taxes on financial and capital transactions	0	0	0	0	0	..	..	..	..	..
4500 Non-recurrent taxes	0	0	0	0	0	..	..	..	..	..
4600 Other recurrent taxes on property	0	0	0	0	0	..	..	..	..	..
5000 Taxes on goods and services	**0**	**431**	**2 281**	**1 574**	**1 676**	**51**	**267**	**0**	**0**	**0**
5100 Taxes on production, sale, transfer, etc	0	0	0	0	0	51	267	..	..	..
5110 General taxes	0	0	0	0	0	0	0	..	..	..
5120 Taxes on specific goods and services	0	0	0	0	0	51	267	..	..	..
5130 Unallocable between 5110 and 5120	0	0	0	0	0	0	0	..	..	..
5200 Taxes on use of goods and perform activities	0	431	2 281	1 574	1 676	0	0	..	..	..
5300 Unallocable between 5100 and 5200	0	0	0	0	0	0	0	..	..	..
6000 Other taxes	**432**	**0**	**0**	**0**	**0**	**0**	**0**	**0**	**0**	**0**
6100 Paid solely by business	0	..	..	..	..	..	..	..	..	..
6200 Other	432	..	..	..	..	..	..	..	..	..
Total tax revenue	**14 929**	**75 761**	**113 076**	**183 968**	**213 712**	**18 003**	**84 830**	**0**	**0**	**0**

.. Not available

1. The Norwegian National Insurance has been integrated into the Central government sector from the year 2000 onwards.

StatLink https://doi.org/10.1787/888934212915

Table 6.28. Poland, tax revenues by sub-sectors of government

Million PLN

	Central government					State/Regional				
	1975	1995	2005	2015	2018	1975	1995	2005	2015	2018
1000 Taxes on income, profits and capital gains	..	**32 774**	**40 398**	**71 381**	**95 153**	..	..	..	..	..
1100 Of individuals	..	23 937	24 518	45 462	60 583	..	..	..	..	..
1200 Corporate	..	8 837	15 880	25 919	34 570	..	..	..	..	..
1300 Unallocable between 1100 and 1200	..	0	0	0	0	..	..	..	..	..
2000 Social security contributions	..	**0**	**0**	**0**	**0**	..	..	..	..	..
2100 Employees	..	..	..	..	..	..	..	..	..	..
2200 Employers	..	..	..	..	..	..	..	..	..	..
2300 Self-employed or non-employed	..	..	..	..	..	..	..	..	..	..
2400 Unallocable between 2100, 2200 and 2300	..	..	..	..	..	..	..	..	..	..
3000 Taxes on payroll and workforce	..	**831**	**2 555**	**4 028**	**4 720**	..	..	..	..	..
4000 Taxes on property	..	**0**	**0**	**0**	**0**	..	..	..	..	..
4100 Recurrent taxes on immovable property	..	..	..	..	..	..	..	..	..	..
4200 Recurrent taxes on net wealth	..	..	..	..	..	..	..	..	..	..
4300 Estate, inheritance and gift taxes	..	..	..	..	..	..	..	..	..	..
4400 Taxes on financial and capital transactions	..	..	..	..	..	..	..	..	..	..
4500 Non-recurrent taxes	..	..	..	..	..	..	..	..	..	..
4600 Other recurrent taxes on property	..	..	..	..	..	..	..	..	..	..
5000 Taxes on goods and services	..	**43 483**	**120 438**	**207 070**	**269 132**	..	..	..	..	..
5100 Taxes on production, sale, transfer, etc	..	42 863	120 036	203 244	264 330	..	..	..	..	..
5110 General taxes	..	21 051	75 783	125 836	172 210	..	..	..	..	..
5120 Taxes on specific goods and services	..	21 812	44 253	77 408	92 120	..	..	..	..	..
5130 Unallocable between 5110 and 5120	..	0	0	0	0	..	..	..	..	..
5200 Taxes on use of goods and perform activities	..	620	402	3 826	4 802	..	..	..	..	..
5300 Unallocable between 5100 and 5200	..	0	0	0	0	..	..	..	..	..
6000 Other taxes	..	**99**	**18**	**0**	**0**	..	..	..	..	..
6100 Paid solely by business	..	0	0	..	..	..	..	..	..	..
6200 Other	..	99	18	..	..	..	..	..	..	..
Total tax revenue	..	**77 187**	**163 409**	**282 479**	**369 005**	..	..	..	..	..

	Local government					Social Security Funds				
	1975	1995	2005	2015	2018	1975	1995	2005	2015	2018
1000 Taxes on income, profits and capital gains	..	**4 896**	**23 093**	**45 697**	**61 831**	..	**0**	**0**	**0**	**0**
1100 Of individuals	..	4 427	17 916	38 512	52 076	..	..	..	..	..
1200 Corporate	..	469	5 177	7 185	9 755	..	..	..	..	..
1300 Unallocable between 1100 and 1200	..	0	0	0	0	..	..	..	..	..
2000 Social security contributions	..	**0**	**0**	**0**	**0**	..	**38 260**	**120 296**	**223 482**	**277 670**
2100 Employees	..	..	..	..	..	..	16 486	49 644	91 163	115 821
2200 Employers	..	..	..	..	..	..	19 097	46 256	87 616	108 672
2300 Self-employed or non-employed	..	..	..	..	..	..	2 677	24 396	44 703	53 177
2400 Unallocable between 2100, 2200 and 2300	..	..	..	..	..	..	0	0	0	0
3000 Taxes on payroll and workforce	..	**0**	**0**	**0**	**0**	..	**0**	**0**	**0**	**0**
4000 Taxes on property	..	**4 370**	**14 723**	**24 637**	**27 851**	..	**0**	**0**	**0**	**0**
4100 Recurrent taxes on immovable property	..	3 579	12 718	22 206	24 326	..	..	..	..	..
4200 Recurrent taxes on net wealth	..	0	0	0	0	..	..	..	..	..
4300 Estate, inheritance and gift taxes	..	44	242	246	299	..	..	..	..	..
4400 Taxes on financial and capital transactions	..	747	1 763	2 185	3 226	..	..	..	..	..
4500 Non-recurrent taxes	..	0	0	0	0	..	..	..	..	..
4600 Other recurrent taxes on property	..	0	0	0	0	..	..	..	..	..
5000 Taxes on goods and services	..	**1 340**	**3 368**	**4 139**	**4 181**	..	**0**	**0**	**0**	**0**
5100 Taxes on production, sale, transfer, etc	..	0	0	0	0	..	..	..	..	..
5110 General taxes	..	..	..	..	..	..	..	..	..	..
5120 Taxes on specific goods and services	..	..	..	..	..	..	..	..	..	..
5130 Unallocable between 5110 and 5120	..	..	..	..	..	..	..	..	..	..
5200 Taxes on use of goods and perform activities	..	1 340	3 368	4 139	4 181	..	..	..	..	..
5300 Unallocable between 5100 and 5200	..	0	0	0	0	..	..	..	..	..
6000 Other taxes	..	**158**	**278**	**647**	**1 080**	..	**0**	**0**	**0**	**0**
6100 Paid solely by business	..	0	0	0	..	..	..	..	..	..
6200 Other	..	158	278	647	1 080	..	..	..	..	..
Total tax revenue	..	**10 764**	**41 462**	**75 120**	**94 943**	..	**38 260**	**120 296**	**223 482**	**277 670**

.. Not available

Note: Including taxes collected on behalf of the European Union.

StatLink https://doi.org/10.1787/888934212934

Table 6.29. Portugal, tax revenues by sub-sectors of government

Million EUR

	Central government					State/Regional				
	1975	1995	2005	2015	2018	1975	1995	2005	2015	2018
1000 Taxes on income, profits and capital gains	**81**	**6 557**	**11 506**	**17 516**	**18 829**	..	..	..	..	..
1100 Of individuals	..	4 691	7 757	12 316	12 498	..	..	..	..	..
1200 Corporate	..	1 866	3 705	5 199	6 331	..	..	..	..	..
1300 Unallocable between 1100 and 1200	81	0	43	0	0	..	..	..	..	..
2000 Social security contributions	**0**	**1 560**	**1 887**	**2 064**	**2 112**	..	..	..	..	..
2100 Employees	..	941	1 629	1 867	1 926	..	..	..	..	..
2200 Employers	..	619	259	198	186	..	..	..	..	..
2300 Self-employed or non-employed	..	0	0	0	0	..	..	..	..	..
2400 Unallocable between 2100, 2200 and 2300	..	0	0	0	0	..	..	..	..	..
3000 Taxes on payroll and workforce	**12**	**0**	**0**	**0**	**0**	..	..	..	..	..
4000 Taxes on property	**12**	**226**	**261**	**202**	**378**	..	..	..	..	..
4100 Recurrent taxes on immovable property	0	0	0	6	144	..	..	..	..	..
4200 Recurrent taxes on net wealth	0	0	0	0	0	..	..	..	..	..
4300 Estate, inheritance and gift taxes	4	57	25	0	0	..	..	..	..	..
4400 Taxes on financial and capital transactions	7	169	236	196	233	..	..	..	..	..
4500 Non-recurrent taxes	0	0	0	0	0	..	..	..	..	..
4600 Other recurrent taxes on property	0	0	0	0	0	..	..	..	..	..
5000 Taxes on goods and services	**198**	**10 402**	**19 638**	**21 488**	**25 552**	..	..	..	..	..
5100 Taxes on production, sale, transfer, etc	187	10 195	19 220	20 881	24 619	..	..	..	..	..
5110 General taxes	52	5 481	11 846	13 745	16 301	..	..	..	..	..
5120 Taxes on specific goods and services	135	4 714	7 374	7 136	8 317	..	..	..	..	..
5130 Unallocable between 5110 and 5120	0	0	0	0	0	..	..	..	..	..
5200 Taxes on use of goods and perform activities	12	178	375	594	927	..	..	..	..	..
5300 Unallocable between 5100 and 5200	0	30	43	13	6	..	..	..	..	..
6000 Other taxes	**2**	**98**	**252**	**578**	**676**	..	..	..	..	..
6100 Paid solely by business	1	18	160	341	411	..	..	..	..	..
6200 Other	0	81	92	237	265	..	..	..	..	..
Total tax revenue	**304**	**18 844**	**33 544**	**41 849**	**47 547**	..	..	..	..	..

	Local government					Social Security Funds				
	1975	1995	2005	2015	2018	1975	1995	2005	2015	2018
1000 Taxes on income, profits and capital gains	**0**	**307**	**725**	**1 246**	**1 284**	**0**	**0**	**0**	**0**	**0**
1100 Of individuals	..	156	298	832	814	..	..	..	..	..
1200 Corporate	..	151	427	414	471	..	..	..	..	..
1300 Unallocable between 1100 and 1200	0	0	0	0	0	..	..	..	..	..
2000 Social security contributions	**0**	**2**	**7**	**19**	**0**	**161**	**5 267**	**11 100**	**14 099**	**17 015**
2100 Employees	..	2	7	19	0	62	2 100	4 053	5 106	5 764
2200 Employers	..	0	0	0	0	97	3 167	7 047	8 993	11 251
2300 Self-employed or non-employed	..	0	0	0	0	2	0	0	0	0
2400 Unallocable between 2100, 2200 and 2300	..	0	0	0	0	0	0	0	0	0
3000 Taxes on payroll and workforce	**0**	**0**	**0**	**0**	**0**	**0**	**0**	**0**	**0**	**0**
4000 Taxes on property	**0**	**599**	**1 532**	**2 105**	**2 485**	**0**	**0**	**0**	**0**	**0**
4100 Recurrent taxes on immovable property	..	310	827	1 529	1 501	..	..	..	..	..
4200 Recurrent taxes on net wealth	..	0	0	0	0	..	..	..	..	..
4300 Estate, inheritance and gift taxes	..	0	1	0	0	..	..	..	..	..
4400 Taxes on financial and capital transactions	..	289	704	576	984	..	..	..	..	..
4500 Non-recurrent taxes	..	0	0	0	0	..	..	..	..	..
4600 Other recurrent taxes on property	..	0	0	0	0	..	..	..	..	..
5000 Taxes on goods and services	**0**	**499**	**971**	**1 132**	**1 363**	**0**	**335**	**823**	**1 179**	**1 065**
5100 Taxes on production, sale, transfer, etc	0	442	837	876	1 079	..	335	823	1 179	1 056
5110 General taxes	0	318	563	629	740	..	276	592	994	824
5120 Taxes on specific goods and services	0	124	273	247	339	..	59	231	184	232
5130 Unallocable between 5110 and 5120	0	0	0	0	0	..	0	0	0	0
5200 Taxes on use of goods and perform activities	0	57	133	256	285	..	0	0	0	10
5300 Unallocable between 5100 and 5200	0	0	1	0	0	..	0	0	0	0
6000 Other taxes	**0**	**3**	**28**	**2**	**4**	**0**	**1**	**3**	**0**	**0**
6100 Paid solely by business	..	0	25	0	0	..	0	0	..	..
6200 Other	..	3	3	2	4	..	1	3	..	..
Total tax revenue	**0**	**1 410**	**3 262**	**4 504**	**5 137**	**161**	**5 603**	**11 926**	**15 278**	**18 081**

.. Not available

Note: Including taxes collected on behalf of the European Union.

StatLink https://doi.org/10.1787/888934212953

Table 6.30. Slovak Republic, tax revenues by sub-sectors of government

Million EUR

	Central government					State/Regional				
	1975	1995	2005	2015	2018	1975	1995	2005	2015	2018
1000 Taxes on income, profits and capital gains	..	**1 993**	**2 968**	**5 542**	**6 370**	..	..	..	..	..
1100 Of individuals	..	695	1 496	2 464	3 218	..	..	..	..	..
1200 Corporate	..	1 166	1 345	2 917	2 943	..	..	..	..	..
1300 Unallocable between 1100 and 1200	..	132	128	162	209	..	..	..	..	..
2000 Social security contributions	..	**85**	**240**	**253**	**410**	..	..	..	..	..
2100 Employees	..	10	104	58	99	..	..	..	..	..
2200 Employers	..	75	136	195	309	..	..	..	..	..
2300 Self-employed or non-employed	..	0	0	0	1	..	..	..	..	..
2400 Unallocable between 2100, 2200 and 2300	..	0	0	0	0	..	..	..	..	..
3000 Taxes on payroll and workforce	..	**0**	**0**	**0**	**0**	..	..	..	..	..
4000 Taxes on property	..	**27**	**28**	**0**	**0**	..	..	..	..	..
4100 Recurrent taxes on immovable property	..	8	9	0	0	..	..	..	..	..
4200 Recurrent taxes on net wealth	..	0	0	0	0	..	..	..	..	..
4300 Estate, inheritance and gift taxes	..	2	1	0	0	..	..	..	..	..
4400 Taxes on financial and capital transactions	..	16	18	0	0	..	..	..	..	..
4500 Non-recurrent taxes	..	0	0	0	0	..	..	..	..	..
4600 Other recurrent taxes on property	..	0	0	0	0	..	..	..	..	..
5000 Taxes on goods and services	..	**2 782**	**6 031**	**8 974**	**10 428**	..	..	..	..	..
5100 Taxes on production, sale, transfer, etc	..	2 594	5 773	8 442	9 847	..	..	..	..	..
5110 General taxes	..	1 616	3 880	5 423	6 319	..	..	..	..	..
5120 Taxes on specific goods and services	..	978	1 893	3 020	3 528	..	..	..	..	..
5130 Unallocable between 5110 and 5120	..	0	0	0	0	..	..	..	..	..
5200 Taxes on use of goods and perform activities	..	189	256	532	581	..	..	..	..	..
5300 Unallocable between 5100 and 5200	..	0	2	0	0	..	..	..	..	..
6000 Other taxes	..	**0**	**0**	**0**	**0**	..	..	..	..	..
6100 Paid solely by business	..	..	..	..	..	..	..	..	..	..
6200 Other	..	..	..	..	..	..	..	..	..	..
Total tax revenue	..	**4 887**	**9 267**	**14 770**	**17 208**	..	..	..	..	..

	Local government					Social Security Funds				
	1975	1995	2005	2015	2018	1975	1995	2005	2015	2018
1000 Taxes on income, profits and capital gains	..	**0**	**0**	**0**	**0**	..	**0**	**0**	**0**	**0**
1100 Of individuals	..	0	0	0	0	..	0	0	0	0
1200 Corporate	..	0	0	0	0	..	0	0	0	0
1300 Unallocable between 1100 and 1200	..	0	0	0	0	..	0	0	0	0
2000 Social security contributions	..	**0**	**0**	**0**	**0**	..	**2 817**	**6 037**	**10 643**	**12 828**
2100 Employees	..	..	..	0	0	..	540	1 377	2 352	3 163
2200 Employers	..	..	..	0	0	..	1 774	3 356	6 124	7 561
2300 Self-employed or non-employed	..	..	..	0	0	..	503	1 304	2 168	2 103
2400 Unallocable between 2100, 2200 and 2300	..	..	..	0	0	..	0	0	0	0
3000 Taxes on payroll and workforce	..	**0**	**0**	**0**	**0**	..	**0**	**0**	**0**	**0**
4000 Taxes on property	..	**84**	**220**	**335**	**369**	..	**0**	**0**	**0**	**0**
4100 Recurrent taxes on immovable property	..	72	220	335	369	..	..	..	..	..
4200 Recurrent taxes on net wealth	..	0	0	0	0	..	..	..	..	..
4300 Estate, inheritance and gift taxes	..	0	0	0	0	..	..	..	..	..
4400 Taxes on financial and capital transactions	..	12	0	0	0	..	..	..	..	..
4500 Non-recurrent taxes	..	0	0	0	0	..	..	..	..	..
4600 Other recurrent taxes on property	..	0	0	0	0	..	..	..	..	..
5000 Taxes on goods and services	..	**17**	**198**	**182**	**193**	..	**0**	**0**	**0**	**0**
5100 Taxes on production, sale, transfer, etc	..	10	9	12	16	..	..	..	..	..
5110 General taxes	..	0	0	0	0	..	..	..	..	..
5120 Taxes on specific goods and services	..	10	9	12	16	..	..	..	..	..
5130 Unallocable between 5110 and 5120	..	0	0	0	0	..	..	..	..	..
5200 Taxes on use of goods and perform activities	..	1	94	17	16	..	..	..	..	..
5300 Unallocable between 5100 and 5200	..	6	95	153	161	..	..	..	..	..
6000 Other taxes	..	**0**	**0**	**0**	**0**	..	**0**	**0**	**0**	**0**
6100 Paid solely by business	..	..	..	..	..	..	..	..	..	..
6200 Other	..	..	..	..	..	..	..	..	..	..
Total tax revenue	..	**101**	**418**	**517**	**562**	..	**2 817**	**6 037**	**10 643**	**12 828**

.. Not available

Note: Including taxes collected on behalf of the European Union.

StatLink https://doi.org/10.1787/888934212972

Table 6.31. Slovenia, tax revenues by sub-sectors of government

Million EUR

	Central government					State/Regional				
	1975	1995	2005	2015	2018	1975	1995	2005	2015	2018
1000 Taxes on income, profits and capital gains	..	**479**	**1 828**	**1 528**	**2 157**	..	..	..	..	..
1100 Of individuals	..	413	1 029	958	1 269	..	..	..	..	..
1200 Corporate	..	54	795	568	886	..	..	..	..	..
1300 Unallocable between 1100 and 1200	..	12	5	2	2	..	..	..	..	..
2000 Social security contributions	..	**38**	**42**	**59**	**72**	..	..	..	..	..
2100 Employees	..	20	24	31	37	..	..	..	..	..
2200 Employers	..	17	15	23	28	..	..	..	..	..
2300 Self-employed or non-employed	..	1	3	5	6	..	..	..	..	..
2400 Unallocable between 2100, 2200 and 2300	..	0	0	0	0	..	..	..	..	..
3000 Taxes on payroll and workforce	..	**14**	**521**	**20**	**22**	..	..	..	..	..
4000 Taxes on property	..	**5**	**3**	**2**	**2**	..	..	..	..	..
4100 Recurrent taxes on immovable property	..	0	0	0	0	..	..	..	..	..
4200 Recurrent taxes on net wealth	..	0	3	0	0	..	..	..	..	..
4300 Estate, inheritance and gift taxes	..	0	0	0	0	..	..	..	..	..
4400 Taxes on financial and capital transactions	..	0	0	0	0	..	..	..	..	..
4500 Non-recurrent taxes	..	5	0	2	1	..	..	..	..	..
4600 Other recurrent taxes on property	..	0	0	0	0	..	..	..	..	..
5000 Taxes on goods and services	..	**1 554**	**3 805**	**5 541**	**6 248**	..	..	..	..	..
5100 Taxes on production, sale, transfer, etc	..	1 524	3 624	5 203	5 844	..	..	..	..	..
5110 General taxes	..	1 192	2 467	3 222	3 768	..	..	..	..	..
5120 Taxes on specific goods and services	..	332	1 156	1 981	2 076	..	..	..	..	..
5130 Unallocable between 5110 and 5120	..	0	0	0	0	..	..	..	..	..
5200 Taxes on use of goods and perform activities	..	31	181	338	404	..	..	..	..	..
5300 Unallocable between 5100 and 5200	..	0	0	0	0	..	..	..	..	..
6000 Other taxes	..	**0**	**0**	**0**	**0**	..	..	..	..	..
6100 Paid solely by business	..	..	..	..	..	..	..	..	..	..
6200 Other	..	..	..	..	..	..	..	..	..	..
Total tax revenue	..	**2 090**	**6 199**	**7 150**	**8 500**	..	..	..	..	..

	Local government					Social Security Funds				
	1975	1995	2005	2015	2018	1975	1995	2005	2015	2018
1000 Taxes on income, profits and capital gains	..	**194**	**559**	**1 019**	**1 173**	..	**0**	**0**	**0**	**0**
1100 Of individuals	..	192	556	1 019	1 173	..	..	..	..	..
1200 Corporate	..	0	0	0	0	..	..	..	..	..
1300 Unallocable between 1100 and 1200	..	2	2	0	0	..	..	..	..	..
2000 Social security contributions	..	**0**	**0**	**0**	**0**	..	**1 795**	**4 354**	**5 924**	**7 009**
2100 Employees	..	..	..	..	..	..	812	2 124	2 879	3 452
2200 Employers	..	..	..	..	..	..	806	1 579	2 112	2 562
2300 Self-employed or non-employed	..	..	..	..	..	..	177	652	933	995
2400 Unallocable between 2100, 2200 and 2300	..	..	..	..	..	..	0	0	0	0
3000 Taxes on payroll and workforce	..	**2**	**0**	**0**	**0**	..	**0**	**0**	**0**	**0**
4000 Taxes on property	..	**53**	**167**	**239**	**275**	..	**0**	**0**	**0**	**0**
4100 Recurrent taxes on immovable property	..	37	122	199	223	..	..	..	..	..
4200 Recurrent taxes on net wealth	..	0	0	0	0	..	..	..	..	..
4300 Estate, inheritance and gift taxes	..	1	5	8	10	..	..	..	..	..
4400 Taxes on financial and capital transactions	..	12	40	29	40	..	..	..	..	..
4500 Non-recurrent taxes	..	3	0	3	2	..	..	..	..	..
4600 Other recurrent taxes on property	..	0	0	0	0	..	..	..	..	..
5000 Taxes on goods and services	..	**7**	**91**	**96**	**93**	..	**0**	**0**	**0**	**0**
5100 Taxes on production, sale, transfer, etc	..	7	43	57	58	..	..	..	..	..
5110 General taxes	..	0	0	0	0	..	..	..	..	..
5120 Taxes on specific goods and services	..	7	43	57	58	..	..	..	..	..
5130 Unallocable between 5110 and 5120	..	0	0	0	0	..	..	..	..	..
5200 Taxes on use of goods and perform activities	..	0	48	39	35	..	..	..	..	..
5300 Unallocable between 5100 and 5200	..	0	0	0	0	..	..	..	..	..
6000 Other taxes	..	**0**	**0**	**0**	**0**	..	**0**	**0**	**0**	**0**
6100 Paid solely by business	..	..	..	..	..	..	..	..	..	..
6200 Other	..	..	..	..	..	..	..	..	..	..
Total tax revenue	..	**256**	**817**	**1 354**	**1 541**	..	**1 795**	**4 354**	**5 924**	**7 009**

.. Not available

Note: Including taxes collected on behalf of the European Union.

StatLink https://doi.org/10.1787/888934212991

Table 6.32. Spain, tax revenues by sub-sectors of government

Million EUR

	Federal government					State/Regional				
	1975	1995	2005	2015	2018	1975	1995	2005	2015	2018
1000 Taxes on income, profits and capital gains	**1 388**	**38 846**	**71 598**	**62 198**	**71 685**	**..**	**588**	**19 503**	**34 814**	**43 391**
1100 Of individuals	897	31 789	38 219	39 659	43 774	..	457	19 104	34 600	43 127
1200 Corporate	490	7 057	33 379	22 539	27 911	..	131	399	214	264
1300 Unallocable between 1100 and 1200	1	0	0	0	0	..	0	0	0	0
2000 Social security contributions	**0**	**2 027**	**3 027**	**3 505**	**3 484**	**..**	**0**	**0**	**0**	**0**
2100 Employees	..	1 017	1 369	1 541	1 438	..	..	..	..	..
2200 Employers	..	1 010	1 658	1 964	2 046	..	..	..	..	..
2300 Self-employed or non-employed	..	0	0	0	0	..	..	..	..	..
2400 Unallocable between 2100, 2200 and 2300	..	0	0	0	0	..	..	..	..	..
3000 Taxes on payroll and workforce	**0**	**0**	**0**	**0**	**0**	**..**	**0**	**0**	**0**	**0**
4000 Taxes on property	**421**	**405**	**77**	**1 197**	**445**	**..**	**4 050**	**19 031**	**10 286**	**12 694**
4100 Recurrent taxes on immovable property	1	3	5	4	5	..	0	2	38	39
4200 Recurrent taxes on net wealth	0	166	38	32	57	..	419	1 246	961	1 146
4300 Estate, inheritance and gift taxes	56	1	24	222	143	..	835	2 315	2 454	2 412
4400 Taxes on financial and capital transactions	364	235	10	6	6	..	2 796	15 468	6 833	9 097
4500 Non-recurrent taxes	0	0	0	933	234	..	0	0	0	0
4600 Other recurrent taxes on property	0	0	0	0	0	..	0	0	0	0
5000 Taxes on goods and services	**1 609**	**32 388**	**71 536**	**89 031**	**98 039**	**..**	**2 556**	**7 956**	**6 553**	**7 722**
5100 Taxes on production, sale, transfer, etc	1 599	32 206	70 895	87 536	96 298	..	2 387	7 637	6 022	7 127
5110 General taxes	990	20 331	51 583	61 839	70 615	..	786	1 980	2 571	3 006
5120 Taxes on specific goods and services	608	11 875	19 312	25 697	25 683	..	1 601	5 657	3 451	4 121
5130 Unallocable between 5110 and 5120	0	0	0	0	0	..	0	0	0	0
5200 Taxes on use of goods and perform activities	10	182	641	1 495	1 741	..	169	319	531	595
5300 Unallocable between 5100 and 5200	0	0	0	0	0	..	0	0	0	0
6000 Other taxes	**0**	**0**	**0**	**101**	**156**	**..**	**0**	**1**	**19**	**11**
6100 Paid solely by business	0	..	..	..	..	..	..	..	..	..
6200 Other	0	0	0	101	156	..	0	1	19	11
Total tax revenue	**3 418**	**73 666**	**146 238**	**156 032**	**173 809**	**..**	**7 194**	**46 491**	**51 672**	**63 818**

	Local government					Social Security Funds				
	1975	1995	2005	2015	2018	1975	1995	2005	2015	2018
1000 Taxes on income, profits and capital gains	**175**	**2 514**	**4 892**	**5 633**	**6 916**	**0**	**0**	**0**	**0**	**0**
1100 Of individuals	131	2 137	3 426	4 637	5 414	..	..	..	..	..
1200 Corporate	0	377	1 466	996	1 502	..	..	..	..	..
1300 Unallocable between 1100 and 1200	44	0	0	0	0	..	..	..	..	..
2000 Social security contributions	**0**	**0**	**0**	**0**	**0**	**3 367**	**49 851**	**106 040**	**119 330**	**137 750**
2100 Employees	..	..	..	..	..	645	7 372	15 332	17 242	20 201
2200 Employers	..	..	..	..	..	2 722	35 137	77 989	86 024	101 271
2300 Self-employed or non-employed	..	..	..	..	..	0	7 342	12 719	16 064	16 278
2400 Unallocable between 2100, 2200 and 2300	..	..	..	..	..	0	0	0	0	0
3000 Taxes on payroll and workforce	**0**	**0**	**0**	**0**	**0**	**0**	**0**	**0**	**0**	**0**
4000 Taxes on property	**26**	**3 759**	**8 869**	**16 372**	**17 173**	**0**	**0**	**0**	**0**	**0**
4100 Recurrent taxes on immovable property	26	2 754	6 038	12 581	13 199	..	..	..	..	..
4200 Recurrent taxes on net wealth	0	177	431	911	983	..	..	..	..	..
4300 Estate, inheritance and gift taxes	0	19	79	114	132	..	..	..	..	..
4400 Taxes on financial and capital transactions	0	166	423	145	207	..	..	..	..	..
4500 Non-recurrent taxes	0	643	1 898	2 621	2 652	..	..	..	..	..
4600 Other recurrent taxes on property	0	0	0	0	0	..	..	..	..	..
5000 Taxes on goods and services	**104**	**6 072**	**12 810**	**13 067**	**14 536**	**0**	**0**	**0**	**0**	**0**
5100 Taxes on production, sale, transfer, etc	104	1 976	5 946	6 846	7 736	..	..	..	..	..
5110 General taxes	95	1 805	4 186	5 068	5 837	..	..	..	..	..
5120 Taxes on specific goods and services	10	171	1 760	1 778	1 899	..	..	..	..	..
5130 Unallocable between 5110 and 5120	0	0	0	0	0	..	..	..	..	..
5200 Taxes on use of goods and perform activities	0	4 096	6 864	6 221	6 800	..	..	..	..	..
5300 Unallocable between 5100 and 5200	0	0	0	0	0	..	..	..	..	..
6000 Other taxes	**0**	**8**	**6**	**69**	**37**	**0**	**0**	**0**	**0**	**0**
6100 Paid solely by business	..	..	..	..	..	..	..	..	..	..
6200 Other	..	8	6	69	37	..	0	0	0	0
Total tax revenue	**305**	**12 353**	**26 577**	**35 141**	**38 662**	**3 367**	**49 851**	**106 040**	**119 330**	**137 750**

.. Not available

Note: Including taxes collected on behalf of the European Union.

StatLink https://doi.org/10.1787/888934213010

Table 6.33. Sweden, tax revenues by sub-sectors of government

Million SEK

	Central government					State/Regional				
	1975	1995	2005	2015	2018	1975	1995	2005	2015	2018
1000 Taxes on income, profits and capital gains	**28 216**	**72 342**	**100 767**	**21 820**	**34 827**	..	..	..	..	..
1100 Of individuals	25 626	22 541	-1 222	-102 059	-102 620	..	..	..	..	..
1200 Corporate	2 590	49 801	101 989	123 878	137 447	..	..	..	..	..
1300 Unallocable between 1100 and 1200	0	0	0	0	0	..	..	..	..	..
2000 Social security contributions[1]	**0**	**50 560**	**212 964**	**180 723**	**206 593**	..	..	..	..	..
2100 Employees	..	0	0	0	0	..	..	..	..	..
2200 Employers	..	49 222	209 370	179 056	205 392	..	..	..	..	..
2300 Self-employed or non-employed	..	1 338	4 639	1 875	1 710	..	..	..	..	..
2400 Unallocable between 2100, 2200 and 2300	..	0	-1 044	-209	-509	..	..	..	..	..
3000 Taxes on payroll and workforce	**5 723**	**17 800**	**62 432**	**194 121**	**245 036**	..	..	..	..	..
4000 Taxes on property	**1 469**	**23 260**	**40 116**	**27 917**	**27 792**	..	..	..	..	..
4100 Recurrent taxes on immovable property	11	15 263	25 139	16 509	15 167	..	..	..	..	..
4200 Recurrent taxes on net wealth	647	3 583	4 998	0	0	..	..	..	..	..
4300 Estate, inheritance and gift taxes	335	1 388	1 092	0	0	..	..	..	..	..
4400 Taxes on financial and capital transactions	476	3 026	8 887	11 408	12 625	..	..	..	..	..
4500 Non-recurrent taxes	0	0	0	0	0	..	..	..	..	..
4600 Other recurrent taxes on property	0	0	0	0	0	..	..	..	..	..
5000 Taxes on goods and services	**31 985**	**237 720**	**355 413**	**511 387**	**590 449**	..	..	..	..	..
5100 Taxes on production, sale, transfer, etc	29 820	233 671	344 393	492 635	570 614	..	..	..	..	..
5110 General taxes	15 806	166 557	250 470	382 712	445 799	..	..	..	..	..
5120 Taxes on specific goods and services	14 014	67 114	93 924	109 923	124 815	..	..	..	..	..
5130 Unallocable between 5110 and 5120	0	0	0	0	0	..	..	..	..	..
5200 Taxes on use of goods and perform activities	2 165	4 049	11 019	18 752	19 835	..	..	..	..	..
5300 Unallocable between 5100 and 5200	0	0	0	0	0	..	..	..	..	..
6000 Other taxes	**260**	**1 438**	**1 347**	**1 356**	**1 926**	..	..	..	..	..
6100 Paid solely by business	0	0	0	0	..	..	..	..	..	..
6200 Other	260	1 438	1 347	1 356	1 926	..	..	..	..	..
Total tax revenue	**67 653**	**404 489**	**773 040**	**937 323**	**1 106 622**	..	..	..	..	..

	Local government					Social Security Funds				
	1975	1995	2005	2015	2018	1975	1995	2005	2015	2018
1000 Taxes on income, profits and capital gains	**38 415**	**265 068**	**435 577**	**635 719**	**726 221**	**0**	**0**	**0**	**0**	**0**
1100 Of individuals	35 269	265 068	435 577	635 719	726 221	..	..	..	..	..
1200 Corporate	3 146	0	0	0	0	..	..	..	..	..
1300 Unallocable between 1100 and 1200	0	0	0	0	0	..	..	..	..	..
2000 Social security contributions[1]	**0**	**0**	**0**	**0**	**0**	**25 756**	**186 992**	**151 019**	**224 129**	**256 745**
2100 Employees	..	..	..	..	..	0	28 989	74 178	108 356	123 661
2200 Employers	..	..	..	..	..	24 203	154 154	74 377	112 589	129 962
2300 Self-employed or non-employed	..	..	..	..	..	1 553	3 849	2 464	3 183	3 122
2400 Unallocable between 2100, 2200 and 2300	..	..	..	..	..	0	0	0	0	0
3000 Taxes on payroll and workforce	**0**	**0**	**0**	**0**	**0**	**0**	**0**	**0**	**0**	**0**
4000 Taxes on property	**0**	**0**	**0**	**15 935**	**18 050**	**0**	**0**	**0**	**0**	**0**
4100 Recurrent taxes on immovable property	..	..	..	15 935	18 050	..	..	..	..	..
4200 Recurrent taxes on net wealth	..	..	..	0	0	..	..	..	..	..
4300 Estate, inheritance and gift taxes	..	..	..	0	0	..	..	..	..	..
4400 Taxes on financial and capital transactions	..	..	..	0	0	..	..	..	..	..
4500 Non-recurrent taxes	..	..	..	0	0	..	..	..	..	..
4600 Other recurrent taxes on property	..	..	..	0	0	..	..	..	..	..
5000 Taxes on goods and services	**149**	**786**	**0**	**0**	**0**	**0**	**0**	**0**	**0**	**0**
5100 Taxes on production, sale, transfer, etc	119	732	0	0	0	..	..	..	..	..
5110 General taxes	0	0	0	0	0	..	..	..	..	..
5120 Taxes on specific goods and services	119	732	0	0	0	..	..	..	..	..
5130 Unallocable between 5110 and 5120	0	0	0	0	0	..	..	..	..	..
5200 Taxes on use of goods and perform activities	30	54	0	0	0	..	..	..	..	..
5300 Unallocable between 5100 and 5200	0	0	0	0	0	..	..	..	..	..
6000 Other taxes	**0**	**0**	**0**	**0**	**0**	**0**	**0**	**0**	**0**	**0**
6100 Paid solely by business	..	..	..	..	..	..	..	..	..	..
6200 Other	..	..	..	..	..	..	..	..	..	0
Total tax revenue	**38 564**	**265 854**	**435 577**	**651 654**	**744 271**	**25 756**	**186 992**	**151 019**	**224 129**	**256 745**

.. Not available

Note: Including taxes collected on behalf of the European Union.

1. From 1985, social security contributions are classified using the SNA definition of Social security Funds which means that a proportion of these payments are shown under the heading of Central Government. Prior to that year, all such payments were classified under the heading of Social Security.

StatLink https://doi.org/10.1787/888934213029

Table 6.34. Switzerland, tax revenues by sub-sectors of government

Million CHF

	Federal government					State/Regional				
	1975	1995	2005	2015	2018	1975	1995	2005	2015	2018
1000 Taxes on income, profits and capital gains	**3 422**	**10 468**	**16 341**	**26 841**	**30 960**	**7 756**	**19 408**	**26 544**	**34 686**	**37 176**
1100 Of individuals	2 712	5 699	7 823	10 567	11 337	6 342	16 182	21 289	27 185	28 821
1200 Corporate	710	2 678	4 519	9 731	11 275	1 414	2 628	4 627	6 294	7 008
1300 Unallocable between 1100 and 1200	0	2 092	4 000	6 543	8 347	0	598	628	1 207	1 347
2000 Social security contributions	**0**	**0**	**0**	**0**	**0**	**0**	**0**	**0**	**0**	**0**
2100 Employees	..	..	..	..	..	..	..	..	..	..
2200 Employers	..	..	..	..	..	..	..	..	..	..
2300 Self-employed or non-employed	..	..	..	..	..	..	..	..	..	..
2400 Unallocable between 2100, 2200 and 2300	..	..	..	..	..	..	..	..	..	..
3000 Taxes on payroll and workforce	**0**	**0**	**0**	**0**	**0**	**0**	**0**	**0**	**0**	**0**
4000 Taxes on property	**463**	**1 703**	**2 703**	**1 674**	**1 413**	**1 428**	**4 116**	**5 523**	**7 191**	**8 116**
4100 Recurrent taxes on immovable property	0	0	0	0	0	60	162	230	349	347
4200 Recurrent taxes on net wealth	89	0	0	0	0	988	2 467	3 683	4 992	5 653
4300 Estate, inheritance and gift taxes	0	0	0	0	0	270	974	824	964	1 058
4400 Taxes on financial and capital transactions	374	1 703	2 703	1 674	1 413	110	103	157	177	212
4500 Non-recurrent taxes	0	0	0	0	0	0	0	0	0	0
4600 Other recurrent taxes on property	0	0	0	0	0	0	411	629	709	847
5000 Taxes on goods and services	**7 431**	**20 257**	**28 941**	**36 076**	**37 188**	**795**	**1 706**	**2 373**	**2 883**	**2 992**
5100 Taxes on production, sale, transfer, etc	7 431	19 763	27 114	33 093	33 788	154	266	447	604	599
5110 General taxes	3 205	12 428	18 429	22 791	23 042	0	0	0	0	0
5120 Taxes on specific goods and services	4 226	7 335	8 685	10 302	10 746	154	236	410	584	579
5130 Unallocable between 5110 and 5120	0	0	0	0	0	0	29	37	20	20
5200 Taxes on use of goods and perform activities	0	494	1 827	2 983	3 400	641	1 440	1 927	2 280	2 393
5300 Unallocable between 5100 and 5200	0	0	0	0	0	0	0	0	0	0
6000 Other taxes	**0**	**0**	**0**	**0**	**75**	**0**	**19**	**23**	**230**	**358**
6100 Paid solely by business	..	..	..	..	0	..	6	7	64	88
6200 Other	..	..	..	..	75	..	13	16	165	270
Total tax revenue	**11 316**	**32 428**	**47 986**	**64 590**	**69 636**	**9 979**	**25 249**	**34 462**	**44 990**	**48 642**

	Local government					Social Security Funds				
	1975	1995	2005	2015	2018	1975	1995	2005	2015	2018
1000 Taxes on income, profits and capital gains	**6 403**	**15 575**	**18 091**	**22 849**	**24 722**	**0**	**0**	**0**	**0**	**0**
1100 Of individuals	5 398	13 340	15 326	18 625	19 609	..	..	..	..	..
1200 Corporate	1 005	1 624	2 316	3 418	3 933	..	..	..	..	..
1300 Unallocable between 1100 and 1200	0	611	450	806	1 179	..	..	..	..	..
2000 Social security contributions	**0**	**0**	**0**	**0**	**0**	**8 111**	**27 831**	**32 318**	**44 073**	**45 861**
2100 Employees	..	..	..	..	..	3 589	13 021	15 125	20 436	21 356
2200 Employers	..	..	..	..	..	3 618	13 032	15 139	20 468	21 394
2300 Self-employed or non-employed	..	..	..	..	..	840	1 778	2 053	3 169	3 111
2400 Unallocable between 2100, 2200 and 2300	..	..	..	..	..	64	0	0	0	0
3000 Taxes on payroll and workforce	**0**	**0**	**0**	**0**	**0**	**0**	**0**	**0**	**0**	**0**
4000 Taxes on property	**1 068**	**2 614**	**3 251**	**4 262**	**4 763**	**0**	**0**	**0**	**0**	**0**
4100 Recurrent taxes on immovable property	182	443	588	789	817	..	..	..	..	..
4200 Recurrent taxes on net wealth	809	1 873	2 393	3 091	3 549	..	..	..	..	..
4300 Estate, inheritance and gift taxes	27	89	79	124	116	..	..	..	..	..
4400 Taxes on financial and capital transactions	50	42	38	52	56	..	..	..	..	..
4500 Non-recurrent taxes	0	0	0	0	0	..	..	..	..	..
4600 Other recurrent taxes on property	0	168	153	206	225	..	..	..	..	..
5000 Taxes on goods and services	**22**	**97**	**78**	**133**	**171**	**0**	**0**	**0**	**0**	**0**
5100 Taxes on production, sale, transfer, etc	17	55	26	63	74	..	..	..	..	..
5110 General taxes	0	0	0	0	0	..	..	..	..	..
5120 Taxes on specific goods and services	17	29	20	15	17	..	..	..	..	..
5130 Unallocable between 5110 and 5120	0	25	6	48	58	..	..	..	..	..
5200 Taxes on use of goods and perform activities	5	42	52	70	96	..	..	..	..	..
5300 Unallocable between 5100 and 5200	0	0	0	0	0	..	..	..	..	..
6000 Other taxes	**0**	**164**	**223**	**569**	**596**	**0**	**0**	**0**	**0**	**0**
6100 Paid solely by business	..	49	67	277	290	..	..	..	..	..
6200 Other	..	115	156	292	306	..	..	..	..	..
Total tax revenue	**7 493**	**18 451**	**21 643**	**27 813**	**30 253**	**8 111**	**27 831**	**32 318**	**44 073**	**45 861**

.. Not available

StatLink https://doi.org/10.1787/888934213048

Table 6.35. Turkey, tax revenues by sub-sectors of government

Million TRY

Million TRY

	Central government					State/Regional				
	1975	1995	2005	2015	2018	1975	1995	2005	2015	2018
1000 Taxes on income, profits and capital gains	..	**433**	**30 324**	**104 699**	**191 688**	..	..	..	..	..
1100 Of individuals	..	330	20 458	75 426	122 312	..	..	..	..	..
1200 Corporate	..	103	9 866	29 272	69 376	..	..	..	..	..
1300 Unallocable between 1100 and 1200	..	0	0	0	0	..	..	..	..	..
2000 Social security contributions	..	**0**	**0**	**0**	**0**	..	..	..	..	..
2100 Employees	..	..	..	..	..	..	..	..	..	..
2200 Employers	..	..	..	..	..	..	..	..	..	..
2300 Self-employed or non-employed	..	..	..	..	..	..	..	..	..	..
2400 Unallocable between 2100, 2200 and 2300	..	..	..	..	..	..	..	..	..	..
3000 Taxes on payroll and workforce	..	**0**	**0**	**0**	**0**	..	..	..	..	..
4000 Taxes on property	..	**49**	**3 626**	**20 211**	**26 475**	..	..	..	..	..
4100 Recurrent taxes on immovable property	..	0	0	0	0	..	..	..	..	..
4200 Recurrent taxes on net wealth	..	0	0	0	0	..	..	..	..	..
4300 Estate, inheritance and gift taxes	..	1	78	379	815	..	..	..	..	..
4400 Taxes on financial and capital transactions	..	29	3 548	19 832	25 660	..	..	..	..	..
4500 Non-recurrent taxes	..	19	0	0	0	..	..	..	..	..
4600 Other recurrent taxes on property	..	0	0	0	0	..	..	..	..	..
5000 Taxes on goods and services	..	**574**	**71 956**	**231 227**	**322 711**	..	..	..	..	..
5100 Taxes on production, sale, transfer, etc	..	567	69 266	222 702	310 851	..	..	..	..	..
5110 General taxes	..	475	30 343	107 451	156 385	..	..	..	..	..
5120 Taxes on specific goods and services	..	92	38 923	115 251	154 466	..	..	..	..	..
5130 Unallocable between 5110 and 5120	..	0	0	0	0	..	..	..	..	..
5200 Taxes on use of goods and perform activities	..	8	2 691	8 526	11 860	..	..	..	..	..
5300 Unallocable between 5100 and 5200	..	0	0	0	0	..	..	..	..	..
6000 Other taxes	..	**259**	**4 181**	**3 779**	**4 159**	..	..	..	..	..
6100 Paid solely by business	..	0	0	0	0	..	..	..	..	..
6200 Other	..	259	4 181	3 779	4 159	..	..	..	..	..
Total tax revenue	..	**1 316**	**110 088**	**359 915**	**545 033**	..	..	..	..	..

	Local government					Social Security Funds				
	1975	1995	2005	2015	2018	1975	1995	2005	2015	2018
1000 Taxes on income, profits and capital gains	..	**63**	**4 011**	**14 445**	**25 978**	..	**0**	**0**	**0**	**0**
1100 Of individuals	..	48	2 706	10 330	16 681	..	..	..	..	..
1200 Corporate	..	15	1 305	4 116	9 297	..	..	..	..	..
1300 Unallocable between 1100 and 1200	..	0	0	0	0	..	..	..	..	..
2000 Social security contributions	..	**0**	**0**	**0**	**0**	..	**212**	**35 321**	**170 282**	**269 932**
2100 Employees	..	..	..	..	..	..	82	12 128	64 214	101 666
2200 Employers	..	..	..	..	..	..	110	16 132	95 067	151 373
2300 Self-employed or non-employed	..	..	..	..	..	..	19	7 061	11 001	16 893
2400 Unallocable between 2100, 2200 and 2300	..	..	..	..	..	..	0	0	0	0
3000 Taxes on payroll and workforce	..	**0**	**0**	**0**	**0**	..	**0**	**0**	**0**	**0**
4000 Taxes on property	..	**4**	**1 627**	**8 371**	**12 466**	..	**0**	**0**	**0**	**0**
4100 Recurrent taxes on immovable property	..	0	1 148	5 882	8 703	..	..	..	..	..
4200 Recurrent taxes on net wealth	..	0	0	0	0	..	..	..	..	..
4300 Estate, inheritance and gift taxes	..	0	10	56	106	..	..	..	..	..
4400 Taxes on financial and capital transactions	..	4	469	2 433	3 657	..	..	..	..	..
4500 Non-recurrent taxes	..	0	0	0	0	..	..	..	..	..
4600 Other recurrent taxes on property	..	0	0	0	0	..	..	..	..	..
5000 Taxes on goods and services	..	**84**	**5 649**	**28 737**	**42 271**	..	**0**	**0**	**0**	**0**
5100 Taxes on production, sale, transfer, etc	..	82	5 295	27 560	40 604	..	..	..	..	..
5110 General taxes	..	69	4 014	13 619	22 231	..	..	..	..	..
5120 Taxes on specific goods and services	..	13	1 281	13 940	18 374	..	..	..	..	..
5130 Unallocable between 5110 and 5120	..	0	0	0	0	..	..	..	..	..
5200 Taxes on use of goods and perform activities	..	1	354	1 177	1 667	..	..	..	..	..
5300 Unallocable between 5100 and 5200	..	0	0	0	0	..	..	..	..	..
6000 Other taxes	..	**73**	**721**	**4 971**	**5 805**	..	**0**	**0**	**0**	**0**
6100 Paid solely by business	..	0	0	0	0	..	..	..	..	..
6200 Other	..	73	721	4 971	5 805	..	..	..	..	..
Total tax revenue	..	**224**	**12 008**	**56 525**	**86 520**	..	**212**	**35 321**	**170 282**	**269 932**

.. Not available

StatLink https://doi.org/10.1787/888934213067

Table 6.36. United Kingdom, tax revenues by sub-sectors of government

Million GBP

	Central government					State/Regional				
	1975	1995	2005	2015	2018	1975	1995	2005	2015	2018
1000 Taxes on income, profits and capital gains	**16 716**	**92 147**	**177 149**	**223 355**	**249 059**	..	..	..	..	..
1100 Of individuals	14 936	71 973	130 135	168 873	192 765	..	..	..	..	..
1200 Corporate	2 310	20 174	47 014	54 482	56 294	..	..	..	..	..
1300 Unallocable between 1100 and 1200	-530	0	0	0	0	..	..	..	..	..
2000 Social security contributions	**0**	**0**	**0**	**0**	**0**	..	..	..	..	..
2100 Employees	..	..	..	..	..	..	..	..	..	..
2200 Employers	..	..	..	..	..	..	..	..	..	..
2300 Self-employed or non-employed	..	..	..	..	..	..	..	..	..	..
2400 Unallocable between 2100, 2200 and 2300	..	..	..	..	..	..	..	..	..	..
3000 Taxes on payroll and workforce	**-1**	**0**	**0**	**0**	**2 604**	..	..	..	..	..
4000 Taxes on property	**619**	**15 730**	**32 583**	**46 622**	**52 766**	..	..	..	..	..
4100 Recurrent taxes on immovable property	44	12 369	19 523	28 389	30 811	..	..	..	..	..
4200 Recurrent taxes on net wealth	0	0	0	0	0	..	..	..	..	..
4300 Estate, inheritance and gift taxes	307	1 441	3 150	4 442	5 301	..	..	..	..	..
4400 Taxes on financial and capital transactions	266	1 920	9 910	13 791	16 654	..	..	..	..	..
4500 Non-recurrent taxes	2	0	0	0	0	..	..	..	..	..
4600 Other recurrent taxes on property	0	0	0	0	0	..	..	..	..	..
5000 Taxes on goods and services	**8 982**	**85 507**	**136 758**	**204 693**	**226 569**	..	..	..	..	..
5100 Taxes on production, sale, transfer, etc	8 502	81 175	131 362	197 250	218 472	..	..	..	..	..
5110 General taxes	3 515	47 539	84 649	133 064	149 078	..	..	..	..	..
5120 Taxes on specific goods and services	4 987	33 636	46 713	64 186	69 394	..	..	..	..	..
5130 Unallocable between 5110 and 5120	0	0	0	0	0	..	..	..	..	..
5200 Taxes on use of goods and perform activities	698	4 332	5 396	7 443	8 097	..	..	..	..	..
5300 Unallocable between 5100 and 5200	-218	0	0	0	0	..	..	..	..	..
6000 Other taxes	**0**	**0**	**0**	**0**	**0**	..	..	..	..	..
6100 Paid solely by business	..	..	..	..	..	..	..	..	..	..
6200 Other	..	..	..	..	..	..	..	..	..	..
Total tax revenue	**26 316**	**193 384**	**346 490**	**474 670**	**530 998**	..	..	..	..	..

	Local government					Social Security Funds				
	1975	1995	2005	2015	2018	1975	1995	2005	2015	2018
1000 Taxes on income, profits and capital gains	**0**	**0**	**0**	**0**	**0**	**0**	**0**	**0**	**0**	**0**
1100 Of individuals	0	0	0	0	0	0	0	0	0	0
1200 Corporate	0	0	0	0	0	0	0	0	0	0
1300 Unallocable between 1100 and 1200	0	0	0	0	0	0	0	0	0	0
2000 Social security contributions	**0**	**0**	**0**	**0**	**0**	**6 540**	**44 397**	**84 459**	**114 067**	**134 986**
2100 Employees	..	..	..	..	..	2 562	18 646	35 159	44 454	52 055
2200 Employers	..	..	..	..	..	4 068	24 210	46 475	66 491	79 240
2300 Self-employed or non-employed	..	..	..	..	..	195	1 541	2 825	3 122	3 691
2400 Unallocable between 2100, 2200 and 2300	..	..	..	..	..	-285	0	0	0	0
3000 Taxes on payroll and workforce	**0**	**0**	**0**	**0**	**0**	**0**	**0**	**0**	**0**	**0**
4000 Taxes on property	**4 127**	**9 303**	**21 255**	**29 943**	**35 650**	**0**	**0**	**0**	**0**	**0**
4100 Recurrent taxes on immovable property	3 978	9 303	21 255	29 796	35 348	..	..	..	..	..
4200 Recurrent taxes on net wealth	0	0	0	0	0	..	..	..	..	..
4300 Estate, inheritance and gift taxes	0	0	0	0	0	..	..	..	..	..
4400 Taxes on financial and capital transactions	0	0	0	0	0	..	..	..	..	..
4500 Non-recurrent taxes	0	0	0	147	302	..	..	..	..	..
4600 Other recurrent taxes on property	149	0	0	0	0	..	..	..	..	..
5000 Taxes on goods and services	**0**	**0**	**0**	**0**	**0**	**0**	**0**	**0**	**0**	**0**
5100 Taxes on production, sale, transfer, etc	..	..	..	..	..	..	..	..	..	..
5110 General taxes	..	..	..	..	..	..	..	..	..	..
5120 Taxes on specific goods and services	..	..	..	..	..	..	..	..	..	..
5130 Unallocable between 5110 and 5120	..	..	..	..	..	..	..	..	..	..
5200 Taxes on use of goods and perform activities	..	..	..	..	..	..	..	..	..	..
5300 Unallocable between 5100 and 5200	..	..	..	..	..	..	..	..	..	..
6000 Other taxes	**0**	**0**	**0**	**0**	**0**	**0**	**0**	**0**	**0**	**0**
6100 Paid solely by business	..	..	..	..	..	..	..	..	..	..
6200 Other	..	..	0	..	..	..	..	..	..	..
Total tax revenue	**4 127**	**9 303**	**21 255**	**29 943**	**35 650**	**6 540**	**44 397**	**84 459**	**114 067**	**134 986**

.. Not available

Note: Including taxes collected on behalf of the European Union.

StatLink https://doi.org/10.1787/888934213086

Table 6.37. United States, tax revenues by sub-sectors of government

Million USD

	Federal government					State/Regional				
	1975	1995	2005	2015	2018	1975	1995	2005	2015	2018
1000 Taxes on income, profits and capital gains	**163 072**	**750 144**	**1 268 412**	**1 882 708**	**1 795 260**	**25 509**	**157 598**	**275 728**	**391 102**	**436 954**
1100 Of individuals	122 386	594 213	948 921	1 553 620	1 647 896	..	128 429	226 576	343 104	387 288
1200 Corporate	40 686	155 931	319 490	329 088	147 363	..	29 169	49 152	47 998	49 666
1300 Unallocable between 1100 and 1200	0	0	0	0	0	..	0	0	0	0
2000 Social security contributions	**0**	**0**	**0**	**0**	**0**	**0**	**0**	**0**	**0**	**0**
2100 Employees	..	..	..	..	..	..	..	..	..	..
2200 Employers	..	..	..	..	..	..	..	..	..	..
2300 Self-employed or non-employed	..	..	..	..	..	..	..	..	..	..
2400 Unallocable between 2100, 2200 and 2300	..	..	..	..	..	..	..	..	..	..
3000 Taxes on payroll and workforce	**0**	**0**	**0**	**0**	**0**	**0**	**0**	**0**	**1 750**	**2 169**
4000 Taxes on property	**4 613**	**14 948**	**24 989**	**20 191**	**22 871**	**3 284**	**16 880**	**28 808**	**31 016**	**34 978**
4100 Recurrent taxes on immovable property	0	0	0	0	0	1 451	7 240	9 037	13 288	14 917
4200 Recurrent taxes on net wealth	0	0	0	0	0	0	0	0	0	0
4300 Estate, inheritance and gift taxes	4 611	14 948	24 989	20 191	22 871	1 418	5 061	5 322	5 088	5 347
4400 Taxes on financial and capital transactions	2	0	0	0	0	415	2 386	11 711	8 614	10 195
4500 Non-recurrent taxes	0	0	0	0	0	0	0	0	0	0
4600 Other recurrent taxes on property	0	0	0	0	0	0	2 193	2 738	4 025	4 519
5000 Taxes on goods and services	**20 773**	**75 553**	**99 411**	**140 342**	**160 821**	**52 032**	**232 033**	**377 795**	**502 508**	**562 656**
5100 Taxes on production, sale, transfer, etc	20 442	75 553	99 411	140 342	160 821	43 960	200 495	323 137	438 456	490 150
5110 General taxes	0	0	0	0	0	24 916	135 132	218 917	289 875	321 450
5120 Taxes on specific goods and services	20 442	75 553	99 411	140 342	160 821	19 044	65 363	104 220	148 581	168 700
5130 Unallocable between 5110 and 5120	0	0	0	0	0	0	0	0	0	0
5200 Taxes on use of goods and perform activities	331	0	0	0	0	8 072	31 538	54 658	64 051	72 506
5300 Unallocable between 5100 and 5200	0	0	0	0	0	0	0	0	0	0
6000 Other taxes	**0**	**0**	**0**	**0**	**0**	**0**	**0**	**0**	**0**	**0**
6100 Paid solely by business	..	..	..	..	..	..	..	..	..	..
6200 Other	..	..	..	..	..	..	..	..	..	..
Total tax revenue	**188 458**	**840 645**	**1 392 812**	**2 043 241**	**1 978 952**	**80 825**	**406 511**	**682 331**	**926 376**	**1 036 758**

	Local government					Social Security Funds				
	1975	1995	2005	2015	2018	1975	1995	2005	2015	2018
1000 Taxes on income, profits and capital gains	**2 635**	**15 795**	**28 272**	**39 437**	**42 382**	**0**	**0**	**0**	**0**	**0**
1100 Of individuals	..	13 308	22 481	31 228	33 637	..	..	..	..	..
1200 Corporate	..	2 487	5 791	8 209	8 745	..	..	..	..	..
1300 Unallocable between 1100 and 1200	..	0	0	0	0	..	..	..	..	..
2000 Social security contributions	**0**	**0**	**0**	**0**	**0**	**85 039**	**510 476**	**831 410**	**1 125 542**	**1 250 370**
2100 Employees	..	..	..	..	..	36 382	221 800	362 829	502 446	568 322
2200 Employers	..	..	..	..	..	45 241	261 805	423 936	561 881	616 078
2300 Self-employed or non-employed	..	..	..	..	..	3 416	26 871	44 645	61 215	65 970
2400 Unallocable between 2100, 2200 and 2300	..	..	..	..	..	0	0	0	0	0
3000 Taxes on payroll and workforce	**0**	**0**	**0**	**0**	**0**	**0**	**0**	**0**	**0**	**0**
4000 Taxes on property	**50 040**	**197 392**	**359 344**	**488 331**	**559 829**	**0**	**0**	**0**	**0**	**0**
4100 Recurrent taxes on immovable property	50 040	195 339	342 203	477 020	547 082	..	..	..	..	..
4200 Recurrent taxes on net wealth	0	0	0	0	0	..	..	..	..	..
4300 Estate, inheritance and gift taxes	0	30	114	226	294	..	..	..	..	..
4400 Taxes on financial and capital transactions	0	50	13 570	6 266	6 928	..	..	..	..	..
4500 Non-recurrent taxes	0	0	0	0	0	..	..	..	..	..
4600 Other recurrent taxes on property	0	1 973	3 457	4 818	5 526	..	..	..	..	..
5000 Taxes on goods and services	**8 389**	**57 507**	**108 696**	**151 277**	**163 457**	**0**	**0**	**0**	**0**	**0**
5100 Taxes on production, sale, transfer, etc	6 518	42 269	76 976	117 939	126 167	..	..	..	..	..
5110 General taxes	4 322	29 316	53 842	85 591	90 455	..	..	..	..	..
5120 Taxes on specific goods and services	2 196	12 953	23 134	32 348	35 712	..	..	..	..	..
5130 Unallocable between 5110 and 5120	0	0	0	0	0	..	..	..	..	..
5200 Taxes on use of goods and perform activities	1 871	15 238	31 720	33 338	37 289	..	..	..	..	..
5300 Unallocable between 5100 and 5200	0	0	0	0	0	..	..	..	..	..
6000 Other taxes	**0**	**0**	**0**	**0**	**0**	**0**	**0**	**0**	**0**	**0**
6100 Paid solely by business	..	..	..	..	..	..	..	..	..	..
6200 Other	..	..	..	..	..	..	..	..	..	..
Total tax revenue	**61 064**	**270 695**	**496 313**	**679 045**	**765 668**	**85 039**	**510 476**	**831 410**	**1 125 542**	**1 250 370**

.. Not available

StatLink https://doi.org/10.1787/888934213105

Annex A. The OECD Classification of Taxes and Interpretative Guide

Table of Contents

A.1 The OECD Classification of Taxes

1. **1000. Taxes on income, profits and capital gains**
    - 1100. Taxes on income, profits and capital gains of individuals
        - 1110. On income and profits
        - 1120. On capital gains
    - 1200. Corporate taxes on income, profits and capital gains
        - 1210. On income and profits
        - 1220. On capital gains
    - 1300. Unallocable as between 1100 and 1200
2. **2000. Social security contributions**
    - 2100. Employees
        - 2110. On a payroll basis
        - 2120. On an income tax basis
    - 2200. Employers
        - 2210. On a payroll basis
        - 2220. On an income tax basis
    - 2300. Self-employed or non-employed
        - 2310. On a payroll basis
        - 2320. On an income tax basis
    - 2400 Unallocable as between 2100, 2200 and 2300
        - 2410. On a payroll basis
        - 2420. On an income tax basis
3. **3000. Taxes on payroll and workforce**
4. **4000. Taxes on property**
    - 4100. Recurrent taxes on immovable property
        - 4110. Households
        - 4120. Other
    - 4200 Recurrent taxes on net wealth
        - 4210. Individual
        - 4220. Corporate
    - 4300. Estate, inheritance and gift taxes
        - 4310. Estate and inheritance taxes
        - 4320. Gift taxes
    - 4400. Taxes on financial and capital transactions

4500. Other non-recurrent taxes on property

4510. On net wealth

4520. Other non-recurrent taxes

4600. Other recurrent taxes on property

5. **5000. Taxes on goods and services**

5100. Taxes on production, sale, transfer, leasing and delivery of goods and rendering of services

5110. General taxes

5111. Value added taxes

5112. Sales taxes

5113. Turnover and other general taxes on goods and services

5120. Taxes on specific goods and services

5121. Excises

5122. Profits of fiscal monopolies

5123. Customs and import duties

5124. Taxes on exports

5125. Taxes on investment goods

5126 . Taxes on specific services

5127. Other taxes on international trade and transactions

5128. Other taxes on specific goods and services

5130. Unallocable as between 5110 and 5120

5200. Taxes on use of goods, or on permission to use goods or perform activities

5210. Recurrent taxes

5211. Paid by households in respect of motor vehicles

5212. Paid by others in respect of motor vehicles

5213. Other recurrent taxes

5220. Non-recurrent taxes

5300. Unallocable as between 5100 and 5200

6. **6000. Other taxes**

6100. Paid solely by business

6200. Paid by other than business or unidentifiable

A.2 Coverage

General criteria

1. In the OECD classification the term "taxes" is confined to compulsory unrequited payments to the general government or to a supranational authority. Taxes are unrequited in the sense that benefits provided by government to taxpayers are not normally in proportion to their payments.

2. The term "tax" does not include fines, penalties and compulsory loans paid to government. Borderline cases between tax and non-tax revenues in relation to certain fees and charges are discussed in §12–15.

3. General government consists of the central administration, agencies whose operations are under its effective control, state and local governments and their administrations, certain social security schemes and autonomous governmental entities, excluding public enterprises. This definition of government follows that of the 2008 *System of National Accounts* (SNA).[1] In that publication, the general government sector and its sub-sectors are defined in Chapter 4, paragraphs 4.117 to 4.165.

4. Extra-budgetary units are part of the general government system. These are general government entities with individual budgets that are not fully covered by the main or general budget. These entities operate under the authority or control of a central, state, or local government. Extra-budgetary entities may have their own revenue sources, which may be supplemented by grants (transfers) from the general budget or from other sources. Even though their budgets may be subject to approval by the legislature, similar to that of budgetary accounts, they have discretion over the volume and composition of their spending. Such entities may be established to carry out specific government functions, such as road construction, or the nonmarket production of health or education services. Budgetary arrangements vary widely across countries, and various terms are used to describe these entities, but they are often referred to as "extra-budgetary funds" or "decentralised agencies."

5. Compulsory, unrequited payments collected by national governments and paid to supranational authorities are also included as taxes under the definition in paragraph 1. Taxes that are collected by national governments and paid to a supranational authority are included as tax revenues at the level of the supranational authority in the SNA2008 (paragraphs 22.60-61, 22.88 and 22.99 refer) and the ESA2010 (paragraph 20.165 refers). In Revenue Statistics, these taxes include customs duties, contributions to the EU Single Resolution Fund, and any other taxes collected by EU member states on behalf of the European Union. They are included in the tax revenue amounts in the country tables (Chapter 5) of the country in which they are collected and are attributed to the supranational level of government (see §101).

6. In countries where the church forms part of general government, church taxes are included, provided they meet the criteria set out in §1 above. As the data refer to receipts of general government and to supranational authorities, levies paid to non-government bodies, welfare agencies or social insurance schemes outside general government, trade unions or trade associations, even where such levies are compulsory, are excluded. Compulsory payments to general government earmarked for such bodies are, however, included, provided that the government is not simply acting in an agency capacity.[2] Profits from fiscal monopolies are distinguished from those of other public enterprises and are treated as taxes because they reflect the exercise of the taxing power of the state by the use of monopoly powers (see §66–68), as are profits received by the government from the purchase and sale of foreign exchange at different rates (see §76).

7. Taxes paid by governments (e.g., social security contributions and payroll taxes paid by governments in their capacity as an employer, consumption taxes on their purchases or taxes on their property) are not excluded from the data provided. However, where it is possible to identify the amounts of revenue involved,[3] they are shown in Table 5.39 of this Report.

8. The relationship between this classification and that of the System of National Accounts (SNA) is set out in Sections A.9 and A.11 below. Because of the differences between the two classifications, the data shown in national accounts are sometimes calculated or classified differently from the practice set out in this guide. These and other differences are mentioned where appropriate (e.g., in §31 below) but it is not possible to refer to all of them. There may also be some differences between this classification and that employed domestically by certain national administrations (e.g., see §13 below), so that OECD and national statistics data may not always be consistent: any such differences, however, are likely to be very slight in terms of amounts of revenues involved.

Social security contributions

9. Compulsory social security contributions, as defined in §40, and paid to general government, are treated here as tax revenues. They may, however, differ from other taxes in that the receipt of social security benefits depends, in most countries, upon appropriate contributions having been made, although the size of the benefits is not necessarily related to the amount of the contributions. Better comparability between countries is obtained by treating social security contributions as taxes, but they are listed under a separate heading so that they can be distinguished in any analysis.

10. The strict dividing line between tax revenues (compulsory unrequited payments to general government or a supranational authority) and non-tax compulsory payments (NTCPs) (payments that are either requited or made to other institutions) is clearly defined. However, within the range of different compulsory payments to governments existing across countries, it is not always straightforward in practice to decide whether specific payments are either taxes or NTCPs. For example, compulsory pension savings that are controlled by general government and that accumulate on an individual account earning a market return or a rate that compensates for inflation would at first sight be categorised as NTCPs as opposed to taxes. However, even these payments might still be 'unrequited' and therefore classify as taxes instead of NTCPs (for example if these pension savings are not paid out when the taxpayer dies before reaching the pension age and the funds are then used to provide a minimum pension to all taxpayers that are insured). These issues result in the social security revenue figures reported for most countries being based on the premise that all types of compulsory payments to general government are judged to some extent to have a re-distributional element. It should be noted that this conclusion is based on a typically broad interpretation of the term 'unrequited' in the tax definition.

11. Social security contributions which are either voluntary or not payable to general government (see §1) are not treated as taxes, though in some countries, as indicated in the country footnotes, there are difficulties in completely eliminating voluntary contributions and certain compulsory payments to the private sector from the revenue figures. Imputed social security contributions are also not treated as taxes.

Fees, user charges and licence fees

12. Apart from vehicle licence fees, which are universally regarded as taxes, it is not easy to distinguish between those fees and user charges which are to be treated as taxes and those which are not, since, whilst a fee or charge is levied in connection with a specific service or activity, the strength of the link between the fee and the service provided may vary considerably, as may the relation between the amount of the fee and the cost of providing the service. Where the recipient of a service pays a fee clearly related to the cost of providing the service, the levy may be regarded as requited and under the definition of §1 would not be considered as a tax. In the following cases, however, a levy could be considered as 'unrequited':

- *a)* where the charge greatly exceeds the cost of providing the service;
- *b)* where the payer of the levy is not the receiver of the benefit (e.g., a fee collected from slaughterhouses to finance a service which is provided to farmers);

c) where government is not providing a specific service in return for the levy which it receives even though a licence may be issued to the payer (e.g., where the government grants a hunting, fishing or shooting licence which is not accompanied by the right to use a specific area of government land);

d) where benefits are received only by those paying the levy but the benefits received by each individual are not necessarily in proportion to his payments (e.g., a milk marketing levy paid by dairy farmers and used to promote the consumption of milk).

13. In marginal cases, however, the application of the criteria set out in §1 can be particularly difficult. The solution adopted — given the desirability of international uniformity and the relatively small amounts of revenue usually involved — is to follow the predominant practice among tax administrations rather than to allow each country to adopt its own view as to whether such levies are regarded as taxes or as non-tax revenue.[4]

14. A list of the main fees and charges in question and their normal[5] treatment in this publication is as follows:

Non-tax revenues:	court fees; driving licence fees; harbour fees; passport fees; radio and television licence fees where public authorities provide the service
Taxes within heading 5200	permission to perform such activities as distributing films; hunting, fishing and shooting; providing entertainment or gambling facilities; selling alcohol or tobacco; permission to own dogs or to use or own motor vehicles or guns; severance taxes

15. In practice it may not always be possible to isolate tax receipts from non-tax revenue receipts when they are recorded together. If it is estimated that the bulk of the receipts derive from non-tax revenues, the whole amount involved is treated as a non-tax revenue; otherwise, such government receipts are included and classified according to the rules provided in §33 below.

Royalties

16. The ownership of subsoil assets in the form of deposits of minerals or fossil fuels (coal, oil, or natural gas) depends upon the way in which property rights are defined by law and also on international agreements in the case of deposits below international waters. In some cases, either the ground below which the mineral deposits are located, the deposits themselves or both may belong to a local or central government unit.

17. In such cases, these general government units may grant leases to other institutional units that permit them to extract these deposits over a specified period of time in return for a payment or series of payments. These payments are often described as 'royalties' but they are essentially rent that accrues to owners of natural resources in return for putting these assets at the disposal of other units for specified periods of time. The rent may take the form of periodic payments of fixed amounts, irrespective of the rate of extraction, or, more commonly, they may be a function of the quantity, volume, or value of the asset extracted. Enterprises engaged in exploration on government land may make payments to general government units in exchange for the right to undertake test drilling or otherwise investigate the existence and location of subsoil assets. Such payments are also recorded as rents even though no extraction may take place. These payments are therefore classified as non-tax revenues.

18. The same principles apply when other institutional units are granted leases that permit them to fell timber in natural forests on land owned by general government units. These payments are also classified as non-tax revenues.

19. These rents or royalties paid to general government should not be confused with taxes on income and profits, severance taxes, business licenses, or other taxes. If the payments are levied on the profits from the extraction activity, then they should be classified as taxes on incomes, profits and gains (1000).

In addition, any severance payments that are imposed on the extraction of minerals and fossil fuels from reserves owned privately or by another government should be classified as taxes. Payments related to the gross value of production should be classified as other taxes on goods and services (5128). Payments for a license or permit to conduct extraction operations should be classified as taxes on use of goods and on permission to use goods or perform activities (5213).

Fines and penalties

20. In principle, fines and penalties charged on overdue taxes or penalties imposed for the attempted evasion of taxes should not be recorded as tax revenues. However it may not be possible to separate payments of fines or other penalties from the revenues from the taxes to which they relate. In this case the fines and penalties relating to a particular tax are recorded together with the revenues from that tax and fines and penalties paid with revenue from unidentifiable taxes are classified as other taxes in Category 6000. Fines not relating to tax offences (e.g., for parking offences), or not identifiable as relating to tax offences, are also not treated as tax revenues.

A.3 Basis of reporting

Accrual reporting

21. The data reported in this publication for recent years are predominantly recorded on an accrual basis, i.e. recorded at the time that the tax liability was created. Further information is provided in the footnotes to the country table in Chapter 5 of the Report.

22. However, data for earlier years are still predominantly recorded on a cash basis, i.e. at the time at which the payment was received by government. Thus, for example, taxes withheld by employers in one year but paid to the government in the following year and taxes due in one year but actually paid in the following year are both included in the receipts of the second year. Corrective transactions, such as refunds, repayments and drawbacks, are deducted from gross revenues of the period in which they are made.

23. Data on tax revenues are recorded without offsets for the administrative expenses connected with tax collection. Similarly, where the proceeds of tax are used to subsidise particular members of the community, the subsidy is not deducted from the yield of the tax, though the tax may be shown net of subsidies in the national records of some countries.

24. As regards fiscal monopolies (heading 5122), only the amount actually transferred to the government is included in government revenues. However, if any expenditures of fiscal monopolies are considered to be government expenditures (e.g., social expenditures undertaken by fiscal monopolies at the direction of the government) they are added back for the purpose of arriving at tax revenue figures (see §66 below).

The distinction between tax and expenditure provisions[6]

25. Because this publication is concerned only with the revenue side of government operations, no account being taken of the expenditure side, a distinction has to be made between tax and expenditure provisions. Normally there is no difficulty in making this distinction as expenditures are made outside the tax system and the tax accounts and under legislation separate from the tax legislation. In borderline cases, cash flow is used to distinguish between tax provisions and expenditure provisions. Insofar as a provision affects the flow of tax payments from the taxpayer to the government, it is regarded as a tax provision and is taken into account in the data shown in this publication. A provision which does not affect this flow is seen as an expenditure provision and is disregarded in the data recorded in this publication.

26. Tax allowances, exemptions and deductions against the tax base clearly affect the amount of tax paid to the government and are therefore considered as tax provisions. At the other extreme, those subsidies which cannot be offset against tax liability and which are clearly not connected with the assessment process, do not reduce tax revenues as recorded in this publication. Tax credits are amounts deductible from tax payable (as distinct from deductions from the tax base). Two types of tax credits are distinguished, those (referred to here as wastable tax credits) which are limited to the amount of the tax liability and therefore cannot give rise to a payment by the authorities to the taxpayer, and those (referred to as non-wastable tax credits) which are not so limited, so that the excess of the credit over the tax liability can be paid to the taxpayer.[7] A wastable tax credit, like a tax allowance, clearly affects the amount of tax paid to the government, and is therefore considered as a tax provision. The practice followed for non-wastable tax credits[8] is to distinguish between the 'tax expenditure component',[9] which is that portion of the credit that is used to reduce or eliminate a taxpayer's liability, and the 'transfer component', which is the portion that exceeds the taxpayer's liability and is paid to that taxpayer. Reported tax revenues should be reduced by the amount of the tax expenditure component but not by the amount of the transfer component. In addition, the amounts of the tax expenditure and transfer components should be reported as memorandum items in the country tables. Countries that are unable to distinguish between the tax expenditure and transfer components should indicate whether or not the tax revenues have been reduced by the total of these components, and provide any available estimates of the amounts of the two components. Further information is given in Chapter 1 of the Report, which illustrates the effect of alternative treatments of non-wastable tax credits on tax to GDP.

Calendar and fiscal years

27. National authorities whose fiscal years do not correspond to the calendar year show data, where possible, on a calendar year basis to permit maximum comparability with the data of other countries. There remain a few countries where data refer to fiscal years. For these the GDP data used in the comparative tables also correspond to the fiscal years.

A.4 General classification criteria

The main classification criteria

28. The classification of receipts among the main headings (1000, 2000, 3000, 4000, 5000 and 6000) is generally governed by the base on which the tax is levied: 1000 income, profits and capital gains; 2000 and 3000 earnings, payroll or number of employees; 4000 property; 5000 goods and services; 6000 multiple bases, other bases or unidentifiable bases. Where a tax is calculated on more than one base, the receipts are, where possible, split among the various headings (see §33 and §83). The headings 4000 and 5000 cover not only taxes where the tax base is the property, goods or services themselves but also certain related taxes. Thus, taxes on the transfer of property are included in 4400[10] and taxes on the use of goods or on permission to perform activities in 5200. In headings 4000 and 5000 a distinction is made in certain sub-headings between recurrent and non-recurrent taxes: recurrent taxes are defined as those levied at regular intervals (usually annually) and non-recurrent taxes are levied once and for all (see also §48 to §51, §54, §55 and §81 for particular applications of this distinction).

29. Earmarking of a tax for specific purposes does not affect the classification of tax receipts. However, as explained in §40 on the classification of social security contributions, the conferment of an entitlement to social benefits is crucial to the definition of the 2000 main heading.

30. The way that a tax is levied or collected (e.g., by use of stamps) does not affect classification.

Classification of taxpayers

31. In certain sub-headings distinctions are made between different categories of taxpayers. These distinctions vary from tax to tax:

a) Between individuals and corporations in relation to income and net wealth taxes

The basic distinction is that corporation income taxes, as distinct from individual income taxes, are levied on the corporation as an entity, not on the individuals who own it, and without regard to the personal circumstances of these individuals. The same distinction applies to net wealth taxes on corporations and those on individuals. Taxes paid on the profits of partnerships and the income of institutions, such as life insurance or pension funds, are classified according to the same rule. They are classified as corporate taxes (1200) if they are charged on the partnership or institution as an entity without regard to the personal circumstances of the owners. Otherwise, they are treated as individual taxes (1100). Usually, there is different legislation for the corporation taxes and for the individual taxes.[11] The distinction made here between individuals and corporations does not follow the sector classification between households, enterprises, and so on of the System of National Accounts for income and outlay accounts. The SNA classification requires certain unincorporated businesses[12] to be excluded from the household sector and included with non-financial enterprises and financial institutions. The tax on the profits of these businesses, however, cannot always be separated from the tax on the other income of their owners, or can be separated only on an arbitrary basis. No attempt at this separation is made here and the whole of the individual income tax is shown together without regard to the nature of the income chargeable.

b) Between households and others in relation to taxes on immovable property

Here the distinction is that adopted by the SNA for the production and consumption expenditure accounts. The distinction is between households as consumers (i.e. excluding non-incorporated business) on the one hand and producers on the other hand. However, taxes on dwellings occupied by households, whether paid by owner-occupiers, tenants or landlords, are classified under households. This follows the common distinction made between taxes on domestic property versus taxes on business property. Some countries are not, however, in a position to make this distinction.

c) Between households and others in relation to motor vehicle licences

Here the distinction is between households as consumers on the one hand and producers on the other, as in the production and consumption expenditure accounts of the SNA.

d) Between business and others in relation to the residual taxes (6000)

The distinction is the same as in c) above between producers on the one hand and households as consumers on the other hand. Taxes which are included under the heading 6000 because they involve more than one tax base or because the tax base does not fall within any of the previous categories but which are identifiable as levyable only on producers and not on households are included under 'business'. The rest of the taxes which are included under the heading 6000 are shown as 'other' or non-identified.

Surcharges

32. Receipts from surcharges in respect of particular taxes are usually classified with the receipts from the relevant tax whether or not the surcharge is temporary. If, however, the surcharge has a characteristic which would render it classifiable in a different heading of the OECD list, receipts from the surcharge are classified under that heading separately from the relevant tax.

Unidentifiable tax receipts and residual sub-headings

33. A number of cases arise where taxes cannot be identified as belonging entirely to a heading or sub-heading of the OECD classification and the following practices are applied in such cases:

a) The heading is known, but it is not known how receipts should be allocated between sub-headings: receipts are classified in the appropriate residual sub-heading (1300, 2400, 4520, 4600, 5130, 5300 or 6200).

b) It is known that the bulk of receipts from a group of taxes (usually local taxes) is derived from taxes within a particular heading or sub-heading, but some of the taxes in the group whose amount cannot be precisely ascertained may be classifiable in other headings or sub-headings: receipts are shown in the heading or sub-heading under which most of the receipts fall.

c) Neither the heading nor sub-heading of a tax (usually local) can be identified: the tax is classified in 6200 unless it is known that it is a tax on business in which case it is classified in 6100.

A.5 Commentaries on items of the list

1000 — Taxes on income, profits and capital gains

34. This heading covers taxes levied on the net income or profits (i.e. gross income minus allowable tax reliefs) of individuals and enterprises. Also covered are taxes levied on the capital gains of individuals and enterprises, and gains from gambling.

35. Included in the heading are:

a) taxes levied predominantly on income or profits, though partially on other bases. Taxes on various bases which are not predominantly income or profits are classified according to the principles laid down in §33 and §83;

b) taxes on property, which are levied on a presumed or estimated income as part of an income tax (see also §48(a), (c) and (d));

c) compulsory payments to social security fund contributions that are levied on income but do not confer an entitlement to social benefits. When such contributions do confer an entitlement to social benefits, they are included in heading 2000 (see §40);

d) receipts from integrated scheduler income tax systems are classified as a whole in this heading, even though certain of the scheduler taxes may be based upon gross income and may not take into account the personal circumstances of the taxpayer.

36. The main subdivision of this heading is between levies on individuals (1100) and those on corporate enterprises (1200). Under each subdivision a distinction is made between taxes on income and profits (1110 and 1210), and taxes on capital gains (1120 and 1220). If certain receipts cannot be identified as appropriate to either 1100 or 1200, or if in practice this distinction cannot be made (e.g., because there are no reliable data on the recipients of payments from which withholding taxes are deducted) they are classified in 1300 as not-allocable.

Treatment of credits under imputation systems

37. Under imputation systems of corporate income tax, a company's shareholders are wholly or partly relieved of their liability to income tax on dividends paid by the company out of income or profits liable to corporate income tax. In countries with such systems,[13] part of the tax on the company's profits is available

to provide relief against the shareholders' own tax liability. The relief to the shareholder takes the form of a tax credit, the amount of which may be less than, equal to, or more than the shareholder's overall tax liability. If the tax credit exceeds this tax liability the excess may be payable to the shareholder. As this type of tax credit is an integral part of the imputation system of corporate income tax, any payment to the shareholders is treated as a repayment of tax and not as expenditure (compare the treatment of other tax credits described in §26).

38. As the tax credit under imputation systems (even when exceeding tax liability) is to be regarded as a tax provision, the question arises whether it should be deducted from individual income tax receipts (1110) or corporate income tax receipts (1210). In this Report, the full amount of corporate income tax paid is shown under 1210 and no imputed tax is included under 1110. Thus, the full amount of the credit reduces the amount of 1110 whether the credit results in a reduction of personal income tax liability or whether an actual refund is made because the credit exceeds the income tax liability. (Where, however, such tax credits are deducted from corporation tax in respect of dividends paid to corporations the amounts are deducted from the receipts of 1210).

1120 and 1220 — Taxes on capital gains

39. These sub-headings comprise taxes imposed on capital gains, 1120 covering those levied on the gains of individuals and 1220 those levied on the gains of corporate enterprises, where receipts from such taxes can be separately identified. In many countries this is not the case and the receipts from such taxes are then classified with those from the income tax. Heading 1120 also includes taxes on gains from gambling.

2000 — Social security contributions

40. Classified here are all compulsory payments to general government that confer an entitlement to receive a (contingent) future social benefit. Such payments are usually earmarked to finance social benefits and are often paid to institutions of general government that provide such benefits. However, such earmarking is not part of the definition of social security contributions and is not required for a tax to be classified here. However, conferment of an entitlement is required for a tax to be classified under this heading. So, levies on income or payroll that are earmarked for social security funds but do not confer an entitlement to benefit are excluded from this heading and shown under personal income taxes (1100) or taxes on payroll and workforce (3000). Taxes on other bases, such as goods and services, which are earmarked for social security benefits are not shown here but are classified according to their respective bases because they generally confer no entitlement to social security benefits.

41. Contributions for the following types of social security benefits would, *inter alia*, be included: unemployment insurance benefits and supplements, accident, injury and sickness benefits, old-age, disability and survivors' pensions, family allowances, reimbursements for medical and hospital expenses or provision of hospital or medical services. Contributions may be levied on both employees and employers.

42. Contributions may be based on earnings or payroll ('on a payroll basis') or on net income after deductions and exemptions for personal circumstances ('on an income tax basis'), and the revenues from the two bases should be separately identified if possible. However, where contributions to a general social security scheme are on a payroll basis, but the contributions of particular groups (such as the self-employed) cannot be assessed on this basis and net income is used as a proxy for gross earnings, the receipts may still be classified as being on a payroll basis. In principle, this heading excludes voluntary contributions paid to social security schemes. When separately identifiable these are shown in the memorandum item on the financing of social security benefits. In practice, however, they cannot always be separately identified from compulsory contributions, in which case they are included in this heading.

43. Contributions to social insurance schemes which are not institutions of general government and to other types of insurance schemes, provident funds, pension funds, friendly societies or other saving schemes are not considered as social security contributions. Provident funds are arrangements under which the contributions of each employee and of the corresponding employer on his/her behalf are kept in a separate account earning interest and withdrawable under specific circumstances. Pension funds are separately organised schemes negotiated between employees and employers and carry provisions for different contributions and benefits, sometimes more directly tied to salary levels and length of service than under social security schemes. When contributions to these schemes are compulsory or quasi-compulsory (e.g., by virtue of agreement with professional and union organisations) they are shown in the memorandum item (refer to Table 5.38 of the Report).

44. Contributions by government employees and by governments in respect of their employees, to social security schemes classified within general government are included in this heading. Contributions to separate schemes for government employees, which can be regarded as replacing general social security schemes, are also regarded as taxes.[14] Where, however, a separate scheme is not seen as replacing a general scheme and has been negotiated between the government, in its role as an employer, and its employees, it is not regarded as social security and contributions to it are not regarded as taxes, even though the scheme may have been established by legislation.

45. This heading excludes 'imputed' contributions, which correspond to social benefits paid directly by employers to their employees or former employees or to their representatives (e.g., when employers are legally obliged to pay sickness benefits for a certain period).

46. Contributions are divided into those of employees (2100), employers (2200), and self-employed or non-employed (2300), and then further sub-divided according to the basis on which they are levied. Employees are defined for this purpose as all persons engaged in activities of business units, government bodies, private non-profit institutions, or other paid employment, except the proprietors and their unpaid family members in the case of unincorporated businesses. Members of the armed forces are included, irrespective of the duration and type of their service, if they contribute to social security schemes. The contributions of employers are defined as their payments on account of their employees to social security schemes. Where employees or employers are required to continue the payment of social security contributions when the employee becomes unemployed these contributions, data permitting, are shown in 2100 and 2200 respectively. Accordingly, the sub-heading 2300 is confined to contributions paid by the self-employed and by those outside of the labour force (e.g., disabled or retired individuals).

3000 — Taxes on payroll and workforce

47. These consist of taxes payable by enterprises assessed either as a proportion of the wages or salaries paid or as a fixed amount per person employed. They do not include compulsory social security contributions paid by employers or any taxes paid by employees themselves out of their wages or salaries

4000 — Taxes on property

48. This heading covers recurrent and non-recurrent taxes on the use, ownership or transfer of property. These include taxes on immovable property or net wealth, taxes on the change of ownership of property through inheritance or gift and taxes on financial and capital transactions. The following kinds of tax are excluded from this heading:

a) taxes on capital gains resulting from the sale of a property (1120 or 1220);

b) taxes on the use of goods or on permission to use goods or perform activities (5200); see §78;

c) taxes on immovable property levied on the basis of a presumed net income which take into account the personal circumstances of the taxpayer. They are classified as income taxes along with taxes on income and capital gains derived from property (1100);

d) taxes on the use of property for residence, where the tax is payable by either proprietor or tenant and the amount payable is a function of the user's personal circumstances (pay, dependants, and so on). They are classified as taxes on income (1100);

e) taxes on building in excess of permitted maximum density, taxes on the enlargement, construction or alteration of certain buildings beyond a permitted value and taxes on building construction. They are classified as taxes on permission to perform activities (5200);

f) taxes on the use of one's own property for special trading purposes like selling alcohol, tobacco, meat or for exploitation of land resources (e.g., United States severance taxes). They are classified as taxes on permission to perform activities (5200).

4100 — Recurrent taxes on immovable property

49. This sub-heading covers taxes levied regularly in respect of the use or ownership of immovable property.

- these taxes are levied on land and buildings;
- they can be in the form of a percentage of an assessed property value based on a national rental income, sales price, or capitalised yield; or in terms of other characteristics of real property, (for example size or location) from which a presumed rent or capital value can be derived.
- such taxes can be levied on proprietors, tenants, or both. They can also be paid by one level of government to another level of government in respect of property under the jurisdiction of the latter.
- debts are not taken into account in the assessment of these taxes, and they differ from taxes on net wealth in this respect.

50. Taxes on immovable property are further sub-divided into those paid by households (4110) and those paid by other entities (4120), according to the criteria set out in §31(*b*) above.

4200 — Recurrent taxes on net wealth

51. This sub-heading covers taxes levied regularly (in most cases annually) on net wealth, i.e. taxes on a wide range of movable and immovable property, net of debt. It is sub-divided into taxes paid by individuals (4210) and taxes paid by corporate enterprises (4220) according to the criteria set out in §31(*a*) above. If separate figures exist for receipts paid by institutions, the tax payments involved are added to those paid by corporations.

4300 — Estate, inheritance and gift taxes

52. This sub-heading is divided into taxes on estates and inheritances (4310) and taxes on gifts (4320).[15] Estate taxes are charged on the amount of the total estate whereas inheritance taxes are charged on the shares of the individual recipients; in addition the latter may take into account the relationship of the individual recipients to the deceased.

4400 — Taxes on financial and capital transactions

53. This sub-heading comprises, *inter alia*, taxes on the issue, transfer, purchase and sale of securities, taxes on cheques, and taxes levied on specific legal transactions such as validation of contracts and the sale of immovable property. The heading does not include:

a) taxes on the use of goods or property or permission to perform certain activities (5200);

b) fees paid to cover court charges, charges for birth, marriage or death certificates, which are normally regarded as non-tax revenues (see §12);

c) taxes on capital gains (1000);

d) recurrent taxes on immovable property (4100);

e) recurrent taxes on net wealth (4200);

f) once-and-for-all levies on property or wealth (4500).

4500 — Other non-recurrent taxes on property

54. This sub-heading covers once-and-for-all, as distinct from recurrent, levies on property. It is divided into taxes on net wealth (4510) and other non-recurrent taxes on property (4520). Heading 4510 would include taxes levied to meet emergency expenditures, or for redistribution purposes. Heading 4520 would cover taxes levied to take account of increases in land value due to permission given to develop or provision of additional local facilities by general government, any taxes on the revaluation of capital and once-and-for-all taxes on particular items of property.

4600 — Other recurrent taxes on property

55. These rarely exist in OECD member countries, but the heading would include taxes on goods such as cattle, jewellery, windows, and other external signs of wealth.

5000 — Taxes on goods and services

56. All taxes and duties levied on the production, extraction, sale, transfer, leasing or delivery of goods, and the rendering of services (5100), or in respect of the use of goods or permission to use goods or to perform activities (5200) are included here. The heading thus covers:

a) multi-stage cumulative taxes;

b) general sales taxes — whether levied at manufacture/production, wholesale or retail level;

c) value-added taxes;

d) excises;

e) taxes levied on the import and export of goods;

f) taxes levied in respect of the use of goods and taxes on permission to use goods, or perform certain activities;

g) taxes on the extraction, processing or production of minerals and other products.

57. Borderline cases between this heading and heading 4000 (taxes on property) and 6100 (other taxes on business) are referred to in §48, §53 and §80. Residual sub-headings (5300) and (5130) cover tax receipts which cannot be allocated between 5100 and 5200 and between 5110 and 5120, respectively; see §33.

5100 — Taxes on the production, sale, transfer, leasing and delivery of goods and rendering of services

58. This sub-heading consists of all taxes, levied on transactions in goods and services on the basis of their intrinsic characteristics (e.g., value, weight of tobacco, strength of alcohol, and so on) as distinct from taxes imposed on the use of goods, or permission to use goods or perform activities, which fall under 5200.

5110 — General taxes on goods and services

59. This sub-heading includes all taxes, other than import and export duties (5123 and 5124), levied on the production, leasing, transfer, delivery or sales of a wide range of goods and/or the rendering of a wide range of services, irrespective of whether they are domestically produced or imported and irrespective of the stage of production or distribution at which they are levied. It thus covers value-added taxes, sales taxes and multi-stage cumulative taxes. Receipts from border adjustments in respect of such taxes when goods are imported are added to gross receipts for this category, and repayments of such taxes when goods are exported are deducted. These taxes are subdivided into 5111 value-added taxes, 5112 sales taxes, 5113 turnover and other general taxes on goods and services.

60. Borderline cases arise between this heading and taxes on specific goods (5120) when taxes are levied on a large number of goods, for example, the United Kingdom purchase tax (repealed in 1973) and the Japanese commodity tax (repealed in 1988). In conformity with national views, the former United Kingdom purchase tax is classified as a general tax (5112) and the former Japanese commodity tax as excises (5121).

5111 — Value-added taxes

61. All general consumption taxes charged on value-added are classified in this sub-heading, irrespective of the method of deduction and the stages at which the taxes are levied. In practice, all OECD countries with value-added taxes normally allow immediate deduction of taxes on purchases by all but the final consumer and impose tax at all stages. In some countries the heading may include certain taxes, such as those on financial and insurance activities, either because receipts from them cannot be identified separately from those from the value-added tax, or because they are regarded as an integral part of the value-added tax, even though similar taxes in other countries might be classified elsewhere (e.g., 5126 as taxes on services or 4400 as taxes on financial and capital transactions).

5112 — Sales taxes

62. All general taxes levied at one stage only, whether at manufacturing or production, wholesale or retail stage are classified here.

5113 — Turnover and other general taxes on goods and services

63. These are multi-stage cumulative taxes and taxes where elements of consumption taxes are combined with multistage taxes. These taxes are levied each time a transaction takes place without deduction for taxes paid on inputs. Multi-stage taxes can be combined with elements of value-added or sales taxes.

5120 — Taxes on specific goods and services

64. Excises, profits generated and transferred from fiscal monopolies, and customs and imports duties as well as taxes on exports, foreign exchange transactions, investment goods and betting stakes and special taxes on services, which do not form part of a general tax of 5110, are included in this category.

5121 — Excises

65. Excises are taxes levied as a product specific unit tax on a predefined limited range of goods. Excises are usually levied at differentiated rates on nonessential or luxury goods, alcoholic beverages, tobacco, and energy. Excises may be imposed at any stage of production or distribution and are usually assessed as a specific charge per unit based on characteristics by reference to the value, weight, strength,

or quantity of the product. Included are special taxes on individual products such as sugar, sugar beets, matches, and chocolates; taxes levied at varying rates on a certain range of goods; and taxes levied on tobacco goods, alcoholic drinks, motor fuels, and hydrocarbon oils. If a tax collected principally on imported goods also applies, or would apply, under the same law to comparable domestically produced goods, then the revenue from this tax is classified as arising from excises rather than from import duties. This principle applies even if there is no comparable domestic production or no possibility of such production. Taxes on the use of utilities such as water, electricity, gas, and energy are regarded as excises rather than taxes on specific services (5126). Excises exclude those taxes that are levied as general taxes on goods and services (5110); profits of fiscal monopolies (5122); customs and other import duties (5123); or taxes on exports (5124).

5122 — Profits of fiscal monopolies

66. This sub-heading covers that part of the profits of fiscal monopolies which is transferred to general government or which is used to finance any expenditures considered to be government expenditures (see §24). Amounts are shown when they are transferred to general government or used to make expenditures considered to be government expenditures.

67. Fiscal monopolies reflect the exercise of the taxing power of government by the use of monopoly powers. Fiscal monopolies are non-financial public enterprises exercising a monopoly in most cases over the production or distribution of tobacco, alcoholic beverages, salt, matches, playing cards and petroleum or agricultural products (i.e. on the kind of products which are likely to be, alternatively or additionally, subject to the excises of 5121), to raise the government revenues which in other countries are gathered through taxes on dealings in such commodities by private business units. The government monopoly may be at the production stage or, as in the case of government-owned and controlled liquor stores, at the distribution stage.

68. Fiscal monopolies are distinguished from public utilities such as rail transport, electricity, post offices, and other communications, which may enjoy a monopoly or quasi-monopoly position but where the primary purpose is normally to provide basic services rather than to raise revenue for government. Transfers from such other public enterprises to the government are considered as non-tax revenues. The traditional concept of fiscal monopoly is not generally extended to include state lotteries, the profits of which are usually accordingly regarded as non-tax revenues. However, they can be included as tax revenues if the prime reason for their operation is to raise revenues to finance government expenditure. Fiscal monopoly profits are distinguished from export and import monopoly profits (5127) transferred from marketing boards or other enterprises dealing with international trade.

5123 — Customs and other import duties

69. Taxes, stamp duties and surcharges restricted by law to imported products are included here. Also included are levies on imported agricultural products which are imposed in member countries of the European Union and amounts paid by certain of these countries under the Monetary Compensation Accounts (MCA) system.[16] Customs duties collected by European Union member states on behalf of the European Union are reported under this heading at the supranational level of government in the country tables (in Chapter 5 of the Report). Excluded here are taxes collected on imports as part of a general tax on goods and services, or an excise applicable to both imported and domestically produced goods.

5124 — Taxes on exports

70. In the 1970s, export duties were levied in Australia, Canada and Portugal as a regular measure and they have been used in Finland for counter-cyclical purposes. Some member countries of the European Union pay, as part of the MCA system, a levy on exports (see note 16 to §69). Where these

amounts are identifiable, they are shown in this heading. This heading does not include repayments of general consumption taxes or excises or customs duties on exported goods, which should be deducted from the gross receipts under 5110, 5121 or 5123, as appropriate.

5125 — Taxes on investment goods

71. This sub-heading covers taxes on investment goods, such as machinery. These taxes may be imposed for a number of years or temporarily for counter-cyclical purposes. Taxes on industrial inputs which are also levied on consumers [e.g., the Swedish energy tax which is classified under (5121)] are not included here.

5126 — Taxes on specific services

72. All taxes assessed on the payment for specific services, such as taxes on insurance premiums, banking services, gambling and betting stakes (e.g., from horse races, football pools, lottery tickets), transport, entertainment, restaurant and advertising charges, fall into this category. Taxes levied on the gross income of companies providing the service (e.g., gross insurance premiums or gambling stakes received by the company) are also classified under this heading.

73. Tax revenues from bank levies and payments to deposit insurance and financial stability schemes are also included here:

- Compulsory payments of stability fees, bank levies and deposit insurance should generally be treated as tax revenues where the payments are made to general government or supranational authorities and are allocated to the governments' consolidated or general funds so that the government is free to make immediate use of the money for the purposes that it chooses. This principle would apply regardless of whether the government is promising to make payments to guarantee the banks' customer deposits in some future contingency.
- If the compulsory payments are made to general government and placed in funds that are earmarked to be entirely channelled back to the sector of the economy that comprises the companies that are subject to the payment, they would still generally be treated as tax revenues on the grounds that the funds would be available for the government and would reduce its budget deficit, the fee is unrequited for an individual entity and the amounts raised could be unrelated to any eventual pay out to depositors or expenditure on wider support for the financial sector.
- Payments to made to the smaller long-standing schemes for insuring 'retail' deposits, where the payment levels are consistent with the costs of insurance should be classified as fee for service.
- Any payments which involve governments realising the assets of a failed institution or receiving a priority claim on its assets in liquidation in order to fund payments of compensation to customers for their lost deposits would be treated as a fee for a service as opposed to tax revenues.
- Compulsory payments that are made to funds operated outside the government sector and non-state institutions backed by the deposit takers and all payments to voluntary schemes should not be treated as tax revenues.
- Contributions made to the EU Single Resolution Fund are also included here and recorded under the supranational level of government in the country tables.

74. Excluded from this sub-heading are:

a) taxes on services forming part of a general tax on goods and services (5110);

b) taxes on electricity, gas and energy (5121 as excises);

c) taxes on individual gains from gambling (1120 as taxes on capital gains of individuals and non-corporate enterprises) and lump-sum taxes on the transfer of private lotteries or on the permission to set up lotteries (5200);[17]

d) taxes on cheques and on the issue, transfer or redemption of securities (4400 as taxes on financial and capital transactions).

5127 — Other taxes on international trade and transactions

75. This sub-heading covers revenue received by the government from the purchase and sale of foreign exchange at different rates. When the government exercises monopoly powers to extract a margin between the purchase and sales price of foreign exchange, other than to cover administrative costs, the revenue derived constitutes a compulsory levy exacted in indeterminate proportions from both purchaser and seller of foreign exchange. It is the common equivalent of an import duty and export duty levied in a single exchange rate system or of a tax on the sale or purchase of foreign exchange. Like the profits of fiscal monopolies and import or export monopolies transferred to government, it represents the exercise of monopoly powers for tax purposes and is included in tax revenues.

76. The sub-heading covers also the profits of export or import monopolies, which do not however exist in OECD countries, taxes on purchase or sale of foreign exchange, and any other taxes levied specifically on international trade or transactions.

5128 — Other taxes on specific goods and services

77. This item includes taxes on the extraction of minerals, fossil fuels and other exhaustible resources from deposits owned privately or by another government together with any other unidentifiable receipts from taxes on specific goods and services. Taxes on the extraction of exhaustible resources are usually a fixed amount per unit of quality or weight, but can be a percentage of value. The taxes are recorded when the resources are extracted. Payments from the extraction of exhaustible resources from deposits owned by the government unit receiving the payment are classified as rent.

5200 — Taxes on use of goods or on permission to use goods or perform activities

78. This sub-heading covers taxes which are levied in respect of the use of goods as distinct from taxes on the goods themselves. Unlike the latter taxes – reported under 5100 –, they are not assessed on the value of the goods but usually as fixed amounts. Taxes on permission to use goods or to perform activities are also included here, as are pollution taxes not based upon the value of particular goods. It is sometimes difficult to distinguish between compulsory user charges and licence fees which are regarded as taxes and those which are excluded as non-tax revenues. The criteria which are employed are noted in §12–13.

79. Although the sub-heading refers to the 'use' of goods, registration of ownership rather than use may be what generates liability to tax, so that the taxes of this heading may apply to the ownership of animals or goods rather than their use (e.g., race horses, dogs and motor vehicles) and may apply even to unusable goods (e.g., unusable motor vehicles or guns).

80. Borderline cases arise with:

a) taxes on the permission to perform business activities which are levied on a combined income, payroll or turnover base and, accordingly, are classified following the rules in §83;

b) taxes on the ownership or use of property of headings 4100, 4200 and 4600. The heading 4100 is confined to taxes on the ownership or tenancy of immovable property and – unlike the taxes of 5200 – they are related to the value of the property. The net wealth taxes and taxes on chattels of 4200 and 4600 respectively are confined to the ownership rather than the use of assets, apply to groups of assets rather than particular goods and again are related to the value of the assets,

5210 — Recurrent taxes on use of goods and on permission to use goods or perform activities

81. The principal characteristic of taxes classified here is that they are levied at regular intervals and that they are usually fixed amounts. The most important item in terms of revenue receipts is vehicle licence taxes. This sub-heading also covers taxes on permission to hunt, shoot, fish or to sell certain products and taxes on the ownership of dogs and on the performance of certain services, provided that they meet the criteria set out in §12–13. The sub-divisions of 5210 are user taxes on motor vehicles paid by households (5211) and those paid by others (5212). Sub-heading 5213 covers dog licences and user charges for permission to perform activities such as selling meat or liquor when the levies are on a recurring basis. It also covers recurrent general licences for hunting, shooting and fishing where the right to carry out these activities is not granted as part of a normal commercial transaction (e.g., the granting of the licence is not accompanied by the right to use a specific area which is owned by government).

5220 — Non-recurrent taxes on use of goods and on permission to use goods or perform activities

82. This section covers non-recurrent taxes levied on the use of goods or on permission to use goods or perform activities and taxes levied each time goods are used. It includes taxes levied on the emission or discharge into the environment of noxious gases, liquids or other harmful substances.

- Payments for tradable emission permits issued by governments under cap and trade schemes should be recorded here at the time the emissions occur. No revenue should be recorded for permits that governments issue free of charge. The accrual basis of recording means that there can be a timing difference between the cash being received by government for the permits and the time the emission occurs. In the national accounts, this timing gives rise to a financial liability for government during the period.
- Payments made for the collection and disposal of waste or noxious substances by public authorities should be excluded as they constitute a sale of services to enterprises.

83. Other taxes falling under heading 5200 that are not levied recurrently are also included here. Thus, once-and-for-all payments for permission to sell liquor or tobacco or to set up betting shops are included provided they meet the criteria set out in §12–13.

6000 — Other taxes

84. Taxes levied on a base, or bases, other than those described under headings 1000, 3000, 4000 and 5000, or on bases of which cannot be considered to be related to any one of these headings, are included here. Where taxes are levied on a multiple base and it is possible to estimate the receipts related to each base the separate amounts are included under the appropriate headings. If separate amounts cannot be estimated and it is known that most of the receipts are derived from one base, the whole of the receipts are classified according to that base. Otherwise, they are classified here. Other revenues included here are presumptive taxes not included elsewhere in the classification system, taxes on individuals in the form of a poll tax or capitation tax, stamp taxes not related to financial and capital transactions nor falling exclusively on a single category of transaction, expenditure taxes where personal deductions or exemptions are applied and unidentifiable tax receipts. A subdivision is made between taxes levied wholly or predominantly on business (6100) and those levied on others (6200).

A.6 Conciliation with National Accounts

85. This section of the tables provides a re-conciliation between the OECD calculation of total tax revenues and the total of all taxes and social contributions paid to general government as recorded in the country's National Accounts. Where the country is a member of the European Union (EU), the comparison is between the OECD calculation of total tax revenues and the sum of tax revenues and social contributions recorded in the combination of the general government and the institutions of the EU sectors of the National Accounts.

A.7 Memorandum item on the financing of social security benefits

86. In view of the varying relationship between taxation and social security contributions and the cases referred to in §40 to §46, a memorandum item collects together all payments earmarked for social security-type benefits, other than voluntary payments to the private sector. Data are presented as follows (refer Table 5.38 of the Report):

a) Taxes of 2000 series.

b) Taxes earmarked for social security benefits.

c) Voluntary contributions to the government.

d) Compulsory contributions to the private sector.

Guidance on the breakdown of (a) to (d) above is provided in §40 to §46.

A.8 Memorandum item on identifiable taxes paid by government

87. Identifiable taxes actually paid by government are presented in a memorandum item classified by the main headings of the OECD classification of taxes. In the vast majority of countries, only social security contributions and payroll taxes paid by government can be identified. These are, however, usually the most important taxes paid by governments (refer to Table 5.39 of the Report).

A.9 Relation of OECD classification of taxes to national accounting systems

88. A system of national accounts (SNA) seeks to provide a coherent framework for recording and presenting the main flows relating respectively to production, consumption, accumulation and external transactions of a given economic area, usually a country or a major region within a country. Government revenues are an important part of the transactions recorded in SNA. The final version of the 2008 SNA was jointly published by five international organisations: the United Nations, the International Monetary Fund, the European Union, the Organisation for Economic Co-operation and Development, and the World Bank in August 2009. The *System* is a comprehensive, consistent and flexible set of macroeconomic accounts. It is designed for use in countries with market economies, whatever their stage of economic development, and also in countries in transition to market economies. The important parts of the SNA's conceptual framework and its definitions of the various sectors of the economy have been reflected in the OECD's classification of taxes.

89. There are, however, some differences between the OECD classification of taxes and SNA concepts that are listed below. They arise because the aim of the former is to provide the maximum disaggregation of statistical data on what are generally regarded as taxes by tax administrations.

a) OECD includes compulsory social security contributions paid to general government in total tax revenues. Imputed and voluntary contributions plus those paid to private funds are not treated as taxes (§9 and §11 above);

b) there are different points of view on whether or not some levies and fees are classified as taxes (§12 and §13 above);

c) OECD excludes imputed taxes or subsidies resulting from the operation of official multiple exchange rates or from the central bank paying a rate of interest on required reserves that is different from other market rates;

d) there are differences in the treatment of non-wastable tax credits

90. As noted in §1 and §2, headings 1000 to 6000 of the OECD list of taxes cover all unrequited payments to general government or to a supranational authority, other than compulsory loans and fines. Such unrequited payments including fines, but excluding compulsory loans can be obtained from adding together the following figures in the 2008 SNA

- value-added type taxes (D.211);
- taxes and duties on imports, excluding VAT (D.212);
- export taxes (D.213);
- taxes on products, excluding VAT, import and export taxes (D.214);
- other taxes on production (D.29);
- taxes on income (D.51);
- other current taxes (D.59);
- actual social contributions (D.611 and D613), excluding voluntary contributions and payments to employment-related schemes that are not social security schemes
- capital taxes (D.91).

A.10 The OECD classification of taxes and the International Monetary Fund (GFS) system

91. The coverage and valuation of tax revenues in the GFS system and the 2008 SNA are very similar. Therefore, the differences between the OECD classification and that of the 2008 SNA (see §89 above) also apply to the GFS. In addition the International Monetary Fund subdivides the OECD 5000 heading into section IV (Domestic Taxes on Goods and Services) and section V (Taxes on International Trade and Transactions). This reflects the fact that while the latter usually yield insignificant amounts of revenue in OECD countries, this is not the case in many non-OECD countries.

A.11 Comparison of the OECD classification of taxes with other international classifications

92. The table below describes an item by item comparison of the OECD classification of taxes and the classifications used in the following:

a) System of National Accounts (2008 SNA);

b) European System of Accounts (2010 ESA);

c) IMF Government Finance Statistics Manual (GFSM2014).

93. These comparisons represent those that would be expected to apply in the majority of cases. However in practice some flexibility should be used in their application. This is because in particular cases, countries can adopt varying approaches to the classification of revenues in National Accounts.

OECD Classification					2008 SNA	2010 ESA	GFSM2014
1000				Taxes on income, profits and capital gains			
	1100			Individuals			
		1110		Income and profits	D51-8.61a	D51A	1111
		1120		Capital gains	D51-8.61c, d	D51C, D	1111
	1200			Corporations			
		1210		Income and profits	D51-8.61b	D51B	1112
		1220		Capital gains	D51-8.61c	D51C	1112
	1300			Unallocable as between 1100 and 1200			1113
2000				Social security contributions			
	2100			Employees	D613-8.85	D613	1211
	2200			Employers	D611-8.83	D611	1212
	2300			Self-employed, non-employed	D613-8.85	D613	1213
	2400			Unallocable as between 2100, 2200 and 2300			1214
3000				Taxes on payroll and workforce	D29-7.97a	D29C	112
4000				Taxes on property			
	4100			Recurrent taxes on immovable property			
		4110		Households	D59-8.63a	D59A	1131
		4120		Other	D29-7.97b	D29A	1131
	4200			Recurrent net wealth taxes			
		4210		Individual	D59-8.63b	D59A	1132
		4220		Corporations	D59-8.63b	D59A	1132
	4300			Estate, inheritance and gift taxes			
		4310		Estate and inheritance taxes	D91-10.207b	D91A	1133
		4320		Gift taxes	D91-10.207b	D91A	1133
	4400			Taxes on financial and capital transactions	D59-7.96d; D29-7.97e	D214B, C	114114; 1161
	4500			Other non-recurrent taxes on property	D91-10.207a	D91B	1135
	4600			Other recurrent taxes on property	D59-8.63c	D59A	1136
5000				Taxes on goods and services			
	5100			Taxes on production, sale and transfer of goods and services			
		5110		General taxes on goods and services			
			5111	Value-added taxes	D211-7.89	D211; D29G	11411
			5112	Sales taxes	D2122-7.94a; D214-7.96a	D21224; D214I	11412
			5113	Other general taxes on goods and services	D214-7.96a	D214I	11413
		5120		Taxes on specific goods and services			
			5121	Excises	D2122-7.94b; D214-7.96b	D21223; D214A, B, D	1142
			5122	Profits of fiscal monopolies	D214-7.96e	D214J	1143
			5123	Customs and other import duties	D2121-7.93	D2121; D21221, 2	1151
			5124	On exports	D213-7.95a	D214K	1152-4
			5125	On investment goods			
			5126	On specific services	D2122-7.94c; D214-7.96c	D21225; D214E, F, G, H; D29F	1144; 1156
			5127	Other taxes on international trade and transactions	D2122-7.94d D29-7.95b D29-7.97g D59-8.64d	D21226; D29D; D59E	1153; 1155-6

			5128	Other taxes on specific goods and services			1146
		5130		Unallocable between 5110 and 5120			
	5200			Taxes on use of goods and on permission to use goods or perform activities			
		5210		Recurrent taxes on use of goods and on permission to use goods or perform activities			
			5211	Motor vehicle taxes households	D59-8.64c	D59D	11451
			5212	Motor vehicles taxes others	D29-7.97d	D214D; D29B	11451
			5213	Other recurrent taxes on use of goods and on permission to use goods or perform activities	D29-7.97c, d, f D59-8.64c	D29B, E, F; D59D	11452
		5220		Non-recurrent taxes on permission to use goods or perform activities			11452
	5300			Unallocable as between 5100 and 5200			
6000				Other taxes			
	6100			Payable solely by business			1161
	6200			Payable by other than business, or unidentifiable	D59-8.64a, b	D59B, C	1162

A.12 Attribution of tax revenues by sub-sectors of general government

94. The OECD classification requires a breakdown of tax revenues by sub-sectors of government. The definition of each sub-sector and the criteria to be used to attribute tax revenues between these sub-sectors are set out below. They follow the guidance of the 2008 SNA and GFSM 2014.

Sub-sectors of general government to be identified

a) Central government

95. The central government sub-sector includes all governmental departments, offices, establishments and other bodies which are agencies or instruments of the central authority whose competence extends over the whole territory, with the exception of the administration of social security funds. Central government therefore has the authority to impose taxes on all resident and non-resident units engaged in economic activities within the country.

b) State, provincial or regional government

96. This sub-sector consists of intermediate units of government exercising a competence at a level below that of central government. It includes all such units operating independently of central government in a part of a country's territory encompassing a number of smaller localities, with the exception of the administration of social security funds. In unitary countries, regional governments may be considered to have a separate existence where they have substantial autonomy to raise a significant proportion of their revenues from sources within their control and their officers are independent of external administrative control in the actual operation of the unit's activities.

97. At present, federal countries comprise the majority of cases where revenues attributed to intermediate units of government are identified separately. Colombia and Spain are the only two unitary countries in this position. In the remaining unitary countries, regional revenues are included with those of local governments.

c) *Local* government

98. This sub-sector includes all other units of government exercising an independent competence in part of the territory of a country, with the exception of the administration of social security funds. It

encompasses various urban and/or rural jurisdictions (e.g., local authorities, municipalities, cities, boroughs, districts).

d) Social security funds

99. Social security funds form a separate sub-sector of general government. The social security sub-sector is defined in the 2008 SNA by the following extracts from paragraphs 4.124 to 4.126 and 4.147:

"Social security schemes are social insurance schemes covering the community as a whole or large section of the community that are imposed and controlled by government units. The schemes cover a wide variety of programmes, providing benefits in cash or in kind for old age, invalidity or death, survivors, sickness and maternity, work injury, unemployment, family allowance, health care, etc. There is not necessarily a direct link between the amount of the contribution paid by an individual and the benefits he or she may receive." (Paragraph 4.124).

"When social security schemes are separately organised from the other activities of government units and hold their assets and liabilities separately from the latter and engage in financial transactions on their own account they qualify as institutional units that are described as social security funds." (Paragraph 4.125).

"The amounts raised, and paid out, in social security contributions and benefits may be deliberately varied in order to achieve objectives of government policy that have no direct connection with the concept of social security as a scheme to provide social benefits to members of the community. They may be raised or lowered in order to influence the level of aggregate demand in the economy, for example. Nevertheless, so long as they remain separately constituted funds, they must be treated as separate institutional units in the SNA. (Paragraph 4.126).

"The social security funds sub-sector (of general government) consists of the social security funds operating at all levels of government. Such funds are social insurance schemes covering the community as a whole or large section of the community that are imposed by government units." (Paragraph 4.147).

100. This definition of social security funds is followed in the OECD classification with the two following exceptions which are excluded

- Schemes imposed by government and operated by bodies outside the general government sector, as defined in §3 of this manual; and
- Schemes to which all contributions are voluntary.

Supranational Authorities

101. This sub-sector covers the revenue-raising operations of supra-national authorities within a country. In practice, the only relevant supranational authority in the OECD area is that of the institutions of the European Union (EU). Tax revenues collected by member countries and paid to the EU are included in the *Revenue Statistics* at the supranational level of government. Income taxes and social security contributions collected by European Institutions and paid by European civil servants who are resident of EU member countries should not be included.

Criteria to be used for the attribution of tax revenues

102. When a government collects taxes and pays them over in whole or in part to other governments, it is necessary to determine whether the revenues should be considered to be those of the collecting government which it distributes to others as grants, or those of the beneficiary governments which the collecting government receives and passes on only as their agent. The criteria to be used in the attribution of revenues are set out in §103 to §106 which replicate paragraphs 3.70 to 3.73 from the 2008 SNA.

103. In general, a tax is attributed to the government unit that

a) exercises the authority to impose the tax (either as a principal or through the delegated authority of the principal),

b) has final discretion to set and vary the rate of the tax

104. Where an amount is collected by one government for and on behalf of another government, and the latter government has the authority to impose the tax, and set and vary its rate, then the former is acting as an agent for the latter and the tax is reassigned. Any amount retained by the collecting government as a collection charge should be treated as a payment for a service. Any other amount retained by the collecting government, such as under a tax-sharing arrangement, should be treated as a current grant. If the collecting government was delegated the authority to set and vary the rate, then the amount collected should be treated as tax revenue of this government.

105. Where different governments jointly and equally set the rate of a tax and jointly and equally decide on the distribution of the proceeds, with no individual government having ultimate overriding authority, then the tax revenues are attributed to each government according to its respective share of the proceeds. If an arrangement allows one government unit to exercise ultimate overriding authority, then all of the tax revenue is attributed to that unit.

106. There may also be the circumstance where a tax is imposed under the constitutional or other authority of one government, but other governments individually set the tax rate in their jurisdictions. The proceeds of the tax generated in each respective government's jurisdiction are attributed as tax revenues of that government.

107. The levies paid by the member states of the EU take the form specific levies which include

a) custom duties and levies on agricultural goods (5123),

b) gross monetary compensation accounts (5123 if relating to imports and 5124 if relating to exports);

c) contributions to the Single Resolution Fund (5126); and

d) Steel, coal, sugar and milk levies (5128).

108. The custom duties collected by member states on behalf of the EU are recorded

- on a gross of collection fee basis;
- using figures adjusted so that duties are shown on a 'final destination' as opposed to a 'country of first entry' basis where such adjustments can be made. These adjustments concern in particular duties collected at important (sea) ports. Although the EU duties are collected by the authorities of the country of first entry, when possible these duties should be excluded from the revenue of the collecting country and be included in the revenue of the country of final destination

109. These are the specific EU levies that most clearly conform to the attribution criterion described in §101 above. Consequently, these amounts are footnoted as a memorandum item to the EU member state country tables (in Chapter 5) and are shown as supranational revenues against each of the tax headings identified in §107.

Notes

1. All references to SNA are to the 2008 edition.

2. See section A.12 of this guide for a discussion of the concept of agency capacity.

3. It is usually possible to identify amounts of social security contributions and payroll taxes, but not other taxes paid by government.

4. If, however, a levy which is considered as non-tax revenue by most countries is regarded as a tax — or raises substantial revenue — in one or more countries, the amounts collected are footnoted at the end of the relevant country tables, even though the amounts are not included in total tax revenues.

5. Names, however, can frequently be misleading. For example, though a passport fee would normally be considered a non-tax revenue, if a supplementary levy on passports (as is the case in Portugal) were imposed in order to raise substantial amounts of revenue relative to the cost of providing the passport, the levy would be regarded as a tax under 5200.

6. A more detailed explanation of this distinction can be found in the special feature, 'Current issues in reporting tax revenues', in the 2001 edition of the *Revenue Statistics*.

7. Sometimes the terms 'non-refundable' and 'refundable' are used, but it may be considered illogical to talk of 'refundable' when nothing has been paid.

8. A different treatment, however, is accorded to non-wastable tax credits under imputation systems of corporate income tax (§37–39).

9. This is not strictly a true tax expenditure in the formal sense. Such tax expenditures require identification of a benchmark tax system for each country or, preferably, a common international benchmark. In practice it has not been possible to reach agreement on a common international benchmark.

10. Unless based on the profit made on a sale, in which case they would be classified as capital gains taxes under 1120 or 1220.

11. In some countries the same legislation applies to both individual and corporate enterprises for particular taxes on income. However, the receipts from such taxes are usually allocable between individuals and enterprises and can therefore be shown in the appropriate sub-heading.

12. For example, "… sufficiently self-contained and independent that they behave in the same way as corporations… (including) keeping a complete set of accounts" (2008 SNA, section 4.44).

13. In Canada — a country also referred to as having an imputation system — the (wastable) tax credit for the shareholder is in respect of domestic corporation tax deemed to have been paid whether or not a corporation tax liability has arisen. As there is no integral connection between the corporation tax liability and the credit given against income tax under such systems, these credits for dividends are treated, along with other tax credits, on the lines described in §26.

14. This may also apply where a scheme for government employees existed prior to the introduction of a general social security scheme.

15. In the 2008 SNA these are regarded as capital transfers and not as taxes (see section A.8).

16. This is the system by which the European Union adjusts for differences between the exchange rates used to determine prices under the Common Market Agricultural Policy and actual exchange rates. Payments under the system may relate to imports or exports and where these amounts are separately identifiable they are shown under the appropriate heading (5123 or 5124). In this Report, these amounts are shown gross (i.e. without deducting any subsidies paid out under the MCA system).

17. Transfers of profits of State lotteries are regarded as non-tax revenues (see also §68).

Lightning Source UK Ltd.
Milton Keynes UK
UKHW020703230221
379194UK00001B/2

9 789264 955561